D1228696

PROPOSED ASSIGNMENT OF JOINT INTERESTS

I Might Inscribe This Book
to
These Surviving Mates of Long Ago
Namely:

WILLIAM J. GILBERT   GEORGE H. GOODMAN
("Butch")   ("Gee")

MATTHEW J. CARNEY
("Bud")

or Include among the Dedicatees
Three
Comrades of More Latterly Days
to wit:

GENE BUCK   A. J. THOMPSON

LEO CARRILLO

But Being the Sort They Are,
I'm Sure All Six Cheerfully Will Transfer Their Proprietory Rights
in This Small Matter
to

My Greatly Beloved Granddaughter
PATRIZIA COBB CHAPMAN

AUTHOR'S NOTE

The author takes justifiable credit for having
written a personal narrative which is unique in
the respects that nowhere amongst the contents
will be found any likeness of the author at any
age whatsoever, nor pictures of his birthplace,
nor group photographs showing him in the act of
favoring famous persons with his presence, nor
facsimiles of laudatory letters from
distinguished admirers.

CONTENTS

CONTENTS—*Continued*

EXIT LAUGHING

PROLOG

You must change your Mournful Ditty
   To a Merry Measure.
I will never come for Pity,
   I will come for Pleasure.

               —*Old English Song*

1

PLEA FOR THE DEFENSE

ONCE upon a time I was returning, by the not-so-roundabout way of Western Europe from South America, where I had been to collect material on a series of articles for the *Cosmopolitan* magazine. My traveling companion was the most perfect of all possible traveling companions and that would be Will Hogg, eldest son of the greatest governor the state of Texas ever had, and in his own right a great man.

So there we were, aboard an Italian liner bound from Brazil to Spain, a lengthy slantwise cruise of the Atlantic. There were only a few other English-speaking passengers and we had to depend rather heavily upon ourselves for company. Even so, the voyage was for me not a lonesome or a tedious voyage. You see, Will was there.

A day or two out from Rio we met an Argentino, a mannerly, middle-aged and very melancholy individual. I've rarely seen a sadder-looking man; he was a model for professional pallbearers everywhere. He had a limited English vocabulary. Will and I had a store of the bastardized Spanish a fellow picks up on the Mexican border. But we all three had hands to gesture with and eyebrows to shrug with and shoulders to lift; and since to the Latin a language is almost as much a calisthenic as it is a spoken tongue, we got along, after a fashion.

He said he was quite alone. He said he had been copiously indisposed, which was obvious. He said he disliked the sea and practically everything about the sea. This was his first extended sea voyage and, God willing, 'twould be his last one. He had been in his stateroom since quitting the land; this was his initial appearance on deck and now, if we would excuse him, he would go below. In his

13

ceremonious South American way he ventured to hope we might meet again and become better acquainted. An unexpected gulp spoiled the stately splendor of his farewell and with speed he skidded down the nearermost companionway. The purser, who was a finished linguist, ranged up and told us the fleeing one was a former member of the Argentine cabinet and a former senator and generally a person of consequence in his own country.

After the ocean swells ironed themselves out, he came up again for air and we did become better acquainted. Vaguely we felt sorry for him—he seemed so weighed down by some private grief. It couldn't altogether be the squeamishness of seasickness which affected him; there must be something else, a mysterious cankering distress. Eventually, when his formal attitude had softened, he took us into his confidence and the unhappy secret came out.

An associate of his, though by no means an intimate associate, had died recently in Buenos Aires. On his deathbed the lately departed had desired that his body be cremated and the ashes be entrusted to this unfortunate confrere of his with instructions to take the ashes and take ship and at the moment of crossing the equator, strew the ashes upon the face of the waters.

With a dignified pathos, the ex-Senator went on to say that so far as might be ascertained, the decedent was not particularly nautical-minded nor would it appear that he'd ever had any romantic attachment for the equator itself. Apparently it was a moribund ambition which had made him put this burden upon a compatriot. But the obligation was not one to be disregarded. So laying aside his business and leaving his family, this poor forlorn gentleman packed up those ashes and quit his pleasant villa and traveled on one coastwise ship from Buenos Aires to Montevideo in Uruguay and thence on a second coaster from Montevideo to Santos and from there had ridden the railroad up to São Paulo and on another railroad line had descended to Rio and at Rio had caught this Italian liner which would carry him clear over to Cadiz in Spain where he must stay until the ship turned around and headed back. Including the return trip, with its various ramifications and delays, at least two months must elapse, and probably it would be nearer three months, from the time he set out on this difficult and most uncongenial mission until he reached home again—and he was already most miserable and was sure would continue to be miserable until the finish of it all.

We extended our joint sympathy which was gratefully accepted. It then developed that he craved a service at our hands. Would we, out of charity, be so good as to join in a special rite, which, by co-operation with the ship's captain, had been arranged to take place at the moment of crossing the equator? That moment, it next developed, would be shortly after four o'clock on tomorrow morning. We couldn't very well get out of it, so we consented and left a call for 3:45 A.M.

It was a small and a subdued and somehow an uneasy and embarrassed company which gathered on the boat deck, well forward, that next morning. An inflammatory tropic dawn should have been painting the east, but there was plenty of fog, and a depressing humidity, like a sort of patina of invisible gloom, lay over everything. The deck-planks were damp and slippery as though the ship suffered from night-sweats; and a wettish heat enveloped us—and we'd had no breakfast. The chief mourner looked his dismal part. He wore the tall hat and frock coat of high occasions, and there was a tremendous broad band of crape on the left sleeve of the coat and a funereal black streamer draped about the hat. To his bosom, with both his gloved hands, he clutched a small bronze canister or urn. The captain was there, wearing a uniform tunic over his pajamas and the ship's chaplain, a small, shy Italian priest, also was present. A sleepy musician with a bugle and a couple of bored sailors stood by. I couldn't help thinking that the group suggested so many bewildered ghosts who had answered the Resurrection trump expecting a large attendance, only to find themselves the first ones up for Judgment Day.

On the minute, as the steamer's bow met the invisible bellyband of the earth, a signal was given and speed fell off to a crawl. The bugler sounded taps. The sailors came to attention. The priest made the Sign of the Cross and said a brief prayer, and our friend, who had stepped to the guards and stood waiting, now unscrewed the lid of the container, and there sifted forth from it and instantly was whisked away, oversides, a scanty grayish powder. It didn't seem possible that an adult body, when reduced to dust, should produce so puny and inconsequential a yield. You would have said any sizable cat ought to render down into a better crop of ashes than that, let alone a grown man.

That was all there was to the matter, or substantially all. As the engines picked up speed, we covered our bared heads. After fumbling the emptied can as though perplexed to know what to do with it, our friend reached a decision and, with almost a suggestion of relief, heaved it outboard. Yawning from emptiness and perhaps other emotions, all hands went below and had coffee and then went back to bed, or at least Will and I did, and tried to catch up on our beauty sleep.

Afterward, reviewing the experience, we marveled at the vanity of a man who, for his own selfish dying ends, would impose so altogether futile and distasteful a task upon another on whom he had no valid claim. And we marveled that only too often, at the end of a life, does the human who reluctantly is surrendering that life devise some such extravagant and outrageous program in a morbid effort to project his personality across the grave, desperately denying to himself even in that supreme final moment the truth of the mighty fact poetically summed up in what was said once about the little dog whose name was Rover, to wit, that while he lived he may have lived in clover but when he died, he died all over.

Yet this gross and exaggerated egotism, this expiring clutch at the intangible when the substance almost is gone, seems to abide with so lamentably many of us. By binding the hands of his posterity to a certain given course one man craves to perpetuate still his mortal works, nearly always with disastrous consequences for the heirs at law and for the institution he left behind. Example: Joseph Pulitzer's New York *World*. Another man puts his dependency for future remembrance upon some elaborate burial mummery or perhaps provides for a lofty costly monument reciting in graven lines the tally of his puny achievements upon this earth. Yet what is a funeral eulogy, spoken into the cold unresponsive ears of the dead, but a belated plea for the defense uttered after the evidence is all in and the verdict recorded, just as an epitaph is merely an advertisement for a line of goods which permanently has been discontinued? For the matter of that, what is an unfilled grave but an open question eternally unanswered and unanswerable?

Yet other men, facing that unrelenting enemy of the species

which is called old age, express their reluctance against being forgotten by turning to the unfamiliar channels of autobiographical works or by hiring ghost writers to do these personal recitals for them. What he has done or seen or said or thought becomes so tremendously important to the poor deluded creature who is faced with the dread prospect that presently he must forevermore quit doing or saying or seeing or thinking. Or rather it acquires importance because he, the belated narrator, was on the spot.

Being naturally prejudiced on the side of the patient it is hardly to be expected that I, myself, should be competent fairly to diagnose my own case but since, for all my life, writing has been my trade, I make so bold as to profess that it is not altogether a yearning to keep on living after I've quit doing so but possibly, in some degree, is merely obedience to an ingrained impulse which prompts me to set myself to the undertaking at hand.

What I mean to write will in no proper sense be cast in the accepted stylistic form—at least I hope not, and at this moment think it will not be. My purpose is to set down, more or less at random, certain memoirs of events and certain likenesses of individuals that have impressed me as being picturesque or fantastic or glamorous, which means that without too much regard for chronological order I shall range back and forth from the recollections of childhood, which are still so vivid, to happenings of comparatively recent occurrence, which last I'd probably forget altogether did I wait many more years before putting them down.

For further excuse I might add that as a reporter, as a war correspondent, as a recorder after one fashion or another of the daily scene for forty-odd years, I've been where interesting things were taking place. I aim to try to tell about some of them and about some trivial things, too.

Anyhow, as Ted Cook said lately when somebody asked him what had become of all the hero-worshipers: "They're writing autobiographies."

2

BUSINESS OF BEING A DESCENDANT

FUNNY, this business of being a descendant. If you believe, as I do, that prenatal influences are the main governing forces within us, then we are agreed that the fused and reconciled traits of his fore-bears form the core of the average man's character, and environment, generally speaking, is no more than the shellac which overlies these passed-on heritages, adding color of personality to the present individual and emphasizing his separate identity, but without mate-rially altering the amalgam of the original pattern. Accepting this basic premise and still not giving our progenitors all the credit nor yet all the blame for what you or I may be, I say it's fair and proper that a man should look to his traceable antecedents for slants and trends when he begins sorting out his reactions to life.

Speaking for myself, I'm sure that my love for the place where I was reared is not altogether due to the circumstances of my being a native son. I'm sure it goes deeper than that for into it enters the elemental fact that on both sides of our family, certain members were among the early residents of Kentucky. They helped to tame the rampaging young commonwealth when it was very young and very rampageous. Their children, and for the most part, their chil-dren's children to the third generation and the fourth even, were born on its soil, lived there and died there and their dust was resolved back into that same friendly mould. I can scarcely remember a time when I did not rejoice in my birthright nor fail to boast of it. In-deed, I was parentally encouraged to do so. People of some of the geographical and national divisions are so constituted. It's part of their ancestral fiber. To cite conspicuous examples, being a Vir-ginian is a profession, and being a South Carolinian is a trade to be worked at in season and out, but Kentuckianism is an incurable dis-ease, a disease, though, to be proud of. On the other hand, I've rarely

heard a man brag about coming from Armenia—or Arkansas. . . .
But a Bostonian of the older stocks would brag, or a Californian,
either of the Forty-niner breed or the Spanish breed; and a Texan,
surely, and likewise a Louisianian, especially one whose people dated
to the first French settlements or the subsequent admixture of the
Arcadian exiles. Practically all Danes are like that, too, and most of
the Scots, and invariably the Irish. Since I'm part Irish and all Kentuckian, I can offer two valid excuses for my vainglorious behavior
in this regard. The world over, the Irish either are boasting of their
blood or spilling it—frequently in other people's quarrels.

The progeny of the first of my discernible ancestors to land in
America spent all of one century and the greater part of another in
backwoods wandering before one multiplying branch of them made
the belated discovery that Kentucky was the fittest of all possible
spots for a permanent establishment. To this day some of their posterity wonder at such blindness and such a lamentable delay.

The original claimable sire, namely, Henry Cobb, was one of
three brothers who came out of the County Mayo in their youth
and bided a while at Norwich, in England, before sailing in 1626
for Jamestown in His Britannic Majesty's realm of Virginia where,
being Irish and therefore naturally inclined to help run a government or tear it apart, Henry Cobb promptly became a deputy of the
general court. When Jamestown Colony fell on evil days the
younger brothers, John and James, stayed behind to breed copiously, first in Virginia and later in North Carolina and Georgia.
There seems to have been a strain of Belgian hare in these prolific
founders. Several counties of Georgia still abound in Cobbs to an
almost unreasonable extent.

Leaving John and James behind, Henry Cobb went up the
empty shore line to Plymouth in Massachusetts; that would be in
1634 or thereabouts. He had been reared within the Catholic fold
but apparently was pliably inclined in the matter of orthodoxy, for
very soon he was being ordained a deacon at a dissenters' meetinghouse. At intervals since then, some of us have returned to the
Ancient Faith. I have a cousin who is a nun and I had a great-uncle,
who, though outwardly a pious Episcopalian for all his days, on his
deathbed sent ninety miles for a priest to come and shrive him, much
to the astonishment of a soundly evangelical household.

Deacon Henry must have had a Celtic sense of humor. By two wives he begat thirteen offspring and named the last one "Experience." For his memory we claim also a traditional distinction. So far as the evidence shows, he was the first man among the English-speaking dwellers on this continent who got a license to dispense hard drinks. The church files at Scituate for 1636 are said to record that "Good Man Cobb being of sober mien and excellent discretion, is authorized to draw spirits."

Some fifteen years ago I was at a private moving-picture showing in a New York home. The telepathic instinct made me uneasily aware that somebody in one of the rows behind was directing a concentrated thought wave at me. I peeped diagonally over my shoulder and there, with a cryptic, intent look on her face, sat a handsome woman. As our eyes met, she flushed, then smiled and gave a small nod compounded of cordiality and embarrassment. When the show ended I made my way toward her and she held out her hand and said:

"I am Mrs. De Lancey Nicoll."

I was saying that I knew her husband, a prominent New York lawyer, when she broke in:

"That's not my excuse for staring at you so hard. What I want you to tell me, or rather, have you confirm it, because I'm practically sure of it already, is that you're a direct descendant, as I am, of Deacon Henry Cobb, who died in Barnstable, Massachusetts, nearly three hundred years ago?"

I admitted the charge and on the strength of it claimed kinship with her as a cousin, a very distant cousin perhaps, but a most charming one.

"Wait," she said, "let me finish. We've met before, many, many times, although never until now did I behold you in the flesh. As a child, at my grandmother's home on the Massachusetts coast, I used to spend hours looking at a painting of the Deacon—a treasured family possession. It fascinated me. He had such a—a—well, let's say rugged face. And I've never forgotten a single line of it and that's why a few minutes ago I almost jumped out of my chair when my glance happened to fall on you. With your hair down to your shoulders and a jerkin buttoned up to your throat and a big flat white collar around your neck, you might have posed for that portrait yourself. I can't imagine a closer resemblance than the one between you and our revered common ancestor."

I told her I wasn't so sure I'd go on thereafter revering the Deacon. It seemed to me his prankish shade, after waiting almost three centuries to play the joke, might have refrained from implanting his image upon a defenseless great-great-and-so-on-and-so-forth-grandchild nine or ten generations removed. I'm relating the incident now for proof that the dubious legacy of a physical likeness may be transmitted out of the past, along with the diluted temperamental essences of bygone beings. By a kind of inverse process, immortality would seem to go rearward. Whether you agree with the theologians that it goes forward across the boundaries of some other world is another thing.*

To judge by the available genealogy, the Deacon's tribe were a restless tribe and a fruitful one. They did their replenishing best to populate Massachusetts and Maine and Connecticut and northern New York State and eventually Vermont. It was at Fairhaven Village in Vermont that my great-grandfather, Gideon Dyer Cobb, in 1799 assembled his brood and added it to an immigrant train made up of twelve neighboring families, most of them of Irish birth or the Irish breed, and practically all of them bound by blood or marriage to one another; and in ox-wagons this little band started on a nine months' trek, first overland and then by barge from Pittsburgh, for the southwestern fringe of the white man's civilization on the near-

---

* Here is another bit of hereditary freakishness which manifests itself in our stock. As far back as we may trace the thing, half of every generation on the Cobb side of the family have been born red-haired and the other half have been born dark-haired and usually the colors are alternately shown. My grandfather was one of eight; four auburn-tops, four black-headed. My father was one of six; same division. I was one of four. My sister, the first-born, had almost the loveliest reddish-gold hair I ever saw. I made my advent with hair so brown as to be almost black and with the thick, bristly dark brows which likewise are a characteristic of the male members of the flock. Then my brother, a true sorrel, came along and finally my other sister, whose hair was chestnut. There is a legend that the Cobb women are never ugly and the Cobb men always are. Well, from time to time it has been brought to my attention that I was nobody's pretty boy.

ermost edge of the Chickasaw Nation. The expedition capably was led by my great-grandmother's uncle-in-law, Colonel Matthew Lyon, that stormy petrel of New England politics whose vote in Congress made Thomas Jefferson president over Aaron Burr, and who now was going, with these few followers of his, to the farthermost tip of the lusty new state of Kentucky, there to form, in a more congenial environment than Vermont's, a defensive and offensive alliance with a rising young firebrand of Tennessee, just over the border, by name Andrew Jackson.*

According to the fragmentary testimony these aliens from a

---

* Under various heads the rugged Colonel Lyon made the front pages of the journals and gazettes of his day. The son of an Irish rebel out of the County Wicklow, who was hanged by the British, he was sold as a bond servant to one of the New England plantations. The price paid for him was a span of steers. Thereafter his favorite oath was, "By the Black Bulls that bought me!" At the taking of Fort Ticonderoga by the Green Mountain Boys he commanded a company under his kinsman-by-marriage, Ethan Allen, and a little later was court-martialed, unjustly he always asserted, for alleged weakness before the enemy. In 1798 he signalized his entry into the national scene at Washington by spitting in the face of a fellow member, Roger Griswold, Federalist from Connecticut, and when on the floor of the House, Griswold in retaliation attacked him with a cane, he felled his assailant, wielding a set of fire tongs which he snatched up from a handy grate. For offering to fight a duel with President John Adams and for assaulting the administration with his tongue and his equally sharp pen he was, as the first notable victim of the odious Alien and Sedition Law, thrust into an unheated dark cell in a Vermont winter. From his dungeon he conducted a successful double-headed campaign for re-election and for the repeal of the obnoxious statute and on the latter triumph was accorded due credit for re-establishing the rights of free speech and freedom of the person in the young Republic. Before he died he had represented three separate constituencies of three separate states in the Congress—Vermont, Kentucky and, toward the last, Arkansas. Only one other ever equaled this record, and that was Shields of Illinois and points both east and west; and Shields, like Lyon, was an Irishman.

The Irish have a certain facility at running for office. This is not an original observation with me. It has been said before.

thousand miles distant didn't remain aliens much longer than it took for them to change the original name of their tiny settlement on the Cumberland River from "Yankeetown" to Eddyville. Politically and socially they were presently of a homogeneous piece with a scattering population of adventurous newcomers from Virginia and the two Carolinas who, by a scanty margin of time, had preceded them to these remote parts. Sixty-odd years later their descendants, almost to the last man and to the last woman, went with the Confederacy, even more unanimously than their kinspeople back yonder in New England went with the Union.

This great-grandfather of mine came poor into the wilderness, but having, I take it, both Down-East thrift and Gaelic adaptability, didn't stay that way long. Almost before the clearings were made he had enrolled himself among that fabulous crew, half-hoss and half-alligator by their own telling—the keelboatmen. On great raftlike "broadhorns" of virgin timbers he loaded the produce of this fecund archipelago—red whisky, already beginning to be known as Bourbon; heavy rank leaf tobacco grown in the so-called Black Patch of western Kentucky and Tennessee; corn, hemp, pelts, hides, pumpkins and hoop-poles, but particularly the whisky and the tobacco—and floated it out to the Ohio and down the Ohio into the Mississippi, past the dens of the river pirates and through hostile Indian country on to the French and Spanish possessions and sold his cargo at New Orleans and broke up his arks for shipbuilding and then rode horseback or walked home again over the Natchez Trace, a more perilous journey even than the water cruise had been. He was a partner in the setting up of the first iron furnace established west of the Allegheny Mountains and benefited thereby, for literally his farm stood on top of a virgin ore bed and coal was to be had out of a near-by hill for the digging of it; besides, he was a metal-worker by trade as his father before him had been, an acknowledged adept at the crudely primitive bloomer process for fabricating steel.*

---

* On at least two other counts, the Cobb-Lyon furnace, as it was called, bulked in border history. It was sold to a factor named Kelly from Pennsylvania; this happened a few years after its establishment.

Kelly did not hold with slavery, so from Canton by sailing ship he brought thirty coolies who were landed at New Orleans and

Previously to this, with logs of his own hewing, he had built the only tavern on the then lonesome lower bends of the Cumberland River, afterward adding on a warehouse for tobacco and cotton, and a store where he purveyed everything from ox-bows and hymn-books to flintlock muskets, mill wheels and painkillers. Also, being elected a magistrate, he took the title of "Squire," and flourishingly used it.

In my possession are various huge ledgers and day books, saved from the rambling brick building which he subsequently erected and which his heirs enlarged until it spraddled over an acre. When this waterside landmark was torn down, forty-odd years ago, some thoughtful soul rescued these ponderous volumes.*

---

fetched overland to this remote Kentucky settlement—perhaps the earliest group of Chinese laborers imported to America. The first man legally hanged in the newly created bailiwick was a negro, for murdering one of these Orientals. Eventually the rest of them were absorbed into the native population. Twenty years ago there still were families in back corners who probably did not suspect that their names were Anglicized versions of Chinese names or that some among them owed their slant eyes and high cheekbones to a Mongolian strain or, if they did suspect it, certainly never bragged on it.

Employed as a clerk at the little plant was a young Englishman named Henry Bessemer. It was here, or so he claimed, that through experiments he discovered the Bessemer process for fabricating steel. To him this brought fame and a title, for he was knighted when he took his invention back to England. But one of the Kellys claimed that he had fathered the germ idea and that Bessemer pilfered it from him. What's more he pretty well established his case. There was much litigation and at least one large book was written— by a Kelly—on the merits of the dispute. Be that as it may, there seemingly isn't any doubt that the formula which revolutionized the whole industry was worked out here in the half-tamed wilderness.

* Some of the very earliest records—those relating to my great-grandsire's exploits as a pioneer navigator—were missing or perhaps no such records were ever kept. If this last theory be true, for it there was possibly a reason. By family tradition he originated the ingenious idea of packing into tight casks the strong black native tobacco, leaf, lugs, dirt clods, stalks, stems, trash and all; and dousing

By them, I can follow the course of the clan's increase through those long-ago periods. One of the very earliest entries deals with purchases for the proprietor's account against the coming of the first of his children to be born on Kentucky soil—my grandfather, it was, in 1804. I can read how my grandfather at twenty-one was taken into the firm; and I know when he married by the tally of nankeen and blue broadcloth and glass buttons and brass buttons and a flowered silk waistcoat for the groom; and here too are included the fineries and fripperies for the bride and her bridesmaids. There is a whole page of such listings. Another page enumerates nails and bolts and hinges and wooden sashes and what-all, so there I fix approximately the date when the young couple built their own home. On the same plot of ground, as affairs prospered with them,

---

the mess with crude sorghum molasses and pressing it to sticky solidity, then freighting the parcels to New Orleans and there transferring them to sailing ships skippered by seafaring State of Maine men who were distant kinsmen of his. These consignees in turn took the chartered cargoes two-thirds of the way around the globe and on the coast of Africa traded for gold dust and ivory; such was the treasured story and it had a most romantic sound, especially that gold dust and ivory part.

But a whispered version which never reached my ears until I was near finishing my growth, was to the effect that what my ancestor's cousins really bartered for was "black ivory," meaning negro slaves, who were brought back and smuggled ashore in lonely coves and disposed of to Deep South plantations—and that was regarded as a nefarious calling, long even before the traffic was by the Federal government outlawed.

I wish I could have got at the secret of that, although certainly my immediate forebears would have deplored such unmannerly curiosity on my part.

Some of the existing entries are revealing. For instance, this one:

"To postage on letter to lady—one bit."

And this one:

"To use of mad stone taken from deer's belly—for curing rabies—$1."

And this:

"To one set of forged neckyokes and chains for slave convoy—$2."

they reared their second house and it the finest in the town, and
they called it White Hall, after her home in the wife's native state
of Virginia.

So you see, we Cobbs were going up in the world and qualifying
for admission to the ranks of the self-ordained landed gentry of the
Border South. Today a state penitentiary spreads its grim cell blocks
across the knoll of shaly limestone which was the site for that homestead; and where my grandmother's rose garden was is the "death
house" and to it poor forsaken wretches are brought to die by the
electric chair.

From the showings in one of these tattered books, it is made plain
that no matter what else a customer at Cobb's Corners bought,
whether for his lady or his children or his slaves or for himself, he
bought also strong liquors—a bottle of this, a demijohn of that, a
gallon jug of some favored potable, a piggin or a whole keg even.
They were giants—lusty, thirsty giants—in those days. Here
through three years one may trace the rise to alcoholic heights and
the ultimate defeat of a certain Matthew Gracey, obviously of the
kith, since both Matthew and Gracey are names interwoven with
ours.

There is a graphic continuity to this tragic epic—like a Hogarth-
ian saga done in paled ink instead of etched drawings. I mark how
that the aforesaid Matthew Gracey inaugurates his career as a
steady consumer by buying each week a quart of domestic spirits.
Shortly his demand increases to two quarts weekly, and then to
three and four and eventually five.

Presently a deeply significant charge is inscribed:

"To Matthew Gracey, Esquire, for breaking four glass tumblers
while drunk—eight shillings."

There comes an hour in this culminating series of purchases all
marching toward the inevitable disastrous climax when, after seven
consecutive sales on as many days, this pregnant line is set down:

"To Matthew Gracey, by slave girl Sukey, four quarts of French
brandy."

Next occurs a lapse of six days and then:

"To relict of Matthew Gracey, eight yards of black bombazine
for mourning."

Doubtlessly the widow could have saved money by just pouring deceased back in the barrel but she didn't, because some two months farther along she is credited with an advance payment on a marble tombstone to be freighted downstream from Nashville. Thus concludes the tale of Matthew Gracey's rise as a toper and his fall—and his fatal finish. He lost the fight, true, but who would say he wasn't trying?

3

THE SON OF JIMMY DRY

My FATHER'S people were canny colonizers, peacefully getting a toe-holt in the alluvial fat river bottoms of our Kentucky peninsula after some at least of the trails slanting downward and westward across the barrens and through the canebrakes to those ultimate boundaries had been blazed. Statehood had come and the gunfire of border warfare was dimming out behind their caravan as they skirted the great central intervale to exercise rights of squatter sovereignty in a place of tall timbers and dense thickets and converging watersheds three hundred miles farther on.

But my mother's people were of the true pathfinding kind and more than two decades earlier, a front guard of them had legged it through "The Gap" to contend for their holdings with red savages and white turncoats where temporarily the onward sweep of Colonial conquest was checked within a crescent of protective blockhouses on the flanks of the old Transylvanian plateau which since became famous as the Blue Grass section.

It seems there was a man-child born in Fairfax County, Virginia, during the opening year of the War for Independence whilst his Welsh-Scotch father was away soldiering with the Continental troops; and his name was James Saunders, but because of a whimsical salty manner of speech which afterward he had, he better was known as Dry-Talkin' Jimmy or Jimmy Dry for short, so that still later on when, by virtue of volunteer service against the malignants in the dangersome wild domain beyond the mountains, he earned a veteran's land grant, the papers read: "To James Saunders or James Dry, as the case may be."

He was bound out to a journeyman tanner, but presently, being by then a lanky young apprentice, he gave up that dullish employ-

28

ment and as a very junior member of a squad of "Long Rifles" struck out toward where the sun went down. It would appear that herein he obeyed the destiny of his breed since already, years before, three of his senior brothers, besides a couple of uncles and a stray cousin or so, had gone upon the same difficult and precarious pilgrimage, following along on the moccasined heels, so to speak, of the first authentic explorers—Boone and Kenton and the rest of that audacious lot. In fact, it is set down on the files that the second Caucasian invader killed by the hostiles in the "Kain-tuckee Country" was a Saunders and a kinsman of his, a young scout from the Yadkin, down in North Carolina. And two of his sisters-in-law already had played a part in the defense of the log fort at Bryan's station on the Elkhorn near Lexington; their names are on the tablet which tells how, in pretended indifference, the women went singing out of the stockade gates and down to the spring under the deceived eyes of the hidden besiegers and fetched up water for the famished fighting men. But this is a story, stiff with proud adjectives, which you'll find in any Kentucky history book.

Now this laconic Jimmy Dry, who did his homeseeking with a fuke in his hand and a tomahawk at his belt, was my maternal great-grandfather. He had come a young ranger into this unmapped and as yet only partially conquered hinterland and he married young as was the fashion for those days. The wife he took was Jane Bartlett, whose people had lately traipsed up out of South Carolina, and at once this couple set in to make a start and raise a family. They built for themselves a slab cabin on a hillocky clearing six miles from Frankfort, the new state capital. A younger son of theirs, born there in 1808 and christened Reuben, was the only one of my grand-parents still surviving when I came to be of a remembering age. He was such a one as would not easily be forgotten either—a tall, sparse, weather-beaten shape of a man with a mouth like a seam but, to offset that severity, a pair of the keenest, kindliest eyes that ever were. He was almost the silentest human being I have ever known—he saved on words as a miser saves on pennies— but he was never dour. He could be stern enough, but there was no glumness to him. Without saying anything at all he added zest to a company and, by listening with a grave serenity, exalted the talkers. Members of my own household have been known to express regret that this ancestral gift for reticence did not fall upon me. We won't go into that.

For nearly half a century, until he passed the age for professional activities, he held undisputed rating as the leading physician—and probably the most beloved citizen—of the town of Paducah where twenty-odd of us, belonging to the first and second generations of his direct descendants, grew up about him. In all essential regards he fulfilled the ideal conception of that now almost vanished species—the old-fashioned general practitioner. I think he must have been born with the healing touch. Family tradition had it that as a child he ministered to crippled animals and sickly chickens and maintained a rail-fenced hospital of his own. And no sooner had he learned the craft of bookbinding—a genteel step upward for the son of a brush rover who barely could read and write—than my grandfather borrowed the money which saw him through medical college.*

Living near by where he lived was an eccentric character called Charles Julian. This eccentricity assumed a worthy aspect. Being a bachelor and being, for that time and place, a wealthy man, this Charles Julian made loans to needy youths who showed promise in some given direction. Kentucky's first notable sculptor and her first notable portrait painter were among the objects of his generosity. By the same token it was he who advanced the funds for the professional education of the young mechanic, Reuben Saunders. In 1873

---

* Some sixty-odd years later, one of his sons-in-law, prowling through a secondhand shop at Cincinnati, found two quaint-looking tomes and bought them. When he got home and showed them to Dr. Saunders, as relics of a bygone time, the oldster grunted. "I've seen them before," he said. "They were almost the first books I bound after I learned my trade at Lexington." He took a scalpel and turned back the leather flap on an outer cover to show his rubric scored in the backing. I have both these copies in my library. They were written by the first Humphrey Marshall, a United States senator and a unique figure in border politics. He called his work *The History of Kentucky*. He devoted practically all of one volume to lambasting his enemies of whom there were a copious supply, and the other volume to proving that Kentucky was the site of the Garden of Eden—a conclusion with which few of his fellow Kentuckians quarreled then or thereafter.

when Asiatic cholera swept the world and invaded America, Paducah was one of the places devastated by the plague; its people died swiftly and by hundreds; the town coffin-maker, working day and night to hammer together boxes for the victims, was himself nailed up in the last box he made. More or less by accident, or rather, by mistake, he being half-dead with exhaustion and lack of sleep from tending the victims about him, my grandfather happened on an injection which proved so effective a check against the scourge's further spread that the formula was named for him and several foreign governments bestowed decorations upon him. That same year word came that his early benefactor, now very aged, lay hopelessly ill upstate. My grandfather carried a little casket containing the medals and the ribbons to his bedside and told the dying man these things properly belonged to him. It was said the casket, by request of old man Julian, was buried with him. At any rate, the decorations were never seen in my grandfather's latter years nor spoken of by him, nor were they found among his personal effects after he died.

In our town were numbers of elderly men who in cold weather wore fringed shawls draped over their shoulders, usually sober gray or dun-colored shawls. But a distinguished two of the oldsters—Doctor Saunders and Judge Dow Husbands—would have none of this. Winter times they swathed their long meager frames in bright blanket-robes just as their daddies before them had done. On a sharp morning it was a familiar sight to see this rawboned pair striding along together, as erect and as taciturn as the dead-and-gone chiefs whose trappings they had borrowed. Judge Husbands' blanket was a brilliant red but my grandfather's was of rich blue broadcloth. He told me once that never in all his life had he worn an overcoat. By dribs and snatches he used to tell me many things about his childhood and his youth, in that rude and husky settlement of his people upstate. To harken during these rare moments when the reminiscent mood laid hold on him was, for me, like reliving with him vivid phases of the pioneering scene, vastly more stirring than any passages one might read on printed pages. I didn't have to imagine what happened, I seemed literally to be experiencing it myself.

Once, abruptly and seeming apropos of nothing at all, he said:

"One of my uncles on my mother's side, Uncle Gip Bartlett, was a master marksman; kept score of the bushwhackings and the skirmishes he'd been in by the scalps he'd taken. He had three— two black-haired ones and a tow-colored one that he'd lifted off a Tory he had the luck to bring down during a running bout up toward the Blue Licks. He set much store by those scalps; would pin them on his old hunting shirt when he turned out for a rally or a Muster Day. He'd always carry along a turkey-wing fan, Injun-fashion."

He stopped there and left me tingling to beat a tuning fork.

Nearly always he reserved these briefened piecemeal recitals for special occasions. On Sunday he liked to drive out to his own farm in the lowlands or to the farms of friends of his where young chickens would be sacrificed for a dinner to his tastes and, in season, watermelons set to chill in the spring. It was a precious privilege when I was the grandchild chosen to accompany him because, aside from the joy of going visiting, I was reasonably assured that somewhere, going or coming, he would be reminded of some stirring frontier episode to which he had been eyewitness or possibly had been a participant in it.

Almost as clearly as I revive the physical picture of my grandfather, I recall the drugstoreish scent of strong medicines which clung always to his garments. So also after all this long, long time I can still piece together out of the scrapbag of my memory sundry related annals which had been embalmed in community folklore.

There was the tradition about the time when a sort of unofficial census showed that in the county were then living more than a hundred juveniles who, having been ushered into the world by his capable hands, had been named for him, so that on certain back roads about every other youngster one met would, if a male, answer to the hail of "Rube" or, if a girl, would be "Reubie" or "Reubina" or even "Reubelinda."

There was the line attributed to the country wag who, commenting on the fact that the old man would have between the shafts of his battered buggy only the friskiest of half-broken colts, said: "Looks like every time Doctor Saunders gits him a hoss, its natchell gait is runnin' away."

There was the narrative of how a half-crazed man, nursing some

vague grievance, armed himself with a great club and on a dark night waylaid my grandfather at his own doorstep. But my grandfather dodged as the murderous blow fell so that it missed his skull and landed on his left shoulder. Accordingly, he drew a horse pistol and neatly shot the enemy in the side with a leaden chunk the size of a scaly-bark hickory nut, then called the servants and had his assailant lugged indoors where he probed out the bullet and dressed the wound before giving heed to his own cracked shoulder blade.

Most often repeated of all, though, was the legend about the lawsuit over a land deal which had been brought against him by a chronic litigant who, through marriage, was distantly related to his house. When the case was called for trial the patriarch appeared in court without an attorney, although one of his sons-in-law was a member of the bar and a majority of its other members were included among his regular patients, or anyhow their families were.

"Doctor," said the amazed judge, "do I understand that you are going into this hearing without being represented by counsel?"

The defendant stood up and scratched among his chin whiskers. I'm sure he must have done so because, to the best of my recollection, he always scratched at those half-moon whiskers before risking speech.

"This is the first time I was ever sued," he stated. "If this land doesn't belong to me I don't want it. If it does belong to me I'm going to have it."

"But, Doctor, what do you expect to do?"

"Testify."

Which he did, and in jig time the jury returned a judgment in his favor. Afterward some maintained that the evidence offered by him on the witness stand that day formed the longest consecutive statement ever delivered by old Doctor Saunders. But they were wrong there. I'm reasonably sure the longest unbroken speech he ever made was made when he was past his eightieth birthday, and made to an audience consisting of one eager-eared small boy. I was that boy and now for the first time I am recording in writing substantially what he said. Until then I'd never heard him utter, at one stretch, two hundred words. Now, having unlocked his lips, he went on, I should say, for ten or fifteen minutes, which in itself, was a wondrous thing.

Thinking back, I can summon up a coherent vision of that autumnal afternoon and two sitting together on a log, the octogenarian and the sapling in his early teens, at the edge of a cypress slash above a little lazy by-creek which loafed along at the back side of my grandfather's shorn tobacco patch. He began, as usual, without preamble. He said:

"One of my father's older brothers took up with a Cherokee squaw. This was soon after he came out to Kentucky, about the time the Revolutionary War ended. I don't know whether he married her. It was a thing the family didn't talk about afterward, although, back yonder, there was a lot of that sort of thing going on. By this Indian woman my uncle had a son who was named Nathaniel Saunders, but while he still was a shaver people took to calling him Bull Saunders: he had such a fierce temper and was so strong physically. Even in a country as raw and rough as that was, he had a hard reputation, from boyhood on up. This is hearsay with me. He was gone from those parts when I came along.

"The explanation was that, to get rid of him, he'd been sent off as a student to West Point soon after West Point was founded. According to the same story, he made a showing up there on at least two counts—his aptitude at military strategy and his quarrelsome disposition. He hadn't been there more than a year or two, they said, when he got into real trouble. The daughter of a man who ran a ferry between Garrison and the Point told her father Cadet Saunders had been intimate with her and the father made threats. A few days later the ferryman's body was found in the Hudson River with the head battered in. That's the next chapter in the tale as I myself got it much later on. Naturally suspicion fell on young Saunders. On the eve of being arrested, he disappeared after telling a classmate that he wasn't guilty, but since nobody liked him he wouldn't stand a ghost of a show to prove his innocence. His father's race had cast him out; he had no friends, was to everybody a wood's colt and a mongrel. All right then, if America was going to cast him out, he'd devote the rest of his life to hating the whole breed of Americans and getting even with them. First thing though was to get away.

"That wouldn't be hard. All he had to do was to climb the mountains behind West Point and strike off into the wild country

to the southwest. Most of it was still Indian country. He was
swarthy and black-haired. He spoke at least one Indian language,
probably had smatterings of others. He'd get along in the deep
woods if anybody could.

"Now then, here's a wide gap in the sequence. We've got to
jump to the year 1836 when the Texans under Sam Houston captured the infamous Santa Anna at the Battle of San Jacinto. Although Santa Anna was a prisoner of the new Republic of Texas,
the Texans, by some mysterious means, induced the United States
Government to take over custody of him. With a guard of dragoons he was carried across country to Washington and later was
sent back on a naval vessel to Mexico. If you'll read up on him
you'll find he was a dictator and once or twice a president of Mexico
and in at least two campaigns was commander-in-chief of her armies
and finally died somewhere down there in obscurity and disgrace.
He was one of the greediest, cruelest men that ever lived on this
continent, I reckon, but he was a scientific soldier and a genius in
his twisted way, and he left his mark in history.

"Well, when Santa Anna and his escort of troopers got as far
as Frankfort, in this state, on their way to Washington, they stayed
overnight in an old tavern that stood on a hill back of town. I was
still calling Frankfort home then, but I wasn't there to see what happened—if it actually did happen. I'd gotten my medical degree at
Philadelphia and was headed for Alabama to start practicing in partnership with another young doctor who was a distant connection
of my mother's people from South Carolina. Eventually we split
up and I came on back to Kentucky and he went to New York.
Read up on Doctor Marion Sims, too, when you get 'round to it,
son. He's called the Father of American Surgery and deserves that
great name.

"By all accounts there was a mighty to-do on the night Santa
Anna got to Frankfort. Among the Kentuckians who'd gone west
to help the Texans get free from Mexico were several volunteers
from that immediate section and to the last man they'd been
slaughtered by Santa Anna's orders at the Goliad Massacre. So a
crowd of the kinfolks and friends of these dead boys decided they'd
just take old Santa Anna out and string him up for a cold-blooded
murderer. They got some of the dragoons drunk and overpowered

the others—that's the way the story runs, anyhow—but at the very last minute they changed their minds about it and there was no neck-stretching.

"The reason why they'd changed their minds, as I heard the explanation, was this: Three men were selected to go into the tavern and fetch the victim out. But as they broke into the room where he was quartered and he sat up in bed, the leader of the delegation almost dropped dead from surprise when the man in the bed called out his name and, as a blood relation, pleaded for mercy. And he professed to recognize the other two lynchers, too, claiming they'd been urchins together in that very neighborhood.

"Under pledge of secrecy he told them that after refugeeing from West Point he had kept on going until he made his way deep into Mexico; had learned Spanish on his way; had twisted his English name around backward and shortened it up so that it became Santa Anna; had given himself a fictitious birthplace in Mexico and a spurious family tree; and had used his earlier training to such effect that he rose to the highest rank in the Mexican Army and eventually was butchering his own countrymen at Goliad and the Alamo and other places. But he excused these wholesale executions on the ground of military necessity. He begged hard. I reckon he must have been a good talker. Besides, he was talking for his life.

"It wasn't mercy though, that influenced the three who'd heard him, so much as it was the thought of the shame that would be put upon their people and their state if this confession got out. And among themselves they agreed to hush up the incredible disclosures they'd just listened to. Then they went back out to where the main crowd was and successfully argued that to hang a man under the protection of the United States flag would probably involve, not alone them, but Kentucky, with the Federal authorities. So the mob broke up and scattered.

"But such an amazing thing couldn't be kept quiet. It leaked out although always there were efforts, by denial or by ridicule, to suppress it, especially on the part of those belonging to our own family. When he was a middle-aged man my father told me the alleged details, not vouching for them but just repeating the version which had been confided to him. I am getting pretty old myself, so I'm passing the tale on to you for what it's worth—if it's worth anything. I never tried to verify it—somehow didn't seem to want to. If by any chance it's true, then that iniquitous scoundrel, Santa Anna, was my renegade half-breed cousin and some of the blood that was in his veins is in yours. If it's not true, and I'm reasonably convinced that it's not in spite of so much circumstantial embroidery around it, then it's mighty clever fiction. . . . Well, son, let's be getting along, it's six miles to supper."

Except for some sketchy inquiries after I'd reached my majority, I made no effort to substantiate the underpinnings of this strange structure. I was afraid I might spoil a most dramatic product by disproving it. However, while I was at Frankfort in 1900 for a Louisville newspaper, covering the assassination of Governor Goebel, the political prototype of Huey Long—who had a career much like Goebel's and died much the same sort of death that Goebel died—I did trace down an admission attributed to one very ancient, very fragile gentleman of the interesting name of Major Pat Major, a creaky but mentally spry connecting link with the past, who was quoted as saying that men he had known were in the mob which surrounded the tavern on that memorable occasion back in 1836, but went on to say that none of them would ever discuss the unexpected outcome of the affair or even admit they had information as to what privily might have occurred after they got there. In a history of certain Blue Grass counties I read that there was much confusion in the town on that evening and that after dark a disorderly and threatening assemblage, with torches and weapons, trooped up the hill to listen to an impassioned harangue by one John U. Waring, a violent-minded orator who subsequently died a violent death, but that it disbanded without offering any indignity to General Santa Anna—which would seem to give some faint color of plausibility to one phase of the account even though it offers no actual corroboration.

I have heard somewhere—but never sought confirmation for it—that contemporaneous Mexican authorities disagreed as to the exact date and place of Santa Anna's birth; also that the Indians claimed he was all Spanish by descent and the Spaniards insisted he was all Indian. Moreover, I've been told that one biographer of the period intimated that in his youth Santa Anna attended the great French cavalry school at St. Cyr which, on the face of it, would

seem to be a manifest error, while another historian contradicted
this and significantly attributed the man's admittedly expert military
skill to the theory that he had been technically trained in a famous
governmental institution in the United States.

So much for that. And seemingly there isn't much more to be
got by turning to West Point itself. At its beginning West Point
had several false starts; was established, abandoned, re-established,
then sadly languished. In 1802 it authentically was reopened—with
ten cadets; but ten years later was without a single authorized in-
structor and students still were being admitted without regular appointment and with no sort of examination and at any age between
twelve and thirty-four.

So if there be any trustful reader who offhand is inclined to
accept the narration on the strength of this fragmentary fabric,
I'll advise that person to shake well before taking. As for me, I
prefer to include it with such shadowy, speculative myths as the
unbelievable one about the fate of the Lost Dauphin and the one
about the escape of Marshal Ney from his executioners and the
preposterous story that John Wilkes Booth was not shot down after
he killed Lincoln, but hid away somewhere in the Southwest. Famous assassins are always escaping death to live out their lives under
assumed names—take Jesse James and Billy the Kid. Eventually
Johnnie Dillinger ought to turn up somewhere.

My grandfather died at eighty-two. You might say he died prematurely, because one of his brothers lived to be nearly a hundred,
and two of his sisters were in their nineties when they passed on.
But before day of a chilly December morning he got up out of a
warm bed and in his nightshirt went forth, carrying an old der-
ringer pistol, to deal with a rooster which, from under his window,
insisted on crowing too shrilly for dawn and too frequently. He
eliminated the rooster at one shot, but he caught pneumonia and
that was the end of him.

The last I ever saw of him was when he had been "laid out," as
the saying went then, with his gaunt form stretched beneath the
canopy of his great four-poster bed. Afterward, the craze for
brass atrocities and gimcracky monstrosities laid its horrid grip on
an aunt of mine who had inherited the furnishings of the old home
place and that massive heirloom of solid rosewood disappeared. A

long time later a local antique hunter reclaimed it. For two dollars it had been sold as junk by a secondhand dealer to an old negress in the county, but it was too big for her cabin so she used it for a roost in her chicken shed. It was covered inches deep with the accumulated droppings of years. I understand the present owner recently refused a considerable sum offered for it by an eastern collector.

4

AWAY BACK YONDER

IT WAS at my Grandfather Saunders' home on what was then the principal street of our town that I was born and there I lived until I passed my ninth birthday. It was a great town to be born in, being a colorful town and one of character and individuality. And surely that flat-faced, high-shouldered old house and what appertained thereto made a grand place for a child to spend a childhood.

My grandfather built it in the early forties, it being then the largest dwelling in town and the finest. Historically it had another hold on local fame. Until I was a half-grown stripling it was known as "the house the Yankees couldn't burn down."

When, early in the War between the States, both sides ran a foot race to violate the legalistic farce of Kentucky's "neutrality," Paducah was the first port on the southern banks of the Ohio River to be occupied by invading troops. With his gunboats and a flotilla of transports, Grant came from Cairo and took it after dumping over a few shells at a Confederate flag defiantly floating from a tall staff on the waterfront.*

---

* Concerning that same flag there was a little epic. The ladies of the town had donated their silk dresses for its making. When Grant's fleet came and the panic-stricken citizens fled, all directions, it was forgotten. So old Mrs. Jarrett—"Aunt Em" she was to half of Paducah—raced in her carriage to the wharf. She had with her a scared negro boy. She forced him to climb the tall pole and fetch down the precious colors. He feared mightily the shells whistling past, but feared more his grim mistress standing down below with the long snapper of her buggy whip flicking up at his naked shanks. So she got the flag and got away with it. Some Northern sympathizers betrayed her identity to the first landing party and a squad

Possibly also one purpose of the brief bombardment was to put the fear of the Lord into the civilian population who by a large majority so thoroughly were anti-Unionist in their sympathies—and their attitudes—that Paducah was known as "Little Charleston" and all that adjacent tip of the state was called "The South Carolina of the West." This seemed strange too, seeing that here along the uppermost bounds of slave territory, one would have looked for countering geographical influences from Illinois just across the river, and from Indiana only a short distance upstream, while in the opposite directions the debatable land of Missouri lay even closer. Central Kentucky was divided and the mountains of eastern Kentucky might be overwhelmingly for the Federal cause, as they were, but these counties down in the toe of the sock showed their sentiments in the latest election before avowed hostilities began, by sending to Washington as their representative an ardent advocate of secession—with a thumping big plurality behind him. To this modern day, Democratic spellbinders love to proclaim that of all the congressional districts in the whole country, this is the only one which, neither when armed troops held the polling places, nor in the Carpetbagger period following, nor in any subsequent political upheaval, ever went Republican, although when Al Smith ran in 1928, it did have rather a close call from going Baptist. Indeed, it was said certain unreconstructable veterans insisted on voting for Jeff Davis every presidential election—until weaned on William Jennings Bryan.

So as I was saying, Paducah, having promptly fallen into Northern hands, seethingly remained in those hands until the end, although twice Forrest invaded it, coming up from Tennessee with his cavalry, and drove the Unionists behind the shelter of their

---

went to her big rambling house up on Island Creek. They came away thwarted. They searched the house and they made threats, but they didn't search Aunt Em who, under her voluminous skirts, was wearing the flag as an extra petticoat. When she died—as a shaver I went to the services—it served her for a shroud. And the two local camps of veterans gave her a soldier's funeral, with all the honors. I remember the bugles playing "Taps" and the volleys fired across the grave. And finally—which wasn't in the regulations—they gave the Rebel Yell.

barracks and temporarily held dominion of the streets while his men collected horseflesh and supplies and the members of one of his units, the Third Kentucky Mounted Infantry, which had been recruited in that immediate vicinity, hugged their homefolks and their sweethearts before the withdrawal southward. At their first time of coming the sweat of fierce fighting yet was on them. That morning they saw their colonel blown in two pieces by a cannon ball within sight of his father's cottage where he had eaten breakfast before leading an abortive assault on the enemy's breastworks. Two weeks more and he would have been a brigadier; his commission was awaiting signatures and seals at Richmond. And some of the ragged gray-jackets who followed him had come back that day to die—as he died—in a rutted byway which as boys they had frolicked through. They still were boys, most of them, with no thatch of beard on their chins; and in that breathing space between the charge and the retreat they whooped and they caroused and told worshiping sidewalk audiences how the blue-bellies had skedaddled from the surprise attack at sunup. Both of my mother's brothers were among those jubilating raiders and one of them, by dint of patriotic perjury, had lied himself into the ranks as a full-fledged buck private before his fifteenth birthday. At eighteen he came out, a top sergeant and a professional gambler of parts.

Let us get back to the main line: On the heels of the original seizure, the churches and the schools, the larger factories and warehouses had been taken over and converted into makeshift hospitals and very soon these overflowed with sick and wounded soldiers, including many prisoners. Being the foremost physician of the community, my grandfather tendered his services to the military authorities and for more than three years, as an unpaid volunteer, he ministered among the sufferers without regard for the uniform which they might have worn. Behold now, how his merciful labors were as bread cast upon the waters.

When, in April, '65, the news came from Appomattox, the commandant of the garrison saw his chance and vindictively he took it. This was a sadistic tyrant whose name almost to this present hour was an abomination in the mouths of the few tottery survivors of those times—they spat when they spoke it. He gave orders that this night every house in the captive but still seethingly rebellious town should be illuminated, top to bottom, in celebration of Lee's surrender. 'Twas a powerfully bitter dose for nine out of ten to swallow but being helpless under harsh bayonet rule, the householders obeyed—with just one classic exception.

My mother often told me how in fear she and her three sisters and her two stepsisters quaked behind curtained and shuttered windows as darkness came on. Presently they were in complete blackness since their twice-widowed father had forbidden that even so much as a tallow tip should burn beneath his roof.

About ten o'clock there was the heavy clunk of marching feet, the rattle of side arms outside, then a knocking on the front door. My grandfather answered the summons. He had been standing by in expectation of it. On the wide porch behind a young lieutenant were ranged a file of soldiers.

"Doctor," said the officer and saluted him, "this is the only house along this street that is not lit up. Perhaps—" his tone seemed friendly, eager almost—"perhaps you did not hear of the order?"

"Young man," he answered, "my two sons are somewhere in the Deep South—if they're still alive.* If they are still alive, I trust

---

* They were still alive. Johnston's broken army having surrendered, they rode home from North Carolina. The elder, Dr. John Bartlett Saunders, who had been a regimental surgeon, went to Honolulu—a tremendous pilgrimage for those days—and having regained the health which had been impaired in service, made a name for himself there doing research on leprosy, and when he died was court physician to the King of the Sandwich Islands.

The younger brother, Lewis, wandered westward and eventually disappeared without trace. First though, according to a tale which filtered back, he did some distinguished gun-fighting in Arizona mining camps and gambling houses. As a youngster I was quite proud of this shadowy reputation of my vanished uncle as likewise I glorified in the more authentic claim that he and a chum of his, "Red" Klaw, the son of a German-Jewish clothing merchant of antebellum Paducah, were the two youngest regularly enlisted volunteers—not drummer boys or couriers, but musket-toting soldiers—that Kentucky sent to the Confederacy. "Red" Klaw had a younger brother, Marc Klaw, who emigrated to New York and became senior member of the great theatrical firm of Klaw and Erlanger.

they still are fighting for the Southern Confederacy. I will not go through with this mockery."

"Doctor, if after this warning, you still refuse to put lights in your windows, it is my painful duty to instruct these men here to set fire to this house. Won't you save me from a most unwelcome task?"

Granddad shook his obstinate head. "I only ask that you give me time to get my daughters and my servants out," he said.

The unhappy lieutenant drew the older man aside, beyond earshot of his squad.

"Doctor Saunders," he said, "you don't know me from Adam, but I know about you. Last year my younger brother was brought here, wounded in both legs. One of these slaughter-house hands they call a contract surgeon wanted to operate on him—wanted to amputate. You stepped in; took him over as your own patient. You not only saved his legs for him, you saved his life. That damned butcher would have killed him. We owe you an eternal debt of gratitude—he does, I do, our old mother up in Michigan does. Doctor, go inside and stay there—you and your whole household. Stay there no matter what you may hear outside here."

Next morning the proofs of what had gone on during the night were revealed in scorched and smoke-blackened patches upon the clapboarded walls. At risk of a court-martial for himself, that Michigan lad had sent a corporal to kindle a blaze against the foundations at the end and the sides, then following along behind the torchbearer, he had, with his own hands, put out the flames. The charred evidences showed that a dozen times he must have done this. Of course, the men under him were bound to know what was afoot. But they must have liked their lieutenant mighty well, for he was not reported on, was never punished.

Verily, it must have been through my two grandmothers that the aristocratic affection got into our strain. For both of them, it would appear, belonged to "old Southern Families." By the way, who ever heard of a new Southern family? Already I think I've made it plain that my Grandfather Saunders was a simple and direct soul, a man without guile and incapable of arrogance. And by all I ever heard, my paternal grandfather Robert Livingston Cobb was genuinely pleased to call himself a commoner. Many of us unwittingly reveal the vanity we would hide under a cloak of falsified humility. In my time I've known men who'd spend congenial hours telling me how modest they were. But in the case of this grandparent of mine I'm inclined to believe his customary attitude did not typify the posings of a secret egotist. He may have taken a suitable satisfaction in his estate as a successful merchandiser and exporter and steamboat owner and, before comparative adversity came upon him, as the wealthiest taxpayer and the largest landowner in a wideish area, but he appeared rather more gratified that his progenitors mainly had been plain yeomen and honest artisans than that on the distaff side certain remoter ancestors had figured actively in the making-over of a neglected poor dependency of the Crown into a sturdy little state. For his mother's grandfather was Thomas Chittenden, first governor of Vermont, and two of her uncles, Martin Chittenden and Jonas Galusha, also governed it; and her father was "Old Rifle" Isaac Clark, a doughty sharpshooter who fought in three wars, once against the French and Indians and twice against the British, and wound up a militia general.

But I'm reasonably convinced that by his wife these somewhat notable personages of an earlier time must privately have been classified as Yankee upstarts—not blue bloods but blue noses. For this high-headed grandmother of mine claimed for herself a line of Old Dominion planters and warriors and statesmen who, in their turns, invariably had wed with seemly ladies. Or at least I've been told that this was the impression more or less subtly conveyed by her in her general walk and conversation. Back in 1811, when there was a tragic break in the gubernatorial succession, her father, Colonel Linah Mims, for a period of weeks had, as a sort of stopgap functionary, bridged the vacancy and occupied the executive mansion at Richmond, and by her estimates one acting temporary governor of such a high-toned commonwealth as Virginia—even though without official title or actual warrant of authority—outranked, for family-tree purposes, any given number of regularly elected governors of such a huckstering state as Vermont.

As a young girl, she was brought over the mountains; grew up in Kentucky; was married there and raised a large family and in the fullness of time died there at seventy-odd, but to the day of her death, did she in her travels meet someone who inquired whence she came, it is recorded that invariably she answered: "I am from Virginia, stopping at present in Kentucky."

Also it was narrated that once a native son, being somewhat nettled by her imperious airs, said: "Mrs. Cobb, you're forever speaking of the First Families of Virginia. Weren't there ever any second-class families there?"

"Oh, yes," she told him, "formerly there were. But they all moved out here to Kentucky."

Tracing the other wing, my mother's mother was a Carolinian by way of Tennessee and she was of the Clan Douglas and like all the Douglases of whom I have ever heard, freely acknowledged direct descent from Ellen Douglas. By all reports, neither was she behindhand in taking merit unto herself for patrician lineage. I imagine it must have been because of her wishes, that my Grandfather Saunders built for her the most imposing house in the then small and straggly river landing of Paducah. I suspect a humbler domicile might have suited him as well, he who had been born in the fringes of a ramping wilderness and reared in most primitive surroundings among people who might have been plebeians but, if they were, didn't know it and would have tied into any superior-minded interloper who dared intimate they weren't as good as everybody else—or just a mite better.

But, for my oncoming generation, his wife's achieved architectural dreams were to prove a marvelous benefaction. Nowhere on the American map, I insist, could there have been a playground more admirably devised to fulfill the cravings of healthy, adventure-seeking youngsters of half a century ago, or thereabouts. Bear with me while I sketch in its manifold attractions: In brief, a farm in miniature set up in the midst of a growing town; two crowded acres within their high planked palings; at the front, facing the street, the angular ten-room house; and packed in behind it and all roundabout such luring joys as the odorous cow shed; the big stable, with a gorgeous grand hayloft; the slatted corncrib—my grandfather kept fearsome pet blacksnakes there to prey on the rats and the mice; fruit trees to be pillaged and shade trees to be climbed; tangles of unshorn shrubbery; a grape arbor and a tool hutch; and at the bottom of the small, compactly planted orchard, a dumpy white structure delicately known as "Miss Jones'." Then also the smokehouse, its sooty rafters jeweled with fat hams like eardrops and pendent strips of cured middling meat and necklaces of homemade sausages; the well house, with its crocks and pans and jugs and buckets submerged in bricked shallow tanks and it such a lovely cool retreat for sultry days; a densely populated chicken yard; lofty manure piles in the horse lot and beneath the corner eaves, where the tin gutter spouts come down from the roof, open barrels to catch rain water and incidentally to provide breeding places for millions of wiggle-tailed larvae, so that, according to their ordained seasons, we had on the premises an abundance of houseflies and mosquitoes of our own raising. There were no wire screens—they hadn't been thought up yet by some ingenious Yankee—but only mosquito nets for the beds and at mealtimes a languid little black servitor to wave a peacock-tail fan above the dining table. She didn't always keep the flies away from the victuals, but she made them nervous and unsettled in their conduct. Those were the good old days before germs were formally recognized.

5

AMANDA GIVEN OF COLOR

Six days out of seven the jumbled enclosure which I have sought to describe yielded forth its pleasures: fit dens for robbers, slanted ship-decks for pirates, delightful ambuscades for lurking Indians. But on the seventh day it turned to a prison compound and reasonably indulgent mothers and aunts were transformed as the keepers of an unyielding and rigorous code. For, mind you, this household then all at once became as straitly blue-stockinged as any to be found this side of Aberdeen. We didn't spend the Sunday; we kept the Sabbath and that, if you'll take my solemn word for it, was a vastly different thing.

Through the morning we were pressed for most unwilling attendance at a certain old meetinghouse. This was a gaunt, slab-sided, hopelessly homely structure with a spire like a chiding finger and an entryway like a dark tunnel and a balcony that suggested an overgrown martin box. It was aloft there that the negro worshipers sat, mostly old family servants who followed the faith of their employers. The window panes were painted a numb cold gray, the idea, I take it, being to shut out the paganish sunshine or perhaps to provide a matching gloom for the spirits of troubled Fundamentalists. Its pews truly were penitential perches for uncomfortable, dangle-legged youth, being high-seated and straight-backed and very hard on juvenile flesh. I don't seem to recall any cushions. But I do recall the passionless congregational singing and the pastoral prayers that ran as serials, and the blistering potbellied stoves in the winter, and in summer the slow-timed hypnotizing movements of a whole forest of palm-leaf fans. If a woman were in mourning or if she were matured in age, the blade of her fan invariably had a border of black tape sewed on it. And always somebody coughing or else a blowing of the human nose in a subdued and half-hearted way.

I place just two patches of color to relieve the drabbed austerity of that antique kirk. One was a pulpit cushion of dark red velvet upon which The Book rested and the other, framed in black walnut and hung above the inner door lintel where all coming hither might see and heed, was a scroll audaciously done in blue and green letters, which read:

GENTLEMEN WILL NOT USE
TOBACCO IN THE HOUSE OF GOD.

By which, of course, was meant gentlemen who chewed. Most gentlemen did, and some there were moreover who dipped snuff.

First off, to the dismal accompaniment of bells sounding from the steeple, came Sunday school and that, or such was the feeling, lasted for month on weary month. Then the smaller children were taken away and Nature or their nurses revived them out of their comatose state. But the rest of us must stay on to be sermonized by Dr. Hendrick. Now he was a dominie out of Scotland herself and behaved as such. He never preached for less than a century. Sometimes, or so it seemed to me, he preached on and on until the present Christian Era threatened to run out before he ran down. He was a dear kindly gentle old man with the face of a saint and delighted in good deeds, and so lavishly he dealt out such doctrinal beatitudes as Infant Damnation and Predestination and on occasion painted a graphic picture of that most awful nethermost pit of the Calvinistic Gehenna wherein demons, all hoofed and horned, stoked the flames, and tormented souls, like squirming frog legs, grilled eternally on the red-hot hobs of a Hell which had no fire escapes to it. I don't believe I could have been more than eight years old, or maybe ten, when some vague adolescent sense of the plain fitness and fairness of things bade me secretly to revolt against a plan of unutterable, unendable punishment for poor faulty fallible mortals, let alone for innocent babes whose baptisms had been overlooked. How kindly folk, otherwise compassionate and charitable toward their fellow creatures, ever swallowed down such bitter theological boluses without gagging is a matter which will

puzzle me as long as I live. But they did, for many a long year, until
a tempered and more merciful interpretation of the Laws and the
Scriptures came to be accepted, and their creed lost some of its
harrow teeth.

From church, with the lardy smell of sinners fried on both sides
still warm in our impressionable young noses, we marched homeward, two by two along the narrow pavement, like so many down-
cast lambkins going into the Ark and, if it were warm weather,
hating every tortured step we took because of our toes that were so
cramped and burning. Except on high days and holy days we boys
went barefoot from mid-April until school "took up" in September
and those thick stockings and those stiff shoes were as penances
added to a routine already distressful enough.

Arriving, we ate of the enormous Sunday dinner—all the
vegetables available, up to nine or ten separate varieties; chicken or
pork products or both; at least two kinds of hot bread, usually fat
biscuits and crunchy corn pones; and dessert and preserves and the
like; and, as inevitable as the cruet stand rising like a lighthouse in
the center and the moored regatta of pickle dishes surrounding it,
a pitcher of New Orleans molasses and a cold-boiled ham. Indeed,
no matter what else might be provided, the molasses pitcher and the
boiled ham were staple fixtures on that table, three times a day,
every day in the year.*

---

* Kentuckians always have been sincere and painstaking trench-
ermen. A hundred and odd years ago, at Whitley Hill on the Old
Wilderness Trail which Daniel Boone traced into the Blue Grass
country, Colonel William Whitley, a transplanted Virginian but
already saturated in the Kentucky tradition, used to run, once a
year, for his guests and neighbors, a series of races over his own
private track starting as soon as there was light enough to see by.
During the early morning, coffee and toddies and hot snacks were
served but breakfast proper ensued as soon as the last race had
been run. As copied from the Whitley family records, this was an
average menu:

Chicken soup with rice . . . Baked Ohio River salmon . . . Bacon,
Cabbage and Beans . . . Barbecued Lamb . . . Roast Wild Duck, apple
sauce . . . Roast Wild Turkey, cranberry sauce . . . Roast Beef . . .
Broiled Squirrel . . . Leg of Bear . . . Baked O'Possum with Sweet
Potatoes; Roasting Ears, Hominy, Boiled Potatoes. Baked Sweet

Howsomever the scope of this vast meal never daunted me. From my earliest recollectable moment I was ever a sincere and earnest eater, and while with age my hair has thinned and the few remaining teeth have become stately ruins, I am proud and happy to announce that my gastric juices are still quite boyish. For me and for my contemporaries the welcomed interlude of dinner ended all too soon because immediately thereafter our gorged and distended warders reinaugurated the grim Sabbatical ritual, with all its abhorent rules and regulations, and this continued through the dragging long "evening." In our vocabulary "evening" began at the turn of midday and lasted until twilight; and after that it was "nighttime." We hardly knew there was so snobbish a term as "afternoon." Certainly we never used it ourselves. That practice was for benighted people from "up North" who naturally wouldn't know any better.

Observe now how Sunday from the nooning on became one prolonged endurance trial: We might not play at indoor games because such would be grievous affronts before the watchful eyes of the late John Knox and all the lesser luminaries of a hand-picked Heavenly Host. We might not cavort about or whistle or make loud outcry. We might not even scratch ourselves, or at least not in an open manner, yet under the twin spells of humidity and monotony, we itched mightily, as who would not? If we sat very quietly, which meant very miserably, we might read books but only such books as contained Bible lessons and godly tales and uplifting examples; or Aesop's Fables which already I knew off by heart; or ponderous history books, or the collected works of certain standard poets, Longfellow and Wordsworth and Sidney Lanier for choice. Once on a bored prowl in the "lumber room" I unearthed a large volume devoted to diseases of the horse. In sheer desperation I read

---

Potatoes, Hot Cakes, Corn Dodgers, Buttermilk, Plum Pudding, rum sauce; Punkin Pie, rum sauce; Log Cabin Pie, Assorted Cakes, Fruits, Vanilla Ice Cream, Coffee, Apple Jack, Claret, Transylvania Bitters, Peach Brandy and Honey, Old Bourbon Whisky, Port and Champagne.

Not even a Kentuckian could think of anything to ask for after that breakfast—unless it might be bicarbonate of soda and a place to lie down.

it through from cover to cover. So I learned about glanders from there, also distemper, farcy and the botts.

As a great concession, one which tottered on the verge of down-right evil-doing and only granted after a grave counsel of our elders, we were permitted to frequent an old and creaky wooden swing which, providentially shielded from the public gaze, stood behind the kitchen. But this boon had its deadening limitations. For we might not "pump 'way up high" or "run under," might not indulge in shrill speech or boisterous antics while thus employed. After more than fifty years I still associate those dolorous summer-time Sundays with a conglomerate of indented impressions—little heat waves jigging in the distance, little dust devils whirling through the slumbering street, and up in the silver-leaf poplars, locusts sawing tiny gashes in the broody silence; whiffs from heat-baked horsehair furniture and various hot varnishy smells oozing out through the slitted parlor door; the snoring of torpid adults as they stretched on sofas or hunched up in tilted chairs; the pangs of prickly heat under our starchy stiff linen collars and down our dripping spinal columns; and always the agonized whine of its warped thole pins as that decrepit swing traveled slowly to and fro, to and fro, while despondently and yawningly one of us "let the cat die."

Once in a while there was a respite for the establishment's har-assed little inmates. My grandfather had a moral ordinance of his own which he lived and which bore no religion's herd mark; and he might select one of us to accompany him on those delectable buggy rides of his. Then again my father would scheme on our behalf, for he had been raised in the Episcopal flock—with Cathol-icism further back—and privately entertained heretical views touch-ing on the stricter dogmas. There were illustrious occasions when he smuggled us out—my older sister, my younger brother and I, and often a swarm of cousins—through a broken board in the high back fence and took us on past the crawfish towers and dried-up mud holes of the simmering municipal commons to a friendly wood-land where we indulged in such heathenish offendings as wading in a branch and chasing minnows across its gravelly shoals and "chunking" at squirrels and in general reverted to a state of riotous savagery. But not too often did he dare repeat this outrageous kidnaping for fear of stout disapproval at home and the criticisms of properly scandalized neighbors.

Still and all, for every seventh day of stiff statutory discipline, there were six compensating weekdays made all the sweeter by contrast, when within limits, we might live our own natural, unruly lives amid the facilities of that cluttered venue. Two who aided and abetted us in these endeavors were Mandy and Uncle Rufus. Mandy was the fractious but affectionate despot of the kitchen department who'd spank us with enthusiasm for trespassing on her domain and then as willingly would gird up her loins and roll up her sleeves and charge out into the alley to lead a counter-attack against any intruders who had annoyed or threatened us. One of the worst whippings I ever got—and I got plenty—was when my mother caught up with me after Mandy, vengefully waving a skillet, pursued me out of her kingdom wherefrom I had just surreptitiously borrowed a piping hot dried-apple turnover—what a benighted ignoramus of a Northerner would call "a fried pie." It wasn't so much for filching the turnover that I was switched; that was but a minor misdeameanor. It was for the infinitely worse crime of calling Mandy "an ole black nigger" as I fled with my spoils.

Right now I can shut my eyes and see her, all gnarled and painfully kinked, and so bossy and loudmouthed and competent. Perhaps because sundry forward-looking sophisticates of her race were inclined to sneer at what they called a "handkercheef-haided darky" she rarely wore a bandana turban. She preferred a puckered skullcap made from the leg of somebody's discarded stocking and for special outdoor occasions a man's battered slouch hat perched on top of this fez-like effect. The moderns were licked then; they had no word for that combination.

She was chronically rheumatic and what was rare among negroes, a dyspeptic, and she was as cranky as all get-out; but for forty-two uninterrupted years she served one branch or another of our family and died, an enfeebled pensioner, in that service. Two weeks before she went where the faithful loving souls of this earth go, my uncle wrote her will for her. The estate consisted of her life's savings—one hundred and twenty dollars in cash. Of this she decreed that one hundred dollars be spent in burying her tired-out body. The residue she left to her "Baby," meaning by that the youngest of my girl cousins who had been her special charge from the hour when the child's mother died. The child wasn't a child any more; was by now a woman grown. But to old Mandy, she still was "Baby."

There was a punitive justice in the disposition Mandy made of her hoard. She left out her only blood kin and for a reason. A few months earlier she went, lamed as she was, on the first extended journey of her entire career. By invitation she went to St. Louis to visit her niece. She failed to return though on the date appointed, nor was there any word from the absentee although letters of inquiry were written. The whole family grew anxious.

Opportunely, a prosperous and highly respected hack-driver called on my uncle at his law office.

"Judge Bagby," he told him, "I knows you-all at your house must be frettin' about Mandy. I found out about her when I was over there last week. Them two low-flung scalawags—her niece and her niece's husband—has practically got that pore ole crippled-up thing under lock and key. She's perishin' to git back here where she belongs at and they won't let her. Mandy never told a shore-nuff downright lie in her life, but I reckin she did talk kind of bigotty about whut-all money she's got laid by and they're pesterin' after her night and day to give a writin' leavin' it to 'em after she's gone or else let 'em have it right away. And she jest natchelly pinin' away frum bein' homesick and fightin' off that there pair of blood-suckers."

"Andy," said my uncle, reaching for his pocketbook, "how soon can you get back over yonder again?"

"They's a train leavin' fur St. Louie about two hours frum now, suh."

"You be on it."

Hackman Andy's warrant was to secure the prisoner's release by threats or main force or, if need be, by appeal to the authorities—he carried credentials vouching for him—and to fetch her home at the earliest possible moment. Late that night he raised my uncle on the long distance telephone.

"Judge," he said, "we're 'rivin', Mandy and me, Sunday mornin'—that's day after tomorrow. We could git there tomorrow evenin' but she p'intedly says we got to wait fur Sunday. And nothin' would do her but I must call you up fust and give you the schedule about her 'rival. I can't make out whut's in her funny ole haid—mebbe she's gittin' flighty—but this here is the way she says ever'thin' is got to be 'ranged. I warns you, suh, they's quite a passel of fussin' 'round to be done."

And so there was. Nevertheless a puzzled household carried out the transmitted directions, just so. Sunday afternoon when the indomitable old crone had been put to bed, and she all worn down bodily, but swollen with a tremendous exaltation, she said to one of my cousins:

"Douglas, honey, go git some paper and some ink and take your pen in hand and write me a letter to that wuthless tore-down limb of a niece of mine. Put it down, word fur word, jest lak I tells you."

Here—and some of us gloatingly can still quote its pregnant passages—is what she dictated:

"Gal, lissen unto me. The chillun meets me at the depot. They teks and loads me in an open carriage behind the two finest w'ite hosses they is in this entire city. They drives me past my church jest ez church is lettin' out so that one and all kin see me ridin' by in due state. They gits me home and a refreshin' glass of blackberry cordial and a bokay of flowers is waitin' fur me on the bureau of my own room. I reclines there, not doin' nothin' a-tall, twell it comes dinnertime and then a feast is made in my honor. I has fried chicken and whut-all fixin's goes with it. I has boughten ice cream and floatin' island and lemon-jelly layer cake. And these is my own w'ite folks that you kept tellin' with your own lyin' tongue they didn't keer nothin' fur me no more. And now, I'se jest layin' back takin' my ease and the chillun is standin' by waitin' on me hand and foot.

"Trustin' these few lines will find you the same, I remains your lovin' aunt that used to be but ain't never ag'in goin' be your lovin' aunt, respectfully, AMANDA GIVEN."

6

WHEN FEAR CAME INTO THE WORLD

OUR SECOND black mainstay and refuge in the time of storm, was cast in a temperamental mold very different from the managerial Mandy's. For Uncle Rufus was tolerant of small transgressions and ready to shield the transgressors. He combined a great personal dignity with a great humility, and that, I'd say, is an admirable consolidation not so common as it might be, in persons of any color. He had belonged originally to my grandfather's second wife, the Widow Lockett of Virginia, and on her death my Grandfather Saunders bought him from the estate to keep a family from being divided. When Freedom came Rufus elected to stay on with his former master. He stayed on long past his time of real usefulness but continued to enjoy all the perquisites. So loyalty was repaid with loyalty.

Aloof and grave, he pottered about the place, raking up leaves, fetching in kindling, running errands—no, that's wrong; ambling slowly on errands—and doing such-like odd jobs. He was tall and almost fleshless but carried his meager shape most erectly. From age his skin had taken on a curious grayish cast like a dusty mold. About his features there was hardly a traceable suggestion of the negroid. He had an aquiline nose and a high narrow forehead and a Coptic profile. You see faces like his on Egyptian mummy cases. He told me his mother had been an "Affikin princess" and how her neck bore scars where she, being of chieftain blood, had fought against her iron collar in the blackbirder's chain gang until the metal bit deeper and deeper into the galled flesh. This may well have been true for in various of his ways Uncle Rufus seemed very close to the jungle.

He rarely would come to the kitchen, preferring to cook messes

56

of his own concoction in the tumble-down one-room cubicle which was the sole surviving unit of what, before Emancipation, had been a short row of quarters for the domestic staff. He lived alone there, fending for himself and resenting intrusion by the other servants. Except in the hottest weather there nearly always were logs burning in his fireplace and although he had a mountainous "feather-tick" on his bedstead and a wealth of gay rag quilts, frequently he slept on the bare floor with his head muffled in a coverlid and his naked feet thrust into the warm ashes. Or he might choose to hunker down by the mantel shelf, for hours on end staring into the flicker of the little bright flames.

Sometimes I found him in that somber posture when, filled with a delicious anticipatory horror, I came in the twilight to make him tell me "buggerman tales" while I squatted at his bony knees and the fire burned lower and from the corners the thickened shadows stole out across the planking, drawing nearer and nearer until I was in a very frenzy of shuddering.

First though I might join him at his eating. Supper in the "big house" never had such savor as when I slipped away from the table, leaving my portion half-eaten, and went to share with him drainings of "pot licker" out of a besmudged and dented kettle, and the hoe-cake which he baked on the hearth and then wiped on his shirt sleeve to rid it of the grit—but never got quite all the grit off; and the roasted sweet potatoes which he raked out from the embers and then peeled with a deft thumbnail. Fingering hot things didn't seem to bother him. I've seen him catch up a blazing spark to light his pipe with, or with the flat of his hand pat down a bank of smouldering cinder-fluff and never wince.

And then, if the mood was on him and after he had been sufficiently teased and pleaded with, he would launch his storytelling. It was through him that fear, stark hair-lifting fear, first came into my world, for he peopled it with all manner of hideousities. Here was no gentle, whimsical fabulist of the Uncle Remus school; here was a realist dealing in the pure essences of Ethiopian nightmare and making dreadful the wild things and the harmless tame things, as well. On a Friday, from noon on, you never saw a jay bird except he were on his way to the Bad Place to tattle to his master, the Devil; and you couldn't kill a rain crow with any bullet except a

silver bullet because he also was under Old Nick's protection. It
was a bad sign, a powerfully bad sign, did an owl light on the roof,
and any bird flying inside a house meant bad luck, too. But a dog
baying under the windows of a sickroom foretold death for the
one who was sick. Cats in general, but black cats in particular,
loved to invade a room where a corpse was laid out and squat on
the coffin lid and squall. Another specialty of a cat was to stretch
itself on a baby's breast and suck the breath of life out of the child
while it slept. Toad-frogs carried pizen bags in their backs—years
later I found out this, in a way of speaking, was a fact. All snakes
whatsoever were highly venomous but especially the hoop snake
which put its tail in its mouth and rolled downhill at you and if you
were smart enough to dodge behind a tree then the hoop snake's
deadly horn, which jutted forth from its head, would stick in the
bark and before sundown the leaves of that tree would all be withered and within a week the wood would start rotting. You couldn't
burn the wood either, it just crumbled away to nothing, leaving a
loathsome stink behind. The little green praying mantis—only I
knew him as a devil's race horse—would bite you in a minute and
make a running sore which never healed; and the most trivial of
lizards, sunning herself on the garden walk, was a dangerous
"scoripin" although perhaps not quite so evilly inclined as some
other members of the menagerie that might be mentioned and, in
their proper order, invariably were.

But far and away the most awful, the most gruesome and grisly
of all were the creatures that wore human shapes. With an instinctive but sure dramatic craft, Uncle Rufus saved back these monsters
for his climax. The proceedings followed invariably a certain rote:
To start with, the perilous parade through the animal kingdom, then
the introduction of such comparatively minor performers as "witch-
in' wimmin" who worked wicked spells and "hoodoos" who brewed
lovers' charms and mixed villainous "goofer-powders." I knew what
would be coming next and shook in all my members, yearning for
and yet dreading the elaborated cataloguing of the prize specimens
of his collection—"ghostes" that walked by moonlight in the burying ground; "hags" that left a hot breath like a gush from a furnace
as they flitted across the road just ahead of some lonesome traveler;
"ha'nts" that throve in deserted houses where a suicide or a murder

had been committed, but preferably a murder, and clanked heavy chains and moaned in the walls and made a door open and close yet with no hand seen to touch it.

And, deliberately held in reserve until the very end, I shudderingly heard again about "Ole Raw Haid an' Bloody Bones" and "Plateye." Raw Haid was a thing that had been flayed alive, no skin left anywhere on him but only twitchy, oozing tissues. He delighted to lurk in dark places and steal up from behind on small boys who had been bad and clamp down on them with his dripping red paws and bear them off to be devoured at leisure in his den underground. Plateye was a ghoul of so frightful an aspect as to be past describing, and anyhow none who ever met Plateye face to face had survived to tell what he looked like. Still there was a rumor that he used burning coals for eyes in his eye sockets and had tushes longer than a boar pig's. He took his victims apart while they lived, snapping their fingers like stick candy and plucking off ears like ripe figs. He then ate the remains and hollered for more, being chronically hungry.

Sooner or later the shouted summons would come—a grief and a shock to my enthralled soul—that I was to go and be put to bed. But ere I quit the dubious shelter of that cabin there was a protective program to be carried out. It couldn't have been more than twenty feet from the tip of the latticed porch of the kitchen wing to Uncle Rufus' threshold, yet before I ventured to travel that short span Mandy or Donie, the nurse, must station herself at the porch end holding aloft a coal-oil lamp and Uncle Rufus must stand in his open door, with the glare of his poked-up logs shining through, and then, with my heart up in my gasping throat and my marrows jellifying from terror, I would dart along the lighted pathway, yelling every step I took, and hurl myself against the legs of her who awaited me, and try to hide my quaking person in her skirts.

And the very next chance I got I'd go back, like a drug addict, for a fresh spasm. I wonder how many years' growth I lost under Uncle Rufus' fascinating treatments.

Here's the right place to make a belated and until now an unrevealed confession. I was past eighteen and upwards of six lanky feet tall and the downy beginnings of the cherished makings of a future mustache were sprouting on my upper lip before I got over

flinching when called on to enter an empty dark room. I had literally to drive myself to it.

Getting drowned, or to all interests and purposes, practically
getting drowned, was another thing which put an even deeper dent
in my brain, for it has endured to this good day. I was perhaps fourteen years old and just learning to paddle "dog-fashion." A number
of us had secured the loan of a skiff without saying anything to the
skiff's owner about it, and cruised over to a sandbar where the Tennessee merged its blue with the Ohio's muddier volume, directly in
front of town. Having waded out to a breast-high depth, I took a
few splashing strokes parallel to the shore and confidently let down
my probing toes to find the gently sloped bottom. There was no
bottom, sloped or otherwise. I was in a "step-off," where the
treacherous current had scooped a deepish cavity among the hidden
shallows. Such unsuspected pitfalls sometimes form in an hour
especially when the stream is in freshet.

In that first disconcerting instant I didn't altogether go into
panic. Very vividly I remember how I tried to bring my legs up by
thrusting with the soles of my feet against the water and how I tried
with my arms to stroke my way back to safety. But a swift cross
eddy had formed above the undermined shoal and this little whirlpool had caught me and was carrying me along. I opened my mouth
to call for help. Half a dozen companions were taking sunbaths not
fifty yards distant, and some larger boys who swam well were sporting about on beyond me. But the water ran into my mouth and
smothered my cries to faint gurglings. I went under, bobbed up,
struggling hard; went under again.

You have heard—you must have heard it because everybody else
has—how drowning persons always come up three times and how
all in a flash their lives pass in review before their despairing eyes. I
am here to testify that these phenomena do not necessarily occur.
At least in my case they did not.

For I'm sure I got my nose above the surface a score of times
and I know my chief mental sensation, aside from a mounting realization of my danger, was resentment toward those others for cal-
lously disregarding my plight. All mixed in with this was a darting
regret that my mother would grieve so when she got the news.
There formed before me a most clearly imagined picture of our

front porch with my mother and one of my sisters sitting there in rocking chairs and a neighbor—it was Mr. Ed Noble, who lived over the way, and I visioned him perfectly—hurrying up the walk to tell them I was dead.

That was the last I remembered except the water going different shuttling colors—red, blue, purple, green—and then shifting to a black pall which very gently, very slowly, enveloped me, so that I quit fighting and let the blackness close over my head. I was going elsewhere and now I didn't much care.

It must have been about that time that the rescuer arrived. One of my mates on the bar finally arrived at the conclusion that not for the fun of the thing was I imitating an agitated fishing cork out in the supposed safety zone but might be in earnest about it. So he raised the alarm and the best swimmer in the lot got there just as I ceased to be actively interested in the proceedings. He saw my descending topknot before it altogether vanished and made a short dive and got me by the hair. He said I grabbed one of his wrists with both my hands as he heaved me up and kept my grip on him until he had dragged me ashore. So he was surprised to note that I seemed entirely unconscious. But of these latter details I was not cognizant. Some ten minutes later my mind began dizzily to function. I was being emptied. Two youngsters, holding me by the legs, had tilted me upside down and a sizable trickle, yes, a streamlet really, was gurgling out of me and I was beginning to hurt amidships where I had been rolled back and front, belly downward on a cottonwood drift-log having much rough bark still on it. Within two hours we were over on the Illinois mainland and I was industriously engaged, along with several confederates, in stealing melons out of a farmer's field, and never felt sprier in my life although afflicted with an incurable thirst which seemed strange seeing how much of the Ohio River I had swallowed that same morning.

The effect of that experience is still a part of me and has been since the hour the event happened and always will be. For timidity is branded into my faculties. I reckon you might call it mental hydrophobia since I am beset by a menace that my intelligence tells me does not exist—which doesn't make the menace any less real. It was years before I conquered that implanted distrust of water in large quantities to a point where I learned to swim, but have remained always an awkward and overly cautious swimmer. I have never dived—and never shall. Over and over again have I tried to. But my obstinate spirit rebels and my shameless will power balks like a mule. Even though I stand flatfooted in a swimming pool and merely try to sink my head under and straighten and strike out, the effort results in humiliating failure. As my nostrils fill and the water pulses against my eardrums I am again a frantic drowning boy and up I come, all quaky and wabbly and cursing my fool self for being so contemptible a craven. I've even made the experiment of kneeling in a filled bathtub and submerging my person, face downward. But it's no use. Besides, the attitude is not dignified and somebody might come in and catch me. I guess you might say that the only aquatic pursuit at which I really excel is gargling.

I take it that courage is a relative term, that in each one of us a lion and a mouse lie down together and under contrariwise impulses one or the other will rise up and show itself and sometimes both together at once. Making the application personal, I'm trying to sift out from a jumble of more or less fixed impressions of boyhood some of my own psychological reactions and reflexes. For an outstanding instance, I was an indifferent not to say lackadaisical fisticuffer. It wasn't so much that I feared the other boy. Nor did the prospect of the bruises and scratches which he might inflict daunt me. Without whimpering too much, I could endure pain as well as the next one. Rather it was the fear of being licked—the mortification of it, the blow to my vanity, and worst of all, the ridicule of the crowd. So inevitably I already was half-licked. Yet beforehand I often welcomed the prospect of conflict. I was forever provoking the issue and then at the crucial moment going suddenly cold with the dread of defeat. I figure I lost fewer arguments and won fewer fights than any boy ever born in McCracken County. I may even have been state-wide champion although modesty forbids my taking in that much territory.

I was not timorous about snakes. Indeed as regards snakes I was a gay and gallus young exhibitionist. Yet any snarly little fice-dog yapping at my shrinking calves could run me up a tree. I was none too happy at most deeds requiring bodily risk though when it came to robbing orchards and berry patches I shone forth as the admitted leader of any foraging party. And so on and so forth.

As a correspondent on the Western Front in the Great War I found out at first hand a good deal about the trait which we call bravery and the inter-related trait which we call lack of bravery. For illustration, let us arbitrarily take a formation of one thousand men, organized for war, and trained for war and now shoved into war. As the tumult breaks upon them, five men, say, out of those ranks cannot adjust their nervous organisms to this imminent prospect of destruction which all at once has confronted them. Under the intolerable strain of it they quit in the face of the enemy and we label them with the foul name of coward and visit all manner of disgrace upon them—even to the point of setting them up as targets for a firing squad. Yet under differing circumstances any one of them might show a prowess which would shame the rest of us—might go into a burning building or leap into a torrent to save a stranger's life while we stand by, wringing our impotent hands.

Five others, let us say, of that same thousand have so little imagination, so little perception of the attendant perils that these dull fatalists automatically will lead forlorn hopes or uncomplainingly perish in last ditches without ever, I think, comprehending the fear element which besets their more sensitive and therefore more rational fellow beings. This abnormality passes for gallantry. Perhaps it is gallantry, but in it an ox-like stupidity must surely be a factor.

The remaining nine hundred and ninety are even as you and I, that is, assumed that you also are of the run of the mill and not one of these cited exceptions to the prevalent type. Before the fever of the fighting, which generally makes ravaging, unreasoning beasts of men, has laid hold on the herd, you are scared, horribly scared. Your bowels gripe and grind under a cruel pressure, your scalp crawls on your skull and the sour taste of terror is on your tongue. You recognize that your leg muscles are turning to limber tripe inside the puttees which sustain those uncertain shanks of yours and nothing to be done about it. Every time a shell bursts behind you, you feel your backbone being shredded into a whisk broom. Every time a bullet whistles past in front, you feel it plumping in among your most cherished vital organs. But about then you discover there is just one contradictory thing which you fear more than death or mutilation and that is that the chap next to you may find out how afraid you are. And he is thinking the same thoughts about you and so you both stick it out, each saying to himself, "I'll stay here and I'll go ahead, too, so long as this idiot alongside me does. But, oh boy, if ever this line does break, if ever the rest of this outfit gets fed up on this foolishness and starts falling back, just watch me. I'll show these fellows some running as is running. But damned if I'll be the first one to quit."

Call it self-respect, call it an egotism stronger even than the voice of prudence and the craving for self-preservation, call it the triumph of the spirit over the body, call it sublimated discipline. Call it a sense of duty or heroism or blind stubbornness or whatever you please. Whatever it is, there it is and there's no getting away from it and this I claim is the main reason why a battle sometimes lasts longer than half a minute.

I hark back to the first time these paradoxical symptoms overtook me. That would be in the early fall of 1914 and the scene was a harried strip of terrain just below the Franco-Belgian frontier. Barring some Democratic primary elections back in Kentucky, I had never before been under direct fire. A pair of flattened insteps, among other defects, kept me out of the Spanish-American mess. I strove to convince the examining surgeon that in case of a retreat fallen arches wouldn't keep me from traveling as fast as anybody else whereas for a cautious and circumspect advance toward the stronghold of the foe I should have a decided advantage. But he couldn't see eye to eye with me there, and I lost the argument and Uncle Sam lost a volunteer.

On the other hand, my present companion was John T. McCutcheon, the famous cartoonist and correspondent of the Chicago *Tribune*. As a newspaper observer, John had gone through some sharp engagements in the Philippines and so, compared with me, he was a seasoned campaigner.

We were skirting the forward edge of a supposedly quiet but rather exposed sector, being then with the German forces under extraordinary permits from corps headquarters. All of a sudden, we realized that a considerable amount of unshirted Hades had broken out in our immediate vicinity. Either we had blundered into an area of active hostilities or from their trenches just over yonder the Allies had decided to put up a show on special account of our little band of strollers.

Now we enjoyed a distinct advantage over the masses of German troops about us. Unless ordered away from there, they must stand fast while we, being merely innocent bystanders, as it were, and likewise citizens of a then neutral country, were as free as birds. Within me the temptation to take my foot in my hand and forthwith depart out of that racked bailiwick was well-nigh overpowering. I trust I was not altogether governed by selfishness in this matter. Aside from the personal equation, what of the future of American literature if anything happened to John and me? But our escorts, a group of staff officers, showed no signs of an intent to fall back although none of them seemed notably happy and one or two seemed downright uneasy. I wouldn't in the least blame them for that. It wasn't their business to be killed; some other day perhaps, but not this particular day. This, more or less, was presumed to be in the nature of a pleasure trip, or anyhow a tour of unofficial inspection for the benefit of a brace of foreign journalists. Besides, in a way of speaking, John and I represented an American republic. Nothing was said but simultaneously, I think, we reached the conclusion that, insofar as we might, it devolved upon us to remain outwardly calm, cool and collected before the eyes of all these Germans. We must dissemble; I only hoped a shell wouldn't come along and dissemble me all over the landscape.

So with a make-believe jauntiness we stayed right where we were. And to prove how carefree we were, how casually disposed toward the whole tiresome affair, each of us lighted up one of those saffron-colored tubular objects which Northern Europeans call a cigar. Inasmuch as they labor under the delusion that almost anything shaped like a cigar must be a cigar these Continentals suffocate themselves on inhalations of dried chicory and dessicated stable-sweepings and the other standard ingredients, including the fumes from the straw which thoughtfully is run through the center of the device to make the flues draw better. Such people never have tasted any real tobacco so why should they know how real tobacco tastes?

Thereby adding materially to the horrors of war, we touched off our respective flambeaux, I gripping the butt firmly between my teeth so the teeth couldn't chatter. Even so something was gone wrong with those clenched jaws of mine. Immediately I was embarrassed, not to say chagrined, to note that my cigar persistently performed the most weird acrobatics. With a little sidewise convulsion, it would dip downward until it pointed like a divining rod at the earth, next jerkily would go into reverse and climb upward, higher and higher, so that its swaying tip threatened to scorch my pale nose. At least it felt pale, my nose did. Vainly I strove to check these mechanical betrayals.

And then I beheld how John's cigar was behaving after an erratic fashion fully as high, wide and handsome as my cigar's behavior. In my whole life I was never so proud of myself.

Freakishly enough or perhaps naturally enough, at that identical moment while our cigars were doing their St. Vitus's dance duet, there popped into my consciousness out of a long-gone time a consoling admission which, as a quite small boy, I heard from my father's brother, Major Robert Cobb, late C. S. A. After Pelham of Alabama fell, a good many military experts rated him as the most brilliant and audacious gunner of the Southern armies. Assuredly his comrades of the famous Kentucky Orphan Brigade so rated him. In '61 he shut up his law office to help enlist in his home county an infantry company which, when its members had stolen four field pieces from the complacent and secretly approving state authorities, became Cobb's Battery. Of the hundred and forty men—and boys—who originally composed that oversized unit, just seventeen tramped home following the surrender; the rest all killed, missing, captured or straggled. And of the six commissioned officers who served with it or died with it, four were by blood or marriage related to our tribe. Uncle Bob emerged as chief of artillery on Breckinridge's staff. For valor and dash he got promotions and citations and frequently was mentioned in the dispatches. Boylike, I worshiped him as a demigod who could never have known trepidation. So it had jolted me in that far-distant past—but now it sustained and comforted me—to hear him say:

"Gentlemen, I went through those four years scared half to death every waking moment of the whole time. On the night before an engagement I couldn't sleep for worrying. My legs would hardly lift me to the saddle to ride into action. I reckon my voice trembled every time I gave a command while the fighting was on. I've always figured that, being constituted as I was, I deserved infinitely more credit for doing my duty and occasionally taking chances than any of those congenital idiots I sometimes met up with who didn't have sense enough to be scared."

This adored Uncle Bob was a slim short-coupled figure of a man with a mop of hair which, until the years frostbit it, was as red as his temper and that was very red indeed. He never exactly became reconciled to the outcome of that war. Once from Texas where he spent his latter days, he wrote me deploring that some of our remote New England kindred had been what he was pleased to call "crazy Abolitionist fanatics." I think I caught an echo there of the handed-on sentiments of his Virginia-born mother who, I have gathered, couldn't quite forgive her husband for being of Down-East parentage. In the very last letter he ever wrote me—it was shortly before his death in 1914—he said:

"Son, I've finally gone lame. The fool doctors here call it rheumatism but I know better. The Dutchman who used to make my boots quit business and I committed the error of buying out of a store a pair made by a firm in Fall River, Massachusetts. Those infernal Yankees waited more than fifty years to cripple me up but, by crackies, the persistent scoundrels finally did it!"

If ever, Over There, Uncle Bob met up with any or all three of his pet antipathies among the Union commanders, to wit, in the order named, William Tecumseh Sherman, Ben Butler and Nelson A. Miles, I'll bet there was a frightful row in the Eternal Old Soldiers' Home.*

---

* Had he been alive when it happened, I suspect Uncle Bob would have repudiated me as a traitor, spoiled by sojourning among the Northern hordes. For actually I dedicated a book to Olga Wiborg Fish, one of the most charming and gracious women I ever knew—and she by way of being a blood-kinswoman of both the Shermans and the Miles'.

7

BEFORE I FORGET IT

SITTING here, looking over my shoulder at what lies so far and away behind me, and fumbling with my pen for a proper place to begin this chapter, I conjure up a panorama which in some parts is keen as copperplate and in others is mercifully beclouded so that only the better side of it stands out. It is as though I looked in a mirror and around its edges the mirror is flawed and blurry but in the main it throws out bright facets—the shifting, varying pictures of a border Southern community as that community reflected itself before a youngster's inquisitive eyes in the tag end of the last century.

The Paducah of the eighties and the early nineties—now there, I'm telling you, was a town. It had its baser aspects and after some hazy fashion I must have been aware of them—the petty feuds, the small pretensions, the spleens and jealousies and all such bilious little spites as thrive like bad weeds in any spot where human beings herd together. And beyond doubt it was a sloven and a leisurely town, one that was untidy and content to be untidy. Outside of prim New England, most towns were like that in those distant decades and some of them, in isolated and insulated localities, still are. It was dusty in summer and vilely muddy in winter. There were no sewers for drainage but only open gutters and except when offended nature sent her cold snaps to seal the clotted scum with ice, those gutters stank to the skies.*

---

* Household garbage was kept in casks against the periodical calls of one who cruelly was known as "Miss Slop" Johnston. This was a stooped and withered recluse of fearsome aspect who consolidated these unsavory leavings on a rickety pushcart and as provender for her drove of half-wild razorback hogs, carried them down

But unless your own childhood was unbearably dreary, I'm sure time has compounded for you, as it has for me, a narcotic to deaden the recollection of inconveniences and shortcomings in the environment which suckled us as cubs. Having loyalty and affection to strengthen this agreeable anesthesia within us, we invoke memory, not as an honest scroll unreeling to expose the less pleasant phases

---

to the bottoms below the "Yankee Barracks" where she lived all alone in a forlorn hovel. She was the unofficial sanitary department—and the only one.

The first odorous warning of the old crone's approach would send me scuttling off to hiding, because customarily I nursed a guilty conscience anyhow and the commonest threat in our neighborhood was that if a small boy flagrantly misbehaved, Miss Slop Johnston would tote the offender away in one of her swill barrels and he would vanish forevermore.

There were tales about her past; one that she was the close kinswoman of a famous Southern general. Another and more commonly accepted legend had it that she was the sister of John A. Murrill, that master-criminal of the century before this, whose genius as organizer and director of murderous, larcenous border ruffians made the Al Capones and the Dutch Schultzes of our own Prohibition era seem, by comparison, like mere bungling apprentices. (What a subject for a historical movie John A. Murrill of West Tennessee would make!) Miss Slop rarely spoke, though when she did, used good English and she was kindly enough, I guess, but if you had seen her on her weekly collection tours you might have understood why I dreaded her more than I dreaded such harmless slack-wits as "Cairo Sam" Vance and "Slobber John" and "Bee" Moss and "Crazy Henry" Herscher and "Waterbucket Head" Walter or even glum, black "Wash" Fletcher—they hanged him eventually for butchering a negro girl and to commemorate his crime and his punishment some black minstrel band wrote a song, which still lives in local folklore with its refrain, "Fly high, ole buzzard, you bound to light, some day." Wash lived in a shanty in the hollow at the corner just below our house amongst the "root-and-yarb" mixtures and the love powders that were his stock in trade; and, as it so happened, these other poor eccentrics either lived on our street or frequently traversed it in their aimless wanderings, which helps to explain why I was so often thrown into a jittery state even though sheltered behind a high picket fence.

of our youth along with the pleasant ones, but rather as a kaleido-scope which we shake and, lo, the prisms are all gracious and gay and all shot through with fine brave colors. Glamor is largely a state of mind, I figure. One man beholds a rain of molten gold in the atmosphere of an Indian summer afternoon; an unhappier wight fears his hay fever is coming back on him.

Even so, I need be no incurable optimist to discern that there was spice of romance and an inherent dramatic quality in that past-tense Paducah of mine. Somehow—no doubt a psychologist could ap-praise exactly how—out of its soil and its setting and its tinctures it bred unique personalities and peculiar institutions, a pungent native wit and a tangy philosophy, and it nurtured a people who were high-spirited and self-sufficient and who loved to laugh. Lordy, how they did love to laugh!* These people may not have known much about

---

* I think I'm not far wrong when I say Paducah produced, twenty years apart, two of the most eminent practical jokers of their generation. First, there was George Muller who drove the horsecar through our street and knew everybody in every house along the route. For a super-treat my older sister Reubie (my other sister Manie wasn't born yet) and my younger brother John and I, the in-betweener, once in a while were loaded aboard George's car and in George's care embarked upon the adventurous round trip to Jersey Bridge and back, each of us carrying a sweaty nickel. Our adored friend George gravely would collect the fares and sort them according to the following plan of distribution: one five-cent piece for the company, one five-cent piece for himself and one five-cent piece for purchasing, at Broadfoot Brothers' grocery, a watermelon to be shared by the four of us at the end of the run, or dependent on the season, a certain large spicy gingerbread square which was a specialty of Fisher's Bakery.

Serving as a Columbian Guard at the World's Fair in 1893, George was trapped in the memorable fire which destroyed the Cold Storage Building and was buried in the ruins and reported as dead. He dug out next day and wrote a classic letter to one of the Chicago papers bitterly disowning the scanty notice which had been given him that morning and demanded, as a matter of common justice, a more fitting obituary, which he got in the next issue.

Alf Stewart, a contemporary of mine, was no more audacious

hygiene—who did, back yonder?—but they knew all there was to know about hospitality. They practiced it as a religion. There were among them those who were ragged and perhaps lacked for rent money but I'm sure none, white or black, ever went hungry, yet if there was such a thing as organized charity except in some hour of emergency, I don't seem to recall it.

Offhand I'd say an average of fully fifty per cent of the succulent treasures stored annually at hog-killing time in my Grandpa Saunders' smokehouse went during the ensuing year, a ham or a shoulder or a whole side of cured middling meat at a time, to individual applicants, without regard to race or color. And often he bestowed the free gift of a young calf or a spare milch cow or a likely mule colt upon some improvident acquaintance in the county. I might add that when he died it was revealed that on his books he had carried a careful tally of amounts due him for professional services rendered to close friends or to needy persons who were not his close friends, but seemingly he had never sought for payment of any of these sums. Some of the uncollected, and as transpired, uncollectible accounts dated back twenty-odd years. Yet for his time and place he left what was called a handsome estate, mostly in real

---

than his predecessor but had a subtle quality to his pranking and a scope which permitted of operations on a broad scale. On a Court Saturday he practically emptied the neighboring small city of Mayfield of its rural visitors by marching forth from the town armory in a captain's uniform, with a sword, and accompanied by an aliy carrying a Bible, and swearing in unhappy countrymen for immediate duty in Paducah where a desperate and sanguinary race riot was said—he said it—to be raging.

Then there was the time when, pretending to be a murderous maniac escaped from the West Kentucky insane asylum, he stampeded a whole revival meeting, evangelist, hired soloist, choir, the saved and the sinners, too. And I remember a night at a wagon yard when I was present and participating, but that tale would make vulgar telling. Alf rounded out his career as assistant adjutant general of Louisiana with the rank of colonel. I'll wager the National Guard down there was a laughing matter while he helped command it.

estate and farm lands. He had a passion for buying farm lands; he had been reared on a farm.*

We had our own "Emperor Norton." This was "Brother" Jackson—if ever I heard his first name I long ago forgot it—a plump, rubicund, strutty, little Santa Claus-looking man, even to the round belly and the tuft of snowy chin-whiskers and the radish-red button on the end of his nose. He was a Londoner born and through sixty-odd years in America never altogether lost his Cockney accent. In the seventies he had been the town's leading hatter and was included among its outstanding philanthropists. He gave to one of the churches its big brazen bell. He lost all that he had though, and thereafter to the end of their days he and his shy little wife lived in modest comfort in a rent-free cottage on the grateful bounty of the citizenship. Did his dapper wardrobe need replenishing, local merchants ungrudgingly saw to it that a new frock coat was provided. Summer and winter he wore the frock coat. Or some stiff-bosomed shirts or a stock of white linen ties or new boots for his amazingly small feet would be forthcoming. Always he carried a gold-headed cane and always wore a high hat which lovingly he polished with a yellowed old silk handkerchief—both cane and hat, not to mention the silk handkerchief, being treasured relics of his prosperity. He was most dignified, always incredibly immaculate, with a pompous, really a pontifical manner, and he was very condescending in a lord-of-the-manor way to those he regarded as his social inferiors;

---

* I have been told that in a much earlier period, if a transient of genteel aspect arrived by stage, or by river, or by horseback, some prosperous citizen promptly would call upon him and explain that it would be unfitting were a visiting gentleman suffered to remain at a mere tavern, and would bear the astonished stranger off, bag and baggage, to his own house and there entertain him for as long as he cared to stay—which must have given the town a fine name among travelers but couldn't have done the local innkeepers any real good. I do know that once a passenger, a New England merchant returning north from New Orleans was fetched, desperately ill, off a steamboat. His young son was with him. There being no hospitalization facilities my grandfather took the invalid to his house and tended him till he died, making no charge, of course, except for medical services rendered. As a guest the lad remained with the family for upwards of a year.

and these folk, entering into the spirit of the thing, humored him as though he had been an indulgent patron instead of the communal pensioner.

Daily he pushed an imperious abdomen down Broadway, his walking stick whirling, a small market basket on his arm. Invariably on his lapel was a wee blossom, preferably a tuberose bud (donated by the local flower-garden man). Invariably a richly freighted breath (donated by representatives of the retail liquor traffic), like a gust from a hot mince pie, heralded his approach. He promenaded leisurely through Market Square, selecting from this huckster's stall a muskmelon or a soup bunch, from that butcher's stand a brace of lamb chops; here a couple of fresh caught fish and there a ration of roasting ears or new potatoes. He so distributed his patronage that no dealer suffered too often by reason of these small raidings. When he thirsted—which was frequently—the courtesies of the Richmond House bar or Don Gilberto's or Boyd and Wash's sample room were his. He never paid for anything. Nobody ever expected him to pay for anything or questioned his right to a moderate share of the town's plenty. Had any tradesman denied him or hurt his feelings, I am sure the offender would have felt the weight of popular displeasure. I am equally sure it never occurred to us that his place was a unique one and, in its way, beautiful.

When he died, after uttering a sonorous deathbed farewell and leaving explicit directions for the stately manner of his earthly disposal, hundreds attended the funeral and subscriptions bought the lot in Oak Grove Cemetery where his dropsical little body was buried. I think it needed a Paducah to protect and cherish a Brother Jackson, just as it needed a great, gracious-hearted San Francisco to tolerate the demented whims and honor the privately issued currency of her immortal "Emperor Norton."

These Paducahans took their politics very seriously and their not infrequent homicidal outbreaks almost casually. A pistol affray was a "shooting scrape" and a killing (among the better families) a "regrettable occurrence." They were unafraid of poverty, which was prevalent and, taking the wealthier class by and large, not overly arrogant in affluence. The surest sign of a vulgarian was apologizing to a guest for a shabbiness of the house or the meagerness of a meal. Except in the very rudest groups—and sometimes even there—

behavior was exact and punctilious. You see the average man went armed, and a suspected weapon on the other fellow's flank was mighty conducive to politeness. You might have called it laziness, but those folk took the time to be courteous and accommodating to the stranger, took time for indulging in small grace notes and complimentary flutings amongst themselves. They read Sir Walter Scott and Lord Chesterfield's *Letters*. They did at our house.

So I'm glad I've forgotten or have almost forgotten about the weeds in the garden; glad I still can smell the flowers blooming along the pathway to all those vanished yesterdays. I reckon it's easy to dream and be a sentimentalist if you have a dependable liver and mine has never given serious cause for complaint.

Until it came to be a divisional center for two railroads, Paducah's main supporting industries were four and all four of them colorful—steamboating, tobacco, lumber, whisky.

Mule-breeding and horse-breeding, tanning and leather-working, furniture-making and grist-milling, wholesaling and job-lotting were lesser commercial factors and these filled in the chinks of a thriving structure which made Paducah the market place and the trading ground and the chief shipping point of a considerable territory.

Time and the changes of time diminished, one after another, the major industries. The multiplying railroads crippled, then ultimately extinguished the packet lines. The sawmillers and the cross-tie cutters hacked away at the splendid stands of virgin timber in that area, of hickory, poplar, cypress, oak, walnut, cedar, eventually even the persimmon and the dogwood, until the bottoms and the flats alike were stripped of their crowns of glory.

Altered tastes, the loss of foreign markets and night-rider troubles shrank the tobacco business down to a fraction of what it once upon a time had been. Automobiles came chugging along and pretty soon there were no livery stables left, nor tanneries, nor harness shops, nor wagon works, nor hub-and-spoke works and mighty few blacksmith shops.

The crowning blow befell when Prohibition went into effect. The blight wiped out the distillers, the rectifiers, the wholesalers and saloons. So the devastated, gallant town had to make itself over into a factory town and a machine-shop town and a shipping center for strawberries and garden truck, and this transformed its whole face.

In my adolescence each downtown quarter had its distinctive smell. By sniffing the air a blind man could tell where he stood—the almost suffocating rankness of the heavy fire-cured weed as the hands sang at their work in the stemmeries and in the rehandling plants, or the marketable product was "prized" on the "breaks," upon the floors of the vast warehouses, to a clattering accompaniment of loosened hogshead staves, and, overtopping that, the chant of the auctioneer and the grunted bids of the buyers; the lovely savor from stacks of fresh-cut lumber and mountain ranges of moist sawdust along a two-mile stretch of river front; the heavy alcoholic reek of "Whisky Row" on Market Street; the all-pervading ammoniacal scent that rose off wagon-yards and mule-trading pens.

Nowadays, through the regimenting uniformity of chain stores and service stations and mail-order agencies and modernistic store fronts, this looks like almost any interior smallish city you'd a mind to think of. And what with soft-coal smoke and monoxide gas and spilt gasoline on greasy concrete, it smells like any man's town. But I love to think and I think I'm right that my town has kept some of its outstanding elements of the former days: the saving grace of tolerance, the joke-loving, yarn-spinning tendencies, the instinctive hospitality, the noble and commendable vanity of its self-satisfaction; the abiding courage under adversity or disaster.

There never was but one Paducah; there never will be but one Paducah. So Paducah's loyal, boastful children claim. I'm claiming it for her, too.

I was well along in my teens before the inter-related steamboating interests ceased to dominate the picture. Until then the river either touched the lives or furnished the living for nearly every household—tragically took its toll from them too. From the very beginnings, when a cluster of log huts sprang up about a woodyard and a hand-ferry at the mouth of the Tennessee, this had been true. Indeed there might never have been any town here at all were it not for three great rivers funneling together within a stretch of fourteen miles to feed into the near-by Mississippi a flow almost as great as the mighty mother stream's. Or if there were a town decreed it would have found its place in the range of low hills farther back, rather than along the flattened lands facing the low banks where floods could menace it and, on occasion, devastate it.

On a single day in the flush years I've seen ten or twelve steamers, lordly deep-bellied sidewheelers and limber slender sternwheelers, ranked two or three abreast at the landing; and the inclined wharf, from the drydocks almost up to the marine ways, literally blocked off with merchandise incoming or freight outgoing—cotton in bales, tobacco in hogsheads, peanuts in sacks, whisky in barrels and casks, produce and provender of a hundred sorts. Transfer boats, and ferryboats and fussy tugs and perhaps a lighthouse tender or a government "snag boat" would be stirring about; both of the squatty scowlike wharf boats bulging with perishable stuffs; "coonjining" rousters bearing incredible burdens and still able to sing under their loads, swearing mates and sweating "mud-clerks"; drays and wagons and hacks and herdics rattling up and down the slants; twin lanes of travelers dodging along the crowded gangplanks; a great canopy of coal smoke darkening the water front; a string band playing on the guards of some excursion steamer; maybe, for good measure, a calliope blasting away from the top deck of a visiting showboat—French's New Sensation, or Robinson's Floating Palace, or Old Man Price's; scape pipes shrilling and engine bells jangling; and, over-riding all lesser sounds, the hoarse bellow of the whistle between this or that pair of lofty stacks as one of the packets gave notice of her departure.

Barring floodtimes with which no human hands could cope, only midsummer brought a slackening-off in these profitable ramifications; not always though but frequently. Those years the channels shoaled and kept on shoaling until the bars stood up high, like great turtles bleaching their backs in the heat, and the "chutes" went bone-dry and in the formerly convenient "cut-offs" only the catfish and the gars and the buffalo fish might navigate—and sometimes even they got sunburnt. Regular liners hunted the bank then and stayed there, and the owners fumed and prayed for torrential rains at the headwaters and the pessimists amongst them lamented that in this accursed business it was always either a feast or a famine; while the crews temporarily transferred to the "mosquito fleets," these being chartered boats of such skimpy draft that, as the saying went, any one of them could run on a heavy dew. But let a general break occur in the weather and the lean pickings would be at an end in a jiffy.

And pretty soon then, coming on the crest of the fall rise, the big towboats from the "Head of the Hollow" would go chugging by out in mid-current, each one shoving acres of loaded coal barges before her squared bows, and their yawls racing in for provisions and supplies, then racing back out to overtake the plodding convoys. This also was an approved season for the lumbermen to drift down the Tennessee with their huge rafts, and the rafts would be broken up and the timbers imprisoned by the thousands within the "gun- nels" of the sawmills and the woodworking plants along shore. Some of the raftsmen got impounded too—in the calaboose. For with all that good log money in their pockets they went on most gorgeous sprees.

Later, when ice had locked the Missouri and the Upper Missis- sippi and the Upper Ohio, the inner two-mile stretch of Owen's Island, for all the way between the lower towhead and the farther tip where it aimed at Livingston Point, would be lined and often in favored anchorage double-lined and triple-lined with all fashion of craft brought hither to "lay up" in the safest winter haven for a thousand miles of tributary waterways—the famous Duck's Nest. And over on the town side, snuggled amongst the protecting fringes of willow and cypress where Island Creek emptied in, would be a jumble of "shanty boats" and "joe boats" populated by amphibious guilds: fishermen and trappers and market-gunners; poachers and foragers; cobblers and tinkers; peddlers, fortune tellers, "root-and- yarb doctors," itinerant preachers of curious creeds; ginseng-dig- gers, tie-hackers; mussel-dredgers; owners of "tintype galleries" and penny peep shows; floating junk collectors, Cheap Johns and Jacks- of-all-trades, dealers in live bait and in notions and knickknacks and dubious patent medicines, all hibernating together until spring sent them voyaging upstream or down, with their babies and their dogs, their trotlines and their gill nets, to spend nine months of pure gypsying.

Now water-farers, whether the water be salt or fresh, have always been a separate subspecies, more picturesque than plodding stay-at-homes. It was so with us. Our deck hands were swaggering bravos who talked a strange professional jargon and counted themselves a hardier breed and a more reckless one than their brethren ashore. Our mates notoriously were trigger-fingered. Once aboard, masters and pilots became imperious overlords. It was a chancy calling which these mariners of ours pursued and they carried themselves accordingly. If you couldn't snap your fingers in the face of danger you couldn't qualify. For the river, which gave these Dunns their daily bread, was not alone an uncertain provider but a most fickle mistress. There was no taming her. She was like a snake which wriggled sluggishly along in seasons of drought, only to strike, like a snake, when the onrushing freshets put a twisting, swirling viciousness into the swollen coils. Moreover, what with boilers to blow up and snags to rip the bottoms out of lightly built hulls and fires to turn the matchwood upper structures into flaming furnaces and some quick fierce storm to capsize a heavy laden carrier, it was a small wonder—it was no wonder at all—that the lines of graves in the cemeteries were punctuated with the headstones of those who had lived by the river and by it had lost their lives.

Sometimes the same surname recurred on the slabs. For there was a clannishness, a sort of freemasonry about the whole thing. If your father "followed the river" it rather was expected that you, growing up, would travel the same lane. For a typical example take my father's case. As far back as 1818 his grandfather, shrewd and forehanded Vermont Irishman that he was, had given up keelboating to buy part ownership in the first steam-driven craft that plied the Cumberland River. At the peak of the family fortunes my father's father controlled a small fleet of short-haul steamers, manned largely by his own slaves. And my father himself was a steamboatman— with a master's license and, for the better part of his life, a place as traffic manager of a navigation company, so that the unbroken span of operations for his people extended through upwards of seventy years.

So it went. If you were a Rollins or a Pell or a Cole or a Beard you almost inevitably were destined to be a pilot. There were eleven Pells who had held pilots' papers, including "Yankee" Pell who, against his private principles, had been pressed to steer a Federal gunboat, and "Rebel" Pell who quit his wheelhouse to fight under Forrest; Slick Pell who was smooth-shaven and Curly Pell who wasn't; Big Ed and Little Ed, Old Charley and Young Charley and Young Charley's Charley, all sizes and ages, but all Pells. The Dunns usually were pursers, just as a young Hoey or a young McMeekin was a potential mate, and a Dozier was destined for an engineer's berth. An Owen inevitably would be in the ferryboat traffic. Through three generations the Fowlers were steamboat owners—the name was renowned from New Orleans to Pittsburgh, for they also owned wharfboats and a "boatstore." And the lives of two of them were sacrificed to the greedy waters. One, before my time, burned to death after a boiler exploded and the other, a handsome promising lad serving his apprenticeship as a junior officer, was drowned doing rescue work when a sinking occurred in the night-time.

My mother's eldest sister was married to one of these Fowlers, who died fairly young from the after-effects of the privations he had endured as a trooper in Morgan's Cavalry; hence, submitting to a cruel edict then prevalent, she wore the mourning garb ordained for widows for almost half a century until the end of her days. Those black folds cloaked a lady whose tongue was a lancet tipped with a mordant and a devastating humor. Most witty women, I've noticed, do carry chilled-steel barbs in their wit. My Aunt Laura stung her victims in a mortal spot and left them where they fell. In her circle of intimates was a rather elderly spinster who so flutter-ingly was taken up with good deeds and club activities that she sometimes overlooked the soap-and-water attentions which a less zealous gleaner in the grape arbors of the Lord might have bestowed upon herself. In her absence—which was fortunate for all con-cerned—someone referred to this devoted Dorcas as being wishy-washy. Up spoke Aunt Laura. "She may be wishy," she stated briskly, "but God in Heaven knows the woman is not washy."

Speaking of Aunt Laura reminds me of a little thing which came to pass on a long-ago Easter morning. Betimes, my mother and my aunt went around the corner to their own church where they were convinced the Almighty naturally would make His headquarters when, as and if, in Paducah. Having worshiped after the somewhat bleak formulas of old-line Presbyterianism, they decided to call in at the Episcopal Church to observe how the communicants there carried on, what with a surpliced choir and altar drapes and, by the standards of these two, other practices bordering on the semi-idolatrous. They expected the worst, seeing that the parish had lately acquired a new clergyman out of Virginia and he was inclined to be High Church or, at least highfalutin, and the rumor was that he had insisted on some ultra-formalistic innovations for the service this day. At the door the pair of them were met by a young-ish vestryman whom they had known all his life. As he ushered them, he murmured, "Good morning, Mrs. Fowler, good morning, Mrs. Cobb"; and then, obviously pestered and as obviously obeying instructions from his rector, he added: "Christ has risen."

"Ah, indeed!" said Aunt Laura grimly, and lifted her nose—she had a gift for nose-lifting—and sniffed a sardonic sniff.

Halfway up the aisle, their abashed escort turned them over to a senior vestryman, Mr. M. B. Nash, who likewise was an old and, ordinarily, a greatly esteemed friend.

Motioning them to places in a pew reserved for visitors, Mr. Nash, also betraying the embarrassing signs of having been re-hearsed, half-whispered:

"Christ has risen."

"Yes," said Aunt Laura in a chilled, far-carrying tone, "so Lawrence Dallam was just telling us—it must be all over town by now."

The titular head of the Fowlers in those times was deep-voiced, big-framed Cap'n Joe Fowler, my aunt's brother-in-law, and on vari-ous counts he enjoyed more than a parochial repute. If he got angry, which he frequently did, or excited, which he did almost daily, or was deeply moved, he stammered to a dead halt and could only re-gain the power of coherent speech by saying "Dam' it to hell!" It wasn't swearing exactly, it was the only prescription he had for getting under way again. Through stress of emotion, he was known to have whipped out a vehement "Dam' it to hell" while endeavoring to utter words of condolence in a household newly bereft. From the stub of a poisonous black cigar he lighted a fresh one. My father had the same habit, and, like my father, Cap'n Joe would chew tobacco while smoking. Although a well-educated man, he generally chose to speak in the pithy vernacular of the harbor front. And he had a fine talent for satire. His favorite loaf-ing place was the front porch of the old Fowler-Crumbaugh boat-store at "Monkey Wrench Corner" whence he could command a view of the union of the rivers. It was from that porch that Cap'n Joe had descended when he saw a lady tourist come up the slope of the land from a south-bound excursion steamer, carrying in the crook of one elbow the first Mexican hairless dog ever seen in those parts—a timorous tiny creature which sounded off in thin treble, rather like an infuriated canary, as he approached.

"Madam," drawled Cap'n Joe and removed his hat with a sweeping gesture, "pardon me, but might I ask what that thing is you're toting in your arms?"

"That," she said, "is a dog."

"Is it your dog?"

"It is."

"Is it the only dog you've got?"

"It is."

"Madam," said Cap'n Joe, "ain't you mighty nigh out of dog?"

I've heard this story attributed to others but I prefer to think credit belongs where I have here placed it.

For me, until I was bigger than frying size, Cap'n Joe had daunting potentialities. It was to him I owed an emotional shock dating back, I'd say, to about my seventh year—a shock so profound that the details of it remained everlastingly inscribed on the tablets of my memory. On a warm evening my father took me "downtown" to the corner of Locust Street and Broadway where the rival bands of two adjacent variety shows were giving what by courtesy were called concerts. Since both bands played at once, each trying to drown out the other, the combined result was most exhilarating to my infantile tastes. We were standing in the doorway of Sweatnam & Rountree's drugstore when Cap'n Joe, who had been talking with my father, broke off to advance threateningly upon Mr. Lev. Singleton, toward whom, for the moment, he entertained a pique. It would seem that warnings had been exchanged so, naturally, at sight of the enemy, Cap'n Joe reached for his hip and out came a shiny, long, brass-mounted six-shooter. But either Mr. Singleton was not equipped for battle or he had lost the desire to shed blood. He whirled and dodged through the store, heading for the rear, with Cap'n Joe lumbering along behind him and, for the fun of the thing, firing into the ceiling while the crowd, catching the spirit of the sport, roared with laughter. But there were at least two who did not laugh—long-legged Mr. Singleton, leaping convulsively at each shot, and short-legged Master Cobb. I was well on my way home before my father could overtake me and I had been tucked in bed and had my head under the covers before I regained a measure of calmness.

Not more than two days later and being still in a jittery state, I was lingering at "Monkey Wrench Corner" with my younger brother John, waiting for our father who was busy at his affairs inside the building. Presently he would join us and together we would go to supper. All at once the bulk of Cap'n Joe loomed in the porch doorway right alongside me. He didn't seem to see us; was staring at something—cluttered shipping of some sort—sheltered under the lea of the island. Suddenly he brought his right hand out from behind his back and I heard a mechanical snap, like a trigger cocking, or so it seemed to me, and I caught a gleam of brassy fittings as he lengthened the bore of an extended, tubular device and brought one end of it up even with his squinted eye, swinging the farther end out into space above my head. I had never before seen a collapsible spyglass, but only two nights before I had seen this fearsome giant going into action with a weapon which, to my stricken gaze, greatly resembled the present barrel-like contrivance except that this one, being larger, presumably would be deadlier and make louder blasts when it went off.

Into my brother's ear I screamed, "Run, run, he's going to shoot!" Not once turning my head to see whether he followed me, I left there; anyhow, being smaller, he couldn't possibly have kept up with me. This time I got all the way home and tore around the house—the front door might be locked—and bursting into the kitchen, collapsed in an exhausted heap at Mandy's feet.

Eventually I got over my aversion to firearms—gunning long since became my favorite sport—but it took time. It took a lot of time.

8

UNCLE JO SHREWSBURY

FOR ME memories cluster thick as hiving bees about that high-swung porch at "Monkey Wrench Corner." It was where I spent many and many an hour watching the shifting pageant of river life or, what had a still greater fascination, I harkened with twitching ears to the true talk of our elder statesmen and the big talk of resident bragsters and the tall talk of some of the most gifted prevaricators then inhabiting the temperate zone of North America. Clever fictionizing was encouraged there, never deplored.

From that perch I saw Tom January, the man-eating mate, rout, singlehanded, a whole mob of rebellious rousters; and I saw that gaunt and gimlet-eyed dreadnaught, Policeman Buck Mount, he who had a nervous mannerism of shooting people, fetch down a fleeing malefactor at a hundred yards, the first shot.* Once after a

---

* Years following this episode, what I shall ever maintain was at once the most restrained and the most admirable example of understatement of which I have had personal knowledge, centered about Patrolman Mount. Caution was a desirable attribute when he was being publicly mentioned. An alien, reviewing his military career before he took on constabulary duties, might have called him an ex-guerrilla, which would have been a risky thing to do. But since he served with Southern irregulars, tact and sectional sentiment dictated that he be spoken of as one who had been a partisan ranger.

Early on a Christmas morning a group of youngsters, I being included, were winding up our pre-holiday festivities. That was one night in the year when I was suffered to roam wild and free with my mates until late hours. We set off fireworks, just as Northern-bred boys did on the Fourth of July, and we pranked with signs and gates as those same Northerners did on Hallowe'en,

skiff capsized, I shudderingly saw two swollen bodies hauled ashore, the stiff arms still interlocked.

I was present on the memorable day that Pilot Eph Ballowe, a renowned and versatile romancer, offered his narrative of the imaginative mule and the crib of stored popcorn—how at the climax of the most terrific and prolonged hot spell in the history of the valley, the sun's rays set that crib afire and it burned up and the popcorn

---

which we never did then, but only on Christmas Eve. We also turned over back-houses.

Returning homeward, exhausted but happy over having worked a volume of mischief and shooting the last of our firecrackers and languidly tooting farewell toots on our tin horns, we came abreast of the Bleeding Heart Restauraw and Saloon for Colored Only on lower Court Street. A spring wagon was backed up to the curb and from the interior a number of subdued-looking colored men were fetching forth the limp body of a short, stocky negro. Pressing forward with a morbid curiosity, I saw that the deceased was shot twice through the heart and in the dim light I thought I recognized him as one who had been known for his truculence, especially amongst those of his own kind.

At the rear of the barroom, nervously wiping his hands on a greasy apron, stood the proprietor, "Sergeant" Tom Emery, a blocky, dignified mulatto. He stood high, as the saying went, with white and black alike and prided himself on running an orderly establishment. Until General Lloyd Tilghman, our chief military hero, was killed leading a Confederate brigade down in Mississippi, Tom had been his body servant; hence his courtesy title.

Through a huddle of strangely silent negro bystanders, I made my way to him. There was much broken crockery about, betokening a mêlée, and a puddle of fresh blood on the floor.

"Sergeant," I asked, "wasn't that Monkey John those boys just toted out of here?"

"Not nobody else," said he with a somber gravity.

"How'd it happen?"

"Well, suh, Little Boss," said Tom, diplomatically weighing his words before he brought them forth, "it seems like he musta antagonized Mister Buck Mounts." (He even remembered to pluralize the name, which was the wont of his race when dealing with an important white person as tending, I assume, to make the important person yet more important.)

popped and fell two inches deep all over a five-acre lot and the mule mistook the white fall for snow and laid down in it and froze as stiff as a board.

Still I think the most vivid picture in the album had to do with the notable occasion—in that venue it remained notable for years on end—when Mr. J. Shrewsbury, late of the Army of Northern Virginia, had his encounter with old Dr. Bell, the talking prescriptionist of Sweatnam & Rountree's drugstore.

Had I the commission and you, kind reader, the patience I could write a whole book about Mr. J. Shrewsbury. For eccentricities, for lovable whims and unaccountable crotchets, for a scalding tongue and a blistering pen and a self-kindling temper, I doubt if he had many peers, if any, among his generation. Certainly his equal never dawned on our provincial horizon.

To my older sister and my younger brother and to me, he was, by adoption, our worshipful "Uncle Jo," more beloved to all three of us, I'd say, than had he been of blood kin. At the wedding of my father and mother he "stood up" as best man and until death divided them, he remained my father's closest friend.

Inasmuch as he had never married and furthermore had renounced most of his people back in the Kanawha River country for siding with the North, whereas until Appomattox he served under General Robert E. Lee, our family was practically his family. For my middle name I bore his last name, so the tie between us was especially close.* From my sixth birthday on until my thirteenth,

---

* They cheated me at the baptismal font. The first intention was to name me for my father whose name was *Joshua*, with *Shrewsbury* for a middle name. The consultant womenfolk accepted the *Shrewsbury* part, as having an aristocratic sound but vetoed the beginning of the plan, they holding that *Joshua* was old-fashioned and countrified, whereas *Irvin*, which an aunt of mine remembered from reading a popular novel of the period, was regarded as poetic or romantic or something. Accordingly they christened me, I being of too tender an age to protest and having no male adult to champion my infantile cause. But had they consented to the original idea—what a name for a writer and especially a writer addicted to outbursts of alleged humor, I would have worn through life—Josh Cobb!

I was by day his faithful tagging shadow; and by night I dreamed dreams about him, wherein he did large heroic deeds and I went along and held his coat and helped bury the unregrettable dead.

He had a small property, enough for his bachelor needs, but because he loved the job he maintained an indefinite sort of affiliation with our chief daily, the *Evening News*, contributing when he pleased to its pages and for his honorariums accepting orders against merchants who patronized the advertising columns. He specialized in two differing literary realms: wrote barbed paragraphs about people and causes he didn't like—there were, oh, so many in this classification—and with equal fervor wrote sympathetic obituaries about people he did like. He was full of such paradoxical traits: a budget of contradictions.

For instance, he never became reconstructed, speaking always of Republicans as "Black Radicals." Nor would he concede that West Virginia, where he had been born, was not properly still a part of Old Virginia. Yet for at least three Union veterans he had a tremendous affection. Only he wouldn't admit it. He said he just kept them for cussin'-out purposes.* Repeatedly he drummed it into my juvenile ears that if I hoped to grow up a true Southern gentleman, I must acquire these cardinal qualifications, to wit: Become a finished horseman (I can't recall ever seeing him on horseback), read, write and speak Latin (he couldn't speak it himself), learn to dance (he never danced), and play the fiddle (he couldn't

---

* At his death—from an overdose of strong sedative taken to ease the after-effects of a spree in celebration of the downfall of a political foe—these same three cronies acted as pallbearers: Captain Ed Farley, from Michigan, who lived down the libelous and utterly undeserved title of "carpetbagger" to become one of the most venerated patriarchs in the county; Mr. Nelson Soule, who, although a Jerseyman, redeemed himself in Uncle Jo's eyes by being a stalwart Democrat; and Major J. H. Ashcraft, a chronic Federal officeholder, except when Cleveland was president, and a native Kentuckian, who took frequent pains to explain that while he had been a Union officer and was proud of it, he was, by Godfrey, no dam' Yankee! The remaining pallbearers were fellow ex-Confederates, namely, my uncle, Linah Cobb, and old Judge Bullitt and Dr. John Brooks. In my Judge Priest yarns Dr. Brooks became "Dr. Lake," and in various chapters of a book called *All Aboard* I made Major Ashcraft a principal character.

play a note). At his knee I took my first stumbling lessons in Latin grammar, and out of his own pocket he paid for dancing lessons, until old Professor Leopard, the chronically tipsy French dancing master, gave me up for a hopeless case, inasmuch as I, being practically tone-deaf, could not keep time, let alone tell a waltz tune from a schottische or polka.

By the same token, I still know nothing of violin music except that sometimes I like it but generally don't; and I am an indifferent horseman albeit with a unique style. No matter what the horse does, I canter. I'm afraid that had he lived I should have been, on at least three of these counts, a profound disappointment to my Uncle Jo, although surely he would have been pleased that, after a fashion, I followed in his journalistic footsteps.

He was fond of music, and particularly of singing. But he had a devastating antipathy for anyone who whistled. The mere sound of a trill issuing from some passer-by's puckered lips would send him off into almost a maniacal fit of rage. Once he deliberately upset a ladder upon which a persistently whistling sign painter was mounted, and cheerfully paid for the patching up of his victim's torn scalp. He said it was money well spent because now the sorry scoundrel would know better than to whistle within earshot of decent people.

In a section where cornmeal in some shape was a daily staple on every table, he never touched it in any shape. Once he told me why. For the last six weeks in Virginia before the Surrender he lived on an exclusive diet of gritty hoecakes and, after the meal ran out, on the parched grains. When from this his gums were so bloody and his teeth so sore that he no longer could chew the ration, he lay one night half-delirious from hunger, in an abandoned stable. A fat rat crept out of the walls. Uncle Jo killed it with a kick, skinned it, skewered it on a borrowed ramrod and ate it to the last bite. "It was the best meal I ever ate," he said. "I've never repeated it, yet I reckon I'd be ready to if the chance came along and I was as near to starving as I was that time. But from that day to this I've never touched cornbread in any form and I don't aim to, either. I've eaten my share of that stuff."*

---

* During the height of the 1913 flood, which pretty well inundated the town, two refugee camps with barracks, tents and mess halls were set up on Buckner's Hill west of the corporate limits;

By the hour he could quote from the classics and ordinarily he used scholarly English. When aroused though he spouted boozing ken language until he ran out of all the stock swear words. Then, under pressure of great provocation he fetched forth oaths of his own coinage—"God-overeaten," a mysterious qualifying adjective, and "Sapinpaw," which was what he used when he couldn't think of any regular noun that fitted the contempt in which he held the ignominious object of his vituperation. He wouldn't waste either of these though, reserved them for high occasions.

He never stirred abroad without his walking stick, a heavy staff of oak with a shepherd's crook handle. At Soule's drugstore, which was his favorite loafing place, there was a particular spot on a particular railing where, when indoors, he invariably hung this staff and woe be unto any individual who either accidentally or with malicious intent, shifted it by the breadth of a single inch. There was a gaping crack in the cane and this crack he regarded with deep affection. Attorney Henry Burnett had been an intimate of his but they quarreled and Uncle Jo, being Uncle Jo, cherished the feud forever. Seeing Mr. Burnett and Judge Jesse Gilbert at fisticuffs one afternoon on "Legal Row," he ran across the street and thrust the cane into Judge Gilbert's hand for a weapon with which, haply, to brain the enemy. The Judge did his manful best but the descending cudgel struck the iron cross brace of a sidewalk awning and suffered a compound fracture. Uncle Jo refused to have the damage repaired. "It's an honorable wound," he said. "The aim was poor but the intentions were most laudable. Let it be."

In pleasant weathers Uncle Jo liked to sit in a cane-bottom chair against a certain panel of the facing of Mr. Soule's establishment— not any chair or panel but inevitably this chair and this panel. As

---

one camp for white refugees, the other for colored. A new resident, a furniture merchant from northern Indiana, was put in charge of the colored commissary and almost immediately had trouble on his hands. The old-timers among his charges struck against the rations. In his ignorance he had made the mistake of serving them with crusty fresh wheaten loaves and they were going to have their corn pones or die in defense of principle and appetite. As long as he lived he bore the affectionate nickname of "Baker's Bread" Rhodes.

with his jealousy for his cane so with his chair. It was a hardy soul who dared to move that chair during the regular tenant's temporary absence or, worse still, sit down on it and be caught doing so. The resultant explosion would rattle showcases and echo against the front of the prescription cases.

On a June morning Uncle Jo was tilted back on his throne chair, viewing the passing show and from time to time acidly commenting on various of the performers in the show. There came along, filling a pony cart to overflowing, a redoubtable matron, the widow of perhaps the most distinguished statesman the district ever had sent to Congress. This formidable personage was renowned for piety on Sundays and for her spectacular outbursts of profanity through the week. In her way she was as corrosive a verbal adversary as Uncle Jo and nursed almost as many prejudices.

At sight of him her hackles rose—if a highborn lady could be said to have hackles?—and she checked her pony to a stop.

"So there you sit, Mr. Shrewsbury," she shrilly proclaimed, "passing remarks on every self-respecting female who goes by."

"True indeed," answered Uncle Jo, rising and making a low bow, "but only the self-respecting ones. Pass, Madam, pass in peace."

The iconoclast rather libeled himself there because toward womankind in general he could be as courtly as any Walter Raleigh. Likewise for children he had understanding and kindliness, provided they showed no signs of growing up to be whistlers.

The negroes at Mr. Stewart Dick's livery stable, on the corner hard by his living quarters, practically idolized him; and when he set out, as on occasion he did, to get ceremoniously tipsy, there wasn't a barkeeper but sought, by subtle dissuasion, to tame his alcoholic impulses.

He dispensed charity upon the unfortunate with a generous hand—indeed a spendthrift hand, his own estate considered. But pretenders and prigs and upstarts and tiresome folks—these were his pet hates. And hotly he railed at religious bigots—a freethinker in the finest sense of the term. Long before I grew out of short pants he was converting me to tolerance for all creeds whatsoever, counseling that I must never set myself against the practice of any faith but only against its narrow-minded practitioners, if any. I'm proud to think that his preachments soaked into me and mixed with the other ingredients and stayed in there.

Since dullards stood high in his gallery of aversions it was inevitable that Dr. Bell, that well-meaning but everlasting bore, should irritate him beyond the bounds of self-control—not that Uncle Jo had much self-control to start with. Dr. Bell was a plumpish elderly man who went about droning futile questions and, did no one else answer, endlessly answering them himself in dreary, maddening accents. He would put you in mind of one of those leftover houseflies, usually they are gross fat houseflies, which in winter crawl out of hiding to buzz against a windowpane. Only Dr. Bell's buzzing knew no season. He wore a high hat the year round, and in summer went collarless and coatless. On sultry days—and Paducah could have some very sultry days and, for that matter, still does—the sight of Dr. Bell pacing along a simmering pavement with the ardent sun-rays shimmering on the bulge of his burnished headpiece and against the armor plating of his shirt bosom, was a thing calculated to make onlookers turn suddenly dizzy and even bring on heat prostrations.

Nor was this the top of his unwitting offending. Breaking off his own conversational flow, he meticulously would tear from a convenient envelope or paper sack a tiny strip, moisten it with his tongue, squeeze it into a pellet and, arising with the gravity of a yellowhammer storing away acorns, he'd find a cranny or nail hole and carefully pack the wad into the crevice and then, reseating himself with the air of having completed an important undertaking, would resume where he had left off.

Once, tempted beyond his strength by a third repetition of this achievement within an hour's space, Uncle Jo bounced up with a hoarse outraged bellow, hauled a *Courier-Journal* from his pocket, crumpled it up, copiously bedewed it with his chew of tobacco, cud and streaming amber included, and snatching Dr. Bell's battered bee gum from its astounded owner's head, rammed the great dripping bolus into its crown and jammed the hat back on the other's pate and literally ran for the open air, uttering choken and intemperate parts of speech. But Dr. Bell took no offense, merely clucking his regrets that a gentleman should be given to such utterly unaccountable displays of temperament. He couldn't afford to take offense—it might cost him an audience.

It was a drowsy torrid summer afternoon. I was hunched on the whittled guardrail of the old boatstore porch aforesaid. Against the brick façade behind me sat three cronies—Cap'n Joe Fowler, and my father, and Uncle Jo. In harmony they discussed some congenial theme, perhaps the military mistakes of Braxton Bragg, perhaps the iniquities of a high protective tariff, anyway some issue on which they were in perfect accord. Without warning, the chubby form of Dr. Bell appeared in their disturbed midst. With his little pitter-patter gait, he had come upon them. He paused in the doorway, beaming upon the company. A quick pregnant hush befell. Daniel had invaded the lions' den, but this Daniel didn't realize his peril.

"Good evening, Joseph," he said formally, as was his wont.

Cap'n Joe grunted morosely beneath his grizzled mustache.

"Good evening, Joshua."

My father nodded and fretfully he plucked at a sandy-red goatee.

"Good evening, Joel."

My uncle said nothing, but under his scowling brows his eyes began to gleam with a baleful light. Here at the very start was a well-nigh unendurable affront. He disliked his Christian name when spoken in its full two syllables; never used it himself, always signed himself "J. Shrewsbury." I expected an immediate combustion, but with a visible effort he held in.

"Warm evening, heh?" continued Dr. Bell, fairly atwitter with geniality. "Or anyhow warmish. Wouldn't you say warmish?"

Nobody said.

Dr. Bell appeared to realize that his debut had been inauspicious. There ensued a somewhat embarrassing stage wait, a foreboding little silence. The new arrival cast his daunted glance about, plainly seeking an object, any object, for monologuing. It was, you'd say, like a drowning man clutching blindly at straws. His hopeful eyes fell upon the packet *Clyde* lying at the wharf just below, where she loaded for her regular weekly trip up the Tennessee. Her name was printed on a flag which hung limply between her stacks. In rich gilt it was painted on her pilothouse. Hugely, in flaring yellow and red with black shadings, it was repeated on the nearer flank of her boiler deck bulkheads, aft.

Slowly Dr. Bell spelled out the lettering: "*C-L-Y-D-E*. Joshua," he inquired, "is that the steamer *Clyde?*"

My father got no chance to reply, even were he minded to.

As though he had been hornet-stung through the seat of his trousers, Uncle Jo sprang up. With one continuing frenzied movement he uncovered himself and dashed his black slouch hat to the floor, then danced upon it in a Zuluish kind of war dance.

"No," he screamed. "No, you God-overeaten old Sapinpaw, that's the Confederate ram *Merrimac!*"

Half a minute later, strangers, if any, along the lower stretches of our main thoroughfare must have been amazed to behold a squarely built, square-whiskered, middle-aged gentleman erratically tacking uptown, now addressing the unresponsive heavens in convulsed accents, now beating with a great clubbed walking stick on hitching posts and signposts, now belaboring the inoffensive wooden Indian in front of Little Hymen's cigar store, now viciously attacking the red-and-white-striped pillar that marked Green Gray's barbershop, and so behaving, ultimately to vanish in the dusty, heat-pulsing distance.

But down on the boatstore porch good Dr. Bell was murmuring in a shocked and sympathetic quaver:

"Dearie me, suzz, dearie me! What has come over poor Joel? Joseph, do you and Joshua suppose Joel's mebbe has a t'ech of the sun? I'd better follow him up and find out."

"Better start in by taming a Bengal tiger and then gradually work up to it," counseled Cap'n Joe. "Or else give that Shrewsbury about six weeks to cool off in."

Well indeed for Dr. Bell that that day he did not overtake Uncle Jo. There might have been murder. Here was one who could be driven just so far.

From my Uncle Jo, who encouraged me to draw pictures—I had from babyhood some crude knack with pencil and colors and my adolescent desire was to grow up to be a sketch artist—and who guided me in my then secondary ambition to write down on paper what I saw, I got my love for a newspaper office and for the smell of a newspaper office—that alluring stench which is compounded, or was in those days before linotypes and manifolding presses came, of the contributary lesser stinks of wood pulp and sour flour paste and dirty type faces and half-molten composition rollers and musty files and perhaps the frowsy garments of a tramp printer or so.

That smell, for upwards of forty years it is now, has abided in my nose or if not actually in my nose, at least in my consciousness, binding me fast to the workbench of the journeyman scrivener. One way or another it has shaped my course for all my days. I have no regrets. It has taken me where the wheels of the world went 'round.

9

A CUB WHETS HIS CLAWS

MY UNCLE Jo had been dead for quite a spell before a disastrous shift in the already tottering and constantly scanty fortunes of the Joshua Cobbs and the necessities of earning a living for myself and helping to swell the household exchequer, booted me out of grade school and into the harsh world, alooking for a job. The stroke annulled a parental ambition for me to go to military college, at my grandfather's expense, and thence to law school and, as it turned out, eventually quenched my own contingent dream of being a cartoonist.

At this optimistic age my calculated futurities forked this way and that. Taking into consideration the natural gifts I should have to bestow upon the world, my normal expectancies seemed moderate indeed. Having acquired success and an independent fortune practicing law and having followed that up with a fling at political eminence, in middle life I would retire to devote myself to big-game hunting, mainly in foreign parts, and to ornithology. In the last-named pursuit I was then and have always been an enthusiastic dilettante. My music deafness has handicapped me. Unless the note is very distinctive—the piped whistle of a meadow lark, the rattling laugh of the belted kingfisher—I cannot often recognize a bird's call. But if I can get sight of the singer I probably know him. And the sight of him has for me an unfailing fascination—always has, always will. It likewise was on the schedule tentatively mapped for my maturity that when not scientifically engaged in nature study, or with matchless aim diminishing the fauna of this and other continents, I would give further proof of amazing versatility to an awed and appreciative planet by dashing off brilliant caricatures of fellow notables. On the whole I had rather a satisfactory program charted out. But now it was a condition which confronted me, not a theory.

I didn't think that I'd care for the teeming marts of trade. I'd tried business; through two summers had driven an ice wagon to earn spending money and by hard experiences on my free Saturdays during the school year, I knew about delivering circulars and collecting bills and watering lawns and raking them. Also I was an adept at capturing flying squirrels and baby 'possums and fledgling redbirds and mockingbirds and selling them. Our stable loft was my menagerie. There wasn't much market for snakes so I kept my snake collection for my own private purposes.* Occasionally one of the more ambitious inmates would get loose and wriggle downstairs and start prospecting; and then Liza Rose Cherry, the cook, would go out in the alley, sometimes via the gate and sometimes over the back fence, and from there would threaten to quit. She stayed with us upwards of fifteen years and that was until she died.

So I turned down an opportunity to be callboy at the Illinois Central shops, figuring that Uncle Jo would have applauded my choice, and, as the prevalent phrase went, accepted a situation—at $1.75 a week—on the very paper with which for so long he was affiliated. I had a smattering of shorthand; had picked that up in between times. And when not writing "items," which was the name for almost anything printable except a "personal" or a "death

---

* I scarcely can remember when I wasn't collecting something—birds' eggs, pressed wild flowers, autumn leaves, cigarette pictures, geological specimens, mound builders' artifacts—mounds of those earliest people dotted the county—postage stamps, tamed pets and, for the past fifteen years or so, examples of the ancient relics and the more modern handicrafts of the original Americans, plains tribes, woods tribes and desert dwellers alike. My hobbies may change, but I have at least one to go along on and running concurrently with it, my abiding interest in bird life. As a boy I was a deft merchandiser in specimens. Classifying, labeling, identifying, swapping off duplicate items and dickering for new ones—these have been joys to me all my life and still are. The man or woman without a healthy fad has surely missed something. What a pleasure Peggy Hopkins Joyce's helpmate collection must have been to her! And one of the happiest men I ever knew was DeWolf Hopper, the Husband of His Country.

notice," I did chalk-plate drawings. Pretty soon though I found out I'd rather write about things than try to illustrate them and through disuse gradually lost my dexterity at sketching, which for as far back as I remembered had been a part of me. My mother insisted that at eighteen months I was making recognizable pictures of bugs and spiders and chickens and she preserved a sheaf of crumbly scraps to prove it, along with my earliest extant photograph showing me lying on my tum-tum and scribbling away. It was recorded in family lore that fretfully I rebelled against watching for little feeble-minded birds to come out of black boxes; but paper and pencil had soothed my temperamental tantrums. We found these things amongst her private treasures after she died.

Anyhow, at sixteen, there I was, a cub reporter for the *Evening News*. At nineteen I was its managing editor. I was the youngest managing editor of a daily paper in the United States, so they said, and in the light of fuller knowledge I'm sure I must have been the worst managing editor of any age in the United States. I was reckless, smart-alecky, careless, gaudy in my enthusiasms, a dynamic builder of lurid headlines. I rarely let dull fact hamper my style. I think a count would have shown that my headlining brought down more libel suits on the sheet than my treatment of the news did and that, take it from this belated confession, was plenty of libel suits. After a few months the owners found out what was the matter with their paper and I lost my epaulettes. I had one high qualification though, when reduced to the ranks. I could work at high-pressure fifteen hours on a stretch, play dime-limit draw poker all night, drink my share of the drinks, and come to work next morning, blear-eyed perhaps and a trifle drowsy, but without a twitching nerve in my body. Until I was beyond voting age I didn't know there was such a thing as a hangover. It was a profound shock to me when I began to lose my immunity. Until then headaches and queasy stomachs had merely been things other people had.

Before the buoyant imaginations of moving-picture producers, as reflected on the silver screen, taught us that all great reporters were drunken geniuses, with a dashing way about them though, and that all women writers were beautiful abnormalities, and that a city room somewhat closely resembled feeding time at the zoo, a favorite fiction story was the one about the despised cub, whom even the copy boys snubbed and the Neroesque city editor sneered at and the rest of the staff ignored; but he went forth and all by himself, through a superhuman stroke of brilliancy, outslicked the supercilious star of the opposition sheet right down to his union suit. This was known as a "scoop." Speaking personally, I never knew of but one such instance of success on the part of a comparative greenhorn when pitted against metropolitan talent. And success there was not to be attributed to the young hero's intelligence. It was due to luck. I know whereof I speak because I was the young hero. In somewhat different words I've told the tale before in a book which, judged by royalty statements, could have sold only a few surreptitious copies, and anyhow the book has been out of print many a year and I figure no one, barring some ancient with an abhorrent good memory, will recall it, and here's hoping he'll be too poor to buy a copy of this work or, if he does buy it, be too feeble to protest that money was obtained from him under false pretenses.

At twenty I was drawing down twelve dollars a week, a topnotch salary for a reporter in a smallish interior city, and I fancied myself an exceedingly bright and capable young man. To strangers I always spoke of myself as a journalist; I always thought of myself as a journalist—never as a mere newspaperman. I rode free on the streetcars and had a season ticket for the theater and carried a pocketful of telegraph franks and annual passes on railways and steamboats. In those days a cub reporter on a country paper could get more free transportation over trunk lines than a railroad president can get now. Also, I was the resident correspondent for a list of city papers as long as my arm. I used to pick up a tidy bit of money out of this correspondence. Sometimes the weekly space bills equalled my salary.

This was the situation when in Chicago there was committed a murder that startled the whole country. A broken-nosed ruffian named Christopher Merry, who posed by day as a potato peddler and by night followed the vocation of burglary, put his faithful wife to death through slow degrees of almost incredible brutality. As I recall the gruesome circumstances, he sewed the body up in a roll of carpet and, with two lesser scoundrels to help him, carried it in a wagon to a secluded crossroads a few miles from Chicago, and buried it there late at night. Then they drove the team back and forth over the spot until the mound was flattened and all signs of digging had been wiped out. One of the three talked too much, was arrested and confessed. Appreciating the characters of the pair, the police threw double loops of men round the block and round the houses where they knew the murderer and his remaining accomplice had hidden. Cautiously they closed in and broke down the doors of Merry's flat. The rooms were empty.

The crime itself, the grisly midnight burial of the victim and the manner of the escape—most of all the escape—made a whopping big story from the Chicago standpoint. A sizable reward was offered for Merry; a smaller, yet a good-sized one, for the other fugitive.

For a solid month they apprehended Chris Merry all over this continent. Every time a country constable saw a stranger with a broken nose he locked him up and wired to Chicago that he had the murderer. At first the Chicago police department and the Chicago newspapers sent men in response to these messages. Finally they got tired of answering false alarms and resolved to remain calm until the real Merry had been overtaken.

Meanwhile Merry and his partner, whose name was Smith, had been working their way south. They were aiming for New Orleans and then for Cuba, where they expected to join the *insurrectos* fighting against Spain and lose themselves somewhere in the interior of the island. It was a pretty good plan and it might have worked except that, as they were stealing a ride on a freight train in Indiana, a sudden cold snap descended upon them and Merry's feet were so badly frostbitten that he became badly crippled. Every step he took must have been agony to him; but he kept going. At the beginning of Christmas week he and Smith crossed into Kentucky. At Louisville they climbed into a boxcar billed for Memphis. Toward dusk a brakeman discovered them and they were thrown off at a little station in the western part of Kentucky, called Fredonia.

That same night a tramp of the harmless variety known as a gay cat crawled into a toolshed back of an empty section house below Fredonia to stay until morning. There he found two more wayfarers. They permitted him to share the quarters with them. They had a bottle of whisky and they shared that with him, too. Pretty soon the evident leader of the pair—Merry, as it turned out—rolled over on his side and went to sleep. His companion and the tramp sat up to finish the bottle. Liquor loosened the clack of Smith's tongue and he began to boast.

"You're just a plain bum," he told the listening gay cat, "but we're both bad guys." He hauled out a revolver and flourished it. "The cops are lookin' for us now for a big job we pulled off in Chi." He produced a newspaper clipping from his pocket. The clipping bore reproductions of pen-and-ink pictures of two men. The names had been cut off, but the likenesses were fair and in them the startled tramp recognized his new acquaintances. He did not say much, but he did a lot of thinking. He craved to quit such dangerous company as soon as he could. Presently the frayed, greasy clipping dropped from Smith's unsteady fingers and he slept too. The other waited until Smith began to snore. Then he rose softly and straightway departed from there—but he took that clipping with him.

The next night, which was the night before Christmas, an unfeeling flagman kicked him off a train into a roaring snowstorm and the town of Mayfield, Kentucky. Half-frozen, he hobbled to the nearest house and begged for something to eat. The head of the house gave him a hot supper and let him thaw out by the kitchen fire. The tramp sought to make his gratitude manifest. He hauled out his treasured clipping and showed it to his host and told how and when he got it.

"I'll bet there's a reward out for them two," he said. "One of 'em's feet is froze and he can't travel far. You better see the sheriff or somebody, and then he kin ketch 'em and you'll git part of the money."

Behold how beautifully the thing worked out! The householder's brother-in-law was Charley McNutt, the town marshal, a man with more than a local reputation as a detective. Straightway the tramp was taken to the town marshal's house. There he repeated his story and surrendered the clipping, and then he disappeared without telling his name. Before daybreak McNutt was on his way up the line to Fredonia. He had compared the pen-and-ink drawings in the paper with two chalk-plate pictures upon a circular on file in his office, and he knew he was on the track of Merry and Smith and a big cash prize.

He took up the trail at Fredonia, tracing the two southward

down the railroad to Kuttawa, a somewhat larger town. There Merry's frost-cracked feet and his endurance had given out and the pair had secured lodgings—grim joke!—in the house of the Kuttawa town marshal, who took in boarders to help out his official income. Already he was on fairly friendly terms with his transient guests "from up north." When the Mayfield marshal sought out his Kuttawa brother privately and told him whom he was harboring, the Kuttawa marshal almost had a fit. Upon hearing the size of the reward, he promptly revived.

These country policemen had better luck than the astute Chicago police department had had. They rounded up the dangerous boarders with ease. Afterward Merry, with a pleased grin, told me how he detected them watching the front and rear of the house in the dusk and how, stealing to a window with his revolver, he twice drew a bead upon the fair target of his host's large white slouch hat. He did not in the least mind killing him, he explained, but in his crippled state he could not hope to get away; so what would be the use? He reasoned it all out, and then he surrendered.

The triumphant officers carried their prisoners a short distance to Princeton, which was a county seat, locked them up in the county jail, and then telegraphed Chicago headquarters that they had Merry and Smith in custody. But Chicago had heard that tale before—many times. It had got to be a joke. Chicago declined to become excited.

That afternoon, though, a special officer of the Illinois Central Railroad chanced to be in Princeton and he went to the jail to see the prisoners. As it happened, he knew Smith by sight, having met him professionally when he, the detective, was a plain-clothes man at Chicago headquarters. He hurried right out and wired to Chicago that this time it was Merry and Smith, sure enough; but, first, he warned the jailer of the dangerous characters of his charges and advised him against allowing strangers to see the trapped fugitives, knowing they had a wide acquaintance among traveling yeggmen.

It seemed that some of the Chicago papers had begun to suspect it might indeed be the far-hunted pair that had been nabbed down in a back county of Kentucky. Two of the papers—I forget which two now—had already started reporters south before the definite word came; but the *Tribune*, which had taken a leading hand in scoring the police for inefficiency and which, therefore, had a peculiar interest in the story, waited too long. The *Tribune's* staffman failed to board the last train that would land him in Princeton in time to cover the story the following night.

So the *Tribune's* acting telegraph editor, as I found out later, wired every one of the *Tribune's* country correspondents within a radius of a hundred miles of Princeton to go there forthwith. He was hoping that out of the lot of them there might be one who would know enough to handle the story in some sort of fashion. One of these orders came to me and, as it turned out, I was the only country correspondent of the whole lot who obeyed. I went.

Princeton was considerably less than a hundred miles from my town, and within an hour after the telegram reached me I was on my way. It was the first time an assignment of such size had been entrusted to me and I was swollen with a sense of my importance. At the same time I had only the vaguest idea of how to set about getting my story, or writing it after I got it. When I dropped off the train at Princeton the station platform was overflowing with townspeople, and at least half of them followed me up the street leading from the station. I felt flattered until one man asked who I was and I told him. Then my escort began to dwindle away. I was lean and tall and I wore a large ulster and a broad-brimmed hat; they had taken me for a Chicago detective who had been expected on that train.

Not knowing exactly what I was to do, except that I was to get an interview with the prisoners—my telegraphed instructions had been most explicit on that point—I marched into the local hotel and registered—the official loafers were pawing over the book to find out my name before I laid the pen down—and then I started for the jail. A volunteer committee went along to show me the way. The jail was a small mildewed-looking brick structure. Viewed from the exterior the most interesting object in connection with it was a gentleman of a stern aspect sitting on the front steps nursing a rifle upon his knees. Across the way two well-dressed young men were pacing to and fro, swearing in a feverish way. Passing them, I gathered from certain remarks that their preconceived notions of Southern hospitality had suffered a severe jolt.

I crossed over to the jail, showed my credentials to the person with a rifle, stated my business and said that I desired to be admitted to the presence of Merry and Smith. He was courteous enough—but he did not let me in. As I now recollect, he said the Twelve Apostles could not get into that jail except over his dead body. It seemed the jailer was a literal person. He had been warned against letting any strangers see his distinguished prisoners, and he was not letting any strangers see them. It made no difference who they were or where they came from; if they were strangers that amply was sufficient for him. I began to understand why the well-dressed pair across the street had shown so much heat. They were Chicago reporters—but also they were strangers.

I stood there a bit, wondering what I would do next. Then I remembered that I knew the mayor of the town. He was a friend of my father's—they had been soldiers in the same regiment during the Civil War. I asked the way to his house. He was at home. He listened to me and then he locked his arm in mine and led me back to the jail—past those two fuming Chicago reporters, past the deputy on guard at the door and into the jailer's office. The jailer was a grizzled old veteran with a gimpy leg. The mayor introduced me to him.

"Zach," he said, "this boy is Josh Cobb's son from Paducah and what's more, he's Bob Cobb's nephew."

If I had been his long-lost son that jailer could not have been any gladder to see me. He had been a gunner in my uncle's battery all through the war. When the mayor explained that I represented a city paper and wanted to see his two charges, Zach reached for his keys.

"That there Chicago officer told me not to admit any strangers," he said, "and I ain't aimin' to do so; but, son, you ain't no stranger—you're homefolks."

He led the way into the body of the jail. It was a smelly un-ventilated cubbyhole of a place, with blank brick walls on two sides and rows of cells on the other two, and a red-hot stove in the middle. Half a dozen ragged negroes—the ordinary occupants of the estab-lishment—were squatted round the stove. My men were in the larg-est of the cells. The jailer was not taking any chances with them. There was an extra heavy lock on the door of their cage, and for added precaution he had put leg irons on them and made their chains fast to the bars.

The jig was up and they knew it. Besides they had the pride of criminals who had outwitted their natural enemies, the police, and they were ready and willing to talk about their achievement. Somewhat haltingly, I told them I was serving the Chicago *Tribune* and wanted to get a statement from them; then I stopped, not knowing what to do or say next, and to cover the stage wait hauled out an impressively large notebook—sure sign of an apprentice hand. It should have been an inconspicuous wad of copypaper.

They did the rest themselves. They guyed my embarrassment and made fun of my broad-brimmed hat and my budding mustache, but they talked. There was no mention made of the murder—by unspoken consent all three of us avoided that painful subject—but they told me how they had watched the encircling loops of policemen closing in on them and how they had broken through those twin cordons. They gave me a circumstantial account of their subsequent wanderings, with the dates and names of the different towns they had visited; and I put it all down just as they told it to me. If I hesitated over the spelling of a proper name one or the other would help me out; and at the end Merry himself took my notebook through the bars and, holding it upon his knee, drew in it a rough diagram of the Chicago streets through which they had fled, indicating the situation of his flat and the blockading lines of the police. He made a couple of dots to show where two detectives had been standing when he and Smith slipped by, not six feet away, and he wrote down the names of those two detectives. He marked the place where they had scaled the structure of an elevated road and so had walked away to safety right above the heads of a dozen watchful officers. For Chicago purposes the stuff he was giving me was worth its weight in gold almost—only I did not know it.

At the end of half an hour they sent me away with a farewell gibe or two. The old jailer wanted me to go home with him for supper; but I declined because in a dim sort of way I was beginning to realize I had the making of a pretty good yarn concealed about me, and I burned to get it unloaded. Going back to the hotel, I ran into the confederated town marshals who had made the arrests, and they supplied me with full details of their part in the drama. One of them, McNutt the Mayfield man, furnished a graphic enough word picture of the vanished tramp who had given the first clue.

The Western Union Company had its office in the lobby of the hotel, and when I got there the two Chicago men were sitting along-side the operator, who was a young nervous-looking fellow, hardly more than a boy in age. They were turning out copy, seemingly by the running furlong, while an admiring audience of citizens looked on over their shoulders. To this day I do not know whether they ever saw the two prisoners, but if they did I know they failed, by long odds, to get as much copy out of the pair as I did. I still believe that blood-dyed villain of a Merry actually took pity on my greenness and gave me a better story than perhaps he would have given to a skilled reporter. Probably I was the only person on earth who felt sorry when they hanged him a few months later in the Cook County jail.

Anyway, there sat the Chicago men writing away like mad, with the lone telegrapher looking decidedly uneasy and fidgety as he saw how fast the scribbled sheets accumulated. Abashed by the pres-ence of these luminaries from the big city, I timidly introduced my-self and announced that I was on hand to serve the *Tribune*. One of them, the younger of the two, merely looked at me with raised eyebrows and a grin on his face and went on writing. The other man was kinder. He was John Rafterey, a distinguished reporter, as I was to learn years afterward.* He stopped long enough to tell me something of the records of Merry and Smith, and out of the clutter

---

* When newspapermen met they used to tell this story on Rafterey: One May night his city editor—it may have been "Mr. Dooley" Dunne—said, "John, you're covering the Decoration Day parade tomorrow. And for heaven's sake cut out the line about 'the thin ranks grow thinner' and the one about 'the boys in blue are getting gray' and the one about 'Hail, heroic saviors of the Union' and all the rest of that time-worn tripe. There must be some new way to start off a G.A.R. story—some angle or slant that hasn't been worked to death. You find it." This made a hard assign-ment instead of an easy one. Fortifying himself for it, John rather overestimated his cubic capacity. As he sat dazedly in the press stand what impressed him more than any one thing else was the astonishingly large number of veterans who came gimpily along Michigan Avenue in brand-new, creaking shoes. So John went back to the office, sat down, wrote one introductory sentence and fell asleep across his typewriter. When they pried him off, this, they saw, was what he had written: "God, how their feet hurt them!"

in his overcoat he dredged up for me a clipped-out Sunday special, which reviewed the killing of the woman and the police end of the escape. The clipping helped me mightily later on; but when I inquired regarding the chances of putting some copy on the wire they both agreed promptly that they expected to keep the operator busy until midnight or later. Neither one of them seemed to think it worth his while to ask whether I had seen Merry or Smith; if they had I should undoubtedly have turned over to them the whole of my story. But they did not ask, and I did not tell them.

I went in to supper, and over the fleet of white-china canary-bird bathtubs containing the meal, I digested the clipping that had been given me. After supper I headed for the station to make my arrangements for filing with the Postal. The Postal man, as I knew, acted as train dispatcher for the railroad, and because the *Tribune's* instructions to me had come over the Western Union I should have preferred the Western Union; but I knew now it was the Postal or nothing. As I was starting I met a man I knew, a chap named Offutt, the circulation manager of a Louisville newspaper. He had been a reporter before he went into the business office. He had an evening off, and through sheer love of the game—and possibly also through pity for my evident inexperience—he offered to go along with me and help me put my material together.

At the station the night operator made us welcome in his little crowded office, but he said he was going to be so busy clearing trains that it would be nine o'clock for sure, and maybe ten, before he could touch anything else. However, he stole time to flash the *Tribune* a synopsis of my story—I did have sense enough to write that—and right away the answer came back. It ran something after this fashion:

SOUNDS LIKE A BIG STORY. WRITE IT FULLY. LEAD OFF WITH STORY OF THE FLIGHT AND THE ROUTE FOLLOWED BY FUGITIVES, SO WE CAN PREPARE MAPS AND DIAGRAMS FROM YOUR TELEGRAPHED DESCRIPTIONS. THEN SEND EVERYTHING IN DETAIL.

My enthusiasm grew; I realized now that I really did have a tale worth telling. I started off with a flamboyant and be-adjectived introduction of half a column or more, and then I settled down to spin out my yarn. Long before the operator was ready for me I was frightened at the mass of copy I had produced. Never before had I done a special of more than five or six hundred words, and here already were two or three thousand words at least—and I just getting started! Could any paper on earth print such a staggering big, long dispatch? Would any paper pay the tolls on it? Suppose the *Tribune* changed its mind and refused to take it? Inwardly I was a scared young person, but I kept right on writing; and all this time, at five or ten-minute intervals, the impatient telegraph editor in Chicago kept flashing inquiries, wanting to know why in Halifax and other localities that story did not come on.

Finally, along toward half-past nine, the operator got his tracks and his wires cleared of railroad business and was ready to tackle my manuscript. He was a dandy operator, too; he fairly made that key of his beg for mercy. It was he who suggested that I break up my story into sections, with a separate dateline and a separate lead for each installment of it, which was a sound idea, because it gave my volunteer assistant, the circulation manager, a chance to write something. He proceeded to write in detail what I had already written in bulletin form—the narrative of the escape and the flight—while I, now altogether reckless of consequences and filled with the unapproachable joys of creation and authorship, turned myself loose on what I conceived to be a thrilling picture of that pair of shackled ruffians, sitting in that little box of a jail, bragging how they had outwitted the whole Chicago police department. I always liked to do descriptive stuff anyway, whereas a recital of plain facts slowed my pen and stifled my fancy. Pretty soon the operator had another notion.

"See here, kid," he said; "I'm sending over a loop directly into the *Tribune* shop; but if I had another man here to help me out he could send into the city office of the Postal and they could hustle the stuff round by messenger and save a lot of time. My day relief lives up the street a piece, near the hotel. Why don't you go up there and roust him out? He'll be glad to come down here and help out with all this jag of stuff that you two are stacking up."

I put on my hat and coat and went. It was nearly eleven o'clock then, and it was snowing a little and the road under my feet was as black as ink. I stumbled along, feeling my way until I came to the hotel, and I went in to ask the clerk the exact location of the house of the man I was looking for.

The clerk had just started to tell me when he broke off and pointed over my shoulder and said, "Why, there he comes now!"

The young Western Union operator had played out. Unused as he was to handling big budgets, his fingers had cramped. It was only a question of a little while until he would have to give up altogether. In this emergency he had suggested that maybe the Postal's day man, as an act of neighborly accommodation, might be willing to help him; and so one of the harassed Chicago reporters had gone to the Postal operator's house and waked him up and was now bringing him in. His face was puckered with sleepiness and he had an overcoat on over his nightshirt. Yawning and stretching himself, he was just sitting down at an instrument when I reached his side and told him I wanted his services too.

Still half asleep, he started to explain the situation while the two Chicago men glowered angrily at me and probably cursed me inwardly for a meddlesome young cub.

"I've promised to help these gentlemen out," he said. "They're in a fix, so they tell me."

I had a flash of sagacity—the only real flash I begot unaided during the whole night.

"Yes," I said, "but this is the Western Union you're working for, isn't it? You're working for them for nothing, but I've got a slew of stuff to go over your own line—the Postal."

"In that case," he said, "it's a different thing."

The Chicago men, each with a great scad of copy yet to be sent, protested and begged and swore; but the Postal man went with me. He was no slouch of an operator either. In five minutes after we two reached the depot my story, or rather our story, for Offutt did his share, was feeding into the *Tribune's* telegraph room over two wires at once. Pretty soon one of the telegraphers broke off long enough to take a line for me and toss it over:

LET IT ALL COME. SPREAD YOURSELF AND KEEP SENDING UNTIL WE SAY STOP.

I spread myself. I wrote and wrote and wrote! I elaborated my description of the jail scene. I piled the local color on by the hod-load. I described the principal local characters in the story—the jailer, his vigilant deputy, the two town marshals, the unnamed tramp who had sicked them onto their quarry. I humped my shoulders and curled my legs round the legs of my chair, and the sheets of copy slid out from under my fingers in a white stream.

At intervals one of the Chicago men would come in and want to know when a wire would be clear; and I, remembering that mossy and venerable yarn so dear to the heart of every green reporter—the one about the war correspondent who sent the Book of Genesis by cable in order to hold the wire against all opposition until his paper went to press carrying the exclusive account of a great battle—I, remembering that tale, would say to him that I could not tell him when I should be through or anyway near through, and then I would go on writing. He would curse and groan and go out and slam the door with unnecessary violence and I could hear him tramping up and down the platform. The operator of the Western Union had petered out altogether along about midnight.

I held my wires—both of them. I wrote everything I could think of and then wrote it over again. I wrote until my fingers were black from repeated sharpenings of my pencil—wrote until my right hand was numb up to the wrist. My head swam and my eyes blurred, but I kept on writing; and the wonder of it was the *Tribune* kept on taking what I wrote. I imagine one of my operators, appreciating the joke of it, must have quietly told the operator at the other end what the situation was; and possibly the *Tribune* people approved the notion of my holding the lines and shutting out my rivals. Anyhow they let me go ahead. It was nearly two o'clock in the morning—Sunday morning—before they finally cut off my torrent of literature. The message read:

THAT'S ENOUGH. GOOD STUFF! GOOD BOY! GOOD NIGHT!

I got up on my feet, stiff and staggering and grimed to the eyebrows with graphite dust; and just then I heard the whistle of the train that would take me back home. I told my friend Offutt I would send him a fair share of what the *Tribune* sent me. Then I climbed wearily aboard the train and curled up in a seat in the day coach; and the next thing I knew the conductor was literally dumping me in a comatose heap off upon the platform at Paducah. I managed to get home and to bed, and there I stayed until dusk that evening. Then I got up and dressed, and went down to the bookstore and waited until the Chicago Sunday papers came in. I bought a copy of the *Tribune*. I took one look and my eyes popped with amazement and pride—but mostly with pride.

The last column of the first page—under flaring headlines—was mine! Nearly five columns of the second page were mine! I had written the better part of a page for the Chicago *Tribune*. True, the copyreaders had pruned a lot of the fruits and flowers off my introductions, and they had chopped out a good many of my most cherished adjectives; but in all essentials it was my story and, what was more, a good share of it was exclusive, as I found by comparison of the *Tribune* with the other Chicago papers. To be sure, I was not responsible really for this exclusiveness. Most of it had been forced upon me, so to speak; and, anyway, I did not value that part of it as an older and wiser newspaperman would have valued it. What mainly concerned me was the length of the story, as measured in columns. I spent a happy evening picking out my literary flights that sailed through the yarn.

On Monday morning I got a letter postmarked Chicago, and opened the envelope to find inside a single sheet of notepaper bearing the heading: Editorial Rooms, the *Tribune*. The following lines were written on it in a somewhat crabbed hand:

Dear sir: You did excellent work in covering the Merry story for this paper, and I wish to thank you.

I have instructed the cashier to send you a check for fifty dollars as a bonus.

Yours truly,

JOSEPH MEDILL

I was tickled naturally to get such a letter; particularly tickled by the second paragraph. But in the abysmal depths of my ignorance I attached little importance to the fact that Joseph Medill himself had written, with his own hand, to express his appreciation of what a stranger had done for his paper. I knew that the editor or the publisher of the *Tribune* was a man named Medill, but by my estimates the only really great editors in America were Henri Watterson of Louisville, Henry W. Grady of Atlanta and Edward Carmack of Memphis, in the order named. A Medill more or less meant practically nothing to me. I carried that letter about in my pocket for a day or two, and then I tore it up or lost it or something. I wish I had it now.

Anyway, when my check came from the *Tribune* at the end of the month I forgot all about the letter. For the fifty dollars was what Mr. Medill had said it would be—a bonus—and in addition to the fifty they had allowed my expense account and given me full space rates for the story. In all it came to something like one hundred dollars. Here in one magnificent packet was as much as I made in salary in two months.* It was the largest amount I had ever owned at one time in my life. It was hard to believe. If a man working one night could make that much off of a city paper how much could he make in a month or a year? The possibility staggered the imagination; anyhow it staggered my imagination. From that

---

* Part of this important money went to buy the handsomest box of superior mixed bonbon chocolates to be had at Gilbert Brothers' drugstore—large bow of lilac ribbon on the cover and pair of stylish embossed tin tongs inside—for a young resident of south Georgia who had come up from Belmont College in Nashville to spend the holidays with two home-town girls, she bringing with her, in addition to various other attractions, the slurred intonations of the lower coast country, which had a fascinating, slightly foreign sound to those who spoke with the twangier, more nasal inflections of the inland river bottoms. (Yankees don't know it but there are fully a dozen distinctive shadings of pronunciation in various main divisions of the South and dozens of lesser subshadings peculiar to this locality or that.) Within four years I had worn the resistance of the fascinating Georgia visitor down to the point of surrender. When the officiating minister bade me repeat after him the words, "With all my worldly goods I thee endow," I said to myself, "Umph uh, there goes my Ridpath's *History of the World* and the plush postage stamp album." True, I had ninety dollars saved up, but that was to be spent in riotous living on the wedding trip, and was. We breakfasted mighty sketchily aboard the diner on the morning we got back.

hour dated my desire to work on a big newspaper, by preference a Chicago or New York newspaper. I wanted to get there before mad extravagance plunged them into bankruptcy.

There is a hitherto unrelated sequel to the tag end of the yarn I have just told, a sort of moral to adorn the tale. It was early in 1904 when I took the plunge. Chicago was the first stop because it was nearer. "Harry" Beach, the A.P.'s top hand, whom I had met while covering the Goebel murder—of which there'll be considerable to say farther along somewhere—took me in tow, vowing to get me a berth or know the reason why. Despite Beach's fervent recommendations there didn't seem to be any openings until we got to the *Tribune* building where "Eddie" Beck, still in active harness and still cutting wide swathes, presided as city editor. On the strength of Beach's endorsement he decided he would take me on. But for complete confirmation he deemed it better to wait until James Keeley, the managing editor, and an Englishman, got back from dinner. While he waited, I was minded to tell them about the Chris Merry story and the complimentary letter I'd had from Mr. Medill, now deceased.

"Well, now, that makes it all the more binding on the plaintiff," beamed Beck. "I guess you're the same as one of the *Tribune's* happy family already."

Presently Keeley returned and Beck went into Keeley's office, leaving us in the city room. Pretty soon he was out again, with a nervous fixed grin on his face and he beckoned Beach aside and talked with him a few minutes. I could see how Beach was frowning and how he gnawed his mustache. Abruptly he broke away and came to me, Beck following along, looking bothered.

"Let's get moving," snapped Beach. "We're through here."

"Now wait," said Beck. "The offer of the job is still open, Cobb."

"Like hell it is!" barked Beach. "You know Cobb's told you the truth and I know dam' well he's telling the truth, but that would only make it all the worse for him. He might make good in your sight and in the sight of man and God and everybody else around here but that wouldn't save him from being gutted the first chance that Cockney scared-cat got."

In the hallway outside he faced me, simmering with vexation.

"You know what?" he growled. "It seems that when Beck told Keeley how you mopped up for the *Tribune* that time, Keeley suddenly remembered that he was acting telegraph editor then and for him to admit, even after eight or nine years, that just once he'd slipped up by failing to get a staffman down there promptly, would be a reflection on his infallibility. It's plain as the nose on your face that that's what he's afraid of. So he tells Beck you're faking the whole thing; that he distinctly recalls sending a man who hit the town as soon as any other Chicago reporter did, and while you or some other local hand might have covered odds and ends that you never touched a finger to the story proper. Well, that would be that cagey Englishman's way. But the tough part is you can't take a place here. Beck couldn't save you long."

So Chicago's loss was New York's gain, not that Chicago didn't somehow contrive to continue getting out daily newspapers. Five months later I'd shipped my wife and baby daughter south to live off my father-in-law and from him I borrowed two hundred dollars—I got down to the last seventeen of those dollars when the break in my favor came—and was off for New York.

10

HOW TO KNOW THE EDITORS FROM THE
WILD FLOWERS

In the first week in August, 1914, I was casting for bass across the lily pads of a stretch of placid waters in southern Quebec where, with Mrs. Cobb and our little daughter, I had been spending the summer. Up the lake from our rented camp at the lower end came a French-Canadian rowing a guide boat. Having first collected his fee for acting as courier, he handed me a telegram.

It was dated at Philadelphia. It was made up of two sentences—a paraphrase from an old darky joke which was in my own repertoire of old darky jokes; that and the tag line of an ancient and honorable wheeze lately resuscitated by the comedian, Frank Tinney.

It read as follows:

"Seems like this here war has done busted right in our face. Your ship sails Thursday."

That was all but for me that was enough. Because it was signed, *George Horace Lorimer*, and by then, having served him for upwards of two years, I was fairly well acquainted with Lorimer's style of doing things.

The same evening I caught a local train for Montreal and that night caught a through train for the States. In the morning, at New York, I was met by one of Lorimer's deputies who had brought along an emergency passport, a sheaf of credentials vouching for me as correspondent of the *Saturday Evening Post*, passage to Liverpool on the American liner *St. Paul* sailing the following day which, sure enough, was a Thursday; also one of those "To-whom-it-may-concern" letters from Secretary of State William Jennings Bryan commending me to the good graces of all representatives of our

113

government in Europe; likewise an automatic revolver, a letter of credit, a sheaf of travelers' checks and a little black handbag containing six thousand dollars in double eagles and weighing nearly forty pounds, this for expense money in case letters of credit and checks were not being honored abroad when I arrived.

Inside of ten days, after various small vicissitudes and adventurings, I found myself bouncing via chartered taxicab into the back edges of a spirited brush between German Uhlans and Belgian cavalry amongst the trampled poppies of a wayside wheat field on the road from Brussels to Louvain. I aimed to show this laconic chief of mine that, in a crisis, he couldn't move much faster than I could; and by a combination of an amateur's fool luck with main strength and awkwardness, I had made out, up to this point anyhow.

Lorimer was like that. He had a tremendous flair for restrained and under-played dramatics. This sense of theatricalism was his by honest inheritance. His father before him was a promising boy tragedian newly come from Scotland who, getting himself converted at a revival meeting in Louisville, studied for the ministry and became the most brilliant pulpit orator of the Baptist church in America. His first charge was at Paducah; the son missed being born there by a scant margin of months. It takes a great actor to be a great preacher. Here was offered testimony that a great natural actor could be a very great editor. Lorimer never had to rehearse his scenes or plot his discreet histrionics beforehand. They came along, just so. But they neither clogged up his judgments nor retarded his functions. He could go to a decision more speedily than any chief I ever had and always that decision was an unqualified "yes" or a flat-out "no," never an "I'm not sure" or a "Let's think it over." Often enough then, if the answer had been yes, he would squint those chilled-steel eyes of his and rear back and patiently, painstakingly prove to the fellow who'd brought it to him that, as it stood now, the idea was only part of an idea and here, jumping full-grown and full-fleshed out of Lorimer's darting mind would be the rest of the notion, the meatiness which rounded it out and made of it a project complete. For that merit I have yet to meet his equal. In the same breath he'd be warmly affectionate in his personal attitude for an associate or a contributor, and coldly, almost brutally severe in his professional dictum on that same individual.

It was as though sundered lobes of his brain were operating independently—like the average Frenchman in the Great War who simultaneously could dedicate half of his being to gallant service and unstinted sacrifice for a beleaguered country and the other half to keeping books on what the Allies were going to owe him for the use of his land and his property whilst they were engaged in helping to save that land and that property from the invader. I'd say the French are the most logical patriots that ever lived. They never let heroism interfere with profits. All of which, I claim, helps to explain why we paid the debt to Lafayette with compound interest within two weeks after the first contingent of the A.E.F. landed on French soil in '17 and the boys started exchanging dollars for local money. There was the time when the national slogan should have been pronounced "*Vive la Francs.*"

First and last and one way or another, I worked with or for a good many outstanding editorial alcaldes during my more active days as a newspaperman and as a writer for magazines and syndicates and book publishers—but still, I hope, remaining in essence a newspaperman. Let's see?—there's a long string of them stretching away:

There was Lorimer, the benevolent satrap, delighting in his deliberately cultivated trick of assigning a man to an important commission with a casual and seemingly an indifferent gesture; his other trick of showing—or rather not showing—his satisfaction for an assignment well done, by a quickly canceled-out grin on his lean shrewd face and in due season, a substantial reward which seemingly never came through his suggestion but on the publishers' initiative. Lorimer was the one who first realized that in a country dedicated to business, fiction with a business background—in other words the romance of business—would make popular reading and capitalized that invention to the agreeable tune of millions of circulation.

There was—and haply still is—roly-poly Bob Davis, formerly Frank A. Munsey's Man Friday (and all the rest of Munsey's worka-day week too, if the truth only were known) and now, spry as a ferret at seventy-odd, the globe-trotting columnist for the New York *Sun*. In his prolonged career as the imperator of divers popular periodicals, Bob Davis yielded plots as the roe shad yields her roe, only Bob spawned close to shore and the sprat all lived and swam off as novels or short stories or pertly up-to-date articles, usually with some other fellow's name on them as author. Whether Lorimer, with his curtly expressed, outwardly careless teachings, developed more new writers and perhaps discovered more in the first place than Davis brought along by his nursing and mothering technique, was for years a subject for discussion when writing people got together, and possibly the cause for some mild jealousy between the two men. On Lorimer's side was the advantage of a generous budget. He loved to pay and pay well, provided the notion of better pay came from Lorimer and not from some chap seeking to dicker for a higher wage. Whereas Davis, who under the niggardly, cheese-paring Munsey system, was sorely circumscribed, had to use blandishments for money and bestow encouraging words in place of fat checks.

Likewise Davis steered his craft, double shifts, with a mighty meager crew, while Lorimer could hire such subalterns as he needed at high prices and moreover he had for his first aide—that's no pun—Adelaide Neall whose name as associate editor still flies at the *Post's* masthead. To my way of thinking she rates with another yet active veteran, Mrs. William Brown Meloney, as a splendidly capable force among women editors. Be all this as it may, Lorimer and Davis, in the matter of spying out fresh talent, were the Christopher Columbuses of their day. And they were twin Burbanks when it came to the nurturing and cultivation of the same.

Then there was the smiling gentle little giant, Ray Long—may the good saints rest his troubled soul!—who, finding life had snarled up on him, looked about for the nearest exit, which was suicide, and took it. I treasure the memory of this dwarfish friend of mine, whose brain was as sharp as his heart was kindly; who could, with a wired message inspire a struggling wight or revive a despairing one, could with a deft hand soothe the ruffled plumage of some successful— and therefore nine times out of ten, temperamental—writer. It was Long who worked such wizardry with type faces that he made captions to tell tales and by-lines to illustrate the text. Here he stood alone. Often I've watched him while he balanced the blurbs and shifted the display letterings until they fairly jumped out of the printed page and said "Boo!" in the reader's face.

There was quiet, shy Harry Burton, with a sense of news values as timely as today's stop press bulletins, who succeeded Long on the *Cosmopolitan;* Arthur Vance who could in advance come as near to interpreting the shifting, fickle intangible thing called public taste as any of his contemporaries; Roy Howard, that grinning small Buddha of journalism who for all his consequence as head of one of our biggest newspaper chains and one of our greatest press services, will never quit being a reporter and a corking good one; Lord Northcliffe,* the most egotistical man I ever met and with a thousand excellent reasons for being the most egotistical man anybody ever met; Colonel Joe Patterson of the Medill-Patterson-McCormick tribe and he having, as the late General Nathan Bedford

---

* I never worked for Lord Northcliffe. I could have, though. He made me a proposition to sign up with his *Daily Mail* before I ever met him—made it through Charley Hand, his American correspondent, on the strength of Hand's gracious words for my coverage of the first Thaw trial. In 1914, in London, he went out of his way to be kind. He procured for me what I'm sure no other man in the British Empire could have procured—interviews with the supposedly uninterviewable Lord Kitchener and dear, doddery, little old Lord Roberts, and he publicly backed the authenticity of Kitchener's words as quoted by me when they were questioned; and twice he reminded me he still had a vacant place waiting in his organization. Again in 1918, during my second journey to the war zone, he mentioned the proposition as a matter for negotiation when the war came to an end. But it never got any further than that.

Some months before, while directing England's propaganda in America he had rusticated for a few weeks in Westchester County, New York—if so restless a creature could be said ever to rusticate? For proof of his inquisitiveness, his almost maniacal passion for prying under lids, he knew infinitely more and had found time to read more and remember more about Westchester County, its history, its topography, its population and its resources than I who, off and on, lived there for fifteen years had picked up. Northcliffe was interested in all things and forgot never anything and sooner or later made use of what was stored away in the smoothly indexed filing-cabinet which functioned inside his bulging skull.

Like Hearst, he dispensed a perfect hospitality. But the satellites kept getting underfoot, the lackeys and lick-spittles, the courtiers and court jesters that crowded the Yes Man's Land of Lord Northcliffe's inner defenses.

Forrest likewise had it, the faculty of being able to figure "Whar hell is goin' to bust loose next and git thar fust with the mostest men"—including staff photographers; Will Lengel, the best first mate that ever stood watch on an editorial bridge, and if some publishing mogul but had the wit to sign him on, what a skipper he'd make, bringing the ship into port laden with rich cargoes!

Next I think of another, one who was as companionable and as simple and gallant and gracious as any human being could be—John Siddell of the *American Magazine*. With a malignant growth gnawing at his vitals, he gave no sign of his agony and his despair to a living soul and carried on until, like a valiant true soldier, he literally fell down and died at his post among the front line trenches. It was Siddell who discovered, for magazine purposes, what Charles Dickens before him discovered—that common people are interested in reading about common people.

In the gallery, I must insert a miniature vignette of Sam Blythe, the sage of Pebble Beach and the grand old man of Pelican Camp in the Bohemian Club's famous redwood grove above San Francisco. Because Sam Blythe later became the biggest Washington correspondent of his day and the keenest commentator on the Washington scene and on national politics (What a nose to smell out shams and what a rapier to puncture gas balloons with!) a good many in our game seemingly have forgotten that, while still a very young man, he was the successful city editor of a daily and the equally successful managing editor of a monthly.

Nor should I overlook the three most notable city editors, barring only the inimitable "Boss" Clarke of the *Sun's* morning edition, who were active in the New York that I learned to love when I went there in 1904. It was O. Henry's New York then, and Richard Harding Davis' and "Chimmie" Fadden's. It was beginning to be the New York of Frank O'Malley and Frank Case and "Bugs" Baer. Odd McIntyre hadn't come along yet but was due any minute. And Will Rogers was being delayed en route.*

---

* With his scalp intact, Will Rogers had escaped from a small Wild West show and, with an educated cow pony and his lariat and his wad of gum and his yearning eyes fixed on the far distant bright lights, had progressed as far eastward as the Corn Belt. It was no longer a "dumb act" as the booking agents say. He was venturing

One of this trio of top-hands was gnome-like Tommy Dieuaide of the *Evening Sun* with his perpetual Monna Lisa smile, and one was that lanky rawboned Kentuckian, Keats Speed of the *Evening Journal*, two men much alike in temperament and method and both blessed with the gift of being able to grow calmer and calmer whilst everybody about them became more and more excited over some whopping news break. And of course the third would just naturally have to be Charley Chapin of the *Evening World* who, for his cruelties, his uncanny discernment, his generalship, his arrogance and his freakishness, is rapidly becoming a sort of Aryan myth in journalistic mythology. Chapin walked alone, a tremendously competent, sometimes an almost inspired tyrant with a kind of occult instinct for detecting an unsuspected or craftily hidden sensation. In him was combined something of Caligula, something of Don Juan, a touch of Barnum, a dash of Narcissus, a spicing of Machiavelli. Features, specials, comics, supplements and all such circulation-getting side issues he despised. By his estimates these merely cluttered up the space which should be devoted to what was immediate, what was exciting or distressing or funny in the day's grist. His idol, and the only one he worshiped except his own conceitful image, was the inky-nosed, nine-eyed, clay-footed god called News. He walked within the shadow of tragedy. You felt it even while

---

some ad-libbed lines. He wasn't sure though that they were funny. It took the laughter of a continent to convince him.

After Will reached the peak of his fame, I acted as toastmaster one night at a big theatrical dinner that was given for him. In introducing the guest of honor I shot him amidships by reading a squib which Drury Underwood, the Chicago critic, aided and abetted by Nellie Revelle, the pioneer of all women press agents, had dug out of the dusty files of some second-string reviewer's comments upon a third-rate vaudeville show on a Chicago side street. It was probably the first authentic press notice Will got in a big city paper. As I remember it went like this:

"Spot two on an otherwise fairish program is assigned to an alleged cowboy from Oklahoma calling himself Bill Rogers. He is supporting a trick horse. He puts the horse through a routine, meanwhile doing some roping stunts and spilling a line of loose chatter. This turn would go better if the cowboy shut up and gave the horse a chance."

you were torn between admiration for his craftsmanship and hatred for his city room meannesses. And when this lurking nemesis caught up with him and he went to Sing Sing under sentence for wife murder and died there, few of the sweated oarsmen who manned Chapin's galleys were surprised, since some such outcome was for such a man inevitable, and I'm afraid not all of them felt compassion for him.

Each one of all these with whom I had direct contacts exhibited certain admirable traits—traits which, I'd say, invariably mark your real editor. If the script turned in by a man who has been assigned to a particular job or who had volunteered to handle it, measurably approximated what had been expected of him, he sent it to the typesetters substantially as it was written, making as few changes in the text as possible and preferably making none at all. To be sure this applied more to the leisurely editing of magazine material than to the chopping-box method of a newspaper shop where the corps work always against that relentless enemy, the clock; where there are trains to be caught and dead lines to be met and a harassed make-up man roaring in to announce that already tons of overset encumber the imposing stones, and stories are spilling out between the column rules. Then, of course, good stuff must be slashed to the quick and the adorable little brain children of the rewrite staff die in windrows on the city room floor.

Especially in the magazine offices the betraying sign of an editor who isn't sure of himself and so can't be sure of anyone else, is that he worries to a lather and drives competent contributors half crazy by futile, meaching little suggestions. Doesn't Mr. Soft Lead agree with him that it would strengthen the introduction were the second paragraph shifted to where the third paragraph now is? He has been fretting over it all night and his poor head is fit to split. Would Miss Fountain Penn consent to the substitution on Page 24 of the word "pale" for her choice "pallid"? With the context, "pale" is stronger, somehow, more emphatic. At least so it seems to him.

Or, on his own daredevil initiative this poor overwrought little Jack Horner boldly takes the plunge and changes a comma into a semicolon and then rears back and puts his thumbs into the armholes of his vest and twiddles his fingers. In other words, to demonstrate that he is an honest-to-God expert with a blue pencil and a throbbing intellect and everything, he must do his daily dozen of footling stunts. Gehenna is paved with good intentions and full of fuss-budget editors.

There were a thousand things about Chapin I didn't like but one thing about him—and most other authentic newspaper editors—I did like. No matter how big the story might be, or with how many ramifications and on-piling developments, Chapin, having set this man and that on the stint, thereafter left them to their several devices. For him was no harassing of the legmen over the telephone, no shouted demands that all concerned make sure every possible pump was being siphoned, every possible rat hole being watched; and, what would have been the worst pesterment of all, no nervous hovering over some hard-pressed rewrite man who, with his fingers askitter on the typewriter's chattering keys, was trying to co-ordinate a dozen angles into his new "Lead All! Love Nest Slaying! Must!" Having assigned to this undertaking the lieutenants and the skirmishers whom he felt were best equipped for it, Chapin plainly figured that it would be a reflection upon his own judgment were he to display uneasiness regarding either the chore or the outcome. There might be brutal rebukes for whosoever failed in his share of the consolidated operations. But that would come after the battle was ended. To a greater or lesser degree all the real commanders-in-chief of daily journalism known to me by direct affiliation used Chapin's stand-offish methods—Charley Lincoln and Bill Thayer and Foster Coates and Jack Spurgeon, for conspicuous examples.

Lorimer though was the master hand at manifesting this quality of restraint. He had no concern for details; results were what he craved. So, like a wise field marshal, he bided calmly at G.H.Q. and didn't pester himself—or them—about what his shock troops were doing. First in '14 and again in '17 and '18, I rambled at random for upwards of a year along the Western Front or immediately behind it, and in all that time I'm sure he didn't send me in excess of half a dozen cable messages and not a single letter; and these cabled messages were invariably notifications that such and such a batch of articles had come safely to his desk. The second time I went across, almost the only thing he added when he called up by long distance to give me sailing orders ran something like this:

"Our boys are in it now, over there. So you better dust along to

France and try to get where things are going on and garner some pieces for us to print in the *Post*. Pieces about the Americans preferably but anyhow, pieces."

Without exception, all the men I have listed expressed, each in his separate way, these characteristics: First and foremost, a never-flagging, infectious enthusiasm for the job underway or the job just ahead, and second, an unappeasable hunger of curiosity about people and things; about what was happening and was likely to happen; about causes and effects; about the whole haphazard machinery of life. To them a human being was the most interesting thing on this earth. In sequence, money might come next, then perhaps love, then crime, then, in order, dogs and elephants and snakes and bugs and the likes of those, but foremost, human beings. And therein, I maintain, largely lay the secret of their success at the tricky trade they followed after.

I figure the same rule might be said to apply to the two biggest journalistic mastodons of their own saffron-tinted era, William Randolph Hearst and Joseph Pulitzer. In fact, I'm sure it might be said. As firsthand witness I couldn't qualify, though, to give the evidence. True, I labored more than six years for Pulitzer on his *Evening World* and under covenant I spent nine years with Hearst's organization, working on various of his monthly publications. But I never beheld Mr. Pulitzer, never heard his voice save once. I'll come to that a chapter or so along. And while, during my term of indenture to him, I had frequent and cordial and altogether pleasant social contacts with Mr. Hearst, I never felt that I'd met the real Hearst.

Mainly I beheld only his outer shell, the protective film behind which lurked a secretive, aloof being whose personal convictions were not to be fathomed, whose private viewpoints were only to be guessed at.

Once in a while the mask would lift for just long enough to reveal, in one quickly eclipsed flash, the prodigious figure who, like a miraculous juggler, could keep a dozen spheres in the air at once—newspapers, radio stations, magazines, syndicates, press bureaus, mines, ranches, real estate, moving pictures, book-publishing, policies, political ambitions, what-all; and yet find time for building fabulous palaces and gorgeous playhouses; for collecting the finest and the largest collection of antiques and art treasures ever assembled by any individual since Lorenzo the Magnificent, which is going a long distance back; for knowing the why and the how and the wherefore of thousands on thousands of separate items among his voluminous possessions, he being an acknowledged authority on such diversified subjects as armor and Old Masters, Spanish glass and Navaho rugs, first editions and Mexican saddles, Frederic Remington's Westerns and Gobelin tapestries. He was powerfully proud of his grasp on his fads; he had excuse for being so.

Or, on occasion, he might offer another facet of his many-flanged personality, an attribute which so many among his biographers, hostile or friendly as the case might be, seem somehow to have overlooked or slurred. William Randolph Hearst has a redeeming sense of humor—not the spurious brand which sees what is ridiculous in other people—but genuine drollery. He can laugh at himself. The joke which is aimed at him or the one which he actually aimed on that target is the one over which he laughs the heartiest and remembers the longest and repeats the oftenest. A million things have been said for or against Hearst, mainly against, I'd guess. Yet not the most rabid of his enemies or the nastiest of his critics has accused this man, who gets fat on denunciations and chuckles under defamations, of having a false dignity or an exaggerated idea of his own sanctity. Hearst may have thought of himself in the agreeable role of the Major Prophets, all melded together, but he has no fetish of infallibility—at least not yet, and he is pretty far along in years now to be taking on the Messiah complex, although, on occasion, he does seem to fancy himself as chosen to be God Almighty's ghostwriter.

However and to the contrary notwithstanding, in his moments of relaxation when temporarily he shifts the burden of a perverse and, generally speaking, an ungrateful world from his galled shoulders, he presents himself as a thoughtful host, and an appreciative employer—provided you deliver the particular brand of goods he hankers for; and a gracious companion abounding in witty, pungent comments on what's transpiring about him and what's happening to him, personally. His manner of speaking enhances the comedy asset. Within a towering, broad-shouldered frame which age hasn't greatly caved in yet, he has a voice that bleats thinly and flatly forth like notes on a child's toy flute. The effect is startling until the hearer gets used to it; as though a steam locomotive hauled off to whistle for the crossing and then gave out in the puny trebles of a penny fife.*

At the top of his success Mr. Hearst spent money, not as some tremendously affluent brother capitalist might, nor yet as the unhampered monarch of a barbaric despotism might, but like a wildly extravagant government. In 1926 he took seventy of us, mostly motion-picture folk, by special train replete with refreshment booths and musicians, from Hollywood to his unbelievable barony up the coast at San Simeon—a night's travel—there to spend the Fourth of July. On the eve of the holiday he announced at dinner in his ninety-foot-long banquet hall—solid silver service but paper napkins and all the known condiments on dress parade down the priceless refectory table—that some of the party had shown a willingness to stay over until the evening of the fifth. He asked a show of hands to divide these guests from those who felt they must adhere

---

* "Jimmy" Swinnerton who for forty-odd years has been drawing comic pictures that really are comic for the Hearst issues, tells a yarn illustrative of all this:

One day when Park Row was perhaps more inclined than at present to do its saloon shopping early—and oftener—Mr. Hearst entered the editorial conference room of the New York *American* and saw a number of vacant chairs.

"Where's So-and-So?" he inquired softly.

"His wife telephoned he wouldn't be down today—under the weather, she says. Well, when I saw him last night in Lipton's bar he was pretty weather-beaten and getting more so, drink by drink."

"Hem. I see Mr. Whosis is absent, too?"

"He's at St. Vincent's—on Newspaper Row." (Newspaper Row was a hospital ward frequently patronized by overtaken journalists. It was suitably named.)

"And how about Thingumbob?" The big chief's bland falsetto was taking on a saddened tone.

"They just telephoned up from Andy Horn's asking where we wanted the remains sent. He's passed out speechless."

"Dear me!" said Hearst. "For a man who's practically a total abstainer, I probably suffer more from alcoholism than any human being on the Western Hemisphere."

to the original schedule, so that suitable plans for return transportation might be arranged. About thirty of us raised our hands. The big man turned to one of the pack of docile soothsayers who trailed him about like so many trained Pomeranians.

"Son," he said, "run, please, down to the dispatcher [there was a private telegraph office on the domain], and tell him to notify the railroad that instead of one train back tomorrow night we'll need two trains—one with accommodations for thirty or thereabouts tomorrow and one for about forty of us, including myself, the night after."

Most of those present seemingly took this as a matter-of-course. They'd been at San Simeon before. But it was my first experience. As I recall, I perspired, but in what I trust was a restrained manner.

At a convenient lull to draw him aside, I said, "Mr. Hearst, far be it from me, a comparative stranger here, to pry into a kindly taskmaster's mental processes but, purely by hearsay, I've gathered that hiring private trains runs into money, what with locomotives and conductors and Pullman drawing rooms and free ice water and all. What's more, a good many of this bunch came west riding brake-beams; they should be grateful for berths to stretch out on. Private cars for us, if you will have it so—I feel I could acquire the private car habit easily—so long as somebody else foots the bill. But why, if I might be so bold as to ask, why a whole private train for our batch?"

"Well, I tell you, Cobb," he said and so far as I could tell spoke in dead seriousness, "if your group had only private cars they'd be parked on a siding at San Luis Obispo station until the regular train came through and you'd be jerked about while they were hitching you on and getting under way again. I used to use a private car going down from here and just about the time I got to sleep that infernal train would come along and bump into us and wake me up. I hate to be bumped around that way. And I figure any friends I'm entertaining hate to be bumped, too."

I still ponder sometimes the problem of how many thousands of dollars it cost him to keep a mixed lot of actors and writers and social climbers and bogus princelings and British remittance men from being bumped.

Now that his vast kingdom somewhat has crumpled through

sheer top-heaviness above and the burrowing termites of debt beneath, his detractors have increased to a host, ringing him in like jackals that snap at the flanks of a sick lion. Paradoxically, I've noticed that frequently the author of one of these screeds interrupts the embittered flow to offer Hearst begrudged praise for a virtue to which he is not in the least entitled. He is credited with having jacked up the average of newspaper salaries in America. Outsiders have been saying this from the long-ago hour when he broke into the business as an audacious and headstrong fledgling, with the wise-acres all predicting that not even old Senator George Hearst's massed millions would keep this wastrel son of his afloat for long in the troubled journalistic waters. It is a fact that all along Hearst had paid his hand-picked favorites more than any opposing publisher ever before had paid anybody; more than his fierce and ruthless competition could induce them to pay now.

It was by dint of this seemingly extravagant but really wise strategy that he raided rival hen roosts for such shrill-crowing editorial roosters as Arthur Brisbane and Morrill Goddard; for Tom Powers and George Luks and other popular illustrators; for petted columnists and coddled comic artists; for paragraphers, for commentators, specialists in all conspicuous lines. But inside our guild he always had been notorious for paying his run-of-the-mill employees as poor wages as any of the metropolitan plants paid, poorer wages than some of them customarily paid in the past. That has been his schedule—game pies and rich pastry for the pampered and widely-publicized stars, and the top union scale for the technical squads—the unions saw to that. But as for the mute inglorious sub-editors and copy-desk hounds and plain legmen, their portions were those of Lazarus in the parable—the crumbs that fell from the rich man's table.

Still and all, Hearst has done but little more sinning in this respect than many have. Even if the pay for the anonymous groups generally is better than it used to be, the truth remains that, considered what they give in ability and energy and devotion, such newspaper-men are as overworked and as poorly paid as any like class in the whole economic frame.

Saying this, I'm not dipping my pen into a font of staled rancor, vintaged out of my own experiences as a toiler in vanished vineyards.

My case was a favored and a fortunate one when compared with most of my confreres of three decades back. Before I quit the daily grind to browse in the less hectic and more succulent pastures of magazine work, I had by painful degrees forced my stipend to a peak where the Pulitzer shop was paying me $150 weekly. These figures wouldn't startle creation today but thirty-odd years ago they constituted a breath-taking salary for one who neither was a departmental head nor an executive. Whether it was true or not, I was called the highest paid reporter in this country and perhaps in the world. In addition I regularly harvested smaller sums for signed contributions to the special pages of the *Evening World* and the magazine section of the *Sunday World*. Moreover, the *World* permitted me to market my contributions in outlying cities through the McClure syndicate. Frequently my income for a single month was upwards of a thousand dollars—and did I count myself a darling of prime luck!

Now, in those times the *World*, on payday, had a way of dividing the sheep from the goats. If a man drew as much as a hundred dollars a week he went to a certain window of the cashier's corridor downstairs and personally was handed a check by old Mr. Angus Shaw, the demure and dapper little Scotch auditor. The check was a symbol of herd importance, proof of high standing on the roster. If he drew a lesser sum he took his humble place in the queue of the common flock and at a second window received an envelope containing his due—in cash.

To keep down heartburnings among compatriots who were not supposed to know how much I earned, my wages were apportioned to three separate payrolls—exactly $99 from the *Evening World*, $51 from the *Sunday World*, and various lesser dribs for my side endeavors. So that, come Saturday afternoon, instead of joining the aristocrats and the gentry at the main wicket, I marched in line to the other wicket and acquired three or more envelopes containing currency and silver bits. This utterly transparent little farce was played out fifty-two times a year during at least two years, everyone concerned keeping a straight face.

It was at the tag end of this profitable period that I met Lorimer. Already I had sold him, by mail, my first efforts at out-and-out fiction. Coming up to New York for an annual banquet of the

American Publishers' Association, he asked me to be a guest at his table. After the dinner, which was quite moist, an exhilarated coterie of us took a drive through Central Park in a squadron of chartered hansom cabs. By invitation I was riding with Lorimer. All of a sudden he broke off his plaintive singing of "Glow, Little Glowworm, Glitter" which was, as would develop, his favored song and his only one for festive occasions, and he said:

"How about hooking up with the *Post* when your time's up at that treadmill down in Park Row?"

"I'd like it," I said and expanded inwardly, the words being sweet music to my ears.

"Well, then, first chance you get, run down to Philadelphia and we'll talk it over."

But when I did run down to Philadelphia, there didn't seem to be much talking-over to be done.

"I'd like to have the call on your time for such suitable stunts as may come along," he stated, "and the refusal of the stuff you turn out on your own hook. I shan't mind you doing a little free-lancing on the side for other shops, but if your output gets by here, I figure we'll be keeping you so busy you won't want to be doing much of that." (And so he did keep me busy, for eleven years.)

"Suits me," I said, "when do I sign up?"

"You don't sign up," he said. "I don't hold with contracts, exclusive or otherwise. Haven't any contract myself with Cyrus H. K. Curtis and never put anybody else under contract. Just verbal understandings—gentlemen's agreements, as they call them. But I reckon that's a joke."

The doubtful lease-hold of a contract, after these six years with the *World*, had gotten into my blood. Perhaps I wasn't cut out to be a maverick ranging the great open spaces? Perhaps I'd worn the brand of a corral boss too long?

"I know what's ailing you," diagnosed Lorimer, seeing how I hesitated. "You're suffering from an occupational disease which is very catching and sometimes becomes incurable. It's brought on by exposure at stated intervals to a salary envelope. It makes a coward of a man—makes him afraid to swap a dubious security for a better chance where he can be more or less independent."

I admitted the impeachment.

"All right then," he said, "I've got a treatment to last till you're restored to health. Every other week, unless in the meantime you've sent in enough acceptable copy to off-balance the sum I have in mind, the cashier will mail you a check for that figure as advance payment against future performances." His face cracked in the reticent Lorimer grin. "And, son, any time two whole weeks go by and you don't beat that guarantee, you're automatically fired."

I went back to Yonkers, where we lived then, and metaphorically spat on my hands and proceeded to beat the haslets out of an already maltreated L. C. Smith machine. And to this hour I don't know what contingent amount, if any, Lorimer had calculated out in his brain on that long-ago afternoon.

11

THE UNBELIEVABLE CHAPIN

Away back in 1905—and that in retrospect seems almost as far behind me as the Old Red Sandstone Period must seem to a geologist—I moved one door over from the *Evening Sun's* squatty home where I'd done fifteen months' close confinement in apprenticeship to cosmopolitan routines as counter-distinguished from the country style formulas which I thought I knew. It was on a fine October morning that I fitted myself into the berth awaiting me in the dingy cluttered tower of the Pulitzer Building alongside Brooklyn Bridge.

This befell in an epoch of part-way transition. Joseph Pulitzer's properties were no longer so blatantly pumpkin-colored as during the preceding decade when Pulitzer strove to plunge as deeply and splash as furiously in the paint pots of Hysterical Journalism as Hearst who—pardon, please, the mixed metaphors—was the proud papa of that misbegotten babykins. At that, in spots, they still somewhat were tainted with the stubborn bilious stain. They were over the yellow fever but still had the yellow jaundice. So my new taskmaster, Chapin of the evening edition, continued to enjoy a fine protective coloration. Sensationalism—even diluted sensationalism—was gravy to Chapin's spoon.

My transfer coincided with a stage when the various Pulitzer agencies had become thoroughly habituated to an absentee proprietorship. After contending for nearly all his life with faulty sight, Mr. Pulitzer was totally blind. Moreover the long fight against his affliction, the entailed curtailment of bodily activities and to top all else, the strain of unceasing, self-imposed toil in earlier days, were taking vicious toll of his physical resistance, not of his mental resources though. His mistreated nerves had frayed until the smallest alien noise was a monstrous torture to the captious recluse. He abode in inner compartments of sound-proofed houses or took long voyages aboard a private yacht having quilted bulkheads and padded floors for the owner's quarters—that same yacht which privately we called "the prison hulk" because of the existence his bullied underlings were presumed to endure while aboard her. We heard tales: His companions spoke in sign language unless they were called on to answer him or read to him. Stewards and mess boys wore felt-soled slippers, and lost their jobs did they so much as let a dish clink. When he craved to hear music—and hired some fine artist to play— no other person could sit with the master during the concert for fear a rustle or a creak might disturb him. Cowed subordinates crept about, pussyfooted, trying to anticipate what neurotic whim might next possess him. In the main his tiptoeing secretarial corps was made up of docile young Englishmen—university grinds and curates' sons and the like. Americans were too likely to revolt against such strict ordinances; they wouldn't linger for long among the stealthy altar boys of that strange diocese. Or at least such were the reports that got ashore.

So Mr. Pulitzer dictated the destinies of his manifold interests at long distance in intervals between seizures when his infirmities utterly incapacitated him—a giant intelligence eternally condemned to the darkest of dungeons, a caged eagle furiously belaboring the bars. Not one in twenty of his employees, and these few all veterans, had ever laid eyes on him, although most there, from the straw-bosses in the private sanctums down to the most callow seminarians of the lower grades, had felt the weight of a heavy displeasure over some transgression of his code or, by roundabout, had praise and perhaps a cash bonus or a quick promotion or both, for a job done smartly and to his autocratic standards. Even so it was bound to be that Mr. Pulitzer could not have cognizance of all the conniving for authority and control that went on; the shabby conspiracies and the jockeying for advantage among his jealous surrogates; the free press notices and the sly puffery for influential people or for favored concerns which, disguised as legitimate reading matter, crept into his papers. The atmosphere was laden with office politics and sometimes was riven by it. Nevertheless, the spirit of independence which had been the cornerstone of the structure he had reared still governed all major policies. For a generation past

Pulitzer had been the people's crusader against entrenched corruption and financial skulduggery. He still meant to be. Not the most ambitious marplot among the bureaucrats dared tamper there. Hence no outside force, however powerful, could intrigue to pervert the color and shape of the real news as the *World* papers printed it.

I witnessed demonstrations of this fine attitude. For instance, once on a time the head of one of the biggest department stores up town—let's call it the Moffitt Store—arbitrarily threatened to annul his very handsome contract unless the *Evening World* omitted the name and purposely confused the locale of the store itself, in its account of a homicide which had been committed that noon in the restaurant that was an annex of the establishment. A husband had crept in amongst the diners and in cold blood riddled his estranged wife, a waitress there.

We found all this out when Don Seitz, at the moment Mr. Pulitzer's chief mouthpiece, came charging up from downstairs and burst into our midst.

"Listen," he called out so every hireling there might hear him, and his words were like crackling whips; "I want the name of that dam' store stuck into the first line of the first sentence of the first paragraph of this shooting story. I want the store's name repeated throughout the story whenever the use of it is warranted and maybe, for good measure, a few times when it isn't warranted. I want the panic among the patrons in the lunchroom fully described—children screaming, women fainting, men trying to climb out of the windows. I want the spot further identified by the number of the main entrance and by mention of the streets which border the store. And across the top of the first page I want this seven-column streamer smeared in the biggest stud-horse type we've got, 'MURDER AT MOFFITT'S.' We're going to teach certain busybodies that when they buy space in this paper they don't buy the paper along with it."

He taught them. The sequel seeped through by grapevine telegraph next day. The chastened merchant had begged Mr. Seitz to reopen the advertising lists to him and kindly let bygones be bygones. The joke of it was that he did not increase his appropriation for lineage in at least two subservient afternoon papers which had obeyed demands like unto those he so disastrously had made upon the *World* shop.

I am constrained to believe that at least one high-geared brisk-talking gentleman who figured in dual capacities might not have attained such prominence had the founder been overseeing things with his own eyes and overseering them with his own hands. This functionary filled a designated place in the directing organization besides which, as a sort of minister without portfolio, he held a vague scouting commission. He was idea man and suggestion maker. Railroad people would have called him a trouble shooter; big business, an efficiency engineer. You'll recall that prior to the Year of the Big Wind in Wall Street nearly every great corporation used an efficiency engineer whose job was to spy out shortcomings and give advice for the betterment of things and generally to find out what was wrong. Following '29, however, this practice languished somewhat. Bankruptcy courts and Federal prosecutors and investigating Congressional committees took over the work of finding out what was wrong with many of America's larger commercial houses.

Our roving ambassador also temporarily occupied the desk of any brass hat who was ailing or on vacation or had over-extended himself in the merry Broadway game called playing saloon. This last didn't occur quite so often though as once it had. To begin with, there were facilities on the premises for indulgence. Doc Perry's snug little deadfall dispensed strong waters on the ground floor and malt beverages abundantly were on tap in the snack-stand up under the dome. Moreover, the old fetish that a brilliant newspaperman performed most brilliantly when in a highly incandescent state no longer prevailed, that is, conceded that it ever did prevail, which I doubt. Those the outsiders called newspaper Bohemians, Park Row commonly referred to as newspaper bums. And an editor would no more have detailed a confirmed inebriate to an important beat than a railway traffic manager would send a drunken engineer out to run one of his passenger trains. By that I don't mean to imply we were absolute teetotalers. But lapses from sobriety were much rarer then—and nowadays—than you would be led to believe by watching these weird conceptions of a city room which moving-picture studios have lately been putting on the screens.

Some of us who had opportunity to study this ranging emissary doubted not only his scientific fitness but his sense of fairness. Among ourselves we privily accused him of inviting volunteered ideas from the staff at large, then summarily turning them down as impractical or unsuitable. But within weeks or even days the same notions, only slightly changed about, sometimes would be launched with this gentleman sponsoring them and by inference at least, taking credit for having thought them up, all by himself. And we suspected that his judgment of news values was not quite as infallible as his cocksure attitude might indicate.

I remember once I took off the telephone what seemed to me about as macabre a little saga as any nightmare-ridden mind could conjure up. Common procedure would have been to give the essential facts in the first paragraph, then follow through with the details in an orderly processional of expansion. But this story, it seemed to me, called for different treatment. For two reasons every capable newspaperman has learned the academic rules of his trade, which are the tools of his trade. He learns them so that customarily he knows how to obey them, and also he learns those rules so that intelligently he may know when and where to break them.

I clicked off this heart-gripping story in substantially the same graphic sequence which had been employed by the efficient legman who relayed it in.

Over in Brooklyn lived, in semi-retirement, a wealthy elderly Jewish manufacturer. For his kindliness and his good deeds he was a sort of neighborhood institution. He seemed to have a greater share of the so-called Christian virtues than many a practicing Christian has. Two weeks before a stray cur had bitten a pet puppy of his. With his own hands he washed the cut and dressed it. He forgot about a tiny abrasion on one of his thumbs.

The injured animal developed hydrophobia and mercifully was put to death. But no such compassion was vouchsafed the man. At the first dreadful signs of infection on the part of the puppy he had taken the prescribed treatments. But it was too late. The virus was racing through his veins and the Pasteur injections could not overtake it.

Now, in hideous pain, he was awaiting the end. His jaws were locked so that he could not swallow solids; barely could speak between his clenched teeth. At first narcotics offered some temporary relief, now they had almost entirely lost their power to dull the agony. Between paroxysms he had called his family in and calmly had bade them farewell; to his attorney and his business associates had given directions for the disposition of his property; had made large bequests to charities—not all Jewish charities, either; then barred from the death chamber all save the nurses and the physicians. Because he fully realized what was ahead of him, he did not intend that anyone he loved should be witness to those expiring torments.

I wound up with this:

"The doctors give him three days, about. They wish they might shorten those three days. They realize what his finish will be like. And the worst of it is, the patient realizes too."

I hadn't elaborated the bald facts, nor pulled out any tremolo knobs. As I saw it there was here no need to thicken the appeal in a thing so poignant and so utterly pitiable. If the reader, reading my unadorned words, sensed what my emotions had been while writing them, why then his own sensibilities and his own sympathies and most of all his own imagination, would fill out the picture in all its pathos more adequately than any high-flown, tear-jerking rhetoric of mine could.

But when the edition was off the press, this man I have been speaking of came to me, an inky damp copy in his hand.

"Say, Cobb," he demanded, "what's the matter with you? I thought that story would get under your skin."

"It got under my skin, all right," I said.

"Then why didn't you cut loose on it? Why didn't you tell what that poor devil's thoughts must be—describe his feelings, describe his family's feelings and the grief and the hopelessness that's passing through their minds."

I couldn't help saying it:

"Listen, please. If I had the power to do that I'd have the ghosts

of such pikers as Robert Louis Stevenson and old man Victor Hugo
reaching for their hats."

He went away, shaking his head. But Chapin, coming on watch
next day had complimentary words to say:

"It got me and I'm pretty tolerably callous. If it got me, I guess
it got the average man in the street."*

Another day the same roving plenipotentiary drifted across to
where I was skimming through a stack of out-of-town papers. I
hadn't been in New York long enough to acquire the average New
York newspaperman's insular and insulated viewpoint. He'd be
concerned only with what occurred in New York or adjacent thereto. I trust I never did altogether take on that pose. Stubbornly I
entertained the belief that beyond Manhattan Island was quite a
sizable stretch of territory where interesting people did live and
interesting things did occur. From a differing angle I was full
cognizant of what seemingly came as a considerable surprise to a
typical East Side Tammany leader who probably never before had
been west of Albany and who, the first morning out, on his way as
a delegate to a national convention in Kansas City, gazed from the
dining-car window into the well-peopled Ohio landscape unreeling

---

* To Chapin's credit be it said, he was never slow at offering
praise or posting special awards on the bulletin board when the cogs
in his machine had meshed smoothly. Also an admirable quality of
his was that when some irate citizen charged a reporter with misstatement or double-dealing, Chapin was never the one to jump at
the conclusion that the impeached man was impeachable. He gave
accused the benefit of every reasonable doubt, standing by the guns
until conclusive guilt had been shown or vindication was offered.
This gave us confidence because a reporter's business is other people's business. And generally speaking, those other people are
conspiring to circumvent him. Hardly a big story breaks but it is
to somebody's interest that the real facts be hidden or, anyhow
glossed over, because somebody is due to suffer shame or ridicule
or punishment if the truth gets into print. So the reporter must
match trickiness against guile, must cook up stratagems if he's going
to fetch in the spoils and not always may he be overscrupulous
about the methods he employs to meet the wiles of those leagued
together to thwart him. He must turn over chips and pry under logs
to find where the bugs are hidden and then stick pins in the bugs.

past, and in tones of mild wonder remarked to Martin Green, of our staff who was breakfasting with him, "Martin, me lad, no matter where you go there's always human life."*

As I was saying, our argus-eyed ranger interrupted me while, in a spare hour, I glanced through first one and then another sheet which I had borrowed from the exchange editor's cuddyhole.

"I've been thinking," he said. "I've been thinking we could do with a little new blood on the magazine page. A new comic series now. I could use another comic series or so if it didn't cost too much. So as you go through these papers, if you run across the work of any chaps out in the sticks that looks promising I wish you'd cut out samples of their stuff and slip them to me. Don't say anything about it, though. I might take on a couple of youngsters, providing they'd listen to reason regarding salary, which they no doubt would, getting a chance to break into New York."

During ensuing weeks I saved typical examples of the daily offerings of an artist on a Louisville paper and an artist on a San Francisco paper. I'd never heard of either of them before. I judged their reputations were purely regional and as it turned out this, for the time being, was true.

---

* Even more definitely confirmed in his metropolitan status was "Smitty," the factotum at Andy Horn's bar, a lifesaving station down under the bridge and much in favor with sailors, longshoremen and thirsty reporters. Smitty had been foaled on Cherry Hill and fetched up in Chatham Square. He had never been outside the five boroughs, so that no matter where he went he was still in the Greater City. But he took a week's leave to visit his sister who was married to a German market gardener living a few miles back of Newark. His brother-in-law owned a car (vintage, about 1906) and he took Smitty on a sight-seeing tour into that strange hinterland lying on the farther side of the Hudson River.

"Well, Smitty, what sort of a time did you have?" inquired a regular customer.

The returned one looked up from where he was refurbishing a brass cuspidor.

"Me, I don't like that Joisey," he said. "Never again for me!"

"What's wrong with Jersey?"

"Too confusin'," stated Smitty. "Why say, Cul, believe it or not, all dem towns over there is got diff'unt names!"

I took my two batches of clippings in to the great man. He thumbed them briskly and then magisterially fired a double-barrelled ultimatum:

"Much obliged, but there's nothing doing here. This first fellow's stuff, this Kentucky boy, whoever he is, is purely small-town stuff, hick comedy. It couldn't possibly go over in a big town. And this second kid—he must be a kid—doesn't know a thing in the world about draftsmanship. His drawings are too crude, too exaggerated—positively outlandish. I don't think he's got any funny notions, either."

It came to pass within the next few years that both these unknowns landed in New York and neither proved a downright failure there. One was Fontaine Fox; the other was Rube Goldberg.

Admitted that I'm somewhat late in making my nomination for the ability instantaneously to appraise ability—or the lack of it—I feel that in Newspaperdom's Hall of Fame, my former mentor is entitled to a niche adjoining the one long since voted by acclamation to the late "Cozy" Nobles. Or at least my candidate should have a wall plaque. Such of his contemporaries as survive will recall that Cozy, being then Sunday editor of a San Francisco paper, summarily refused to buy at prevalent space rates—approximately six dollars a column—an unpublished tale which had been offered to him by a diffident, spectacled young Anglo-Indian writer newly arrived out of the Far East and needing the money. As the accepted version ran, the story was declined as lacking in literary merit and human appeal and anyhow it was too confoundedly long-drawn-out with descriptions of things which readers in this country didn't know about and wouldn't be interested in. The name of this story was *The Man Who Would Be King*.

There is, I now belatedly confess, but one blemish on the scintillating splendor of this historic episode and that, as you might say, merely a technical flaw. In 1913 Mrs. Cobb and I were making our first trip abroad and we spent a day as guests of Rudyard Kipling at his home in Sussex. At lunch I asked Mr. Kipling for the circumstantial details and, with a shading of pensive regret in his voice, he told me he would be glad to furnish them except for the drawback that to the best of his recollection and belief the thing never happened at all. He had not made this disavowal before, he said. As a romancer himself, who was he to mar a conception of such pure and classic beauty? Nor, as far as I recall, did Cozy Noble, as the other principal concerned, ever deny it. Why should he? Vicariously, he shared in a famed Kiplingesque tradition. It gave him eminence, distinction. I never heard that it hurt his professional reputation. Every good marksman is entitled to one clean miss of the bull's-eye and Cozy had some high scores to his credit.

Returning to Chapin, I'm willing to make affidavit that I never saw him miss any targets. And truthfully I could say that for scarcely any other man put, as he constantly was, in a station where offhand sharpshooting at illusive marks was necessary. To watch him, whether in action or at ease, made a fascinating sport—this malign, vulpine, competent creature. I didn't know while I studied him, didn't know it until years later, but I was storing up material for a whole series of fiction tales centering about a thinly disguised portrait of Chapin.

Physically, he was a treatment in dulled granitoid tones: his hair faded to dun; his skin the color of wet wood ashes, as though overlain by some strange unwholesome patina; his face that was an ashlared gray paving block with jaws as square as a lynx's jaws and as tight; his eyes which suggested disks of polished flint. The shallow light in these eyes never seemed to come from within but always from without. His voice seemed to match the rest of him and to be a proper part of him. It was part whine and part snarl. Big game hunters have told me that a hostile leopard has a voice like that.

All day long, crouched in lonesome state behind his big flat desk on a slightly raised dais, this prodigy ruled his dukedom—ruled it pitilessly but most exceeding well. And all day long, except when he ate, which was phenomenally often, he kept a cigar clamped at the corner of his taut cross slot of a mouth. He ate ice cream, pies, doughnuts, cakes, orders of pickled cherries or canned peaches, jam, candy, sticky nut bars, and swigged coffee that would be half sweetening. In one of his rare bursts of confidence he told me that as a strolling actor in his youth and later when he took on newspaper work in Chicago, he had been a heavy drinker and that still through every waking hour there was a craving for liquor inside him which he could mitigate, but never entirely quench, by feeding those fires with sugars and starches which fermented alcoholically in his stom-

ach. He told me also about the time in Tombstone—or perhaps it
was in Dodge City?—when he took potshots at another itinerant
trouper, one Edward Fitzgerald, subsequently called Eddie Foy.
They were playing in rival repertoire companies and pique between
them arose over a frail sister of the community. To prove his versatility he boasted that sometimes, when *Uncle Tom's Cabin* was the
bill, he had played Simon Legree and sometimes Uncle Tom. Now
though he was Simon Legree and, by the unwinking stare in those
snake eyes, you could tell when he contemplated attack on some
unlucky Uncle Tom whose inefficiency or whose slackness had
infuriated him. He would carry such a grievance for days though,
hugging it to him like a possession dear and fragile, before he loosed
the vials of his wrath on the condemned man. He was something
out of a storybook. And knew his business like nobody's business.

Chapin had dealt with flaring headlines so long that automatically he thought in headlines and unconsciously spoke in headlines.
"Barton Currie," with the rubber transmitter still at his ear he would
call across the city room, "take Johnny Haggerty off booth number
two. 'Tiny Tot With Penny Clutched In Chubby Hand Dies Under Tram Before Mother's Eyes!' Rush along three sticks of it,
will you, and make it snappy, Barton? We need something to
brighten up the front page of the Home Edition with."

Without any affectation, he dealt conversationally in such copy-
reader's stand-bys as "Probe," "Foe," "Rift," "Fray" and "Slay,"
"Dragnet," "Prey" and "Rack" and "Pact." Quite seriously he
told me he rather liked a certain popular murderess of the moment
because she had a nice short name, one that would fit into almost any
top caption.

He had the faculty—not acquired I think, but probably his by
nature—of being able to sink any private sympathies he might have
into his unremitting greed for the news. While the story was running, human beings were not human beings. They had been flesh
and blood creatures before, they might be again. Now they were
just copy. Senior members of the staff used to tell how on the day
of that appalling holocaust, the burning of the overladen excursion
steamer *General Slocum* in East River, case-hardened reporters were
made sick with revulsion almost to vomiting as Chapin gloated over
the mounting totals of death and horror that poured in by telephone

and in the volleying cylinders of *City News* flimsy. "Women and
children jumping overboard with clothing on fire!" he would shout
exultantly. "Water full of charred bodies!" And between these
outcries he would be pacing back and forth humming a simmering
little tuneless tune. But next day, they admitted, he gave a week's
salary—and it was a fine large salary—to the fund for the sufferers.
He was fond of money but fond also of spending it.*

Making up for early hardships, he reveled in luxury as a cat
would, rolling in a catnip bed. He lived in a suite at one of the most
lavish hotels. He had owned a span of trotting horses and had
raced with the best of the harness drivers on the old Speedway.
When I knew him he owned a beautifully equipped sloop and sailed
her himself, almost always alone. He liked good clothes and wore
the best clothes—and the most foppish—that tailors could make. He
was vain of his compact, straight figure, so he walked all reared

---

* Johnnie Goldfrap was an Englishman, a jaunty, foppish,
happy-go-lucky person with a streak of real brilliancy in him. With
Chapin he maintained a sort of sleeping feud. In spare times he
wrote dime novels under a pen name, invariably describing somewhere in each yarn a horrible-smelling, revolting secret compound
used by murderous conspirators and most infernally deadly. It was
called "Chapinite." Chapin wouldn't fire Goldfrap because he was
too valuable a reporter but occasionally when Goldfrap played
hooky, or reported for duty in a weaving way, Chapin suspended
him without pay. Johnnie was on one of these disciplinary vaca-
tions when Chapin fell ill. The report got about that he was critically ill, which wasn't so. Somebody's wish must have been father
to the rumor. In the midst of his illness his birthday came along and
a hand in the shop—probably a new hand—started a fund to buy
some flowers suitable for a birthday, and likewise for an invalid,
thereby, as it were, aiming to kill two birds with the same stone.
Down in Doc Perry's snug little bar-room on the ground floor of the
Pulitzer Building the originator of this thoughtful design was way-
laying incoming and outgoing members of the staff as they stopped
by, and garnering from them assessed shares in the purse, when
Johnnie meandered groggily in.

"Say, Goldfrap, you're just in time," hailed the collector. "How
about slipping me a couple of dollars to help buy some flowers for
the Boss?"

"Great notion! It's a positive pleasure," gurgled Johnnie and

back, with his heels coming down like drumsticks on a snare drum.
Having probably not a friend on earth—how would the Chapins
of this earth have friends?—he longed for and cultivated the company of the rich and the talked about, paying for the boon of their
society with flattering write-ups which, as supervisor of the news
streams, he could smuggle into type. Indeed scandal had it that in
part his ultimate downfall was due to the calculated treachery of
a distinguished capitalist. A member of this man's family had become involved in some rather smelly legal and domestic complications and Chapin, it was alleged, guided the underground campaign
which saved the family name from much unpleasant publicity—and
did not lose anything by it, either. Not content with the rewards
he received, it was said he applied the screws to his patron for more.
It was all done within the law so you couldn't call it blackmail. At
length the secretly resentful victim tipped Chapin to put his remaining capital into a certain speculative stock and then through his
brokers, rigged the market so that Chapin lost about everything he
owned, besides funds he didn't own, these being legacies entrusted
to him for investment by women relatives. Parts of this sordid tale
undoubtedly were true; the extra brocading was office gossip.
Women troubles also contributed to the final tragedy. Chapin
openly gloried in his prowess as an elderly flirt, while still showing
an incongruous but apparently sincere affection for the faded delicate wisp of a woman who was his wife, the same wife that he shot
in her sleep, then hung a "Do Not Disturb" sign on the outer door-
knob and waited five hours for the life to run out of her.

I hold it was entirely characteristic of the man that personally he

---

hauled out his contribution. "I'll not be present at the funeral," he
said, rocking on his heels, "but I heartily endorse it."

"This isn't for a funeral," explained the busybody.

"Don't tell me that Chapin's not dead," pleaded Johnnie. "Let
me have my little daydream."

"Matter of fact, he's better."

"Hold on," demanded Goldfrap, suddenly turned suspicious.
"What are these flowers for then?"

"Why, for Chapin's birthday."

"Half-wit," cried Johnnie, "hand me back those two bucks
before I knock your block off."

utterly lacked a sense of humor yet was spry to note and play up to humor in the news. Of all the store of yarns that focused about him, none is more familiar than the very ancient one of the reporter who was sent to ask a large and brawny Irish contractor why his wife had eloped with a Chinese laundry boy. Some hours later the battered youth, dragging himself to a telephone, recited the melancholy score of what dreadful things had befallen him, then plaintively added, "And, Mr. Chapin, he says if he ever lays eyes on me again, he'll kill me."

"Is that so?" shouted Chapin, who for all his bullying and bluster notably was a coward. "Well, you go right back there and tell that big ruffian he can't intimidate ME!"

I was present when a staff photographer dashed in with one of the most ghastly snapshots that ever was published in an American newspaper before the first of the tabloids taught us how far beyond bounds of common decency the debased art of pictorial realism might be carried. Mayor Gaynor had been wounded by a crazed assassin on a Hoboken pier as he was preparing to sail for Europe. At that precise instant our photographer had his camera aimed on the mayor and his friends. The developed negative showed the stricken man collapsing in the arms of "Big Bill" Edwards, with horrified bystanders stampeding in the background.

Chapin fairly caressed this atrocity when it was thrust into his hands.

"What a beautiful thing!" he called. "Look—blood all over him! And exclusive, too!"

Late one hot Sunday night, Russell Sage, that ancient thimblerigger who was so envied for his piled-up dollars and so despised as a miser and a merciless money-grabber, died rather suddenly. Now for years and years Chapin had played attendant coyote to Sage's gray wolf, for he was by way of being the octogenarian's nephew and, as all of us knew, had been encouraged to believe that for services rendered in print and elsewhere, the old man meant to leave him a considerable fortune, at least half a million, according to the account.

Sage's body hardly was cold when at our shop rumors from more or less authentic sources percolated in to the effect that various persons, also related to the unlamented Midas, were preparing to contest the validity of his will on grounds of mental incapacity. This was before noon of Monday. The bare facts of the death had been flashed in an early edition. Now the story was being expanded.

All in a dither Chapin darted to my side. I was throwing together the main account.

"Cobb," he rasped nervously, "do a new introduction, quick as you can. Play up the fact that in spite of his age, Uncle Russell had one of the keenest brains of any man in Wall Street—clear as a bell up to the last moment—knew exactly what he was doing and saying—everyone who saw him marveled at his grasp on things. And a few paragraphs along press this point again. It's only fair to his memory. And only fair to the rightful beneficiaries of that rugged, misunderstood old soul that a gang of disappointed bloodsuckers shouldn't be given encouragement in any dirty scheme they'll try to cook up. Get me?"

I got him. No doubt about it, I got him. Chuckling to myself, I proceeded to pound out a bill of mental health for deceased. I was just polishing it off when Chapin emerged from a telephone booth, a sorely stricken apparition. He was trembling all over. He rushed over to me. I think he would have cried except that rage was choking back the sobs. After that I was ready to accept the story that crocodiles had been seen to weep.

"Throw away that new introduction," he ordered. "I've just heard—well, something has come up that changes the whole aspect of this sanity business. I was wrong. Why, Cobb, there isn't any doubt about it that miserable old ingrate was doddering, senile—in no shape to dispose of his affairs—putty in the hands of any unscrupulous scoundrels who wanted to enrich themselves at the expense of those who are really entitled to a suitable share in his fortune. Just so much putty! So write another lead, bringing out this fact. And intimate pretty strongly that already a number of the surviving relatives are taking preliminary steps to fight in the courts for justice and what's rightfully coming to them."

My private guess was right, as it turned out. There was a leak. Some lawyer who so soon was on the prowl to secure clients in the threatened litigation, or possibly it was a not entirely disinterested member of the Sage menage, had passed the word along that by the terms of Sage's latest will, Chapin's legacy had been reduced to a

sum no greater than the bequests specified for numerous other relatives and very, very much smaller than the amount of his expectations.

But almost at the last moment before press time and after more
frenzied telephoning by my distressed superior, came the third
switch. The original lead, the one which so fulsomely praised Sage's
testamentary capacity, was hurriedly rescued from the wastepaper
basket and printed as written.

So speedily, it seemed, a compromise had been framed, Chapin
having been guaranteed that if he lined up with the principal beneficiaries and used his influence to discourage the filing of any law-
suits by the rest of the kinfolks, ways and means clandestinely would
be found to increase his inheritance out of some special fund or
other. At least so the whispered rumors went.

Thus we see how, behind the scenes, the news may be hewn to
order when the hand of some privileged highbinder is doing the
carving. In behalf of an honorable and usually a scrupulously conducted industry I ought to say though that such hatchet-man's tactics are no longer common. I doubt they ever were common except
in the departed epoch of violently partisan politics when it was
deemed ethical to say anything, however preposterous and unfair,
about the hated opposition. Even then rabid party loyalty and not
a selfish or venal design generally steered these bygone pen-pushers.
In the face of subtle temptation, which may or may not be backed by
the promise of private enrichment, the modern brethren nearly
always keep faith with the public. Mind you, I'm not ascribing
to my fraternity purer motives than the motives of trusted men in
any legitimate line of endeavor you might care to name. Not necessarily as moral principles but as sound business methods which make
for prestige and public confidence and the acquisition of that precious, unbuyable asset known as good will, they have found out, as
millions of other merchandisers have, that honesty is the best policy
and virtue is its own reward, not to mention that only too often the
chickens hatched of bribery came cackling home to roost, with
income tax snoopers or a grand jury shooing them along.

Getting back on the main line, it was some months later and
apparently apropos of nothing which immediately had gone before,
when Chapin took from a locked drawer in his desk six deposit books

and showed me he had opened comparatively recent savings-bank accounts aggregating $150,000. Perhaps he read on my face what suddenly was in my mind. So he made the somewhat hurried explanation that he merely wished to prove to me how gratifying the fruits of laudable thrift might be, by indirection indicating that he thought me overly inclined to spend my earnings before I earned them. But I still was just skeptical enough to suspect that a different purpose might be hidden behind the gesture—a sort of testimonial to the success of an expert mercenary's coup, now confidentially revealed before the understrapper who had been dragooned for co-operative spade work in digging out the loot.

In those six years and more of my service on the *Evening World* I saw Chapin visibly discomforted only once. But this once was devastating in its immediate repercussion upon that brassy and previously impregnable front.

Surreptitiously, Chapin had gone about separating from the pay roll a well-meaning but blundersome and irritating worker. While he was nursing his wrath to keep it warm, "Red" McLaughlin, better known as "Wurra Wurra," the high-tempered and sweet-natured and occasionally irresponsible head of the copy desk, learned what was afoot. Behind the old freebooter's back he interceded to save the intended sacrifice. McLaughlin had an instinctive sympathy for underpups and singed cats and the courage to champion their causes. Chapin in turn found out about this checkmating maneuver. Nobody ever fooled Chapin for long—except Chapin.

Alongside his desk we saw the two men heatedly threshing out the issue and as McLaughlin, having said his say, went back to his slot in the copy desk, Chapin sung out, purposely lifting his voice: "Red, you're too mushy-hearted, too sentimental for your own good." Then, and may heaven forgive him for saying it because we who listened never did, he spoke words which were true and brutal prophecy: "You'll never get ahead in this game, never get an inch past where you are now. And when you die, you won't leave a red cent to bury you with."

"True for you, Chapin!" retorted McLaughlin. "But when *I* die there'll be a hell of a lot of people will come to the funeral."

It was as though an unexpected broadside had blown a quarter-deck right out from under the feet of some cocky bucko mate.

We saw Chapin wince and go white as a flour mask. For an hour he sat there, staring at nothing and chewing the dead stub of a cigar to sodden pulp, a shriveled and blighted shape. I have stated already that I believe Chapin was psychic. With that sixth sense of his I think perhaps he was tearing apart the veil of the future, no longer beholding himself in the flattering mirror which usually he held before his deluded eyes but in an honester light. I think perhaps he saw a man being slowly stripped naked of power and perquisites; a man growing older and losing his grip; colleagued against for his job by envious interlopers; deserted by men who despised him and no longer feared to disguise their feelings; his lady loves gone, his credit gone, his hoarded money altogether gone; the prospect of prosecution for misappropriation of other people's money becoming hourly more menacing; he saw a despairing man secretly buying a lot in a Washington burying ground and ordering a tombstone on which he had his wife's name engraved and his own, with a blank left where the date of the two deaths would go; next the murder committed and suicide almost committed, but the killer turning craven so that he could not force his finger to press the trigger again; then the final scroll unfolding on a lifer's cell at Sing Sing and a wan bent figure of a man in convict gray feebly pottering among the glorious flower beds which he had created behind those harsh walls with nothing better to start on than some dime packets of flower seed and a three-dollar set of gardening tools donated by Father Cashin, the prison chaplain.* I was sorry for

---

* When they checked Chapin in at Sing Sing he was assigned to edit the prison paper, the *Star of Hope.* He made it so popular it choked to death of its own popularity. Then he was made clerk in the library where he had perhaps fifteen busy minutes in a day. He wrote an autobiography there. It was mostly alibis and extenuating circumstances. Still in some of its chapters he neither spared himself nor anybody else. Even yet there were crackling embers of the dictatorial heat which after his arrest led him to give out interviews from his cell in the Tombs criticizing as shoddy writing and bad reporting the spreads that were being printed about his crime.

With the book done, inaction preyed on him until he became a melancholiac. Warden Lawes, a wise man and a skilled criminologist, one who can be kindly without turning maudlin sentimentalist, ordered him to quit brooding in dark corners and get

Chapin, watching him that day. I'm sorry for him now as I review the picture he made for us that day.

When he got up to go, his feet dragged a little and his shape, always before so jauntily carried, was drooped so that his shoulders were no longer firm, like stiff mansards, but sagged down like gables. Or so it seemed.

Coming in next morning, he somewhat had lost the blasted look. He halted in the doorway, obviously anticipating the reprisal. We guessed he had been awake in the night thinking up some shaft of retarded repartee.

"Red!" he barked out. "Red, when I got uptown last evening I

---

outdoors. Chapin wanted to know what he would do when he got outdoors. "Make a garden," said Lawes, offhand. "What with?" said Chapin. "That's up to you," said Lawes. "I can furnish you with all the rough labor you need but no money." In the library Chapin found, of all things for such a place, a florist's catalogue two years old. He studied it. Presently he had a whole squad of helpers digging out the rubbish which paved the filled-in enclosures and fetching in topsoil from vacant state property near by. And he was learning about floriculture—cultivating, irrigating, fertilizing.

The story of what he was doing found its way into the news and Ray Long read it and sent me up to do an article for the *Cosmopolitan* about it—how the bleak compound, covered with smelly garbage cans that had been the last sight on which a condemned man's wistful eyes rested as he was led into the Death House was a glorious tulip bed; how specimen roses, the gifts of rich men in the neighborhood to whom Chapin mailed begging letters, now by hundreds lined the walkways; how the glass-roofed hut where formerly autopsies were performed on the scorched bodies of those who died in the Chair had been converted into a conservatory and aviary. As a result of the publicity we gave to the story, thousands of dollars' worth of rare plants and tropical exotics came as donations from all over the country and from countries as far away as Australia and South Africa; and an elderly Jewish philanthropist, who specialized in rehabilitating ex-convicts, came to see me. He had heard I was on excellent terms with Governor Al Smith and said if I would ask Smith to ask the Pardon Board to move up Chapin's name on the list of applicants for parole, and Smith complied with the request, then as soon as Chapin had

told Mrs. Chapin what you said here yesterday afternoon. And you know what Mrs. Chapin said, Red? She said, 'How Irish!' "

Everybody roared, and McLaughlin was roaring louder than any. All pouter-breasted and springy, Chapin, like an old gray cock pigeon, strutted to his place on his platform. He didn't often misinterpret things but this time he had misinterpreted. He thought the laugh was on McLaughlin.

---

been freed, he would pledge himself to give the released man employment as assistant foreman of his extensive gardens. I told him I would be glad to co-operate provided Chapin agreed to the plan.

"Agreed?" he asked in astonishment. "Who ever heard of a prisoner who didn't want to get out of prison? I've been dealing with convicts for years and never heard of such a thing."

"You haven't been dealing with Chapin," I said.

I telephoned the Executive Mansion at Albany and told the Governor I might drive up next day to make a personal request—perhaps. In the morning I stopped by Sing Sing and was taken in where Chapin superintended the building from scrap material of an annex to house his rapidly growing collection of caged song birds.

"Listen," he stated in his old peremptory way, "give that gentleman my thanks, but beg him please, not to bother me again until I give the word. This job's not half finished—I've got a lot of plans—and I never yet quit a job until it was finished. Anyhow, I don't fancy the idea of being a pensioner on some millionaire's bounty, coddled one day and the next being pointed out as Chapin the life termer. If I change my mind I'll let you, or him, hear from me. So far as I know I'm the only man here who hasn't either put in a petition for parole or pardon or isn't fixing to do so. It makes me unique. Well, if that's all, good day and much obliged, Cobb. I've got to keep this sloppy gang busy."

As I went away, bound for New York now, and not for Albany, he was snapping out orders like a drillmaster. I never saw him again.

He bossed his squads and tended his flowers and his pets almost until he died when he was nearing seventy, and found time to compile material for another book, mainly made up of correspondence with a sympathetic woman penologist, which was published posthumously. I reckon there never was another quite like Chapin.

12

WORDS BY JOSEPH PULITZER

REMEMBER, don't you, the old story of the professional jail-breaker who boasted that no prison could hold him? So they interred him in an underground cubicle which was guaranteed to be escape-proof. A great reputation was at stake. He tried all the tricks in his repertoire. But the steel grill at the venthole above, the smooth stone walls and the seamless floor defied him. Years went by—one version has it that twenty years went by—until on a certain day it happened that absent-mindedly he pressed against his barred door and it swung open. It had never been locked at all. The easiest possible way out was the way which, by reason of its very simplicity, had never occurred to him. With modern improvements, and the stamp of verity upon it, this, substantially, is going to be a repetition of that ironic little yarn.

There was hell to pay and no pitch hot around the *World* shop during one throbbing month of 1908. The Pulitzer papers, aided and abetted by the plucky Indianapolis *News*, had laid bare, item by item, the monumental intrigue which pyramided up from the negotiations for our purchase of the strip across the Panamanian isthmus. And it stank like the tropical muck out of which it sprang and was as oozy.

These allied intelligencers plied lancet and scalpel ruthlessly. Long before they were done with the job a most noisome cadaver had been dissected and men high in the councils of the Republican party had been plentifully flayed. Daily, self-assembled statesmen and self-anointed diplomatists were being invited to explain this and that. Kingpin lobbyists and political adventurers were hunting their burrows. There was, for instance, the curious matter of a $40,000,-000 payment by the United States Treasury to J. P. Morgan &

Company for delivery to the stockholders in a shadowy domestic corporation called the New Panama Canal Company which, back in 1894, took over the wreckage of the original De Lesseps project that had gone bankrupt, swallowing up $260,000,000—the life savings of 600,000 Frenchmen.

The messy thing walked right into the White House grounds. A close relative by marriage of President Theodore Roosevelt was caught under the skinning knives and listed as a participant in certain aspects of the deal. The President, feeling himself aggrieved, went so far as to sue the *World* and the *News* for felonious slander. The Supreme Court dismissed the cases. Despite two congressional investigations, soft soap and whitewash so effectually coated the main facts that the names of those share owners who had divided amongst themselves that delectable forty-million-dollar chunk of manna from heaven were not revealed and never have been. In our justifiable pride over the magnificent achievement of digging the big ditch and tying together two oceans and driving plague and pestilence out of the jungle, most Americans have forgotten that the undertaking was conceived in international sin and whelped in a wallow of Latinized chicanery, Yankee double-dealing and governmentally encouraged injustice to at least one sister republic, namely, helpless little Colombia.

What particularly affected the Pulitzer ménage was not that certain besmirched and castigated dignitaries were covertly said to be seeking Federal indictments for criminal libel against the publishers of the *World* and the *News*, first off in the states of New York and Indiana, and then in all the states where the defendant papers circulated by mail, which would have covered the entire Union like a circus tent. They were confident this plan of reprisal would collapse from heft of its own manifest unfairness, which promptly it did. Not even a vengeful Administration could force such wholesale sniping as that.

For the *World* the guerrilla warfare struck closer to home, which meant closer to the person of Joseph Pulitzer. Counsel for President Roosevelt's kinsman demanded of William Travers Jerome, the spunky, explosive district attorney of New York County, that under the state law governing malicious misstatement, a warrant be issued and Mr. Pulitzer be arrested and arraigned and, as the lawyers hoped, indicted and put to trial, these punitive actions to be separate and apart from any similar prosecutions in the Federal jurisdictions.

Now here was Jerome's chance to flog an enemy as with whips of scorpions, and Jerome, mind you, was no slouch at cutting and slashing. Lately the *World* had passionately railed at him for alleged breaches and torts in the conduct of his office. Just a short time before it had been especially scathing in its comments on his treatment of George W. Perkins, formerly of the Equitable Life Assurance Society, and a person prominent in financial circles and in society. A serious charge was lodged against Perkins. Instead of taking him formally into custody, Jerome permitted Perkins to appear, unescorted, in court for preliminary pleading. Incidentally, if memory serves me right, Perkins never stood trial; the accusation was not pressed or was dropped or something.

The *World* seized on this episode for ammunition in the duel of lashing recriminations. Jerome terrifically was lambasted. Were there two kinds of law in the land—handcuffs and patrol wagons and the barred pen of the committing magistrate for ordinary culprits and velvety consideration for an entrapped nabob? Wasn't sauce for the proletarian goose sauce for the plutocratic gander? And so on and so forth, with the scolding going to overdone limits, so many folks thought.

Now, all of a sudden, with the circumstances sliding in parallel grooves, was Jerome's chance to humiliate Pulitzer as Pulitzer insisted that Jerome should have humiliated Perkins. If you knew Jerome, you knew that while on occasion he might go fairly bloodthirsty, he'd never be guilty of so inhuman an act as to subject an old man and one blind and sick and practically prostrated to such unnecessary indignities as sending policemen to fetch him from his home and before the eyes of the town make a shameful, quaking spectacle of him. Moreover, it was reasonably sure that Jerome, being Jerome, would resent any pressure from the Washington crowd to use him for its cat's-paw in a scheme which, many people were beginning to say, smacked of persecution and the fear of further exposures. Any time Jerome raked chestnuts out of the fire, they'd be Jerome's chestnuts.

But since Mr. Pulitzer was concerned, Mr. Pulitzer's higher-ups, the big ones and the medium-sized ones and the little teeny-weeny ones, went straightway into dire panic, having horrid visions of flatfeet pounding their way into his retreat and dragging the invalid forth like some dangerous malefactor turned fugitive. In their frightened ears they heard the rattle of manacles and the slam of the steel door on the detention cell.

The course which Jerome elected to follow only prolonged their consolidated sufferings. For what surely must have seemed to the *World's* janissaries four of the longest weeks since the Dawn of Time he remained absolutely mum regarding his intentions. Figuratively, he retired to an inaccessible tower of silence and brooded on top of it, as aloof and as inscrutable as an owl—no, that's a faulty simile and bred out of mythological error. Many profoundly stupid creatures, including owls, get a bogus reputation for being smart merely by being inscrutable or, let us say, dumb. People say that if ever such a one did deliver, the pent-up wisdom of the ages would gush forth. And at least these counterfeits do have sense enough to keep their mouths shut and merely look thoughtful. Jerome was in no fashion owl-like; rather he was a swooping falcon. But owlishly now he spake not a word, neither yea nor nay, nor go to Hades!

The contagion of anguish affected Mr. Pulitzer's lawyers. He had two sets of lawyers. He had his regularly retained firm and another firm of impressive-looking and important-acting and highly costly gentlemen. These lawyers in turn hired special investigators and private detectives whose task it was to find out what Jerome was or was not intending to do. And the detectives went their extravagant gum-shoed ways as is the habit of detectives wherever found, and turned in large expense accounts but nothing else. And the lawyers ran around in rings, assuredly in a dignified and judicial manner, but nevertheless running around in rings. From the strain Mr. Pulitzer was said to be on the verge of a complete collapse where he refugeed in his house on upper Fifth Avenue. So his chamberlains and his chancellors were panting like lizards. And the bill kept mounting up to figures which would have made history in any previous frugal day before the dispensation of the New Deal taught us to think airily in terms of billions instead of paltry thousands and puny hundreds of thousands.

Four weeks and better the tightening suspense continued. Intolerably it dragged on to turn the corner of the fifth week, with the whole establishment, from the greatest down to the least, feeling the tenseness of it. The quavering antenna touched the working staffs more or less remotely but to the humblest minion on the premises, we could feel it.

This was the situation when one day I walked into the city room. My trick started at 9:00 A.M. Before I could hang up my hat John Tennant, the managing editor, pounced at me. I use the verb advisedly. Mr. Tennant was a chubby man but on this occasion he pounced.

"Hop right downstairs," he bade me. "The big bosses want to see you about—well, they'll explain to you. And you needn't show up here again until they turn you loose."

So by elevator I hopped right downstairs to the main floor. Tennant must have telephoned that I was on my way because at the foot of the shaft a clerk was waiting to escort me into an inner office of the business department.

The regime's three chief mouthpieces were there, looking powerfully anxious, viz: Messrs. Don Seitz, Florence White and Bradford Merrill. Always there were three chief mouthpieces. Here the blinded hermit had borrowed a plan successfully used by Richard Croker, King of Tammany Hall. When Croker went away once for a longish spell and wanted to make sure the organization would be intact and all his when he returned, he named a triumvirate to carry on while he was gone, giving to these keymen even authority. And Croker in turn was indebted for the idea to the early Caesars who, departing for the wars, caused the Roman senate to name from its ranks three men, presumably equal in power, to conduct the Imperial affairs during the interim. There was never just one of these pro tem administrators, because that might permit such a one to seize the Empire for himself; and never two, since two might plot together to the same end, but always three, so if two conspired, the third tribune almost inevitably would be a jealous spy on them and by the same token, a dependable servant of the departed master, striving in season and out to circumvent the majority and confound their knavish tricks and therefore save his own pelt against the day of retribution. It is an excellent policy of accident insurance for any absentee seignior of a domain to carry; not perfect protection, because nothing on this faulty planet is quite perfect, but fairly safe.

Well, I have just said, the current proconsuls were convened in that inner office when I was ushered into their presence. I forget whether it was then or a bit later that we were joined by the eldest of the three sons and heirs of the dynasty, young Mr. Ralph Pulitzer, a bookish, kindly, retiring gentleman, more fitted, I think, for the life of a poet happily scribbling pastoral verses in the proverbial garret, than to be a cog in the racketing grinding powerhouses of a great newspaper shop. Until the final downfall of the undermined edifice years later he woefully was miscast for the role he had to play. But as a gracious human being he was until his death in 1939 an outstanding success.

The bluff, self-assertive Seitz acted as spokesman. There was no preamble. Mr. Seitz did not hold with preambles, in print or out.

"Mr. Cobb," he began, giving me formal title as though to add the ceremonial touch to an already serious moment, "we have just heard that you are a close friend of District Attorney Jerome. Is that correct?"

"Well, sir," I said, "I wouldn't go quite that far. Since I came to New York I've gotten to know Mr. Jerome fairly well—covering criminal cases which he prosecuted, and so forth. And I've been with him on numerous social occasions. There have been times when, off the record, he gave me his confidence—and so far I haven't knowingly abused it. I admire him for a lot of things, and I like him. I hope he likes me. I think perhaps he does."

"That's a frank enough statement," he commented. "You know, of course, that owing to his persistent refusal to commit himself one way or another in the matter of these recent Panama Canal disclosures—the demand that Mr. Pulitzer be arrested forthwith for libel, et cetera, et cetera—we have all been in a state of great uneasiness?"

To myself I said: "Uneasiness, eh, when several dozen people around here are as jumpy as a troupe of trained fleas? That's being conservative for you."

Aloud I said: "I've gathered as much."

"And doubtless you also know that we've spent a great deal of time and a great deal of money in efforts to induce Mr. Jerome to state his position? To put it baldly, we've exhausted practically every expedient, every available resource we could think of—we and our lawyers and our other representatives—and without success. A grave emergency exists. Mr. Pulitzer is in a very depressed, very harassed state. The possible consequences to his health are dangerous—most dangerous. So as a last resort we are asking your co-operation. Can we count on you—for immediate action?"

"Just a minute, please," I put in. "Gentlemen, am I to approach Mr. Jerome on a purely personal basis, as a friend, or am I to act as an ordinary reporter on a routine assignment in the line of regular duty?"

"That," said Mr. Seitz, "is for you to decide." The rest nodded in chorus like so many gloomy mandarins.

"Very well," I said. "Then are there any specific instructions?"

Somebody handed me a typewritten sheet.

"Here," said Mr. Seitz, "are three questions designated A, B and C. What we are hoping above all things is that you can induce Mr. Jerome in his official capacity, or otherwise, as the case may be, to answer these questions."

I glanced at the paper, folded it and put it in my pocket.

"I'm ready to get going," I said.

"Splendid! Take as much time as you please on this proposition—you will make your reports to us here and nowhere else. If you desire the aid of anyone to assist you, from the top to the bottom in this organization, you have only to mention his name and he will gladly work with you or under you until further notice."

"I think I'd better begin by tackling the stunt alone," I said. "Later I may yell for help. It all depends."

"That is for you to say. Oh, yes, one more thing: Your expense on this work is unlimited. No one in the cashier's department or elsewhere will question any item of any size which you care to charge up."

(That following Saturday I derived a peculiar and perhaps a malicious satisfaction, turning in my "swindle sheet," which is the trade term for an expense statement. It was as follows:

Special assignment, W. T. J. matter:

To carfare up Center Street .... 5 cents
To carfare down Center Street.................... 5 cents
                                                  _____
Total ....10 cents)

At the Criminal Courts Building I quit the trolley. County Detective Al Thomas, a witty, saturnine Irishman was on guard duty at Jerome's office. By Thomas I sent in my card. In a jiffy he was back.

"The chief's busy," he said. "Says for you to slip across the street to the Back Room. He'll be along in about fifteen or twenty minutes."

The Back Room at Pontin's Restaurant, over the way, was a semi-private retreat reserved for judges, certain court officials and a selected group of lawyers and newspapermen. I went over there; the refuge temporarily was empty. It was a bit late for before-breakfast drinkers and a bit early for pre-luncheon drinkers.

I sat and waited. In about a quarter of an hour Jerome breezed in. I have a right to use the word "breezed" here. He had a gusty way of speaking and a rolling, forward-lunging gait almost like a man climbing the slant of a boat deck in half a gale. He ordered cocktails for two as he came through the door from the public bar.

He flung himself into a chair facing me. There was a quizzical, meaningful twinkle in his eye. Jerome could peer as far into a grindstone as the next one. As the greatest cross-examiner of his time and one of the greatest that ever tried a case in any time, he had reason for being so visioned.

"Well, Kentuck," he said, "what's on your mind—if anything? Not that I couldn't make a guess."

"Mr. Jerome," I said, "I've had the option of coming to see you either on a purely personal basis or impersonally as a reporter for the New York *Evening World*. I've decided to come as a reporter."

"That simplifies the equation. Well, Mr. Reporter for the New York *Evening World*, you may fire when ready."

"Thank you, Mr. District Attorney. I have been asked to put three questions to you. What you may tell me in reply is not necessarily intended for publication." He chuckled and winked. He knew as well as I did that whatever he might tell me would never see print. "But that is none of my business. My business is to put these questions to you and report on the results to my superior. Here they are." And I hauled out the paper which meant so much to so many people and to one sorely distressed man in particular, and uncreased it and laid it on the table before him. Slowly he read it through, reread it and then he said:

"Before we go any further I want to tell you something. You may use your own judgment about repeating it to any interested party or parties. That's up to you. If you do repeat it I figure you might think it expedient to modify my language although for the good of Joseph Pulitzer's soul I could hope that you quoted me exactly.

"I don't like a hair in that man's head. He has attacked me viciously, violently and, as I see it, without due provocation. He never hesitated—or his papers never did—to hit below the belt and gouge in the clinches. Even so, I never intended to make either a burnt offering or a martyr out of him. If it had been John K. Jones, ordinary citizen, who was involved in this thing, the *World* would have gone about covering it in an ordinary way. But no. Because it was His Imperial and Sacred Majesty, Pulitzer the First, those dam' stuffed shirts down on Park Row couldn't handle it that way. They had to make it terrifically portentous, supremely important. They had to build it up into a breath-taking, world-shaking crisis. They had to turn creation—or their addled part of it—upside down. And so for four weeks they've had their crepe-heeled flunkeys dogging my steps and shadowing my people. Mangy dicks have tried to seduce my clerical force, have tried to pry secrets out of my assistants and my secretaries, have spent dough in great gobs and perspired blood. Whereas, if any properly accredited reporter from the *World* had come to me, as a reporter, and had looked me in the face and had asked what my intentions were, I'd have told him— that is, as soon as I made up my mind which was within forty-eight hours after the complaint was first lodged with me. So, because of all that and for nothing else, I've let King Pulitzer—and his gang of sycophants—stew in their own juice.

"Got a pencil? . . . O.K. You'd better write down what I tell you, just to make sure. My answer to this first question is 'No.' My answer to the second question is 'Yes.' I decline to answer the third question but if any of those ponderous pundits down where you work has half the intelligence God gives to young grasshoppers— which in view of recent occurrences I rather doubt—he can add up the first answer and the second and get a fairly clear idea of what my answer would be to the third question if I cared to commit my-self that far."

I had already worked out the simple but significant mathematics of it. Mr. Pulitzer was not going to be prosecuted, was not going to be molested or personally inconvenienced in any legal way what-soever.

I pouched my precious paper and stood up.

"Thank you, sir," I said. "I think I'd better be getting back. Could I buy you another cocktail?"

"I've had my mornin's mornin'," he said with a little half-grin on his mouth. "Besides somebody might claim you'd been corrupting a judicial officer of New York County with a fifteen-cent drink."

I timed myself. I had been away just fifty minutes when I returned to the room where I had left the three high priests and the crown prince. All four of the conferees were still in a huddle and one of the four—I believe it was the silky-voiced, light-stepping Mr. Merrill—sat at the telephone, apparently holding the line open. I don't think he could have been holding it open on my account be-cause surely none there expected me back so soon.

The look on my face must have told them the news I brought was good news. I rather liked my part. I was Michael Strogoff, the Courier of the Czar; I was the chap, whoever it was, that carried the word from Aix to Ghent; I was the messenger to Garcia, all rolled into one, I fancied. But I didn't delay the revelations and for proof of what I bore, showed the scribbled words on the paper.*

"Quick," ordered somebody, "get on that wire there. One of Mr. Pulitzer's staff is waiting at the other end—at the mansion up-town—for any developments."

"Hello," I said, into the transmitter.

It was Norman Thwaites who answered back. Thwaites, a

---

* No official notice was ever taken of this performance. I was pledged not to mention it myself. But at intervals for weeks there-after and upon the slightest provocation my name would go up on the bulletin board as the recipient of a cash award for merit—usually on the strength of some commonplace story covered according to commonplace rote. The thing got to be an office scandal. Fellows went around calling me "Teacher's Pet" and wondering how I ac-complished such larceny.

charming young Englishman, was more than a secretary. He served
as a trusted liaison officer, maintaining contact between his employer
and the various executive heads. When the World War broke he
entered the British Intelligence Corps in this country and did brilliant work there and was made a major and now is Sir Norman
Thwaites, still capably filling posts in his nation's diplomatic service.

"Thwaites," I said, "I've just seen Mr. Jerome. I was instructed
to ask him three questions and—"

"Yes, yes," he broke in, "we know about that. Go on, please."

So I went on and told him the glad tidings and I could hear him
excitedly repeating them to someone who evidentally was quite
near him. When I was done there was a little pause, while he must
have been holding his palm over the transmitter, and then he said:

"Cobb, Mr. Pulitzer is sitting here beside me. He has just asked
me to express his deep appreciation for the service you have rendered. A great load has been lifted off his mind—off the minds of
all of us. But as we understand it, you only undertook this commission a very short while ago?"

"That's right," I said, "a little less than an hour ago."

"Just a minute more, please," said Thwaites. Another tiny stage
wait. Then from him:

"Mr. Pulitzer is desirous of knowing how this most gratifying
result was accomplished so speedily?"

I could hear him repeating, word by word, my reply:

"Well, it's like this," I said and was I enjoying my brief moment
of vainglory! "I got on a surface car and I went up to the Criminal
Courts and I sent in word to Mr. Jerome that a reporter from the
World wanted to see him and when he came out to where I was, I
asked him—and he told me."

Now for the first, last and only time in my life, I heard the voice
of Joseph Pulitzer. In a tone which was high-pitched and yet, so it
seemed to me, just a bit gutteral on certain syllables and with the
slightest possible slurring of accent to it, this sentence came trickling
to me over the wire:

"Well, I wish I might be God-damned!"

One object in describing this incident at such length has been to
advertise my coup, easily accomplished though it was. Another has
been to demonstrate by actual illustration that my only method of

approach as a newspaper reporter was the direct approach. No matter how difficult the problem might be or how devious its meanderings, I always walked toward it by the straightest possible path and with neither camouflage nor subterfuge inquired after the facts. I claim no honorable mention for this. My brain was so convoluted that I couldn't think of any subtle course to pursue.*

---

* I'm sure it was Chapin who first showed me the value of such tactics. There was a young ex-policeman, handsome and soldierly, well educated and of good family, who was in the Tombs awaiting transportation to state's prison. As a fireman he had won a lifesaver's medal. As a patrolman he had a spotless record. But being put in plain clothes and transferred to the well-named Vice Squad he succumbed to Tenderloin temptations and got caught. While being arraigned, he attempted suicide with his own service revolver. At his trial, by exposing others, he might have saved himself. He obeyed the unwritten law of the underworld and took his dose—and a bitter dose it was.

On the afternoon before this poor fellow would ride up the river, chained to some other felon, Chapin bade me go and see him in his cell.

"It's the psychological moment for that boy to talk. He's ruined and disgraced. Remorse has got him and if he's ever going to try for revenge on the crooks that let him take this rap for them, now is the time. Don't fool around with him. Shoot when he shows the whites of his eyes. Tell him we'll give him a fair deal if he'll come clean. And my guess is he'll break down."

Wise old Chapin had mixed the right medicine. The prisoner neither spared himself nor, what for our purpose was better, did he spare his accessories. If he didn't tell all the names, he told me the names of men, on the force and off who, under pressure, might themselves confess and implicate others. He told me where to look for hidden evidence.

I sat up half the night writing the first of a series which I fondly fancied would shake the town until divers human rats were flushed out of their holes in the wainscoting of the castle of police graft. Howsomever this same night was chosen by Harry Thaw to enact "the crime of the century," as we immediately took to calling it; and the next day my opening volley against mid-town villainy had about as much chance of making the front page as a scholarly article on explorations among the cliff dwellers of New Mexico would have had.

By contrast at least two of my confreres of those days delighted to match their wits against the wits of any who might be leagued to choke off news streams at the fountain heads. The first of these was Winfield Sheehan who afterward rose to first rank as a moving picture producer and became the ruling force in the great Fox Studios and now is a Hollywood millionaire several times over; and the second was Raymond Carroll, who disarmingly suggested a rather diffident theological student. He left the *Evening World* to become a roving writer for the Curtis publications, daily and weekly, and at this time of writing is at the head of a Washington bureau. Carroll almost yelped in his eager joy to take over some complicated assignment where conniving elements sought, with red herrings or aniseed bags, to divert him from the true scent. The crookeder and more confused the trail, the happier would be young Master Carroll, with his falsely credulous baby-blue eyes and his misleading air of utter candor. He was a relentless bloodhound disguised as an innocent turtledove, which many a dissembling—and eventually discomforted—actor in some big news break found to his scarified cost. These twain, the purring, round-faced Sheehan and the soft-treading Carroll, were the prize beagles of Chapin's pack. Couple them and the enemy had not the chance of a defective mechanical rabbit on a dog track. What wonderful graduates for any Jesuit college that pair would have made!

Elsewhere, I have narrated something of Sheehan's shrewdness at unraveling close-skeined mazes. But somehow, in no article or book which I wrote did I deal with any of Carroll's kindred exploits. This next chapter would seem to be a good place for making amends on that oversight.

13

OUT OF A CORRESPONDENT'S MEMORY
BOOK (1918)

OVERSEAS, early in the spring of 1918, I formed a defensive and offensive alliance with Carroll and with that inventive and most capable veteran, Martin Green. So close was the partnership that other war correspondents took to calling us the Pulitzer Cadets even though Green, who had been my old teammate in Chapin's rewrite battery, was the sole one of the three remaining on that roster. He still was anchored there, showing fumbling sophomoric youngsters how a postgraduate did the work, when the riddled *World* properties finally fell apart years afterward. He died whilst I was doing the final chapters of this book. Carroll now—I mean in 1918—served the Philadelphia *Public Ledger;* I was back again at the front for the *Saturday Evening Post,* having as I've already stated, been over there in 1914, at the beginning.

As regards the A.E.F., the accredited representatives of American prints were free, within rational bounds, to bore freely into or through our lines anywhere between the base camps and the forward trenches. Cars and drivers and, if needed, guides were generally at our disposal. But to penetrate or to cross sectors held by the Allies, and notably those held by the French was, as they used to say down in west Kentucky, a gray horse of a mighty different color. Especially the French doubted the dependability of journalists, their own journalists included. To their high command it seemed incredible that members of our tribe might keep the faith when entrusted with important information even had there been no censorship to clamp down on us and curb our enthusiasm.

But actually to deny the American writers access to their more or less active spheres of operation; that was not to be thought of.

'Twould be entirely contrary to the native system of carrying on a war—or possibly almost anything else. The French, being, as all know, a most polite race, had a reliable system for governing such contingencies. They never uttered either a downright *no* or a flat-out *yes*. But so distressingly often the qualified yes turned out to mean an unqualified no.

For instance, there were then in Paris two separate and out-wardly antagonistic agencies to which foreign correspondents might apply for special touring privileges. One was the Maison de la Presse, an all-civilian organization, and the other was a bureau manned exclusively by soldier-men in shining gear. The prevalent fiction was that these two shops practically were co-equal in authority, each able to invoke from some supreme source a counter-mand for the actions of the other, and each supposedly intensely jealous of the other. Behold how admirable—from the French standpoint—and how sound were workings of this dual device.

You would ask the genial force at the Maison de la Presse, let us say, for a permit to circulate in some given area up toward the front and observe what went on there. No sooner said than done—wait, that's wrong; no sooner said than undertaken. There would ensue the flurry of excitement which marks any official function, whether in peacetime or wartime, in almost any country of Europe, except-ing in England or in Scandinavia. You could wreck an American bank in less time than is required to cash a check in almost any pro-vincial bank on Continental soil.

So all over the Maison gentlemen in frock coats would be darting hither and yon in a kind of happy, typically Gallic frenzy. There would be a great pother made of stamping documents and signing names and affixing seals, and eventually there would be bestowed upon you a whole sheaf of passes done on paper of the softer tints— heliotrope, beige, sepia, robin's-egg blue and mauve predominating. The display would put you in mind of an Easter hunt. You would say that this collection should take you wherever lovers of the pastel colors might be found. Then would follow an exchange of saluta-tions, felicitations, bows from the hips and affectionate farewells.

This would be the first act of the farce. It would change to trag-edy when, within a few hours, and before you left for the battle zone, there appeared at your lodging place a devastated grandee, to break the rueful news that those insufferable imbeciles of the rival branch had interposed to countermand the permissions. To be sure the interruption was but a passing one—means speedily would be found to offset this entirely stupid delay. But for the moment—only for the moment though—his esteemed patrons of the American press must possess themselves with patience. He seemed torn between conflicting impulses; couldn't decide whether to break into tears of chagrin and let them run down among his whiskers or buss you on both cheeks. It was a beautiful little drama, beautifully staged.

Or the other way about, if instead you went to the military office, the performance followed the same routine except that now it was a shoulder-strapped, heel-clicking mourner coming in dismay to inform you that, due to the unwarranted and impertinent objections of the accursed civilian outfit, your departure temporarily must be postponed. You were not to despair though but rest tranquil. Those *sacré bleu* specie of a kind of cabbage would be put in their places and you would be free to go wherever you pleased.

In either event, the upshot was that you stayed on right where you doggoned were and futilely kicked your heels, while yearning to kick something else—the seat of a pair of exquisitely tailored Paris pants for preference.

When I joined them in '18, Green and Carroll who had had saddening experience of the thing, warned me to beware of rainbow dreams. They impressed this whilst taking me to make the customary ceremonial call at the Maison de la Presse. Even so, I was almost swept off my feet by the warmth of the greeting of the chief figurehead there, as I was entranced by the boskiness of his verdure. His lesser compatriots mainly wore the landscaped or trellised whiskers. But his whiskers roved, as it were, wild and free and enmeshed him to the cheekbones as with a luxuriant fleece. He made you think of a man trying to climb out of a fern bowl. And so flattering, so gracious was he.

He had heard of me—oh, many, many times. He recalled with deepest gratitude what immortal, resplendent words I had written of France in 1914 and 1915. He appreciated the immensity of circulation and the scope of influence of the incomparable *Saturday Evening Post*. And here and now he swore that whatever favor I might ask at his hands, no matter how extraordinary, it should be mine. Others might be refused but never the distinguished *Messieur Ivan Cope* whose name was a household word in the land.

So despite the skeptical and sarcastic comments which Green and Carroll spilt with some bitterness on the way back to the Rue de Castiglione, I decided to keep him, as our native vulgarians phrase it, for my ace in the hole.

Within two weeks, the Germans launched their final great offensive—the desperate Big Shove which crumpled up General Gough's army, tore a gaping V-shaped hole between the shattered remnants of his corps and the French defending forces to the right and brought the enemies back into a wide deep terrain which had been wrested from them at bloody cost the year before. That, you may recall, was when Haig admitted that the British fought with their backs to the wall. The French were rushing up half-grown, half-trained boys of the class of 1917 and labor battalions of grizzled, middle-aged Territorials. The English were shoving in the last of their reserves—convalescents from field hospitals, orderlies, stretcher-bearers, musicians and headquarters clerks, the ragtags and the bobtails of the forces to stiffen the bending line already broken on one salient. The American First Division had not yet moved up against the vast high tide of gray coats.

Now, we three decided in a council of war, was the hour to cash in on the glittering pledges that voluntarily had been made across the river at the Maison de la Presse. If we could move northward through French-held territory as far, say, as Soissons, we figured that our standing luck ought to do the rest. At least we would be near the top edge of the area at which the onpouring Germans threatened to launch their next thrust. There were scattered Yankee detachments somewhere up there in that imperiled wedge. They would welcome us, and ration us, and shelter us, give us help if possible. Best of all, to our knowledge there were no correspondents at all in the upcountry district over which we hoped to do our discreet ranging. The other two would bring back material for cabled dispatches; I ought to be able to gather plenty of word pictures to be mailed across. And so far as the English-speaking races were concerned our copy would not only be vital and most timely but it would be exclusive.

Carroll shaped the necessary strategy and by unanimous vote we adopted it. Here's what we did: In a body we descended upon the Maison de la Presse. On reaching the palpitating heart of the institution, I made proclamation. Reminding my arboreal friend of his recent grateful avowals, I asked, on my own behalf and on behalf of my two associates then present, for passes which would open the railroad north to us and permit us to move at will after we reached its temporary terminus at Soissons, it being our intention, I told him, to go on the mixed troop and passenger train leaving at 7:00 A.M., the following day. I emphasized our desire to take the morning train, explaining that it would require until then to make ready for the journey. I conceded that, under the circumstances, the favor I craved was a tremendous one, and unique and no doubt without precedent now or in any previous emergency.

Impetuously he broke in on my eloquence. What we desired was to be ours. Granted, the boon might cost him his official head. What of it? It was as nothing. Behold now:

In a miraculously short time—that is to say, miraculously short for that place—the final visas had been imprinted upon our sheafs of confetti-colored traveling permits and the entire staff lined up to congratulate us and wish for us a marvelous experience and a safe return. As a slight token of our appreciation we begged that our benefactor be the guest of honor at a small dinner that evening at eight at the Café de Paris. We would feast, we would drink to one another's good health, we would offer toasts to his country and ours. And please remember the hour—eight o'clock. He consented to be there.

It was then past noontime and now we were operating on schedule. We dusted out of the building into a sun-drenched day and hurried around the corner to where a chartered taxicab awaited us. In the cab were our musettes, fully packed, our gas masks, steel helmets and overcoats. We already were in khaki uniforms with field boots and Sam Browne crossbelts. All who had the right to do so—and a good many who hadn't it—wore uniforms in Paris that spring. And at one o'clock or thereabouts we were pulling out of the Gare du Nord aboard the afternoon train—an almost empty train on which we were the only foreigners and obviously the only non-belligerents.

The denouement was exactly as Carroll had calculated. When in the cool of the evening the bebearded one, all breathless and heartbroken, arrived at our hotel to tell us that those brass-hatted scoundrels at the war office had succeeded in having our papers canceled—an outrage for which they would suffer dread penalties—the gloating proprietor, M. Lotti, who was in on the sweet secret and who, being an Italian, enjoyed a joke where the laugh was on Frenchmen, handed him a note—Carroll forethoughtedly had written it prior to making our call on him. And the note said that we had been able to leave that same day for the front instead of waiting until the morrow, as originally intended, and that the dinner at the Café de Paris would be held on some jointly convenient date when we got back. With love and kisses, or words to that effect.

Hurrah, boys, hurrah, it was then too late to overtake and detain us by wire! We were in Soissons, having at the last walked in. Our train had halted five kilometers out, for the already racked and ravaged city was under bombardment. The Germans being a methodical and a painstaking people, their guns were subjecting it to the customary afternoon strafe. So we finished the pilgrimage afoot, laden like sumpter mules with our duffel and our kits. Incidentally that was the last train in or out of Soissons for several months. Within three days it was in hostile hands, remaining so until the Yankees drove out the invaders—this time for keeps—in the big summer counter-attack; the Château-Thierry campaign, as it was called for convenience.

Refugees were streaming out as we trudged in. We entered a crooked street, plainly a main residential street, for it was lined, both sides, with handsome houses behind tall masonry fences. There met us, tramping in the opposite direction, two French infantry sergeants, heavily burdened. We judged they were going on furlough. Under their packs they moved with a jaunty swing and their lined, sweaty faces were smiling as they saluted us. They hardly had passed the first twisty corner behind us when a shell, a big one, to judge by its sound, fell just beyond the bend and not a hundred yards away. When the reverberation had died out and the spattering debris had fallen, we went back to inspect the damage.

The shell must have scored a direct hit upon that hapless pair. There was a yawning smoking hole in the narrow pavement, a

destroyed gateway in a pocked stone wall and, at first glance, no
sign of the soldiers. We looked closer and there we saw what was
left of them and their equipment. I shan't go into details but you
could have put all of it, every scrap, in a quart jar. Unless you had
been there with us you'd never be able to conceive that any mortal
force contained in a metal cylinder six inches thick so completely
could abolish two full-grown human beings. I had seen and was yet
to see many men being killed in that war, and many, many more
after they had been killed, but nothing to equal this.

At their headquarters in an old barracks, the French commandant and his staff were packing up to move out. They seemed astonished to see us; and for that might very well be excused. They
weren't expecting visitors from a southerly direction and certainly
not Yankee visitors. They admitted the validity of our credentials
but, when we hinted that we might be disposed to fare even farther
than Soissons providing we could secure transportation facilities,
there was a lifting of eyebrows and a shrugging of shoulders. That
would be our business, not theirs. There was left only a skeleton
garrison. They were shifting the bulk of their troops out of that
immediate vicinity, some of the regiments retreating below the river
Oise, some hurrying westward to reinforce the imperiled lines
toward Noyon. Perhaps we did not know that the Boche outposts
were within eight kilometers of the town, that skirmishers had been
seen in its suburbs and that its occupation within days or perhaps
hours was inevitable? Would we not be content to watch the exciting spectacle of an ammunition dump being dismantled and then
return whence we had come? We might have told them that this
would be no treat to us—when you'd seen one ammunition dump
being dismantled you'd seen them all.

We gave thanks and expressed regrets and excused ourselves and
went and looked up an American hospital unit in the northern edge
of the beleaguered city. Here the surgeons and nurses were evac-
uating their patients, mainly French casualties, with a few straggled
Englishmen, wounded or utterly exhausted. These last were strays
from the rout of Gough's army. Another group of our people were
emptying a schoolhouse which had been converted into an auxiliary
supply depot. These fellow countrymen were glad to see us, even
though they must have regarded us as a nuisance but, when we

brought up the subject of possible vehicular assistance to further us in our ambitions, they just laughed. Every available automobile and truck and camion and commandeered farm wagon was in use. At daylight next morning the last overloaded American ambulance would be heading south. For all they knew Paris might be the next stop—if the Heinies kept on coming and nobody checked them.

It seemed that for us there was but one route open, and that route rearward. Moreover, we must decide pretty soon what we meant to do, else face the prospect of being mighty lonesome. In any event it behooved us to get out before the Germans moved in. An orderly guided us across a little plaza to the Golden Lion Inn, an ancient gabled place famous for its flageolet beans and its tripe and other good things. The proprietress, a brisk smiling little woman, and her two pretty daughters extended to us the hospitalities of the house, apologizing for the fact that things were a bit upset, a wing of the building having been blown to flinders the day before. They had lived through one captivity and with a bland fatalism were ready to live through another. We left our impedimenta there and, the shelling having ceased, presumably so the German artillerymen might enjoy their customary five o'clock *Kaffeeklatsch,* we visited the Cathedral. A palsied old priest showed us through the hideous hash which was the interior of one of the most venerated churches in Christendom and, before war came, architecturally one of the loveliest. So far, it was being spared any further mutilation in the renewed punishment, but previous bombardments had left little more than an ugly shell to show where beauty and spiritual glory had been. There were great jagged holes in the lofty vault of the roof and one side altar was entirely demolished. The sunset sent its slanted rays through gaping breaches in the walls to touch heaps of parti-colored shards and fragments—all that remained of the famous and priceless windows, resplendently stained by a process of the old monks forgotten centuries ago, and impossible of reproduction. At every step our boot heels crushed glass splinters into crumbs and in that glancing light the crumbs were like rubies and emeralds and sapphires and opals. Here was a finished and a perfect tribute to the efficacy of modern war. Of course, we're doing better in the present great European war; scientific improvements are coming out all the time.

We dined and, incredibly, dined well at the Golden Lion. We were the only diners barring the members of the family, except that in the middle of the meal there drifted in, quite casually, a rather bewildered but cheery young Yorkshireman, Captain William Pepper by name, with a fresh machine gun wound through the palm of one hand and a confused idea of where he had been and what he had been doing the past few days and nights. He had been caught up on the ground swell of the enemy onslaught, and carried along, like a chip in a freshet, eventually to be tossed off sidewise into a riverside littoral where there were no Englishmen but only Frenchmen. So far as he knew he was all that was left of his company or indeed his battalion. And at the table he was the life of the party. Excusing certain class distinctions, he was cut off the same piece of goods as a stunted Cockney corporal whom we picked up that very next day three miles below Noyon, just after the Germans took it. With this corporal was the sole remnant of his platoon—a stubby-nosed East End private, with adenoids and a chronic snuffle and a chronic whine. Both of them were gray with fatigue, staggering from hunger and sleeplessness, but still carrying on, since insofar as they might note, they constituted the entire strength of His Britannic Majesty's forces in those parts. We fed them on bone-dry sandwiches and gave them coffee laced with cheap rum to drink, and promised to deliver them to the nearest English command off toward Compiègne, if any such there might be, and just before he fell asleep on my lap in the front seat of a crowded jitney, one of these runty little Londoners said in a husky, gulping croak:

"Sir, we've been a bit knocked abaht. But we shall 'ave the best of them yet. You know, sir, the barstards carn't fight!"

Which, I'd say, was for all purposes a sufficiently typical utterance and helped to explain why his Empire wins so few battles and loses so few wars.

But I'm getting ahead of my yarn. We slept—or at least in sketchy intervals I did—under the Golden Lion's roof and about twelve o'clock the night shift went on duty in the enemy's batteries. The big guns belched shells at Soissons until nearly daylight and a squadron of airplanes came over and dropped bombs here and there. One bomb hit a medieval wattle-and-daub cottage just off the square and turned it into a job for a janitor with a dustpan; and clouds of

powdered plaster sifted in at the window of my room on the upper
floor and settled on everything, so that when I got up before dawn
for breakfast and lighted my tallow dip and looked in the little
flawed mirror, I thought for a moment I'd turned a circus clown.
Eyebrows, eyelashes and all, my face was a pasty dead white.*

When I turned in I figured that for all our contriving, we surely
were at a dead end. I reckoned without Carroll's genius. Because
just before I slipped off into my first cat nap, he came up from the
cellar where wine was being opened by the sparrow-like, bustling
little landlady for the other guests of the establishment and, grinning like a Cheshire cat, he said:

"Well, it's all fixed, kid. Leave an early call. The carriage, me
lord, will be waiting at the door at five o'clock sharp."

"What do you mean?" I asked. He couldn't be in earnest.

"A few minutes ago a young bird from Texas blew in out of the
evening dews and damps. He didn't know it—he doesn't realize it
yet—but he was sent as a blessed angel from On High."

"Are you delirious?" I said, "or starting to drink after all these
years on the wagon?"

"Wait," he admonished me. "You don't know the half of it.
This lad's got a lovely little tin Lizzie with a Red Cross sign on her

---

* I acquired an entirely undeserved reputation for indifference
to danger because I could sleep, intermittently, at least, through
heavy bombing, with the result that I sought my bed or my bunk
whereas others mainly went to some underground *abri* and were
uncomfortable and jittery while the hullabaloo lasted. I found this
out when Zeppelins raided London early in 1918 and I lay sick abed
at the Savoy Hotel. In France and Belgium later the thing recurred
often enough to constitute a case. The first high explosive, going
off in my vicinity, made me drowsy, especially after nightfall. A
succession of such crashes sent me off, much as though I'd been
drugged.

One Sunday when I lunched with General Sir Douglas Haig at
his headquarters, General Sir Arthur Sloggett, chief of the British
Medical Corps, who was domiciled there, told me he had encountered two similar types—a rare sort of narcotizing effect created, he
thought, by the atmospheric disturbance which with most victims
brought on shell shock and, thousands of times, a complete nervous
or mental upset.

windshield. That's what makes him angelic. Seems he went into the Red Cross when they shut him out of regular service. The recruiting surgeon found some physical defect—a tendency toward receding gums or dandruff, or something. So as soon as I found out he had that Ford, I started making love to him something scandalous. Say, he gave down his confidences like a cow with a new calf gives down her milk. He knows this country around here like a book—has driven every mile of it between here and Flanders. And the Frogs all know him by sight and they let him go through almost anywhere without being too fussy about it."

"I begin to get your drift," I said and by now I was sitting up in bed, hugging the pillow. "Pray proceed, Brother Esteemed Leading Knight."

"I went to flirting, like I said, and pretty soon he was baring his fondest ambitions which are two in number: He wants to be a lieutenant in this man's army and he wants to get a batch of his poems—he's addicted to that secret vice; sort of a privy poet, as you might say, but otherwise quite normal—wants to get some of his poems printed in a magazine having a large popular circulation. So that's where you and I come into the picture. I'm to speak to Pershing about his commission—that part is as good as done, he thinks, and you are going—"

"Wait a minute," I said. "You've only met Pershing once."

"With me once is enough," he said. "I'm just like *that* with Black Jack. Those captivating ways of mine, you know. And you are to attend to the rest of his desires. In fact, you've practically attended to them already. I looked out for that. You get his poems printed in the *Saturday Evening Post*."

"But how—"

"He's somehow got the impression that you pass final judgment on all poetry printed in the *Post*. Maybe it was something I said. Anyhow, don't be so darned technical. You literal-minded people give me the pip.

"The point is that once you get through the outer lines, the boys on sentry duty quit bothering you so much. You know that. They figure you've got business—a special mission, or a special observation party—or you just naturally wouldn't be up there in the first place. And what's more, if we'll hit for the approximate spot where the

British are trying to re-form their disarranged lines up against the French, naturally the Frogs will assume the Limeys let us through and the Limeys will think the French did it and leave us be. And you'll be sitting in a front seat all bundled up in that swanky field marshal's overcoat of yours that you bought in London, and you'll be smoking a big cigar and, as you already have put it, trying to look like U. S. Grant with a clean shave. And if any young squirt of an officer gets inquisitive and tries to flag us down you just outrank him with a hard look and an imperious wave of the arm. So before sunup tomorrow there'll be a Red Cross driver gone A.W.O.L. and a pot-metal car, temporarily or possibly permanently playing hooky from where it belongs, and you and I and our beloved pal, M. Green, Esquire, will be en route by private conveyance to the present seat of disturbance."

It all befell as he had said. And that was how and why the Pulitzer Cadets and their Texas charioteer were probably the only English-speaking noncombatants who traveled at will in and out of the backwash of the Great Retreat and with their own eyes saw the first checking of the tidal wave of the Great Attack.

As some foul plagiarist remarked shortly before I got around to thinking it up myself, there are several ways of killing a cat besides choking it to death with butter.

14

STILL FARTHER ASTERN (1914)

IN ALL my years as a reporter no attempt at influencing me through an offer of cash or other valuable consideration to hide facts or sneak deliberate falsifications into my copy was ever made by an outsider. Or, for that matter, by any insider. There were numerous occasions when someone of higher rating more or less delicately intimated that I impart a certain coloring to what I might be writing. I cited an example of this—Chapin and his Uncle Russell Sage's will—in a preceding chapter. When this sort of suggestion came, naturally I obeyed just as any well-broken private would try to obey the desires of his commanding officer. Privates in the ranks are not expected to ask questions. It's enough that they know the answers—or can guess at them.

Usually the implication was—and oftener than not it was a true one—that the paper's policy or the public welfare or a sense of genteel restraint required a specific shade of meaning or a slantwise inference to be given to this or that aspect of the news.* Under the

* In every great criminal case, every great scandal exposé, there are certain aspects which never are published. To this rule I am sure there never have been any notable exceptions. So when a newspaperman who has not been working on some piece of big news meets a second newspaperman who has been working on it and asks for the "inside story" he means that in confidence he wants to know the unprinted or the unprintable part—elements believed in but not legally provable as facts; details which voluntarily have been withheld because it would be against public decency or public morality to print them or because it would mean injury to the feelings of innocently involved individuals; revelations of bestiality or perversion; things like that. There is no such restriction as direct cen-

seemingly slack but actually rigorous discipline of a newspaper shop, the hint, dropping like a seed on fertile ground, was amply sufficient. A reasonably conscientious reporter would strive to keep his personal prejudices and private piques out of any story, especially a story susceptible of differing interpretations. That frequently he failed here was no evidence of venality. Merely it proved that he happened to be a human being.

I'm speaking more directly of efforts of interested parties to buy a reporter off from his bounden duty. Of course, reporters have been corrupted. I've seen them caught with the spoils and exposed and put on the blacklist. Summarily they were driven out of the business and most of them, however repentant they might be, never got back into it, either. But as for me, either the opportunity to fatten my purse at the cost of my self-respect never happened along or else I was too dumb to recognize a cloaked bribe when it spread itself before my eyes. By that I don't mean I never was tempted. But it was the temptation to print what already I believed to be true rather than to suppress the truth. Now to a newspaperman I know of no greater bait than that, though it be to break faith with a friend, or betray the admissions of a confidant, or make use of some pertinent disclosure which has reached him through other than the proper channels. It means credit amongst his fellow craftsmen; the bubble reputation of having achieved a noteworthy coup; it may mean advancement and a boosted salary. To keep one's professional honor clean against such luring prospects is no easy thing to do. I'm saying this as one who knows whereof he speaks and yet my case was no different from the cases of ninety-nine per cent of my contemporaries. Ours is not quite so piggish a calling as you might assume from reading some of the fiction written about newspaper people— mostly by persons who know nothing about newspaper people—or from viewing films which purport to picture the average life of the average reporter. Most newspapermen die poor but powerfully few of them need die afraid.

I'm thinking back on some of the opportunities I had to make a nine days' sensation by sacrificing an indiscreet or over-trustful indi-

---

sorship practiced here, nor is such needed. Of their own accord the editors and the publishers strike out the obnoxious and the noisome particulars.

vidual or an entirely innocent third person. Any veteran of our profession could siphon up like memories from the caissons of his own experiences.

For instance, days before the story broke out with a crash, I learned through intimate sources of the disappearance of Dorothy Arnold, a mystery which was never to be solved and which, owing to the distinction of the persons involved and the almost incredible governing circumstances, ran for months on the front pages of the American press. Because of the manner in which the tip came to my ears I kept silent until after the police, at the request of her stricken family, had put forth a general alarm for the vanished heiress. But I'll have to confess I used to lie awake nights sweating with the urge to scoop this large earth on the strength of what already I knew.

It was years later, to be exact, in mid-October of 1914 at Aix-la-Chapelle on the Rhineland border that John McCutcheon, the cartoonist-writer and world rover of the Chicago *Tribune*, and I made the acquaintance—and a pleasant and profitable acquaintance it proved—of a staff officer of the German High Command, a major temporarily detached from such service because of a heart ailment. He had been a military aide of his government at various embassies. Both as a diplomatist and as a soldier-man, he knew how to deal with American journalists. Perhaps this helped to explain why so opportunely he turned up to volunteer as our adviser and friend whilst we were waiting for the permission which ultimately we got, to revisit the German front lines in northern France. We had been down that way before, as uninvited spectators—just trailing along on the motive power furnished by some mighty dubious credentials, which is a tale I have told in another book called *Myself To Date*.* Now

---

* Constantly I experienced a curious sensation during that first more or less unauthorized expedition of ours in August and the first part of September, a haphazard journey which included the fall of Louvain, the completed phases of the occupation of Brussels, an unwitting side trip into the back edges of the Battle of Mons, the taking of various towns, and finally our arrest when we were within a few miles of the Maubeuge fortresses on the very day when they capitulated to German attacks. It was mental, but there was about it something almost physical. It encompassed me all through those thrilling days of our wandering down across a triangle of

we hoped to return to the battle lines under more orthodox auspices, as shortly we did. During our enforced stay at Aix-la-Chapelle the solicitous and thoughtful major was kind to us in a hundred ways. He had charm which he could turn on or off like a spigot. For us he kept the spigot turned on full head.

At this particular time, in the third month of the Great War, the official German communiqués were loaded with alleged details of triumphs directly attributed to the Crown Prince. He was given personal credit for at least two victories, one of them an important victory. In the inspired bulletins it was "the Crown Prince's Army" this and "the Crown Prince's Army" that. Across the dinner table one night the name of that young martial prodigy came up. A few days before our major had introduced to us a compatriot of his and had vouched for him. This was an invalided officer who spoke excellent English. He was in almost constant pain from a recent wound and he used alcoholic stimulants to dull the pain. On this night he was the guest of McCutcheon and myself. Before either of us realized how near he was to being intoxicated he bent forward and said:

Belgium and along the borders of France. Weary as I was, it made my sleep restless. After an almost sleepless night I asked a companion if he felt what I was feeling—or was it just my over-excited imagination? "Am I?" he said. "The damned thing is driving me nutty." The others with us admitted to a realization of the same intangible and undefinable manifestation. We decided then—and I'm sure we were right about it—that an enormous psychic force was being focused upon the immediate spots where we chanced to be; that all over the civilized globe millions on millions of human beings had their thoughts concentrated where, behind the smoke screens of gunfire and the veils of manufactured secrecy, a new kind of warfare—a warfare of engines and machines and anonymous units—now was being carried forward on a scale never before dreamed of by mortal minds. I don't think it affected the enormous hordes of fighting men who crawled like gray larvae across the landscape. They were too busy playing—and dying—at the new game of mechanized war. But we, the truant onlookers and for the moment almost the only neutral spectators, were being shoved against by telepathic pressures—literally squeezed and flattened like autumn leaves in a drying press.

"My friends, to you I tell something which few know. We have all love and respect for our Crown Prince. He is a brilliant young man and most brave. But we have in our army older men of great attainment and wide experience in warfare. Moreover, some day, Gott willing, he will be the Kaiser of all the German people. His life, you see, is too precious to be risked needlessly. Now about these battles which the dispatches given out at our headquarters say he is winning. Listen, please. I have been in those battles and I know. On the evening before such a battle he is made quite content in some captured château well behind the lines. Toward nightfall the next day, if all has gone well, he is escorted to the scene and to him the chief of operations says, 'Highness, behold what with the aid of the brave troops under you, you have this day done for the Vaterland.' And he looks about him and he says, 'So? It is good, fine, admirable. Comrades, see to it that tomorrow we do again as well.' And he returns to his château for dinner feeling most content."

Here suddenly he checked his clacking tongue but the damage was done and the Crown Princeling's Prussian cat was out of the bag. Did we two put into the mails what this tipsy sick man had just let slip, the proud pretensions of that vulpine-looking young hero would have been laughing stock for all the Allies and for the world at large or anyhow, for all the world except in Germany where *lèse majesté* was akin to blasphemy and blasphemy was akin to downright treason. What's more it would have been easy enough to accomplish this stroke, because at the Dutch border only a few miles away we were smuggling out uncensored mail stuff.* We could

---

* When first we arrived in Aix-la-Chapelle, on a train of wounded and prisoners, our warders, figuring now we safely were cooped on German soil, turned us loose to watch us, I think. They couldn't make up their minds whether we really were what we professed to be, a group of strayed American newspapermen who had been doing the best we could against conditions highly adverse to newspapermen, or a handful of half-wits who had escaped from some asylum and blundered into their battle-zones, or, possibly disguised pro-British observers. It didn't take long though for us to readjust ourselves in the eyes of the resident authorities, especially since by now they had dropped the initial disastrous policy of secrecy regarding their western campaign and were beginning to realize the

arrange with our editors that the story be held back until we two safely were in another country.

But for our companion of that evening and for the major who had sponsored him, the ultimate publication surely would have meant the ruin of two honorable careers. Clumsy as the German secret service was, one or the other or both of them inevitably would be suspected of divulging the secret to us. So inside our

---

value, as propaganda amongst outside nations, of press accounts done by disinterested journalists.

I happened to know our ambassador at Berlin, Judge James Gerard; the year before Mrs. Cobb and I had been entertained by him. Being appealed to by wire, he vouched for us in all regards and offered, if desired, to come to Aix on our accounts. Luckier still for us, it turned out that the American consul at Aix was a veteran newspaperman who had served alongside McCutcheon in earlier Chicago days and he made us free of his quarters and in divers ways gave us council and support, along with a clean bill of health.

Presently, from an unlocked desk drawer in his private office there mysteriously disappeared quite a number of consular envelopes and consular seals. Moreover, he had a German clerk, a serious young man, who every day carried a pouch of consular mail, which was free from censorship, across the near-by Holland border and there posted it. This young man proved to be amenable to argument—as soon as he became convinced that in nothing which we wrote did we mean to deal unfairly with the German cause. Perhaps also he was influenced by the fact that the consul saw in it no impropriety that his clerk should accept suitable sums in payment for his help, as drawn from our expense accounts.

Thus, shortly it came to pass that at weekly intervals or oftener, large, tight, properly labeled, properly stamped consular folders were, without let or hindrance going overseas, bearing the following superscription:

G. Lorimer, Esq.,
Manager *Post* Manufacturing Company
Curtis Building,
Independence Square,
Philadelphia, Pennsylvania.
U. S. A.

(Consular samples without value)

respective selves McCutcheon and I bottled it up. We came near
to bursting from the pressure of it but it stayed bottled. Months
later, back in Philadelphia, I told George Horace Lorimer about it
and all he said was: "Quite a sweet little yarn, eh? But to launch it
properly and make it sound authentic you'd practically have to
identify your stewed friend, wouldn't you? So considering the way
you got it, I can't quite see you writing it or the *Saturday Evening
Post* printing it. Some day, maybe, but not now."

To this episode there was a sequel which made another notch to
be cut in my gunstock tally of killed-off stories. In this case, however, professional ethics did not enter into the equation. It wore
an altogether different sort of face. In it the instinct of self-preservation was a dominant factor.

A few weeks after the occurrence which I have just described,
McCutcheon and I were making ready to quit Germany and, by a
roundabout detour, to head for home. In our articles we had striven
to be fair to both sides, seeing that our country then was outwardly
at peace with everybody and our President, Woodrow Wilson was
urging Americans to remain, in deed if not in spirit, absolutely
neutral. I had proof that within my temperamental limitations I was
fair, because as my articles came out in print I was accused by over-
zealous lovers of the Allied cause with favoring the Central Powers
and by equally bitter German-Americans with being pro-British
and in British pay. So by that I knew I was sitting steady in my little
journalistic boat and not rocking her either way. From the venomous standpoints of these partisans the plain unvarnished truth as
he saw it was the worst thing a war correspondent could write.

By now we had a feeling that we were beginning to wear our
welcome out on German land. The punctilious surface cordiality
had frayed a little along the seams. There had been embarrassing
moments there, embarrassing to our hosts as well as to ourselves. We
spoke American and the Rhenish burghers mistook that tongue for
English—something which the English never do—and speaking
English on the streets of a provincial German town in those times
was a risky thing to do. The Germans hated the English so much
that the very sound of their language—or a kindred language, such
as ours—made madness in their souls and occasionally some of them
would get nasty about it.

Preparing to depart, we didn't exactly give out plans and speci-
fications regarding our itinerary. For politic reasons we strove to
create the impression that we were aiming to reach the coast of the
Netherlands and take passage on some Dutch steamer going to
America and calling en route at no British or French port. You see,
we had very lately left the theater of active German operations;
had seen Rheims Cathedral bombarded and had toured at pleasure
to and fro over the Western Front; John had been up in a warplane
and I'd taken an ascent in an observation balloon above the battle
lines along the river Aisne. If so minded, we might leak information
of conceivably possible value into the ears of their enemies. So we
figured it was just as well did none in Germany know our real intention, which was to get to the seaboard as speedily as might be
and ferry across to England on a channel steamer. Otherwise we
feared obstacles would be put in our way; that we might be detained
—courteously enough, to be sure and with profound apologies for
the delay, but nevertheless detained.

On the night before we took the train which, by way of Maes-
tricht just over the adjacent frontier, would move us as the next step
in the general direction of the coast, our helpful associate, the major,
and a very pretty Saxon lady asked us to join them at a farewell
dinner. Over the coffee and the liqueurs, he said to me:

"Herr Cobb, I wonder if I could impose upon your good nature
for a most great favor? I have a friend, a very close friend, in Washington. To that friend I desire to send a most important and most
confidential communication. I dare not entrust it to the transatlantic
posts since the damned English fleet is beginning to stop westbound
ships, no matter under what flags they sail, and rifling the mail
pouches. Above all things I desire that this letter shall not fall into
their piratical hands. Could I ask you to take it with you, on your
person preferably, and when you reach New York send a telegram
to the one whose name and address you will find on it and that person either will come up from Washington to receive it or send a
messenger?"

Now, from the gossipy but attractive American-born consort of
a former Scandinavian minister to the United States, who lived at
our hotel with her husband, we have heard that the major, during
his service at the German embassy in Washington, was said to have

had a romantic affair with the wife of a certain senator from the Middle West. In fact, we rather gathered there had been a mild scandal. Immediately I jumped at the conclusion that the major's letter was intended for the flirtatious lady. I didn't exactly fancy playing the role of go-between, even though an innocent one, in anybody's love affair but we were under abundant obligation to the major and, for private motives already pointed out, I couldn't very well say no, so I said yes.

At the station on the following morning the Saxon girl was there with little nosegays for us. But there was no sign of the major. When the train almost was ready to go, his orderly, a big, smartened-up non-com hurried along the platform to us. He saluted and handed me a flattish parcel and the young lady translated what he said:

"The major sends his compliments and his affectionate regards and his best wishes for a safe and uninterrupted journey to America. Most of all he sends his profound regrets that he cannot come personally to bid you gentlemen good-by. But this morning his heart is distressing him very much so that he dare not leave his room. Besides, he sat up for most of the night preparing the letter which the corporal has just given you."

It was more though than just an ordinary letter. With a sudden sinking sensation at the pit of the stomach I noted that when we had cleared the border and were in Dutch territory. I took it out of my breast pocket and hefted it and considered its aspects and I didn't in the least like the looks of it. To me it looked more like T.N.T. than a billet-doux.

To begin with, there was a large outer envelope of tough parchment. By touch I could tell there was an inner wrapper, apparently of oiled silk, and within this, in turn, my fingers told me there were many, many doubled sheets of very thin onion-skin paper. I could guess—it didn't take much guessing—that what was written thereon would be in cipher. I looked at the superscription: a man's name, without official designation or title, and a residence number on a Washington side street. Well, that detail might be simple enough. Perhaps the man to whom the budget was addressed would be some trusted emissary previously coached to see that such missives as this one reached the intended recipient without interruption and without arousing jealousy in any quarter. But the name itself—that name clinked with a faint familiarity against some cell in my brain.

"John," I said, "this may be only an overgrown mash note but I begin to doubt it. My bet is that it's done in code. I may be toting a whole skiffload of potential dynamite into dangerous waters. Did you ever hear of a man named von Papen—he's the chap this plump package goes to?"

"Did I ever hear of him?" he echoed. "I'll say I have. He was smeared all over the last American papers I saw two, three weeks ago. He and a pal of his named Boy Ed. They're attachés of the German diplomatic outfit working under von Bernstorff the ambassador and no doubt in cahoots with Doctor Dernburg, the Austrian. And they are beginning to get some unfavorable publicity on account of the kind of propaganda they're trying to slip over—not to mention the suggestion of even smellier underground activities. I'd say these fair-haired lads were very good people to leave strictly alone. Might I inquire what you intend to do with that jolly little infernal machine you've got cuddled to your bosom?"*

---

* After this long last quarter of a century and better, the ubiquitous von Papen still at intervals steals the limelight. Of the meddlesome trio, Dr. Dernburg, the Austrian legate, was the first to be recalled, by request of the American government. It was he who had the bright idea of bringing on a Mexican invasion of Texas—as though Texas didn't have two full companies of rangers, ninety men to a company. As may be remembered amongst the oldsters, von Papen and his accomplice, Boy Ed, the half-Teuton, half-Turk, were ousted together for overt acts against our national peace and dignity, including alleged sabotage. This was quite a spell before we severed our already sorely overstrained relations with Germany. The pair returned to their native land and, I think, to military duty under the Hohenzollerns. During the Revolution and subsequent lesser upheavals nothing was heard of von Papen. Apparently he crawled under some convenient log in the Black Forest. Anyhow he sang—if at all he sang—very soft and low. All of a sudden he, who was an aristocrat and a member of the Junker military caste and presumably an Imperialist at heart, emerged to bask in the beaming sun of the Nazi day. He qualified as Hitler's pet and was for a season an alert lieutenant and pious idolator of Der Fuehrer, holding this office and that, only to lose his peacock feathers and be cast again into outer darkness at the whim of the fickle God-head. More

"What else can I do but take it along, anyhow as far as I can? I promised the major to get it through. And you stood by and practically endorsed the idea."

"He didn't tell us that it was intended for a man—a man who's already under scrutiny in America."

"No, and we didn't tell him we intended to go home by way of England. If there's been any double dealing we're as guilty as he is. In case of a jam or the prospect of one, I'll just destroy the blamed thing and drop the major a line sometime telling him complications impended and I used my best judgment. Meanwhile, we'll just have to let nature take its course, I reckon."

"Where do you get that 'we' stuff?" he demanded. "If anything happens this is your proposition." But I knew he was teasing. There is no record in peace or in war where any yellow ever sprouted amongst the tailfeathers of that weather-beaten old cock bird from Indiana. He became my friend in that campaign of nearly a quarter of a century ago. I'm proud to say he has been my friend and I, I trust, have been his friend ever since.

At Flushing that night, by good luck, we boarded an outbound channel steamer. It was the last channel steamer that made the westward passage for months, so we heard later. It was meant to take perhaps two hundred passengers. It was filled to the gunwales now with upwards of a thousand bewildered Belgium refugees—old men and old women, mothers, children, and nearly all of them in pitiable plight. It was a full cargo of misery that chunky little craft carried.

We gave up our smelly small stateroom for which we had paid wartime rates, meaning exorbitant rates, and on the two narrowed bunks babies slept in cross rows, packed like kippers in a kit, while

---

recently still he blooms forth in the Nazi ambassadorial corps. Unless he be liquidated in some future purge—a fate he narrowly escaped in the 1936 massacre—this smooth opportunist may be depended upon, at the next swing of the pendulum, to reappear in some new role unless by then too aged and stiff in the joints for any more quick changes. As a turncoat, von Papen seems to have qualified for the all-time Prussian championship and, by the available records, that took quite some doing. Well, even in a totalitarian state it's awfully hard to keep this type of chipmunk on the ground. Long may he waver!

their mothers crouched in the narrow strip of flooring between. We two stretched ourselves in a decked-over companionway among men and boys and at intervals went topside to save ourselves from being suffocated on foul air.

For nearly all next day we ran through mine beds, threading a tortuous course amongst the mazes of those deadly things. Twice we saw contact mines which had slipped their moorings and come to the surface and were drifting along in the current. Our route was being conned for us by a petty officer of the Royal Naval Reserve who had been aboard one of the mine layers that sowed the North Sea with these touchy devices. When the prevalent jeopardy had abated we got acquainted with this competent person. Once beyond the danger zone he could take his ease—and a drink or two. Barring ourselves and certain members of the crew and Donald Thompson—"Thompson of Kansas"—a young cameraman who had made a reputation with his war photographs, our pilot was the only English-speaking person we met on that parlous trip.

It was drawing on to sunset of a raw drizzly November evening when we edged up to Tilbury Docks. With the navy man, McCutcheon and I fought for footing on the inner side of the overburdened steamer, we two straddling our hand baggage which was the only baggage we had. We were wedged against the guardrail by the press of hungry, weary passengers behind and about us.*

Below on the landing quay were uniformed policemen and Red

---

* This was the period when all England bowed down and worshiped before the shrine of a more or less imaginary image which might well have been called "The Heroic Belgian." Nothing was too good for the emigrees that had fled before the advance of the enemy or had been expelled from the homeland. They had only to reach England. There great country houses welcomed these unfortunate expatriates as honored nonpaying boarders; mass meetings were held to extol their Spartan virtues, of which they had some, and their patient endurance, of which they had plenty. But in a little while the enthusiasm began to cool and pretty soon it was quite cold. The trouble was that the Belgian tradesmen being logical creatures and the Belgian peasants being of a shrewd breed and, like so many farmer folk the world over, a selfish breed, accepted this generous gesture not as a temporary relief measure but as an agreeable permanent plan. They settled down like swarms of

Cross workers and men and women of various auxiliaries waiting
with food and hot drinks for those poor wretches and with cars to
take them away to temporary billets. Also we saw down there a
squad of chunkily built gentlemen in bowler hats and thick-soled
boots. There was no mistaking them. A plain-clothes man is a
plain-clothes man wherever found. They blocked the gangway;
they clumped in pairs along the pier. There was an unpleasantly
businesslike air about them.

"Scotland Yard operatives," explained the steersman, seeing
where my suddenly apprehensive gaze rested. "We're having a real
spy scare. Nothing like that ever happened in my time—not in
England. But silly people have got the wind up and so they're
searching the luggage and sometimes the persons of those who
come in from over the way. You gentlemen being fresh out of Germany, they'll probably give you quite a going-over when your turn
comes. Stupid, I call it. Stupid and annoying, too. Still there's a
war on. . . . Well, I must be off—if I can get there—to report to the
harbor master. Cheerio!" And by main force he shoved into the
massed multitude. Almost instantly though he was caught fast, un-
able to move either way. We could see him futilely wriggling and
frailing away with his elbows and his knees. He might as well have
been between the jaws of a vise.

My first impulse was to get that accursed parchment casing out
of my breast pocket and tear it and the enclosures to bits and drop
the bits into the narrowing strip of sea water below. But no, that
wouldn't do. Those downward fluttering fragments would instantly
quicken the suspicions of hundreds of pairs of vigilant eyes, and
volunteers would be going overboard to salvage the evidence. It
would be equally futile to try to sift the scraps down about my feet.
It was my time to think and think fast.

I managed to stoop and undo the clasps of my biggest bag. Worse

---

locusts and were content, like the locusts, to live off the country.
When their hosts intimated that gainful pursuits were available for
the able-bodied among them the common attitude was, "Work is
for working people. We are refugees." When next I landed in
England more than two years later, it was hard to find a Britisher
but had a tale to tell of ingratitude and sorry greed on the part of
some pampered Flemish guest of 1914.

luck, it was a brand new German-made bag. I pulled its jaws widely agape and on the top layer of its wadded-in contents I laid the letter to that lively picaroon, von Papen.

"John," I said in what I've no doubt was a panic-stricken whisper, "there's the hellish thing in plain sight. And you are to bear witness—I'll call on the cops to bear witness too—that the bag is wide open and that there is no attempt at evasion or hiding it. I'll demand that I be given an opportunity to explain how the stuff came into my possession. You're to back me up there. I'm sure to be arrested—probably I'll spend the night in some fuzzy cell. If they don't take you into custody too—and let's hope they won't—your job will be to get up to town as fast as you can and hustle around to the American embassy and rout out Ambassador Page—he knows both of us—and have him land the U. S. Marines and get the situation well in hand."

"Meanwhile let us pray," said John piously. "Pray for the best and be fortified for the worst. They tell me the firing squad at the Tower of London works up its appetite for breakfast by shooting somebody at sunrise every morning. And sometimes they're that hungry they just can't wait until sunrise. By the way, do you belong to any established faith? And what's your favorite hymn?"

I could tell though that he was deeply worried. And why not? But we have the word of Holy Writ for it that the prayers of the righteous avail mightily. And, lo, very soon was the Scriptural promise to be fulfilled. Because so many of the forlorn creatures about us were falling down from exhaustion where they stood and because to examine the poor belongings of all of them would have required hours on hours, some humane authority cut the red tape and gave orders that the uncongenial search and seizure procedure should be foregone. Englishmen have an instinctive aversion to meddling with the liberty of the subject anyhow. So without individual examinations the shuffling swarm of wet and famished fugitives were admitted, amid cheers from the sympathetic crowds. When our turn came, the detectives at the foot of the gangway merely glanced at our passports and our correspondents' credentials and checked us through—us and our baggage.

But when we'd ridden to the city—by the way, we halved a railway carriage with a pair of Scotland Yard men—our troubles were not over by a long shot. London was convulsed with its new-born spy panic. All fashions of aliens were being herded off to concentration camps or to prison. Lumbering old "Beefy" the internationally known factotum of the Savoy Bar, he of the three-tiered chin and the greasy Bavarian accent, had been lugged away to gaol, and next day they locked up one of the managing directors of the hotel, a naturalized German; and in general, outlanders of whatsoever degree, and more particularly outlanders recently arrived from the Continent, were being watched with a vigor such, I'm sure, as had not been visited on strangers since William the Conqueror landed.

In this crisis I remembered my Edgar Allen Poe. Instead of committing the folly of trying to conceal amongst my belongings that large rectangular menace to my own security, I balanced it against the mirror of the dressing table in my bedroom where to one entering the room for any purpose it conspicuously would be in view. It held that position for the ensuing three weeks, until we sailed on the *Lusitania*. I presume the chambermaid shifted it daily when she tidied up my lodgings. The valet and the floor waiter must have seen it almost as often as she did; perhaps they handled it, too. It hardly could escape the cursory notice of anyone calling upon me. If, in my absence, the room was searched—and I rather am inclined to think it was, at least once—nobody attached any significance to an object so prominently displayed.

On the *Lusitania*, the same being a British-owned ship, remember, I kept it propped against a bulkhead of the cabin where McCutcheon and I stayed. Or rather I stayed there and was acutely indisposed for most of the voyage and that low-combed Hoosier game cock smoked large black cigars and ate enormous meals—and bragged about them—and was disgustingly healthy and almost unbearably cheerful. Nothing else of moment happened except that I had occasional recurrent attacks of jitters; that would be while I lay suffering and supine, and saw the room steward dusting off the big envelope.

As soon as we got to New York I wired to the Washington address and before nightfall an egg-shaped embassy clerk with double lensed spectacles and a haircut by the Fuller Brush Company, came up and got that hateful packet from me.

In the spring of 1915 a considerable number of kindly disposed persons gave me a dinner at the Waldorf-Astoria, presumably in celebration of the fact that I had gone on a lecture tour during the winter and had escaped alive. (I always got out of town before popular indignation could crystallize.) Count von Bernstorff and sundry members of his entourage came up from Washington and took a table for the blowout and after the oratory a lynx-eyed, foxy-faced gentleman ascended to the speakers' dais and introduced himself as Herr Captain von Papen and expressed undying gratitude for my kindness in bearing to him information which he said was of almost inestimable value and expressed the hope that I had experienced no material inconvenience in so doing. Huh, he didn't know the half of it!

To round out the previously unwritten annal of this adventure I feel I should add one sentence: This will be to the British government the first intimation that twenty-five years ago I, without malice aforethought, brought into the realm and safely out of it, an exceedingly high-powered contraband of war.*

---

* Having had plenty of wartime contacts with specialists in espionage and counter-espionage, I am impelled to discount much that is written about the wondrous sagacity of these nosey ladies and gentlemen.

To my way of thinking the English do not make especially clever spies—or clever spy catchers, either. Perhaps the fault lies in the Englishman's inherent distaste for prying into other people's business. Or perhaps by their racial temperament the English are less adapted for subterranean work than are the more subtle races.

In my opinion what applies to the Englishman applies in even greater degree to the German. For the German is by nature an honest and straightforward creature. He thinks along direct lines rather than by obliques. He's such a clumsy liar; that's why he so often fails as a diplomat or as a professional lie-monger. And when he essays to dissemble he generally makes of himself a figure of fun.

I couldn't say what happened in the latter years of the First World War but I can testify that at the beginning the German secret agent actually advertised himself for what he was—or fancied he was—by wearing a uniform. If, a hundred yards away, you saw an earnest-looking party dressed in knickerbockers and a Norfolk jacket and vivid golf stockings and with a pheasant feather in his

[*Footnote continued from previous page.*]

deer-stalker's hat, you might be reasonably sure you were beholding a member of the military secret service. If, on closer scrutiny, you observed, as frequently you did, a green cord showing above his collar at the back of his neck you knew you were right in your diagnosis because inside his shirt, attached to that green cord, was a large metal disk bearing his identification number. Undoubtedly the object was to delude outlanders into the belief that this merely was a citizen on a walking tour. But here the purpose was defeated, by reason of the fact that he spent so much of his time not in walking but sitting down in cafés and railway stations and other places of public resort and, with obvious intensity, watching for suspects. It took Germanic psychology to conceive the notion of dressing up the accredited Peeping Toms in a regalia which anyone could recognize.

During the first week of our stay at Nagel's Hotel in Aix-la-Chapelle in 1914, McCutcheon and I were dogged by an unmistakable member of this simple-minded fraternity of patriotic snoopers. His shadowing methods were beautifully transparent. He even got himself a room adjoining the suite we occupied. And we presently had cause to believe that he spent most of the daylight hours listening where a screw cannily had been removed from a hinge of the locked door between his quarters and ours. So we took to spending our leisure time at a table close by the partition and in loud clear tones we would speak well of the German army and the German people, always though expressing our profound aversion for one particular individual. The gentleman plastered up against the wall between us was bound to know who we meant. We went into details regarding the obnoxious manners and the physical shortcomings of the mysterious stranger that we saw stealthily gliding through the hallways on our floor and popping out into the side corridor every time we stepped forth. He stood the bruising strain for a week and then he moved out, suffering, we figured, from an acute attack of earburn.

On the other hand, by then his superiors had concluded we really were what we professed to be, to wit: itinerant American correspondents who had been caught up with as we went vagabonding along behind their armies, and not low-down scoundrels on English hire.

15

VIRTUE AS ITS OWN REWARD—
AND ITS ONLY ONE

It was while we were in London during this time that I've been telling you about, namely, the early winter of 1914, when one of my most tempting chances to make journalistic history presented itself and, purely on ethical grounds, was declined with most sincere regrets. Within a week after our arrival McCutcheon and I went to luncheon at the town house of Lord and Lady Northcliffe. The only other guests were James Barrie (afterward Sir James Barrie), the Scotch novelist, and Dr. Jameson, the Transvaal raider who lighted, somewhat prematurely, the fuse which ultimately set off the Boer War and added South Africa to the British Crown. Here, in their respective ways, were two as interesting folk as one would care to meet—the shy, gentle Barrie and the grizzled soldier of fortune. We wanted them to talk about themselves—a thing which Barrie probably never did much of, whereas under ordinary conditions Jameson would, I'm sure, have spun some gorgeous yarns of adventure. On the other hand they wanted us to talk about what we just had seen of the war. They won—with not too great a struggle on our parts.

Next morning I was in my bed at the Savoy, keeping company with the von Papen letter, when the telephone rang. The owner of the voice at the other end of the line, it being a secretarish sort of voice, said he was speaking from the *Daily Mail* offices in Fleet Street. "Lord Northcliffe wonders if you would care to see Lord Kitchener this morning?" he said. "If so, Lord Northcliffe will be very glad to arrange it." Inasmuch as Lord Kitchener was supposed to be, to all newspaper people whatsoever, as inaccessible as the Grand Lama and as mute as the Sphinx, I figured that this invitation probably meant the privilege to sit on sidelines somewhere and watch the Field Marshal riding past on parade; or possibly he was going to dedicate a new recruiting station.

I was starting to say such a prospect did not particularly excite me, but the speaker in a shocked tone made correction. "I'm afraid I put it awkwardly," he amended. "What Lord Northcliffe means is that if you can find it convenient to be at the War Office at ten o'clock today, Lord Kitchener will receive you. Perhaps there are some questions you might care to ask him. And no doubt there are some questions which he might care to ask you." I gulped my thanks and my acceptance. Not since the war began nor, so far as that goes, for years before it began, had Lord Kitchener given an interview for publication. And here was a chance, as I saw it—and so it turned out—to trade with him for some mighty printable material. Anything he said would make nutritious reading. Now comes the explanation why the two most significant things he said were omitted from what I did write.

I spent forty minutes with Lord Kitchener. We were for all that time quite alone. No one interrupted us. Afterward, to account for some of his attitudes, it publicly was stated and never denied that in those last few months of his life he drank heavily. Be that as it may, there was on this morning nothing about him to suggest over-indulgence. As an administrator he may have had his shortcomings, but as a figurehead to attract volunteer enlistments he earned ten times over the praise which his country bestowed on him only a short while after that, when he died by the sinking of the war vessel which was carrying him to Russia. I knew, as all the world did, that he had been a very great soldier. Facing me now from behind his desk he impressed me as a very great gentleman, and, saving one blurted slip of the tongue, a gentleman with a most proper sense of the proprieties.

At the outset he told me he had heard from Lord Northcliffe something of the rather special concessions a companion and I had enjoyed within the German-held areas; and since we so lately had come from there, he meant not to seek to draw from me such facts as might have fallen under my direct observation or any facts such as might have been confided to me, touching on the Germans' actual operations, or their intentions, or the disposition of their forces along the Western Front. If his zeal for his country's interests led him inadvertently to cross this border line he trusted I would forgive him—and decline to answer. But as regards the morale and the general conduct of the enemy's soldiers, their spirits, their hardihood or the lack of it, their discipline and their treatment of the inhabitants of the occupied lands—here he thought it entirely proper to probe for knowledge from one who had studied these things at firsthand within a matter of days or weeks. In return, he stated, perhaps there were questions I might care to put to him which, if considered by him to be reasonable questions, he should be very glad to answer. Within these bounds of his own making and strictly along the specified limits the dialogue progressed.

Almost at once and of his own volition, he expressed his belief that the war would last for at least three years and that the people of Great Britain should prepare for a prolonged struggle. Since most of the so-called military experts, both among the Allies and the Central Powers, were then predicting a decision within a few months, this statement alone, coming from such a source, was deserving of screaming headlines in any newspaper anywhere. Also without any prompting from me, he spoke condemningly and contemptuously of the new fashion of trench warfare. I inferred that he rather regarded trench warfare as being, so to speak, unsportsmanlike and unbecoming of brave men. Along here he became obviously excited. His face was a red glow by now. Tamping with a huge clenched fist on his thigh, he called von Kluck, the capable generalissimo of the German right flank—an ass. "A stupid ass" were the words he used. In the next minute he voluntarily was introducing into the conversation the alleged torturing of wounded or captured men and more particularly the alleged ill-treatment of the civilian Belgian populace by the invading Germans. This, you should recall, was when so many unprovable atrocity stories were being circulated—and believed in. Vehemently he declared that the behavior of the German forces during or following engagements and in the occupied areas might well be likened to the excesses perpetrated by the savages he had fought against in his famous Soudan campaign, and he added that in his opinion the Germans were as undeserving as the Mahdi's followers had been, of being regarded as civilized beings operating under the common rules of civilized warfare. He set forth the comparison without any qualification whatsoever. It was a flat-out indictment of a whole people—and made on prejudiced hearsay testimony besides.

I took no notes on what he said whilst he was saying it; at least I took none save mental notes. I was too old a hand at this interviewing game to be fetching out paper and pencil. But I had naturally a good memory and it was a memory trained by long experience. As soon as I got back to my hotel—and I got back as quickly as a cab could carry me there—I carefully set down, so nearly as I could recall, the exact language he had used. I am conceited enough to think I was reasonably accurate in these quotations.

On the voyage home, once I was over my seasickness, I wrote out the story of my call on Lord Kitchener in precisely the same form in which it shortly thereafter appeared in the *Saturday Evening Post*.

But despite the temptations to do otherwise, I reluctantly eliminated from the story what I regarded as his two most graphic and provocative declarations. I believed that on sober reflection he would not have called one of his chief adversaries a stupid ass. And he was being given no opportunity to strike so pregnant a sentence from my copy. Accordingly I did not include his reference to von Kluck.

Moreover, it was to be recalled that, in his famous North African campaign, Kitchener had issued orders to kill without mercy all Soudanese lying injured on the field following an action, since these crippled fanatics made it a cheery practice to feign helplessness until British surgeons or stretcher-bearers approached them and then to butcher the very men who would have given them aid. And to top that, I seemed to remember that back yonder in 1896 on the march of Kitchener's column to the relief of Khartoum, mighty few prisoners were taken alive. So I reasoned that if either the British or the Germans or both took literally his most unguarded and unqualified charge that the Germans were guilty of such bloody offenses as the Soudanese had been guilty of—and were to be judged by the same barbaric standards—there might be slaughter of soldiers who had in good faith surrendered and there might be planned massacres of disabled men. I wanted no such burden of hideous reprisals and retaliations on my soul nor did I for a moment believe that Lord Kitchener, upon fuller consideration, would have consented that the responsibility for any of these murderous contingencies be saddled upon his shoulders, either. So I elected to leave that part out, too.

My reward for my forbearance was that I got in a pickle. Under the title "Forty Minutes with Lord Kitchener" the *Saturday Evening Post* printed the article. It preceded by two weeks another narrative, likewise procured through Lord Northcliffe's good offices, which I called "A Day with Lord Roberts" and which, by chance, appeared almost coincidentally with Lord Roberts' death in France, where, at eighty-odd, he had gone to visit some beloved veterans of his own bygone training among the native East Indian contingents. But the Kitchener story was the one which made the sensation. The press agencies distributed sizable extracts from it all over this continent and other continents too. The resident correspondents of British and Colonial papers sent by wire to their journals condensations ranging from a few salient paragraphs to as many as fifteen hundred words, so that on the day following the original publication, these dispatches had been broadcast to all parts of the English-speaking world. Without positive knowledge on the subject I assume that correspondents of foreign language papers, notably French and German papers and South American papers, likewise picked up portions of the interview for distribution by cable.

Some forty-eight hours later the English War Office issued a bulletin, one not signed or sponsored by any individual, saying in effect that while it was true on a certain date I had seen Lord Kitchener and talked with him, some of the language attributed to him was not used by him and, by indirection at least, this anonymous fugleman for the War Office repudiated the authenticity of the whole thing.

Immediately, in the columns of that great thunderer of British opinion, the London *Times*, Lord Northcliffe stepped into the controversy. If the dispatches forwarded from America contained spurious phraseology or misleading statements why, he asked editorially, did the War Office, which exercised strict censorship over all incoming press matter, not squelch the libel as soon as it had reached English soil? Wasn't the properest time to scotch a snake before it started wriggling? Why did the War Office suffer the interview to go along to scores of morning papers in the British Isles and then wait until all the afternoon papers had opportunity of reprinting it before impugning, in part at least, its validity? He went on to state the publisher of the *Times* was in position to say that on divers occasions Lord Kitchener had employed substantially the same terms which I had attributed to him. He intimated rather broadly that the War Office deliberately had permitted the British public to hear certain things which it were well for them to hear, notably Kitchener's prophecy as to the duration of the war, and then, to appease English journalists who were resentful because a Yankee had been granted admission to Kitchener's presence—a boon refused to them—now belatedly threw out this part-way disclaimer as a sop to the disgruntled ones. I was powerfully glad and powerfully proud too, and still am, that before Lord Northcliffe gave forth this defense of me and, inferentially, of his own part in the teapot tempest, American publishers were rallying around, saying in print that I had the name of being a reputable newspaperman and that, before hearing any more, they were prepared to accept my explanation of the circumstances and the accuracy of my reporting. So far as was shown by the bales of comment which the press-clippings bureau sent to my apartment there were just two newspapers in this country that chose to condemn me without a hearing. One was a New York City paper which was very much on the Anglomaniac side, and the second was a daily in a small middle western city.

However, all things considered and not even excepting the *affaire* Kitchener, I'd say the loveliest openings I ever had for scoring reverberating beats—and didn't avail myself of—came during the first of the two trials of Harry Thaw for the murder of Stanford White.

16

WM. GOEBEL: HE KEPT TRYING

HOWEVER, before telling my own heretofore untold chapters of the Thaw case, I deem it incumbent upon me to hark back to another and almost equally amazing case, the one which centered about the bushwhacking from cover of Governor Goebel of Kentucky. For it was while covering the Goebel trials in 1900 that I acquired a celerity at recording testimony in long hand, which accomplishment served me most excellently well when, for the New York *Evening World* seven years later, I wrote running accounts aggregating more than 600,000 words during the first trial of Harry Kendall Thaw, the great all-American profligate, for the murder of Stanford White, the great architectural genius, over the affections of Evelyn Nesbitt, the great international beauty. I might as well say it now and smirk and get it over with, that I never met any reporter who could cover copy paper with more lines of script in a given space of time than I could.

Because of the elements and the individuals involved, and the fact that it had a cosmopolitan setting, the Thaw-White-Nesbitt affair will live in retrospect as perhaps the most spectacular criminal case, not even excepting the kidnapping of the Lindbergh baby, that ever sucked dry the descriptive reservoirs of the American press. You see, it had in it wealth, degeneracy, rich old wasters; delectable young chorus girls and adolescent artists' models; the behind-the-scenes of Theaterdom and the Underworld, and the Great White Way, as we called it then; the abnormal pastimes and weird orgies of overly aesthetic artists and jaded debauchees. In the cast of the motley show were Bowery toughs, Harlem gangsters, Tenderloin panders, Broadway leading men, Fifth Avenue clubmen, Wall Street manipulators, uptown voluptuaries and downtown thugs—a bedaubed, bespangled Bacchanalia dizzily revolving about that newly risen Playboy of the Western World, Harry Thaw of Pittsburgh, and his young wife whose glory of a face had adorned a thousand billboards and gladdened the hearts of a million lovers of so-called art calendars. Charles Dana Gibson had painted her and James Montgomery Flagg sketched her and Archie Gunn and a score of others had drawn her likeness. In her latter teens and her early twenties she was, I think, the most exquisitely lovely human being I ever looked at—the slim, quick grace of a fawn, a head that sat on her flawless throat as a lily on its stem, eyes that were the color of blue-brown pansies and the size of half dollars; a mouth made of rumpled rose petals.

On the other hand, the Goebel killing, occurring at the turn of the century, is well-nigh forgotten, outside, that is, of my own state and, in the main, only faintly remembered there. For it concerned neither money nor any woman whatsoever. But it did have in it for a prime performer one of the most monstrous and one of the most brilliant shapes that ever played out a tragic, somber role in the national scene.

Since he passed, I have met a good many of the distinguished men of this country, and of other countries, too, but I have yet to meet one who impressed me as being mentally superior to William Goebel, that son of a poor Pennsylvania German mechanic, whose dreams and whose death—and the manner of it—practically plunged Kentucky into civil war. Here was a Mussolini of politics if ever one lived. He had audacity, ruthlessness, a genius of leadership, an instinct for absolute despotism, a gift for organization, a perfect disregard for other men's rights or their lives where his own wishes were concerned; the brain to plan and the will to execute. Had he lived I am firmly convinced he either would have ruled the Democratic party in the nation or he would have wrecked it as already he had half-wrecked it in Kentucky. He loved power as drunkards love their bottle and he would have waded through blood up to his armpits to have his way. One man—Colonel John Sanford—stood as a lion across his path and Goebel shot him to death in the city of Covington. Sanford tried to draw, but Goebel who deliberately had fostered the quarrel between them, and who crossed a street to put himself in Sanford's path after having hideously insulted Sanford in print the day before, beat him to it. It was claimed he had his revolver already drawn; had it hidden under an overcoat folded over his left arm. Next, foreseeing the day when he would need it, he forced through the Legislature, of which he was a member, a measure that bore his name, the Goebel Election Law, the most cruelly, blatantly unfair device for defeating the popular will that had been enacted since Reconstruction days in the Deep South. Even so, there is no doubt but that Goebel aimed at the ultimate betterment of plain people; the trouble was that his good motives and his clear reasonings were cankered by a lust for authority which gnawed at the man day and night, making him a malignant and a menacing force.

There were those who blindly followed him, those who hated and despised him, those who feared him mightily, but I do not believe he had an intimate friend, one with whom he was on terms of confidence, and I am sure no living creature read the inside of that dark and sinister and lonesome being of his.

In a belated biography written nearly forty years after Goebel's murder, the lately deceased Urey Woodson, a Kentucky editor of parts and a devoted aide of Goebel in his lifetime, called him "The First New Dealer" and undertook to prove that Goebel had been a pioneer in trust-curbing legislation, antedating the elder La Follette and likening him, in his program of proposed social reforms, to Franklin D. Roosevelt. But I'd say he rather was the political forebear of Huey Long, except that the Louisianian had a born demagogue's knack for rabble-rousing and an almost miraculous sense of mob psychology appraisal, whereas Goebel, with no warm impulsive gift of personality, mainly worked his mischief from behind the scenes, like a skilled operator manipulating a troupe of marionettes. Moreover Long had human qualities—human faults, too, while Goebel made me think of a synthetic, self-assembled mechanism. It was remarkable, that both should have had careers much alike and that both, on their respective Statehouse grounds, with complete success for their biggest schemes within clutching reach of their greedy hands, should have fallen before the assassin's bullet.

By a great many of the members of the old and enfeebled oligarchy of the state—which finally he overthrew—Goebel was called an intruder and an interloper and a presumptuous, ill-mannered upstart. These contemptuously dubbed him poor white trash—another parallel to Long. They abhorred him piously. They had reason to—he brought their already tottering political aristocracy smashing down in scraps about their heads and did it, too, while defying all traditions of office-seeking and office-holding which those fathers of the faith, the pampered Confederate brigadiers and the Bourbon colonels and the oily understrappers, had been building up since the War between the States ended. He had none of the hand-shaking, pat-'em-on-the-back, ask-about-the-family tricks of the typical Kentucky job hunter. He belonged to no lodges or clubs. He was no orator—another point of difference between him and the crown princes and high priests of our reigning political dynasty. He had no social graces. There was no woman in his life, ever. It was said he was a celibate. They say the same thing today about another dictator of Teutonic blood, to wit, Adolph Hitler. In mixed company he was embarrassed and showed it. He was cold and secluded, an aloof, clammy figure and a malformed one; I think it was always snowing in his wintry soul. He had lieutenants to do his bidding. But in "The Dutchman's" camp there was only one commander—and that would be William Goebel.

I never saw a man who, physically, so closely suggested the reptilian as this man did. He had a curious yellowish cast to his skin as though stale suet rather than live flesh lay beneath it. Under stress he would grow tallowy pale but no flush to betoken red flowing blood ever showed in his face. His hair, which was black and very slick, lay plastered against a small, slanted skull that was strangely flattened at the rear. His eyes were glazy, shallow, coal-black; except when he was stirred an ophidian film was on them. His throat was disfiguringly swollen, with loose folds of skin overlapping the collar line. It was very like the throats of certain lizards. In repose he would put you in mind of a coiled snake, in action, of the snake about to strike, and when he did strike, lashing out viciously, you almost could see the spattered venom fly. He was a daunting yet a fascinating creature to study.

His star brightened and soared across the troubled Democratic firmament, at an hour when an already split and disrupted party cried for more modern leadership. Four years earlier—and divers homeless bureaucrats still were shivering from the dreadful shock of it—the Republicans, aided by fifty thousand disgruntled Democrats, had carried the state for the first time in its history. It was more than a shock; it was a cataclysm, a convulsion of outraged nature. Not so long before that Colonel Bob Ingersoll, casting about for a comparison to express the absolute impossible, had said that he would think of turning Christian when Kentucky went Republican. But the Free Silver issue had made a widening cleavage in the entrenched organization and the Populist movement ate deep sunders in agrarian strongholds, and the current administration wasn't so popular any more. For a crowning disaster a group of the biggest men in the state, men nationally known, several of them—Secretary of the Treasury John G. Carlisle, U. S. Senator Lindsay, Colonel W. C. P. Breckinridge, the silver tongue; "Marse Henri" Watterson, the editorial trumpeter for the whole South; the Haldemans and the Knotts, publishers of our largest newspapers; ex-Governor Simon Bolivar Buckner and that smouldering little live coal of a man, Basil Duke, both former Southern generals of distinction; practically all the bankers, and hundreds more had gone, temporarily at least, over to the other side. Even so, the earthquake which sifted a lot of veteran officeholders out of the capital and slid a lot of astonished strangers into it, was a tremendous surprise to the average voter. The slate of Republican nominees had been patched together while seemingly there was no chance for its success, a list mainly made up of lowland nondescripts and petty chieftains from the high ranges who, as usual, were expected to hold a synthetic machine together for the ultimate sake of Federal patronage. It was headed by William O'Connell Bradley, a former Democrat and, surprisingly, a member of an "old family"—the only candidate of outstanding ability on the ticket. The landslip carried onward to the highest bench in the state a bushy and somewhat incredible old gentleman whose signboard when first he opened an office at his native crossroads had read:

WAKE SNAKES AND COME TO TAW
B. L. D. GUFFEY WILL PRACTICE LAW

You couldn't call him an impossible person because that's a snobbish way of putting it but it was generally conceded that he was highly improbable. You had to see him to believe him and frequently then you couldn't, like the yokel's first view of the giraffe. The new attorney general was one William Sylvester Taylor, a well-meaning but a poor enough creature; and born for trouble as the sparks fly upward. His profile suggested some ungroomed and dandruffy Hapsburg—perhaps a seedy uncle of King Alfonso of Spain. Upon viewing him sideways one understood why his neighbors in a cruel but graphic flight of foothill humor, had christened him "Hawg Jaw" Taylor. Not nine tailors nor nineteen could have made his clothes fit his frame. To use a good but shelf-worn simile, he was, in the hands of stronger men, just so much putty. It wasn't very high-grade putty, either. Tragedy lay in wait for him. She stacked the cards so that after this one term as attorney general, and in the ensuing fight for the gubernatorial place, he should be set up, like a frightened puppet, against the iron-willed, the resourceful, the relentless Goebel. When the crowning crisis came after the assassination he, a trapped and foredoomed plotter, lost what remaining shreds of resoluteness he had and fluttered about in an impotent state of complete bewilderment, defiantly threatening his tormentors one minute, abjectly pleading for mercy the next. To top all, he sprouted a dress of yellow tail feathers and ran away when he should have stayed put. Kentuckians of whatsoever shading never cared much for dunghill cockerels. After that, most of those who had voted for him, and, if the count had been fair, overwhelmingly had elected him to the governorship, gagged at the very mention of his diminished name.

When I first knew Goebel he was a state senator and an aspirant for the gubernatorial nomination. By trick and device, by main strength and brutal force, he wrested the nomination from a badgered convention and tore the party into two fluttering pieces. At the election, on the face of the returns and despite his iniquitous election law, he was defeated by the aforesaid William Sylvester Taylor, he whose undistinguished candidacy had been so heartily backed by a great multitude of rudely unsocketed Democrats. Goebel contested the result before the General Assembly and, having coerced and conquered it, was about to be seated when a hired mercenary shot him down from a window of the Executive Building on the old Statehouse Square at Frankfort. He lingered five days—long enough to take the oath of office as governor—and left

as a malign legacy to his people the active seeds of a partisan upheaval which endured until a whole generation had died off.

I followed Goebel through his outrageous campaignings before
the nomination and after it. I sat at one of the press stands on the
stage of Music Hall in Louisville where the convention was held,
and from that dangerous perch, not once but half a dozen times, I
saw six-shooters drawn and ducked under the table and flattened
myself to be out of the road of the crossing bullets. I heard the shot
that felled him on a cold January forenoon of 1900 and, hearing it, I
ran out of the Legislative Hall and was one of those who helped to
carry the stricken man away. There was blood on my sleeve and
blood on my hand when we put him down. I did not send the first
bulletin of the assassination but I think I did send the first coherent
story of it. From the bodyguards who had been with him when he
dropped—Colonel "Eph" Lillard and Colonel "Dirk Knife" Jack
Chinn—I got the hurried details while we were bearing him those
three blocks through the street to the old Capitol Hotel, and rushed
them over the wire to my paper, the Louisville *Post*. On the way he
fainted and we thought him dead but he very soon revived.

I started back toward the Square then, to fatten out my story
and caromed off a company of State Guards (Republicans) hurrying to intercept a hastily armed civilian group (Democrats) who
threatened to mob their nested enemies in the Capitol; so I detoured
through a comparatively quiet byway just in time to see "Cash" Ireland (heartily Democratic), who was a leading sportsman, perforate
a negro (name unknown but naturally a Republican) for committing, so 'twas claimed, the lethal sin of declaring that Goebel had got
what he deserved.

This was only noontime and I still had all the afternoon and
evening before me to record the making of much exciting history.
Subsequently—say, three weeks later—I gave a paragraph in my
daily dispatch to the triumphant acquittal of Mr. Ireland, the negro
having in the meanwhile died without benefit of any newspaper
mention whatsoever. I was a witness for the defense at the trial
which lasted nearly forty minutes, having to testify that at the
moment when Ireland's revolver spoke there was a small smear of
blood on his face, proof—so the jury held—that he had been struck
before he opened fire.

As the weeks went on I covered the captures, under exciting circumstances, or the voluntary surrenders of several of the men accused of confederating to murder Goebel, and I covered the first trials of three of these alleged conspirators—Caleb Powers the Secretary of State, Henry Youtsey a clerk, and James Howard a rifleman from the east Kentucky knobs, naming them in the order of their importance. First and last, I worked on some phase or another of the Goebel story for upwards of a crowded year.

For instance, one phase, insignificant in itself but possessing a value of grim humor, had to do with Goebel's last words. Several hours after he expired, a newspaper proprietor of literary pretensions came forth to where the newspapermen of the "death watch" lingered and from a scrap of paper read what he solemnly, almost tearfully proclaimed to be the farewell utterance of the deceased. It was: "Be brave and fearless and loyal to the great common people." Duly we all telegraphed this sentence in to our shops—with our respective tongues in our respective cheeks. The thing sounded entirely too oratorical, too rhetorical for Goebel to have uttered it and besides, he had been a master of plain-spoken, straightforward English. Not even on his deathbed could we conceive of him as using two words meaning precisely the same thing—"brave" and "fearless," where either one would have served. So, not for publication but for our own private information, two of us did a little snooping. This was the actual fact: Shortly before he went off into the final coma, Goebel expressed a craving for oysters—his favorite dish. His case was hopeless anyhow, so they let him have one. He spat it out and looked up at an attendant physician and whispered: "Doc, that was a damned bad oyster!" I wonder how many of the last words of swooning idols have been manufactured to order by high-pressure salesmen of propaganda?

It was at the outset of the campaign which immediately preceded the contest, and the killing and the trials and all the rest of it, that I heard what I still think, after four intervening decades, was, everything considered—scene, moment, setting and all—the most devastating retort I ever did hear. It was delivered by Theodore Hallam, a battered-looking, hard-hitting, hard-drinking, little Irish lawyer, and an ex-member of Morgan's Rangers—and *that* for nearly half a century qualified a man for social and political distinction anywhere in the border South and particularly in Kentucky. Despite a high, strident voice, Hallam was perhaps the greatest natural orator in a state of natural orators and had a tongue pointed with a darting, instantaneous wit. Had there been for him a metropolitan background, with newspapers waiting to broadcast his quips, his memory would have endured along with the memories of such other masters of spontaneous repartee as Billy Travers and Wilson Mizner and Joseph Choate and "Mr. Dooley" Dunne.* But his fame was local. It might have been local, but it was deserved. The same with enlargements might also have been said of Charley Russell the cowboy artist. (I'm making a mental note now that elsewhere along in this book, as I go bouncing from one unrelated topic to another, I must bring up Charley Russell and some of the things he said. Nor must I overlook Oliver Herford, one of God's favorite fools.)

* Dunne was notoriously a procrastinator. He might write better humor and more pungent philosophy than any of his active contemporaries—and so he did—but he was almighty slow about the actual creation of it. One day Frank O'Malley and Frank Garvan and I ferreted him out in the hidy-hole which, in his semi-occasional working hours, he occupied at the offices of the *American Magazine* where he served, when run down and made captive, on its editorial board and where he did, for his delectable department called "In the Interpreter's House," an article once a month. He heard us following the trail through the hallway and tried to lock the door but we were too quick for him. "Get out!" he bade us. "Get out and go entirely away from here." "We merely want to take you over to the Waldorf for lunch—just an hour and no longer," said Garvan. "I've got a day off from the grind down at the district attorney's office and I'm in a mood to celebrate." "Not a step!" proclaimed Dunne virtuously. "You can't tempt me. I go out with you hounds of Satan and I won't be back for ten or twelve days. It's happened before. I don't stir an inch from this spot till I've finished this job. I've made a sacred pledge to John Phillips, the poor, patient, long-suffering man, to lay it on his desk by a set and specified time and I'm a man of my word, once I pass it." "Oh, thunder," said O'Malley, "let's see if we can't figure an out someway. Of course dead lines are dead lines and we've got to respect them but—say, look here, Pete, what is absolutely, positively the last minute when you have to turn this stuff in?" Dunne glanced up at a wall calendar. "Two weeks ago last Tuesday," he said sweetly.

Hallam lived in Covington, where Goebel likewise lived, and as a comrade in war and an ally in peace of Colonel Sanford, the Conservative whom Goebel pistoled to death, he hated Goebel mightily. Having bolted when Goebel seized the gubernatorial nomination by craft and device—and at the last moment, by open violence—Hallam promptly took the stump against him and went about over the troubled commonwealth joyously sowing dragons' teeth and poison ivy.

The seceding wing of the party picked on Hallam to open its fight, and chose the town of Bowling Green as a fitting place for the firing of the first gun, Bowling Green being a town where the rebellion inside the ranks was widespread and vehement. But Goebel had his adherents there, too.

I could fairly smell trouble cooking on that simmering-hot August afternoon when Hallam rose up in the jammed courthouse to begin his speech. Hardly had he started when a local bravo, himself a most handy person in a rough-and-tumble argument, stood upon the seat of his chair, towering high above the heads of those about him.

"I allow I want to ask you a question!" he demanded in a tone like the roar of one of Bashan's bulls.

One-third of the crowd yelled: "Go ahead, Black Jack!" The other two-thirds yelled: "Throw him out!" and a few enthusiastic spirits suggested the advisability of destroying the gentleman utterly, and started reaching for the armpit or the hip pocket, as the case might be. Despite the heat all hands were wearing their alpaca or their seersucker coats which, if you knew our sturdy yeomanry in those parlous days, was a bad sign.

With a wave of his hand Hallam stilled the tumult.

"Let it be understood now and hereafter, that this is to be no joint debate," he said in that high-pitched shrill voice of his. "My friends have arranged for the use of this building and I intend to be the only speaker. But it is a tenet of our faith that in a Democratic gathering no man who calls himself a Democrat shall be denied the right to be heard. If the gentleman will be content to ask his question, whatever it is, and abide by my answer to it, I am willing that he should speak."

"That suits me," clarioned the interrupter. "My question is

this: Didn't you say at the Louisville convention not four weeks ago that if the Democrats of Kentucky, in convention assembled, nominated a yaller dog for governor you would vote for him?"

"I did," said Hallam calmly.

"Well, then," whooped the heckler, eager now to press his seeming advantage, "in the face of that statement, why do you now repudiate the nominee of that convention, the Honorable William Goebel?"

For his part Hallam waited for perfect quiet and at length got it.

"I admit," he stated blandly, "that I said then what I now repeat, namely, that when the Democratic party of Kentucky, in convention assembled, sees fit in its wisdom to nominate a yaller dog for the governorship of this great state, I will support him—*but lower than that ye shall not drag me!*"

From then on the only thing which interrupted Mr. Hallam was applause.

Incidentally, I, still sappy-green, had now my first contacts with some of the big men of my trade—such outstanding notables as Charles Michelson, then of the Hearst outfit and now, as I write this in 1940, the marvelously effective head of the Roosevelt publicity bureau at Washington, being the Alexander Hamilton of the New Deal; Homer Davenport, who'd quit cartooning Marc Hanna and the high dogs of Tammany Hall for long enough to come down there among us and do some masterly character sketches and courtroom pictures; J. Murray Allison of the Cincinnati *Enquirer*, who afterward in New York became a producer of musical comedies and was my close friend; "Harry" Beach, star of the A. P. staff at Chicago, one of the sanest, surest, shrewdest newspapermen that ever lived; plump, slow-moving "Jersey" Chamberlain of the New York *Sun*, looking deceivingly like a master plumber of a Sunday. And there was one who forevermore is marked in my memory by a blazing red asterisk—that redoubtable Washingtonian, the Kentucky-sprouted but Texas-ripened Colonel "Bill" Sterrett.

The brindle-topped, amber-squirting Sterrett was a stalwart Democrat but he had not been for Goebel alive and, most outspokenly, was not for Goebel dead, as witness a bellowed remark he made while four of us were returning, via hired hack, from the services at the state burying ground up on the wintry peak of Cemetery Hill overlooking the town. It had been a bitter, miserable day, first thawy, then freezy, with spates of rain and snow mixed. We had remained, we reporters, while U. S. Senator Joseph Clay Stiles Blackburn, from amidst a dense damp pack of active and honorary pallbearers, delivered the stately official oration. Considered that a few years ago he had stood by the open grave of John Sanford demanding vengeance on the slayer of his fellow soldier and life-long friend, and now stood alongside that identical slayer's coffin demanding the same measure of punishment for whoever had killed *him*, Senator Blackburn acquitted himself very well. Somebody was unkind enough to say he lifted eloquent and heart-moving quotations from the Sanford tribute and bodily incorporated them into the Goebel eulogy, all with such deftness that you hardly could detect the seams.*

Quickened by the prospect of imbibing copiously of hot whisky toddies, the quartet in our carriage were just decanting ourselves in front of an outlying barroom when a dripping pedestrian hailed the impatient foremost of our little band. There was about this gentle-man nothing to show whether he was pro-Goebelite or anti-Goe-

---

* To guard Goebel's grave, his faction hired two worthies ac-counted as competent for the job, to wit: Mr. "Bad Bill" Smoot of the adjacent Blue Grass section and Mr. "Silent Bob" Wolfe from up in a higher county. In midnight hours when he deemed the tomb safe from vandals, Bad Bill had a way of slipping down to the hotel bar and taking refreshment. Late one evening three of us, in a rol-licksome mood, went clattering and whooping down to that cosy retreat. But I, who chanced to be in front, quit rollicking as Bad Bill, starting up from a chair, poked deep into my yielding dia-phragm the muzzle of a chunky, short-barreled gun which to my goggling gaze looked to be about as big around as a standard can of tomatoes. Explanations followed; it appeared that Bad Bill, sud-denly aroused from slumber and being perhaps a trifle jerky, had jumped at the conclusion that the hostiles were upon him and he meant to sell his life dearly. So the thing was laughed off. But I would say my laughter was of the hollow or artificially forced variety. As I recall, I hurriedly took a drink of straight whisky, immediately followed by another of the same, but didn't seem to care for any of the free lunch.

belite, and just about then ordinary folk were careful of saying things which might arouse antagonism either way.

"Well, suh," he asked, "how did the obsequies pass off?"

"Most beautiful sight I ever beheld!" boomed Sterrett in a tone which could have been heard half a block away. "One infamous sonverbitch being buried and a couple of hundred equally infamous sonverbitches catching their death of pneumonia at the funeral."

There never was the least doubt where Sterrett stood on any proposition. He used spraying tobacco juice to punctuate with. And when he spewed the quid out, that would be an exclamation point.

For me, at the impressionable age of 23, there were so many distinctly thrilling moments in that twelve months' experience. Here's one I recollect that carried distinctly a personal touch: Some three months after Goebel was shot, a group of us one afternoon were sitting in front of the telegraph office discussing—as usual—the crime in one or another of its phases. A member of the Frankfort police force, a fat, good-natured man named Wingate, joined us. The talk eddied back to the day of the assassination. Each of us told what he did that thrillsome morning. My turn came. I said:

"I was in the washroom on the first floor back of the library. I had just taken my coat off and rolled up my sleeves to wash my hands when I heard the shots. To me they sounded as though they had been fired in the narrow strip of yard between the Legislative Hall and the Executive Building. Bareheaded and leaving my coat behind, I ran out of the side door to see what had happened. Everybody was expecting trouble and plenty of it. Three men had picked up Goebel and were hurrying with him back toward the main gate. I remembered there was a picket out of the iron fence about halfway up the block toward the corner of the Square. So I took a crosscut. I ran diagonally across the lawn, passing directly under the windows of the Executive Building where the shots had come from, but I didn't know that then, and squeezed through that gap in the panel and was out in the street just as the men, with Goebel in their arms, reached that point. That was where I joined them and—"

"Say," broke in Policeman Wingate, "say, listen: Now I know who the fellow was I came so blamed near taking a few wing shots at. Me, I busted out of the front door of the Hall less'n half a min-

ute after the shootin'. I knew already who it was that was shot—a
fellow had just bumped into me, yellin' that Goebel was murdered.
So I pulled my gun and bulged for the open. As I came out on the
portico between them tall columns the first thing I saw was a long-
legged fellow, in his shirt sleeves, and no hat on, with his hair flyin'
behind him, tearin' acrost the grounds. It looked to me like he was
tryin' to get away from there as quick as he could. I said to myself,
'That must be the fellow that did the shootin'.' So I drew a bead
on him. Somebody ran against me by accident and knocked up my
arm. I pulled down again and was just about to let go when a representative grabbed holt of me and said, 'Hold on, don't shoot. I
know that kid.' Before I could ask him who the kid was he'd darted
away and then when I looked again I couldn't see the bareheaded
fellow any more. And now, by gum, I find out it was you I came so
near pluggin'. Because I'm a better'n medium shot. All this time
I've been wonderin' in my own mind who the devil that long-legged
youngster was? Say, boy, I'm right glad I didn't plug you that day."

I was right glad, too.

17

ALONG HERE, AMONG OTHER THINGS,
A WEDDING

A COUPLE of months or so before the Goebel case was advanced to the point of prosecuting the alleged assassin and his affiliates in that gory whirligig, we turned our attentions for the time being to something in the nature of a by-piece. This was the trial for manslaughter—and the triumphant acquittal—of Colonel David Colson, the central figure and the hero of a flare-up marked by some mighty quick mortality. Burning powder fanned it to a red-hot climax in the lobby of the principal Frankfort hotel only a few days before the major tragedy of Goebel's undoing was to befall just around the corner, as it were. This lesser affair was not related, except distantly and collaterally, to the larger factional controversy, but dated back rather to the Spanish-American War when Colson had surrendered his seat in Congress to lead a volunteer regiment which boiled internally for the entire term of its enlistment and frequently boiled over. It did its only fighting in camp at Anniston, Alabama, making a showing there which would have boded considerable ill for the enemy in Cuba, provided the Fourth Kentucky Infantry had got that far.

First to last, the actual gunfire in this cribbed and confined hotel battle lasted less than ninety seconds; final score: Three dead, those being ex-Governor Bradley's truculent nephew, Captain Ethelbert Scott, and two bystanders accidentally slain; and four wounded, including that master marksman, the Colonel, and a Northern traveling man who, on his first trip south of the Ohio River, had arrived only that day and was having his shoes shined at the head of the steps leading down to the basement, when the im-

promptu duello began. So he vaulted over the stair railing and as he
sprawled on the half-landing below, with a smashed ankle crumpled
under him, Captain Scott, all riddled and dying on his feet as he fled,
came tumbling down and fell across him, while the vengeful Colson
followed on behind, with a fractured right arm dangling but with
his left hand briskly throwing lead into the quivering back of his
adversary. When I arrived, having heard the racketing blasts from
just across the street, the traveling man was still lying there, crying
out:

"My wife begged me not to come to this wild country. She
begged me. And what happens? No sooner do I get here than
everybody goes to shooting everybody else and then when I jump
down here and break my legs they start piling dead men on top of
me."

The place was a shambles: bullet pocks in the wainscotings;
dribbles and dots and stippled trails of red on the tiles; separate red
puddles here and there; shattered plate-glass windows. In the middle
of the floor, under a bright blue raincoat and an overturned chair,
was the slight body of Assistant Postmaster Demaree of Shelbyville.
I happened to know him and helped to identify his remains. There
were two holes through his thin breast. Scott, who inaugurated the
fusillade and probably died repenting of it, had used this hapless onlooker for a living shield. Behind the clerk's desk was a deputy manager in a faint. I headed along a cross hall, seeking for scattered eye-
witnesses who might be able to furnish particulars, and one of the
overlooked casualties, a mountaineer lawyer named Golden, with a
puncture neatly placed right between the rear buttons of his long
frock coat, pulled away from a wall against which he was leaning
and collapsed in my arms. He was Scott's friend and the theory was
that, finding the occasion grown perilous, he had turned to retreat
and Colson deftly had flung one sidewise shot and plugged him as
he ran. I got Golden disposed of and came abreast of the open door
of a sample room just as another uncounted victim, who had dragged
himself in there, a tobacco planter named Julian from out in the
county, finished bleeding to death through a severed artery in his
leg. On Mr. Julian's account there was much local indignation, his
being the only Democratic name on the fatalities list. It would seem
that fourteen years before the event, I was being tutored—but of

course didn't know it—for service as a correspondent on the western battle fronts of the First World War.*

Oh, yes, I almost forgot the farewell sequel to that particular day's happenings: Without notifying anyone, numbers of the colored help had gone hurriedly thence, but the remaining members of the staff succeeded in tidying up after the massacre in time for Honorable William Jennings Bryan, the Peerless Perennial, to speak there that night. It was a good speech, naturally; it being his regular one, with tremolo interpolations where he endorsed the Goebel contest, of the merits of which he knew only one side and that sketchily. After that he ran again and again for the presidency.

So far as court proceedings were concerned, this Colson interlude proved a short horse and one soon and satisfactorily curried. With it behind us, we young gentlemen of the press again could give ourselves over to the multiplying developments of the greater event. These followed swiftly, one on the heels of another and frequently overlapping.

Had Goebel succumbed instantly to his wound, or even within a few hours, the situation immensely would have been simplified for those who fostered and encompassed the killing and our own labors might have been shortened. But, as I've said, he lived long enough to be declared by legislative majority the truly elected governor and he was sworn in, with the rest of his ticket and, as he sank into the

* Kentucky has calmed down considerably since those times. It's not yet as calm as Vermont, say, or Delaware, but its leading citizens are not so pettishly inclined as once they were. Even so, there is in certain areas a tendency to become fretful over polling-place eventualities. On the presidential election night in 1932, I forgot that my state had now a law by which, presumably to lessen this peevishness, it was provided that the count of the ballots cast should not be begun until twenty-four hours after the voting ended and as I entered our New York apartment where the family were listening to bulletins coming in over the radio, I said, "Any news from Kentucky yet?" "Yes, Dad," my daughter answered gently, "the first scattering returns just arrived: Nine dead and fourteen injured. Additional figures are expected later when more outlying precincts are heard from." My daughter, being only half-Kentuckian sometimes manifests a regrettable tendency to gibe at institutions which to her aging father are sanctified.

shadows, with a stiffening hand he signed one official document. Immediately then his running mate, young John Crepps Wickliffe Beckham, who had been the Democratic candidate for the lieutenant-governorship, took oath as his successor; which actions, if sustained, would seem to make pretenders of Taylor and the other lately installed Statehouse incumbents and render their subsequent acts null and void. On this outcome much depended. For no sooner did the county grand jury indict a group of alleged principals and accomplices than Taylor, not to be outdone, issued blanket pardons for the whole batch, himself included, for, generously, the grand jury had shuffled him in along with those accused of promoting the murder. The State Court of Appeals—by a strict party vote—confirmed the General Assembly's dictum, which automatically set aside all those job-lot pardons. Accordingly the issue went up to the Supreme Court of the United States, the Republican usurpers meanwhile holding the fort at the Capitol and defying attempts to serve warrants on them, but the temporarily houseless Democratic administration doing the bulk of the functioning.

It was known that on a certain spring day the Supreme Court would pass on the appeal. I got confidential word from my managing editor that Taylor was to slip away to Louisville to await the decision on Federal property where presumably he would be immune from arrest by the local constabulary until at least the ruling was handed down. So I followed to bide with him in that parlous hour of waiting. It so happened I was the only reporter who sat in the private office of the postmaster on an upper floor of the Louisville Custom House from eleven o'clock on that morning. Our tip had been exclusive. Slipping in, I had taken note of the two city detectives at the lower front entrance; they were supposed to be ready to take him into custody at the proper moment.

It is no pretty sight to see a grown man go gelatinous from pure terror; literally to disintegrate, whilst you watch him, like so much molten jelly. Continually Taylor walked the floor, his bony arms flailing the air, the skirts of his dismal coat flapping like black distress flags, his famous underslung jaw adroop until it seemed ready to come undone and fall off, and his haggard eyes streaming. One minute he weepingly would demand to know why he, the undoubted choice of the people for the noblest office in the commonwealth, should be persecuted with threats of imprisonment, of the gallows even? The next moment, with a great beating of clenched fists on a concave chest, he would be swearing that he'd face what dire things might befall—a felon's cell, a felon's fate—all in defense of principle and high dignity and honor.

"I'll never run away," he quaveringly shouted at me and at the fat, stolid postmaster, as though we had accused him of such an intent. "I defy them to do their worst!"

It was now eleven fifty-five and even as he spoke his piece he fell into a racking tremor and began edging toward the door. In another instant he was gone—gone by the back way, as we found out a little later, and into a closed carriage and while the flashed bulletin from Washington was coming in—the ruling went against his cause and his pretensions—he crossed by one of the vehicular bridges to the northern side of the Ohio where the Governor of Indiana gave him asylum and declined to honor a requisition for the fugitive's return to Kentucky jurisdiction, for which attitude he and his successor subsequently received the hearty endorsement of President Theodore Roosevelt, who had a chronic fancy for poking his nose into other people's business. Even so, I think he made more mistakes as a politician and fewer mistakes as an American than any president we've had since Andrew Jackson.

Taylor lived out the remnants of his broken life in Indianapolis and died there not so many years ago. I think yet our authorities deliberately made no honest effort to apprehend him before he quit Kentucky soil, preferring rather to turn the runaway into a contemptible figure than to run the risk of making him a possible martyr.

This vain foolishness of wholesale pardoning being satisfactorily over and done with, and the jubilating Goebelites comfortably installed in the berths left vacant by the ousted losers, I went back to Frankfort for the trial of the first of the jailed defendants, that of James Howard, one of Clay County's most facile and seasoned sharpshooters. Howard hadn't waited to be run down or be besieged. Of his own accord he came out of his mountain hiding place where he was reasonably secure from arrest and gave himself up. He was a personable chap, quite handsome and very silent. He was fairly plump, too, whereas most of our American highlanders used to be sparse-framed. He was by way of being a Democrat in a heavily Republican bailiwick. He had no grudge against Goebel; indeed he had supported him in the election six months before. Still politics makes estranged bedfellows. However, with Howard this issue was on purely a commercial basis, so the prosecution purported to show. He had been out on bail pending appeal from a murder conviction in his home district, for having emptied the contents of a repeating rifle into the body of a certain man, old and helpless, but a member of an embroiled family and therefore, by vendetta ethics, fair game. The burden of the present charge against him was that, for extinguishing Goebel, he had been promised by Taylor the Pardoner a full and free legal clearance of that annoying upcountry verdict and, on top of this, was to receive as a special inducement eleven hundred dollars in cash which had been left over from the Republican campaign fund—a nourishing sum by mountain standards. It was alleged that by arrangement he came down to Frankfort on the night before the appointed date and unostentatiously had repaired to the Executive Building betimes next morning; had been made welcome and congratulated on his promptness and escorted to Secretary of State Caleb Powers' private office and there had made a choice of three rifles offered for his expert consideration; had built on a window ledge a balanced rest for his rifle by piling up—gritty irony—divers bound volumes of *The Revised Statutes of the Commonwealth of Kentucky;* had bided there, taking his ease and smoking his morning's smoke, until three men, walking abreast, turned in at the gates of the Square and came up to the middle walk; had thereupon inquired which one of the three was Goebel and, on being told it was the center figure, put his pipe aside and bored that figure through the right breast with a single cartridge, then rapidly several times discharged a revolver into the air to make plausible the theory that a number of shots had been fired, after which, according to allegation, he sedately strolled to the station and caught the next train traveling upgrade to the back districts—the unhurried conception of a hired man serenely aware of having been worthy of his hire. On the strength of all this it now was proposed to unjoint his neck for him.

But Commonwealth's Attorney Bob Franklin couldn't quite cooper his staves into a doubt-proof cask. The testimony leaked, so to speak. Anyhow that was what we reporters said among ourselves. We didn't figure that the accused would be let go. That, community pique being what it was, was asking too much. We figured on a mistrial as the most likely result. So it was a jolt to all present that the jurors, having gone out to deliberate, returned in an unexpectedly short time to tell the court they found the feudist guilty as charged and fixed the penalty at death. I was stationed very close to Howard whilst the grizzled foreman read the findings. Not by the slightest quiver, nor by any change of countenance, nor by any quirk of rigidity did he betray his feelings. Only his left eye suddenly crossed. It would seem that when he was still but a coltish youngster, with no worth-while homicidal record yet accumulated, a thoroughly irritated partisan of the opposing clan had clouted him over the head with a clubbed Winchester. The reversed hammer made a permanent dent in his skull so that after that under emotional stress one set of optic nerves would go askew. Now he put his lips close to the ear of his counsel, who was himself credited with having in youth earned the right to cut a pair of notches on his own gunstock, and in the casual, almost indifferent tone with which a man might mention the weather, he remarked: "Well, now say, Jeems Andy, I didn't think those dam' fools would do that."

On a plea of prejudice, change of venue to the near-by Blue Grass town of Georgetown was granted for the ensuing trials of Powers, the alleged head and front of the murder plan; and of Youtsey, the complacent lackey boy who, prior to the shooting, did everybody's bidding and went about blithely manufacturing future evidence against himself. In a convenient court recess I took advantage of the opportunity to go southward to Savannah and get married with a compact, small personage named Miss Laura Spencer Baker, five feet-one of steadfastness, wholesomeness and spunk, who had a family tree which, for martial fruitage, made mine look in comparison like something that had sprouted down cellar, although I wasn't exactly ashamed of our own record in that regard, either. Her great-grandfather, Colonel John Baker of Middle Place on Colonel's Island just off the coast, was that courtly figure in Revolutionary lore who, having been chosen to head a squadron of his fellow planters and tidewater neighbors against the Britishers, lined up the command and removed his hat in a sweeping salute, and in this language uttered an order which was destined to become immortal: "Gentlemen of the Liberty County Guards, kindly come to attention!" Most of these recruits were kinsmen of his, after one fashion or another—Stevens, Quartermains, Dorseys, Bohuns, Bacons, Bullochs—President Theodore Roosevelt's mother was one of these selfsame Bullochs—from the Colonial settlement about historic Old Midway Church.

The conclusion of the War between the States found my wife's Prussian-born but Prussia-hating grandfather, at the age of sixty-three, serving as captain of a forlorn company for home defense made up of elderly heads of households, schoolboys, convalescents, conscripts and semi-invalids. It also found her father, Marcus S. Baker impatiently awaiting his fourteenth birthday so that he too might volunteer as a musket-toting soldier, just as his five older brothers had done in '61. One of the five was already dead and another grievously maimed. But it was to the memory of her mother's young brother, Private John Frederick Krenson, that his womenfolk, in the time when I first knew them, wove their biggest garlands of white and red blossoms on Confederate Memorial Day.

Before he was eighteen, this John Frederick Krenson enlisted in the Oglethorpe Light Infantry, with the rest of "Bartow's Beardless Boys," as the local papers proudly called them. With his regiment, the Eighth Georgia, he went under fire at First Manassas and was shot through the lungs. After long nursing in Virginia he was, greatly against his will, mustered out of service as unfit for even the lightest duty and shipped home to die. He had developed tuberculosis. For months he lingered about the town—a gaunt, coughing shell—trying vainly to re-enlist. Finally he started north alone, tramping afoot and feeding on what scant forage he could gather. A year and a day after receiving his wound, he rejoined the survivors of his old outfit just as they were coming to grips with the Northerners in front of Richmond. Empty handed, he followed behind them on the advance. When a soldier dropped, young Krenson picked up the fallen man's gun and pushed forward into the ranks. He was disabled by a half-spent, glancing Minié ball. The injury seemed superficial but already he was perishing from weakness and exhaustion, and so he lived only a few hours. When his racked and wasted body was returned to Savannah for burial there came with it his honorable discharge. There was a stain of dried blood on the folded paper. He had carried it, in a breast pocket, into the charge and the fight.

As soon as we got into the World War my wife's young cousin and, like her, a nephew of this John Frederick Krenson—the lad's name was Fred Krenson, too—qualified at training camp for a commission but when he came up for his physical examination was turned down as being underweight. He asked for another chance and on the morning of the second ordeal trained for it by choking down an incredible number of ripe bananas and drinking almost enough water to cause suicide by drowning as an inside job. On the scales, he passed the test by a scant half-pound and thereupon gave the Rebel Yell for himself, dashed outdoors and put a finger down his throat and turned into a spouting human geyser with banana soufflé effects. This determined stripling went to France as a second lieutenant and on his first round of duty at the front caught trench fever and was sent back, kinked like a pretzel with rheumatism, to spend nine months on the flat of his back in a military hospital. But he was content; in him the tribal ritual had been fulfilled.

Mrs. Cobb and I are proud that in our daughter's veins and in the veins of our two grandchildren runs the strain of that stock. If anything, she's a mite prouder than I am. That Georgia stuff comes from her side of the family.

On our bridal tour we went to Washington in the merry, merry month of June when the asphalt melted to chewing gum in the streets and the draft horses wore straw hats and fell down in their tracks and the salamander in the zoo perished by a heat stroke. I think they saved the Arizona Gila monster by packing him in ice. Niagara Falls was cooler probably, but it was farther off and I didn't have passes on any railway line going that far. I ended our suffering by curtailing the honeymoon and bringing my sweetheart with me back to Georgetown and there, scrooged in beside me at the press table while I turned out running reams of copy, she followed the forward march of that most absorbing, most breath-taking of all dramatic spectacles in all the world—the fight by the due credo of the law for a human life. Together for six weeks we harkened as the testimony unreeled in a bedaubed and evil scroll and the opposing legal batteries volleyed and thundered, for nearly every outstanding criminal lawyer in the state and at least one highly vocal imported mouthpiece had been retained by either the commonwealth or the defense. The summing up at the finish required upwards of a week but that was because the attorneys for one side were so busy vituperating their personal enemies on the other side that for hours on end they forgot the prisoner at the bar, young Caleb Powers.* He was a man who seemed to have some ice water in his veins. He was cold and reserved and wondrous shrewd, with an unbreakable front. Apparently he was more concerned by the embarrassment of wearing steel cuffs on his daily trips between the jail and the courthouse than by the mass of proof banking up against him—proof tending to make him out as the guiding and contriving force in the conspiracy. The jurors filed in one steaming afternoon and said it would be a hanging matter and he merely glanced indifferently at them, meanwhile sniffing delicately a rosebud which a young woman in the crowd had given him. He was quite dandified and very good-looking—and a widower.

After a briefened interim then, they fetched up the little Oriental-looking Youtsey for judgment by his peers. Here was a sight to evoke your pity, no matter what your sentiments might be—this

---

* After a successful appeal and a retrial and a reversal and a trial again, Powers finally was freed. Promptly his district, which predominantly was Republican, sent him to Washington—the sole member of Congress, living or dead, who ever had thrice been in jeopardy of the scaffold for murder in the first degree. During his terms of service no Southern member of either House barring a small delegation of Republican representatives, mainly from the high country of Tennessee, North Carolina and the two Virginias, ever had anything to do with him, except under official necessity. Sometimes I don't think we take our politics as seriously now as we did in the good old days. Youtsey was the only one of the condemned trio whose conviction stood up. That would be his luck. Still he did dodge the noose; was vouchsafed the dubious mercy of a life sentence and glad to take it. I saw him once in the penitentiary. Always pale, he had now a complexion like the belly of a dead eel. His pin-point black eyes were glazed; the eyes of a sleepwalker. For some infraction of prison rules he was dragging a heavy ball and chain riveted to one of his ankles. He sat down against a wall in the exercise yard and played with the links of his chain.

poor weakling who had been the cat's-paw for desperate, bloody-minded men and who now was their beleaguered scapegoat, twisting and wriggling like a mink with a snare on its leg.

When Youtsey's trial was perhaps a third done, and fall coming along, the judge fixed a date on which, following the local procedure, the prisoner, the jurors and one lawyer from either side would go to Frankfort in a body to view the scene of the crime and the surroundings. I knew the regular Frankfort correspondent of our paper would cover the Frankfort end, and I desired greatly to steal a holiday and take my "Miss Laura" up to Cincinnati for a day. I went to see Judge Cantrill, and Judge Cantrill told me that after the return from Frankfort, court would probably not reconvene, since it would be late in the afternoon when the party got back. So I felt perfectly safe in slipping away with the new Mrs. Cobb.

The day at Cincinnati stretched into a day and a night. Mary Mannering, a gracious lady who afterward became our very dear friend and was then at the height of her career as an emotional actress, was playing a dramatized version of the most popular novel of the hour at one of the theaters and, since I had this assurance that nothing would be happening at Georgetown, we decided to stay over, see the play, and catch an early train which would land us where we belonged in time for the opening of court. When we reached the station the next morning, I bought a paper. It was the *Enquirer*. In those days the *Enquirer* ran to large, deep, single-column headlines. I took one look at the last column of the first page and my knees knocked together.

Under a Georgetown date line I read that, unexpectedly, an adjourned night session of the trial had been arranged. About ten o'clock, Arthur Goebel, the younger brother of the murdered governor, had taken the stand as a witness and had proceeded to tell for the first time in any court of a detailed confession of the crime and the conspiracy, as related to him by Youtsey four months before in Frankfort jail on the day of Youtsey's arrest—a confession of which no one on earth, with the exception of a few persons in Arthur Goebel's confidence, had any knowledge. Even to the newspapermen it had come as an absolute surprise. But this wasn't all. As Arthur Goebel, acting out the scene in the jail with minute detail, reached the point where he began, word for word, to repeat

Youtsey's admissions, Youtsey leaped to his feet, screaming out that Goebel was not dead and all the devils in hell couldn't kill him, and then, as the court officers jumped forward to overpower him, fell on the floor writhing about and frothing at the mouth, finally going off into a seeming cataleptic stupor and lying like one dead. It was good acting but here was somebody acting for his very life. Youtsey's young wife had gone into hysterics at the sight of her ostensibly frenzied husband fighting with the officers and being held down and manacled. Several women had fainted. In a stampede to get out, a number of persons had been crushed at the second-floor doors and on the narrow twisty stairs. And then, while that wily malingerer Youtsey, mute and pretending unconsciousness, played 'possum on a cot alongside the witness stand, with his shoe-button eyes set in his head and his chained hands crossed on his breast, Arthur Goebel who had not moved once during all the uproar, went calmly on with his amazing, totally unexpected testimony.

All that had happened at Georgetown the night before with a new reporter on one of his biggest assignments ninety miles away in Cincinnati, Ohio. Because the hour had been so late and the wires so crowded, the story in the morning paper was little more than a series of jerky bulletins; but my paper, the Louisville *Post*, was an afternoon paper, and I knew the editor would be expecting a complete account of the whole thing, testimony and all, for the first edition, going to press at 11:10. The routine A.P. account wouldn't do. This stuff must be translated according to the editorial policy the *Post* was pursuing.

The train was one of those things misnamed an accommodation train, which meant that it stopped at all stations and hesitated in between. I walked the aisle of our car in a condition which fluctuated between a fever and a chill. It seemed to me that only slow, fat old ladies got off and only slow, debilitated old gentlemen got on.

Like a contemplative caterpillar, the train dawdled across the autumnal-tinted landscape. It crawled and crept, it stammered and faltered. It was due at Georgetown at 10:30. Following the usual custom, it was late. It was ten minutes after eleven when the locomotive whistled for the stop. As we ambled into the station, a newly married newspaper reporter, basely deserting his bride of a summer, leaped

off the rear platform, ripped up the cindered right of way with his
toes and knees, gathered himself up and tore through Main Street
toward the Western Union as fast as a moderately long pair of legs
would carry him. I was slim and limber and very agile those times.
As I fell panting in at the open door of the telegraph office, the manager looked up, startled.

"Where in thunder you been?" he demanded. "Looky here—
I got about a thousand messages for you from your shop already this
morning," and he held up a sheaf of little yellow envelopes.

"What did you do?" gasped a despairing voice which I recognized as slightly resembling my own.

"Well," said the manager with appalling deliberation, "I couldn't
find you and I couldn't find any of the other boys that had time to
help out—all of them too busy with their own stuff. And your
folks calling for copy from you every half minute and not getting
a smidgen."

"Oh, Lord!"

"So, not knowing what else to do and feeling that something
had oughter be done, I took a chance. I went up to the hotel and
got a dupe of Clarence Walker's transcript of what happened last
night, and about three-quarters of an hour ago I put it on the wire.
It was sort of long—over four thousand words, I guess; but I
couldn't think of anything else."

"Let me see it, quick."

"Too late now," drawled the manager. "Bancroft's just feeding
the last part in over your leased wire."

I ran around behind the screen and scooped up the pile of typewritten sheets which lay just under the operator's elbow. I ran my
eyes through one page, through another, part way through a third,
and my heart, which had been a cast-iron hitching post down in the
pit of my stomach, jumped back in my chest where it belonged and
turned into a vital organ again. Songbirds began chirping in the
cage of my ribs. The sunshine was as molten gold. For it was a
great story that had gone into the shop. Done in the methodical
style of the official court stenographer it was all there—the oaths,
the screams, the inarticulate cries, the shouted orders of the judge,
the well-counterfeited but obviously artificial ravings of Youtsey,
the damning account of young Arthur Goebel—everything—and

told so it made a more graphic picture of the scene than any written-out, adjective-laden account could possibly have been.

I went back and found little Mrs. Cobb and resumed normal breathing. Later in the day, I got a telegram of congratulations from my managing editor. With a two-hundred-word introduction, written in the shop, the stenographic narrative had run in the paper exactly as it came in over the wire. And it had been the talk of the town. So far as anybody in Louisville knew, no paper had ever before covered such a story in such a way. The admiring managing editor wondered how I ever came to think of it. To the day of his death he was still wondering, I reckon. Because he certainly never found out from me.

Hence it was thus and so that I qualified for the task of covering the Thaw trial which for so many roundabout paragraphs I've been stealing up on. But in the intervening years a considerable amount of water was to pass over the mill wheel. To be, for the moment, chronological about it, I stayed with the *Post* another year and worked up to a salary of eighteen dollars a week, plus what small cash perquisites I could glean by sending condensations of pilfered A.P. telegrams to various small dailies over the state. Then I went back to Paducah, to become the editor of the same afternoon paper upon which I'd cut my reportorial milk teeth; was to have a child born, to my abiding joy, while having plenty of grief with my job, for we got out six week-day numbers and a pretentious Sunday edition and a weekly issue and I toiled about eighteen hours a day except when I toiled longer. I never fell down but there were times when literally I went to sleep standing up and many a night I staggered from fatigue like a drunken man. I stood it until 1904; was to give up this man-killing labor then and go to New York and after certain small vicissitudes, break into the game as they played it there; was to serve a year and a half on the *Evening Sun* and for the *Evening Sun* to help cover Theodore Roosevelt's personally super-vised peace conference between the Japanese and the Russians at Portsmouth, New Hampshire, and write a series of perfectly incon-sequential articles on the local color and the side views of the pro-ceedings and the parties most prominently present; as a result of the publication and the syndication of these articles was to get a consid-erable raise in wages and offers from other papers. I picked the

Evening World—it offered the most—and sweated between decks in Chapin's slave ship until I got my chance to use the facility with a running-and-jumping lead pencil which I had acquired in Kentucky. That would be when the Thaw case broke on a steamy summer evening before the eyes of a typically smart first-night audience at the opening of a musical comedy featuring Billy Rock and Maude Fulton, the prize dancing team of that era, on a new roof garden atop of Madison Square Garden which was the architectural masterpiece of the brutally murdered Stanford White—it stood as his monument until it was taken down. It herewith is conceded, I take it, that for purposes of immediate and abiding notoriety, the Thaw story got off to a fairly good start.

18

"—AND SAID, 'WHAT A GOOD BOY AM I?'"

THEY said I broke some kind of a record during that first trial of our nation's champion spendthrift for the unprovoked killing of his wife's older suitor. In the autobiography which he wrote from his lifer's cell in Sing Sing, Chapin stated that regularly I turned out at least twelve thousand words per working day and that my reports were as full and comprehensive as those printed in any of the rival afternoon sheets, each of which had from two to five men collaborating in the descriptive matter, the new leads for succeeding editions, the interpretative treatment of developments needing explanation, and the gist of the running testimony and the speech-making. Partly he was wrong there. I didn't average twelve thousand words a day. But there were days, when my output went to a higher volume than that, notably while the witness chair was occupied by Evelyn Nesbitt Thaw, spuriously decked out in a reefer jacket and demure flat collar and big bow tie, and looking the part of a virginal schoolgirl innocently caught in a hideous web of circumstance.

At the beginning after a day or two of fumbling experimentations with helpers, I asked Chapin that he provide one boy to run with my copy, sheet by scrawled and sprawly sheet, down to a basement corridor of the Criminal Courts Building where capable Johnny Gavin of our city-room crew would read the manuscript over a private wire to a stenographer in a telephone booth at the shop a mile away on Park Row—a real stroke of journalistic enterprise for that day; and provide another boy whose sole job it would be to stay just behind me at the press table and keep me supplied with freshly sharpened pencils. (Our weekly pencil bills must have been as added stabs in the bowels to Mr. Pulitzer's frugal treasurer. He suffered from acute financial cramps anyhow.)

Under these conditions I told the boss I'd try to swing the proposition singlehanded. I preferred to have it so, being vain of my agility at hand galloping and champing to show off before other disciples of my calling. At the finish, Cousins-Hardie, one of the foreign correspondents on the assignment, graciously gave me a laudatory paragraph in his wired account, praising quality as well as quantity. There was no doubt about the quantity, anyhow. I think his paper was the *Daily Dispatch*, anyhow one of the big London papers. Cable tolls were costly then and Cousins-Hardie had a big reputation, and I strutted about, treasuring the clipping that arrived from overseas. So far as I know this was the first time my name had ever been mentioned in print outside the United States and Canada. For in those days an assignment man rarely signed a news story no matter how much fancy language he might have milked it for. That distinction was reserved for halo-wearing feature writers and for specially hired celebrities—popular novelists and professional criminologists and technical sharps and the likes of them. An anonymous umbra enveloped the rest of us—us and our most ambitious literary footage—as with a horse blanket. And not such a bad idea either, when you consider some of the by-lined effusions which, upon the slightest provocation, go shriekingly into print nowadays.

To the contrary of Chapin's estimates, there were days when my totaled grist would fill only a very few columns of double-spaced, double-width type under the blazing scareheads and the black-faced introductions for, no matter how dull the material, the make-up editor, at the behest of the circulation department, would play the tale for all it was worth. These breathing spells for the press gang came while long-winded counsel engaged in the customary flatulent quibbles over some legalistic precedent as far remote from the problem involved as it was possible to get without squabbling one another clear off the judicial reservation. Or else, only this would be toward the last after our patience with such solemn farces had frayed thin, the pleasant intermission would come when a chosen member of one or the other opposing herds of trained tame alienists responded to his mahout's prodding and put on a display of intricate and, very often, self-contradictory verbal acrobatics. (They call them psychiatrists now but the breed has altered very little, although shrunken somewhat in number and greatly in gainful employment.) These elephantine intellects had been procured for this exhibition without regard to expense and—judging by results—sometimes without much regard to scholarly background. Glibly, they knew all the stock answers, but under cross-racking the questions distressingly would upset them. Rarely though did one of them lose his gravity, which was specific and dense, or his air of infallibility, which almost was suffocating. To do so would have been unethical, it might even have set the populace to snickering. Better in moments of stress to take refuge, like the octopus, in an impenetrable inky screen of nonunderstandable jargon.

In this regard, Thaw had the best collection of talent that the general market afforded and money could buy. For the People of the State of New York, as the quaint term went, there daily appeared —at so many hundreds of dollars of the taxpayers' money per appearance—a mighty array which Dexter Fellowes of the Big Show probably would have billed as a Phenomenal Peerless Processional of Ponderous Pachydermic Prodigies Pluperfectly Presented in Peculiar Pageantry and Plastic Performances. Through experience District Attorney William Travers Jerome knew full well he could depend upon this mastodonic drove. They'd been many a time and oft on his pay roll and never had failed him yet. On previous occasions he had seen them adroitly swallowing their own profound deliverances when the strategy of the fight called for an abrupt shifting of tactics; had heard the slight nervous rattling as they swapped ends like so many old-style celluloid cuffs. Thaw's high-priced pets were equally adaptable, equally accommodating. And if you think I'm exaggerating, consult the files of any metropolitan paper during the decade, 1900 to 1910 or thereabouts, with particular reference to this affair and to the famous Robbins case.

In this trial the alienists of both wings rose to new heights of flexibility. Today—and the strange thing was that nobody laughed out loud—good old Dr. J. Mumble Viceversa, the snuffy, owlish ex-keeper of this public or that private madhouse in the adjacent area, would be adjusting his double lenses and smoothing his waistcoat and demonstrating by a mysterious patteran, studded thick with infirm Greek and limping Latin, and likewise by quoting substantiating extracts from medico-legal authorities, that Thaw had been wildly insane when he shot White although now was miraculously and absolutely restored to complete sanity. But tomorrow, provided the policy had about-faced overnight to meet the nimble opponents' double-back somersault, he'd be proving beyond the scintilla of a doubt that the man had never been at any hour of his life insane, or else, that from birth on he'd always been an incurable, a hopeless and a dangerous defective. It depended on which flavor the kind floor manager desired. Just give the spigot a slight turn of the wrist and out it gushed—strawberry, vanilla, sarsaparilla. From that debased and disillusionizing period, I think, dated the decline and fall of faith in the integrity of bought-and-paid-for testimony in litigation affecting degrees of mental capacity and, to an even greater extent, in proceedings under the criminal code. For you can't fool all of the people all of the time, though P. T. Barnum said that frequently there are twin suckers born; but eventually chickens will come home to roost and the proof of the pudding is that the burnt child dreads the fire, while the pitcher which travels too often to the well butters no parsnips. The reader may go on from there as far as he likes.

As I now recall but two benefits—unless you'd include getting a hung jury for Thaw—accrued from the scurvy, sweated smear of pseudo-scientific poppycock which was spread, like batter on a hot griddle, all over the fraud-tinged transcript. For one thing, those former Pooh Bahs of the popular lunatic asylums along our eastern seaboard collected their fat retainers, meanwhile, I suppose, like the Roman augurs in the Forum, avoiding one another's gaze for fear of a betraying giggle; and, secondly, the native tongue eminently was enriched by passages of newly coined phraseology. "Brain storm" was a notable mintage. "Dementia Americana" was another. "Sob sister" became the aptly alliterative title for any over-heated young female who mistook flowing hysteria for a true reportorial viewpoint. It is still in use and deservedly so. Being recalled to the stand, an impressive pundit from over New Jersey way outdid his best previous metaphorical efforts. He likened a person suffering from a given type of delusion to "a rudderless ship adrift on an uncharted sea without any balance wheel." For some reason—probably just an oversight—he failed to mention "caught like rats in a trap." To describe Evelyn Thaw and her inevitable companion, a diminutive brownie-like ex-actress, somebody thought up "the Wounded

Bluebird and the Broadway Sparrow," and that line was good until repetition wore it brassy.

As regards the merits of the rival camps of alienists I would say the score stood even-Steven. But, except in gross tonnage, Thaw fared infinitely less well in his choice of lawyers than in the personnel of his experting department. Here the state's attacking force was greatly outnumbered but by no matter of means outnoodled. Jerome was then at the crest of his prowess as a prosecutor which is the same as saying he had no superior anywhere in the land and perhaps no equal. He was murderous at cross-examination and malignant at invective, as quick as a panther to spring and as ready to strike as an adder; always keeping an eye skinned for the advantageous main chance and having the probing, boring abilities of a crawfish to undermine his adversary's strained and weakened levees. His principal dependency was his able first assistant from upstairs, Frank Garvan, who afterward served as Custodian of Alien Property in President Wilson's second term and as a rich man, a philanthropist and a deservedly admired patriot, died a few years ago. Of course the district attorney had behind him the resources of his own powerful organization and at his beck and call all the manifold police agencies of Manhattan Island, but his chief strength was in himself.

Studying the opposition line-up, the one which Thaw had pieced together to save him from the consequences of his jealous fury, I couldn't doubt but that he still was quite mad. No sane man would have picked such a conglomeration. The whole thing stank of money but, other than that, there wasn't much you could say for his layout. The attorney of record was a tall, raw-boned emigree from the Turpentine Belt, with the characteristic accent that Northerners so often mistake for a dialect, which it is not, but merely a sort of labial laziness. It was rumored he owed his present elevation to the fact that he had been Thaw's frequent partner at bridge in an expensive card club which they patronized. Nearly everybody excels at something. Doubtlessly this gentleman played a snappy game of bridge. Second rating among the resident coterie went to a paunchy nonentity who was in the nature of a landmark: he was one of the last stands of the North American side whisker, scarce then and now practically extinct. He distinguished himself—and visibly con-

vulsed his astounded affiliates—by putting to the very first defense
witness, who was a stodgy general practitioner of medicine from
Pennsylvania, a hypothetical question based altogether on the accumulated testimony of the state—a maneuver which, I'm sure, had
never before been executed anywhere. After pushing through this
novelty to its chaotic conclusion, he relapsed and was again just so
much scenery. Next in order was grizzled Roger O'Mara, former
chief of detectives of Pittsburgh, whose functions, if any, remained
undisclosed, unless looking inscrutable was one of them. Also there
was a youngish sprig of the law whose name I have entirely forgotten, not that it makes any difference. His principal tasks, apparently,
were replacing the divots, so to speak, following intermittent family
disagreements and in more peaceful intervals running errands for his
imperious if sorely frightened client or for the client's austere elderly
mother or for the brother or for either or both of the sisters, the
Duchess of Yarmouth, but separated now from her noble husband,
and little shy Mrs. George Carnegie who had married in amongst
the opulent ironmongering Carnegies. He was quite competent
for such duties. Occasionally too he was told off to act as liaison
officer between the family group and Evelyn Nesbitt who sat yards
removed from them, with her drab little Broadway friend for a
sole companion, and except through this intermediary, had no contact whatsoever with anybody. So there were cliques inside the
courtroom just as there were noisy antagonistic claques outside in
the hallways.

A financial arrangement had been made; we all knew about that.
For so much down and so much in continuing installments Evelyn
Nesbitt was to do her level best to keep her husband out of the
electric chair, and a very good job of it she made when you figured
what she had to go on; but no amount could beguile her to maintain
outward friendly relations with her husband's people.

To be the sun god of the strange galaxy of eclipsed legal lights
with which the defendant had encircled himself; to bear the heaviest
burdens of the fray and, when the proper hour struck, to undam
great floods of persuasive, pent-up eloquence, the Thaws had imported from his native West at a reputed tremendous cost, one
Delphin Michael Delmas, who in his prime, which now was faded
and past, had scintillated as the most gifted *Boco d'Oro*—to give the

proper Spanish flavoring—before the San Francisco bar. This was a crowning error on their part; on his also. To the sympathetically inclined, a practically extinct crater which still fancies itself an active volcano is a pitiful sight for to see. Lamentably in this instance, or maybe it was a blessing disguised, the victim hadn't heard the bad news yet. Perhaps nobody had the heart to tell him, and certainly not the closely attached satellite whom he had brought across the continent with him. This adhesive retainer was a silent reserved individual, with the melancholic look upon his face of an elderly fox hound, whose only duty seemed to be packing in a pile of lawbooks each morning and toting them out again at evenfall. If he ever spoke, I didn't catch it.

Mr. Delmas' repertoire included all the old tricks of all the old tricksters. He stemmed from the obsolete Clay-Webster-Calhoun-Yancey school, wherein a reputation might be made by an epigram or slain with a slogan. As reckoned against the brisk staccato routine of any eastern courtroom and the rapid-fire methods of a Jerome prosecution his fashion was so outmoded that almost you could see the lichens forming on the back of the neck and the tendrils of ground ivy creeping out of his shirt collar. He had a vocal register which could be dropped at will from the gusty roar of the Nubian lioness yearning for her mate to the softly plaintive notes of the lowing herd which poetically is alleged to wind slowly o'er the lea. But a typical New York jury would rather you totted it up like a cash register than that you stretched it out into a harp solo. It was said that he never discounted, but rather encouraged, circulation of a report that he was an uncertified yet nonetheless authentic descendant of the late Napoleon III, Emperor of the French. Outwardly he possessed most of the essential props—an educated forelock which on the slightest whim of its master fell in a sweeping cascade off the forehead and into the eye; a dapper foot in a dapper bootee, a set of opulent gestures; unfailing benignant courtesy to one and all; small and beautifully garnished hands, there being huge seal rings on at least three of his fingers. By rights and to support this regalia of personality, the visiting gladiator should have been fashioned in the image of the towering redwoods of his own Pacific slope. But, alack, he was in stature as some stunted scrub oak is—approximately five feet six inches of pudgy grandeur. And that

stubbiness hurt his style, and style was almost the last shot left in
the veteran smoothbore's locker.

It was a carnival of mayhem and maltreatment. It might be joy in
a butcher shop but here it wasn't even funny and Lord knows wasn't
sporting. It was the sharp corner of quick Broadway repartee suddenly thrust in to dent the rounded period which had traveled
across with the prairie schooner of the pioneer fathers and now had
come creakily back to be flattened as by a city steam riveter. It was
the medieval play of rusted rapiers against the very newest thing in
the line of Gatling guns. It was a spectacle which always I shall
remember.

By devastatingly quick counter-blasts, by cruel indifference to
the sufferings of an elder, Jerome preyed on his cornered but still
gallant adversary as a famished tramp might prey on an unguarded
free lunch. With almost a sadistic fervor he ate him alive, bite by
wriggling bite. Jerome always was like that. Once let him taste
blood and he'd turn tigerish and have no mercy. It was the one weak
joint in his armor. For this ferocity created the sympathy which
might defeat the ends of justice.

Certainly there was no fairness in the use of such tactics here.
Before ever he arrived poor Delmas was most sorely handicapped.
Lured by the price which was dangled before his eyes, he'd come
hurrying to the slaughter pits, utterly unaware of what he was being
let in for behind the bulwarks of that purse-proud but terribly
tangled defense. It was common gossip that old lady Thaw, she
being imperious and temperamental, bullied the runty, thwarted
little man shamefully. Furthermore, we gathered that behind his
back envious traitors among his confreres conspired to hamstring
him and blunt his best designs and generally make a mock of him.
When the debacle was over he had but one crumpled laurel leaf to
rest upon. "Dementia Americana" was his very own; he publicly
had authored it. He could take that puny consolation prize away
with him; that and a gross check expressive in dollar signs of the
mess of pottage for which he'd sold his birthright of dignity and
honorable distinction.

Aside from this cruelly circumvented relic of early California,
there was one person in the curious Thaw entourage who strove to

give the worth of the money paid to him by his distracted employers. They could never justly complain that they didn't get value received from Dan O'Reilly, "the Irish Cupid of Park Row," as the newspaper fraternity called him. He was a plump, juicy jelly roll of a man, handsome and debonair and witty, always in high spirits, always boisterously good natured, always beautifully groomed and shaven to the pinky underpelt. I never knew a man who had a sweeter smile than Dan, nor one who flashed his smile oftener. To him was assigned the secret sifting out of talesmen called for jury service, the finding of undercover witnesses and the moulding of testimony, all highly essential to the prisoner's interests and calling for shrewd and shifty handling. Dan could qualify there. His father had been an old-time city magistrate and his pretty wife was the daughter of a wise retired police captain. He had been weaned on a Tammany teething ring and fetched up in the back alleys of criminal law and he knew his way in and out of many a darkened maze of chicanery there. When Nan Patterson the Floradora chorus girl killed Caesar Young the English athlete in a cab, Dan got to her first at the nearest precinct stationhouse and saved her from her just deserts by making away with the scared young woman's pair of elbow-length white gloves—with a telltale back spit of burnt powder grains in the crotch of the right-hand glove. After that she could claim Young had shot himself while she contended with him to take the gun away. Everybody liked Dan, barring Jerome. There was between them an old falling out dating rearward to a time when Dan slipped an especially captivating bit of skulduggery over on the district attorney's office. But Jerome couldn't see the joke and picked at his sores and swore to get even.*

---

* Jerome got even all right, just as he did with that wise little wizard among the shysters, Abe Hummel. An excellent long-distance grudge-keeper was Mr. Jerome. Patiently he nursed his wrath to keep it warm until he trapped O'Reilly in a palpable breach of the codal provisions, and, applying here the fate of Hummel, had him disbarred and sent away for a term in the penitentiary on Blackwell's Island. (They fixed it up later on with the politer name of Welfare Island.) Hummel weathered his humiliation and went to Paris to stroll and pose on the boulevards, but being of a softer

On an evening in the second month of the trial I stayed on at
the reporters' room in the courthouse to do an installment of an
allegedly whimsical series which appeared thrice weekly on the
magazine page of the *Evening World* and for which I was paid five
dollars apiece and very glad to get the money. Somehow even while
transcribing each day's proceedings, I contrived to turn out these
contributions although frequently it meant getting up at 5:00 A.M.,
and being jocular—or trying to—on an empty stomach, or pegging
away after adjournment when already I was poisoned from exhaustion.

This evening, with a finished screed in my pocket, I dragged my
weary frame downstairs and at that moment Dan spiraled out of
Pontin's Restaurant diagonally across the way. He barely was able
to stay upright. It had been a hard grind on him too, that day.

I managed to load him into a hansom, a wild extravagance for me,
but he was almost past navigating afoot and getting him aboard the
subway or an L train was out of the question. We lived quite near
each other in Harlem's remote wilds so the cab fare wouldn't all be
a total loss. He drowsed for a mile or two while we jogged up the

---

fiber, Dan was destroyed utterly. I'm sure if ever a man died of a
broken pride this was a true case. He had been one of the few
honorary guests who by special invitation sat with the working
reporters at big league games in New York. His fellow lawyer,
Bill Fallon, the "Great Mouthpiece" of Gene Fowler's fine book,
was one of these, and Louie Mann, the comedian, was another and
Jim Corbett and George M. Cohan were two more. And a fifth
was a spick-and-span young song writer ("Will You Love Me in
December As You Did in May?" and other hits) named James J.
Walker who had turned politician and was going to the State Senate
and although nobody suspected it then, except possibly James J.
himself, would climb to the job of mayor of Greater New York,
sitting like Humpty Dumpty on top of the wall and like Humpty
Dumpty having a great fall. A few days after Dan's sentence was
finished I was passing through a private passage on my way to the
reporters' enclosed perch back of home plate. In the semidarkness I
bumped into a man lurking irresolutely alongside a pillar. He'd
been hiding there, he told me while the tears streaked down his face,
trying to make up his mind to show himself openly in the stadium
above; he loved baseball like a schoolboy and especially he loved to
watch John McGraw's Giants at play. His padding of flesh was

street, then all at once roused in a mood of maudlin self-pity. He put an arm about me and rested his wobbly head on my convenient shoulder.

"Time like thish a fellow needs a friend, Irv," he mumbled. "Yeshur, now's time for all good Samaritans come to the aid of the party. And I'm the party. Get so tired fighting with a bunch of ignorant, conceited rich nuts that want to raise hell, day in, day out. 'Nuff to run a fellow nutty himself. Say, Irv, lemme tell you about some things that happened—one jusht yesterday, one jusht day before yesterday. Mosth incredible things ever did happen, I guess. Gotta tell somebody or bust or c'mit shuicide or something. Say, Irv, ole pal, lishen. On my word of honor, it's all Goshpel truth, s'help me!"

From then on there was no stopping him. Nor, to be honest about it, did I try to stop him. Such a thing was not to be expected of any normal human being. And especially not from a professional news gatherer.

For serio-comedy effects, the event of the day before yesterday, deftly put into shape for printing, would have been priceless copy,

---

quite entirely gone; his once-fat cheeks were gaunt hollows with gray shadows in them. I hugged him and soothed him and made him go with me upstairs where such shameless rascals among the sports writers as Bozeman Bulger and Damon Runyon and Charley Van Loan, reinforced by such calloused low-downs among the actor folk as Hap Ward and DeWolf Hopper and Digby Bell, made much of him before the eyes of several thousand Manhattanites. As he left us after the game, slightly tipsy and crying a different kind of tear now, he whispered to Bulger and me: "Boys, I didn't believe I could ever be this near to being happy again." But this poor make-believe happiness was not let to last long. The next day a certain staffman of a certain paper, who sometimes wrote a condensed diary in the style of Mr. Pepys—it wasn't O. O. McIntyre, praises be, but a very dissimilar person—ran in his column something like this: "To the Polo Grounds where a mighty throng of outdoor lovers and in the press stand behold Master Daniel O'Reilly, the unfrocked barrister, with the smell of the prison still upon his garments." It was about six weeks later that a few of us buried Dan's shrunken body in a Catholic burying ground. I used to wonder if the man who wrote the sentence I just quoted was uneasy in his sleep on the night following the funeral?

absolutely priceless. For it had to do with a battle royal—properly you might almost call it that—which Dan said had been staged at a hotel-room conference of all hands concerned, following a court session when their cause had suffered by reason of bobbles and backsets. One pair of bearded cheeks had been soundly slapped; smoking epithets and blistering denunciations for inefficiency had been exchanged and, for an unapproachable climax, an object of decoration in the nature of an urn or vase, being flung with accuracy by a feminine hand, had been dashed to fragments—so Dan repeatedly averred—against the high and domelike brow of the golden-throated Delmas, no less.

By itself, a circumstantial account of this free-for-all melee would have made, as you must allow, most satisfactory reading in any live journal. But it faded to a pallid triviality when set up alongside Dan's stumbling and repetitious but, in spite of all that, tremendously graphic recital of the alleged affair of the day before. Some of the parties to it still are alive; and it wouldn't be fair and might be libelous to undertake, even at this late date, the publishing of names and the story of an event for which there probably exists no actual substantiation, although I hadn't then nor have I now the slightest doubt of O'Reilly's veracity. I'm safe though, I'd think, in saying this much: In a cell block of that gloomy prison, the well-named Tombs, there had been a fiendishly planned and only accidentally averted attempt at cold-blooded homicide. In it had figured a Judas kiss and a weapon made from an iron bunk support, and an unsuspecting victim saved by chance—or so this supposed eyewitness to it all now most vehemently proclaimed.

To publish this, especially with the public taste already whetted to the watering-at-the-mouth stage would have been the newspaper coup of many a year. It would have altered much of the integral fabric of the defense; it would entirely have annulled other equally important factors. It surely must have precipitated a mistrial since it was an impossibility to prevent the jurors from learning what would have been trumpeted in the public prints. And inevitably it would have ruined, professionally and otherwise, this babbling tattletale who lurched and floundered beside me in that confessional box of a hansom cab, and breathed his hot alcoholic breath in my face.

Verily I say unto you, the Devil had taken me up on a high mountain and promised me the world. And I sat there and perspired a cold dew and wrestled with temptation and finally—but it almost tore me in two—got a hammer lock on my demon and threw him down flat. Before Dan quit his gabble and relapsed into sleep, I knew what my course would be. I took no special credit to myself for it; my decision was what the decision of any reasonably self-respecting newspaperman, similarly placed, would have been. But to this long-after hour, thinking back on it, I like to hand myself an imaginary bouquet of rosemary—and that's for remembrance—although personally I would regard spring onions as being superior for re-creating reminiscent effects.

At his address the cabby and I got my sleepy co-passenger out and propped him against his door and rang the doorbell and ran. I was calm again—calm and sadly resigned—when I disembarked at our forty-four-dollars-a-month apartment on West One Hundred and Forty-third Street which then was as far north as the hardy traveler could go by subway or surface line. From then on, in wintry weather, you took dogsleighs and put your faith on the good monks of St. Bernard having a hostel in the unexplored reaches of the uppermost Bronx, or at least so the quip-writing paragraphers of the period delighted to intimate.

I didn't sleep very well. I was awake at six o'clock in the morning when the telephone rang in our form-fitting living room.

"Irvin," came Dan's shaken, agonized voice over the wire, "Irvin, for dear Christ's sake, what have I done?"

"I don't know what you've done today, it's still sort of early," I said. "But what you did last night was to go on a sincere toot. And I delivered you home like a laundryman with a jag of wet wash. The cab bill was four-eighty, in case you're interested."

"Don't kid with me," he pleaded. "I recall—I recall what I told you last night, driving uptown. I was pretty drunk then, but it's all come back to me. Irvin, tell me what I told you, before I go crazy?"

"Dan," I said, "if you told me anything unusual last night I've entirely forgotten it. I'd advise you to do the same thing and take something for your nerves and get your clothes on and go to court."

"Then you aren't putting it in the paper?"

"How can I print anything about anything that I can't remember anything about?"

"Oh, thank God!" he said and he was sobbing now. "And oh, thank you!"

"Let it go at that," I said, "we'll split the credit between us— me und Gott. You can buy the lunch today, and pay for half that cab bill."

Neither of us ever again mentioned the thing to the other. Nor till just now when I sat down to tell this tale, have I mentioned it, except in a very few private ears.

I'd like to add that I'm still a little pleased with myself that more than once when I put in my journalistic thumb and pulled out a forbidden but delectable plum, I put it right back in the pie. I may have done some bleeding inwardly. But I put it back.

19

MR. HARRY THAW IS DISSATISFIED

AT HIS second trial, Thaw's chief counsel, Martin Littleton, providentially was picked for him by somebody else and Littleton, with his slow drawl and his deceitfully gentle aspect, conducted the defense practically singlehanded and, for once in a misshapen life, Thaw got his rightful share of the breaks. Let the going be placid and slick, and stocky, curly-headed Littleton—he suggested pictures of the young Stephen A. Douglas—could be as smooth as custard and seemingly not much solider. But it were just as well not to start smacking the custard around. Because, when he flared up, he put me in mind of the story told of a resident of Littleton's own East Tennessee ridges who, testifying as a character witness for a somewhat combative friend from across the adjacent gap, said: "Yas, suh, Jedge, ef you don't rile him, Shep here is milder'n the new-bawn lamb and ez full of sweetness ez a bee-tree. But I must say he's a powerful onlikely fellow to prank with." *

* Grantland Rice took me one night to a dinner of one of the Southern societies in New York where Littleton, who had been elected to Congress from a Long Island district, was to be the principal speaker. He came in late and it was evident that somewhere along the road to town he had been badly enveloped in liquor. He slumped into his seat at the top table and took a few lackadaisical bites and let his drowsy eyes close. Arising to introduce him, the toastmaster, who figured himself pretty good at satire, apparently felt it would be safe to take some caustic liberties with the guest of honor, which accordingly he did, while the target for his shafts sank deeper and deeper down inside the collar of a rumpled dress shirt. In concluding he said: "And now we are to hear this gifted friend of ours who is never at a loss on an occasion like this. The formula is simple: Down goes his dinner and up comes a speech." Littleton

From the outset Littleton took over absolute command of the rudderless ship which had no balance wheel. What browbeating as was done within Fort Money-Bags, he did; and the flaunting plutocratic flag came right down off of its parapet and a savor of humility arose from within the casemates. He hammered the relatives to rebellious acceptance of the fact that if he were going to save their black sheep from burning, they must fortify their souls to the prospect of seeing him locked up, either in a madhouse or a state's prison. In other words, they couldn't eat their cake and have it, too. Moreover if, in pursuance of this plan, family skeletons must come forth from family cupboards, why let 'em come. They came. There ensued quite a rattling of brittle dried bones as sundry ancestral cadavers passed in review. The imperious Littleton reduced the welter of wordage of the alienists and curtailed the stupid shilly-shallying of the first trial. Because the papers had begun to ridicule what obviously had been a masquerade, he stripped Evelyn Thaw of her last season's "testimony clothes" and dressed her in the sackcloth and ashes of a chastened repentance. True the sackcloth had been cut along smart juvenile lines and the ashes were appliquéd on in the best mode of Fifth Avenue. On the stand he reduced her smoothly rehearsed tale to its least common devisors. For it was a year old now and beginning to go rancid; even the part relating to seduction under duress and drugged champagne. It nearly always was drugged champagne in those days when seduction seemed to require more apologizing for than it does at present. Littleton faced the scowling Jerome, jowl to jowl, and gave him back snap for snarl. And the upshot was he made twelve tired jurymen believe that at the hour of the commission of the crime and, in the language of the statute, "defendant did not know the nature and the quality of his act and did not know that the act was wrong." So Thaw side-stepped by a margin of inches the death house at Sing Sing and went instead to the State Asylum for Criminal Insane at Matteawan, a few miles farther up the Hudson River. In no time at all he was much dissatisfied with the accommodations and craving to depart therefrom. His was ever a restless spirit.

was instantly on his feet; all the befuddlement was gone from him. "How different the case with your toastmaster," he said. "Down goes his speech—and up comes your dinner!"

Common sense and hopes for their own peace of mind would have dictated that the Thaws leave well enough alone. But almost before the ink was dry on the commitment papers they were financing a campaign to win again to their collective bosoms the prodigal son. Some months passed, presumably spent in making ready the fatted calf and then they lighted the light in the cottage window and came out in the open with a petition for his release on the premise that while he had been insane in a certain tragic bygone hour, he now was sane and therefore entitled to his freedom. In the month of May the cause was tried at the seat of the county in which Matteawan is situated and that was Poughkeepsie, the historic site of Vassar College and the original home of the deathless haired-over Smith Brothers—Trade, with the classically Gothic whiskers, and Mark, who on the package, wears a chaste Doric set.

A whole squadron of us—newspapermen, wardens, lawyers; Jerome and his caravan of pet testifiers; Thaw, in close custody, also with his entourage of savants, subpœna-servers and messengers went upriver for the hearing. It lasted one week, from a Monday morning to a Saturday night, and it was on Saturday night that the elaborately built-up pleadings of the Thaw expedition exploded right in their faces and canceled all the Welcome-Home-to-Our-Harry plans. But that's getting ahead of the narrative. All through that week Thaw's alienists, the same pedantic and pompous ones who regularly had served him, expounded the old familiar parrot talk and babbled those identical platitudes which already had been worn clear to the quick. A daring chance was taken when Thaw, for the first time, briefly went on the witness stand and was permitted to give semi-incoherent answers to a few cautiously framed questions. It was a repetitious procedure and calculated to wear a fellow down. But the reporters liked the presiding justice's looks and his attitude; he at least yielded us some copy. There was a most unlawyer-like directness about him as he cut through the traditional verbiage which drapes the English common law and probed straight to the core of things. Nor had he any hesitation whatsoever about kicking holes in the moldy though venerated foundations of the centuries-old Home for Decayed Precedents, so beloved of most of his fellow judges through the land. He had started life at a mechanic's workbench and worked up the hard way. Almost any state in the Union could do with a few like him on its highest bench.

Late one night, along toward the middle of that boresome week, I dropped into a little groggery on the main street for a noggin of ale. Other than a sleepy barkeeper, the only person present was a rutabaga-looking, middle-aged man. He was an underkeeper, an Austrian, I guessed, or maybe a Saxon, who had been sent along from Matteawan to guard Thaw. I've always had a theory that prolonged association with demented people sooner or later will cut up didos in almost anybody's brain, especially if the party of the second part hasn't any too sinewy an intellect to begin with. And this individual, you'd say, had from the start belonged to one of the pithier species of the vegetable kingdom.

"Say," he hailed me, "you been over yonder at the courthouse efery day, ain't?"

"Yes," I said. "For my sins, I've been there."

"Sure, I seen you. Reporter, huh? Say, Meester, ain't it a shame the way that Jerome crowd is trying to keep on keeping that poor boy Thaw locked up? Uf he vas gone I vould miss him but vot of it? The things I could tell you aboudt that boy—how nice he is, how free mit his money. Von thing in particular vot chust goes to show I'm thinking aboudt right now while I am standing here. Meester, if nothing else, you shouldt hear aboudt them Easter lilies und them vanilla éclairs."

"Come on down to this end of the bar," I said with a sideglance to make sure the barkeeper wasn't eavesdropping. "What's yours going to be?"

"Straight whisky," he said. He had been drinking beer. I waited until the order had been served and the barkeeper had gone back to his former station.

"You were speaking about Easter?" I prompted.

"Sure. I ain't told nobody aroundt here aboudt it. Somebody might say, vot is it your business? Und me vorking for the state."

"That's right," I said. "But, brother, you could tell me. I'm not a state employee."

"Say, that's right, ain't? Vell, first you should know how that boy loves vanilla éclairs. Chocolate éclairs sometimes und caramel éclairs ulso, but mostly vanilla. Always he is eating them, aivays hafing them sent in from oudtside. Vell, vot does he do this last Easter morning, chust four-fife veeks ago? Nobody suggests it to him, mindt you. Oudt of his own head exclusively, he thinks it up. Listen, meester, und den you tell me vasn't that a beautiful thing to do? Almost to my eyes it brought tears. On Easter morning for breakfast vot does efery single solitary inmate in the whole place, even the violent ones, find at his place as a gift from Harry? On this side here, a lovely Burmuda lily—you know, on account it's Easter—und on that side there a nice fresh vanilla éclair! Vot a pity the chudge here don't know aboudt that. Quick then I'll bet you he vould turn that boy loose."

"You said it," I agreed. "Have another drink. Two more of the same, please, Mr. Manager. Naturally you couldn't be the one to slip the word to the judge—your job being at stake and all that. You just leave that part to me. Without you being dragged into it, I'll see to it that he hears about it not later than tomorrow morning. So until then don't you whisper a word of this to a human soul."

For all that he promised, I stood watch and ward over my Teutonic prize package until he safely was bestowed at his boarding-house close by the county jail where Thaw was lodged. Then I sat up another hour at the telegraph office writing a substitute lead, dealing mainly with lilies and éclairs, for my story which would appear in the early "Lobster Trick" edition of the *Evening World*, on the streets and in the mails at 9:30 A.M. It was a gorgeous beat. It was the spiciest beat, and, in fact, the only real one which enlivened the dragging routine of the hearing clear on to its unexpected and sensational conclusion on Saturday night.

Chapin, as city editor, wired me his congratulations, but when I turned in my expense tally for the trip, Tennant, the managing editor, sternly questioned my entries of half a dollar for hack fares between Poughkeepsie station and the hotel when for a nickel either way I could have ridden on a trolley car. These contrasting actions were characteristic of the two men. Under his contract, Chapin was the highest salaried city editor in New York. Tennant, his supposed ranking superior, drew a smaller wage. Still, by his penny-wise vigilance he probably lopped as much as seventy-five cents off the expense items, some weeks, while in hidden retaliation on the part of the staff, it couldn't have cost Mr. Pulitzer over five or six thousand dollars a year. Because if any green reporter didn't know how successfully to pad his "swindle sheet" there was always a veteran handy by to teach him.

On Saturday, as I've said, the unexpected befell. In the afternoon the lawyers for Thaw closed their case. It was expected that, for offering his rebuttal and making his summing-up, Mr. Jerome would require several days anyhow. To expedite matters, His Honor ordered a night session, with more to follow. But when court reconvened at seven-thirty o'clock, Jerome fairly blew the Thaw crowd out of water by announcing that he would rest his case on the testimony already offered by them and would waive the right to present any counter-arguments against such speeches as his esteemed antagonists might choose to make. There was nothing for the bewildered adversaries to do except acquiesce and decline the opportunity to orate. Whereupon, with great promptness and a remarkably few words, the justice disallowed the petition and remanded the petitioner back to his place of confinement at Matteawan and there he remained until scads of money, plus a misguided persistency and at the end a suspicious court decision turned him free to go his scandal-studded way before age slowed those unwholesome activities of his.

I'm anticipating though. At supper that evening at the Nelson House I was engaged in rescuing the last bite of my second stack of delectable wheat cakes—a specialty of this excellent old hotel—from drowning in an ambrosial puddle of genuine maple syrup, when the proprietor edged up behind me and said in an undertone: "Have another helping? No? Then if you're about done there's a gentleman waiting just outside the side door who wants to see you by yourself. I'd go out kind of quietly, if I were you."

I finished mopping the platter clean and stepped out on the innerside of the dining-room wing, the side farther away from the street. There was a grape arbor there running alongside the extension and bordering it a vacant lot and on beyond that a little public park and in the deserted center of the park a small pagodalike bandstand. There was some moonlight, not much though. Under the interlacing of naked grapevines was a shortish, heavy-set man with a soft hat drawn down well and the collar of his light overcoat turned up. I looked closer and saw it was the presiding justice.

"Good evening," he said and held out his hand. "Feel like taking a little stroll before we go back to court?"

Wonderingly, I fell into step with him. He steered me across the empty lot and into the empty park, saying nothing en route except to ask me if I'd care to smoke. We came to the bandstand which was in a sort of circular clearing well away from any trees or heavy shrubbery, and sat down there. It was rather chilly with a keen wind blowing up from the river. There was no one else in sight.

He cleared his throat, then asked me whether I belonged to a certain secret order. I said I didn't.

"No matter," he said, "tell me, do you regard yourself as a fairly close observer? I've been told that you were."

"Well, sir," I said, "ever since I was sixteen—and I'm in my thirties now—I've worked at a trade which is supposed to sharpen a fellow's powers of observation. Besides, I started out with a healthy natural curiosity, which I've cultivated deliberately. I figure that ought to help."

"Just so," he said and went on with his catechizing: "How long have you had an opportunity to study Mr. Harry Thaw?"

"Ever since the day after the shooting," I told him. "And that's going on into its third year now. Under various circumstances and conditions, I expect I've reported about every phase of his case."

"And as a result of this scrutiny did you arrive at any fixed opinion as to his sanity or the lack of it, speaking, of course, strictly as a layman?"

"I was bound to."

"And what is that opinion, may I ask?"

"Judge, he's as crazy as a creek crane."

"I'm not familiar with creek cranes. Still, I think perhaps I get your general drift. Do you regard him as being of a dangerous type?"

"Well, he shot down one defenseless man in cold blood."

"Hum!" He puffed at his cigar which smelled like a cheap cigar and drew badly.

"Here in my court this week has anything about him or his demeanor caused you to modify your belief as to his mental state?" he asked next.

"You've watched him yourself," I said. "Judge, I came from a horse country. If I owned a horse with an eye in its head like the one Thaw's got, I'd hire somebody else to drive it."

"This isn't much of a horse country," he stated dryly. "And in my judicial capacity I try not to permit myself to be too greatly swayed by outer impressions. Well, I guess that's about all." We stood up. "Oh, yes, another thing: What do you think of so-called expert testimony?"

"Sir," I said, "I've seen the pick of the whole New York crop in action for weeks at a time. I've seen nearly every one of the present bunch on either side of this case reverse his own position so often that, as the fellow says, you'd almost expect him, coming in, to meet himself going out. Judge, it's a poor expert witness that won't work both ways."

"Um hum," he murmured. "I suggest you return by the route you came. I'm going to take a short cut off yonder. Thank you and good night. One final thing: I see no impropriety in our having this little intimate chat. Still, I'd suggest that you treat it as strictly confidential between ourselves." He didn't ask for my pledge or my word of honor. I liked him the better for that.

I've treated it as confidential until now and that means for thirty years and a little the rise. I figure there's no harm in telling it now.

20

FROM WATTERSON TO WINCHELL

ONCE a newspaperman always a newspaperman. I assume the same generalization may relate to crippled lion tamers and pensioned-off letter carriers, but I like to think that for such as me its application is special and explicit. Excusing childhood memories which, I take it, are the dearest of all, my most cherished recollections pertain to the calling I principally have followed.

When the *Titanic* sank I was weaving warp and woof in a complicated fiction story with design to mend my still wobbly purchase on magazine work into which I newly had been projected. I left that imperative job on the loom with its loose ends flapping and dusted into town and borrowed a police card and as an unpaid assistant helped the men regularly detailed on the assignment. I interviewed rescued passengers as they came ashore from the liner *Carpathia*, got the accounts of crew members, gathered up various odds and ends of news—the whole thing was news, big news—and for two days and nights had a gorgeous time.

The day the *Lusitania* was torpedoed was my seventh day following an operation. At the Polyclinic Hospital my quick rise in temperature was attributed to something I had eaten. But I knew better. My blood pressure also went up till it matched my golf score. It was because I couldn't betake my bandaged belly out of that place and hit a straight line for the nearest newspaper shop and ask them there whether they could use a hand willing to work for nothing.

On the night before the Tomb of the Unknown Soldier was dedicated in Washington, I was marooned at a cabin in an isolated cleft of the Adirondacks, waiting for a spell of bad weather to abate. I suddenly had a notion for dressing up the next day's story;

not altogether an original notion because the germ idea was pilfered from Jim Keeley's patterning of the Iroquois Theater horror for the Chicago *Tribune*, but departing sufficiently far from the structure of that masterpiece to give it, I think, some merits of its own. Why not get from the files of the War Department the complete list of names of American soldiers, reported as missing in action or presumably dead but never identified, and on the front page run that list under the simple caption: "He's One of These"? This roll call of honor, I figured, would include men from probably every state, men of all races and of many nationalities. And all over America the Gold Star mothers would be reading it and each one to herself saying: "It might be my boy. Perhaps it is my boy. O God, grant that it is my boy!" But the woods road out of the notch was washed away and the telegraph service from the nearest town, even if you could get to it, temporarily was nullified and there was no long-distance telephone so I couldn't offer the suggestion, gratis, to any of the news agencies, as I had hoped to do.

To this good hour I detect myself reading the paper, first for the news and then for the pleasure of re-editing the news by processes of absentee treatment. I redraft headlines; I shuffle the make-up and I contrive "boxes" and "ears" and parallel column displays for contrasting or agreeing yarns; arrange the picture layouts differently and occasionally rewrite a whole story in my mind. Only here the other day I ran across a reprinted paragraph which, aside from the tear-wringing pathos that was in it, was the overlooked text for a grand feature article stemming from about the most magnificent single swift flash of advertising genius I ever met up with. It told of a morning in May and two blind men tap-tapping along the same city street a few rods apart. A pedestrian following them noticed that one of the pair got in his tin cup only an occasional coin. But the one in the rear was faring better. Passers-by would glance at him, halt, spin on their heels and hasten to put money into his hand. The watching citizen, his curiosity stimulated by this small mystery, overtook the two unfortunates. The first one had on his front the conventional painted sign asking for alms. In sprawling letters on a crude homemade cardboard plaque which hung upon the second man's breast was this legend: "It's Springtime—and I'm Blind."

What a flower-decked Sunday special might have been twined over that trellis!

I don't believe it altogether is attributable to my own background that I find the company of newspapermen more interesting than that of any other specifically bounded group I can think of. The fact is, that when newspapermen talk shop it always is somebody else's shop that they talk. (*Note to proof-reader: Leave me alone. I know it should be written "somebody's else" but nobody could say it that way without taking a dead rest.*) For you see, a newspaperman's business is other people's business; his most imperative task to ferret out what is obscured or hidden or unsuspected and fetch it forth for the world to behold. Sometimes though, so it seems to me, contemporary newspapermen in the talkative mood are more matter-of-fact, or perhaps I should say not quite so sprightly as were their predecessors of fifteen or twenty years ago. This might be due to staff regimenting which has evolved from the packaging and the canning of news by press associations and chain-store newspapers, all of them more or less uniform, except for local news coverages. Or perhaps it is the wistful pessimism of my own rearward-cast thoughts that fills me with this impression. As we grow older the "good old days" which may have been plenty bad, become, as more and more they recede into distance, the best of all possible days. With the youngster romance is something which hasn't happened yet; it's just around the corner. With the oldster it is something which already has happened. One lives for the rainbow-striped promises of tomorrow; the other looks lovingly back to his departed yesterdays and repaints them in glowing colors.

Going for the moment entirely reminiscent, I say that within the span of my activities in the game, I witnessed the passing of three distinctive and predominating journalistic phases and the rise of a fourth which still is the prevalent one. Judging the refulgent lattermost of these by its transitory and now effectually diminished predecessors, I regretfully am constrained to give it as my humble opinion that, except mechanically, there has been no great improvement in American journalism as it expresses itself in the present culmination.

My own beginnings coincided with the fag end of the age of the flaring editorial voice. Then a newspaper's power and its repute

were gauged by its "leaders." Popularity was part and parcel of the
personality of a single pen-smith's day-to-day output. By reason of
his utterances—invariably unsigned though they were—the sheet
throve or it waned. Horace Greeley was long gone, but old-line
Republicans seemed to believe that his whiskered ghost still walked
between the column rules of the New York *Tribune* and continued
to renew their subscriptions. Charles A. Dana of the New York
Sun whose editorial glands secreted the sourest of bile one edition
and the creamiest of sweet milk the next, would pretty soon be
going. Frank I. Cobb of the Detroit *Free Press,* and later of the New
York *World*, hardly had pipped the journalistic shell and Walter
Lippmann was a fledgling, and his immature or summer plumage, as
the naturalists say, was still in the pinfeather stage. But from Cincinnati, Murat Halstead thumped his editorial pulpit until the dust
flew all over the upper Ohio Valley and at Louisville Marse Henri
Watterson took time out to dictate the final drafts of Democratic
national platforms when not thundering on the organ keys of the
Courier Journal. And Samuel Bowles of Springfield and Brann of
the Texas *Iconoclast;* Henry W. Grady of the Atlanta *Constitution*
—more orator than editor but at that, great editor—fire-breathing
young C. P. J. Mooney down in Tennessee and Bob Burdette of
the Burlington *Hawkeye;* these were golden names on a golden
scroll. Today William Allen White of Kansas is almost the only
working survivor of that illustrious company whose editorial fulmi-
nations give to the sheet which each one served, an influence far in
excess of the natural limits of its circulation. Emporia is a smallish
prairie town but it's Bill White's town and Bill's audience is national
and when Bill spits on his hands and stokes the furnaces of the
Gazette, Emporia's fame warmly is enlarged thereby.

The Time of the Great Editor waned and faded. The Time of
the Great Reporter succeeded it and for a season flourished and bore
the fine fruits of fine writing. I'm glad that I moved to New York
before the heyday of the top-hole reporter was past. On the news-
writing side was where the reputations were being made then—at
least within the ranks of the craft. Julian Ralph and Richard Harding Davis had done their shares at breaking trail for this epoch.
Jacob Riis was another of the pioneers. Riis's reputation so largely
was builded upon his impassioned fights for civic and social reforms

and his successful wars to clear out breathing places for dwellers in the slum jungles of Manhattan, that afterward people were prone to forget he had been a brilliant reporter.

By reading a story the sophisticates inside the profession would recognize the handiwork of Sam Blythe or "Ham" Peltz of the *Herald* or Johnnie O'Brien or Tommy Ybarra of the *Times*, or Lindsay Denison or Al Thomas, even though none of these stories carried the signature of its author. Long after today's paper had become something to wrap up tomorrow's lunch in, we remembered Will Irwin's "The City That Was," a full page of word pictures of the old San Francisco that went up in the smoke of The Fire and the whole thing written in eight hours. And we remembered Frank O'Malley's column of concentrated heartbreak, his interview with the old mother whose son, a young cop, had in the line of duty been wantonly killed by an amateur thug. Or, as proof of the ability of seasoned reporters to change pace it might be O'Malley's immortal whimsey of the "Good Ship *Wabble*" or Irwin's side-splitting yarn about Broadway's growing tendency toward calmness on the advent into its midst of Bat Masterson, who as a stripling had been valiant among the besieged buffalo hunters at the Battle of the 'Dobe Walls and who lived to be almost the last of the trigger-fingered peace officers of the Old West.*

---

* In his outward contours Bat didn't in the least answer to the formalistic image of those tall, spark-spitting regulators of the formerly untamed cattle-capitals. He wasn't tall which was just one of the disqualifying counts against him. He didn't even look the role of a U. S. deputy marshal, which was the job that had brought him east.

To come right out with the disillusioning details, Mr. Masterson was sawed-off and stumpy-legged, with a stub nose and a tedious sniffle; wore a flat-topped derby similar to the one worn by that symbol of civic virtue, Mr. John D. Rockefeller, Sr., and in doubtful weather carried an umbrella. He was addicted to seltzer lemonades and tongue sandwiches; and in general more nearly approximated the conception of a steamfitter's helper on a holiday—a steamfitter's helper who has been dissipated but now is reformed—than the authentic person who'd helped to clean up Dodge City and Abilene with a Colt forty-five for his broom. Two things betokened the real man: his eyes. They were like smoothed ovals of

Not all the resplendent reporting was done by the men who actually wrote the stories. It might be, and very frequently was, that a leg-man, so-called, covered an active occurrence and telephoned the facts in to a rewrite man who fashioned them into copy. This co-operative system still prevails. As a time-saving expedient it scarcely could be bettered. A good leg-man does not stop with

gray schist with flecks of mica suddenly glittering in them if he were roused. But you might not notice the glint in those eyes unless you looked closely—it came and instantly was gone. And some of the men who faced him through the smoke fogs of cow-town melees hadn't lived long enough to get a good look.

With his broad-brimmed hat and his hawk's beak and his ropy, pendant mustaches that were like a catfish's mustaches, the character known as Appetite Bill came nearer to resembling the typical two-gun man of fiction than Bat ever had. Yet Bill probably never had been west of Hoboken, or at least, not intentionally.

Appetite Bill was a gastric phenomenon who favored popcorn. He could eat two pounds of popcorn for a digestive bracer before dinner—if somebody else provided the popcorn and if there was any dinner. He was the recognized bunco-steerer emeritus of the Upper Tenderloin and an ever-famished fixture of the original Considine Boys' Metropole bar which Bat also frequented.

This congenial establishment had many picturesque habitués, especially after the theater let out. Among those customarily present: Playwright Henry Blossom of whom 'twas said he used to drop into the tailor's and pick out material suitable for a fancy vest and then have a whole suit made off of it; "Honest John" Kelly and he just as honest as any professional gambler is who calls himself Honest anything; Jim Thornton, the monologist, looking remarkably like a presiding elder secretly addicted to alcohol and, because of frequent stumbles from sobriety, causing himself to be billed for vaudeville engagements thus: "Next Week James M. Thornton— Perhaps."

Likewise to be encountered here, almost any night were "Ren" Shields and "Vince" Bryan, Broadway's comic commentators who usually stalked their prey as a teamed menace; and surely there would be Ben Hapgood Burt, wit extraordinary and clever song writer, towering, and sometimes teetering, above the crowd like an amiable totem pole; and Herman Rosenthal, for whose murder five men were to die in the Chair; and Kid McCoy, who like Blue Beard had nine wives and went to San Quentin for killing one of them;

transmitting the details. He dresses his narrative up with swiftly phrased descriptive bits, local color, touches of human interest— all the things which will make the yarn a pictured reality rather than a statistical trestle of words. It takes two to achieve this desirable effect. The rewrite man must have the ability to catch the spirit of the leg-man's hurried recital. It is a partnership as intimately co-

and, once in a while, Caruso, who lived across the way at the Hotel Knickerbocker.

One met here, too, the cream of the crop of pugilism and the allied arts; and now and then some deep-sea fishermen (card sharps who rode the ocean liners) straying down from Dave the Dude's place up at the far end of Longacre Square, where their fraternity congregated; and sprinklings of jockeys, touts, promoters, trainers, bookmakers, horse breeders, politicians, criminal lawyers, theatrical producers, stage directors and press agents and wine agents; and almost inevitably the two Dans—"Dumb Dan" Morgan and "Gabby Dan" McKetrick—who were the child wonders among prizefight impresarios. It was the conversational Dan who, upon a memorable occasion, ran a bluff on Bat and got away with it, he being on his own stamping ground and Bat two thousand miles from his. Still they did say, under their breaths, that once in the good old days at whatever town as was for the moment at the top of the Chisholm Trail, John Wesley Hardin, the Texas preacher's son turned stinging lizard, made Bat hunt his hole and snuggle up in it whilst in the street below J. Wesley rode to and fro, reeling in the saddle and dolorously chanting, "I Am a Good Old Rebel," that border ballad being for him what rattling is to a rattlesnake just before it strikes. Anyhow this was the scurrilous tale which rumor had borne to us. But then all heroes have their detractors along with their worshipers.

Considine's was where I saw lots of things started and saw some of them finished. You were reasonably sure of at least one thrill and one good laugh—if you stayed late enough. Two-thirty in the morning was just the shank of the evening for Pete Dailey, master funny man from Weber and Fields' Music Hall down the line, who used to tell the rising sun howdy when he went to bed and the setting sun good-by as he ate breakfast at Jack's about five in the afternoon; and for Raymond Hitchcock, the eccentric comedian, who must have been part hoot owl. Or probably he was part goldfish, because who ever saw a goldfish with its eyes closed? Most sleepless of all that sleepless coterie was Alfred Henry Lewis, Bat's

ordinated as that between the catcher and the pitcher of a big-league ball game.

The greatest leg-man, which, within its technical limitations means the greatest reporter, I ever teamed with, was Max Fischel, a self-effacing, shy man who died in 1939. He started his newspaper career when he was nine years old as copy runner for district re-porters at Old Police Headquarters, 300 Mulberry Street. He spent the next fifty-eight years of his life in newspaper work. How many thousands of stories he covered nobody ever tried to compute. And yet by a vicarious paradox born of the system, Max Fischel wrote no single word that ever went into print. Here was an artist who never touched brush to canvas, a sculptor who never had a chisel in his hands, a master musician who played on his instrument only by proxy.

He had all that it takes—a passion for accuracy, a faculty for terseness, the knack of plucking drama, tragedy, comedy, pathos out of the shuffled, shifting panorama of the news. He had a memory for the past as quick as his enthusiasm for what would be happening next. He was Jacob Riis's mentor and guide while Riis was gathering the material for the journalistic crusadings upon which Riis's reputa-tion was based. With his intimate knowledge of policemen, their plots and their pitfalls and their problems, he became a trusted confidant of Theodore Roosevelt when Roosevelt was made police commissioner. Roosevelt publicly acknowledged his indebtedness to Fischel. So did Riis. So, in his turn, did Lincoln Steffens when he came to write his autobiography. I'm glad of the opportunity to add my small tribute to theirs.

I remember one story we jointly handled. He was then head-quarters man for the *Evening Sun*. I, who had lately joined the staff, was editing the "Lobster Edition," on the street at 9:30 A.M., and between times was filling a fair part of the humor page of the Saturday issue.

One autumn morning just before dawn, Max called up with the story of a brutal murder—a stabbing affair that had been committed

official historian and author of Wolfville yarns and also eminent as the world's premier coffee drinker. He could sit and swig it by the quart—that is literally true—black and scalding hot, until you mar-veled that the live steam didn't come singing out of his ears.

after midnight in a tawdry bat-cave called "Toby's Slide," which was down in a basement on Twenty-ninth Street, just west of Broadway, in the midriff of the old Tenderloin. There was for the moment no rewrite man available; we had only two such on the lobster staff. Besides, only a few nights before on a slumming trip, I had spent an hour in the smelly drinking den under the sidewalks. So I took Max's yarn off the wire and stitched it together. I didn't have to do much stitching. Practically I wrote it as he told it to me. I was re-seeing the dive and its sordid, sloppy patrons through Fischel's eye. And all day the tale ran as written on the front page and readers liked it and on the strength of it I got offers from three other papers. But Max didn't get any offers, which wasn't fair. A few months later when I had moved over to the *Evening World* I kept dinging it into Chapin's ears that he should have Fischel on his force and before long Chapin hired him away from the *Sun* and again Fischel and I together covered many an assignment, he ranging out-side the shop, I collaborating from the inside.

Not so very long ago, as measured by those far-distant times of our association, I decided I might do a magazine article about Max's peculiar place in the field. But when I asked him for permission he begged off. He said outsiders wouldn't understand the mechanics of our game. I attributed his attitude to modesty. But later I heard that some relation of his—perhaps his old Jewish mother, or perhaps a sister—believed that he was the actual author of those grand yarns which he had sponsored and he did not want to undeceive her. I still think I would have had a fine title for a yarn—"The Ace Reporter Who Never Wrote a Line."

To match the merits of the succulent stuff which they whittled into space limits, there were deft copyreaders competent to adorn the moral and point the tale with their gay or their graphic head-lines. Often they framed top decks which served, really, as supple-menting illustrations to the text. Few among the graying old-timers will forget the time when George V's poet laureate brusquely de-clined to be interviewed by the ship news reporters on his steamer's arrival, reputedly because the American press had dealt somewhat critically with his rhymes—it seemed to be not such a lush season for British poets; and the *Morning Telegraph* came out with "King's Canary Refuses to Chirp."

At frequent intervals the inimitable "Boss" Clarke of the *Sun's* city room obliged with captions having within their enforced brevity, the real poet's touch, like "A Little Child in the Dark" for Ed Hill's poignant story about the drowsy five-year-old walking to death in her sleep from the roof of a tenement house on a hot night; and for a piece which summed up the tragedy of immigrants held at Ellis Island for possible deportation, he did this one: "Those Who Sit at the Gate."

There was a Pastor Wagner, a pious but commonplace minister who wrote a pious but commonplace little homily, an elaborated sermon, really it was, and he called it "The Simple Life"—and it certainly was simple, the way the esteemed author epitomized it. But President Theodore Roosevelt liked it and temporarily gave it a tremendous vogue by endorsing it. On his recommendation hundreds of thousands of people bought the work and were disappointed to find in it platitudes where beautitudes had been expected. Pretty soon hawkers were selling paper-backed editions of this prosy preachment for ten cents each, the market being sluggish even at that reduced tariff. A small boy was arrested in City Hall Park for stealing two copies from a vender's stack and Boss Clarke, with ironic economy, reduced the story to a paragraph and labeled it: "Tempted beyond His Strength." An added passenger in the person of a brand-new infant having suddenly arrived on a crosstown trolley car, his line was: "Born While Her Mother Was Away from Home."

There was a partnership of contractors doing a big building job for the city. The firm got into financial difficulties and its two members, who pleaded insolvency, were had up in supplementary proceedings where attorneys for the creditors brought out that while the bankrupts themselves lacked for tangible assets their respective spouses had become all at once gratifyingly prosperous. Boss Clarke topped the account after this fashion:

"WE'RE BROKE," SAYS HOGAN
"We Are," Says Slattery, "But
Our Wives Is Doin' Well."

But I liked best his treatment of the benign announcement of "The Bishop of Wall Street," a self-inducted chaplain who established himself in the Stock Exchange district. On dull days he unwittingly produced semi-satiric copy for the financial reporters. They had given him his ecclesiastical title; they frequently quoted him, embellishing his utterances with little jabs which sometimes bordered on outright scandalizing. But the worthy exhorter, taking himself seriously, took with equal seriousness these veiled gibes of sacrilegious pressmen. He expanded himself accordingly, growing positively pontifical. He issued for publication a pronunciamento, stating he had deigned to set aside certain afternoon hours once a week when to his improvised confessional hard by the Curb Market, world-weary souls seeking easement from the grind of money-changing and dollar-grabbing, might repair for consolation and uplifting admonitions. To the *City News* flimsy, just as it came across his desk, Boss Clarke gave a front-page position under these words: "Bishop Bilkinson Will Be Sympathetic on Thursdays, from Four to Six."

Variety's flashing streamer in its issue for the week of the Big Crash of October, 1929—"Wall Street Lays an Egg"—was an inspirational hark-back to that bygone period when a glorious audacity in the treatment of news was in the ascendancy; when any minute an episode might be turned into an epic.*

To a greater extent even than the news columns, the sports department was a show ring for the display of reportorial extravaganza —still is, for that matter, and a very good thing for the levity of the world that this is so. Because of this freedom of individual expression, which not only is permitted but encouraged, the sports page has been the Alma Mater for an array of distinguished graduates into wider fields. Well back yonder there were such notable alumni as Charley Dryden and Paul Armstrong, subsequently a success as a

---

* There are some veterans who think that the streaming across-the-page headline came in with Yellow Journalism. But when I was in my teens I remember how an ordinarily staid Southern newspaper was moved under emotional enthusiasm to break column rules. I forget now whether it was a Louisville newspaper or a Memphis newspaper. Ben Butler, most hateful to Southerners of all Union generals, having passed on, this paper came out with this screamer: "Praise God from Whom All Blessings Flow, the Beast Is Dead!"

playwright; George Ade, Bozeman Bulger, Charley Van Loan and Grantland Rice. Later classes turned out Ring Lardner and Damon Runyon and "Bill" McGeehan and Heywood Broun; and still more recent refugees from the constant grind of sports-writing have been Westbrook Pegler, Paul Gallico, John Kieran, the memory wizard of "Information Please" on the radio; and that sprightly youngster Henry McLemore, the parson's boy from Georgia. Reading after him though, you wouldn't take him for a parson's boy.

Glory be, in those bygone days of which I've been telling, if a new hand plucked a grain of original comedy from out the daily grist, they didn't try overnight to make a job-lots humorist of him. In the first place, he might not be able to repeat. Book publishers and editors, especially editors of periodicals, will tell you that the casualty lists of popular literature record the sad brief obituary of many a gifted young pullet that laid one lovely double-yolked egg in the barnyard of letters and under the strain of creative labor gil-flirted itself so it never could lay another. Then too there was the danger that the forced strain of endeavoring to wring laughs from sober facts day after day might destroy a sweet fancy. The New York *World* almost ruined Frank Sullivan, one of the choicest wits of recent growth, by trying to make a departmental cutup of him. When the best of them doesn't feel funny, which is most of the time, he just doesn't feel funny and that's all there is to it. That in-destructible prodigy "Bugs" Baer who has made a cosmic record by producing a string of acceptable wheezes seven days a week, fifty-two weeks a year, for twenty-odd years, is a lonely exception. The Bugs Baers do not occur in bunches, like grapes; they occur singly, once in a millennium, like the blooming of a century plant. For the run of the breed there never has been sadder work for mortal hands to do than to turn out humor even when the turning out is good. Wasn't it Grimaldi, the greatest of the clowns, who forever trembled on the verge of acute depression? It's the lachrymose Hamlet who jokes over Yorick's skull, not the first and second grave-diggers, though they were written into the script for comedy pur-poses. Shakespeare might have been a trifle shy on geography and the use of standard drugs, but he knew his human nature. And Charley Chaplin suffers from spells of black despair. Because, in its essence, humor merely is tragedy standing on its head with its pants torn.*

While I was on the *Evening Sun*, Tommy Dieuaide, the diminutive city editor—we called him the Little Big Giant—would glide over to a fellow's desk, treading as noiselessly as a cat on a plush carpet and with the semi-apologetic air he always wore, softly

---

* Taking humorous writing in its broader and more enduring aspects as distinguished from the ephemeral humor hurriedly turned out in a print shop to catch an edition, there is, I think, this to be said: It has a trick to it; there's a catch in it. Very often is presented the case of a writer whose satire is keen and whose ability to recognize the ridiculous is sure. But the world refuses to hail him as a real humorist. The trouble with him, the curse which destroys him, is that he is like some great unapproachable, unassailable seer rearing his Jovian head in a rarefied atmosphere of intellectual purity and occasionally stooping to impale on a pin point one of the inferior bugs scrabbling at his feet, and hold it up and spin it about and while it writhes, laughingly tell it and its fellow bugs of its blundering imperfections. It is such a one who says, "What fools *you* mortals be," never, "What fools *we* mortals be." On the other hand a man of less merit may win a humorist's place in the popular estimation because that somewhere in whatever he writes he says to his readers, between the lines: "My poor friend, you're an awful ass, addicted to all manner of nonsensical performances. But in your most assinine moment you never came anywhere near to being the ass that I am. So in all humility, as one ass to another let's sit down here together and talk about ourselves and our failings. For the Lord knows we'll have plenty to talk about."

Mark Twain developed this captivating artifice to a point approximating perfection. In somewhat lesser degree Bill Nye and Opie Read knew its value. Among present-day humorists Bob Benchley notably utilizes this caper in his writings and in his screen skits, too. Donald Ogden Stewart had it before melancholy—the dread type of melancholy born of moving-picture script writing—claimed him for her own.

Almost without exceptions—I think only of Sophie Kerr and Gracie Allen, the radio artist—women lack this trait of subjective analysis. A woman may have a witty tongue or a stinging pen for the foibles of her sex or mine but never deliberately will she laugh at her own individual shortcomings. Dorothy Parker's sallies, bril-

would purr: "Here's a little squib out of one of the morning papers.
Strikes me as being down your alley. Maybe I'm wrong. If you
think you can squeeze some sap out of it—you know, good-natured
kidding—all right. If not, just throw it away."

See, there was no prompting, no forcing about it. The result
was that sometimes nothing came of the suggestion. And then
again, there would be a carbonization of ideas and from the humdrum coverage of the next edition some amusing conceit would
shine out like a diamond in a hod of anthracite.

Chapin might be a trifle more insistent about it—he always suspected his boys of wanting to loaf on him—but generally he could
be convinced. However, having no sense of humor as regards himself, he was none too sure of his sense of humor so far as outside
subjects were involved, the consequence being that occasionally
the pages of the *Evening World* would droop under the burden of
synthetic and unfunny whoop-de-dees. But with that astigmatic
side to him, Chapin would set much store by these labored effusions.
Anything which even partly was his acquired importance accordingly. It does with most of us.

By evolution, one era overlapping and intermingling with the
other until eventually it more or less superseded it, came the next
rearrangement of journalism's constellations and its heavenly bodies.
Good reporting didn't perish; it never will perish until radio or television, or some more cunning invention as yet undreamed of, has
done away with daily papers. Yet there came along a time when
people at large—and certainly the advertisers whose money is the
lifeblood of the press—began to think less of well-turned-out news
stories and more of the consolidated impulses and the dominating
influences of executive directorship. Call it the Age of the Publishers. For that precisely was what it was: the age of Hearst and
Munsey—only Munsey prospered as a journalistic undertaker and
buried more papers than he let live; the age of Colonel Nelson in

---

liant and pungent and searchingly wise though they be, always are
fired at somebody else. When she turns introspective, self-pity
wells up in her small dainty body like an artesian gusher and it takes
a tank to hold her tears.

I wouldn't exactly define it as over-sensitiveness, or even call it
an abstract vanity. It's due to being a woman.

Kansas City and the Elversons in Philadelphia; of Patterson and McCormick, the temperamental heirs of Joseph Medill, as they also were his legal heirs; of Adolph Ochs of the New York *Times*, Paul Block, Roy Howard of the Scripps-Howard string; and Clifford Copley and Frank Gannett and Bernarr MacFadden and lesser men than these.

Still, to the public eye, there isn't much that is glamorous in being the king of a countinghouse or even the head steersman of a commercial fleet. We, the many-headed, find more of human interest in the stokehold, and amongst the stevedores and the sailor lads and the deck hands. Let us pass along then to the phase which, so far as the reader interest is affected, now tremendously is in the ascendancy. It is the phase taken over by the disciples of St. Stylites, he who so contentedly sat at the top of a column.

21

LUSTY SONS OF ST. STYLITES

TODAY a newspaper is known by the columnists it keeps. It is the day of the departmental-allotted pabulum, the warmed-over semi-editorial pap with an illustrious name tacked on to give it weight; the volunteer moralizer, the self-elected philosopher, the featured scientific contributor, the fashion arbiter, the last worder on etiquette or housekeeping or dressmaking or affairs of the heart—or all four at once; the authority upon legal matters and the adviser on health, diet and the care of the teeth; the social wiseacre, the whist wizard, the untiring traveloguer, the perambulating diarist, the veterinarian dealing with diseases of our domestic pets; the played-up paragrapher, the cocksure interpreters of foreign events, the technical observers of domestic relations expounding wisdom in large gobs from their political watchtowers in Washington; the financial prognosticator who with almost godlike precision predicts the next market crash within two weeks after it occurs—or anyhow as soon as he comes to.

For the price of a jitney you may have your horoscope cast, your investments fixed up, your palm read, your love life psycho-analyzed, your stomach ulcers identified and your reluctant liver expertly prescribed for.

Of course newspapers always have had columnists. The success of one great publishing house in its formative stages is attributed to a single departmental adjunct, a column devoted to women's more intimate problems, and a novelty for those days. But now newspapers have so many columnists that often you can't see the woods for the trees and average news stories are merely the solder which binds the joints between the columns. Once on a time when a fellow failed at everything else he sold life insurance—until he ran out of insurable prospects amongst friends and relatives; or he took orders for enlarged crayon portraits. At present he does a column.

Be sure of one thing though—if the paper keeps the columnists, the columnists help to keep the paper endowed with circulatory health. Some of them are more than stars. They are major luminaries of journalism's refashioned planetary system. They don't ask you what you think; they tell you what you must think—if they happen to be political commentators. And the most popular of the columnists—the one who deals in scandals—never doubts but that you are tremendously concerned in his quarrels with some other gossip-pander over which scored an exclusive beat on the progress in pregnancy of some decent woman, or which precipitated a divorce or wrecked an engagement by harping on the misconduct of some truant husband or frivolous wife, or—most important of causes for a deadly feud—the burning issue as to which is entitled to the credit for having coined a twistified word that was a blemish on proper slang to begin with. There must be millions on millions of Americans who crave to read of the slightest doings and the silliest sayings of those who for the moment are notorious. There must be a tremendous audience for disclosures of unhallowed minutiae which in former times would never have seen print unless the author were willing to accept the risk of attending his own funeral. For in the South they'd have shot him and in the West they'd have pistol-whupped him into a yellow omelet, and in the East they'd have sued him. There must be countless subscribers in Peoria and Pawhuska and San Pedro who can hardly wait for the carrier boy to arrive with the hottest flashes from New York's night spots and Hollywood's play places. Otherwise some newspapers wouldn't give these matters equal prominence with, and sometimes more space than such comparatively unimportant things as—well, say the drowning of whole nations in the tears of their women and the life blood of their sons; the dissolution of a civilization; the abolishment of a whole plan of life; the wreck of all the landmarks by which mankind has sought to con its courses through the last two centuries.

Newspapers may seek to lift the popular taste to higher cultural standards; and the best among them do continually and persistently try to, but no newspaper can fly in the face of the popular desire and stay alive. It must offer to its readers what its readers demand.

And yet—and yet—Arthur Brisbane with his skillful aptitude for making sky-piercing mountains of drama out of inconsequential news nubbins and insignificant molehills, sold his timely stuff in every corner in this country; sold it without having to stick his nose into the private lives of his fellow citizens. Dorothy Dix is beloved and believed in by the women of this country as no other syndicate writer is, but she never in all her life has dealt with personalities. And when O. O. McIntyre died, his daily column, the backbone of which had been friendly chatty jottings about people, was being printed in more than three hundred newspapers in the United States and Canada, but if once this kindly town crier peddled nasty hints or barbed innuendoes or unpunishable libel; if ever he entered into vain disputations with competitors over what didn't amount to a whoop in Hades to begin with; if ever he pantingly dished out obstetrical bulletins direct from the bedside, the records are incomplete, for they fail to show it. Nor should due credit be denied to divers living columnists who deal in such trivia as McIntyre did and, what's more, enjoy reasonable success at it without ever having to demean their talents to the level of fat garden slugs trailing smears of fresh slime behind them.

However, to one who is just old-fashioned enough to view their outputs with the jaundiced eye of disfavor it seems only just to admit that here lately some of North America's more bumptious Peeping Toms have shown a tendency toward restraint. Members in good standing of the transcontinental garbage collectors' union aren't easily cured of what ails them. That's expecting too much, but the symptoms in certain metropolitan areas do seem less violent. Maybe some got columnist's eyestrain by squinting through keyholes; some perchance have developed knee callouses from chinning themselves on transoms and climbing into butlers' pantries; or leg weariness making the rounds of boudoirs, toilettes, lying-in hospitals, back alleys and servants' entrances. Maybe one or two got beaten up or harkened to threats of bodily harm. When a worm does turn he may turn to a fighting worm. Possibly the stinky flow from the scandal sewers has run low through over-pumping. Anyhow it strikes me that of recent months the allusions put forth from this quarter of the compass are not so open and the insinuations are more cloaked than formerly. And occasionally one of the scavenger boys partly redeems himself for transgressions against all common ethical codes by injecting into his copy, like a hypodermic shot in diseased tissue, a piece of real news—and then brags about it for a week or two.

Still and all, the lads must lose their following if they continue for too long to reform their journalistic manners. You can't feed the customers on stick dynamite and then wean them on stick candy. The dog must return to his vomit and the snouting pig to the swill pail.

Out here in the movie colony, on the edge of which these lines are being written, is where the privy patrol is still at the top of its pristine naughtiness and its provocative implications find the readiest encouragement. To be sure, Hollywood is a place of extremes, so perhaps it is only to be expected that here would flourish the most unrestrained among the Nosey Parkers and the Paul Prys and the Meddlesome Matties. When, tucked in among the legitimate and well-bred writers of movie news, you observe, as now and then you do, one who thrives by fomenting domestic differences, by putting the worst possible construction on what may be innocent flirtations or honest friendships, by gleefully, gloatfully telling how some one-time leading man now is making his living, or trying to, as an extra—as though that were news and not a cruel exposure of a fellow being's extremity—then, I claim you are looking at a running sore on the leg of American journalism.

Several of the resident pus-pockets are said to enjoy large incomes through their laudable contributions to contemporaneous literature.*

---

* From the viewpoint of a captious few of us, some American newspapers may be overly kind in their indulgence of certain types of journeyman columnists but on the other hand there isn't any denying that, generally speaking, they exercise an increasingly close supervision over the character of the paid advertisements which they print. The same is true of nearly all the slick-paper magazines. But I have in mind one widely circulated paper which has gone just the other way. Once, as I recall, it was reasonably careful to exclude from its columns advertisements for obviously dubious com-

[*Footnote continued from previous page.*]
modities. But when I picked up a copy of it the other day I found
whole pages given over to the fraudulent blurbs of fortune-tellers
and soothsayers; the cure-all promises of unmistakable charlatans
and quacks; the bids of loan sharks and suspectable installment
houses; the specious claims of get-rich-quick promoters and salesmen of highly speculative stocks, especially gold-mine stocks and
oil-well stocks. If the buyer was willing to pay space rates I'm
inclined to think that particular sheet would run a glowing testimonial to the late John Wilkes Booth.

22

PRESIDENTS AS THEY PASS

IF, AS I ventured to claim in a chapter before this, newspapermen, conversationally speaking, are the peartest of segregated groups, then for my money the dullest are those who under a democratic form of government constitute our ruling class. I'm talking now about the professional office-seekers and the professional office-holders; the silver tongues and the handshakers; those two most prolific types of so-called leadership: (1) the overly cordial, outwardly frank, paternalistic generalissimo who carries his entire stock of goods in the show window—"open his front door and you're in his back yard"; (2) the despotic or silent variety, letting reluctant monosyllables dribble from one corner of his mouth and disposing of the destinies of men and measures with a cryptic lift of the eyebrow or a judgmatical shrug; then, still lower down the scale than these, the hangers-on, the lickspittles, the thimbleriggers, the smug lobbyists, the mealy-mouthed evangelists of buncombe, the buffoons and precinct clowns and legislative pimps—in short all that pretentious greasy procession which through every campaign follows this or that self-ordained prophet across the Promissory Land of partisan politics.

Our false Moseses are so appallingly serious. That's just one of the things about them that're wrong. In their purview, a sense of humor always is dangerous, frequently is fatal to the owner of it. What's more, they have taught the public to believe that any man capable of jesting, either at himself or at the follies of this lamentable but ludicrous world, is unfitted for high authority. Tom Marshall, one of the keenest little men who ever came out of that former haunt of the fur-bearing vice-presidents, to wit, the state of Indiana,

was denied his proper elevation in party counsels, as likewise in national affairs, because he dared to indulge himself to the extent of
an occasional japery. Job Hedges was almost the most alert, most
dependable politician I ever knew, and he lost the governorship of
New York for the unforgivable offense of being witty. Take Congress, which is the chief assembling plant of coagulant dullness.
How much of conscious gaiety comes out of there in a session?
Through fifty years three examples of real mirth have illumined the
pages of that encyclopedia of solemn mediocrity, the *Congressional
Record*. At least I recall but three—Proctor Knott's tribute to
"Duluth, the Zenith City of the Unsalted Seas," Private John Allen's
plea for the establishment of a fish hatchery at his home town of
Tupulo, and Speaker Tom Reed's thrust at the impassioned breast-
pounding patriot who declared he'd rather be right than president—
"the gentleman need not worry, he'll never be either." Were the
last lingering sparks of whimsicality quenched when jovial, storytelling Nick Longworth died and "Uncle Joe" Cannon bid a sardonic farewell to the House and all its stodgy works, and went
ambling out with his Wheeling stogie top-tilted at that saucy angle
between his store teeth, and his wise, puckered old eyes atwinkle?
Such laughter as does infrequently resound within those sacred
walls—must it forever keep on being as the crackling of thorns
under a pot?

And politicians have such an awfully poor sense of dramatic
values. As a staff correspondent or as a contributor to syndicates I
went to a succession of national conventions of both the major
parties and likewise to the second and last convention of the Bull
Moosers, but this one hardly counted, since ex-President Roosevelt,
its sole reason for being, abandoned it to return to the succulent
fleshpots of orthodox Republicanism and from then on it exhibited
merely the spasmodic twitchings seen in a batch of frogs' legs on
being sprinkled with salt. For proof of the inherent stupidity of
the master minds, I would point out that while going about the
somewhat important project of choosing the men who will guide
this nation for the ensuing four or eight years, or, since we have
endorsed the third-term idea, for as many as twelve years,
thousands of ordinarily rational human beings, including here and
there one deemed to have some degree of statesmanship, will pack

themselves in a festering, sweltering mass within a large hall and behave for days on end like so many dancing dervishes gone drunk on hemp. If only there were a few sprightly innovations, a tendency to get a little further away from Dan Rice and a little closer to Billy Rose, there might be some excuse for all the ballyhooing and the whoop-de-deeing and the hog calling. But there never is.

If you turn out a forty-piece orchestra to meet your candidate on arrival, we have ours serenaded by a glee club of at least one hundred weary voices. Or consider the impromptu ovation which marks the mention of my man's name, it being about as impromptu as a patent tabulating machine. Under applications of artificial respiration it lasts for a built-up and stretched-out forty-five minutes. There are timekeepers to clock it and cheer leaders to stimulate the laggard supernumeraries and squad bosses to pump oxygen into the pinchbeck fakery of it. Therefore the sham demonstration for your man must run a full hour or you're not the super-showman I thought you were. Do you import Scotch bagpipers with plushy shanks, I show down a trump hand of drum majorettes who have an even more attractive line of twinkling legs to offer and not so much nap on 'em, either. Let your outfit bring along a troupe of reservation redskins to parade for South Dakota's favorite son, whereupon, on behalf of Alabama's glamour boy, we come right back at you with a flush in spades of Plantation Jubilee Singers direct from Harlem, while the Arkansas delegation, not to be overlooked, opens a fresh crate of Ozark Mountain Holy Rollers and old Missouri unleashes her famous pack of non-rekickable hound-dogs.

Is it any wonder then, that the serfs in the press box, drugged on bad air, bad oratory and bad stage management, welcome with whoops of joy any genuine unrehearsed interpolation—a young William Jennings Bryan cavorting in from the West, to stampede the assembled wild asses of the prairie with his Cross of Gold and his Crown of Thorns? Or, as I once beheld, a soused enthusiast falling out of the balcony squash on a militant bishop of the African M. E. church, serving as alternate delegate at large from Mississippi, and plenty large, at that: two hundred and ninety pounds, tare weight, to be exact? Or a pretty girl in red with a bright red parasol to juggle up and down, and a voice like a brass bugle, to scream, "We want Teddy!" for three-quarters of an hour without once stopping? (The winner of this long-distance endurance record was, by the way, an expatriate Paducah damsel and we were properly proud over her but if she really wanted Teddy, it was more than a large majority of her late fellow townspeople did.) Or, as in 1940, people—just people—taking a national Republican convention away from its proprietors and nominating a comparative stranger and a political greenhorn for president?

I mind one convention at Chicago through which I lingered in a comatose state, but recovered or I wouldn't be sitting here now. This was a nice, noisy old-fashioned three-ring circus, a throwback to the early Ringling Brothers era, with grand entrees at every performance and hippodrome effects and side shows just bursting with freaks and human oddities. For its ringmaster it had the newly-elected junior senator from Ohio, the Honorable Warren G. Harding, who looked so much—on the outside, that is—as a true genie of statecraft should look. Being the presiding officer, he delivered what is known in trade circles as the keynote address, which here was a misnomer because—excuse, please, the double-headed pun—it keyed nothing and was without note. Little did Temporary Chairman Harding dream, as he stood there, gavel in hand and age-hallowed rhetoric rolling off his facile tongue, that four years later he himself would be the presidential nominee of the party. In fact, it is reasonably certain that he neither dreamed it little nor dreamed it much nor dreamed it at all. Under like circumstances practically no one, in dealing with some implausible contingency of the future, does dream it. Yet folks go on writing that line just as we mid-Victorian stylists reel it trippingly off the pen point that for Gwendolyn to reach the opposite window was but the work of a moment when what we intend to convey is the idea that Gwendolyn was fairly brisk about getting across the room. I marvel why we hang on to the worst of the old clichés and discard the apter ones? Maybe it's reverence for authentic reliques.

The only bright spots in that back-number convention were three, and none of them was on the program. It was the unexpectedness, the spontaneity which gave to each its spicy savor, against that backdrop of cut-and-dried pretense. One of these happy innovations came when a pretty woman, beautifully gowned and with a fine stage presence was called to the platform to speak. She had been an actress; had quit the theater to marry a rich man who was a delegate from West Virginia. Unless I'm wrong her stage name had been Jewell. Slim and fragrant and poised, she loomed over that sweaty, disheveled milling herd of shirt-sleeved and collarless men like a hollyhock rising above a hog wallow. And she had something to say and said it in her own charming way and not the way Demosthenes or the late Henry Ward Beecher would have said it. The remaining bull's-eyes were scored by superannuated wheel horses, octogenarians, both of them. One was former Senator Chauncey Depew looking the personified essence of the Union League Club, Fifth Avenue, New York City.* The other was former Speaker Cannon, and he seemed highly emblematic of some

---

* In 1919 when a contingent who had been overseas with the A.E.F., came back to Westchester County, ex-Senator Depew, being the most distinguished native-born citizen of the county, acted as chairman of the Welcome Home Committee at Ossining. He was nearly ninety then. Seated in the improvised reviewing stand, he turned to my neighbor and close friend, the late Colonel B. B. McAlpin and to me, and he said:

"Gentlemen, today I believe I am enjoying a distinction which probably is unique in this country. As a very small boy I was brought here by my father from our place up at Peekskill to a military reunion at which for special guests there were three very aged veterans of the Revolutionary War. A number of men who had served in the War of 1812—probably six or eight—also were present. A few years later and still quite a youngster, I saw a turnout in honor of men who had been to the Mexican War. Following the close of hostilities in our Civil War I was once more here, in the uniform of an army paymaster, to make a speech of greeting to soldiers returning from the Southern battlefields to be mustered out. I had the same experience, after the close of the War with Spain in 1898. And today, gentlemen, again I have come to join with you in honoring our local heroes. In other words, from this same little town square, I have witnessed the march-past of survivors of every important war in which this republic has been engaged since before it was a republic. Well, here come the boys. Let's stand to salute them, gentlemen."

And he was the first one on his feet, the first to sweep off his hat, which was a high hat and one burnished to a grand and glistening polish.

quiet residential district of Danville, Illinois; and these twain, having
their political careers behind them and no ill consequences to fear
if they committed the dire transgression of spawning a few honest
laughs, could afford to be witty and they were. A revitalization
which was ageless had taken hold on both. For them this was hail
and farewell, it was their consolidated valedictory. And they knew
it and we all knew it. But there was no repining, no reminiscent
gloominess, no suggestion that a little moaning of the bar would be
in order when this team put out to sea. Everything about them
carried the implication: Forgive us our trespasses as we long ago
forgave those stuffed shirts who trespassed against us; and now
stand back and give us room to cut up in, because the bridle is off
and the kicking straps are unloosed and before we're through we
may even blaspheme against the name of that holiest of the fetishes
in our temple, the sacred white elephant, Queen G. O. P. herself.
No veteran troupers could have asked for better exits.

The night following Harding's nomination was a hard night for
United States Senator Hiram Johnson of California. He had been
euchred out of the nomination by the party Warwicks who at 3:00
A.M. sat in that historic "smoke-filled room," as one of those present
afterward described it, and decided that it should be Harding and
not Johnson or Lowden or Leonard Wood. So Johnson, who probably was the real choice of the delegates, now was sulking in his
tents. A punster might have said, sulking in his past tense. Because never again would he have so fair a chance to be president of
the United States.

"Jimmy" Montague was a close friend of the Senator and of
Mrs. Johnson, affectionately—and aptly—known as "the Boss,"
a tiny woman, quick as chain lightning and a shrewd politician.
Jimmy rounded up Ring Lardner and me, both of us being in Chicago for the same syndicate which had him on its staff as a poetizing
contributor.

"Come along down to the Blackstone," he said. "We're going to
sit *shivah* with the Johnsons. They need company."

We went along. In the Senator's suite there were only Senator
and Mrs. Johnson, their son and a private secretary. You could cut
the gloom with a butter knife, it was that thick. In the interests
of harmony and for fear he might bolt and upset their apple cart,

the bosses had for hours been importuning Johnson to take second place on the ticket—the place which went next morning in the getaway hour to Coolidge of Massachusetts. Had he taken it he would have succeeded to the presidency when Harding died and our subsequent national history might have been a very different story.

There wasn't much to be said, but the secretary brought out a bottle of Scotch and we joined the Lodge of Sorrow, offering silent sympathy and sharing the Scotch.

Presently the telephone rang. The secretary answered the call and reported that Colonel Theodore Roosevelt, Junior, was at the other end of the line craving a word with Senator Johnson. We could guess what that implied. Because in the first Bull Moose campaign, Johnson had been the senior Roosevelt's running mate, those floundering leaders, as a last resort, were invoking young Teddy's influence to induce Johnson to change his mind and accept the rejected vice-presidential nomination.

"Tell him I'm not swapping idle conversation with anybody this evening," growled Johnson. "Tell him I've gone to bed—tell him anything."

"Hiram," said Mrs. Johnson, "for his father's sake if for no other reason you must listen to him. And he's a fine boy and I'm fond of him. So are you."

"This is no time for sentiment," he snapped. "I'm more in a mood for murdering a few people."

Nevertheless he went to the telephone. Listening from the adjoining room, we heard his share of the dialogue. It ran about like this:

"Hello, hello. . . . Johnson speaking. . . . No . . . no, not in a million years. . . . No, I tell you, no. . . . Oh, yes. . . . *No, sirree.* . . . For the last time, damn it to hell, *NO!*" And he slammed up the receiver.

As he stomped back in, red as a fire truck, Montague softly said, "Senator, there wasn't any doubt as to what you meant by all those 'noes.' But that solitary 'yes' in the middle of 'em—just here in the bosom of the family, would you mind telling us why you stuck in that lone 'yes'?"

"Oh, that?" said Johnson and for the first time that night the makings of a wry, sardonic grin were on his face; "that was when the young man asked me if I was sure I heard what he was saying."

Following his election I came to know President Harding fairly well and with all my heart to like him and before very long with all my heart to pity him. I think I never met a kindlier man or a man of better impulses or one with more generous and gracious opinions of his fellow men.

It was at a small non-political luncheon given in his honor soon after his nomination that I met him. As I appraised him then, he was bewildered at the immensity of the task that would be put upon him should the Republicans win at the polls in November, but still exhilarated by the bright lights of publicity and popularity which focused on him. The applause of the mob was sweet music to his eager ears; seemingly he even believed the self-seekers and the syco-phants who jealously hedged him in, were honest in the praise with which they slathered him. He wistfully was desirous of doing a workmanlike job if the voters chose him. And he was a wee bit tipsy on the heady wine of a spurious and a manufactured adulation.

Perhaps eighteen months later I spent part of a week end with him on the Eastern Shore of Maryland, at a hunting lodge. Playing truant, he had slipped out of Washington on a respite from official cares. In the afternoon there was duck shooting and in the evening we played poker, which was a thing he dearly loved to do. And there were good Eastern Shore dishes to be eaten and though the hydrant-headed specter of compulsory Prohibition shadowed the chastened land, there were comforting drinks to be drunk. Those eighteen months had worked a change in him; with half an eye one could see that. All his old-time warmth and geniality abided with him yet. He still craved to like everybody and to be liked by everybody in return; still figured the run of mankind to be above-board and dependable, but nasty little worms of doubt were nibbling at him. As I diagnosed his altered attitude he was beginning to be fearful for his own capabilities and, what was still worse, to the peace of mind of a man of his temperament, he had become dubious of the good intent of some of the gang of gay freebooters and greedy opportunists with whom, out of the goodness of his heart and to pay off campaign pledges, he had ringed himself in. For a political figurehead he had two cardinal defects; had had them all along, for that matter: He wanted to make no enemies, which was bad enough, and, of all things, he had a sense of obligation toward those who had put him where he was. Now of these two, I'd figure the latter sin to be, from the standpoint of practical politics which means heartless and conscienceless politics, the greater sin of the two. For in our national setups and usually in our lesser setups, gratitude is a vice and not a virtue; and pre-election promises are but frail things and meant to be broken, and that man who means to go clear to the top must use the necks of his friends for the rounds of the ladder he climbs on. Or anyhow that's how the thing usually seems to turn out.

When the poker game was over we had a snack of broiled oysters and Canadian ale. Some of the party put off to bed. These were the gunners who would be called at the bleak hour of 4:00 A.M., to keep rendezvous with a flight of wild fowl that also were feeble-minded enough to be up and about before sunrise of a chill November morn. The rest sat chatting. Without warning and apparently not regardful of anything that had been said or done, the President burst forth with an avowal which, by reason of its frankness and its unexpectedness and its self-searching analysis, was startling even to these men who were his intimates.

I'm quoting him now by another's account, but I was careful to ask for his language as nearly as my informant could recall it and I am reasonably sure that in substance this is the utterance, practically in the words that were used:

"Boys, I guess maybe I got too big for my breeches when I let a lot of smarter fellows than I am—fellows like Penrose and Smoot and Jim Watson—edge me into this spot. Because it certainly is one tough spot. I was all right, running a country paper out in Ohio. It's a doggoned good paper, if I do say it myself. No, sir, I wasn't biting off more than I could chew back yonder in Marion. And through the grace of God I even got by, being a member of the United States Senate. But I'm a small-town product. My horizon is limited; it doesn't stretch out internationally. Problems of involved diplomacy, and of intricate foreign relations, and the problems of financing a government—well, they keep bobbing up and I haven't either the intuition or the experience to swing them. So I have to let Jones or Smith or Brown do it and if the thing succeeds

I get the credit and that's not fair to the faithful lads hanging around the palace. I've been fearful all along about my ability to hold down the job and I'm not getting any less afraid as time passes on." He smiled a rueful smile. "Boys, don't any of you ever let anybody you care for get elected president of these United States."

For the last time I saw him briefly in a crowd at a ball game in New York. His cabinet was crumbling and his administration was a discredited tottery thing. That measly miserable crew of parasites who had surrounded him and buttered him with soft words and cajoled him to a make-believe security while they battened on the public fund, fighting one another for a good hold on a front teat and sucking hard lest the udder go dry before each got his fill— they now were abandoning him like pirates who quit a scuttled hulk. The Teapot Dome scandal and the Forbes scandal and the Dougherty-Fall-Denby mess were smeared all over the front pages, and on the wind there actually was talk of his impeachment for malfeasance in office. Gossip had it that to set a national example and to please the triumphant and dictatorial Drys who had laid their unenforceable darling of sumptuary legislation in his lap for enforcement, he had stopped drinking; I know he was frightfully nervous. He looked dazed and distracted, like a man not yet rallied from knockout blows, looked terribly old, too. His once splendidly proportioned and erect figure had folded in on him like a collapsing framework and on his face was unmistakably the death look, which is so recognizable and yet so indescribable. This was just before he took train for the transcontinental journey by which he hoped to rehabilitate himself in the eyes of the people, and from which he would return in a coffin, sincerely mourned, as a well-intentioned failure sometimes, and justifiably, is.

I think Harding will go down in our history as a man to be sorry for; a loyal, honest, trustful weak man; a man befooled, belittled, betrayed by a host of Iscariots; and, at the back of all that, a man most woefully miscast for the role to which ruthless expediency and the complacent selfishness of party nabobs assigned him. They wanted a pliant and a credulous and a not overly shrewd man; a man who would stand hitched, as the saying is; who could be cozened or bulldozed into playing the game and go along, docile as old Dobbin and blind as a mine mule, but taking care en route of the organization boys. Well, they got him and it almost was the undoing of their supposedly foolproof machine. But it was his utter destruction. I guess though that didn't much grieve them, they being busy taking to the lifeboats.

Harding had his capabilities. He would have made an ideal chairman of the entertainment committee at an Elks' reunion. He'd have succeeded, no question about it, as the manager of a smart country club; as a resort hotel proprietor, superb! But aside from a profile fitted to be steel-engraved on postage stamps, he probably had fewer qualifications for filling the presidential chair than any man who ever did fill it.

Once only and then fleetingly, I interviewed Grover Cleveland, finding him a wasted-away, listless, broody husk of a great man, disillusioned and persistently disappointed over the Free Silver split and the resultant repudiation of his leadership and his policies by the dominant wing of the Democracy. He was sickening then for his last illness.

And once again, but that would be years later, on a steaming hot night I boarded a way train on a jerkwater side line which, seemingly to avoid giving offense to fastidious folk by any display of boisterous haste, was winding worm-like across the sun-blistered littoral of southern Ohio. Already that night I had changed cars twice; must change again before we crossed the river and slanted off through eastern Kentucky. I climbed aboard a day coach, to be greeted by the familiar scenes and smells—dust clouds sifting in the open windows and ashes and acrid smoke and gushes of humid heat; fretful, sour-looking babies crying; men and women crowded together and curled up in tortured attitudes; snores and choked grunts; and underfoot, trampled food fragments and slimy fruit peelings, and a heavy sprinkling of anthracite cinders which made a crunching, gritty sound when trodden on; and the superimposed layers of fine grime so deeply imbedded in the faded upholstery that putting your cheek to it was like pressing against some sort of furry sandpaper. I found a vacant place, the last one available, and hunched down in it. Leaving the next stop but one, I was aware of the very broad back of a man who stood in the aisle a little forward of me. He straddled a heavy suitcase which he must have lugged aboard without aid, for his globular sides were heaving and he was

giving little grunts and panting sounds. Automatically he was swaying to the swing of the train as it bounced and stumbled and reeled
along an inconceivably rough and crookedy track. I don't believe
there had been any changes made on the roadbed since Morgan's
Cavalry passed this way in 1863. They tore it up. Where he had
halted I couldn't see the new passenger's face, but from the wearied
slump of the rotund form I figured he wasn't young.

I tried to forget the figure he made; I was pretty tired myself
and powerfully drowsy and most earnestly desirous of catching
forty winks or so. But the sharp elbow of conscience kept nudging
me. I had been reared to have respect—and some consideration—
for my elders. I bent forward and touched him and he turned a
ruddy, sopping-wet, dirt-streaked face upon me and it was William
Howard Taft. If any of our fellow travelers ever before had seen
him, or his picture, they either had forgotten or, seeking their own
ease, chose to ignore his presence. Yet here he was, only a few years
out of the White House. Gamely, he chuckled the inimitable
deep-throated Taft chuckle as he protested against taking my seat;
chuckled thankfully when I wore him down by my persistence;
chuckled because no one else had recognized him, and chuckled
over the compounded discomforts which the two of us must undergo, for both were filling speaking dates on the same midsummer
Chautauqua circuit. I thought poorly then, and still do, of a government which finds billions to sow broadcast in all directions yet
is too niggardly to make provisions for our ex-presidents in their
latter years.

When a naked July sun was rising to suck up the scanty dew
like a sponge and burnishing to twin silver streaks the steel rails
where they met in a distant V among the reawakened heat waves
on beyond, we parted company at what might be described as a
secretive railroad station which unostentatiously, indeed almost
furtively, was keeping two cornfields from merging. He got off
here while I went along to fulfill my dismal destiny at a fragile,
frame-built West Virginia town I'd never heard of before. He
chuckled a sympathizing adieu and waved a plump hand as he
faced about to meet the yawning local reception committee which
had arrived and was stumbling along the warped crossties. A very
gallant gentleman, carrying on without lament or grousing, was
William Howard Taft.

I think Colonel Theodore Roosevelt had for so long cultivated his personality complexes—his fixations of voice and gesture and mannerism—that they had become part of him, calling now for no prior cueing. Always on leaving him I found myself wondering whether he relaxed, even for just a little bitsy bit, in his sleep. I doubt it. But his behavioristic buoyancy was not exhausting upon the spectator as so often is the case when one of the strenuous ones of this earth is putting on an act. On the contrary, there was an exhilarating and almost a contagious quality about it. You marveled that you also were not grinding and grating the back molars, nor pummeling space with a clenched fist, nor clenching your own jowls until the jaw muscles knotted like angleworms in a can. From every pore he excreted a stimulating charm, an almost daunting enthusiasm, the forcefulness of an indomitable will, a monumental combativeness. You might not agree with him. I'd say he'd rather you didn't agree with him so that he might pound you down with his violent and vociferous rebuttals. He looked for a thundering good fight as more pacific souls seek peace and quietude. But whether you would agree with him or whether you wouldn't, you had to give him credit for believing what he said—at least for the moment.

Almost the last time I saw him was in 1917 at a luncheon given for a small company which mainly was made up of his devoted admirers, at the home of Julian Street the fictionist, who, along with Charles Hanson Towne the poet, and George Barr Baker the publicist, and Porter Emerson Browne the playwright, were the chief image bearers in Literary Auxiliary Number I, New York Chapter, of the True Blue Flock of Roosevelt Worshipers, the grand hailing sign of the order being, I'd say, "Our hero right or wrong—only he's always right!" At this time the Colonel was as restless as a chipmunk's tail over being kept at home when his country was at war elsewhere and he still seethed with indignation that President Wilson had denied him a commission to go across in command of a division of his own raising and staffed with a personnel of his own selection. With truly consistent Rooseveltian inconsistency, he could see no impropriety, no upsetting of discipline and morale and orderly procedure, but only a personal spleen and a personal jealousy in Wilson's refusal to accept the request that he, of a military experience confined to that burlesque campaign of ours in Cuba twenty years before, should be taken out of the civilian class and jumped in rank beyond scores of men who had given their lives to the service; and furthermore, that he should be permitted to strip the National Guard of this colonel and the small standing army of that general. He named the men he would have chosen—the pick and the prime of what stuff we had on which hurriedly to build an expeditionary force for answer to the urgent call for help from overseas.

Along with his wayward obstinacy, and his unconquerable optimism, he exuded an all-enveloping, stupendous love for his country; a versatility of viewpoints, a vigorous if somewhat lopsided grasp of public affairs, a universality of comprehension regarding what had interested him—and seemingly nearly everything had: ornithology, ethnology, Egyptology, anthropology, books, his own prominently included; big-game hunting, exploration, nature in general, the habits of red ants, and the quaint peculiarities of the Arizona hydrophobia skunk. He had, besides, a boyish exuberance, plus an intolerance for shams and snobs (and for opposition); and a compassionate sympathy for all mankind, excepting that contemptible segment of it which couldn't see eye to eye with him. Most characteristic of all, there stood out his uncompromising, unalloyed Americanism and his yearning to dedicate his remaining years to upholding America's principles and America's ideals. If, in pursuance of these laudable purposes, it became incumbent upon him to beat out some stubborn idiot's brains or here and there to burst a luckless opponent's eardrums for him, or trample a few sets of toes to pulp, what of it? That's why darkies were born. By casual contrast even, you caught the infection of his spirit. You might put it in a line: You had to hate the Colonel a whole lot to keep from loving him. And when you reckoned the one man against the other, it took no great sapience to understand why it was inevitable that a whole nation—yes, in large degree, the habitable globe—should hail him as "Teddy," while at the same time realizing how incredible it would have been had anybody, even in his youth, called Woodrow Wilson, "Woody." We nickname the spouting geyser or the frolicsome whirlpool, never the gelid glacier.

Seemingly, sojourning in the chief executive's chair had a tendency to broaden and strengthen the common touch in Harding and Taft and the two Roosevelts, but to dry it up in Coolidge and Hoover and Wilson. It was not until after he finished his tempestuous tenure of office that Mr. Hoover developed the humanized qualities that speedily made him the first citizen of California, as in the estimation of sundry millions of his fellow Americans, who appreciate him for his patriotism, his wise and tempered judgments, and his tremendous organizing and directing faculties, he is the first gentleman of America. He still is a shy man and often is fumbly and inarticulate when most he craves to bespeak his feelings, but he no longer impresses you as one who is all intellect. You speedily discover that he has a very great heart to match a great brain. He may not wear it on his sleeve but it's not very far up the cuff.

It wasn't always so. In the second fall of his administration when the Depression had settled down to spend the winter with us—a whole succession of winters, as it turned out—the flustered President seemed disposed to pass on nearly everything that was troublesome to personally-picked investigating groups with powers to snoop and ponder and jot down notions and generally to fiddle about while Rome burned. Returning from a gunning trip on lower Chesapeake Bay, a quartet of us felt that Mr. Hoover needed cheering up and we decided to send him, with our compliments, a bag of game. It would be in the nature of a bipartisan testimonial since General Coleman Du Pont, who had been our host on the expedition, and a political standby of his from Delaware were Republicans while the remaining two, a Maryland sportsman and myself, were old style, Model-T Democrats. So, a waggish mood possessing us, we packed up six brace of lusty canvasback drakes and forwarded them to the White House, labeled with a card bearing our four signatures with impertinent directions on it, reading as follows:

"*One dozen wild ducks. To be eaten, NOT referred to a Commission.*"

Our blithe, brave little whimsy died aborning. We didn't even get a formal acknowledgment. Well, the President was particularly not in the mood for jollities at that moment. I think it was just about then that the Wickersham fact-finding body reported back that the Eighteenth Amendment would be an unqualified success, if it weren't such a horrible failure.

Toward the tag end of President Coolidge's second term, he

journeyed up to New York to read a paper on our relations with
the Latin-American republics at an annual banquet of the American Newspaper Publishers' Association. That spring it was the turn
of the United Press to sponsor the party and, as a sort of low
vulgar relief to the serious note which the President was expected
to sound forth, Roy Howard, chairman of the board of the U. P.,
asked me to make the only other talk on the program.

The presidential party was late in arriving. The twelve hundred
members and guests on the floor, and the long rank of us who sat
like so many waxworks on the platform, had worked deadly havoc
to the fronded celery and the iced olives before there was a flutter
of secret service men at the door and a backwash of hotel functionaries and then, in the wake of this groundswell, Mr. Coolidge advanced, prim-lipped and frozen-faced, with a tight scroll of manuscript clenched to his breast. No base miscreant was going to get
those chosen remarks away from him without a struggle. There
were loud cheers and scores rose up to intercept him with greetings
on his way across the room and scores more swarmed to the dais
to pump his free hand and to be seen in the act of doing so.
Eventually the pestered little man was permitted to sit at the right
of Karl Bickel, president of the U. P. who would be toastmaster.
Beyond Mr. Coolidge was Roy Howard. I was at Bickel's left.

As we all settled down and the waiters began charging in with
the over-due first course, Roy Howard leaned backward and in
a half-whisper said to me:

"I notice you didn't shake hands with the President. Any feud
on, you dirty rebel?"

"No," I said. "It just so happens I never met him—in fact, never
saw him before tonight."

"Let me introduce you?" he suggested.

"Hold on," I said.

I knew how a man feels when he has a speech churning around
in his system and is wondering whether it is going to come sloshing
out, rich in proteins and butterfats, or just clabber inside of him
and produce nothing but a thin whey. He doesn't want to be
bothered. I was feeling that way myself, right then.

So I said to Howard, "When he is through with his address
which is important to a whole hemisphere, and I'm through with

mine which is important only to me, and possibly Mrs. Cobb, I'll be proud to have you present me to the president of my country. But not before then."

Apparently oblivious to the dialogue going on behind his back, Mr. Coolidge was baling out his consommé cup and between sups glancing at his precious typed passages, when a certain individual of practically everybody's acquaintance came, like the chamois of the Alps, skipping between the tables and uttering his character-istic flute-like hunting call. This gentleman was more than a char-acter about Broadway; he was in the nature of an institution: a small but broadish person, suggestive in shape and temperament of an agreeably flavored sweet gherkin. (The reader may have noted that I am prone in these writings to take liberties when describing the physical idiosyncrasies of others. As one who perhaps justly has been acclaimed the homeliest man of his weight and age on this continent, I claim the right to deal as harshly as I please with con-tenders for the title. I shall hew to the line; let the upstarts fall where they may.)

Well, here, by leaps and bounds, came this elfin celebrity who, following the death of Diamond Jim Brady, had become illustrious as the most persistent, sincere and indefatigable banquet-fancier in Manhattan borough. He belonged to all the clubs, most of the soci-eties, and many of the sodalities, leagues and associations. He went to their blowouts; also to the large subscription and invitational affairs. He was a highly thought of executive in a concern of great importance and was kindly and generous, and always was doing people favors. The whole midtown endorsed him as a worth-while and useful citizen. But it was not to be denied that our small pickle-shaped friend was just a trifle limelight-struck.

The stage was set for his entrance; he had the scene to himself and he meant to squeeze it dry. He wrested the soup spoon out of Mr. Coolidge's grip and imprisoned the limp hand in both of his hands just as they used to do in old-fashioned melodramas but don't any more, probably because we don't have old-fashioned mel-odramas any more. He recalled to the President's attention their last meeting before this one and the one before that and tendered his regards and his compliments; and he asked after Mrs. Coolidge's health and begged to be remembered to her. By that time the waiter with a deft stroke of the legerdemain common to waiters, even while wearing those dank, white cotton gloves with the thumb tips on them which are like wilted morning-glory buds, had whisked away to some secret cache the presidential soup cup and substituted therefor a section of that pale and flabby species of fish which so often is served on large formal occasions such as this one was, and which invariably comes to the feast immersed in a pallid sauce of a prevalent gruel-like consistency: one might say a sort of edible library paste. You never see these fishes in the water, alive; only at banquets, dead. And if you are smart you leave that sauce be.

As the interrupter moved off, radiantly victorious and looking back our way and smiling, I tilted myself on the hind legs of my chair and, speaking on past Mr. Coolidge's unyielding spinal column, never dreaming he would hear me or take notice if he did, in an aside I addressed Howard, one seat beyond him.

"Roy," I said, "I reckon the only way to avoid meeting Luke the Cuke at dinner in New York is to eat at an owl wagon."

Instantly the President jerked about and to me he directed the only words uttered by him that evening, excepting when he read his message to our Pan-American cousins.

He clasped my hand, shook it with great fervor and spoke as follows:

"Oh, thank you!"

23

RECIPE FOR MAKING WARS PRETTY

UNTIL President Wilson made his bid for a second term I had never met him. I had brewed a tremendous admiration for the man, as an intellectual force and as a master of rhythmic English and an apostle of good intent. Very soon I was saying to myself that the only man who ever could convince me that Woodrow Wilson wasn't the safest shepherd our government had had since Lincoln, would be Woodrow Wilson. And so he did, but it took quite some time for the disillusioning process to set in.

Above all, I admired him then for his struggle to preserve our threatened neutrality. You see, it had not been so very long before this that in Flanders and in France I had seen War for what it is— the next morning of drunken glory. I had seen it stripped of all the spurious passementerie in which the stay-at-home exploiters of quickened young flesh and supple young bones delight to dress it up. I mean the profiteers and buccaneers; editorial incendiaries and street-corner agitators and professional saber-rattlers; peddlers of the paper-soled shoes and purveyors of the shoddy blankets and canners of the spoiled meat-scrapings; mousy diplomatists and swinish contractors; and behind these, the enterprising munition-makers seeking commerce in any governmental market whether it be friendly to their nation or avowedly hostile to it, so that English-built machine guns manned by German crews even then were mowing down Englishmen, and German shells fired from British ordnance had been killing German troops. I mean just the whole kit and caboodle of that buzzardly flock which flops on ahead and mops up behind the insatiate vast engine which we call modernized warfare.

In various of its aspects, I had seen the workings of that hateful machine and had assayed it and attested to it as the most obscene, the most suicidal, useless, wasteful thing, and nearly always the most unnecessary thing that has ever degraded this afflicted planet. I had seen the flower of the youth of Europe being turned into pestilential carrion and decent men reduced to the level of the beasts. I had seen in newly consecrated cemeteries the lines on lines of little white crosses and came to know that these crosses were merely as so many gratifying plus marks on the profit page of the ledgers of the affiliated traffickers in murder, mortality and mutilation. How the nicely alliterative words do come clanging forth when one has such an engaging topic! And by the same token I was aware that the spilt red blood of all the silent sleepers in those already over-crowded burying grounds had not been spilt in vain if only no red ink marred the stock accounts of—let's see now, what was that quaintly winsome name which the speculators and the rejoicing brokers in Wall Street and the investment bankers and the bucket-shop boys had for them?—Oh, yes, War Babies.

If you think that in this institution there is any part that is beautiful to the senses, or a balm to the soul, arrange to visit a battlefield before they've had time to gather up all the dead and tend all the wounded. Or drop by a front-line dressing station while the fresh casualties are being hurried in, and the churned mud at the doorway is a sticky brownish paste and the stretchers look as though they had been dipped in dye vats of a certain color. Or frame your plans so that you may call at an asylum ward for shell-shocked veterans during a thunder shower. Twenty-odd years after the event we still can furnish an abundance of these finished products of the industry as it then was geared and meshed. Since then, of course, many beneficial readjustments have been made in the agen-cies for mangling human beings into messy chunks and scraps and perforations. If, in this machine age, we anywhere are ap-proaching the perfect in fabrication it must be at the factories where they turn out planes and tanks and bombs and the chemical drenches and the cute new notions in gunnery. Should we not be proud to reflect that every time civilization produces a formula to prolong the normal span of life, science, for a counterpoise, evolves a way to shorten it with painful abruptness? Too bad to have to wait until an oncoming generation, which is the sacrificial raw material for the mills, has grown up to killing age before the various plant units may be speeded to top capacity. The trouble is the outgoing generation, who lived through the last successful revival of this business on a world-wide scale, have such vivid memories of what happened then. It hurts trade to have these long lapses between the boom seasons.

When I think of war I do not think of marching columns and cheering multitudes and Junior Leaguers wrapping Christmas boxes for the forces, with their skirts so arranged that the photographers command a fine view as far up as the knees anyhow. I do not think of massed flags or the sunshine glinting on shifting lanes of bayonets or orchid-mounted debutantes toasting The Blessed Cause at the ladies' cocktail bar in the Ritz, or troopships pulling out for foreign parts while some damned brass band plays jubilee tunes instead of the dirge it should be playing.

When I think back on that other war I think of certain little detached pictures, miniatures of despair, I suppose you might call them, rather than of the great panorama of a major engagement, or the colossal sweep of waste and ravishment and suffering at the hinder end of a major retreat. I think, for instance, of an abandoned seminary standing on captured territory just above the Belgian-French border, and it at best a bleak and comfortless barracks of a place and made over now into a temporary hospital; and there on filthy stinking pallets, side by side upon the tiled floor, I saw fourteen men together dying in the unspeakable agony of lockjaw because the tetanus antitoxin had given out.

I think of a walled-in courtyard behind a little nunnery which also had been taken over by the Germans. Once on a time it must have been a cloistered, peaceful spot, with the robed sisters walking in pairs along the graveled paths and under the plane trees French schoolchildren playing in their funny little blue and black apron-smocks. The day I passed that way it was tenanted by men, almost boys, some of them were; and all their eyes had been shot out by bullets or eaten out with infection; there being both Germans and Frenchmen among them and one Austrian artilleryman and a turbaned black legiondaire from northern Africa. But they forgot about having lately been enemies, seeing how they were so busy now learning to grope with timorous faltering steps into the darkness which would be their joint portion forevermore.

And I think of one more small episode, only this happened shortly before the Armistice and came to me at secondhand. On my spare evenings that year I went touring about to the cantonments and rest billets, opening up my little box of tricks for Americans and for Britishers and Colonials.* I'd recite a range of dialect stories, but mainly what the Englishmen, who liked them, called "Blackamoor" yarns, meaning by that, skits on negro life. In the course of these excursions I met a fellow worker in the same field, a knowledgeable, clever fellow. He was a singer of ballads and a

---

* During the disturbing time when Big Bertha, the great German long-distance gun, co-operating with German fliers, was subjecting Paris to frequent strafes, I spoke one night to a big crowd of our men in a hall near the Madelaine under the auspices of the Knights of Columbus or the Jewish Welfare or the Y.M.C.A.—I forget now exactly which it was, but anyway one of the three. All of a sudden the *alerte* was sounded and there broke out the heavy crunch of dropped explosives and the brisk cracklings of anti-aircraft guns in the suburban defenses. We were probably just as safe as we could have been in some damp underground *abri* crowded with panic-stricken Parisians and beyond doubt much more comfortable. So we stayed, all of us, where we were and I spoke over—or rather under—the tumult until the enemy had been driven off and the all-clear signal was sounded.

A doughboy came up to the platform then and addressing a buddy who had just arrived, he said: "Kid, next time Mr. Cobb is spielin' his stuff anywheres 'round where you are, don't miss it—if you can!" After twenty-two years I'm still wondering whether I was being complimented or criticized. I put the puzzle to Wilson Mizner and he couldn't solve it, but he did give it circulation.

Again that spring I went up to the Picardy front where our First Division was helping the French and British repel the final Great Push of the Germans. On a comparatively quiet evening at a little village south of Compiègne I had for an audience a battalion of the Twenty-eighth Infantry to which temporarily I was attached. The party was staged in a huge communal barn used in peace times by a co-operative association for storing unmarketed foodstuffs. During the afternoon a regiment of French soldiers of a class just

teller of folklore tales. He was originally from New Zealand. He got disabled at Gallipoli and now was doing his bit by entertaining groups of former comrades behind the lines. He told me of having motored out from London one night to a sumptuous country house which had been handed over by its owners to the government and made into a convalescent home for invalided officers. He gathered, in some rather cloaked and roundabout way, that the patients here differed from the run of such. In fact, he had been warned to prepare himself for a shock when he faced his audience. So he was fortified for a distressing encounter with drastic surgical cases, perhaps, or possibly blinded men or men with their faces blown away,

---

called up had marched in to be billeted in the same town. Mostly they were fresh-faced boys of seventeen or eighteen. Very few of them, I'd say, were as old as twenty. Presently they began to drift into our meeting. They grinned in a puzzled fashion when the American lads laughed and if there was applause they showed their good manners by joining feebly in it. None of them, I think, knew any English. And my knowledge of French was powerfully bad and powerfully scanty. But I craved to tell a yarn especially for their benefit. I explained my dilemma to their chaplain who spoke some English and asked him to ask his lads to supply any missing word when I paused for lack of it.

I had dredged up from my memory a mildly naughty little anecdote which I figured had a Gallic flavor. Indeed I'm not sure it wasn't French to begin with; it sounded like it. Helping out my halting, fumbling delivery with pantomime, I got under way. Instantly the French lads caught the spirit of the effort; they made a jolly big game of it. When I hesitated over a word they roared it out in chorus.

The story was the one about the man suffering from a bad attack of laryngitis in a strange place late at night and he went along the street looking for a physician's house where he might get relief for his sore throat. He saw a sign over a doorway and he went and knocked at the door. The physician's wife, in her nightdress answered. "Is the doctor here?" he asked in a strained whisper. "No," she said in the same undertone, "come on in."

When I got to the point of it, those French boys almost lifted the roof off that storehouse. But the chaplain set me aright. It was, he laboriously explained, not the tale at which they laughed. It was my pronunciation.

of whom there were many. But his tongue froze stiff and the breath choked in his closing throat when he stepped through the curtains of the theater which had been improvised in a fine big dining hall and saw before him rows of men, mostly youngish or very young men, it seemed to him, and in all but the front row every man among them had lost either a leg and an arm or both legs or both arms. But in the front row were men in basket-chairs and these men had been hewn down into truncated remnants of men, having now neither legs nor arms. They called themselves "The Oysters" and for a still grimmer jest pretended a ribald contempt for those with less extensive amputations than theirs.

The teller of the tale went on:

"For a moment, standing there looking into the faces of those fellows, and some of them of public-school age, mind you, I felt that I could never begin my feeble little program, let alone go along with it. And then I said to myself, 'You cheap crocked-up quitter! If these living fractions of men, these maimed fragments, can sit here and smile up at you and clap their hands—those that have hands, and stamp their feet—those that have any feet left to stamp with, you can pull yourself together and carry on. And by the living God, you will!'

"But the last straw, the final touch of sheer heartbreak that sent me out of there blubbering like an overgrown baby was when a kid subaltern was wheeled up alongside and in the cheeriest fashion you could imagine said with his clipped university accent: 'You may have noticed, sir, that a chap who has only a left hand, like me, for example, sat tonight next to a chap who has only his right hand. We always do that, you see, sir, so we can applaud in pairs.'"

My New Zealand friend got out his handkerchief and made a fussy ceremonial of blowing his nose. "It appeared," he stated, with just a suspicion of hoarseness in his voice, "that this was a standing joke among those chaps."

So these, as you might say are examples—not quite so efficiently conceived and by no means up to date, but nevertheless samples of the goods now being offered for inspection over Europe's torn and tortured map wherever the wholesalers of pure hellishness show their latest wares to the customers. This morning's papers abounded in tidings direct from the main abattoirs—various slaughters accomplished, bigger and better slaughters arranged for.

It would seem that this current one is not such a prettified war either.

I must lack for esthetic appreciation, must be shy on the artistic fundamentals. Even though I beheld it at close hand never was I able to look upon war as pageantry or majesty or spiritual transformation. Only, at the back of my brain always has been the conception of a bloated abortion with dollar marks on its flanks to denote its sponsors and a dripping steel snout and knuckles of brass; a ravaging monster which never is emptied yet never is filled up; and it dragging its gross belly across the face of the land, rending and spoiling what all it does not devour.

Since 1914 the romanticists have been deploring the passing of cavalry attacks and bayonet charges. With the elimination of the hand-to-hand struggle and the knightly open combat, they lament that the ancient beauty of it, its poetry and its chivalry, soon must altogether vanish out of battle. Since I have, alas, no such rose-colored glasses to look through I sometimes wonder whether after all there ever was so very much romance in mass massacre, or mass starvation for women and babies, or mass decomposition of the corpses of the young men?

Yet—and this is set down on the small chance that anyone should be interested in hearing how I feel about this matter—it is no bleating nonresistor who said what just has been said. Admittedly, we have the Scriptural promises that the meek shall inherit the earth and the peacemaker is blessed, for he shall see God. Mankind being what undeniably it is, I fear that in the hour of the invasion and the hateful time of the conquest, the meek are likely to inherit the earth in the proportion of six feet six, by three feet three per meek one—unless burial should take place in the common ditch. And since the cannon has no eyes to distinguish between armed belligerents and gentle pacifists the peacemaker may go to behold his Maker prematurely and in a manner entirely uncalled for. So for this one, please, no membership in the Lowly Lodge of the Turned Cheek; no plea for admission to the Soft Answers Society.

For we know that the dream of universal disarmament is a fog screen behind which mad leadership keeps right on planning reprisals for old grudges or grabs at the coveted resources of weaker neighbors. We know how despotism abominates democracies, and how Totalitarianism and Communism would tear down all that constitutional forms of government can build up. And the demons of greed and envy possess some rulers as they possess some individuals; and divers Great Powers go armed for vengeance and hungry for territorial increase, while lesser states are defenseless to keep their geographical boundaries intact or their citizens safe from destruction. Knowing these things, would any sane creature preferably put himself in the fix of a wealthy city which gets rid of its police force and sends to the near-by criminal classes missionaries bearing tracts and sweet preachments? There likewise are such things as the instinct for protecting our national integrity and preserving our national self-respect and our national honor, although the jingoes and the trouble-smiths are rather prone to overwork these phases.

But until driven to take the final plunge over the precipice, we still can hope that, even at that eleventh hour, plain sense may find a way to reconcile embroiled races so that, only as a desperate and mutually ruinous last step, will peoples resort to the Supreme Arbitrament of the Sword, as they've been calling it through these bloodied centuries. With what lovely language do its apologists dress up so fetid and filthy a device!

For one, I pray that never again may we see this country descend slothfully and blandly into the deluded state of a fat, rich, flabby oyster without a shell in a sea full of famishing sharks and sharp-clawed crabs. But until we are over-driven into the abyss we may at least strive to regard the articles and the acts of war for what truly they are and not view the thing according to the falsified image pictured by the soap-box Ciceros and the peddlers of tainted propaganda and the lie-spreaders and the malice-mongers and those who are by far the most insidious of all such merchandisers of potential human misery: the internationally minded financiers who'll always be right there to pat your grandson or mine on the shoulder and bid him strike a blow for his flag—and their dividends.

How generous these persons are—with other people's boys.

24

KIND OF A SMOOTH-FACED MAN

HAVING the sentiments I had, I felt that our champion's line, "Too proud to fight," should be nailed in letters of flame across the national firmament and kept burning there. At St. Louis on the night of the renomination I sought out Secretary of the Navy Josephus Daniels. I told Mr. Daniels I was not especially concerned over purely domestic policies and didn't know enough about them to discuss them but possibly I might transmit to some of our people a faint visualization of what war really was like when it struck in the door-yards of unoffensive nations and at their towns and upon their countrysides, and I said I would like to make a few speeches, if so be the national committee could use me. The national committee said yes, it could—said it with alacrity as soon as it found out I meant to pay my own expenses. I spent three weeks in New England and upstate New York, speaking at least once every night and some nights oftener than once.

After his re-election the president wrote a whimsical little note in which he said that to the best of his recollection and belief I was almost the only volunteer worker for the ticket who neither had filed a telegram nor sent a special delivery letter offering congratulations and delicately intimating that the writer's efforts on the stump or at headquarters materially had contributed to the successful outcome. He said he appreciated the evidences of my friendly interest and hoped opportunity might enable him to repay the favor. There were just two paragraphs. He signed himself:

"Gratefully yours,

THE SMOOTH-FACED MAN"

This was a little joke between us. On the heels of the opposing nomination of Mr. Justice Hughes, the only full-bearded member of

the Supreme Court—who had however many fine offsetting qualities—a dinner was given at the New York Press Club for President
Wilson. Since the Press Club was assumed to be strictly a non-
political club, all the lesser speakers, myself included, were warned
to avoid any mention of party issues. When my turn came I told
the company I had no intention whatsoever of making partisan
references or calling names in a gathering of men of all shades of
opinion, but in passing merely wished to state that my candidate
happened to be kind of a smooth-faced man.

Somewhere along here I collaborated in doing President Wilson
a good turn. At any rate my confrere and I thought it was a good
turn. He never knew about it, as the reader will understand if he
reads a bit further. My publisher, George H. Doran, was also our
closest neighbor. The bungalows stood back to back in Park Hill,
a subdivision of Yonkers.

Yonkers always was much easier to take if you cut it up into
broken doses.

Together, morning and night, we commuted to the city on an
ignored, I might almost say an abandoned spur of the New York
Central system. This appropriately was known as the Putnam
Branch. You will recall that General Putnam attained fame in
connection with a riding adventure on an abrupt and bumpy pathway slanting at steep, difficult grades, excepting in his case, crude
stone steps took the place of the crossties which slowly were dis-
integrating on his vehicular namesake. Little Orphant Annie also
would have been a suitable name. I would not be quoted as saying
the Putnam was the first feeder of a trunk line built in the lower
Hudson Valley because there I might be wrong but I believe I am
reasonably safe in assuming that it was the first one to be entirely
forgotten by its parent. Sharing the daily hazard of round trips over
this neglected foundling made a further bond between the heads of
the two households. Moving from Yonkers to near Ossining we
again had adjoining places.

After prolonged negotiations and at a considerable initial outlay
Doran purchased from the divorced wife of Professor Peck, who
was a member of the university faculty when Wilson went as
president to Princeton, the publication rights on a series of letters
written by Wilson over a period of years and mainly during the

lifetime of the first Mrs. Wilson. The remaining half of the correspondence—Mrs. Peck's replies to these letters—were of course
not included in the sale, being presumably in Wilson's custody if
indeed they existed. Now in both his races for the presidency
attempts to create the impression in the popular mind that there
had been a secret love affair involving Wilson and this lady, while
she still was living in wedlock with her former husband, had been
set afoot by libel-mongers and very properly squelched. The heads
of the Republican campaign committee, remembering the boom-
erang effects of a somewhat similar attempt to besmirch Grover
Cleveland more than thirty years before, refused to circulate the
scandalous tale, either anonymously or under sanction; in fact,
refused to touch it in any form, which was not only good taste but
mighty good judgment. Because in the letters which the former
Mrs. Peck had now disposed of to Doran there was not a single
syllable even remotely suggestive of any impropriety, committed
or contemplated. On the contrary every one of them was eloquently
expressive of a congenial and comforting companionship between a
brilliant man and a sympathetic and discerning woman. If you could
believe these letters, and reading them any unprejudiced person had
to believe, here was evidence of an understanding and an uplifting
friendship, that and that only. But some of them were packed with
political dynamite. Occasionally Wilson had bared his real opinion
of certain of the men who through party expediency were members
of his official family. The Cabinet itself was not spared. On at least
one page Secretary of State Bryan was described in terms which by
no elastic stretch of charity could be called complimentary.

One evening Doran brought over to our house the manuscript
of the proposed book which, according to the format agreed upon,
was to be composed almost altogether of the letters, with a brief
forword and explanatory or chronological paragraphs sandwiched
in.

"Cobb," he said, "as you know, I've acquired this material at
a good stiff price and now I'm in a quandary. In it I can see nothing
but proof of an intellectual communion—a spiritual and not a
fleshly thing and,I think, a very beautiful thing expressed in beautiful
prose. But you know the ugly talk that was bruited about only a
little while ago. False inferences can be put on almost anything,

however clean. You're a congenital Democrat. I'm an incurable Republican. I'm a Canadian-born and while I've been a naturalized citizen during most of my active life a good many of my contacts, both social and commercial, have been with England. Perhaps without realizing it I've acquired some ultra-conservative British viewpoints. You're all unadulterated American for a good many generations back—and you're a devoted advocate of President Wilson. You'd approach the situation from another angle than mine. As a favor—a confidential favor—read this copy and give me your advice as to handling the problem that's arisen in my mind: the problem of when and how I should handle the actual publication. I won't tell you beforehand what my own conclusions may be. I don't want to influence your judgment."

I sat up for long hours that night reading those letters of which there were a great many. I agreed with Doran as to the highly honorable interpretation which was to be put upon them. And there could be no question as to the facile and graceful choice of language. Next morning I gave him my views and there was gratification on both sides when it developed that we were as one.

The decision was this:

Wilson was President of the United States. That meant something. He was facing the almost certain contingency of war. It would be unfair to the office he held and to the man himself were he subjected to any unnecessary discomfort while concerned with the mountainous task before him. Under conditions insuring absolute secrecy the manuscript was to be put in type and the type cast into duplicate plates and the plates stored in separate safety deposit vaults until such time as President Wilson quit the White House. Then immediately the book would be released.

But when Wilson quit the White House it was as a broken-hearted, broken-bodied, dying man. At heavy financial risk—and as it turned out, heavy cost to himself, Doran very generously elected to postpone printing until after the ex-President had passed on. Then, when a decent interval of time had elapsed he would go to press with his first edition. But almost immediately following Mr. Wilson's death, the attorneys for the second Mrs. Wilson, having learned from some source of what was planned, served legal notice forbidding the George H. Doran Company to publish the text of her late husband's letters. This embargo was laid under the law which gives to a recipient the physical possession of a private communication but debars him or any assign of his from publicizing the contents, without he first obtain the consent of its author or, in case the author be dead, the consent of decedent's next of kin. In other words the sheets of paper upon which the lines originally were written may belong to the present holder but the power to broadcast the lines themselves is the exclusive right of the original composer or his heirs. Strictly speaking, here you have property which is not property. So Doran was boxed in to the tune of a good many thousands of dollars put out by him in advance royalties and preliminary mechanical expense.

25

FRIENDS OF WOODROW WILSON

It was during the stormy period which followed so closely his second inaugural that I tried to cash in on President Wilson's self-acknowledged debt for elocutionary services rendered. For a little while I was a trifle vexed at being turned down but, thinking it over, I decided I had no right to quarrel with his attitude. This was when at last we had broken off relations with the Central Powers and the beginnings of the A.E.F. were trickling across the Atlantic Ocean.

I was under no illusion as to the joyous fascinations of going to war or of being in a war or having anything of a risky nature to do with a war. It might be glamor to some but to me it was heavy labor without the advantage of union hours and pay for overtime. But so far as the available files showed, members of our line had fought in all preceding wars of any consequence, including the Colonial wars, in which Americans were engaged. With one or two exceptions they did not make conspicuous warriors, but on the other hand there had been among us no recorded shirkers or deserters. So when hostilities against Spain began in '98, I, as the first-born son of my generation, was desirous that the family scutcheon continue to be unspotted of the slacker taint, and this despite my private convictions touching on the dubious pleasures of toting a gun and carrying a load which no humane man would strap on a mule colt. Accordingly I tried to enlist in the Second Georgia Infantry which was being recruited to strength at Savannah whither I had repaired to do some intense courting of the future Mrs. Cobb.*

---

* We celebrated our fortieth wedding anniversary just the other day, but I hold she deserves no special credit for such hardi-

The examining surgeons turned me down, partly on account of an abnormally oversized lung which they said was a standing invitation to any home-seeking pneumonia germs, but mainly because of a set of flattened insteps, also considered by them to be serious obstacles to a military career. I tried to argue that, as I understood the rules, I would not be called upon to stamp any Spaniards to death. I still maintain there was merit in my conten-

---

hood. Any woman who lives more than eighteen months with any man has gone numb and her reflexes won't respond. At the party, as a gesture to remembrance, we hauled out of storage some of the marriage presents, mostly cut glass and very massive. For our love story ripened at the very apogee of the cut-glass era when on high occasions the legs of the dining-room table might give 'way unless reinforced to carry all that extra weight. Also there were five fish slices which had been more than sufficient. During the first years of our housekeeping whenever we had a fish course it would be sardines.

After a while, though, we got socially ambitious and branched out. I often review a memorable fete night when a pair of roast Long Island ducks was the main dish. The controversy took on an embittered aspect when I got tired of prying off mere slivers and inflicting only the slightest of flesh wounds upon the glazed bosoms of the unconquered upstarts. They were by now flinching a little under punishment but not actually in retreat. Inwardly I said, "A truce to all this shilly-shallying. Who's the boss around here?" And with that I went to a clinch and started infighting. The opening round wound up with one partially intimidated duck hiding where it had slid under the corner whatnot but the other defiantly was nestling in the lap of our most cherished guest. I'm not exaggerating beyond the moderate limits to which a reformed fiction writer may go. I beg the reader to believe that while the basic facts may be dressed up a trifle fancifully they remain facts and can be substantiated by surviving ring-side spectators.

I'd say a fair decision would have been to declare the bout a draw. My late antagonists were still intact, somewhat frayed about the torso to be sure, but not badly scarred elsewhere, while I was very disheveled and painfully chafed under the collarband. I also was on the verge of exhaustion and was breathing heavily and my white vest needed changing. But you can't do much changing when you have just the one white vest until Saturday comes and with it the laundry. Fortunately the wallpaper was of a neutral tone, har-

tion. It has been my observation that more male adults have been
slowed up by fallen women than by fallen arches.

Owing to the stubborn attitude of those doctors the army
somehow got along without me. It already had the picturesque and
dashing Rough Riders and, as it turned out, the not quite so dashing
but highly competent Tenth Cavalry (Colored) to do the mopping
up behind the Rough Riders at San Juan Hill. And it had Richard
Harding Davis and James Creelman to advise the generals how to
run their war. So I went on with my courting, unexposed to the
typhoid epidemics that swept our horribly unsanitary camps at
Tampa and Chickamauga, and later at Montauk Point, and was
remote from the perils of "embalmed beef," that being the pet name
for a ghastly broth which some of the public-spirited packing
houses sold by carload lots to the commissary department—hunks
of gristle and stringy meatless fibers and putrid scraps, with preserva-
tive douches to glue the noisome mess together. Of course there
was an investigation or, as the headliners like to put it, "a stern
probe" which is the polite term for hunting the lost key of the
stable door after the horse is out. There was a great hullabaloo in
the newspapers but nobody went to jail, the sickened ones having
been for the most part enlisted men and very few of them of any
financial or social standing. Secretary of War Alger was eased
back in the lumber business—he knew about lumbering—and the
stockyard companies kept right on paying their gratified shareholders the customary rates of interest. If all the investigating committees chosen in this country to inquire into public rascalities and
private grafts and preventable disasters were laid end to end it
would be a shame not to leave them that way.

Taking stock of my most conspicuous physical defects in the
early summer of '17, I found that the intervening nineteen years
hadn't done me any real good. To be sure, I had not yet reached the

---

monizing with the gravy; a sort of giblet-colored tone, as you might
say.

For quite a spell thereafter when we had company we had liver.
That's when I acquired my present skill. With none of this skid-
ding business and practically no backing and filling to worry about,
I can carve liver against anybody.

age where a man begins swapping his emotions for symptoms. But thirty superfluous pounds of settled weight had pressed down on my ankle joints so that now, when going barefoot, I left prints in the beach sand like a pair of fried pies, out for a stroll together. Also in '14 I had acquired a small umbilical hernia while fetching maimed men out of hospital trains at the northern French city of Maubeuge after the litter bearers on duty there dropped from utter exhaustion.*

---

* The Germans had turned the captured railway buildings here into dressing stations, figuring on caring for a maximum of eighteen hundred cases a week. During twenty-four hours while we stood by, a total of more than three thousand men, coming up from the battle lines along the Aisne, were unloaded at that malodorous place for treatment. In the halted freight cars and cattle cars were dead men, dying men, men rolling in the festering stained straw from the pangs of untended and mortifying hurts. The trains came around a curve a hundred yards to the south and it was a fact that we could smell an approaching train before we saw it. The floor of the waiting room was knee-deep in a smeary snowstorm of discarded bandages. Buckets of carbolic acid solution sat about and iodine was available by the gallon. The only two nurses still able to stand on their feet tottered back and forth, sometimes holding to solid objects for support. One was a widowed baroness from Cologne, a handsome gray-haired lady of sorrows. She had lost a son at Liége in the first days of fighting. The other was a Magdelene, even to the red hair and the lovely compassionate face. She was a fashionable prostitute from Berlin whose lover, we were told, was a major of Uhlans at the front. The pair of them, carrying on in a common sisterhood of mercy, seemed more like the figment of a tale than a partnership drawn together by the tentacles of war out of real life.

Because intervals befell when there was no one else to do it, the orderlies being either played out or engaged on similar duties, my companion and I bodily lifted men out from where they wallowed in their own filth and half-dragged, half-led them indoors and there we stripped off clotted first-aid dressings and mended infected wounds and even performed minor operations under the eyes of the surgeon in charge, a frail middle-aged Saxon who had given out along with nearly all the members of his staff. He was stretched now on a refreshment counter where a coffee urn and beer pipes still remained. He was too weak to get up but able to direct our

Yet the quickening touches of the patriotic impulse—or maybe it was just the Cobbesque vanity—reawakened my long-slumbering ambition to get into the service. I figured that through Executive influence I might detour entirely around prying medical boards and, practically under false pretenses, win me a pair of shoulder straps. I aimed as high as a berth in the Military Intelligence Section, feeling that I could hook my riding spurs in the top drawers and do the bronco-busting act on a skittish rolltop desk as well as the next one. Or perhaps I might insert myself into some other niche suitable for a fat man to fill, and from there call upon the shades of my ancestors to bear witness On High that a Cobb was wearing khaki even though wearing it did make this gallant tribesman of theirs look a good deal like a covered wagon in search of its missing ox team. To complete the illusion all I'd need would be a hound dog walking under me and a spring mattress tied on behind.

Over long distance, I was promised an audience by Joe Tumulty, the President's secretary and such an ultra-diplomatic, ultra-competent secretary as rarely was before or since, I calculate. The guileless smile of an Ah Sin was there; and behind the smile, the wiliness of a Cardinal Richelieu. When I reported at the designated hour, which was late in the afternoon, Mr. Wilson was engaged. Washington was humming like a stirred beehive and, for some reason, dense crowds stood on the sidewalks flanking the Mansion grounds, peering in through the guarded gates.

"The Governor," said Tumulty, "is going to see you as soon as he gets rid of a lot of boll weevils, mostly long-winded babies from up on Capitol Hill. Their idea of a conference is a week-end party. So sit down and rest your face and hands . . . . No, be gee, I've got an idea! An excursion outfit of nice people from out in the Wheat Belt—Nebraska, Kansas, somewhere out there—have been hang-

---

awkward ministrations. I aided at setting a cracked shinbone in straw wrappers which we stripped from mineral water bottles, with flat strips of boxwood for the reinforcing splints; and from the shattered hand of a young Hessian private two of us sheared away three fingers so far gone from gangrene they looked like rotted bananas; and the soldier stood there while we were doing it and made little whimpering sounds, little mewing sounds, like a complaining sick kitten.

ing around for hours hoping to get a glimpse at the Governor. They want to go back and tell the folks they saw him, anyhow. Until this minute it looked as though they were going home disappointed. But now—well, you come along with me."

Immediately I found myself in the President's own office, seated at his big flat desk with my back toward the door. That conniving Tumulty made sure the top of my head showed above the curved high back of the arm chair in which he had placed me.

"Now start fiddling with papers or something," he bade me. "Pretend you're signing state documents—that would be a nice touch. But whatever you do, for the love of Pete, don't turn that face of yours sideways. That'll kill the show and what's worse, maybe get me killed, to boot." He went out, leaving the door ajar.

In a minute or so I heard the shuffle of slow-moving feet in the corridor behind me, heard a murmuring of subdued but excited voices, heard the ushers urging the thrilled procession to keep going and I know those worthy burghers from out where the profiled grain elevators cut the sky line were watching their President at work, patiently fighting their war for them, long after quitting hours for ordinary folk and, for all they knew, would still be there on past the sunset and far into the stilly night.

The traffic abated and President Wilson came in, stepping snappily. He bade me sit down alongside him and told a hovering attendant we were not to be disturbed and wanted to know what was on my mind. He looked fit and fine-drawn, trained down like a racing whippet. His eyes were not dulled even after a long and arduous day, but were swift and keen behind his glasses. His scholarly lean face showed no heavy lines of fatigue and hardly any suggestion of strain. Here you would say was a man unafraid, a man whose mind was fortified to grapple with any emergency and whose shoulders were squared for any burden no matter how grievous.

Somewhat shamefacedly, I told him what was on my mind. All at once my small desires, born as they were of a mistaken pride, seemed petty and trivial, as though a tumblebug had asked Barnum and Bailey's parade to slow up while it crossed the road.

"See here," he said when I somehow had got it out, "as commander in chief of the armed forces of the United States I could issue you one of those phony commissions. (*Phony* was the word and I laughed to myself that the great pedagogue, the elegant purist, employed a word so un-Wilsonian.) Until you got too ashamed of yourself to stay there any longer, you'd be moping about, doing futile clerical jobs and perhaps running errands for some brass-hatted bureaucrat. I've discovered that there are a large number of persons in departmental jobs around here who think you can win a war, no matter what else is lacking, if only you have plenty of red tape handy and an abundance of paper work for the boys to do. You tell me the *Saturday Evening Post* is going to send you back to the front, in case I didn't give you an appointment. Well, you forget this foolishness and go on back. You can be of some account to your country over there, writing about our effort, our spirit, our boys—most of all about our boys; writing stuff for the mothers and daddies and sisters and wives and daughters to read. That's where I'm telling you to go. No, that's where I am ordering you, as a loyal citizen, to go.... I've got fifteen minutes to spare. Tell me how you approximate things as you go about over the Union? What people think about? What they talk about? And next time you want something at my hands let it be something worth your having and worth my giving." For a second he brushed around my shoulder with his bent arm. I don't believe many men were hugged that summer, even fleetingly, by Woodrow Wilson. I came away with an enhanced chest expansion and went to the Hotel Shoreham to find my canny old shooting mate, Charles R. Flint, the veritable reincarnation of a State of Maine privateer, and tell him that I would be off to Europe pretty soon. Somewhere later on there must be more about Charles R. Flint. American business hasn't produced many personalities more picturesque than his.

So that night at the famous old Dower House just outside the District of Columbia there was a sort of going-away party. Miss Eleanor Wilson, the President's youngest daughter, was there and Miss Helen Bone, the White House's social director, and Mr. Justice McReynolds of the Supreme Court and George Creel, who as wartime press censor was beginning to crackle briskily in the sizzling fires of editorial disfavor. But sacrificing himself as a burnt offering for forlorn hopes and unpopular reforms was and still is a pastime with the crusading Creel. Saint Lawrence the Martyr, usually depicted by the Old Masters as looking smilingly up to Heaven while being broiled on a gridiron, undoubtedly is George's patron and pattern. They shared the same hobby.

The Maryland cookery was as good as Maryland cookery can be. No better beaten biscuits and spoonbread had ever been fabricated than the biscuits and the spoonbread we ate; no sweeter fried crabs had ever been fried.

The affair was notable in one almost unprecedented regard. When, amid deafening applause, a second helping all around of the sweet potato pie was voted, Mr. Justice McReynolds did not file a dissenting opinion. (All joking aside, some among us are glad that since the Supreme Court was reconstructed to conform somewhat nearer to the Executive heart's desire, Mr. Justice McReynolds chose to ignore the age for retirement and kept right on disagreeing with the majority approval of practically all the New Deal's legislative protégés. This naturally has thrown him on the opposite side from the recentest appointees, and notably from Mr. Justice Black.

A year later and I couldn't have got into the White House with burglar's tools. For I had committed the unpardonable offense of daring to disagree with its chief occupant. There was this about Wilson and it was ingrained in his inflexible and schoolmasterish ego: if you refused to accept his judgments as true judgments then that would be proof of one of two things: Either you were a besotted idiot or you were a deliberate traitor and in either event you were ripe to be cast into the outer darkness. For he had become as the viceroy of the Almighty; the fetish of infallibility enveloped him like a mantle.

In my luckless case the sinning was cumulative under various heads: To begin with, I thought he made an atrocious mistake when he sent to the Paris Peace Conference a commission made up of men of the same political faith. I thought it should have been a coalition commission with such men on it as Chief Justice White of the Supreme Court, a Catholic, a Confederate veteran and a conservative Southerner; ex-President Taft, representing in the Republican party that which White represented in the Democratic party; Secretary of State Lansing, to be spokesman for the administration (Colonel House would have been a perfect choice here except that he had no official connection with the government); John Bassett Moore, the great international lawyer, instead of Elihu Root, whom many favored; and finally, Henry Cabot Lodge, chairman of the Senate committee on foreign affairs. Three Democrats and two Republicans—so the completed group would have stood. And if the mission succeeded the Democratic party could take the main credit and if it failed the Republicans would have to share the responsibility for the failure. And that, to some of the President's friends, seemed sound political strategy. Best of all, Lodge, the bitterest enemy of Wilson's post-war policies in either branch of Congress, would have been damned if he declined the appointment and tied hand and foot if he accepted.

In the second place, I entertained, along with a great many others, the profound belief that President Wilson should never have been chairman of that commission. For, like the country boy headed for the city slickers' poker game, he was going across to be cast into the arena, and the odds four to one, against conniving diplomats of European powers—and one Oriental power—who knew the intricacies of foreign politics as no American ever might hope to know them; to see his beloved Fourteen Points whittled down to shoe pegs; to become signatory to a treaty which neither was just to the losers nor agreeable to the hungry, vengeful winners and which, like an evil sow, farrowed a litter of lesser wars and finally this Great War of 1939-1941. Whereas, had he bided at home, these others must have come to him. Far remote from the jockeying and the turmoil, he would have had time for deliberate and reasoned decisions instead of being called upon to say yea and nay while the dust of combat filled his nostrils and blinded his eyes.

But the head and front of my offending was that I couldn't accept his adored League of Nations, the rock on which ultimately he broke his spirit and his heart and because of which, as I veritably believe, he died before his appointed time. In my small way I did my best to combat the League of Nations plan not only in magazine and newspaper articles which I wrote, but through the winter of 1919-1920, as I went about the country making talks for federated lyceum bureaus. From the moment I took this position, inconsequential though my opposition might be, he turned from me the light of his countenance. I was either a small-time Benedict Arnold or I was a congenital idiot and it didn't make very much difference which. The next time I saw him—it was an accidental meeting—he frigidly ignored my outstretched hand and gave me a nod so congealing that I found my shrunken shape encased in shore ice. It took hours for me to thaw out to a degree where I was ready to take my place in the Wilsonian doghouse, which already sheltered the abashed forms of several really important inmates and, before the final chapter was written, would be enlarged to take in several more.

Not counting various minor occupants, like myself, the thing grew into an impressive bench show or should we say, kennel club? We might start with "Billy" McCombs of Arkansas, who literally wore himself out in Wilson's service and almost by main force kept Wilson in the race for the 1912 nomination after Champ Clark had built up an apparently irresistible strength—McCombs who was flung aside like a soiled dish clout when he dared expect a Cabinet portfolio for his earned reward. There was Colonel George B. Harvey, editor of J. P. Morgan's *Harper's Weekly* who discovered Wilson in the academic tanglewoods of Princeton and guided the novice's footsteps to the governorship of New Jersey and thence along the thorny pathway to the presidency. Colonel Henri Watterson went simultaneously into the discard. He had the effrontery to resent Wilson's cold-blooded repudiation of Harvey when Harvey's affiliations became an embarrassment.* There were the city bosses

---

* I was privileged to hear more of that breach; privileged to hear a lot about a lot of things. Not very long before Colonel Watterson died, George H. Doran who was publishing the Colonel's memoirs, gave a luncheon for him at the old Union League Club on Fifth Avenue. Besides the guest of honor and the host there were only three of us present. The food included favorite dishes of the venerable gourmand, and to drink he had what he loved best of all for, contrary to popular belief, he preferred brews to distillations. It was Prohibition time but Doran had managed to smuggle in a case of real Canadian ale. Marse Henri's one good eye shone like a star under his cocked bushy brow at the sight of the foaming bottles. He did the talking. And for a full three hours how he did talk! And nobody dared interrupt except to refill his glass for him. Listening to him was like turning back the pages of our history through three-quarters of a century and finding previously un-

who served as means unto Wilson's ends: Roger Sullivan and John Hopkins of Chicago, Charles Murphy of New York and United States Senator "Jim" Smith of Newark. The first three might have been mercenaries conscripted under the draft laws of expediency to tardy and reluctant support of the nominee. But from the outset Smith was an ardent proselyte, with the zeal which always marks your true convert, and to Wilson's forlorn hope in those earlier days he sacrificed his prestige and his private purse and through his persistency in the cause finally saw his machine disintegrate. For when Smith got his Irish dander up he was a last-ditch fighter. Because of the faith which all four of these men followed, it was alleged that some sour theological bilge was belched up from the bottom of Wilson's soul to give him an acute distaste for them and their works even though by their works he had profited himself. But they had had that same faith when they were bullying their reluctant cohorts to rally round the flag before the first election and he accepted their help then. And their faith was the faith of the human being who was closest to him, Joe Tumulty, and the faith

---

detected passages, yes, whole pages of unsuspected disclosures. As a child he had been taken to Washington and lived there while his father, Ewing Watterson, was serving as a Congressman from a Tennessee district. He, who seemingly never forgot anything, now was moved to remember Franklin Pierce and Roger B. Taney and Calhoun and Jim Lane of Kansas—and told things about them; their vanities and their follies—bits of character, bits of scandal, illuminating bits of personality that none of us ever before had heard. He revealed private chapters in the efforts of Secession leaders to seduce President James Buchanan—efforts of which he had first-hand knowledge. He told of the private sinfulness of Thad Stevens of Pennsylvania and the lapses of Stephen A. Douglas. He told of his experiences while he was editing a traveling newspaper for the Confederacy in the West. Then, as more good malt poured into him and more remembrances poured out, he would jump to happenings of last week or last year or twenty or thirty years ago and then jump again back to the beginnings of things. He knew the extent of Grant's drinking habits and Sherman's relentlessness as a military campaigner. He lamented the vacillation of Braxton Bragg which had delivered over Kentucky to the Union Armies and he said, approvingly quoting George Wendling a famous orator of his time, that the Almighty decreed the South should not prevail

likewise of the two laymen that he chose to go to Europe early in 1918 to be his civilian eyes on military operations—Martin Egan, the old Associated Press war correspondent, and James Kerney, the Trenton newspaper publisher.

So I don't believe any part of that tale. I think a blurted statement attributed to Wilson and dealing with the quality of his rigid Protestantism either was wilfully perverted or accidentally garbled in the retelling. It was inconceivable to think of him as a religious bigot although surely he was an intellectual bigot, having, I'd say, the disdain of a book-taught man who'd got his education off library shelves for men who got theirs on street corners and in the back rooms of family liquor stores. He would have been at home at a salon. But he'd never on this earth have been the soul of gaiety at a Tammany chowder party. (Theodore Roosevelt would have been equally at home at either or both functions, and prepared on a moment's notice to convert the Tammany festival into a salon—a one-man salon; or vice versa, in which latter event not only would the

---

and so reached forth His hand and plucked from their saddles the two men who would have made it victorious—Albert Sidney Johnston and Stonewall Jackson. (As regards Jackson I was told practically the same thing in 1914 by Lord Roberts.)

The Colonel chuckled appreciatively as he repeated what a rival editor said when he chose as a topic for a lecture "Money and Morals." The rival said Watterson was as well qualified to discuss morals as he was to discuss money, seeing that he never had had either. He gave us inside facts on the theft of the presidency from Samuel J. Tilden. He told—and I'm sure he never before had told it in its entirety—of the unbitted outbursts which passed between him and Grover Cleveland when Cleveland upbraided him for having taken the young bride of the White House, Frances Folsom Cleveland, behind the scenes of a Washington theater to meet a popular actress of the middle eighties. And of what he called the "God-damnable and contemptible perfidy" of Woodrow Wilson's dismissal of Colonel Harvey, he spoke in words that seemed to catch on fire as he spewed them out. By virtue of a magic resident in his recital, we were made to see the best that was in some of our biggest figures and the worst that was in them, too.

A stenographer hidden behind the window curtain of that private dining room could have recorded ten thousand dollars' worth of precious copy before the afternoon was over.

outing have been a tumultuous success but he'd have been the biggest clam in the chowder.)

In succession the ranks of the untouchables were increased by such one-time court favorites as Bryan—but then Wilson never did like Bryan and no more did Bryan like Wilson; and Lansing, a rubber stamp of a man, it is true, but one obedient and dependable; and Colonel House of Texas, whose wise counsel, unselfishly given, had been from the very beginning a weapon for Wilson's offensives and a bulwark for his protection—House, who was at once a sword and a shield.

Last of the ousted captains and offering the most lamentable case of all, was Joe Tumulty, surely the most loyal, the most resourceful, the most worshipful Man Friday that ever abode after the rest were gone with an imperious Crusoe on the desert island of Crusoe's own devising. As Pythias to Wilson's Damon he made the original Pythias seem but an indifferent and wavering reed. When in violent displeasure Wilson branded Tumulty as unclean and drove him away, Wilson was through; there remained no more of those who once stood close to the throne to be driven away.

I figure there never died a lonesomer man than Woodrow Wilson, twice President of the United States.

Thinking back on it I'm not regretful that I refrained from sticking my nose into politics. Twice after I moved to New York I could have had congressional nominations in Tammany districts, the nomination in those snug bailiwicks being equivalent to election. Your future constituents need not even know who you were. Nor need they care and they didn't. Few of them would ask, "What's the name?" They merely marched up and voted straight Democratic and in you went along with the rest of the ticket. And much further behind than that I had my first chance.

Back home at Paducah whilst I was making up my mind whether I should try to break into the newspaper game at Chicago or farther east, the tempters came to me saying: "That vacancy in the legislature from this county—we'll put you in it. Play the game as representative for one term and we'll shove you right on up into the state senate—you'll be old enough by then to be eligible. Along about that time Ollie James will be going to the United States Senate (it turned out that way, too) and if you've kept your nose clean and strung along with the right crowd in this district, there's no reason why you shouldn't succeed Ollie as congressman. After that it's up to you."

I was being stretched between two impulses. In this bemused state I sought out my long-time friend, Hal Corbett, who'll get more mention—and surely on his merits he is deserving of more—a chapter or so farther along. I asked Corbett what he would do if he were me, which by the way is always a stupid thing to do because you, with your different background, your different experience, your different temperament can never be me any more than I can ever be you, to think as you do and govern myself as you govern yourself. Still I asked him.

"I don't know anything about journalism in a big city," said Corbett. "And I do know you're being worked to death on the job you're in. But when I was about your present age and trying, as you are now, to decide whether I'd stick to my trade or start trying for office, I went to see that old spavined-up war horse, Major Blank; went out to Ballard County, where I was born, especially to see him. He was about a third cousin of mine, you remember. He was sitting on the front porch of a tumble-down boarding house hugging a stingy little strip of shade and fighting off half a million flies with a palm-leaf fan. There may have been more than half a million flies. I only counted up that far and then quit. I put my proposition up to him and he borrowed a cigar off of me and lighted it and studied a spell and then he said, 'Hally, my son, I started running for office almost as soon as I quit running from the Yankees. You might say I came out of the Confederate Army a candidate. In the past thirty-odd years I've held about every office there was around here—from railroad commissioner to deputy county clerk. And one of the net results of this career is that in the twilight of my life I'm called on three times a day to do a loaves-and-fishes miracle, trying to make two fried rabbits, or some such niggardly trifle, feed a tableful of jack-leg counter jumpers and one-gallused tobacco buyers, while the dear, saintly white-haired wife of my bosom is back yonder in a hot kitchen, helping a lot of no-'count darkies to dish up supper, and steeling herself to listen to the whiny complaints of people who aren't fit to tie the latchets of her shoes. And we're sleeping under a leaky roof and two mortgages, and the foundations are rotting out from under this wreck of a house as we sit here—and no money to have them mended, besides which I'm practically out of sweetening drams and chewing tobacco.

"And Hal, the only other asset I have to show for my long experience in west Kentucky politics is this: I have a small circle of lukewarm friends and a large and growing coterie of sincere enemies."

So I took the Major's handed-on warning even though Hal didn't—and by failing to do so he spoiled what might have been a brilliant career at the law. I rarely have known a man who had so much confidence in deuces back to back and so little faith in his ability to earn a living without trying to be elected to something.

26

MOSTLY ABOUT ME

As ALREADY I have stated, with perhaps more unction than either the importance of the post or my brief tenure in it justified, I was at nineteen probably the youngest managing editor of a daily paper in the United States. But I was nearing sixty before I tried to be an actor. At sixteen I was a fair shorthand reporter—if the witness didn't go too fast; and like almost every scrivener I wrote my first play when I was quite young. At twenty-five I was callow enough and credulous enough to believe it was a play. Entertaining this belief made me the entire membership of a club which never grew any larger. Yet I waited until I was in my thirty-seventh year—an age when many adept practitioners of the craft have sense enough to quit—before I turned my prentice hand to out-and-out fiction writing.

For a longish spell before that I had nursed the urge to write imaginative yarns, but drafts on my time and my energies, begotten of the somewhat arduous jobs I held and the pressing necessity of earning a living for one family and, part of the time, two families, checkmated me. Always though, it seemed the half-smothered impulse was ticking away like a little watch which never required rewinding, at the back of my skull. Well, as far rearward as the short pants period, in the second of the seven ages ordained for the male sex by Shakespeare, prophecy had been made that I would one day turn to fictionizing.

I was about eight, I'd say. Anyhow I was old enough to fix the facts in my memory so that now as I write it down, I recall the affair distinctly. A forlorn little caravan of Indians, from somewhere east by south of us—Eastern Tennessee or North Carolina, for choice—were camping at Fisher's Garden up on Island Creek. They

were being taken west by agents of the Interior Department; presumably they were a lingering remnant of the Cherokee Nation
on their way to reservations beyond the Mississippi, there to join
their exiled brethren of that terrible enforced trek of earlier times.
In any event, they must have been thoroughly cowed, and thoroughly dispirited, and of course satisfactorily impregnated with the
dispensations of the white man's civilization, including drunkenness,
disease, dishonesty and a choice of eight or nine brands of religion,
each in active conflict with the remaining seven but all Heaven-
bent to confer on the diffident aborigine the revealed guarantee of
a blissful Hereafter, plus the temporary discomforts of remaining
saved through the present interim of his earthly span.*

But to me Indians were Indians. I was born two days before
Custer and his men were wiped out, and in shuddering fascination
heard gory details of that disaster almost as soon as I was able to
have some infantile notion of what it was about. (It was, of course,
much later, that I came to understand that if Indians in fair fight
killed off a command of white soldiers, as at the Little Big Horn, that
was a massacre, but if white soldiers slaughtered a band of partially
unarmed and mainly defenseless Indians, including women and children, as at Wounded Knee, that was a battle and congressional

---

  * I might be wrong there. Possibly some of those forlornly
herded migrants had been so perverse as to reject any and all of the
variegated theologies of their white brethren and so should have
been classified as heretics, apostates, backsliders, idolaters or, to use
the most favored word in the indictment, heathens. Now *heathen* is
the ugly label which we Christians plaster on parties, generally of
darker complexions than ours, who prefer their own faith, which
probably is infinitely better adapted to their spiritual needs, rather
than to embrace a choice from among the variegated assortment of
creeds which we so generously offer them. By reason of this application I regard it as the cruelest word in the language—barring one.
That one is the word "wild" as used to describe the lower animals.
For there would be no wild things, whether the fowls of the air or
the beasts of the earth, had man not made them so. Cease for but a
few years, even a few months, to pursue them, to harass them, to
destroy them; provide them instead with sanctuaries and refuges,
and the wildness altogether will be gone from them. By demonstration it has been shown that only a few quickly succeeding genera-

medals of honor were bestowed; also that a barbaric raid if carried out by Indians was equivalent to a punitive expedition on the part of our heroic troopers. In these matters a considerable advantage accrues to the side which writes the history books.)

The newspapers in which Donie, my nurse, taught me to spell out words, dealt with campaigns against the Cheyennes, the Sioux and the Apaches. Sitting Bull and Crazy Horse and Geronimo were fearsome names made familiar through the talk of my seniors. By day I played at Indian fighting and by night the war whoops and the war drums spoke to me through my dreams. If the supply of game held out I fully intended to grow up to be a scalp-lifting, rootin', tootin' Indian fighter, a sort of dashing consolidation of Buffalo Bill and Daniel Boone—"Sure Shot Irvy, the Boy Scourge of the Comanches." But there was no rush about it. For the present I could take my Indians or I could let them be, preferably not in the order named.

And now, at this formative juncture in an impressionable young life, my beloved but misguided Uncle Jo Shrewsbury, who just couldn't leave well enough alone, has to send word that the following afternoon he will call by to take me to visit these bivouacked redskins up at Fisher's Garden. I recall how troubled was my sleep

---

tions are required to cure the creatures of the fear and the hate implanted in them through all the countless centuries since the cave man learned the taste of meat and his dame first craved a set of silver fox furs to wear to church. Some of that brute kingdom may remain shy and aloof, which is their way; some may prefer to avoid our company, for which one hardly could blame them, seeing how we have behaved toward them in the past; but there will no longer be man-terror amongst the birds that fly nor among the flesh-eating creatures nor yet among the deer and the timorous hares and the antelopes.

Look who's saying this, will you? None other than a persistent and confirmed killer of what we call game, makes this confession on behalf of himself and his murderous kind. I have my moments of remorse. Yet by a strange coincidence, these qualms of repentance beset me only during the closed season. But, shuckins, why should one practice what he preaches so long as he can enjoy the virtuous satisfaction of having preached—and find other people who are so weak-willed as to do the practicing?

that night, how increasingly besetting my secret misgivings during the next forenoon and how inwardly I quaked while my mother scrubbed me, getting the top soil out of my ears and off the back of my neck in preparation for the excursion. But for the moment, boylike, I was more fearful of being exposed in my fright than of the cause of the fright.

I must have greeted Uncle Jo in an abstracted, not to say distracted manner. Dragging my leaden feet like a deep-sea diver, I had progressed with him from the front porch to the front sidewalk when pretense fled and the elemental instinct for self-preservation unashamedly asserted itself.

I wrested my clammy hand from his and twined myself into a firm coil about a hitching post at the curbing.

"Uncle Jo," I gasped, improvising desperately, "I—I don't think I'd better. Once I got in a fight with some Indians, some place away off from here. I didn't go to do it—I just wanted to scare 'em. But I killed a couple of 'em. This—this—might be the same gang. So I don't believe I'd better."

"Madam," said Uncle Jo, when he had regained the powers of coherent speech, but still holding for support to a fence paling and addressing my mother who stood in a window, choking back her laughter in sympathy for her unhappy child, "Madam, in his maturity this boy may not be distinguished for truth and veracity. But mark my word for it, he'll succeed as a romancer."

The average story writer is addicted to morbid descriptions of his or her literary birthpangs, much as though a steam hatchery might feel that it had a remarkable personal ordeal to relate. It always has seemed to me that the achieved output is the thing which the author should hope may prove interesting rather than a recapitulation of his genitive throes before and during delivery. These are called the pains of creation and we love to proclaim that of all the creative arts ours is the most laborious, the most heartbreaking and the most exacting. But I claim that when writers speak of creative art really they mean the intertwined lesser arts of assimilation and choosing and reassembling. Powerfully few of us ever have been creators. Because creative geniuses aren't spawned in clumps, like shad roe. They come along at wide intervals like the seventeen-year locusts but unlike the locusts they come one at a time. The rest of us merely have the facility for absorbing a master's product and digesting it into our systems and regurgitating it, somewhat altered by our own personalities and adorned with our own small inventions. And if perchance one has innate good taste, meaning by that a sense of proportion, a natural restraint, a faculty for discrimination, and, most needful of all, a feel for the proper weight and color and shape of words—for words have dimensions and densities just as clouds and flowers have them—then we say that person has style in his writing, which is true. Nor do I believe there are such abnormal creatures as born writers, any more than that there are born wire walkers and born concrete mixers. Some are born with the impulse to write. Some learn readily to write; some try and try and never become writers; some become writers only by strenuous and prolonged effort. But every writer must learn his trade just as every paper hanger must.

Now if you are saying that writing is the most laborious and wearing of the so-called (and miscalled) creative arts, there I'll agree with you and, what's more, I'll prove it: When not giving concerts, a musician finds joy in playing for his own delectation. An actor not professionally engaged delights to take part in benefits. In his off hours a portrait painter does water-color sketches, largely to amuse himself. And I assume that an architect on vacation enjoys making drawings to show how he could have improved on the design for the Taj Mahal. But show me a writer who, when not writing for pay, deliberately writes for fun or for self-expression, and I'll show you one of the rarest cases of freakish misapplication in the entire dime museum of the human race.

Touching on plots, I always have worked by a sort of haphazard systemless system. I'd get the scenario of a theme out of a newspaper or from something I saw or something somebody told me or, infrequently, something I thought up out of my own head; and I'd stow it away in my mind and at intervals fetch it out, as a pet crow might fetch a bit of shiny bright salvage from a hiding place, and turn it over and take something away from it, maybe, or add something to it, and then put it back where it came from and keep it until it either got ripe or got mildewed. Or, the other way around, I'd either conceive a character or, commoner still, I'd borrow one out of real life and put him or her through the same developing processes until a story, starting first as a nebulous thing and gradually solidifying, had formed around this character. I have carried a yarn in my head for years before I got to the point actually of writing it, or it might be that I carried it there no longer than a few hours. I have turned out a short story of sixteen thousand words—a novelette really—in eight days and then again I have toiled and moiled and sweated over a five-thousand-word story for a solid suffering month. In rare instances I have been satisfied with my first draft of a complicated yarn but have rewritten a comparatively simple-seeming tale half a dozen times. They say Thackeray labored three weeks over a single paragraph and then threw it away. Throwing it away was where he showed a judgment which we lesser contenders lack.

I might take advantage of this opportunity to state that, regardless of the length of the incubating season, I have never just dashed off something. Once somebody wrote me asking me whether I didn't just dash off some of the things I wrote. Possibly he got a dash confused with a blank; they look rather alike in print. I told him I'd like for him to come around some morning when I was in the mood for dashing off something and watch me as I sat there dashing it off at about the same rate of speed attained by the Muir Glacier, which moves upwards of eighteen inches a year, some years.

Even so, and to a degree, the job is facilitated by reason of the fact that I do not bother at trying to keep up with the unaccountable vagaries of spelling books. I spell by ear altogether, spelling a word the way it sounds, which frequently is much simpler than the way these academic sharps put it together. They sprinkle in stray consonants and absolutely unneeded vowels and I leave them out. Long before the modernistic and the futuristic crept into the plastic arts and the graphic arts, I freely was employing the same forward-looking system in my spelling. I am not claiming any special attention for being a pioneer in the field, but merely ask that credit be given where credit is due. Moreover, I have noted that the individual who offhandedly and smirkingly—drat 'em, they always smirk!—correctly can spell the most difficult word isn't fit for many other purposes, if any. It is his one gift to mankind; let the poor wretch make the most of it.*

For my working schedule I have had only three sets of rules: (I) I have never waited for inspiration. (II) I go to my desk at a certain hour. (III) I stay there a given number of hours. If for long enough I look a sheet of paper in its reproachful but otherwise empty face I know that sooner or later I'll cover it with words, not necessarily the choicest or the handsomest words in the lexicon but, nevertheless, words.

My competent former secretary, Mrs. Olive Sullivan, who through fifteen patient years reduced my phonetic eccentricities to hackneyed and humdrum forms more in accordance with the ritual of the literalists, wrote once on the margin of a sheet of manuscript, "Dear Mr. Cobb, I think you have beaten your own best previous efforts. In a word of four syllables you have misspelt five times." As I recall, the word was *rhododendron* or it may have been the first name of the Hungarian poet who won the Nobel prize that year. His name was just a series of fascinating typographical errors. But Mrs. Sullivan didn't dare express her opinion of the merits of anything I wrote. Not that I didn't respect her opinions and not that I shouldn't have taken them. The trouble was that I'd take anybody's opinion. No need that the carping critic be a professional carper. If the janitor ventured an adverse view on a newly born brain child of mine I would agree with him absolutely and probably tell him to throw the monstrosity in the ash can. If, however, he liked it, and was kind enough to say so, I immediately would be convinced that here was a classic for future ages. I reckon a hen is never the best judge of her own egg.

One thing more, please, and then I shall be done with this thesis

---

* His is a soul akin to the chaps who can fabricate the perfect salad dressing—you know, whether the ingredients should actually be anointed with the garlic or the garlic chewed by the operator who then breathes on the mixture, and which brand of vinegar should be used: Flotsam, Jetsam or Tarascan; and a dissertation on the criminal depravity error of ever washing the wooden bowl; and so forth and so on—get him off of salad dressings and what have you? Nine times out of ten you have on your hands for the balance of the evening a human vacuum with traces of olive oil on its vest.

which every fiction writer delights to expound—on the methods which he or she uses to produce his or her priceless contributions to English letters. For years I pecked out my own enrichments to our store of deathless prose on a typewriter, two-finger style, like a little girl taking her first piano lessons. Finally I decided that with increasing facility I traveled too fast; my wordage outran my thinkage. I tried dictating and the ease of it made me even more careless in my grammar than I had been before that. A wag low down enough to indulge in puns could have said: "Be sure thy syntax will find thee out." So at length I went back to longhand. The contents of this book will all have been done with ink and a stub pen. Kindly excuse blots.

The sources from which plots are extracted is another matter. It interests me to think back on my small adventurings there; possibly it might interest some others. Anyhow, if so be the reader has borne with me thus far it might be said that by now we jointly are committed to going along together and seeing the undertaking through.

The first short story I ever wrote was written on a bet, a bet with my wife. Whilst I still was on the *Evening World* I covered the trial in Federal Court of Charles W. Morse, former head of the iniquitous Ice Trust and a notorious Wall Street marauder whose manipulations got him snarled up with the law pertaining to national banks after the baby panic of 1907-1908. (Unless panics last ten years or longer, we don't count them any more.) He was found guilty, as he should have been, and condemned to twelve years at Atlanta. We reporters were sure he wouldn't stay there long. And he didn't. He was too smart to stay there. President Taft let him out in the mistaken belief—all shenanigan, by the way—that Morse was dying of some organic disease and the conniving little sharper lived long enough to get himself indicted again following our entry into the World War. Morse's bearing at the earlier trial—his wise handling of his own defense, for he practically took the case out of the hands of his lawyer, former Congressman Littlefield from Morse's own State of Maine; his masterly fencing from the witness stand under cross-examination by the government's prosecutor, Henry L. Stimson, afterward in two Cabinets; his disdain for the public disfavor in which he was held; and, most of all, his defiance before the judge who, in passing sentence, denounced him for his proven peculations—these things set me to wondering just what could defeat a trapped felon of such chilled-steel nerve and so much mental agility. After months I answered my own question to my own satisfaction. Assume this hypothetical premise: On the way to prison a collision occurs between the train carrying him south and another train; the deputy marshal accompanying him is killed in the wreck; but the convicted man, uninjured, is flung by the force of the impact out of the shattered coach and, obeying a mechanical impulse, slips away unnoticed into the adjacent woods where he spends the night. Next morning, figuring that ultimate escape for him is impossible, he starts back for the railroad to give himself up. As he reaches the tracks a handcar passes and from it one of the crew tosses an extra of a city paper. Glancing at its rumpled front page, he reads that a badly mutilated body has been identified as his body. He turns then and flees back into the thickets, filled up and exultant with hope of deliverance from punishment. He has money in the bank; four millions saved from the crash following his arrest. He has no legal heirs but he has smart lawyers still under retainer. He will get in touch with those lawyers; will change his name, change his appearance; will bide in hiding somewhere until his beard has grown out. The authorities can have no further interest in a malefactor supposedly dead and buried. He will steal off to some remote land, some South Sea island where requisitions do not run; he will buy himself a yacht and cruise in tropic waters; will have women again, and extravagances and luxury; will repurchase life, liberty and the pursuit of happiness. The rest of the story concerns itself with his misadventures, his discomfitures, his physical sufferings, his efforts to further his plans, each one defeated by hampering circumstance, and finally the surrender to a country constable of the exhausted, starving, beaten fugitive—a man with four million dollars who has been licked by a pair of four-dollar handcuffs. I called it "The Escape of Mr. Trimm" and Lorimer bought it and so I broke into the magazine game.

But before I wrote it I told Mrs. Cobb what I intended doing: "I've got a vacation coming—two weeks with pay. We'll go where it's quiet—and cheap. The first week I'll play about with you and the young one. The second week I'll write a short story that's been bouncing around in my mind for months now. Maybe it will help to get us somewhere before I blow up, working until my tongue hangs out, for Chapin."

"It will be a humorous story, of course," she said.

"It will not. Unless I'm wrong about it, it will be a fairly grim story."

"But all the signed things you've ever written for the paper—what little reputation you have—that's all based on humor. You'll never sell it, I'm afraid."

"I'll make a bet with you," I said. "I'll bet you a cold million, first, that there won't be an intentionally funny line in it and, second, that I'll sell it somewhere. Because it just can't help being salable—with the plot I've got lined out. No matter how amateurish I may be at putting it together, the story is there. It can't miss."

I won the wager and while the principal stands unpaid to this good day, I collect daily interest in harmonious companionship from the loser.

Once I dreamed a story. This never had happened. It never has happened since. I wish it would. I wish I could remember what I ate the night previous. Usually when I dream I say to myself, in my sleep: "As soon as I wake up I must put this down—it's wonderful stuff." At least that is the impression which afterward is left in my mind. But when I do wake up every figment has vanished out of my consciousness, or else that which remains is a meaningless hodgepodge of fantastic and disassociated nonsense. But this time was different. I dreamed a story which was complete even to the names of three of the four main characters; a story which had a brisk beginning and progressed straight through to a climactic finish. Now that was as it should be, since a short story is like a railway train. It must start from somewhere, taking along with it various passengers. While things are happening aboard it passes through certain settings and eventually reaches the appointed destination. Thus it was in the case of this dream of mine. So vivid was the conception that it brought me sitting up in bed, wide-eyed. There was no need for me to get up and make notes. I knew the whole sequence would be clear enough at my proper rising time—and so it was. Before I got to the breakfast table I had added a third twisti-fication to the already double-pronged plot and had provided a name for my fourth character. On my regular morning walk down Park Avenue a matching title, one which had an O. Henryesque quirk to it—"Three Wise Men of the East Side"—popped into my brain.

Many times I have had this varied experience: I would dress up my imagined actors, assign them their parts and set to work to put them through their paces only to find that one of them, usually the main member of the cast, refused to do my bidding. He—or she—stubbornly insisted on behaving in a manner entirely differing from the planned order, insisted on uttering speeches unlike the speeches already tentatively drafted and proceeded to take the trend of the thing over a route mapped out, not by me but by this rebel, leaving me nothing to do except to follow along and putty up the cracks.

But this fully developed product of my subconscious self did not in any regard depart from its visioned outlines. I've never thought I was occult. Occasionally I've been bilious but not to my knowledge psychic. But here in this instance it was as though I were a medium through which the story flowed and my task was merely the task of putting to paper the scenes, the lines, the denouement which an unidentified force dictated. I'm not undertaking to explain but only to state on my word of honor that the phenomenon came to pass after the fashion in which I have described it.

A young man named Grannis wrote me from Chicago where he was employed by a gas company. He detailed a tremendously dramatic thing, an actual occurrence, he claimed. It had occurred in Montreal where he was then living and in it he had played what might be called a secondary role. He thought it might be worked up into a short story. If I agreed with him he would like to sell me the idea for the price of an overcoat? How about it, then?

By return mail I wrote him that I did agree with him, unanimously. I would convert his experience into a short story and if I sold it—as I was confident of doing—he'd get his new overcoat and, along with it, as good a suit as could be bought in all Chicago.

Now nearly always an occurrence out of real life requires a lot of busheling before it is tailor-made into acceptable fiction. Fiction must be plausible; facts do not have to be plausible and frequently aren't. An actual happening may be the beginning of a short story, frequently it is the middle part of it, rarely is it the proper conclusion. But as it stood, this young Mr. Grannis' tale practically was complete. I put a cowcatcher in front, hitched on a caboose at the rear end to carry the moral along in, and within a week the job was being typed.

Feeling highly pleased with myself I went that night to a dress rehearsal of a play which Roi Cooper Megrue and I together had written. In a lull while Megrue, who was a practical working drama- tist, which I most distinctly was not, worked with the electrician over some tricky light effects, I sat out in the body of the darkened theater with Theodore Dreiser, the novelist, whose brother was in the company; and with Bob Davis and Charley Van Loan. Being full of the subject, I was moved to tell these three about the tale I had that day completed. Though I thought I made the recital brisk, I was annoyed to see, in the half-light, Davis and Van Loan exchanging winks and grins. I lost my temper.

"Say listen, you two," I demanded, "why all the merriment? This isn't supposed to be a funny tale."

"So far as you're concerned we know darned well it's not funny," chortled Van Loan who dearly loved a joke but like the average practical joker couldn't stand being joked himself. (There was a ton of sweetness in Van's huge frame, but in his perverse mo- ments, as when, say, a hoax had exploded in his face, he would put you in mind of Kipling's little brown brother who was half-devil and half-child.) "No, sir, for you, it's powerfully sad." And his derisive whoop made the people upon the stage stop whatever they were doing and turn to stare our way.

"Hold on," said Davis with a deceivingly soothful air. "What did you say you call it?"

" 'Heart of Lead,' " I said.

"Well," put in Van Loan, "that's a better title than it had when *Everybody's Magazine* printed it here about three years back, eh, Bob? They called it 'The Lead Dollar.' But otherwise substantially, the same identical little old yarn."

"And very much as it was years before that when some English magazine ran it," amended Davis. "That version of it, as I recall, was named 'Bad Money.' But no matter what alias it goes under, it's getting to be an old friend of mine."

They weren't trifling with me. What they said was true as my sorrowful trip next morning to the Public Library proved. So I tore up the script that I'd been so proud of, and I fired a blistering telegram at Grannis. Hardly could I conceive, I told him, of a man who for the sake of getting an overcoat deliberately would scheme to make a man who had done him no harm commit the deadly literary sin of plagiarism. Back came a wire begging me to suspend judgment and saying a letter of explanation would follow. The letter did follow. Grannis confessed that the basic event was not of his own personal experience; he had added that part merely to give the narrative an air of firsthand authenticity. But, he protested, he had it straight from a Montreal friend of his, a Major Smith, serving then with a Canadian contingent, and Smith, he swore, was the man who had figured in the event. Smith at present was home on leave. So would I please wait until I heard from Smith? In due time I had an entirely satisfactory and convincing statement from Major Smith. In only one regard was Grannis at error, he said. Smith was not directly concerned in the basic episode, but a reputable acquaintance of his was, and Smith had had the story from this third person and had repeated it in Grannis' presence, believing it to be true. He still believed it to be true.

There was a sequel to the mix-up, in fact a couple of sequels. Some years later I was on a lecture tour which took me through the South. At Birmingham, Octavus Roy Cohen took me to luncheon at his country club. With us was the city editor of a Southern paper who was visiting the Cohens. The pair of them, one supplementing the other, told me about a young woman of their acquaintance, the plucky daughter of a desperately poor family who had an underpaid newspaper job. Between stints she had written her first short story and now was supremely happy because she had sold it to the *Popular Magazine* and received in payment the largest sum of money she had ever at one time owned in her life.

"We're proud of that game little kid," declared Cohen. "She's sort of a joint protégée of ours. And it's a smooth piece of writing she's done. With a perfectly corking plot. Listen while I give you the general idea."

I didn't have to listen long. Almost before he was through with the preface I broke in on him.

"Just one minute," I said, "and I'll tell you two fellows the plot of this tragedy. Because it's seared into my sensitive soul."

They sat there, goggle-eyed, while I checked off the high points—how in a poker game a newspaper reporter won a dollar and how, for a joke, the banker paid him off with a counterfeit coin; how with only that bogus dollar in his pocket he started home and on the way, in a lonely spot, bumped into a weeping penniless country girl who, under false promises of marriage, had been lured to the city and then deserted by a scoundrel; the reporter believed her sobbed story and handed over to her the contents of his change pocket and pointed out to her a third-rate hotel where for a dollar she could get a night's lodging and a breakfast. In the morning he would come with funds borrowed from his more affluent room-mate and lend her the money with which to pay her way back home. But when he came to the shabby hotel, he learned that she had been turned away because when called upon to pay in advance, she tendered an obviously worthless coin. And so on and so forth, up to the climax when he is sent out to cover an inquest over the body of a girl suicide taken from the river and the coroner opens her stiff hand and clutched in it is that spurious dollar.

We worked fast to save the little newspaper worker from the fatal consequences of what Cohen and his guest said must have been an innocent larceny. Indeed, all three of us assumed that the theme must have been repeated to her, purportedly as an authentic happening, and she in all good faith had made use of it, as I did. Over long-distance we got hold of "Pop" McLean, the kindly editor of the magazine and explained the circumstances, taking care to absolve the girl of any blame. He snatched the story out of the forms—a few hours more and it would have gone to press. And we three signed a day letter to the unlucky author, urging her immediately to return to McLean the amount of the check he had sent her, with the added intimation that if she had spent the money or any considerable part of it, ways and means would be found by the undersigned three to make up the balance.

Our reward was the customary one for the well-meaning busybody who takes it upon himself to correct mistakes for other people. The young woman, so Cohen wrote me, became highly indignant at our interference. The plot was her very own, she insisted. She didn't know whether it was malice or envy which had inspired established writers to try to spoil her career at its outset but she despised our motive and she repudiated our evidence.

Four years ago, the same yarn, complete in all its essentials, appeared in a reputable American periodical. This time the author was a French-born writer. He had and has a deservedly high standing and in my mind there isn't the least doubt that he likewise was imposed upon as to the sources of the material. I'm watching now for its next reappearance, because unless steps are taken to check this durable staple from further circulation, it will be making more farewell tours of hospitable America than the late Sarah Bernhardt did and almost as many as the sad little tale which sprang up twenty-four years ago and now is enjoying a popular revival. It's the heart-moving one about the German housewife who writes a letter to her kinfolks in America that everything is just dandy in the Vaterland but suggests that the stamp be soaked off the envelope for a souvenir, and when the stamp is soaked off there underneath are the words, "We are starving." I don't know how we'd get along without that standby every time war breaks out in Europe.

Bringin Birmingham into these recordings reminds me of another experience I had there. But out of that one I garnered the usufruct of salable copy. In May of 1916 the United Confederate Veterans held a reunion at Birmingham. The members were getting pretty feeble, most of them, so the innovation had been inaugurated of inviting the son of some old soldier to deliver the annual oration. That year I was the old soldier's son who had been chosen.

The town was swathed in martial bunting—that and a prematurely early heat wave. The outnumbered veterans were practically swamped under a foaming and fragrant tidal wave of preening, prancing womankind. From every nook and glade of the South they had fluttered in. Bebadged matrons of honor were apparent in multitudes amounting to a host, and sponsors, maids of honor, blossoming junior auxiliaries, majestic dignitaries of the U. D. C. enticing damsels unattached, who had just come for the junket. And hundreds were sugar-sweet in their gowns of billowy white with pipings of bright red—the Confederacy's colors; but others of the sisterhood came grandly forth displaying somewhat feminized uniforms of Confederate gray, gold-braided and brass-buttoned up to the snug military throat latches. The wearers of these patriotic liveries did not seem to be suffering from the prevalent weather. No woman who fancies herself becomingly dressed ever does seem to suffer by the rigors of climate. It is the triumph of self-content over fleshly misery.

There was a great tin-roofed convention hall and here on as hot a night as you'd care to live through was where I delivered my speech. The windows were set high in the walls and flags and banners intercepted such air as might otherwise have entered. The place was packed to the rafters with simmering humanity. You could have poached eggs in my hip pockets.

To make a speech to this audience was not too difficult a thing. You came to attention and said, "Comrades of my father," and the crowd would cheer for two minutes, more or less, and the massed bands behind you on the platform would blare forth with bars of "Maryland, My Maryland," or "Swanee River," or, as in this case, "My Old Kentucky Home." You ended a paragraph on the name of Robert E. Lee. (Great and prolonged applause, with appropriate music: "Old Virginny, Never Tire.") Another paragraph to introduce the name of Wade Hampton and up and down the aisle the South Carolina camps would be putting on an impromptu parade, with stiff jig steps interpolated. And so on and so forth. And when you reached your peroration and topped it off with a reference to "the Lost Cause which could never be lost so long as Americans reverence valor and devotion"—well, you got no further than that because a thousand cracked old voices, wispy but defiant, would give the Rebel Yell, and some folks would cry and some would stand up on their chairs and, with catches in their throats, try to cheer; and the bands would play "Dixie"—it couldn't be anything but "Dixie" now. Perhaps to an alien it might have been all pretty silly and banal and dripping with the saccharin syrups of a vain bathos, but for these tottery old gaffers and the white-haired grannies who sat with some of them, and to their children and even to their children's children, the clanging years were turned back like a page and the vanished legions marched again and Johnnie was gone for a soger!

So the speaking part was made easy. But long before it was over my high linen collar was flat as a matzoth and the starchy plastron of

my shirt front had become a sopping, sticky ruin. I could feel the
perspiration sloshing in a new pair of patent-leather pumps and
lather might have been wrung from the shoulder paddings of my
dress suit. Moving in a separate low-pressure humidity belt of my
own, I made my way off the crowded stage and went out by a side
entrance and was standing in the door ledge there waiting for a traffic
break so that a car could navigate a way through the jam and take
me up to the mountainside home of Lieutenant Governor Gray
for a cool drink and a bite to eat.

I felt a grip close upon my wet sleeve. It was not like a hand
clutching. It was like the talon of a bird, fumbly and faltering; as
though I were being clawed at by some debilitated hawk. I looked
and there alongside me was the shriveled-up framework of a man.
He was whiskered high on his cheeks; more whiskers seemed to foam
out of his neckband and from his ears. He was bareheaded, and a
sparse long fringe of white hair streaked his skull on which the scalp
was drawn so tightly it seemed about to split. A frayed, stained old
butternut jacket hung loosely on him with its absurd little peak
of a tail sticking out behind; and on the breast of his collarless
hickory shirt was pinned a badge almost big enough to make a hand
towel of. He was never a large man to start with. Now this fleshless
shell of him couldn't have weighed an ounce over ninety pounds.
And he was ninety years old if he was a day—a rack of bones with
a skin that was like a seamy dried parchment stretched tautly
over it.

"Son," he squeaked in a shred of a voice—it was a feeble voice
and yet somehow spry—"I heared you in thar jest now. You spoken
my sentiments frum who laid the rail."

"Thank you, sir," I said, "I'm glad you approved. And I'm much
obliged to you for telling me so."

"Yep," he quavered in that chirpy, birdlike way of his; "it was
purty fair in spots, the way you putt it." He peered up at me with
his rheumy dim eyes that were like dulled agates under the cadaver-
ous frontal. "Son," he asked, "whar you hail frum?"

"I came here from New York," I told him. "That's where I
live now. But I was born and raised in Kentucky."

"Tha' so?" The skeleton shape straightened just a wee bit.
"Well, I'm a' Alabama boy."

Alabama boy! Texas boy! Missouri boy! All the boys and all of them still boys! From the edge of the grave the Old South calling back to the New South! That now—that, better than a dozen history books or fifty songs or a hundred poems, told why they had fought four years against the odds they did fight against and then, amid the ruins of their social and their political and their economic structures—and oftentimes the ruins of their homes, too—had fought the twinned iniquities of Carpetbaggery and Scalawaggery through ten more years of Reconstruction.

I was sniveling—as though I weren't sufficiently damp already— as I climbed into Lieutenant Governor Gray's car. But before we passed the next corner I was contriving the ground plan of a short story synopsis with the Alabama boy patterned into the motif, as in due time he was.

27

STIR IN THREE AND SKIM OFF ONE

VERY early in my belated salad days as a short-story writer I wrote one called "Words and Music." It was buttressed on a courtroom scene which had taken place shortly before the turn of the century in a town in Tennessee just below the Kentucky line. It was to have been an isolated and individual yarn. But who was I to say? It became the first of a series of nearly seventy more or less inter-related short stories and besides there was a novelette and then a novel-length mystery yarn, all having for their axis and their pivot a character called "Judge Priest."

Now Judge Priest, who became a mainstay and a breadwinner for the Cobb family over a stretch of thirty years or longer, was a consolidated likeness, into which I diagrammed elementary parts of three separate persons. In him, as he ambled across a border south-ern terrain, was a trace of my father, but only mental attitudes here, not bodily aspects; and an occasional touch taken from my former fellow townsman and crony, Hal Corbett, who made a briefened appearance among these strolling memories chapter be-fore last. But predominantly he was a reincarnation of the late Judge William S. Bishop and physically almost altogether was Judge Bishop—the high bald forehead, the pudgy shape, the little white paintbrush of a chin whisker, the strident high-pitched voice which, issuing from that globular tenement, made a grotesque contrast, as though a South American tapir had swallowed a tomtit alive and was letting the tomtit do the talking for him. The habits and the traits embodied in this triple-sided composite portrait mainly were his too: his exterior dovelike gentleness under which deceiving surface lurked a serpent's shrewdness; his deftly concealed manipu-

333

lations of local politics; his cultivated affectation of using a country
jake vernacular when off the bench and his sudden switch to
precise and stately English when on it; his high respect for the
profession that he followed and for the office that he held so many
years; his divine absent-mindedness; his utterly unreasonable fear
of thunderstorms.

Touching on these two last-named peculiarities, tales were
told. Once when company was present in his home a sudden
forked flash in the murky heavens and a great thunderclap sent
him fleeing to an umbrella closet under the front stairs where he
fastened the door behind him and cowered among the galoshes.
His wife pursued him there and through the keyhole she said:
"Judge Bishop, I am ashamed of you—you a brave soldier of the
war, to behave like a veritable coward before our guests. Don't
you know, Judge Bishop"—the good lady was very religious—
"don't you know that if the Lord wants to smite you dead He will
find you, no matter where you hide?"

"Maybe so, Madam, maybe so," came back the muffled answer.
"But by Gatlins, I'll put Him to as much trouble as possible!"

In midsummer he went to a bar association meeting upstate.
As he was leaving, Mrs. Bishop said: "Judge, I've packed six clean
shirts for you and six clean collars so don't you go mooning around,
like you usually do, and forget to change every morning." (In
those days, before pajamas were ever dreamed of and nightshirts
were regarded as being fussy, not to say effeminate, many a cultured
Southern gentleman slept by night in the hard-bosomed back-
buttoning linen which he had worn through the day.)

When he came home she was waiting for him at the depot with
the family buggy.

"You look warm," she said.

"Warm?" he echoed. "I'm parboiled. I'm cooking in my own
gravy. I'm broken out with nettle rash like a baby. I think I'm
fixing to die."

"Why, the weather here has been very seasonable," she said.

"It wasn't too warm in Frankfort, either," he said. "That's
the funny part of it. Seemed to me I got hotter and hotter all the
time. Maybe I'm sickening for a stroke or something. Right now
I'm sweating like a free nigger at election."

"Right now? Why there's a cool breeze blowing. . . . Judge Bishop, bend over here and hold still!"

She undid a wilted collar and ran an exploratory finger down inside his neckband—down inside six neckbands, to be exact. Obeying orders, he had each morning put on a clean shirt. Only one detail had he inadvertently skipped. He forgot to take off the shirt he'd slept in.

But the bit I liked best of all the treasured folklore relating to the patriarch had to do with a time when he had quit the bench to become, as the papers liked to call it, the dean and the Nestor of the local bar. There was a country blacksmith, a gangling tall sycamore from the Massac Creek bottoms, all gnarls and knuckles and joints, and this knobby artificer got tired of bending mule-shoes and shrinking iron tires on warped wagon wheels, so he packed his belongings in an overcoat pocket and moved up to Paducah with intent, as the phrase runs, to "read law." It appeared to him that lawyers were a privileged class. So far as he was able to note they sat, in pleasant weather, in splint-bottomed chairs tilted back against the brick walls along Legal Row, and on hot afternoons cut watermelons and frequently strolled north to Billy Gray's sample room or south to Jim Sherrill's place and presently came back wiping their mustaches; and sometimes they had a marble game of "Plumpin' Boston" in the dusty street, or paired off on the sidewalk for bouts at checkers; and every four years about one in three of them ran for office.

In consideration of his doing the dusting-off and the sweeping-out at my uncle's office, he slept in the back room there, and by the same mysterious means attributed to the ravens of Scripture, he ate at irregular intervals, growing gaunter all the time; and day by day he absorbed professional lore, as it were, through his pores. After sundry months of this preliminary training, he applied for a license to practice law. There being no Board of Regents in those times, Judge Bishop's successor named a committee of the bar to examine into and pass upon the applicant's capabilities and appointed Judge Bishop as the chairman. On a sultry afternoon the committee met in the circuit court chamber where the candidate appeared before them wearing, not only his customary celluloid collar but for this momentous occasion an experimental necktie.

Also he wore a Prince Albert coat, formerly the property of my uncle; but my uncle was of medium height and was sparsely built besides, so that the sleeves rode almost up to the elbows of the present wearer and pinched him so tightly between the shoulders that he couldn't get his arms down, and so somewhat suggested a muscle-bound penguin, trying to flap and not getting anywhere at it.

"Elijah, my son," squeaked Judge Bishop paternally, "before we can qualify you to follow after this most jealous mistress of us all, the Law, it devolves upon us to test you out—*ahem*—touching on your qualifications for entering our brotherhood. Air you ready for the questions?"

"Yas, suh," assented Elijah. "I reckin I'm as nigh ready as I ever will be."

"I take it then that in pursuance of this most laudable ambition of yours, you have grounded yourself in the teachings of Blackstone?"

"Which, Jedge? I didn't ketch the name."

"Blackstone, generally acclaimed the father of the English common law."

"Don't know as I ever heared tell of him, suh. Couldn't a been he ever lived around here."

"No, I regret to say that he didn't. Perhaps then you have specialized in Coke, also regarded as quite an authority?"

"Oh, that feller? I ain't bothered none to speak of with him."

"*Hum!*" grunted the old man, fondling his tufted chinpiece. His tone grew shriller, and yet was silkily beneficent. "Elijah, son, you'll excuse me for my seeming inquisitiveness, but since we have a solemn duty to perform here I'm moved to inquire whether you went as far as to acquaint yourself with the Constitution of the United States of America and the Constitution and Bill of Rights of the sovereign Commonwealth of Kentucky?"

"To tell you the truth, Jedge, I ain't got 'round to them yet, neither."

"*Hem!* Again begging your pardon for seeming to pry into your affairs, son, and assuring you that this is not mere morbid curiosity on the part of my learned associates and myself, would you, in confidence, as it were, mind telling us just what reading, if at all, you have done and just what preparation, if any, you have made in connection with this aim of yours?"

"Well, suzz, thar's one book in Jedge Bagby's office, a kind of a big heavy saddle-colored book, that I been readin' off and on and I kin remember a right smart of whut it says. It's called 'Vol. Seventy-three, Revised Statutes of Kentucky.'"

"Elijah, my son," wheezed Judge Bishop, "I sorely fear that's not going to do you much good. The next legislature is liable to meet and repeal every dam' thing you know."

Nevertheless our Elijah did not long remain null and void; he got his license. He had always voted the Democratic ticket, it appeared, and his daddy had belonged to Forrest's Cavalry and his granddaddy was a Campbellite preacher; obviously the man had his just claims to a liberalized consideration. Thereafter he flourished mightily in small litigations, appearing almost exclusively in magistrates' courts. Ancients back home still treasure the precious memory of a summing-up delivered by him out in the Clark's River district. Here he represented the bereaved owner of a family cow which, browsing between the rails of the Paducah, Tennessee & Alabama Railway, met an untimely end when a freight train came along and distributed her for a considerable distance along the grassgrown right of way. But to hear the argument of the plaintiff's attorney one might have been led to believe that the locomotive of a soulless corporation deliberately had left the tracks and went charging over the disrupted countryside seeking that which it might destroy. He pictured his client's distress, he dwelt on the magnitude of the loss the poor man had sustained; and at length came to the terminal jewel of this gem-studded oratorical outburst, and it was as follows:

"Finally, squire, I would say this: Effen the train had been ran as she should have been run, and furthermore, effen the whistle had been blowed as it should have been blew, and effen the bell had been rang as it should have been rung—both of which they done neither—this here cow would not have been injured at the time she wuz killed."

It took Paducah, as the laughingest town in the state and the laughingest of its size upon the face of the habitable globe, to develop and nurture a Hal Corbett. Georgetown, up in the Blue

Grass, might be more aristocratic, Henderson richer, Bowling Green more cultured and Lexington a greater source of blooded horse-flesh. (It is true that within one year and in two counties then adjacent, the western portion of the state produced an Abraham Lincoln and a Jefferson Davis. But on the other hand we never have bred a Derby winner.) Owensboro outranked us in distilleries' output and Hopkinsville ran ahead of us as a dark tobacco market, but we excelled in pone-bread philosophy and pot-licker humor. Our acreage of story tellers was prolific and never failed; always a new crop coming on as the older ones petered out. I think in all fairness our town might have been called the buckle on the national story-telling belt which extended west from Tidewater Virginia and upper North Carolina athwart the Mark Twain and Gene Field and Charley Russell country, having first taken in southern Indiana with an upward loop, and then dipped down across Arkansas and through Texas and wound up in the deep Southwest.

And Corbett, with his full-moon face and chunky frame and his Kris Kringle belly; with his parrot-like gift for mimicry, his pretended bucolic simplicity and his persuasive river-bottoms drawl was for a generation the top of the heap of the fun-makers down our way. Soon after I moved east he wrote me that he was coming to New York on legal business and asked that I engage a room for him "at the tavern where I stopped the last time I was up there—the one that's got the trestle running past it so if I get lost I can light out under the tracks and come moseying back." (He meant the Imperial Hotel near the Sixth Avenue elevated road.) It so happened that two of his closest friends, Judge "Bill" Reed, who had succeeded Judge Bishop on our circuit court bench, and Attorney Campbell Flournoy, then of Washington but originally from Paducah, were in New York, so the three of us met him at the ferry—there was no Hudson tunnel yet—and escorted him across town. After warmly shaking hands with a perfectly strange room clerk and inquiring as to that astonished young man's health, Corbett registered and then he said: "Gentlemen, this reunion of kindred spirits on a foreign soil calls for a celebration. Besides, I'm fixing to buy, which serves still further to make it a historic occasion. Gentlemen, where is the grocery?"

This suited our plan for there was a conspiracy to deal our

newly arrived compatriot a severe jolt. With alacrity, we led him to the bar downstairs and lined up with him before the wide mirror.

"Judge Reed," said Corbett, making a ceremonial of it, "you are the senior here. What is your pleasure?"

In his deep basso Judge Reed said:

"A seltzer lemonade."

Corbett gave a start.

"Judge, are you ailing, by any chance?" he inquired.

"I am not," said the older man.

"But you said—I could hardly believe my ears—did I understand you to say—"

When so moved Judge Reed could rumble like an elephant's stomach. He rumbled forth some of his most reverberant notes now:

"Since when, Mr. Corbett, does one Southern gentleman have to explain to another Southern gentleman his preferences in the matter of potations? Furthermore, I am, in a way of speaking, your guest. You invited me here and I accepted the invitation. I think you heard what I said but in case deafness is afflicting you, along with other infirmities of age, I shall repeat it. I crave, with your permission, a simple seltzer lemonade."

"Certainly, certainly," hastened Corbett. "This venerable gentleman will have a seltzer lemonade," he told the barkeeper, and in a stage aside added: "He's turned experimentalist, evidently. Don't make it too strong of the lemon. At best this is bound to be a shock to his system. He's failing fast."

He addressed Flournoy hopefully.

"Well, Campbell, my dear old comrade, what about you?"

"Ginger ale," stated Flournoy, firmly.

"Ginger ale—and what else?"

"Just ginger ale—if you don't mind, Mr. Corbett." Flournoy's tone was belligerent.

Corbett put both arms about my shoulders and looked deeply into my eyes. "Pardner," he murmured, "this is an hour of sorrow for us. One of these unfortunates became violently deranged and the other caught the disease from him. Pardner, through thick and thin—only neither one of us is thin any more—we've stood together since you were a mere lad and I was in the full flush of my brave young manhood. A hundred times, under circumstances more or less similar to these, you have never yet disappointed me. Dearly beloved, what's yours going to be?"

"Buttermilk," I stated; "a small glass of buttermilk, Hal."

Corbett took off his broad-rimmed Stetson and cast it upon the floor and trod upon it vehemently.

"Mr. Wine Clerk," he announced, "I'm going to be in the fashion whilst sojourning in your thriving city, if it kills me. Gimme a bottle of bluing!"

So, in concocting the character who contributed for so long to the support of the Cobb family, I added to every gallon of Judge Bishop, a full pint of the peart and chubby Corbett and from time to time poured in about a gill of my father's personality, then stirred the mixture freely and let simmer on the back of the stove until another short story boiled up. My red-haired, pink-freckled father was a very small man but unlike most opinionated small men he managed to convey the impression of forcefulness without either strutting or working on his chest expansion. I never heard him use an oath or a dirty word or tell even a mildly suggestive anecdote. He would blush like a schoolgirl if any impropriety, however innocuous, was attempted in his presence and, dependent on where he was, if another used foul language he either would betake himself away or sternly admonish the offender. He avowedly was timorous in some regards. As a lad he had never learned to swim, nor would he ride a spirited horse, or climb on high places, or in any like fashion risk his life and limbs. It was a standing joke at Monkey Wrench Corner that when he captained one of the boats of the packet line in the absence of her regular skipper, he would, at the first sign of a threatened storm, order her to the shore until the wind lulled and the clouds lifted. Because of this over-caution on his part, and because he never blustered or swore or raised his voice beyond a certain level pitch I, as a small boy, felt a secret shame for what I deemed to be his lack of courage until I learned how, armed only with a fire ax and singlehanded, except for Big Foot Willis, the faithful black "cap'n of the watch," he had quelled a riot—at the expense of several broken Afro-American heads—on the steamer *Gus Fowler* after drunken negro excursionists had overpowered the two mates and driven the lower-deck crew to barricade themselves in the engine rooms.*

I didn't hear of this, or of similar acts of his, from my dad though. He might boast of his ancestry and of his parents' onetime affluence but never of himself. And while I sensed that he rather would have gone on being an appraiser and classifier of various grades of tobacco—a quality at which he had been an acknowledged master—he never complained because necessity made a riverman of him.

Here, crowing not for vanity of himself but for vanity of his people, was a small, proud, intolerant gamecock. The simile suits— I never see one of those perky little red bantam stags but I think

---

* This business of courage—and its brother, fear—takes different people different ways. A few years ago my daughter Elisabeth, better known as "Buff," traveled three weeks with the Barnum & Bailey Ringling circus getting material for one of her novels, called *She Was A Lady*. The following year when the circus had opened its season at Madison Square Garden she invited some of her friends among the performers and executives to be the guests of honor at a buffet supper in her apartment. Literary folk also came and either set marveled at the quaint behavior of the other set, so it was quite a pleasant party. Gene Tunney was present. Gene still held the heavyweight championship, I think, or at any rate only recently had surrendered it; and was just beginning to suffer from his first violent attacks of nervous culture. He had not reached the point where he could find suitable intellectual companionship only in Einstein, George Bernard Shaw, Mahatma Gandhi and Nicholas Murray Butler—and I wouldn't be too sure about Dr. Butler qualifying. He still spoke words not too unabridged for a layman's understanding and altogether was a model figure as a great athlete and an ambitious young American intent on keeping his body fit and his mind open. One of the show-folks spent a bedazzled half-hour harkening while Gene told of his ring victories and then this enthralled listener burst into a group in the next room crying out: "Gee, it must be great to have as much nerve as that Tunney fellow's got!" The author of this tribute was youthful Mr. Clyde Beatty, whose job, twice daily, was to go into a steel-barred cage and master a snarling, rebellious collection of forty full-grown lions and half-tamed tigers.

of my dad in the days of his prime before the curse of heavy indulgence bedraggled his plumage and bleared his straightforward gray-blue eyes. In part I'm sure it was an affliction for those eyes which drove him to liquor. In 1862, as a young lieutenant, he was in temporary command of one of a fleet of supply boats on the lower Cumberland River. Where camp had been made on the shore, he bent over to light a cigar and a pistol cartridge fell out of his belt into the fire and the explosion filled his face with red-hot embers so that he had to quit the army. Long afterward the injured tear ducts began to disintegrate so that continually his eyes wept and the lower lids became thickened and inflamed and painful. About that time a change in steamboating ownership lost him his place and the salary which was the sole source of support for his family; and that added stroke completely broke his morale. He had left only an insurance policy and it carried an anti-suicide clause. So very deliberately, as I believe, he set about drinking himself to death so that we might have something to live on until my Grandfather Saunders' estate was distributed and my mother got her share. He had health though and was strong, and to accomplish this took four hard years. They were four hard years on my mother, too. The memory of them still is like a scar burnt in my brain. I was twenty when he died. We buried him on a Christmas Eve.

He, who had been a rich man's son was for most of his life comparatively a poor man. I marvel how my mother managed so well on so skimpy an exchequer. True, servants cost almost nothing as measured by domestic wage scales of today. Food was incredibly cheap. We owned the house where we lived; my Grandfather Saunders had deeded it as a gift to my mother. But there were taxes to be paid and wardrobes to be bought and replacements of worn-out furnishings to be provided against. Most of all, appearances must be maintained; we must hold our heads up, as the saying went, since ours was a "leading family." What was worse, we had kinpeople who by the moderate estimates of that period were accounted as wealthy and this put an added strain upon my mother; her children must be as well dressed as were their affluent cousins. Life for her meant contriving and long hours of needlework; often it meant depriving herself of bits of adorning finery which she craved, for she had been a very beautiful girl and a belle of the town. She kept traces of that beauty until the day of her death, and she dearly loved pretty things.

Nor was my father behindhand in personal denials. Still he had a few, a very few extravagances, in which he indulged himself no matter to how low an ebb the household finances might have dropped. He smoked, through nearly all his waking hours, the best five-cent cigars that money could buy. He had always a starchy and spotless white linen vest for Sundays. His footgear was made to order by the most expensive bootmaker in town; his feet were the smallest I ever saw on a grown man and his hands were tiny, too, and he was vain of them. He usually could find funds with which to attend a Confederate reunion or a waterways convention. And once a year, when the circus came to town, he went on a real debauch, an orgy carried through to its triumphant conclusion without regard for cost.

He believed, with almost a passionate fervor, that every child should go to the circus. So he took his own children; and he took the children of neighbors who through religious scruples or for other reasons, couldn't go themselves. He collected from all over our part of town children whose parents had not the means with which to buy tickets, and on the way to the show grounds usually managed to pick up a few more penniless urchins. For these two latter groups he would provide at his own expense. His appearance under the big-top, shepherding along his flock of gaping, happy youngsters, was an anticipated event. Sometimes it was marked by a spatter of applause which made the show-folk wonder why there should be this small sudden outburst of hand-clapping when the performance hadn't even started yet.

We sat, all of us, on a racked-up rank of narrow blue planks. The flap-backed reserved seats were not for us. Anyhow he must husband his resources since red popcorn and parched goobers (roast peanuts to you) must be provided. Because what would the circus have been without goobers and popcorn? I figure that the total expenditure must have equaled a week's income for my father, but I'm sure he counted it as money wisely invested.

When the performance was over he would shuffle them out— his convoy of tired, gorged children—and distribute them at their several addresses. Then, he would repair to the Palmer House, two "squares" down Broadway from our house and pre-empt a private place at the far end of the bar and, drink by drink, get gently but firmly tight. He might not touch liquor after that for another year.

In the brooding peace of the twilight he'd come home, stepping carefully and humming to himself his only drinking song, which consisted of but one verse. The words to the tuneless refrain were as follows:

"I jumped aboard the telegraph;
I steered her by the triggers.
The lightning flew and 'lectrified
And killed ten thousand niggers!"

Often I get to thinking about those long-gone circus days. I get to thinking that of all the wasteful and wanton excesses to which men are addicted, my father's was about as excusable a one as ever was. I used to hear of an aged Kentuckian named Hill, a man who as a boy knew Lincoln; and this old Mr. Hill had, in his later life, a belief that Paradise was a place where a man did forevermore what he had done best and most contentedly on this earth. Now he had been a grist miller up in Hardin County. And he was sure that in the life to come he would turn out for the Lord's dinner table and for all the host of the saved, the finest hominy grits, the whitest wheaten flour, the tastiest water-ground cornmeal that the Celestial populace ever had seen. It seemed to me that this was a pretty satisfactory conception of eternity—better than some of the pictures painted by some of the preachers when they seek to describe the glories of the Kingdom. And—meaning no irreverence—if old man Hill, the grandfather of my dear friend George Goodman, had the rights of it, then I like to picture my sorrel-topped, spry-stepping little dad, rounding up the overlooked cherubim and the neglected seraphim and taking them with him to some Heavenly circus where the bareback riders are all lady angels and, in the grand entry, Gabriel as the drum major leads a saintly brass band playing an *umph-pah* tune thrice around the hippodrome track; and the gentlemanly Apostles will pass among the blest, selling tickets for the grand concert and minstrel-carnival or after-show.

I must have been, even at that distant time, quite a sincere young individualist, my age considered, for once I actually balked at going to a circus until I could wear my old hat. I barely remember the affair being, I figure, about six years old, but my mother loved to tell about it. My oldest hat must have been a very old hat indeed; its straw crown was caved in and its ribbon was gone and the torn brim lopped down in a disgraceful manner. But it seemed that I would wear no other. To this good day I like an elderly hat. So that year when we set out on the regular pilgrimage to the circus, my mother took advantage of my mounting excitement to slip upon my head a nice new shiny hat, and I went along docilely enough until just as we were entering the menagerie tent a gust of wind made me clutch for my toppiece and I became aware of the wicked deception which had been practiced upon a trusting child; and I yelled and whooped and kicked and carried on until an adult member of the caravan hurried me home—luckily our house wasn't far away—where I was given my beloved old wreck of a hat and a good spanking and we got back to the lot before I quit whimpering.

It was on a subsequent circus day—I was probably ten or twelve years old then—that a thing happened, which still abides in my memory, as about the finest example of spontaneous humor I can think of. That year, at the last moment, two old ladies unexpectedly joined Captain Josh Cobb's personally conducted caravan. One of them lived across the street from us and the other just around the corner. Mrs. Lawson, the senior of the pair, was exceedingly deaf. She used one of those old-fashioned, flexible ear trumpets with a tip at one end and a bell-like aperture at the other. Her crony, Mrs. Rohm, had a high-pitched, far-carrying voice.

On a blue-painted seat, with the old ladies at one end, my father and mother at the other, and the customary row of youngsters in between, we watched the unfolding pageant. The time came for the crowning feature of a circus of those times. Perhaps the reader is of sufficient age to remember what this was. Elephants and camels and horses would be close-ranked at the foot of a springboard. Along a steep runway, which slanted down to this springboard, would flash in order, one behind another, the full strength of the troupe. The acrobats would tumble over the backs of the animals to alight gracefully upon a thick padded mattress. The clowns would sprawl on the backs of the living obstacles. Always there was one clown who, dashing down the runway, would suddenly halt and fling his peaked cap across. There was another, dressed as a country woman, who, as he somersaulted, lost a pair of bifurcated white garments, while the audience whooped its delight.

This season, a culminating treat had been provided by the management. The lesser gymnasts had done their stunts. Now, to the head of the runway mounted the premier tumbler. He stood there, grand in his rose-colored fleshings, his arms folded across his swelling breast and his head almost touching the sagging canvas of the roof. The band, for the moment, stopped playing. The ringmaster mounted the ring-back and proclaimed that Johnnie O'Brien, foremost athlete of the world, would now perform his death-defying and unparalleled feat of turning a triple somersault over two elephants, three camels and four horses. For many this announcement had a special interest; they knew Johnnie O'Brien was a native-born son of our town, as was Cal Wagner, an equally famous kinker.

An expectant hush fell upon the assemblage. Mrs. Lawson turned to Mrs. Rohm and in the silence her voice rose as she asked:

"What did he say?"

Mrs. Rohm brought the blunderbus end of Mrs. Lawson's ear trumpet to her lips and, through its sinuous black length, in a voice so shrill that instantly every head there was turned toward the pair of them, she answered:

"He says that there pretty man up there with the pink clothes on is goin' to jump over all those critters yonder without hurtin' himself!"

On the sawdust, in his baggy white clothes, squatted one of the clowns. On the instant he leaped to his feat, ran to the head of the larger elephant, and in both hands seized that creature's long black dangling trunk which now, as everyone saw, looked so amazingly like Mrs. Lawson's ear trumpet, and raising its tip to his mouth, he shrieked out in a magnificent imitation of Mrs. Rohm's falsetto:

"He says that there pretty man up yonder with the pink clothes—"

If he finished the sentence, none there heard him. From every side there arose a tremendous gasp of joyous appreciation and, overtopping and engulfing this, a roar of laughter which billowed the tent. Strong men dropped through the seats like ripened plums from the bough and lay upon the earth choking with laughter. The performers rolled about in the ring. The band members laid aside their instruments and whooped.

And through it all Mrs. Lawson and Mrs. Rohm sat there wondering why the band did not play and why the pretty man in the pink clothes up at the top of the runway didn't go ahead and do his death-defying feat but instead seemed to be having a convulsion.

28

GOLD IS WHERE YOU FIND IT

To SUPPORT Judge Priest in his fictional aspects, I drew heavily on actual personalities in the Paducah I had known as a cub reporter. Real men and women, somewhat idealized perhaps, were made to play the auxiliary roles. For my choruses, for the bit players, I grazed through the negro community and there found fallow fields rich in types and topics. Bear with me whilst I call the roll of some who, as supplemental deputies, have filled in many a background for me:

There is Connie Lee, still the town's leading chiropodist and the only survivor of all the individuals, white or black, who marched across my manuscripts. He was the original of Judge Priest's private retainer, the one I called "Jeff Poindexter." It was Connie who, seeing his first passenger plane come zooning across the Ohio River, southward bound, remarked that, so far as his race was concerned, he didn't believe it ever would be necessary to put on a Jim Crow section.

There was "Major Jeems" Williams, as dark-complexioned as Mammoth Cave, and "Sis" Josephine, his chatty little yellow wife, who advertised themselves as the "beatenest team in Dixie at housecleanin'." Once the "Major," having been impressed to do coachman duties, was driving my aunt and my mother through Oak Grove cemetery. They came to a heretofore unexplored addition where up-ended bottles and bargain-counter crockery marked otherwise neglected graves. "Jim," inquired my aunt, "who's buried here?"

"Jest odds an' ends, Miss Laura, tha's all, odds an' ends," he explained.

There was Albert, the headwaiter at the Palmer House, who carried, except in the very dead of winter, a palm-leaf fan; carried it even in the hotel dining room, where he used it upon his underlings as a sort of symbolic baton, an emblem of authority. For some especially flagrant offense the long suffering proprietor, Captain Reed, with harsh words told him to pack his belongings and get out of his sight and off the premises and stay off forevermore. "Cap'n Charley," answered Albert in his affectedly shrill voice, "I been here longer'n you is 'cause I moved in befo' they had the roof all on an' you didn't. Ef anybody moves out it'll have to be you. 'Cause, not meanin' no disrespect, I most p'intedly ain't never gwine do so. So please, suh, kindly don't mention no mo' about it." As he switched away with a defiant flirt of his hips—Albert undeniably was on the effeminate side—his employer turned to a grinning group of lobby loafers and said resignedly: "Well, I reckon that settles that. But, gentlemen, I must say things have come to a pretty pass when a man can't fire his own darkies."

Whenever I went back home I could be sure that between my last visit and this present one, my mother would have treasured up some increases for my store of local folklore. She had the rare faculty of being able, seemingly without effort, to draw intimate disclosures from black people—and black people, as you should know if already you don't know it, can seem to be the most artlessly outspoken and yet, as regards their own private affairs, remain inwardly the most guarded and the most reticent of all peoples. A constant source of material was her laundress, Aunt Minerva Victoria Machen. Under crafty indirect prompting this formidable pillar of independent thought in church circles and lodge circles yielded her confidences to my mother, and to my mother only.

For instance, one Saturday night Aunt Minerva Victoria, having fetched the week's washing, had taken a bite of supper with the cook before setting out for her cabin on Plunkett's Hill. Her impressive bulk was spread across the kitchen doorstep and her broad flat soles were turned up sidewise, like two smoothing irons, in the posture described as "favorin' the feet," when my mother came forth on the back porch and with due caution proceeded to sound out the old woman on the subject of her current pastor, knowing that no matter who the current pastor might be or however recently installed, Aunt Minerva Victoria already would have a standing feud with him.

"Lawsy, Miss Manie," she boomed, "ain't it cu'ious you sh'd mention that, 'cause I been layin' off, very fust chance't I had, to tell you 'bout my latest do-see-do with that overbearin' lil' ole preacher-man? Last Tuesday evenin' I wuz settin' on my front porch in the cool of the day, when 'long come the Rev'n Rogers, big ez life. An' he stop an' rattle the gate latch, sort of significant-like, an' he clear his throat, same ez a ole bullfrog, an' he say to me, he say, speakin' Bibical, 'Sister Machen, could't I have speech with thee?' Miss Manie, I don't 'low nobody even ef it's a minister of the Gospel to use mo' stylish language than whut I kin. So I say right back at him, kind of Scriptural: 'Rev'n,' I say, 'draw nigh an' ye shall be heard.' So he come on in an' he ain't no mo'n start talkin' 'en I sees whut he's aimin' to talk about. It's 'bout that low-flung, tore-down limb of a daughter of his'n, Psyche May Rogers, that got herse'f in trouble with a high-yaller guitar-pickin' boy name of Fishface that come here frum Nashville on the packet *B. S. Rhea;* an' account of her bein' a preacher's daughter the scandal is all the worse. So now he gwine 'round lookin' fur sympathy in the con-'ergation. So I uplifts my hand this-a-way an' I say to him, I say, 'Rev'n, hold! Rev'n,' I say. 'Last year when my husband, Isom, at the age of seventy-fo' when he should have knowed better but bein' whut he is, didn't, wuz makin' hisse'f permiscus with not only one but two of the lady members of our flock an' I went to you an' ast you ez the pastor to 'monstrate with him, jest because he give you five dollars fur the new church organ fund you tole me shut up my blabby big mouf an' go 'long home an' mind my own business. Rev'n,' I says, 'ez you sows that mo'over likewise is whut you reaps. Rev'n,' I says, 'pass on!' "

Nor would the credit list stand as a thing rounded out and complete unless I included a small vignette of Uncle John Matthews. Uncle John was a wizened little dark-brown man with a shrewdly squinted eye in his head and tufts of snowy white wool in front of his ears and aged legs as bowed as a set of hames. Just before the war he had for a few months belonged to my Grandfather Cobb, so that made me belong to him from the time when I reached what might be called a contributing age until he passed on.

My train from the north arrived at 3:45 A.M.—when it was on time . (The man who compiled the I. C.'s passenger time tables in those days was a gifted fictionist.) Frequently I came unexpectedly.

Not even my mother and sisters might know beforehand I was coming. Possibly nobody at the station except the night porter and a sleepy hackman or two was aware of my arrival. There is such a thing though as the "Affikin telegraph." Invariably when I went downstairs for breakfast Uncle John, dressed in his Sunday best, and an old bandana tied about his scrawny neck with the ends flaunting in a sort of gala effect, presumably for my exclusive benefit, would be hovering near the back door waiting to collect his proper dues. As late as May he has "ketched Chris'mus gift" on me and accepted his belated holiday dividend. As early as October he might anticipate the customary New Year's donation on the theory that I would not be on hand then. Forehandedly he was peering into the future.

Like Albert, the lady-like headwaiter, Uncle John was a staff member of long standing at the Palmer House. His particular mission was to attend the poker game which went on, year in and year out, in Parlor 202. When the grand jury met, the commonwealth's attorney, on a fishing expedition to get indictments against our more prominent gamesters, often would summon Uncle John to give evidence. He would try cajolery, threats, heated language, but the witness' stock answer was: "Boss, I don't remember." Once a special prosecutor from another district who had been assigned to local service thought he had the old man trapped. "Not six weeks ago," he thundered, "I was in that room when a game was being organized. Before I came away I saw you there, waiting on a number of gentlemen. You recall seeing me, don't you?" "Seem lak I do, now you mention it, suh," admitted Uncle John. "Well then, you stop this monkey business and tell these grand jurors the names of those other gentlemen present." "Boss," said Uncle John, "I'se feared I can't do that." "Well, if you recall me, why can't you recall who they were?" shouted the zealous inquisitor. "Boss," expounded Uncle John, "dem gen'elmen always has a few rounds of toddies befo' they starts doin' somethin'. Some of 'em leaves some sweetenin' in the bottoms of the glasses. I drinks that. Once't in a while some gen'elman decides he's had enough an' leaves his glass mighty nigh full. Natchelly, I drinks that. An' so, suh, by the time the card playin' does git started—*ef there is any card playin'*— I'm so drunk ever'thing is a puffect blanket befo' my eyes."

After that the white folks just quit pestering Uncle John. In the

billiard room at the Palmer House some admirer hung a small square
of black-painted tin, with a neat frame enclosing it; and upon the
upper crosspiece of the frame these words were carved:

"Picture of John Matthews' Memory."

Of another outstanding account he had institutional rating.
Once a year he accompanied the members of two local camps to
their reunion, sporting Confederate colors and carrying on his shoulder a live rooster in token of having been a kingpin among the
foragers. Also once a year, wearing the blue uniform and the
bronze button in his lapel, he attended a G. A. R. encampment somewhere. In fact, he was an inmate of a Federal old soldiers' home in
Illinois during the last years of his life.

I prevailed upon him to explain this two-way distinction of his—
not that much prevailing was required. There was conscious pride
in Uncle John's bearing as he said:

"Tain't many people kin brag of bein' a veteran on both sides
lak I kin. Heah's the way hit came to pass. When the Big War
bruk out, I wuz jest 'bout grown an' workin' ez a hand in your
grandpappy's tobacco warehouse up yond' in Lyon County. So
he loaned me out to your cousin, young Mister Lieutenant Harry
Matthews, that wuz the son of my old marster, an' wuz in your
uncle's battery, so I goes 'long with him to be his body servant.
Well, young Mister Harry he gits hisse'f kilt at Shiloh, but I stays
right on with my white folks, rustlin' up vittles fur 'em an' the likes
of that. But in the campaignin' 'round Nashville seems lak I gits scattered away frum the command an' next thing I knows I'm heels over
haid amongst them Yankees. So ruther'n have any rookus, I
jines in with them an' does cookin' fur one of the gen'rals till the
war's over. An' then I drifts on back an' moves down yere
to Paducah whar your pappy's folks has done resettled they-
selves.

"Well, one day Doctor Brooks meets me on the street an' he says
to me, 'John,' he says, 'the Yankee gover'mint done made me the
pension 'zaminer fur this town. God knows why they done it, me
bein' an' unreconstructible Rebel, onlessen 'twuz 'cause they
couldn't find a Republikin with sense enough fur to handle the job.
Anyhow them folks up in Washington is passin' out pension money
right an' left to ever'body that kin even halfway qualify. Me, I

believe in supportin' home industries,' he says. 'John,' he says, 'I'm goin' to git a few of us old soldiers to club in an' betwixt us we oughter be able to furnish you with a record that'll elevate you into the money classes.'

"So him an' Major Tom Moss an' Cap'n Dick Barber an' some of my other Confed'rit friends, they fixed up the papers fur me an' lo' an' behole, fust thing you know I draws down fo'teen hund'ed dollars in one sweet lump sum an' I been gittin' my pension ever' month ever since an' I suttenly is mouty grateful to all concerned an' mo'overly always will be."

I was luckier than Arnold Bennett, the English novelist in opportunities to refurbish my mental images through revisiting the home community. On the occasion of his one trip to America I asked him how frequently, in order to freshen up his local colors, he went back to those smoky Five Towns of his, about which he wrote so graphically and with such minute detail.

"I don't dare go back," he said. "I fear I might not have an agreeable reception. You see, so many of the characters in my books are my own relatives—thoroughly unpleasant lot they are for the most part, quite—and the likenesses are so lifelike they feel a bitter resentment, I'm told. So I depend on my memory which, if I may say so, is an excellent one."

"By the way," I said, "did you ever study medicine?"

"Oh, no," he said, "I was a solicitor's clerk but I never studied medicine. Why did you ask?"

"That book of yours—*Clayhanger*," I said. "In it was such a marvelous description of the disintegration, physical and mental, of an old man suffering from some rare and incurable disease. Reading it made me feel as though I were standing right there watching a surgeon literally dissecting the poor old chap alive. So I thought—"

"Ah, yes," he said, with an understanding nod. "You see, I had rather exceptional opportunities of studying such a case. From my father, you know—he died so."

So I remembered an old aunt of his—he already had told me she figured rather disagreeably in another of his books—and I asked how she was getting along.

"Oh, fairish," he answered, "for one of her age, fairish." But I thought I detected a hopeful gleam in his eye and to myself I said that should Auntie pop off some day with heart trouble, she would be good only for a short story but if she had the good taste to get something painful and lingering—that would be more satisfactory.

Deep down inside where he communed with his innermost fractions, I'm sure Bennett remained a solicitor's clerk till the end of his days. Mentally, I think, he was forever pulling his forelock to the highborn, forever looking up to his betters. I dislike the smug and cantish phrase, "lower middle-class," that so often and so trippingly falls from the tongues of his fellow countrymen, but there doesn't seem to be any other term competent to sum up the station in life to which so many folk—they themselves coinciding—are assigned. And Bennett betrayed a consciousness, a secret acceptance of his designated humility by a very evident awkwardness in mixed company. For him to accomplish some such small matter as buying a round of drinks became rather an uneasy and botched proceeding. He was overly brusque toward those he deemed to be his inferiors, nervous in the presence of persons of large consequence. Yet here was an authentic artist with fine achievements to his credit and no reason for kowtowing to anybody. Because of the inflexible caste system of the English—a plan of selection lacking among the Irish and more or less among the Scotch—it is difficult for one of them to escape from his type grouping. Materially, he may rise up into the sunshine, but spiritually he accepts his predestined place in the cellar. On his home island he even is addicted to dressing himself according to his status, in uniforms of sorts, so that, lacking the expected demarcations in manner and speaking voice, it still would be easy to distinguish the clubman from the "City" man, the village chemist from the village publican, the valet from the butler, the workingman from the costermonger and the costermonger from the corner loafer.

It is hard for an American to understand this. For, being constantly in a condition of flux, none among us stays put. Our social geology is not a series of banded strata. It always is in a state of violent upheaval. Almost without exception we go up from the surroundings wherein we were born, or else we go down. That's why you can't segregate mass from class in this country, seeing that yesterday's class man is tomorrow's mass man and vice versa.

For all his shrewdness as a copy-gatherer Bennett had an ingenious, naïve side. He stayed here a few weeks, never got west of Indianapolis or north of Boston or south of Baltimore, I think, and then went back home and embalmed his observations in a volume which he called *Your United States*—a broadness of classification only equaled by George Ade's father, who in the early days settled in a remote Indiana hamlet, and opened up for business in a one-room building under a sign reading "The National Bank of North America."

But what Bennett did see he remembered—and utilized to the last ounce. None of us but found his likeness, not always a flattering one, in the book. He quoted our daughter Buff copiously, leading off with a thing which happened when he was having a home dinner with us. She was then at the inquisitive age—say seven or eight—and in dealing with a neighboring family's idiosyncrasies, Mrs. Cobb and I spelled the key words. Buff stood this as long as she could and then, having slipped down from her chair, she said, as she slammed out:

" 'Scuse me, Mr. Bennett. I'm going over to Marjorie Allen's. There's too dam' much education in this house!"

He called her a saucy chit. She was—and still is.

Some months after Mr. Bennett's departure from these shores, Mrs. Cobb and I were spending an evening at the apartment of Oliver Herford, that puckish droll who, along with the late Don Marquis, and Rollin Kirby, the cartoonist, and others that were blessed of the gods, used to make evenings at the Players' Club notable to the grateful listeners. Ollie's brilliant wife Peggy and his equally brilliant sister Beatrice the impersonator were playing bridge against Mrs. Cobb and "Sissy" Loftus the Irish comedienne, while Ollie and I, over in a corner, talked of cabbages and kings, not to mention sailing ships and sealing wax.

The dialogue drifted off at an aimless tangent until we found ourselves discussing the merits of various contemporaneous literary figures in Ollie's own tight little islands. He was Irish-born but of English rearing. And here he delivered himself of a sentence in which, I claim, was summed up the very essence of the average reviewer's professional viewpoint.

I had asked him what he thought of Bennett as a novelist or as an essayist or both?

Now before he delivered one of his devastatingly funny mots Herford had a disarming trick of half-closing his eyes and sinking his voice to a drowsy undertone.

"I tell you, Cobb," he droned, "something I once wrote about him—in a critical way—so prejudiced me against the man I could never bear to read any of his works."

Ollie wore the cap and bells of his jester's motley so well, yet so unassumingly; a gentle, shy, utterly improvident creature who took no heed of tomorrow, being too busy sipping the joyous juices from today's honeysuckles. The only time he was ever financially embarrassed was once when he had money.

29

SHOPPING AT LIFE'S FIVE-AND-TEN

First and last, I've done my share of cruising around among the bargain counters of professional endeavor and, I might add, enjoyed every minute of it. One way or another I had my whack at the direct main sources of a scribbler's income and at most of the by-products and the offshoots. Not alone the staple goods but the notions, findings and trimming attracted me to small departures off the regular route. I have gone in for radio and for public speaking, have dabbled at advertisement writing, have been in and out of the syndicates for thirty-odd years, have done movie scripts and here latterly, have played parts in movies. This nibbling about has kept life from becoming monotonous and, believe me, life can be pretty monotonous to the literary truck horse that grazes always in the same pasture and feeds always at the same trough and ploddingly draws always the same kind of load along the same familiar roads.

I should include playwriting in the category of my branching-out efforts. For from time to time I stuck my nose in here and each time got it pinched in the crack. I should have had better sense than ever to have gone down that detour and spang up against dead ends. For some it might be an easy avenue to affluence and fame, but to me it was a difficult and a rutty lane, a blind alley on a dark night. To recapitulate my fundamental handicaps, the behind-the-scenes end of it never had for me the lure which it has for so many people. I was bored by the companionship of actors who, being actors, wanted to talk about themselves while I greatly preferred to talk about myself. In the next place, try as hard as I might, I could not bring myself to imagine a sentence as it might sound when spoken within the framing of a proscenium arch, with all the facilities of lights and sets and make-up. I viewed it only as it would scan on a printed page, which was a fatal defect.

Among theatrical people it is an axiom that the play which reads well rarely acts well and that is quite right. Not often is the finished dramatist's dialogue overwritten. It will be terse, staccato, almost choppy. For he appreciates how a lift of an eyebrow, a shrug, a sigh, a grunt, any well-devised bit of by-play, will emphasize the meaning he wishes to convey so clearly that further language is superfluous. Whereas the novelist, or the essayist, seeking for sonorousness in his prose, for the sensuous effect of fine writing, may be as discursive as he pleases. Regardless of its length or its brevity a phrase for the stage should do one of three things: advance the motive, strengthen a characterization, or produce an emotional reaction—laughter, thrill, what not—in the minds of the audience. If it accomplishes one of these three things it is good; if, as happily occurs once in a blue moon, it accomplishes all three of these things, why that's perfection. I have a theory that a line in a play should be either the caption over a picture, the text under that picture, or, infrequently, the obituary for the picture uttered in the brief pause after it was erased. Perhaps if I had been able to follow my own deductions I might have fared better at the box office and at the hands of the blitzkriegers of the daily press, those conscientious firing squads who serve the public weal by machine-gunning bad drama to death at sunrise.

As I seem to recall having said a few pages back in this chronicle, I wrote my first play at, I hope, an excusably early age. I started it—and the Lord only knows how I found the time—when I was carrying the back-breaking burden of directing a woefully understaffed country daily in Kentucky. I finished it during a lonesome winter in a boarding house on West Fifty-seventh Street, working away there, night after night, in a form-fitting hall-bedroom, with a smelly gas stove and my homesickness for company; and lovingly I laved it in nostalgic memories of more congenial surroundings. There was a whale of a difference between Paducah and New York City. You wouldn't notice it so much at Paducah, but the fact certainly did impress itself on you in New York.

I sent my darling brain-baby out to producer after producer. Each one detected flaws in it but never the same set of flaws. Finally it became to me merely a series of overlapping, superimposed and closely interwoven flaws and I interred the outcast in the bottom tray of a tin trunk. That trunk is somewhere around the premises now, having accompanied us in our devious wanderings. Some day my executors will open it and, as they lift the lid, will wonder why I should have kept a vintage Limburger cheese mouldering there through all the years.

While vaudeville prevailed I wrote a number of one-act sketches, some of which enjoyed a moderate, a very moderate, success, but most of them were sickly from birth and soon succumbed to infantile debilitation. When Ed Wynn decided to quit being either a single performer or half of a double team, I wrote his first starring vehicle, a skit elaborated into a farcical tabloid. The playlet died abruptly but Wynn survived, which only went to prove that a true comedian, no matter how juvenilish, could triumph over any obstacles. I assisted Bayard Veiller in an adaption of some of my stories and we named the result *Back Home*, that being the title of the book in which the stories had appeared; and after a six weeks' struggle Heaven was its home. The second-act curtain had to do with a circus parade and Selwyn Brothers, who in a thoughtless moment had produced the piece, spared no expense to make the scene realistic. They even hired a live elephant. The verdict of the newspapers was that the elephant had been badly supported.

I did the book—and some of the lyrics—for an ostensible comic opera which was written around the scenery and the wardrobe that had been left over from a previous failure. Every time I had a notion for some sprightly chorus number, the backer, a stealthy, cat-like gentleman who several times had gone broke putting on shows, would check me. "Stick to the props and the costumes we've got," he said. "Don't start making me spend money on any outside dew-dabs when already we got aplenty."

The mainspring of the plot was not exactly original but it had tradition behind it. Owing to the physical limitations, including a shopworn cherry orchard—with cheesecloth cherry blossoms—and a wrinkled backdrop showing Mount Fujiyama, the prima donna just naturally had to be a Japanese maiden and the tenor a United States naval ensign—we had to pick a tenor who could wear the ensign's uniform, so his voice didn't much matter. Nor did it. And the basso was an admiral and the comic was a singing and dancing marine in love with a stowaway chambermaid. If the reader has a memory which stretches sufficiently far back into the Dark Ages of musical extravaganza in America, he may go on from there, unaided.

For an agreed advance royalty of five hundred dollars, which I never received, I wrote this offering in five days and it ran five lingering weeks at the Casino Theater and played to a total of less than five hundred paid admissions during the concluding two weeks. Attendance did pick up nearly fifty per cent though on the very last night—the ushers all brought their wives. On no provocation except that the word had a Japanesy sound, we christened the pariah *Funabashi* which gave the chortling reviewers a welcomed excuse for a wordplay—"Fun Abashed." As I recall three of these brilliant minds used it simultaneously. But Alan Dale of the *American* said the only bright thing about the show was the electric sign across the front of the theater, which clever remark made my wife cry until her pillow was soaked. Who was it said nobody ever saw and nobody ever will see a monument erected in grateful memory of a critic?

Broadway was Broadway then. Decadence hadn't begun to spread along it like some insidious creeping gangrene. Seeing it today—by daylight anyhow—it would be hard for anyone to re-create from this shabby ghost the vision of Broadway as it was in the first decade of the century. For that would be before time and the tarnishing processes of time—and still later, the golden temptations of Hollywood—had dimmed its spangles and corroded the tinsel and taken away most of its more famous habitués. And death and high taxes took the rest.

Then Broadway had the indefinable but very obvious something which certain other streets have; and which certain cities such as San Francisco and New Orleans and Charleston and Boston have; and as Vienna had before it went Nazi, and Paris, before Hitler stamped with his goose step on her lovely face. There are rivers, like the Connecticut and the Rogue and the Susquehanna, which likewise have this intangible charm, this peculiar individuality—oh, you know what I mean without me trying to describe it. Because the more I'd try the worse I'd fail. By night it was a gorgeous glittering anteroom to all manner of fascinating places and by day a

parade ground for promenading notables, a setting for the outstanding *boulevardiers* of the nation—Miss Lillian Russell and Frankie
Bailey of the faultless legs and buxom Trixie Friganza; with Diamond Jim Brady* and Oscar Hammerstein and David Belasco and

* The truth about this paragon doesn't sound like truth. It
sounds like allegory—his fabulous capacity for chambering food;
his balloon-like proportions; his tastes in haberdashery and fair
ladies; his love of precious and pretentious gems; his prodigal spend-
ings; his prowess as a salesman. He sold railroad equipment, a hundred locomotives at a clip, or a thousand freight cars; or would
somebody care to buy a nice suspension bridge?

One Sunday four of us, including three who had covered the
Portsmouth Peace Conference, were having a breakfast at the old
Café Martin on lower Madison Avenue, the others being Sam Blythe
of the *World's* Washington bureau; Charley Hand, perambulating
correspondent for Lord Northcliffe's London *Daily Mail*—about
as big as a minute, Charley was, but keen as grated horseradish; and
Carl von Guttberg, staff star of the Berlin *Anzeiger*. Both these
famous peregrines were lame, Hand from a Boer sniper's bullet
which bored his thigh in the South African campaign and von
Guttberg from an accidental lance thrust that he got during
maneuvers while he was a captain of Uhlans. When the first World
War broke he joined his old command and was disabled in the
second week of fighting on the East Prussia front. Hand died,
nearly blind, a year or two ago. I had a letter from Blythe yesterday, full of Blytheisms.

As a trencherman I fancied I had acquitted myself rather well
that fine September morning. Though in those far-away days I
was as lean as a shikepoke, I had commodious storage bins. In the
middle of the vittles, Blythe, who was himself no trifling consumer,
nudged me. "You think you're some eater, eh?" he said. "And you
think William Jennings Bryan is pretty good, too? Well, you are
and he is. And Boise Penrose is not so bad. But yonder comes the
champion of the ages. Watch him, you puny piker from the sunny
Southland—watch him and weep."

Although this was my first sight at the approaching phenomenon
there was no need to ask who it might be. His gross displacement
was awe-inspiring. He had a huge frame to start with and fat was
draped upon it in creases and in folds. He had three distinct chins
and the nethermost one ran all the way round his neck as though,
being fearful of punctures, he was carrying an extra spare on

Dave Canfield and the Gondorff boys, kings of the wire tappers; with Charlie Dillingham and George Ade and Arnold Rothstein, who was just coming along as a gambler but destined to reach an eminence where murdering him would seem advisable to some of his close friends; and Nick the Greek, crapshooter extraordinary; and Bet-you-a-Million Gates, and that rising young assemblyman, Al Smith, dreaming of bigger things.

That was the Broadway where I longed to see my name pricked out in sparkles of light upon a marquee—and the audience crowding in and the ticket speculators thick on the sidewalk. And so, despite the promptings of a still small voice which kept telling me this was not for me, I clung to my forlorn hope.

I collaborated to a limited extent on an expanded version by Charles O'Brien Kennedy of a short story of mine called "Boys Will Be Boys." It struggled along for two months to an untimely end at a small theater on West Forty-fourth Street, which has been a veritable Death Gulch for much ambitious drama. When those who witnessed its performances had decided not to carry the grudge any longer, Will Rogers played the piece for the silent films and in

---

behind. His coat was of a shrieking checked pattern, needing only the name of the stable across the rear to be a blanket for some racing filly—and about the right dimensions, too. It being the Sabbath day he was content to wear his comparatively unobtrusive star sapphire set: matched stones the size of plover eggs in his cuff links, on his watch fob, upon two of his dropsical-looking fingers, down his shirt front, in his vest buttons and, if rumor had it right, mounted also in his front and rear collar studs, his suspender buckles, his gold penknife and his sock supporters. When Diamond Jim ran amok with jewelry he ran a very fierce mok indeed.

A whole relay of waiters, sure of nutritious tips, fluttered in his wake like gulls following a Turnverein excursion barge. He was given a table near us and while we looked on spellbound and von Guttberg reverently muttered, "Gott in Himmel!" and other praying words, they brought him a quart of orange juice in a tall pitcher, a huge pot of coffee and an over-sized cream jug. Next, arriving on a silver platter suitable for a roast turkey's accommodation, there appeared a quadruple portion of corned-beef hash, mounded like an igloo and shingled over with at least eight poached eggs. Maybe there were more than eight—anyhow, practically a setting of eggs. With this order came a towering edifice of hot cakes. Like a fast

that form it went fairly well, but that didn't do Kennedy and me any good because we had sold our interests for a lump sum. Not a big lump. It didn't even suggest lumpiness.

Even then I wouldn't admit that I had sufficient punishment, and several more years passed, intermittently marked by small misadventures along the shores of those tantalizing theatrical waters into which some of my close friends dived so easily and from which they dredged up such succulent prizes. Finally though, after one more attempt, I took the cure and I've stayed cured ever since.

That very last play now—that was certainly a sick headache for all concerned. I produced the seed corn for it in the shape of a theme. Roi Cooper Megrue supplied the more technical fittings, he having written several successful pieces. At the end of the second act, sure as you are born, it looked like a million dollars; just another *Within the Law*, that's all. At the end of the third act you almost could hear the horses pawing impatiently in the alley, waiting to carry the corpse away to that cemetery of expired theatrical hopes, Cain's storehouse. In fact, after Act II Sam Goldwyn— only his name was Goldfish then—who had just sold out his original

---

workman double-tiling a bathroom, he tessellated that mighty dome of hash with two layers of hot cakes, fitting them on top of the poached eggs. He then sluiced the ensemble with large quantities of melted butter and maple syrup, and using a carving knife and fork—no ordinary table tools would have served—he chopped the whole thing into chaos. And then, by Saint Appetitious I swear it, then with a dessert spoon he ate it to the last bite and the last lick. Sam discounted the suggestion that Mr. Brady might be putting on airs for our benefit. This was just average for him, he said. I figured he must have a waiting list of at least eight tapeworms.

Diamond Jim used to go to all the important dinners, always taking covers for two and eating as two, for himself and for the imaginary guest alongside him. And banquets were banquets in old New York—eight, nine, even ten lavish courses. Then he would wallow pensively down to the grill room and for a savory, as the English say, would have a tenderloin steak measuring about fourteen inches from tip to tip, with mushrooms and the fixings; also a tall tankard of orange juice. He never drank anything stronger.

When finally his bunker spaces pulled loose, the surgeons at Johns Hopkins found he had a stomach which was as big as six normal stomachs—and still hadn't been big enough.

movie interests for a packet and come to New York looking for
investments, offered then and there to buy a piece of the production. Megrue and I liked Sam so we advised him to wait until the
show was over and then renew his offer—if he felt so inclined. At
the dress rehearsals we had seen the poor thing break apart amidships. When the final curtain fell Sam was gone. Possibly that was
the night he coined his famous and typically Goldwynesque ultimatum: "This is where I include myself out."

Here was the fatal defect: Our notion was to hang the play on
two pegs—prison abuses and prison reforms. Leading up to these
goal posts, we approached by the medium of an hour and a quarter
of corking good melodrama: dark cells, cruel guards, stupid warden, innocent inmates, pretty young woman playing Nemesis to
wicked Wall Streeters. Our lead—George Nash played him—was
a ruthless financier, addicted to despicable banking and large black
cigars, who, having been sent to Sing Sing, proceeded to put that
institution on a business basis, not because he loved his fellow convicts or pitied them, but to prove his oft-repeated boast, "Boys,
you can put handcuffs on a man's wrists and steel bars in front of
his face—but you can't lock up brains."

Well, we must have locked up ours. Because we had the halves
of two entirely dissimilar plays riveted together. We packed ramping heroics and villainy and virtue into the front half; but we spaced
out the latter half with preachy, moralistic stuff.

What a frantic to-do there was, trying to save that listed ship
from sinking in the Red Ink Sea! We could see a fat fortune running out, like a squeezed handful of ocean sand, from between our
clutching fingers. Every morning we tinkered with that infernal
last act; rewrote it entirely sometimes, partly rewrote it every time.
And every afternoon the bewildered company would rehearse the
new business and learn the new lines and every night would try the
fresh-laid version; and next day we'd start the redrafting operation
all over again. Months after the accursed piece had ceased to breathe
on a hand mirror, Megrue said to me, "Cobb, what idiots we were!
If only we'd forgotten that prison reform guff and written a fast
new first act to precede the good old Jim the Penman hokum that
we already had, you and I would now be cutting up a couple of

hundred thousand dollars in royalties and the Selwyn boys would be organizing about six road companies."

Two enthusiastic unknowns, both of them youngsters, effectively played bits in the foredoomed opus. Both are in California at this writing and doing fairly well, in case anybody should ask you. One is Thomas Mitchell who scored so heavily as Gerald O'Hara in the screen adaptation of *Gone with the Wind*. And the other is still an eager little round-faced fellow of whom you may have heard, under his stage name of Edward G. Robinson. This Robinson won a prize of ten dollars for naming the play, the name being *Under Sentence*. I think those ten dollars meant more to him then than some of the Rembrandts and Goyas he buys nowadays for his private gallery.

So you see, it took me a distressingly long time of baiting and angling and praying for bites and spitting on the worm before I admitted to myself that I didn't have the dramatic touch which, by the by, is something you cannot acquire in easy lessons by mail. Had not the stubborn persistency which is born of conceit made blinkers for my eyes, I might have seen, through two little off moments of mine, that in judgment of matters theatrical I was not what you would call absolutely infallible.

For a third of a century James O'Neill played *Monte Cristo* up and down this country. He trod the boards stampingly, a heavy tragedian of the orotund school, all bombast and gesticulation. Upon his retirement he reverted to his proper and natural self, which would be another way of saying he was a simple, gracious, unassuming old gentleman. The few elocutionary flutings that he kept out of his former repertoire were as so many agreeable oddities to adorn his conversation. At the Lambs' Club I spent a good deal of time in his company. One afternoon he said to me, rather diffidently, "I wonder if I might ask a favor of you? My son Eugene—he's away now on a sea voyage—but at Harvard he studied under Professor Baker, and he has written some playlets—dramatic sketches, I suppose you might call them. Now I have read them and I confess I'm in doubt about their playability. I've brought them along with me—" he hauled some rather meager-looking folios out of his pocket—"and I'm taking the liberty of asking you to read them and give me your opinion on their possibilities. In strict confidence, of course. He knows nothing of this."

"I'll be glad to give you my opinion for what it might be worth, Mr. O'Neill," I said, "but why not submit them to some of the regular playwrights around here—this place crawls with 'em?"

"You are my friend," he said, "and you're a writer."

I tried to explain to him that as between writing stories and writing plays a wide gulf intervened—that in a way of speaking it was like the distinction between laying bricks and laying eggs; both laying operations, but different functional activities were involved. He insisted, and sat near by, sipping his cocktail while I read what the young man had written.

Before I turned the first page of the first script I could understand why this old-time melodramatic star, trained in the noisier mode of a vanished era, might be puzzled by the revolutionary technique of his junior. I read them through—there were four scripts. And then, stirred to my very marrows by the brute strength here expressed, I reread them.

"Mr. O'Neill," I said, then, "alongside some of the candy-store tripe that's being produced these days, this stuff is like a slab of fresh beef hacked with a cleaver on a butcher's block and slapped down on top of jelly beans and gumdrops. This has got raw, crude life in it—blood and muscle and guts. Worked over into short-story form it might go—if you picked the magazines that would dare to print it. But as play material—well, I don't believe you'd ever find a manager to produce it or a critic who'd endorse it or a public that would go to see it."

"Exactly what I thought myself," he said, resignedly.

Included in the batch was a one-act play called *The Moon of the Caribbees* and one called *Bound East for Cardiff* and, unless my memory is wrong, the remaining two afterward were expanded into *The Emperor Jones* and *Anna Christie*. Much later than this I was stopping over in New Orleans on my way to the Louisiana marshes on a duck-hunting expedition and to my hotel room, with intent to interview me, came a reporter from one of the papers, a young transplanted Tennessean named Roark Bradford. The thing got switched around so that pretty soon I was interviewing him. He told me about a plan he had in mind to do a sequence of stories embodying a rice-field negro's conception of Biblical scenes and of Heaven itself. I thought I could see great possibilities there and I urged him to go ahead with the undertaking.

So he made the book, *Ole Man Adam and His Chillun,* and in advance of its publication sent me, with his compliments, a set of page proofs and I wore the sheaf ragged toting it around East-hampton down on Long Island where we had a summer place, and reading selections to whosoever would lend an ear. I believed then as I do now that here was a genuine contribution to American humor, moreover one which dripped with color and carried a superb understanding of negro psychology.

In some quarters I probably made a nuisance of myself, but not at the home upon the sand dunes of that gracious lady, Olga Wiborg Fish, whose passing left a void in this world for so many, many people in high places and in low. Over a week end she had for a house guest, Robert Sherwood, one of the deftest playwrights in this country and, beyond peradventure, the tallest playwright in any country. (I wonder if bull bats don't bother him of an evening, flickering around up there where he is? I know if I were as tall as that, I'd be afraid to look down for fear of being seized by an uncontrollable desire to leap off and end all. But luckily for theater lovers, dizzying altitude doesn't seem to affect either the quality or the quantity of output; certainly it hasn't in this case.)

At our hostess' instigation I hauled out *Ole Man Adam and His Chillun* and read aloud extracts from it, notably the delectable chapter about Cain and the Gorilla Gal and the priceless one dealing with the adulteration of Ole King David.

"Grand going!" pronounced the longitudinal Sherwood speaking down to the assembled company out of the void away up aloft yonder.

From his heights he went on enthusiastically: "Look here, Cobb, you ought to throw in with your friend Bradford before somebody else beats you to it. Together you two should be able to cook up a corking play based on this stuff. You're both Southerners; you ought to make an effective team. And, if you handled the thing the right way, I guarantee you'd mop up a potful of dough."

"Not a chance," I said sapiently, and with the utmost assurance. "These are disconnected episodes. How'd you hitch 'em together?

And made into a play, this treatment of sacred topics would give offense to a lot of overly sensitive, over-reverent people who wouldn't catch the spirit of what Bradford is driving at. Such a play would be chased off the stage in a week."

"I don't agree with you," he said. "If you don't mind, I'm going to try to interest somebody in the notion—this joyous stuff is too good to be lost to the stage."

"Help yourself," I said generously and I reached up and gave him Roark Bradford's address.

Pretty soon there was a play called *Green Pastures*, done by Marc Connelly, on the foundation of Bradford's writings. I've forgotten how long it ran on Broadway and how many road companies there were, and how many performances of it have to date been given. I imagine it is being played somewhere tonight. And if it isn't being played somewhere tonight, then it should be.

Incursions into radio have lasted longer and have paid better than various of my shoppings but there's a disappointing side to this. Some broadcasters profess to be stimulated by the telepathic communications that come from the millions out on the wave lengths who are tuned in. To me though it always has seemed that the microphone was the beginning and the end of the transmissions. That is why I like an audience in the studio when I go on the air; not so big an audience as to be difficult to control, but a wieldy, compact, tolerant audience. If I register with the group that are present I have a reasonable hope that part of what I say may be registering with those unseen hearers along the network stations.

In parentheses I might append that nearly always legitimate actors are noticeably more nervous at their radio debuts than are novices of the non-professional types. The actor has been used to protective coloration provided by grease paint, costume, footlights, scenery; and other actors to throw him his cues and in turn to respond to his delivered lines. Being deprived of these accessories, he quivers like an aspen in the barren surroundings of a sound-proofed studio. I saw the legs of that seasoned adept, DeWolf Hopper,go wobbly under him the first time he was a guest artist on a radio program and I was told of a distinguished actress who fainted dead away at the mere prospect of an ordeal which many an acolyte found to be no ordeal at all. Incidentally it has struck me that over the radio it is easier to recognize latent or undeveloped talent and harder to detect the fraudulent note in the voice of a practiced demagogue than would be the case if there were no mechanical bar between auditor and performer. Or is that just my delusion?

Radio, its devotees say, still is in its infancy. Some skeptical ones think that, barring the values for dissemination of spot news and for discussion of public issues which it acquired as it evolved, radio passed right out of its infancy into its dotage. Whether or not its second childhood overlapped its first, of this I am sure: The reason why broadcasts are so pure—and often so puerile—is because those who edit the continuities have such dirty minds. In so much that is natural and normal they discern only nastiness. Thus insipidity gains at the expense of what merely is decently realistic and intrinsically suitable for listener consumption.*

---

*I believe radio, in conjunction with cinema or television or some outgrowth of these, is yet to come into its own. Its time of greatest usefulness will follow when it is the voice which complements the visual adjuncts of the other two for popular education and religious training. I think I see the schoolroom of the future: The teacher will be a monitor and a disciplinarian and the lessons will be more than repetitious dreariness and the oral dingdonging of facts and figures into bored young brains. A historical date then will be more than merely a date. For before his eyes on the screen which will be a part of every classroom's equipment the pupil will see projected a moving picture of the event which the date commemorates; will see trained actors playing the parts, will see accurately reproduced backgrounds, will hear battle cries or triumphant choruses or funeral dirges or wedding chants. And that thing will stay in his memory long after supposedly instructive statistics or tiresome rote would have been forgotten; and lessons will be entertainment, with the informative part all sugar-coated.

For the church I see the pastor there only to carry on the ritualistic side of the service, while coming through the air to the congregation, will be an address by some great denominational figure, or some great ethical teacher, and on a film the embodiment of the speaker will be shown before the worshipers' eyes. Or perhaps there will be enacted illustrations to supplement and make more vivid the meaning of the transmitted discourse. In that way fewer good people will sleep through the sermon and forget the text before night.

Measured by the same yardsticks, it would seem that to a considerable extent, this likewise is applicable to moving-picture supervision. No reasonable onlooker can deny that except for the sterilizing intervention of such agencies as the League of Decency, the pornographic propensities of a few swinish offenders among the producers would by now have degraded the cinema to depths even lower than prevailed before outraged public opinion was organized to curb such excesses against good taste and common decency as were being committed in the name of art. There is no art in it when a dirty-minded little boy writes short and dirty words on an alley fence. There is no art in smut and filth acted out before a camera and flung upon a screen. There is no art in parading homosexual implications or triumphant adultery before a mixed audience—or any other kind of an audience. For decency's sake it was well that Mr. Sammy Sodom and Mr. Jasper Gomorrah should have been restrained.

But then again, the matter of restraint may be overdone through blinded zeal or through the bigotry of censors who, being prurient-minded themselves, see pruriency where no such element exists. Among the English-speaking groups, about once in so often, with a profound feeling of shock, we become aware all over again, that there are such matters as carnal impulses and atavistic throwbacks, whereas most other breeds long since made the discoveries that sex had been going on for quite some time and that really there wasn't very much they could do about it.

Take it or leave it, the average European race, possibly barring the German race which is in the same boat with us, long ago developed a moralistic ideology of its own and adheres to it. This likewise is true of the Oriental races, who being fatalists, accept what is for what it is.

Narrow the comparison with the Britannic stocks to the more culturally developed Continental countries: On the Continent a nation's moral code is like a plumb bob. It may joggle a trifle now and then but uniformly it points one way. Our code is a pendulum which, once in so often, oscillates in a wide and upsetting arc; and in between is never quite sure to which angle it will swing next. Trace this record of vacillation back through the centuries: Bloody Mary's frightened people walk a strait and narrow path beset with canonical traps to snare the straying feet of heretics and wantons; Elizabeth's happier subjects celebrate their merry freedom by reveling in loose living and loose talking and loose writing; in wenching, dicing and other tolerated lapses. The licentiousness of the coxcombs and the gay ladies who flourish under the first Charles is balanced off by those dismal strict proprieties which are enforced through the Cromwellian days. Under the next of the Stuart line is more profligacy, more flaunting sinfulness, and the King's chief prostitute, Nell Gwyn, is the adored of the masses; then, for offset, comes a revival of hypocritical puritanism during the reign of William of Orange and his sour-pussed queen. In the Georgian successions misbehavior is ramping and raucous and the commoner takes encouragement for his bawdiness from divers royal examples. Victorian smugness follows, with prissy modesty and priggishness for its handmaidens. That era goes out with the first World War; and after that and from then on till now and still prevalent, we have the frankness and—too bad to have to say it—the flaunting unrestraint of the post-Edwardian period, a period which has been typified abroad among the set led by H.R.H., the Duke of Windsor, and extending its ramifications and multiplying its repercussions in London and pretty much all over metropolitan America. The social barometer seems to indicate a change, perhaps a change toward a more discreet day. But aside from long skirts and high bodices and corsets—somehow women's fashions always pave the way for these stylistic upheavals—there aren't many portents of it as yet visible on the horizon. So the movies, like the radio, are damned if they do and emasculated if they don't.

With all this conceded, I still decline to add my voice to the chorus of those who think the present generation is practically a total loss. When one takes into consideration that within the scope of a quarter of a century our generation has managed to bring about the two cruelest and most wasteful wars of recorded time, not to mention the greatest industrial depression, the greatest man-made famine and the greatest mass massacre—those latter two were Russia's contributions—and perhaps the greatest volume of revolutionary unrest in all history, we scarcely can blame our immediate descendants for having disdain for the opinions of the elders and a sneering disregard for their admonitions.

Pessimism regarding the future is the inevitable tendency of the retiring members of any old established firm, anyhow. When we get past a certain age we begin to fear that when we, with our superior wisdom, are called on to quit, anything else that's worth while automatically will suspend operations too. There isn't any doubt in my mind that Father Adam, sitting in the Garden in the cool of the day and observing the boorish antics of his hairy whelps, turned to Eve and said: "Mother, this world has done fairly well under our control. But Lord help it when these crazy kids of ours take over. Why, it's plum' discouraging to think about."

So perhaps we complain overmuch regarding the slackness and the laxities of our immediate descendants when we should bear with them. But bless their little hearts, and sympathetic though I be, I do get to wishing sometimes that they had better manners.

30

ONE MAN IN HIS TIME

TALKING for hire, another sidesaddle which I rode at intervals for years, was the natural outcome of experimentations, previously carried on and persisted in. As though it were a series of steeply dropping stairs, I can trace my downward course to the ultimate depths—first storytelling, then after-dinner speaking, then, at the farther end of the trail, the lecture game—a special tour to begin with; and after that Chautauqua circuits, lyceum dates, college engagements and the like. Let's go back to the beginnings.

Always the effort to shine at anecdote telling—especially anecdotes in various vernaculars—was a sort of fixation with me. I early discovered, or perhaps the knowledge came more or less instinctively, that storytelling was an elemental phase of dramatic expression, calling, among other expedients, for a proper sense of rhythm and a use, but an economical use, of decorative frill-work. Here's what I'm getting at: One man stands up to tell an anecdote. His phrasing suits the subject, his timing is right, his imitative powers are well stressed. You laugh at his points, you appreciate his mimicry, you feel that his accent is good. But something still is missing, something the lack of which has marred the general effect. Another man tells a story, telling it no better, so far as accuracy of dialect is concerned, than the first man did; but in his case he scores because by a roll of the eye, a grimace, a gesture, a glance, some such small but crafty artifice, he made you forget him altogether so that at once it was as though you saw and heard the characters in the story as flesh and blood embodiments. You see, he sank his own personality out of sight, by merging it into Pat and Mike, or Jake and Lee, or the Swede and the Greek pushcart peddler or whoever his actors were. And yet it was his erased personality operating, so to speak, from behind the scenes, which so successfully put the illusion across. Ventriloquists follow exactly the same formula. It is the dummy which takes on human qualities and dominates the act, practically to the seeming eclipse of the performer. But in the case of the first man you continually saw him and not his imaginary stooges and that spoiled the nuances.

Nor need a schooled storyteller hesitate to tell an old story, provided he dresses it up in modern garb or even if he knows how to tell it smartly. Old stories must have been good to begin with, else they would never have endured amid changing modes and changing tastes. Their ethnic antiquity attests their everlasting excellence.

I can testify to the ripened age of at least one anecdote. I was writing a supposedly light-hearted article on food, and somewhere in it, with intent mildly to be facetious, I said that on the average Englishman's dinner table there were but three staple vegetables, to wit, boiled potatoes, boiled cabbage—and another helping of the boiled potatoes.

Shortly after the publication of this article I got an indignant letter from an Englishman transplanted on Australian soil. I couldn't make up my mind whether he was the most literal person in the Antipodes or a subtle satirist. For he began by stating that I was woefully astray on simple arithmetic since I had mentioned three vegetables and then had listed only two. For further proof of my abysmal ignorance he pointed out that there were ever so many edible and nourishing growths common to the British Isles. He must have had access to a seedman's catalogue for he enumerated a long string—the beetroot, the mangel-wurzel, the scarlet runner bean, the turnip—four kinds of turnip; the vegetable marrow and thus alphabetically right on down to watercress.

I was running then a syndicate department of my favorite jokes. (It started out to be a series of fifty jokes but because of the forbearance of the American public, it ran for over seven years, six days a week.) So next day in my space I repeated the line which had provoked my Australian correspondent to wrath and quoted his letter in full and tacked on a confession. My modest effusion, I admitted, was merely a paraphase of an old joke. I had twisted around and revamped the time-encysted wheeze about the teacher who asked a pupil to name six animals encountered in the Arctic regions and the pupil had replied, "Three walruses and three polar bears." I went on to say that as a small boy I had heard this from my father and I presumed it was fairly hoary at that time.

In a day or two along came a letter from a professor of economics at Cornell University who said that like most bookish men he had a hobby. His hobby was tracing the genesis of popular jokes. A morbid pursuit, if you're asking me, and calculated to pierce to the very vitals of the storytelling profession. But, by his own confession, that's what it was.

He added, "You say you suspect the joke regarding the fauna indigenous to the polar regions possibly was old even when your father recited it to you. By virtue of my investigations I am able to confirm this suspicion on your part. The item in question is even older than your father's generation. If you will consult Josephus, the historian on Jewish antiquities, in such and such canto and on such and such a page of the standard edition of his works, you will get further illumination as to my meaning."

So I looked in Josephus' great tome where the professor indicated I should look, and I came on a passage to this general effect: "It is inscribed among the earlier chronicles that in ancient Thebes a sage, addressing one of his followers said, 'My son, name for me six quadrupeds peculiar to Ethiopia?' Whereupon the disciple with promptness answered, 'Master, three water-horses and three camel-opards.'"

So it would appear that at the time Josephus gave this durable evergreen further and revived circulation—and Josephus was born twenty-odd years before the beginning of the Christian era—the little trinket already was venerated as a classic. The proverb-maker, whoever he may have been, evidently didn't mean to include jokes in his category when he said the good die young.

From storytelling in informal companies to after-dinner speaking was an inevitable step in my descent toward vocal infamy, the transition from chrysalis to larva being marked by a most painful experience. I had been in New York perhaps four or five years when along came an invitation to speak at a large banquet in honor of Abraham Erlanger, the head of the all-powerful Theatrical Trust. I had never tried to make an after-dinner speech but I had heard a lot of speech-making done at dinners which I covered as a reporter; and as I sat down to compose my maiden remarks, it appeared to me the task before me should be comparatively easy. It had seemed almost ridiculously easy when such jugglers of badinage as Sim Ford and Job Hedges and ex-Ambassador Joe Choate were making even the bus boys whoop with joy.

So I was full of confidence when I emerged from the cocoon stage and joined the customary aggregation of white-fronted nightingales at the head table on the evening of the Erlanger blowout. I do not wish to boast but in all sincerity I must state that in the entire record of formal dinners in Greater New York during the past thirty-five years no tyro ever scored a more monumental failure than I did that fateful night. Various things contributed to my downfall: I was as nervous as a teeter snipe. I, the downiest of neophytes, was on the same bill with such polished journeymen as Lew Dockstader and "Ren" Wolff the newspaper wit, and Wilton Lackaye the actor, and Patrick Francis Murphy, and Chester Lord of the *Sun* and Melville Stone of the Associated Press. I had a bad spot on the bill. I was away down toward the foot of the list when many of the diners had lapsed into one of two classifications—those who had drunk too much and gone to sleep, and those who had not drunk enough yet and were working like Swiss Bell Ringers, trying to catch up. And finally what had appeared to be bright and airy chaff when I memorized it, proved on exposure in that overheated hall to be as cold as yesterday's batter cake—and fell as flat, or flatter. It was long after midnight when I took the mortal remains home to distant Harlem. By right I should have traveled in a hearse, holding a lily in my waxen hand.

It was bruised vanity now which definitely set my feet on the slanted path. I told myself there were hidden quirks and curlicues to this business and I would learn them and prove to the world that I had learned them. With a thoroughness of intent which should never have been wasted on so futile a campaign but reserved for something worth while, I set about educating myself in the debased science of after-dinner spouting. I accepted all manner of invitations from all manner of clubs, societies and fraternal bodies. The Amalgamated Pants Pressers' Union heard my voice uplifted in briskened persiflage and the members of the Bronx Chowder & Literary Association came to know my store of apt divertisements. By such laborious practice I acquired a glib facility, and incidentally built up a Frankenstein's monster which has pursued me ever since. With advancing age I have more or less taken the veil but there was a mid-period when I'd say to myself, "My word, what on earth am I going to do with myself tomorrow evening—I'm not due to speak anywhere?"

Through progressive degrees I mastered certain essential rudiments. For instance, I came to understand that the most dulcet music which has ever uplifted the human soul is the sound of a speaker's voice in his own enthralled ears but, so far as hearer resistance is concerned, he achieves his higher marks if he can but force himself to shut the flow of oratory before he has gone too far. In other words, he should quit before the crowd quits him. He must be a terminal, not a roundhouse. And keep away from sidings and spur tracks. And not blow too often for the crossings. No speech can be entirely bad if it is brief enough. And the person who cannot say what he has to say within the bounds of a reasonable brevity should never be allowed to say it. The Gettysburg Address was delivered in about two minutes, they say. But in the judgment of authorities it seems to compare favorably with the four-hour speech of Senator La Follette—the first La Follette—at the annual dinner of the Periodical Publishers' Association in Philadelphia on a tragically memorial occasion. I was there with a thousand fellow sufferers. At 2:00 A.M., when I told the waiter to give me an eight o'clock call and drifted off, the Senator was getting right well along into his subject.

Also I learned that there is no substitute for spontaneity. The line which has been carefully thought up, and properly rehearsed and given out at just the right moment and in just the right tempo may be the very brightest line that ever was on land or sea, but it never gets the response that is bestowed upon a retort or interjection intrinsically much less humorous, which springs from something that has just happened or something that has just been said by the toastmaster or by the preceding speaker. There, if one values such baubles, is where an after-dinner speaker scores his best bull's-eyes.

Betty Rogers, Will Rogers' widow, and in her own right a very wonderful person, has insisted that there be included here an incident which she was moved to write about when I told her here the other day that I had it in mind to touch on this topic in this book. She thinks her contribution serves to illustrate the point I would make. So, with all proper acknowledgments to Mrs. Rogers, here is what she wrote:

There generally was an added free show at a banquet where my husband and Irvin Cobb were included among the speakers, for each was apt to forget the object of the party, if it had any, in order to poke fun at the other.

I remember attending one big affair where Irvin seized his chance to score at Will's expense. Every winter the Friars, which numerically was then the biggest theatrical club in New York, gave at least one dinner, always in honor of some notable in the entertainment world. This time there were to be three guests of honor, the overlords of as many fields of organized amusement.

George M. Cohan was the general master of ceremonies but his function as the presiding dignitary was briefly to introduce the introducers. First, DeWolf Hopper was "press agent" for Judge Kenesaw Mountain Landis, the czar of baseball and, of course, had to recite, as no other living soul could, the immortal poem of "Casey at the Bat." Next, my Will wittily presented Will H. Hays, head of the moving-picture industry. At the tag end of his remarks, evidently feeling that he should return the compliment for the kind things which had been spoken about him, Mr. Hays said: "It didn't take long, ladies and gentlemen, after Bill Rogers came here, a rope-throwing, gum-chewing cowboy from Oklahoma, for New York City to discover there was something under his old slouch hat besides hair."

On that he sat down and in the same instant Irvin stood up. Irvin's job was to introduce playwright Augustus Thomas, the mouthpiece for the legitimate stage. But for the moment he had something else on his mind. With a meaning downward glance at Will's head which, as usual, was fantastically tousled, and before George Cohan could get a word in, Irvin drawled:

"I'm awfully glad Will Hays just said what he did about Bill Rogers having something under his hat besides hair. It's high

time somebody in this country spoke a kind word for dandruff."

I was watching from just a few seats away and for Will I
must say that no one in that great dining hall at the Hotel Astor
seemed to enjoy that thrust more than he did.

From that day on, when the two of them were on the same
dinner program, which was frequently, Irvin would never
speak first. Will said this was because Irvin wanted to steal his
ice cream, but Irvin confided to me that he was taking no
chances by letting Will follow him.

"I'm not inviting murder, thank you," he said.

31

IN A WAY OF SPEAKING

THROUGH ten years I went along on my misguided course, speaking often for my supper but never under hire. Then, without warning, the third stage eventuated and down the ramp I slid into the ranks of the bought-and-paid-for brethren. It was the winter of 1914–15. I was just back from the Western Front—almost the first neutral observer who had actually witnessed operations to get back. As a guest I went one night to the Greenroom Club, since defunct, but then an active theatrical organization rating with the Lambs, the Players and the Friars. After the supper I was called upon to say something, it being suggested that the members preferably would like me to tell about my recent experiences in the battle lines of Belgium and France and behind them. That was easy prompting; I thought of little else than what I had seen, dreamed of little else, wrote of little else. I went serious. I forgot the small mannerisms and masked subterfuges of after-dinner speaking. When I was through, I learned, greatly to my surprise, that I had been on my feet for an hour and a quarter. They made me an honorary life member of the Greenroom and I thought that would be the end of it.

But before I quite finished breakfast the following morning, Edgar and Archie Selwyn, commonly known along Broadway as the Good Brother and the Bad Brother, were at the door of our apartment, both of them grinning like dentifrice ads and wiping imaginary canary bird feathers off their lips. I thought of Tweedledum and Tweedledee.

"Well," said Archie, he being the bad one, "how soon can you come by our office and sign up?"

"Sign up what?" I asked.

"Sign up the contract to go on a lecture tour," stated Edgar.

"Who told you I was going on any lecture tour?" I said.

"Nobody told us. We're telling you. It's our own cute little idea—we took turns hatching it out going home from the club last night," explained Archie.

"But I never made a lecture—you know, a set talk—in my life," I expostulated.

"We never handled a lecturer, either—only regular shows," stated Edgar. "It's as fair for one as it is for the other."

"Listen," said Archie, "it's like that old yarn about the East Side kid who joined the army and they sent him out west and stuck him in a cavalry troop and when he landed at the remount station he told the top sergeant he never had been astraddle of even a gentle plug in his life and he hoped they'd make it easy on him until he kind of got the hang of the thing. So the tops led him to a corral where a man-eating tiger of a broncho with a Roman nose and a wicked eye and a set of front teeth like an alligator was trying to tear the pen down. And the sergeant said to him, 'Looky, kid, you say you ain't never rid no hoss. Well, that there hoss yonder ain't never been rode. You two amateurs can start in together.' Get me?"

"I get you," I said, "but you're sweeping me off my feet. I've got to think this thing over."

"Think it over on the way downtown," said Archie. "You're going to say yes anyhow and that'll save time."

"We've got a cab waiting downstairs," said Edgar.

"Here's your hat," said Archie.

"Let me help you on with your overcoat," said Edgar.

It was perfect teamwork and prevailed.

In a sort of daze I sat while a pen was put in my hands and certain papers were spread before me to be autographed on the dotted line. I was introduced to "Pink" Hays, who would direct the tour from New York, and to "Si" Goodfriend, who would be my personal representative on the road, and to my traveling manager and the advance agent and the second publicity man back with the troupe. Crosby Gaige, the third member of the Selwyn firm suggested that perhaps I should go up to Carnegie Hall where the music teachers and the dramatic coaches and the teachers of expression clustered in numbers amounting to a Bedlam and take a few hurried lessons in stage delivery. We waived that or rather, I waived it. No studied gestures for me, no voice effects; if anybody insisted on that we'd just tear up the documents and I would take my doll-rags and go home. Here at least I was firm as adamant about it.

Within ten hectic days we opened our season. We opened in Brooklyn on a snowy night at a huge building which contained several assembly halls. For the tryout, Pink Hays had meant to rent one of the smaller halls, he fearing a small audience in a big place might discourage a beginner. There was a mix-up though and at the last minute, we found he had engaged the main hall, a big cavern of a place full of echoes and cross drafts. We sold every seat; we sold standing room; we sold sit-down space on the stage and in the wings. And with deep regrets we refused admission to four hundred latecomers. A great light shone in our astounded faces. Next day we were busy as trap drummers revising our schedule. We canceled all that we could of our percentage dates. Whenever possible we surrendered our calls upon medium-sized theaters. On a straight renting basis we booked buildings having augmented seating capacities—convention halls, coliseums, auditoriums, armories, exposition dromes. And everywhere for ten weeks, until I had to quit to undergo an operation for that small abdominal rupture I'd got overseas, we stood 'em up—to use showman talk—and most nights we turned 'em away.

It wasn't my compelling eloquence which packed our houses. I had no grace of eloquence to start with and I fought against acquiring any semblance of the same. When I caught myself growing rhetorical, indulging in rolling metaphors and sonorous periods, I cut it all out and swung back to the colloquial and the conversational. I figured it out that if, talking informally to half a dozen people, I held their interest I'd try to talk after exactly the same fashion to a hundred or a thousand or five thousand people. This sounds easier than it is, for after a fellow gets used to the role the temptation to go oratorical is almost irresistible. Almost immediately I picked up another bit of routine which proved workable. As I came out on the platform and stationed myself along our stage settings consisting of (1) a small table; (2) a pitcher of ice water; (3) a glass; (4) a small American flag, from the lines of patrons various faces immediately would catch my eye—a boy down here directly in front of me, an old man yonder in the box, a girl up in the first balcony, an elderly woman back there in the tenth row. Between us then there was a telepathic joining; this handful at least radiated friendliness and sympathy and I would catch myself saying to myself, "All right, ladies and gentlemen, I get you. You're for me and I'm for you. So I'm going ahead and speak my piece for you folks. And if all these other people here care to listen that's their privilege—they've paid money for it."

Here's another thing I very soon discovered: You must like your audience if you hope to have them like you. Step upon the stage out of sorts or in an ill humor over some minor irritation and instantly the psychic waves transmit the fact to those who sit waiting and their attitude shortly reflects yours. But school yourself to the conviction that in coming hither these kindly folk have paid you a tremendous compliment and are entitled to the best you can offer and they'll know it and across the footlights to you will come pouring a gush of friendliness so cordial that it is as though you walked out of a chilly night into a hospitable house and stood warming your hands by a cheery crackling fire.

Traipsing up and down the map and across the latitudes I found out in what states and cities are the liveliest, most responsive citizens. And I know, roughly, the boundaries of the elbow-shaped stretch of territory wherein the dullest ones live—good Americans, good citizens, listeners, but a trifle slow on the uptake. Never mind where that section is, but I know.

In those ten weeks we took in more cash receipts than any show on the road did in the same period with the single exception of Ziegfeld's Follies. We were all proud of our showing but for one I was under no illusions touching on the underlying reasons for the success. Every full-witted man, woman and child in the United States yearned to hear at firsthand the experiences and the observations of an authentic eyewitness. When we were reported as missing and again when the exaggerated story spread that for three weeks we had been cruising in a chartered Belgium taxicab in the backwash of the German invasion, the newspapers had splashed these matters across their front pages. And at frequent intervals my signed articles had appeared and still were appearing in the *Saturday Evening Post*, which wasn't exactly what you would call bad advertising for our little gabfest.

It was in the run of the luck that some of the most disconcerting incidents piled up at the beginning of my swing around the country when I was not yet insulated against these sudden shocks or fortified with the confidence which came later. It was at the end of the first week that I appeared in one of the near-by Connecticut cities in a municipal auditorium that was so new it wasn't finished yet. The vaulted roof was of iron and either it had been put on temporarily or nailed down very sketchily, because about the time I got going a sharp windstorm came up and these long thin sheets of metal billowed like tide rips and crackled like thunderclaps and threatened any minute to fetch loose from the fastenings. Under these distractions the audience was uneasy—perhaps downright apprehensive— and as for the speaker of the evening, that person was as jitterized as a Mexican jumping bean.

At the height of the uproar from above, a fresh interruption came out of another quarter. The apron of the balcony sloped at an acute angle. At the top of the slant had appeared a very large, very broad, very groggy gentleman who stood swaying on his unstable pins. For a space he wavered there and then—it was part a stagger, part a fall and part a slide—he coasted down the incline in a lunge which left his limber form decanted across the guardrail at the bottom, and he breathing heavily and threatening any moment to topple entirely over and land on the heads of those below. While some of the customers stood and while all of them craned their necks, two ushers hurried to him, upended him and guided him back up the steps to the point from which he started his tobogganing acrobatics. Watching from where I stood, I saw one of them put in his hand some money obviously to repay him for the gallery seat he had purchased, and then they steered him out of sight, he not saying a word all this time, but making up for that by much clunking footwork. As he vanished I sighed with relief and tried to splice up the snapped thread of my tale. But in my ears my voice sounded as artificial and strained as the notes of an off-stage bird's song in a woodland scene and that, I'm sure, must be the most utterly artificial and unlifelike sound there is.

In another minute or two I was appalled to behold our tipsy friend advancing toward me in a teetering fashion along the downstairs center aisle. Having been ejected from the balcony exit, he had blundered back into the building via the main box office, evidently under the impression that he was patronizing another establishment altogether. Automatically, and with the frozen look of a somnambulist upon his face, he advanced until he reached the footlights and from that point he stared unblinkingly up at me across a distance of six feet or so, and then a semi-conscious light shone in his glazed eyes and in the fixed tones of a hopeless resignation, he delivered his first and last utterance while in our hypnotized midst.

"'S'no use!" he cried out hoarsely. "No matter where a fellow goes in thish town, the same dam' foolishness is goin' on."

Already we had discarded the plan of enlisting the good offices of some prominent citizen at each stand to present me to my hearers on the time-honored theory that otherwise they wouldn't have the least idea who it was they'd paid their money to listen to. The designated introducer was apt to be long-winded, a somewhat common failing among prominent citizens wherever found, and that would add to my nervousness. Or, with the best intentions in the world, he might say what we thought was the impolitic thing, sentiment being acutely divided then as between favor for the Allies and favor for the Central Powers. To walk the tightrope of a strict neutrality was a sufficiently difficult task already, without the peril that some outsider might inadvertently deliver himself of a prejudiced prolog. If, for example, I admitted that punitive reprisals of a cruel sort had been perpetrated in invaded Belgium, that was an affront to every pro-Teuton in the audience, while on the other hand, did I deny that hideous atrocities against civilians and prisoners had taken place—or at least hadn't to my personal knowledge and to the best of my belief—any violent British partisan was likely to denounce me as a lying apologist in German pay.

So the rest of the troupe elected Si Goodfriend, my so-called personal representative, to do the introducing and Si qualified admirably for the role. He was one of the last of the old school of traveling press agents, the kind that specialized in personal contacts and a nation-wide acquaintance. I think he knew every managing editor and every dramatic critic in temperate North America. He was courtly and friendly—a natural friendliness and not one professionally acquired—with a scholarly profile and beautifully schooled Vandyke whiskers. And he dressed the part according to the ancient code—a black broadcloth overcoat trimmed with baby lamb's wool, fawn-colored spats, an end-man's collar and a lovely high hat polished like a new base-burner stove and tended with loving care by its devoted owner. You could almost hear Ponto purr—we had christened the pet Ponto—as he stroked the ruffled nap back into place. In the entire tour I never saw him at any hour, day or night, when it was not either on his head or resting in the crotch of a protecting elbow. I would not go so far as to say he was born wearing it but I was quite convinced that, in accordance with a tribal rite of his people, when he was nine days old a rabbinical deputy came to the house and blocked Si's high hat.

So Si became our introducer and imparted to the proceedings an atmosphere of dressiness and culture which otherwise would have been lacking. But going into Detroit for a Sunday afternoon's engagement, he inconsiderately developed acute bronchitis and his voice became a croak. We wired an appeal to the resident manager, asking him to invite some local orator to open the meeting after the customary formula, but impressing it upon the manager what he in turn would please impress upon the gentleman chosen, namely, that we hoped the later would in his remarks mercifully be brief since we had to catch a train leaving at 4:30 P.M., or thereabouts, in order to reach St. Louis, which was our next stop, on the following morning.

A young blizzard greeted us on our arrival and our hired cabs had a struggle getting us across town through the driving snow storm and the gathering drifts. The place where I was to speak turned out to be a converted skating rink. But it wasn't entirely converted because it still looked a good deal like a skating rink. I went in by the improvised stage entrance and the manager took me into his cluttered little coop of an office and there I met the kindly soul who had agreed to help us out—a prominent and a most generally respected member of the highest court in the state. Even so, at sight of him my heart sank. Unmistakably he had the look about him of a sincere and earnest, not to say determined, orator. Moreover he was wearing a double-breasted frock coat and by past experiences I knew that only too often is the seat of eloquence found under the tails of a double-breasted frock coat.

Quakeful with forebodings, I followed him out upon a platform to face an overflow audience of three thousand and I sat down in a chair trying to look dignified and sociable at the same time, and the judge advanced to the front and after a few preliminary words, to my complete surprise, he said:

"Night before last in the sister city of Pittsburgh I sat in a great hall, crowded to the doors as this hall is, and there I heard Mr. Cobb depict in vivid phrases some of the dreadful scenes, the thrilling moments, the heart-rending scenes he lately has witnessed in that mightly conflict overseas. For instance, I heard him describe this moving episode."

And then, for thirty of the most horrible minutes of prolonged torture undergone by any poor wretch since the Spanish Inquisition folded up, I heard him give a somewhat condensed but on the whole satisfactory version of my speech. He had an excellent memory, even for minute points. I must, in fairness, say that for him; and his delivery was more finished than anything which I, with my limitations, could ever hope to achieve. And I squirmed there on the rack in muted agony and at each successive part of his rendition I desperately whispered to myself, "Well, that beloved little story is out. Not even these snowbound citizens would care to hear it twice in the same afternoon, especially since His Honor, gosh dern him, is reciting it ever so much better than I can. But, oh Lord, help me to decide what am I going to stick in instead?"

And when he finished, amid loud and deserved applause, I stood up, the broken wreckage of a once-strong man and with my brain reeling and my eye on my wrist watch and counting the racing minutes until train time, I had to think up, in shaky, disconnected chunks, an entirely new talk to take the place of the one which had just been rattled forth there under the vault of that reverberant cave of the winds. For the structure had peculiar acoustics of its own. A fellow's voice would go out into the void and then break up into a whole bevy of small persistent echoes and they, like little homing pigeons, would come winging back to the author of their being and murmur confusingly in his ear.

From hippodroming under the auspices of a producing firm to traveling a summer Chautauqua circuit and then to filling lyceum engagements were natural transitions. Because of a variety of blighting causes—the spread of radio and the movies; the building of good roads and the universal adoption of the automobile as an essential

part of farm life, the Chautauqua as it once prevailed is vanishing
from the American scene, which seems a pity, for it was so entirely
and so exclusively a native institution. More than once have I
sleepily crawled out of a train at an inhuman before-day hour alongside an empty way station of which perhaps I never before had heard
and, beholding hardly any houses roundabout, nor even a watering
tank, have said to myself: "Well, the booking office certainly pulled
a boner this time. There may be something here which will pass
muster for a town some day, but they haven't got around to building
it yet. Or else I made an awful mistake and got off at the wrong
whistling stop and here I am, lost in the midst of a vast and practically uninhabited wilderness."

But before I could decide which standard method I would
employ for committing suicide, some friendly individual would
materialize out of the gloom and take me and my luggage in charge.
If he was one of the inexcusable sort who are merry and bright before breakfast, I would be tempted almost past endurance to commit
murder, but if he knew enough to remain good and glum, it wasn't
so bad as I wedged myself into a buggy seat alongside him and his
team went clop-clopping along the turnpike and the smell of dew-
drenched earth came up to us and the sun rose, all coppery-hot, and
wreathed like Salome in shreddy veils of soft-colored mist, and the
cock quails started piping from the top rails of the fences. Nearly
always we drove to my escort's home, for some of these places were
too small to support even the most modest of hotels and where there
were hotels they nearly always were such frightfully bad hotels.
(Having more varieties of food to eat than any people on earth,
our country hotel-keepers know as little about preparing it as
any people you'd care to mention.) And that afternoon I would
be taken to a campground that had become a tented village and
there under canvas or tin, in a temperature which might range
well above the hundred mark—and frequently did—I would speak
my piece to an audience numbering into the thousands. And this,
mind you, had been going on since the beginning of the week—
three entirely different shows a day—and would continue to go
on thus until the end of the week. Once a year the marvel of
it came to pass and once a year a bucolic constituency would
gather in from all over that particular area—men, women and

children in teams and wagons and cars, and travelers by special excursions—for a spell of outdoor gypsying and for their one annual contact with the outer world: talks on the problems of the farmer and his wife; concert singers, choirs, tabloid operas and condensed dramatic productions; freak acts but each with a high moral tone; all manner of entertainment by all manner of entertainers. And tons of dust would be churned up daily, and hundred-weights of chewing gum would be chewed, and dozens of nursing, prickly-heated babies would be crying all at once under the jammed pavilion while a fellow was trying to do his bit. For the agencies it was the safest form of amusement-purveying that ever had been devised. They got in advance fees sufficient to cover all costs, including salaries of "talent," while the local Chautauqua society, which had guaranteed these expenses, passed the fiscal burden along to the merchants who in turn peddled tickets to townspeople and countrypeople at cost or less, and figured on getting their money back through increased volume of trade. Generally, there still was a fair margin of profit to be split proportionately among those who had assumed a joint risk by underwriting the proposition. Chautauqua performers never had to walk back home, although some of them should have been chased back home.

Just as vaudeville and before that, variety and burlesque, had been springboards for youthful ability, Chautauqua was a life net for declining substars of the legitimate stage. As big-town audiences grew weary of Shakespearian spouters and they tearing emotion to pieces and mouthing the pieces, there was room for them out on the horse and buggy routes, far remote from scornful cities and snooty sophisticates, and what's more, the pay-in-advance arrangement meant for these galled and hobbling derelicts a security which they never had known in the precarious times of shoestring city producers and fly-by-night road shows. Yet there was scarcely a one of them, man or woman, but would gladly have swapped the bread-and-butter fatness of the Main Streets of the Polkvilles of the land for the uncertain rations which awaited second-raters and down-and-outers on Broadway. They were homesick for the place where there were no homes, hungry for the glittering district which yielded semi-starvation for such as they. It made you think of a prisoner who had been freed from a comfortless jail, clamoring to quit his present green fields and shady lanes and get back again into the musty cell block. I ran across scores of such cases and never ceased to marvel at their discontent with their present well-cushioned berths.

As his masters of ceremonies, each circuit mogul engaged for the season two gentlemen who leap-frogged each other from town to town, so that the "*artistes*" re-encountered them on alternating weeks. Almost without exceptions these functionaries were either ministers of the Gospel on leave from their congregations or county school superintendents picking up extra money during the summer vacation. And somehow they all seemed to look alike and they all behaved alike. For instance, in presenting an entertainer it invariably was announced that the person in question "brought an inspirational message." The formula never varied. The party waiting to do his stunt might be a "lame duck" lately outsted from Congress with a dreary hour of shopworn bamboozle and flapdoodle about public questions to unload; or the proprietor of a troupe of educated cockatoos; or a young woman imitator of the notes of wild birds; or an ex-clergyman featuring a worked-over version of one of Spurgeon's or Beecher's sermons. No matter, he or she had brought a message and it was inspirational. I think it was in the contract of the official herald with the parent bureau that he drag in that poor fatigued phrase by the hair of its head.

On a lyceum tour the audiences were more citified and more sophisticated than Chautauqua audiences but no whit more attentive or considerate. Here the train connections and the hotel accommodations were superior, which lessened the strain of travel for the "attraction"; but on the other hand, the social burden was heavier upon him even though he took drastic steps to fend off this load, as I did, after one winter's experience which left me gibbering and jittery on the raw edge of nervous exhaustion. By nature as gregarious as a seed tick and garrulous as a guinea hen, I nevertheless was driven by the stark instinct for self-preservation to armor myself in a shell of isolation, and this at the risk of seeming unappreciative and churlish. Even so, I preferred dying by natural causes to being killed with kindness.

An elaborate defense mechanism was worked out: At the signing of the contract for my appearance it expressly was stipulated that because of the need of privacy and the likes of that, on no account could I accept invitations from hospitable citizens or civic bodies. Two weeks before my arrival the local management received a form letter from the home office calling attention to this requirement and two days before a telegram of the same tenor was sent. But without fail, as I climbed off the steam cars, there would be waiting a volunteer delegation of well-intentioned, stubbornly persistent fellow creatures intent on bearing me away to a luncheon of Kiwanis or the Greeters or the Lions or the Commercial Club, where I'd have a golden opportunity to talk for thirty or forty minutes and for twenty minutes more shake hands with strangers, including always the local Sampson who tries to crush all your finger bones to pulp in his splendid grip, this muscular feat being regarded by him as evidence of a manly virility. . . . "Oh, yes, Mr. Cobb, we know what you wrote on ahead about being so busy writing pieces and so forth that you couldn't go places. Well, that might do for some towns but say listen, Irvin S., this town is different. We've got one fellow here—Fred McBaxter, our leading mortician—that's funnier than Will Rogers ever dared to be. And there's a chap named Heiney Schultz—only we call him Dutch Schultz—that'll knock you cold, playing on a juice harp. Just hear him doin' 'Sweet Hallie' with mockingbird trills and you'll never forget it. . . . And oh, say, Cobb, meet Mr. Hostetter, our leading banker and owner of the handsomest residential property in town. Mrs. Hostetter wants you at a literary reception and tea she's giving this afternoon so you can meet our most prominent ladies, besides several local authors. She wants you to come early so she can take you through the house. . . . And in between the luncheon and the reception, we'll find time somehow to drive you around and show you the sights of the city. We've got a new public library that's a darb and the biggest soda-bottling plant between Omaha and Chicago. Irv, you can spend an hour there and not see half of it."

Vaunting is foreign to my nature, but I feel it to be no more than asking my proper due that I should state I went through an entire lyceum season, covering all parts of the United States and Canada, and never attended a single club luncheon and never once saw the inside of one of the Hostetterian mansions of either land, nor ever uplifted my voice for God, for Country and for

International Rotary. This, I believe, constitutes a record without parallel in our continental annals.

For some reason that was a fruitful season for visiting English novelists of the two commoner migratory varieties, i.e., the one who gave readings of selected passages from his own works, and the one who lectured, in a spirit of charity, on the artistic shortcomings of contemporary English novelists such as Galsworthy and Barrie and George Moore. From the British Isles in the past we have suffered divers invasions that we might have done without and yet been no worse off. At a much earlier time they exported over to us the English sparrow and the English starling and between them they took the whole country excepting Hollywood. Later, in flocks which darkened the noonday sun, came the English actors and they took Hollywood.

But the time of which I specifically would speak was the time of the touring British writer and particularly the kinds that did their touring for pecuniary motives. To offset this visitation we had and continue to have as visitors some of the most charming and most engaging writer-folk who have inhabited this planet during the past quarter of a century. I think of the modest Somerset Maugham, with his fascinating stammer and his nice wit; the dumpling-built Chesterton, who was so wise and yet dressed his wisdom in a quiet simplicity; the genial, understanding H. G. Wells, a great novelist and a greater constructive thinker, and he starting life as a draper's assistant in a provincial town and, unlike most of his countrymen who have emerged from "trade," not ashamed but justifiably proud of those humbler beginnings (which a Yankee wouldn't regard as humble at all); the sprightly Anglicized Michael Arlen, making glittering profitable things out of a deft trickery of words, and the only Armenian I ever met who didn't try to sell me a rug. I think of E. V. Lucas with his smooth intriguing humor and his placid philosophy; and Seumas MacManus the Irish poet and Irish patriot, wearing a burning fine genius under the cloak of an innate humility and dividing his time between California and his beloved native hills of Donegal; and James Stevens, the spiritual reincarnation of one of his own shy leprechauns. I think of Lord Tweedsmuir, late governor general of the Dominion of Canada, but I knew him first and best as plain sturdy John Buchan, writing classic tales that qualified him for immortality with such fellow Scots as Sir Walter Scott and Robert Louis Stevenson, and he an ardent fisherman who pictured for me trout burns and salmon pools in his Highlands and harkened while I, in turn, told him about Oregon rapids where the steelheads ranged and lily pads sheltering small-mouthed bass and the lusty ounaniche in landlocked northern waters. And of course I think of P. G. Wodehouse who came to be as much American as Britisher, the only man alive who can write the same story over and over again, using the same scheme and the same theme and the same only slightly altered set of characters, with the same situations and the same climax, and yet at each time of writing make it even funnier and more appetizing than it was before. Heaven grant that P. G. never changes the plot! For if he does millions of his faithful readers will be horribly disappointed.

By way of contrast with these men I revive reminiscences of a couple of altogether different persons belonging to subspecies of the breed. There was one who was the house guest, for a spell, of my publisher and neighbor. He had ability, no doubt about it, great ability for a certain microscopic analysis of human characteristics, and what he saw there he meticulously put down on paper, but he made the mistake of believing that calculated rudeness was an outward evidence of genius. Or possibly he had, as the saying is, been raised up that way. I'm not assuming either that in his own country he lacked for manners but as I interpreted his attitude, civility was as good as wasted when extended to inferior races, and all races except natives of his island were to him inferior, especially including those whom he referred to as "Colonials." (I wonder why the mere fact of one being a Canadian or an Australian so irritates an insular Englishman.)

To express his disapproval of things—and in an uncouth non-conformist country such as ours there were bound to be many such—he had a way of thrusting forward the upper front teeth, rather like an incensed whistling marmot and making choked snuffling sounds down in his throat. He made these sounds in a slightly lower key when not antagonized; in fact, he used them to punctuate with. For Britons never will be slaves except to their adenoids.

His sniffling apparatus never worked better than on the occasion when George Horace Lorimer gave a luncheon in his honor.

To Philadelphia for the party went one group from New York, and from Washington another group came up so altogether it was quite a party, and Lorimer, who knew a lot about entertaining people, had put the big pot in the little one. There was a private dining room at the Bellevue Stratford and it literally was upholstered in bronze chrysanthemums and flaming autumn leaves. For the first course the maître d'hôtel proudly chaperoned in a huge tureen and when the silver lid was lifted so that he might ladle out the contents, an aroma went up from those contents which set twenty expectant mouths to watering. A poor family could have made a fairly satisfactory meal on the smell alone.

As a big soup plate of the gorgeous concoction was placed in front of the principal guest, he fretfully agitated it with a spoon and he inhaled, and then he sniffed and sniffed again, not aggressively however as was his wont, but rather in the fashion of an apprehensive patient going under the ether and he spoke to Lorimer, sitting alongside him:

"I say, what's this 'strordinary stuff?"

For an instant Lorimer stiffened, then he unbent.

"That's terrapin stew, Philadelphia style," he explained. "I thought you might like to sample what we regard as a distinctive American dish. So I got the management here to send down to Chesapeake Bay to make sure we'd get the genuine article and not 'sliders.' A slider's a sort of illegitimate cousin to a terrapin."

"Yes, yes, quite so," the great man's tone was impatient, petulant rather. "But I mean to say what specifically is this precious thing, the terrapin?"

"It's a salt-water creature with flappers instead of feet and a lot of tender meat under its shell. I suppose you might call it a variety of seagoing tortoise. And when we blend it with—"

"Oh! In other words then, a sort of turtle, eh?" He pushed the plate under the boskage in the middle of the table as though wishful to get the obnoxious mixture out of sight. "I shan't touch it."

Lorimer who congealed readily under provocation, froze solid. In fact, a general chill fell on the assemblage, but our critic from overseas took no heed of this if indeed he noticed it, he being engaged in a monologue on the deficiencies of the American sleeping-car system as compared with the European sleeping-car systems. It would appear that he had become seriously estranged toward the Pullman company two nights before and still felt embittered.

The glacial proceedings were perhaps a third of the way done when he shoved back his chair and stood up. Until then there had been no suggestion that he was going to let us struggle along as best we could without him.

"Must be barging off," he said. "Engagement at three o'clock to go to see the Widener art collection. Might be worth while, who knows? Well, cheerio, all!"

And on that he was gone from us. A hush befell. It was broken by a Washingtonian getting upon his feet.

"Brother Lorimer," he said, "complete as this luncheon has been in all other regards, one detail was overlooked at the very beginning. You neglected—inadvertently I'm sure—to ask someone to invoke the divine blessing upon the food of which we were about to partake. Now, speaking for myself, I was reared in a pious household and we always said grace before meals. With your permission, gentlemen—"

He closed his eyes and in fervent tones spoke as follows:

"There being no longer any English novelist among us, *let us thank God!*"

I'm not striving here for effect. Without exaggerating or straining, I do but state the facts in the case.

Nor am I overstressing as I next deal briefly with a second eminent British writer who quit writing in order to cruise about America giving readings from what he had written. The Cobbs were invited one Sunday morning to come to a near-by home where he was being entertained and meet this distinguished personage—for he *was* distinguished. Impressively he descended a flight of stairs into our expectant midst and impressively he acknowledged our presence. But hardly was the ceremony of introductions over when, with a certain bluff, country-squire manner, he said:

"Frightfully hot here—frightfully. So many of your houses are so frightfully overheated over here. Think I shall have the weskit off."

And while we were all still gasping, he whipped out of his coat and vest, revealing that he was wearing a pair of those London-cut trousers which extend so high up and snuggle so closely under the armpits as practically to constitute a princesse style, except that in this case the garments did not button at the back. In addition to a very stout set of elastic braces or, as we would say in our silly Yankee way, suspenders, he also wore a belt snugly girthed on about ten inches above the normal waistline, like a surcingle that had worked up. It would appear that in the matter of keeping one's pants up one was a bit of a pessimist.

Now I'm sure that back home in the stately manor house of his feudal line at Stilton-on-Rye cum Colman, one would not have done one's stripping-down act in the drawing room. But here and now, in a crude half-savage country—well, one asks oneself?

I had subsequent contacts with this famous figure. I was adequately proportioned, I thought, but in his presence I somehow lost all the self-assurance which usually goes with brawn and bulk. I felt strangely shrunken, overpowered, futile. You have seen in the published snapshots of African big-game hunters the one entitled "Two-horned rhino with attendant tickbird?" Well, I was the tickbird.

For all that he so largely filled the beholder's eye, the celebrity was very easy to control when it came to paying for such things as meals, drinks, cab fares, hotel accommodations, railroad tickets, theater admissions, etc., etc., etc. A little child could have wrested from his nerveless clasp the tab at restaurant or night club. Frugal, that would be the word for it. Indeed I may say this was beyond doubt the frugalest man of any nationality I have met as I went along through this world.

Somehow the subject of his family connections kept getting itself crocheted into the motif of the conversation. It developed— and kept on developing—that there were titled members. For instance, frequent mention of an uncle crept in. It would appear that uncle was an earl, a belted earl, no less, although presumably preferring for informal occasions to wear his old school tie.

From time to time the nephew has returned to us to fatten his purse with the debased currency of this semi-barbaric land. I ran into him not long ago. Time had mellowed him. He now was generously free to admit that a few of his brother novelists had begun to evince some fleeting traces of merit—transitory, perhaps, but on the whole commendable as showing worthiness of effort. And he merely touched in passing on our significant shortcomings as a people; merely mentioned them casually instead of developing the thesis as formerly. And what was even more indicative of a softening tendency was that while still content to let you settle for the dinner and tip the waiter and fee the major-domo, he'd fight you like a tiger for the hat check.

32

WHAT A PAIR TO DRAW TO!

In my platforming pursuits I manfully faced a plentitude of agents'
tunts, on the theory, which I regard as a very sane theory, that
when a fellow temporarily is engaged in cashing in on his notoriety,
any publicity is so much silver in his purse and friendly publicity
is as pure gold and only complete absence from current prints is
lead. I balked though at the suggestion of one press bureau that a
roster of performers hailing from various parts of the Union be
called a national galaxy and that in it I be labeled "The Typical
Kentuckian." In the first place this galaxy billing would be a sort
of symposium and I constitutionally am opposed to symposiums.*

---

* One of the crying needs of this country is a symposium to
end all symposiums. By my way of thinking the same drastic treatment should include anthologies, an anthology being a cute plan
devised by somebody who can't write himself to assemble selections
from the works of those who can write and put them in a volume
and put out the volume, emblazoned with the fiat of his approval.
And why shouldn't he approve? He collects the royalties, doesn't
he? The authors sweated blood over these brain products. All he
needed was a pair of scissors, a paste pot, a potential publisher—
and his nerve.

Hatched from a similar egg is the editor of the new magazine
which is going to be a different kind of magazine and which, as
soon as they become acquainted with its unique and transcendent
merits, will have an overpowering appeal for discriminating readers
who until now have felt a great void in their literary appetites
though not realizing before how that craving for better and brighter
things might be realized. However, until the venture firmly is
established in the public estimation, the promoters are just a little
bit shy of ready cash to go along on from month to month. There-

In the second place I doubted I could measure up to the role of the Typical Kentuckian as the public outside of Kentucky has been taught to know him. By practically all the ancient fictional precedents this candidate was ineligible. And even according to the imitative methods of the cinema I hopelessly was *déclassé*. The cinema has a way of picking up a sentimental tradition about the time the romantic writers have discarded it as worn-out and frazzled. Your dramatist of twenty years ago had his choice of two standard themes for a Kentucky play. One was wrapped around a horse-racing episode dealing with a crooked jockey and a Blue Grass maiden named, for choice, Madge or Virginia May; and a likely filly—the last nag in Colonel Buckingham Shelby's stable. And this is the filly that wins the Derby and discomforts the Yankee interloper who covets the Colonel's broad acres, and saves from foreclosure the beloved old homestead with its white portico and its mortgage and its decrepit, burnt-cork retainer who'd rather work for nothing for Old Marse than draw regular wages from rich white folkses. The second of these dependable stand-bys had a feud for its featured background, with the aristocratic scions of one family gunning through the generations for the scions of the neighboring family and the fairest daughter of one clan falling in

---

fore, if Mr. So-and-so will kindly send in gratis for the first number one of his characteristic scripts, the editor will be very grateful indeed and when the periodical finds its place, as undoubtedly it speedily will, the obliging Mr. So-and-so will have in it a steady market for his wares.

If an author heard of a shoe store which was a new kind of shoe store and sought to get on its feet by inducing the manufacturers and wholesalers of shoes to stock its shelves with original and distinctive designs in shoes, free of charge, on the promise that if the shoe store succeeded it would be pleased to consider making future purchases of the same goods, why in that case the author would probably say this was material for a humorous screed having for its text the incredible credulity and guilelessness of shoemakers and shoe jobbers. Yet there is many a recorded instance where he has succumbed to an identical lure when it was dragged across his nose. It has been said that as a rule writers are not good businessmen, which is indeed true. On the other hand, if they were good businessmen they'd have too much sense to be writers.

love with the outstanding profile of the other clan, a formula which was well established when Shakespeare built a play called *Romeo and Juliet* on that same enduring foundation. Within the past eighteen months one of the movie companies insured double success by combining both these orthodox recipes into a large and soppy six-reel dose. The facts that the district which produced the enduring feuds never produced any first-rate race horses and that the district which produced the horseflesh never produced any Grade-A feuds, didn't matter in the least to the two gifted young Southerners—one from South Brooklyn and the other from South Odessa—who turned out the script. P. S.—The picture was widely acclaimed as true to life and grossed several millions.

And, of course, on other counts I hopelessly was out of the running. None of my forebears bred a handicap entry or bushwhacked a tribal enemy from behind a brush fence. Nor was there among them a single one who sat on the infirm porch of a tumbledown mansion, cursing the blue-bellies and trimming his goatee and his frayed cuffs with a pair of hedge shears. Lacking the proper traditional credentials, I likewise lacked in my own self, the requisite qualities. For behold, I am an indifferent equestrian. As a tipple I prefer beer to Bourbon. I never bet a tobacco crop on a single hand of poker; never owned a tobacco crop and if I did own one wouldn't bet it all on a single hand. The other fellow might hold better cards and I have a Scotch strain in me. I never shot anybody although once or twice I've been shot at while traveling at a high rate of speed. (I was going so fast that had I been hit I'm sure the bullet would have caused only a slight flesh wound.) So far as I have been able to judge, my blood is no hotter than the blood of the run of Northern-born persons. At least I've never felt any sensation as of passionate boiling in my arterial system. I've been mad but I've seen persons from other sections, from New England even, who seemed to be able to get just as mad as I did.

I never thought of myself, nor ever have spoken of myself as either Colonel or Major despite having four commissions as an honorary colonel—governors' staffs or such like—and one commission as major—Military Intelligence Section, O. R. C., U. S. A. I believe those embellishments should be worn only by those who have earned the right to wear them in the service of their country.

And where would your Typical Kentuckian be without a single martial title to his name?

Here is the most fatally disqualifying handicap of all: I do not recall ever having referred, either within earshot of him or behind his back, to a negro employee as "a kinky-headed black rabbit" or a "trifling old he-coon." In my youth I was discouraged—forcibly, if necessary—from indulging in such pleasantries and of recent years, since the race grew more aggressively race-conscious, I should have restrained any such latent impulses, even had I had them, on the grounds of prudence, if not on the premise that needlessly to hurt the feelings of a fellow creature isn't smart, isn't even decent.

Running true to type is frequently so difficult, imposing as it does a severe strain upon the candidate who wishes to be typical and yet lacks the expected characteristics. Stonewall Jackson, the Southern infantryman, was in temperament, religion, habit of life and all his Cromwellian qualities the absolute personification of Puritanism, while George Custer, the Northern cavalryman, with his dash, his long hair and his bizarre uniforms, might have posed for the idealized portrait of the ideal Cavalier. Excusing political convictions and his way of pronouncing divers words, my friend of many years, Charles M. Palmer, the veteran newspaper broker, has all the conceived attributes of the perfected Southern gentleman: his reverence for women, his chivalric courtesy to every human being with whom he comes in contact, his charitable estimates, his generosity, his love of the outdoors, his gracious hospitality; and yet C. M. was born in Wisconsin of Vermont parentage, had divided his active life between upper California and northern New York State and principally knows the South by what he sees as a winter visitor to fishing waters among the Florida Keys. On the other hand, I know a citizen of the Deep South, his people having been Southerners for several generations, who with no make-up, could play the flinty-hearted father in any Down-East rural drama— you know, the iron-jawed, saw-voiced old codger with an eye in his head like an undertaker's night bell, who can hardly wait for a driving snow storm to throw an erring daughter out into.

Reviewing the lists of those whom I intimately have known, I think of but two men who, in every outward regard and in every inner quality were flawlessly representative of their respective types: Will Rogers the actor and Charley Russell the artist, the closest of friends in this life and in death destined eternally to be comrades still, for Will's statue stands in Statuary Hall at Washington and Charley's will be there keeping it company, as soon as his state comes to realize who her greatest adopted son was.

In a way these twain were so alike and yet, if you knew the differential shadings of the real West, each so distinctively marked by his sectional environment and his separate mode of upbringing. Both were true philosophers, though Will's philosophy was worldly-wise while Charley's horizon was more or less parochial. Will was part Cherokee—on both sides of his family—but did not in the least suggest a man of Indian blood, whereas Charley, who was of the pure Anglo-Saxon breed, needed only to dye his long hair and put brown-red paint on his face to be as Indian-looking as Tecumseh was, or Kicking Bear. Both were humorists; not wits or wags, but true humorists. Charley's chief forte was in storytelling and in coining homely epigrams. America knows him as the only rival Frederic Remington had as a painter of the vanished border country, but some of us knew him—and still mourn him—as probably the greatest repositor and expositor of the frequently ribald but always racy folklore of forgotten mining camps and plowed-under cattle trails that ever lived. Some of his deftly fabricated yarns, part fact, part fable—"Piano Jim and the Impotent Pumpkin Vine"; "Shep the Sheepherder versus the High Velocity Cheese"; "Kalispel's Tubercular Horse Thief and the Compassionate Stranger"; "Rawhide Rawlins' Indisposed Bobcat"—these and a dozen more are classics and deserve to be. The pity is there is none left who can render them as Charley did.

Will never told an out-and-out anecdote in his life. He told me he never had tried. But at deft turns of speech and racy metaphors by which a whole cosmic aspect was summed up in a small mouthful of tangy words, he had mighty few equals since Benjamin Franklin, and fewer still since Abraham Lincoln. Will loved speech-making and no wonder, for he was a wizard at it. Charley probably never talked standing up in his life. He hunkered on his heels and let wisdom seep out of the squeezed corner of his lips like sugar dripping from a sugar tree. Will liked crowds and excitement and the glare of the limelight. Charley sought the solitudes and hated being fussed over. While Russell lived he admired Rogers as he admired hardly any other and when Russell died, Rogers wrote, as a preface to a posthumorously published book of Charley's writings, one of the most beautifully simple, most loving and lovable tributes that ever was penned in memory of a departed comrade.

Will was absolutely the Oklahoman. No mistaking that if you were familiar with the fenced-in prairies and the tidy homesteads of modernized Oklahoma. Charley was the very embodiment of the open range men of the high country, before barbwire came, and nesters to rip up the buffalo grass by the roots and spoil the grazing forever and grow one good grain crop and two poor ones and then see the harrowed land become a Dust Bowl. His drawl still bespoke the Missouri of his boyhood, but his sentiments and his prejudices and his affections were those of the early Montanan. Will rejoiced that the former Indian territory had oil wells now and sky scrapers and scientifically rotated crops. Charley bemoaned the passing of the unbitted Northwest, nor ever could reconcile himself to dude ranches and paved roads straddling the passes between the peaks. He proclaimed that a transplanted Corn Belter was akin to the clods his plowshare turned up, and that moving-picture cowboys were stains on a decadent civilization.

To him intensified agriculture was another name for intensified destruction. For proof of this contention he pointed out how by unneeded irrigation projects and reclamation schemes the immemorial roosting beds and breeding places of the wild fowl had been spoiled to create farms where already there were farms being abandoned, and how the thickets which were the natural sanctuaries of the four-footed creatures had been shorn away so that soil erosions followed and noxious weeds sprang up on the bald clearings. Even the deserts had been irrigated until they broke out with a nettle rash of garden truck—artificially forced harvests which in bad years failed to return a profit and in other years produced so great a yield that the surplusage rotted in the furrows for lack of a market. These may not have been Charley's exact words but they were planks in his platform of protestation, and helped to explain why he so loved the craggy uplands. Meddling mankind might pick and potter at their bases and mess up their lower slopes with its sapping and mining operations but hadn't yet found a way, he said, to mar the mysteries and disfigure the shapes of the main range; that he figured would come with the forward march of industry and progress. So he spent at least five months of every year in the shadow of the still unspoiled Rockies.

Playing the part of a rival steamboat captain, I worked with Will in the last picture he ever made, the one called *Steamboat Round the Bend*. For our first day together we joined John Ford, the director, at Sacramento aboard a superannuated broad-beamed stern-wheeler which had been camouflaged in an effort to make her resemble an old-time Mississippi river packet.

"Gentlemen," said Ford, with just a whiff of sarcasm in his tones, "I don't suppose either of you has gone so far as to read the script for this production?"

"Who, me?" said Will, in pretended surprise. "When did I ever read one of those fool things? I been too busy roping calves and romancing around."

"How about you, Mr. Cobb?" inquired Ford, formally.

"Oh, I took one glance at it," I said, taking cue from Will. "And then I quit. I could write a better script than that with one hand and Eugene O'Neill tied behind my back."

"Permit me to explain—if I'm not boring you?" said Ford. "In the opening sequence you, Mr. Cobb, are in the pilothouse of your boat *Pride of Paducah*. Will comes butting in to tell you he's just bought the *Claremore Queen* which is a little old wreck of a condemned ferryboat. So you start twitting him about being stung on the deal. And so on and so on, back and forth for about four minutes. Now then, I might suggest that you rehearse the routine along that general line, just ad libbing as you go."

"Listen, Cobb," said Will, "let's humor the poor Mick. But to keep down heartburning and ill feelings, I'll make up all your speeches for you and you make up all my speeches for me. F'rinstance, you'll say, 'William, how does your corporosity seem to segashuate this mornin'?' or something original like that. And then I'll come gallavanting back at you with some gag that's just as snappy."

So for twenty minutes, while a large and expensive cast and a technical crew seventy-odd strong fidgeted about, and several hundred extras in costumes simmered pleasantly under the ardent sun of a California midsummer, we raked each other with cross fires; at the end of which time Ford held up his hand.

"That's fine," he explained, "that's certainly mighty fine dialogue. This show is supposed to be laid along back about eighteen-ninety and so you've brought in the New Deal and Madame Perkins and Aimee Semple McPherson and Mae West and Dizzy Dean and a lot of other interesting topics, for all of which I'm naturally grateful. Please though, do me one small favor. Just once in a while mention the plot, won't you? With your gifts I'm sure you can work it into the conversation naturally and casually." His voice changed from a soothing Celtic monotone to the sharp-cornered accents of the Maine coast where he was born and fetched up: "And now, you two crooks, you'll play this scene and play it right or I'll have you thrown into the river—and I hope neither one of you can swim."

Even so, a good many of the lines that percolated into the sound tracks of that picture did not come out of the book. On the last day of shooting, back at the studio, I came off our set to find Will sitting on the running board of his car with a portable typewriter balanced on his knees, pecking out his daily syndicate stint. I tried to slip by him unobserved.

"Hey, hold on," he said. "I been waiting for you. Let's go to Santa Monica Canyon and ride up to the back end of my ranch. I want you to see the new cabin I'm building back in the hills. We'll dedicate it some night soon by sleeping in it; you and me and Leo Carrillo and Fred Stone—if those two suckers'll promise not to snore."

I explained that I had a writing job on the scaffolding at home and must do some carpentering and joining on it.

"Aw, come on," he begged. "I'll even let you ride Soapsuds. And I'll follow along behind and watch you. There may be some people who think you're kind of humorous. They oughter see you straddling a bronc on a rough trail. That's where you're shore-nuff funny."

I waved my hand in farewell and hurried off. I was afraid I would succumb to temptation.

"Better change your mind, old-timer," he called after me. "I may not be seeing you again for quite a spell."

He was right about that. Two days later he and Wiley Post started off for their Alaska trip in Post's plane.

Since Will's death some people have popularized a statement attributed to him as characteristic—so in their guilelessness they think it to be—of his attitude to life. They love to quote the line, "I've poked fun at all of the big men of my time but I never met a man I didn't like."* Now I am in position to testify that he couldn't possibly have designed that this should be interpreted literally. Every person who enjoyed close contacts with him could testify to the same effect. Will Rogers was as shrewd a judge of human nature as I have known. His estimates almost invariably were generous and his philosophy was colored by his innate kindliness and in print he refrained always from blasting at individuals, contenting himself rather with ridiculing the issues for which they might stand. But he neither was sappy nor overly sentimental. His charity was deep as a well, but it wasn't as wide as the ocean, nor should it have been. He had his favorites and his antipathies and privately he never hesitated to express these judgments in salty language. During his most tolerant moments I can no more imagine him having a mushy softness in his soul for the kidnaper of the Lindbergh baby or for Hickman the child-killer, or H. H. Holmes the wholesale murderer, or "Old Creepy" Karpis, or Jesse Pomeroy the torturing

---

* He was quoted as saying that were this line carved on his tombstone, he would come back after he was gone and read it. But I make so bold as to say that a fitter epitaph for Will or for Charley or Kin Hubbard or Don Marquis or Oliver Herford or that grand old mountain of a man, Opie Read, or any one of a precious departed coterie that I have known, would be found in those vainglorious words—vainglorious but bespeaking to a fuddled universe oh, so laudable an intent—the words which Shakespeare put in Jaques' mouth, to wit:

". . . Motley's the only wear. . . . I am ambitious for a motley coat. . . . I must have liberty withal, as large a charter as the wind, to blow on whom I please; for so fools have. . . . Invest me in my motley; give me leave to speak my mind, and I will through and through cleanse the foul body of the infected world, if they will patiently receive my medicine."

fiend, or Mrs. Guinness, the marrying Indiana lady who killed off husbands partly for sport and partly in the line of a thriving matrimonial business—conceivably all of them persons he might have encountered in their lifetimes and in his lifetime—than I can imagine one of these degenerate worms as being worthy of the regard, let alone the pity, of decent-minded people. I'm sure that what Will intended to say was that he had met all the big men of his time, but never met a man (among those big men) that he did not like.

I think one of the happiest summers I ever spent was the summer we had a cottage on Lake McDonald in Glacier National Park. Charley Russell and Nancy Russell were in camp down at the foot of the lake, six miles below the cottage we had leased from John Lewis, proprietor of Lewis' famous hotel. When Charley wasn't painting a picture or modeling in clay or writing one of his designedly illiterate humorous sketches, he was likely to be sitting on our front porch at the edge of the water, where the Rockies were humping up their spiny backs like angry cats behind us, and across to the south was a view of the saddle in the mountains where the transcontinental trains dipped through. Sitting there one afternoon he held up to the light a pair of smeared and blurry glasses and said to his wife:

"Hon, why is it these here specks of mine always look like windows in a hen house?"

"When did you wash them last?" she inquired.

"Only yestiddy," he stated. "Or maybe the day before."

"Too bad you don't wash your thumbs at the same time," she snapped tartly. The Lady Nancy had a clever tongue of her own.

In a parched but breezy August a forest fire threatened the middle gateway to the Park. Every able-bodied adult at the entrance joined the fight of saving the splendid timber which clothed those notched foothills under the shoulders of the Great Divide. Day and night men worked to check the roaring, swirling, mounting façade of flames; worked until all of them were black as sweeps and choked with resiny fumes, worked until some dropped in their tracks and might have burned to death had there been no volunteer rescue crews to drag them away. Under a false twilight of smoke, the women trudged back and forth in the defending lines, with sandwiches and coffee and drinking water and some of them carried

first-aid kits for blistered faces and streaming eyes, and some risked
their lives by venturing deep into the imperiled pinelands with
rations for the front skirmishers.

A change in the wind saved the little settlement of Belden, on
the state road piercing the main gap. The nearermost sparks were
beaten out at the back side of the Russells' stable yard. That was
how close a call the village had. On that last day the park rangers
evacuated everybody in the colony and brought the lot of them up
to Lewis'. Hundreds slept in the hotel that night, and strangers
were stretched on pallets upon every spare foot of space on the
floors of our cottage and temporarily homeless families were quartered in a double row of log cabins along the lake shore on beyond us.

The Russells, with their adopted son Jack, occupied one of these
cabins. Just across the narrow footpath from them, a Belden transient, an itinerate photographer by trade, was domiciled. Having
been compelled to abandon his shop, this refugee arrived, it would
seem, in a state of low spirits and, presumably to comfort himself,
he spent practically the entire night practicing on a slide trombone
which he had fetched along with him. The selection chosen to
lighten his gloom was the hymn "Nearer My God to Thee," an
appropriate choice, the governing circumstances considered. But
since the saddened instrumentalist knew only the first bar of "Nearer
My God to Thee," he played it over and over again a thousand times,
and never seemed to get any nearer.

Next morning after breakfast I came along the trail between
the twinned lines of cabins. Charley, worn by a sleepless night
and with a murderous glint in his reddened eyes, was sitting on the
slab doorstep of his cabin. He hailed me:

"Old Cobb,"* he said, "would you maybe like to buy one of
these here slip horns at a bargain?"

----

* Charley was twelve or fifteen years my senior but he always
called me "Old Cobb." But to Andy Mack, the singing comedian,
I was, for no reason that I could fathom, "Sheriff." A third friend,
Charles R. Flint, taking advantage of the fact that I had been given
honorary degrees by Dartmouth and by the University of Georgia,
thereafter gravely hailed me as "Doctor," while no doubt chuckling
inwardly at the joke of it. And when I was a boy I gathered nick-
names as a cow's tail gathers cockleburs. I think in various stages of

"Well, now, Mr. Russell," I said, "you take me by surprise but on first thought I would say, with a reasonable degree of certainty, that at present I am not in the market for a slip horn."

"Better think it over," he said. "There's a man's hide goes with this one."

One of the most engaging of the near-by sojourners was an ex-cowman who had wandered afar from his native Panhandle, with a string of ponies. His father must have been somewhat of an extremist as a patriot, for he had named his four sons after four of the cities of his beloved state—Waco, Dallas, Austin and Tyler. Our neighbor was Dallas—Dallas Desbro. From him I purchased four travel-worn Texas ponies and for the season he threw in the use of bridles and stock saddles. I think he rather overcharged me but the Cobbs, like the elephant, never forget and in the fall before we left I got even with him. I gave him back the four plugs and left him stuck with them and winter coming on and the sucker crop gone from Glacier. It was indeed a fiendish revenge.

My steed was a reformed cowhorse, a steep-gabled high-ribbed structure which, being of a prevalent biege tone, would anywhere in the West inevitably be known as "Buckskin." But because of a certain attribute he shared with a lifelong comrade of mine, I rechristened him "Bob Davis"—he ate everywhere he could stop and stopped everywhere he could eat. In his youth, it was said, he had been a snaky and unpredictable animal, freely addicted to scolloping, sunfishing and swapping ends with himself. But the years were supposed to have sapped his enthusiasms.

One afternoon I decided to go for a ride on the government

---

my youth I must have worn a dozen different ones, none of them exactly complimentary, either. I've been proud though of two of my extra names, both gifts from red tribesmen. By formal adoption into the Blackfoot confederacy I wear one of the oldest tribal names "Petok Pekos"—Eagle's Rib. Catlin painted the portrait of the first Eagle's Rib. But because a clever little squaw scored on me when I tried to be smart at her expense I more familiarly am known on the northern Montana reservations as "The Fat Liar." In New York State I'm qualified to call myself by the Iroquois entitlement of "Rohni Kon Riyo" but—accuse me of being coy and hoydenish about it if you choose—I'm not translating the meaning of those three words.

highway then building up toward the great ramparts of the towering Garden Wall. The remaining members of the household were
otherwise engaged and so when I mounted Bob Davis and undertook to ride him out of the improvised corral behind our cottage,
he balked; he didn't want to leave his three mates at the feed rack.
I raked his corrugated withers with a pair of inefficient Central
Park spurs and slapped him between two stubbornly cocked ears
with my hat—and lo, he had left in his usually sedate system a few
unexpended bucking gestures and, without warning, he arched his
spine and sank his head and put them on, with intent pronto to pour
me out of the saddle.

The first stiff-legged lunge jolted me so high aloft I could see
distant peaks I never had seen before. I had ample time for deciding
where I would come down, so I decided to come down somewhere
on his upper plane surfaces. So I alighted on his rump, away back
by his tail roots, and slid forward. And the next trip down I straddled his neck and slid backward; and next time after that I descended solidly in the center of him and I could feel some of his
vital organs fetching loose from their moorings and seemed to
hear these detached contents sloshing about inside of him. So to
make a mutually painful story no more painfully prolonged than
needs be, when he quit, with his quivering legs widely braced and
his sides heaving like a captive balloon and his humiliated nose in
the dust, I still was aboard.

All through this Charley had been perched on the top rail of
the fence, intently eying the proceedings. Now he climbed down
and calipered on his bowed legs over to where I sat, breathless
but triumphantly enthroned, and he took my free hand and warmly
he shook it and said:

"Old Cobb, you've been norratin' around that you're no fancy
rider. Me, I claim after seein' this here exhibition, that you're better'n average. I admit your system is different from any I ever saw,
but there ain't a way for any four-legged critter to beat it. I figger
you must be part eagle. Why, you just natchelly hover over a
hoss!"

That winter, on Mrs. Cobb's urgings and with Mrs. Russell reinforcing the effort, he came to New York to consult a specialist
about the thyroid trouble which at a time not far away was to kill

him. He came against his will for he didn't like New York. He said that by the processes of methodical evolution, springing out of the Machine Age, the future resident of New York wouldn't need a brain because everything automatically would be thought out for him from a central powerhouse; and he would have only rudimentary traces of legs since walking would be abolished; would have eyes like a Mammoth Cave fish, since groping in the eternal gloom between the skyscrapers would have dimmed his sight; would consist, in short, of a mechanical steering apparatus, a shrunken stomach and one enormously overdeveloped thumb—for pressing push buttons with. Nevertheless, Charley stayed for a couple of homesick weeks and made a picturesque sight in what his fellow artist from the West, Ed Borein, calls "cattlein' clothes"—circus-ring hat, spindle-heeled Justin boots, loose-collared shirt and a woven Navaho sash cinched about his middle. Entirely without self-consciousness, he wore these trappings wherever he went and was oblivious to the rude stares of the city jaspers.

Through some curious quirk, he desired the experience of riding on the subway. He kept hinting that he figured one trip would satisfy his yearnings but he wanted that trip. So choosing a time when the rush hour would be at its horrid worst, I led him down into a maze of those underground miseries and rammed him aboard a local which already contained twice as many human kippers as it was meant to hold. I dragged him off at the first express stop and rushed him across to the opposite edge of the jammed platform and by main strength inserted him into another train. At Brooklyn Bridge station I plucked him forth from the press of massed, mashed and mishandled passengers and brought him up into the blessed resurrection of daylight. I waited while he rubbed his trodden-on toes and smoothed down his rumpled mane and then I asked him how he liked it and would he prefer to go back to Times Square by the same tube, or take a taxi?

He seemed not to hear me, but peered down the smelly bore of the dreadful sap-work from which he had been delivered. Presently he spoke:

"Well, sir, Old Cobb, it's funny, but sometimes a stranger can happen along and work out a thing that all these millions of poor unfortunate shiftless people that live in this town have just allowed themselves to be plum' licked by. Well, I guess they're feeble-minded to start with or they wouldn't go on livin' here. So we mustn't blame 'em for overlookin' the bet. Now you take this here tunnel that's weevelin' along down under us. Me, I go for just one ride on her and I figure out a scheme for gettin' a seat on a subway train that nobody else ever thought of. It's simple: All you got to do is find out where they build the cars and go get aboard one before it's finished."

When he and Nancy started west it was agreed that next year we would have a reunion in Pasadena, where they spent their winters. That following autumn Mrs. Cobb and I went to Italy and stayed there until our granddaughter was born. On the night our ship docked, we having already planned to start for California almost immediately, friends met us on the pier with the news: Charley was dead and all the flags in Great Falls were half-masted and the hearts of all those people out there were at half-mast too.

So another one was gone who made a hole in the world when he left it.

33

THIS AND THAT AND TUMBLEWEEDS

I KNOW that Charley Russell, the salt of this earth that he was, took with him into the On Beyond his pet aversions—dislike for the well-meaning homesteaders who hadn't been content to bide on in their flat Middle West and grow tall corn and the succulent wheat, but must invade his beloved stamping ground and eternally ruin its free grazing with their farming ideas. And he nourished a positive hate for the mistreatment by government functionaries of the beaten hapless fragments of the Indian tribes, those agency prisoners who were the miserable remnants of the haughty Blackfeet and the fierce Sioux and the fighting Crows, the same once-proud braves that he so loved to put upon canvas in colors that glowed like polished jewels.

On a certain night a trainload of officials of the Great Northern Railway and their guests from the East were being entertained in the huge lobby of the Lewis Hotel at Lake McDonald. A little group of Blackfeet, who had been imported from the Browning reservation to provide local color for the visitors and to cadge nickels and dimes out of those visitors, were putting on a pitiable imitation of some of their tribal rites. They offered the hybridized Owl Dance and corrupted bits of ancient sun chants, and half-hearted demonstrations of that most beautiful and graphic of oral manuals—the sign talk of the plains people. The finish of the dreary routine (excepting the passing of the hat for contributions) was according to formula, which meant that one by one the bucks stood up in their bedraggled war bonnets, and through the interpreter repeated the same sorry patter: how glad they were to welcome the beloved white brother to this, their former hunting ground in Glacier Park, and to share with him its beauties and how grateful they were to the Great White Father at Washington and to the Interior Department for this opportunity to express their heartfelt sentiments.

Last of all there rose up on his crooked pins, old Eagle's Rib, an authentic chief of the Piegans, and a confirmed irreconcilable. He straightened his rheumatic back and tightened his blanket about his withered loins and for a moment stood in silence and looked us over. Magically his degradation seemed to slip from him. He lifted his seamed old face above the heads of the crowd and spat out a string of harsh gutterals, then abruptly squatted down again, his brooding eyes fixed on the floor boards.

The interpreter, a Carlisle graduate, was embarrassed and sputtered for a moment and then blurted out that Eagle's Rib agreed with what his fellow tribesman had said; whereupon Yellow Wolf's widow and Night Shot's squaw made ready to take up the collection.

"Two Stabs is coverin' up something," whispered Russell to me where we stood at the back of the audience. "That's not what Eagle's Rib said—not if I read the look in his face while he was sayin' it. Wait until this fool mummery is over with and we'll find out."

When the excursionists had scattered, we cornered young Mr. Louis Two Stabs. "Come clean, boy," said Charley. "Give us the right translation of that last speech."

This, by the interpreter's way of telling it, was the true version:

"Eagle's Rib says that he has heard this false talk about love for the white brothers until his ears hurt. Eagle's Rib says that before the white man came the Siksika [Blackfoot Confederacy] owned these mountains and these valleys as they always had owned them. They did not give them away, they did not sell them. These lands were stolen from them because they did not know that the white man talked with a tongue that forked two ways, like the snake's tongue; and because they did not know they were being cheated out of this land which had come down to them from their fathers.

"Before the white man came the Indian was a free man. He went where he pleased, hunted and fished and camped where he pleased. He was free like the buffalo and the elk. He was as free to range as Anikos [the antelope]. When he dreamed the spirits talked back to him from across the Sand Hills and Napi [Messiah] walked with him in the daytime; and the Seven Peculiar Persons [Pleiades] helped make light for him to walk by in the night-time.

"Now Anikos had been slaughtered and Napi had gone forever and the Indian is not his own master any more. He must mind the agent, must mind the schoolteacher, must mind the white coat [doctor], must do what the black robes [preachers] and the Cross men [priests] tell him to do. He must ask leave to come and go. He is penned up like the sheep and herded like the cows. There is a fence in front of his face. There is a gate that is locked.

"Before the white man came the Indian lived on real food [red meat]. *Now he eats carrots!"*

"And if you know how an Indian hates carrots you begin to get the rough idea," said Russell to me. "Well, I hate 'em myself. I'll go over and congratulate the old boy. I don't know many words of his language, and probably he doesn't know mine—although you never can tell about that among Indians—but he'll understand. In our hearts we speak the same thoughts."

I judge he was right because a minute later I saw him with his arm about the old man's shoulders and that dignified red conservative did not push it away, either, although I'm sure he would have resented such a liberty if taken by any king or potentate.

Charley reserved the most sulphurous corner of his private Gehenna for tourists—not for all tourists but for the tourists who defiled beauty spots with their leavings of banana peels and dillpickle butts and Sunday supplements and empty pop bottles. Also the tourists whose carelessness in the matter of campfires and lighted cigarette ends had turned thousands of square miles of virgin timber into smutted desolations. And the tourists who desecrated natural grandeur by splattering their inconsequential names on noble landmarks and tall cañon walls—well, for these offenders language failed him. Likewise and most especially he abhorred the tourists who strolled, without being asked, into the lodges and the houses of the Indians and fingered what to the dwellers there were private things and holy things, and poked with insulting thumbs the breastbone of some veteran warrior and said, "Heap big chief, huh?" And then went hence and told their fellows that it must indeed be true—

what people said about the Indian being inscrutable and taciturn and never smiling. Naturally they wouldn't know, that sort wouldn't, that the members of one of the most talkative, most gossipy races on earth—under suitable conditions—and of a race that love a joke and amongst themselves love to laugh—might resent having their privacy profaned and their most sacred possessions pawed over by impious hands; and might show that resentment, not by speaking their minds, being a courteous and dignified breed except for those sycophantic few amongst them who had picked up the white man's manners, but by going into the silences.

After spending the summer on the grounds of a resort hotel I was ready to cheer when Charley sprinkled the self-recharging vials of his vitriol on these pesky parties. Indeed I could broaden my indictment to cover a wider territory than his because I had been abroad and there had opportunity to observe characteristic subclasses of the tourist tribe, including several commoner American varieties, whereas Charley's studies now were confined to domestic specimens. But he took my word for what I had seen various curious bipeds do and say; and between us we agreed that a certain type of tourist, whether encountered locally or on foreign soil, might very well be likened to the tumbleweed of our western prairies, a weed which is innoxious enough so long as it stays put and only begins to attract unfavorable attention when it starts traveling.

To flee from a locust-like visitation of clacking round-trippers into the hidden refuges off the public trails was a balm for the bruised and pestered spirit. But when the big excursion trains had disgorged their patrons into the park, a fellow might have to bore deeply into the untrodden places and endure some fairly rough traveling before he could be sure of his escape from the autograph hound and the snapshot fiend and the plain or common old-style open-face gawper. Yet the brooding peacefulness of it when finally he arrived compensated for the small hardships of getting there.

You would penetrate the range to where some great naked, unnamed peak thrust its snowy pinnacles high above the lofty trackless pine-clad escarpments at its base, offering sanctuary for the golden eagle and the hermit thrush—the "lonesome bird" as the lumberjack calls him—and for the wild sheep and the wild goat, but defying puny, prying mankind to invade its ridged preserves. And to yourself as you stood there, inviting your soul, you would say that when the human poachers had trespassed upon all accessible spots on the face of the hemisphere this, the matchless handiwork of the high gods, still would endure through the centuries, unscathed and unmarred, inviolate and unassailable.

Then though would come a discomforting thought: What's the use of daydreaming a pleasant future for this mountain? Sooner or later Gutzon Borglum is bound to find it.

Since civil war smashed it and Franco took over the broken shards of it, I don't know whether this commendable distinction still applies to Spain, but ten years ago it was to me the most attractive country in Europe because of being mercifully free of ultra-aggressive tourists out of Britain and America, those children of a spurious prosperity who had infiltrated into the rest of the Continent and were slathering their money about regardless. Depression diminished this flood to trickling runlets and took some of the gallus cocksureness out of the chastened survivors, but even before hard times decimated their ranks Spain comparatively had escaped the invasions of these modern Goths and Vandals. Seemingly she preferred the dignity and peace of her poverty, her rags and her hunger to sponging on the bounty of the prodigal foreign hordes. Outside of the larger cities, no concentrated effort to draw the transient trade was evident. Even in the cities, once one passed beyond the smartened shopping zones and the garish big hotels, one found the unsullied habits and customs of the poor, proud land of Old Spain still firmly established. Enter some small shop in some crooked, quiet bystreet and rap smartly on a showcase and snap out with, "Say, Mister, a little quick service here if you don't mind," and the woodbine would be trailing over you before either proprietor or clerk gave you more than an indifferent glance. But open the door and sweep off your hat and say, "God be with all here," and this one would hasten to dust off a chair for you and that one would be offering you wine or coffee, at least the weird infusion which these people mistook for coffee; and the sonorous *r* would be rolling grandly forth as though issuing from the throats of cock pigeons. And the utterly unimportant detail of selling you something could wait until the social amenities had been exchanged.

It was a grand sensation to feel that nobody was in a swivet to charge you three prices for an article or hornswoggle you out of your small change or wheedle and cringe and beg in an effort to unload on you additional commodities that you didn't want. From Andalusian grandee in flowing cape and flat black sombrero to barefoot gypsy beggar wearing no shirt at all and only part of a pair of trousers, everyone was a gentleman who wasn't a lady—or anyhow had the bearing of a gentleman.

I recall a small illustration of the point I would make. Will Hogg and I were motoring northward along the Spanish Riviera. Above Barcelona, in the thickening gloom of a rainy afternoon, we came upon a big expensive car canted far over sideways, with two of its wheels, one fore and one aft, bogged to the hub in a loblolly of tough yellow clay, the other pair being on a one-way ribbon of new concrete where workmen had been tearing up and replacing with modern paving the road that Augustus Caesar built by the labor of Iberian slaves. Obviously the passengers in the tilted car must be English. Who but English people would load the roof of a tonneau three tiers deep with so many portable belongings—cases, trunks, hat boxes, carryalls, Gladstone bags, steamer rugs in rolls, golf bags, paper parcels, collapsible bath tub, tea caddy, lunch kit and probably a framed steel engraving of the death of Lord Nelson, just to give a homy touch to a hotel suite? All the impedimenta were here which any well-to-do English family would carry along if embarking on a whole fortnight of travel. Inside were two rather overdressed and highly prosperous-looking women, an oldish one and a youngish one: mother and daughter, you would have guessed. A Cockney chauffeur, his smart uniform smeared with grime, was in the mire up to his shanks, hopelessly poking at a mud-bolstered tire. The seemingly aimless pilgrimage which toward sundown invariably fills a Spanish road no matter how deserted it may have been in the foreparts of the day, was drifting by—peasants and laborers on donkey-back, on foot and on creaky two-wheeled carts, all wearing the red stocking-cap of the Catalan country and nearly all the old men with short side whiskers bracketing their iron-hard faces which were such faces as Velásquez loved to paint. The head of the halted party, a stumpy-legged, short-coupled individual with new-rich Londoner written all over him, was stationed behind his stalled Rolls Royce sulkily regarding the passing caravan and cursing in a despondent way.

We halted in their rear. We had to halt even had we desired to keep going. For their shipwreck blocked the channel.

"Brother," said Will in his friendly Texas fashion, "it looks sorta like you're in the middle of a fix."

"Bloody awful!" lamented the little man in the catarrhal whine of his native East End. "This ruddy ass gets us stalled and 'ere we've been for an hour an' a 'arf. I've made signs to these blighting perishers trooping past. And look—" he hauled out of a pocket of his plaid knickers a fist full of paper currency—"I've waved all this under their silly noses time and again, but do you think a single johnny would try to 'elp us out of this mess? Not a bloody one of 'em. Just look at me as though I was something unpleasant, if you get wot I mean. And keep on going. Wot a country!"

"Maybe you didn't go about it the right way," said Will.

"Wot!" He fairly shrieked it, and capered about. " 'Ow much more money do these burglars want before they'll condescend to 'elp a chap?"

"That's probably the trouble," said Will. "You keep that bankroll out of sight while we go into a huddle with this boy here," indicating the driver of our chartered car.

Our driver was a German who knew a little Spanish and some English, not much though. We made it clear to him that he was to stand by and piece out the conversation if Will's linguistic repertoire broke down on him.

Honestly, I didn't think he had it in him. But their place in Texas history during the past hundred years proves the Hoggs are a resourceful breed. From an approaching clump of twenty or thirty foot passengers Will singled out a thin little priest in a shabby gown and bowed to him. The priest bowed back and all his fellow pedestrians pulled off their caps too and Will braced himself and made oration, with the German lad now and then throwing in a needed word.

The gist of the speech was as follows: This visiting nobleman and his ladies, engaged on a tour of the beautiful land of Spain, had met with an accident, as was plain to see. Therefore they entreated the assistance of these courteous passers-by—here with a wide-armed gesture Will included all the tattered laymen within hearing—in extricating them from their difficulties. For any succor which the assembled señors might in the goodness of their hearts be moved to offer, the beneficiaries thereof would eternally be grateful.

The padre set the example by tucking up his own skirts and kicking off his buckled shoes. But, with all respect to him, the squad elbowed him aside. They threw themselves at the foundered car, laid hold on it, set a convenient timber under the rear axle and found a purchase for it, and with one great gruntful heave they bodily lifted the whole thing out of the quagmire and back once more on solid footing. The Londoner hauled out his handful of bills again, but again Will checked him.

"Not like that," he warned. "Want to make these nice people mad after the way they came to your rescue? You can't tip them for a service like this. Lemme handle this, pards."

From the roll he stripped the outer layers and as he slipped the largess into the little cleric's grasp he somehow haltingly explained— and now I was prouder of him than ever—that nothing would give the visiting don more joy than to accompany the company to the nearest *bodega* and there join with them in a suitable libation on the altar of friendship and international comity. But alas, his two donnas were greatly fatigued and most desirous of reaching their destination before night set in. So under the circumstances he was asking the good father to lead the flock to a suitable place of entertainment and there, at his expense and in his name, drink a toast to their respective countries. *Viva* Spain! *Viva* England! *Viva*— Will threw it in for good measure—*viva* the imperial Lone Star State and its queen city of Houston!

To all of which the priest, as chairman of the rescuing committee, agreed after first taking a vote on the proposition so elegantly set forth by the visiting *hidalgo's* competent spokesman. With every head bared they cheered us wildly as we chugged away.

It couldn't have happened anywhere except in rural Spain. I wonder if now it would happen even there. Fascism kills good manners, I'm told.

Even if we hadn't remembered sleepily crossing the border

late that night, we would have had no doubt as to exactly where we were next morning. For the hotel which at 2:00 A.M. had taken us in—and continued to take us in all the while we stopped there—was one of those typical provincial hotels where the lavatory is always in use and the elevator never is. And the cashier, usually a dowdy female with a carefully tended pet mole on her chin, can make twenty bookkeeping mistakes a day, but never one which costs the house a single sou markee. And the proprietor is an unrepentant former bandit who quit banditry because catering to the non-resident trade pays better and is much safer. When Will found five separate and distinct overcharges in the bill covering lodgings and a meal apiece and when, in the lobby without, we heard a medley of the characteristic nasal tones of Lake Michigan's south bank uplifted in complaint that these crazy foreigners never had heard of ham and eggs for breakfast and wouldn't know a buckwheat cake if they met it in the middle of Michigan Boulevard; and what was there to see around this rube dump anyhow except some mouldy old cathedral or a bum art gallery or maybe a bunch of those lousy Roman ruins?—why, then, by this and by that, we were aware that we must be back once more in the Tourist Belt.

During the ensuing month we encountered and—for our amusement catalogued—the component variations of the species as noted among our fellow countrymen who congested the avenues and rattled through the sight-seeing districts and bought out the stocks of the luxury shops faster than the clerks could reload the shelves. For, as I have said, this was in the forepart of 1929, when the brokers and the bankers were doing so beautifully well for all the lads and lassies, and the only way to lose money in Wall Street was to stay out of Wall Street, and speculation wasn't really speculation, but merely investment against the future blossoming of a prosperity which could never wane; and we could take Uncle Andy Mellon's word for it, with Charley Mitchell and Wiggin and all the other true prophets of high finance to back it up; and such Happiness Boys as Charles M. Schwab and Owen D. Young and Roger Babson and General Hell-and-Maria Dawes coming in strong on the chorus. President Hoover likewise caught the contagion of joyous optimism. As I recall, he interpreted the break as a mere flurry to be followed by a temporary period of readjustment and

sifting out of true values from false. He said this even as the first
earthquake shook such great cracks in the beautiful castle of infla-
tion. That was more than eleven years ago and upwards of seventy
or eighty millions of us aren't what you'd call entirely readjusted
yet. We're resigned by now, but that's as far as it goes.

But I'm digressing. I recall the rough cataloguing Will Hogg
and I made that spring amongst the ranging tourist bands. From
memory I put down here some of the listings in our imaginary file
cabinet. For instance:

The gentleman who, after traveling three thousand miles to see
them, had been disappointed in the chastity belts at the Cluny
Museum, but partly was reconciled on finding the recent issues
of dirty photographs to be purchased along the Rue de la Paix
were up to his expectations. The Crash, when it came, was not altogether an unmixed catastrophe, for it sent this party back down the
toilet-trap to join his brother cockroaches.

The inflexible stalwart who couldn't find it in his heart to forgive the English for failing to recognize the fact that the only
proper treatment for a digestive tract is to drench it at least three
times a day, and preferably oftener, with ice water. Did they know
enough to put enough ice, if any, in a highball? And had they
ever heard of iced tea or a properly chilled cantaloupe? Hell, most
of 'em hadn't even heard of cantaloupes! If you weren't familiar
with this variety, you would think his father had been a Polar bear
and mama a refrigerator car.

The poor lady who was trying to absorb thirty centuries of
accumulated Old World art in ninety days; culture by speedometer,
as it were. Monday, see Venice; Tuesday morning, see Florence;
Tuesday afternoon, see Bologna; all of Wednesday and half of
Thursday, see Rome. When she wept at the tomb of Napoleon
it wasn't because she was sorry for Napoleon's folks. It was because her feet hurt her.

The compatriot who marveled at the roguish impulses of French
telephones and the obvious eccentricities of English dentistry as
compared with what Keokuk or Cripple Creek could offer. Despite
my prejudices against his kind, I cherished the observation of one
of this band: "After lookin' 'em over, I figure a feller in this country
gets himself some false teeth the way a man buys theater tickets

back home. Just walks up to a guy in a box office and slaps down eight bucks and says, 'Bo, give me a couple of good ones down front.'"

The English tourist, holding himself rigidly aloof from all casual contacts, maintaining indifference to all surrounding points of interest and silently but heartily abominating the perversity of a people who insist on speaking their own language when they might better employ their spare time learning English and copying English institutions which, being English, were, of course, incomparably superior to all other institutions.

The rich Argentino, whose wardrobe evidently was fabricated by a Parisian woman designer and whose reckless and profuse taste in jewelry was that of an impulsive Pullman porter.

The German tourist, stalking on ahead with a guide book and a meerschaum pipe while his *Frau* followed along carrying the heavy baggage.

The East Indian visitor of high degree whose Brahman tummy appeared to be in a state of active revolt against European cookery or possibly it was a cultivated affliction, since seemingly he regarded belches as apt retorts and a series of hiccoughs as an after-dinner speech.

And clustered thick along the French Riviera, the American-born expatriates, tourists once, but then numbered among the Mediterranean's scenic fixtures: Ambitious widows with marriageable daughters who hadn't yet spent all of father's life insurance money and still were hoping against hope for a pickup in the titled husband market; ladies of uncertain age but large fixed incomes and weather-proofed complexions and bracelets up to the elbows, zealously attended by gigolos and courted by moth-eaten princelings and by exiled pretenders to European thrones and by holders of dubious patents to nobility; American millionaires' sons who seemingly had taken an oath never to get sober again until Chollie Knickerbocker was elected President of the United States; kept husbands, fetching and carrying for imperious wives and reaching their top height of usefulness when taking Pompon the French poodle out for her evening's evening; former beauties of stage and screen vainly battling to fight away crow's-feet and pouchy chins by face-liftings and massages and reducing treatments and dyes and cosmetics, so that the fading blonde was painted all pinky pink and glossy white, like the wrapper on a cake of old-fashioned toilet soap, while the sepia shellac on the restored brunette imparted to her the glazed effect of a Chinatown duck.

The horrors of a war in Europe, terrible though they be, slightly are softened by the fact that then the eastward-flowing tourist tides turn around and run back the other way. However, the places of some of our homebound tumbleweeders were taken in the latter part of 1917 and even in the early part of 1918 by enthusiastic patriots who might better have stayed where they were, so really for a while there was no improvement to speak of in the crop. This was while we yet were amateurs at the thing, and our government still labored under the delusion that, in a general way of speaking, war was a game to be played at.

Indeed the truce of November, 1918, had been declared before some of our administrative bigwigs became entirely reconciled to the idea that on the whole war was by way of being a fairly serious undertaking. Almost up to Armistice, personal pulls, political influence, the weight of pressure groups among fraternal organizations and religious bodies, were being invoked to sanction the sending across of inquiring bands of well-meaning but bothersome non-belligerents, and with these, individual fuss-budgets, scramble-brains, notoriety-seekers, logrollers, thrill-hunters, so-called civilian observers and miscellaneous busybodies who looked on the gory proceedings as a sort of glorified peep show. They consumed victuals which might have stayed the stomachs of fighting men, and got underfoot and demanded attention and generally pestered the already sufficiently weary and bedeviled defenders of France; and what was worse still, by their blundering interferences they frequently hampered such functioning auxiliaries as the Red Cross and Y. M. C. A. and the K. C.'s and the Salvation Army.*

---

* Until I beheld with my own eyes what this devoted little band did for our boys overseas, it had appeared to me as I think it had appeared to many whose training had been along orthodox lines, that about the Salvation Army there was something trashy and vulgar, something designedly bombastic in its methods. But now I know better and the lesson abides with me. Since 1918 it has never seemed that the breezy, livening hymns of the street-corner meeting

There were four personable young women who turned up on that crucial hour when the hopes of the Allies were at the lowest ebb. They were trig as trout flies and streamlined like chimney swallows and beautifully glossy as to their complexions. None of this dull domestic finish for them. They wore striking uniforms obviously designed according to some Fifth Avenue dressmaker's idea of proper regalia for a lady ambulance driver and the way their Sam Browne belts fitted was something to write home about. But unfortunately they had forgotten to bring any ambulances along and I don't believe they'd have known how to drive them if they had. They had not qualified for nursing duties and one gathered that mere hospital chores or canteen jobs were beneath them. Eventually though they found their places, which was more than some of their discouraged fellow volunteers did. Against terrific competition by local practitioners of a very old profession, they set up as independent operators and flourished until their hotel proprietor asked them to leave. A lot of Americans have wondered what people have to do to be put out of a French hotel. Personally, I have always suspected that in this instance the established boulevard talent threatened to picket the establishment as unfair to home industry.

There were arriving at intervals congressional commissions de-

---

had cheapness in them, or that the spirit of consecration was any the less inspired because of drum-beatings and flag-wavings—yes, or that the Cross could lose one whit of its sanctity for Christians of any communion by association with the tambourine. For its limited funds—it had only dimes to spend where certain other service agencies had double eagles; for its small personnel; for the facilities given it, its Salvationists, with the doughnut for their wartime emblem and smiles to match the hot coffee they ladled for tired boys at the very edge of the trenches, accomplished absolute miracles. This is a statement to which I believe every veteran who lives today and has his memories of those days, will subscribe. Having seen them Over There, I have taken occasion to watch what they did afterward on behalf of broken and needy humans over here, especially in the no man's land of life—the places where despair and degradation otherwise would thrive like unregarded weeds. And wartime or peacetime, I stand ready to salute these people as what surely they are—the Shock Troops of the Lord.

manding official recognition and plentiful attention and being just
as futile as they might have succeeded in being had they stayed put
in Washington. There was one wealthy young woman of exalted
social station along the eastern seaboard who as early as the autumn
of 1917 had wangled her way across, prepared to be a veritable
deaconess of good deeds but lacking practical training or special
aptitude in any field. It wasn't long though before she had a corus-
cating idea. To signalize her country's belated participation in the
mess and as a gesture typical of our institutions, she proposed, at
her own expense, to provide a great Thanksgiving dinner in Paris—
a feast at which all the American aviators would be the honorary
hosts and to which all the French and British aviators would be
brought as special guests. She would scour France for turkeys. She
would import cranberries for sauce and the traditional pumpkins
for the pies, from America itself. She would feed the young heroes
until their outjutting stomachs pushed them back from the table.
She had launched the preparations when someone suggested that, as
a formality, it might be well to obtain the approval of the commanding generalissimos of the three armies. What was her chagrin
to discover that the mean old things could not see their way clear
to endorsing the scheme on the specious and, to the fair donor,
utterly silly ground that if all the air forces moved into Paris
for Thanksgiving Day, the Germans, a race known as lacking in
all the finer sensibilities, would be uncouth enough to come skyhooting across the unguarded lines and just naturally bomb the
stuffin' out of everything. So Lady Bountiful up and left the war
flat on its back. She departed for New York by the next steamer
in what often has been spoken of, but never adequately described,
as a high dudgeon.

There was—I seemed fated to encounter them here and there
for months—a vigilant and zealous delegation composed of supreme
counselors of the Loyal Order of Moose, it being importantly
headed by "Puddler Jim" Davis, afterward a cabinet member under
Hoover and presently a United States Senator from Pennsylvania,
and by a former congressman from Ohio named John Lentz, and
by a third imperial potentate whose name after this lapse of time
escapes me, but he was just as loyal a Moose, with just as wide an
antler spread as the best and biggest of 'em. As nearly as I could

glean, these unselfish gentlemen had dared the growling menace of the vasty deeps and the perils of conflict on embattled foreign shores to make sure that no Loyal Moose, while serving his flag, got the worst of it from anybody right on up to the general staff— and that went for Black Jack Pershing, too. Such a dastardly outrage would be perpetrated only over their dead bodies, and that indeed would take some hurdling for at least two of the trio rather ran to bodies, just as all three of them ran to elocutionary intensities.

34

THE SAGA OF BROTHER BROADUS

WHILE cheerfully according merit for nuisance value where merit for nuisance value is due, I still think the flower of our overseas product, so far as I could take note in 1917 and 1918, was embodied in one to whom I shall refer through this chapter as Brother Broadus, which was not his real name but near enough to it for all practical purposes. Shortly after we had entered the war the British Government saw the necessity of providing a sort of cushion by which the prevalence of so much company from Yankeeland dropping in from time to time might in a measure be mitigated for the troops actively engaged. With this end in view it took over in France a property which immediately became known as the American Visitors' Château. It was a genuine château, too, a feudal structure with exceedingly feudal bathing facilities, and with battlements and escarpments and watch towers and a keep; and plumbing which dated back to the reign of Clovis when there was no plumbing. It also had—and this classicized feature alone made it unique even in the château country—a moat around it, a deep, wide, scummy moat full of water and swans and waterweeds and French period garbage. And to go with the moat and to obviate wading in and out of the house, there was a workable portcullis. It was fascinating to watch the portcullis come flapping down, like the placket on a sailor's pants. But sleeping below the level of the moat was not much of a treat, as I myself found out during my stay there, unless the guest was part amphibian and enjoyed writing his initials in the damp trickling down the stone walls of his bedchamber. It was like sleeping at the bottom of a leaky churn. It was while sojourning there that I acquired recurrent twinges of what variously has been diagnosed as arthritis and as neuritis and as the symptom of

a more uncommon branch of the itis family with an unpronounce-
able first syllable. But I'm just stubborn enough and back-dated
enough to go on calling rheumatism rheumatism.

On the boat train going down from London to Calais another
correspondent and myself shared a compartment. It was in the
regulations that we both must be filtered through the screen of the
American Visitors' Château before we'd be let free to go where
things really might be happening. Presently Brother Broadus moved
in on us and made himself known. He was a subject who repaid
study. He was short of stature and in spots inclined to be lumpy,
and especially abdominally. Past a certain age the average man
either stays thin and becomes a trellis for his varicose veins to climb
on, or he takes on a contour which, being viewed sideways, suggests
that he swallowed a parasol and after it got down in him it blew
open. Brother Broadus belonged in the bulgy category. His pudg-
iness was offset though by a certain assurance of manner and snap-
piness of speech and by his tonsorial embellishments. He had a
roguishly pointed goatee under his twirled mustaches and his hair
was abundant and long and inclined to be wayward. He also wore
a rakish, wide-brimmed hat and puttees and altogether would have
been a sort of abridged edition of Buffalo Bill, provided you could
imagine that shortly before Buffalo Bill was born his mother had
been badly frightened by a Shetland pony. It was hard to believe
that Brother Broadus, with his wind-tossed locks and all, hailed
from New England and not from the great uncurried open spaces,
but it developed that such was the case; also that he had come over
as the expressly designated plenipotentiary at large of affiliated
branches of the Northern Baptist church in the United States. He
wasn't an ordained clergyman, he explained, but a lay reader. There
was something about him indicative of the possibility that his real
intent was to compile material for a lecture or lectures; but he professed that his mission was to go to and fro, making sure of the
welfare and well-being of members of the Northern Baptist connection among the forces. To us it occurred that this might be an
undertaking fraught with difficulty. Because you put a Northern
Baptist in uniform and stick him in a division with thirty thousand
others similarly attired and even the practiced and discerning eye
of a veteran lay reader might be nonplused, temporarily at least,

to distinguish him from a Seventh-Day Adventist or a Unitarian or a Mormon, or even a Roman Catholic. But we didn't bring up that issue; Brother Broadus had the air about him of a man who rarely or never would be at a loss for word or action.

I didn't see him during the crossing, being otherwise engaged. One undersized transport vessel was ferrying through those mine-infested waters nearly two thousand British officers returning from leave to their posts. Some there were of us who preferred the possibilities of being washed overboard by the roily Channel chops to the horrors of the crowded cabin where hundreds of men were violently and simultaneously ill. So we were roped together on deck, ten or twelve to a batch, and our lashings were made fast to the stanchions so that we were indisposed in relays, like so many fish being seasick all on the same stringer. The zigzagging course we followed was supposed to be infested with enemy submarines but we saw none. Personally I was too busy elsewise to be looking for one. I was looking for some trees or a windmill. Even a small island would have done.

At Bordeaux where invalided officers took us over, Brother Broadus rejoined my friend and me. It seemed he also had been concerned with his own disarranged gastric juices during the trip and so hadn't found time to tag any British Baptists who might be aboard. To reach the Château we rode for forty-odd miles over treacherous ice-glazed roads through a ferocious sleet storm, arriving more than two hours behind our scheduled time. We skittered across the lowered portcullis and with one final skid drew up in a walled and cobbled courtyard where batsmen waited to ease our cramped, chilled frames out of the automobiles. And on that instant the double doors opened wide and within, in a brilliantly lighted salon, was a long table laden with every imaginable potable, British and American and French. And hot water for rum punches was steaming merrily and orderlies were lined up behind the ranked mugs and glasses and the tall flagons. In the foreground, waiting to greet us, were our hosts, the resident corps of war-damaged veterans especially detailed to such hospitable service and jolly well fed up with it, too, if anybody should ask you. 'Twas a vision calculated to make a bronze statue of the late Andrew Volstead water at the mouth.

I don't think Brother Broadus got off to a flying start in that venue. For when Major Norrie, the shot-up ranking soldier there, ushered us in and said, "Gentlemen, welcome! We'll have the introductions a bit later. Right now I know you must be cold—and thirsty. So what is your pleasure?"—and with that waved his arm toward the laden table, our compatriot drew himself up to his full five feet five, and in clear ringing tones, using the proper Boston accent, he said, "My dear sir, I have never learned the taste of strong drink."

I was in the act of telling him I'd guarantee to teach him in not exceeding two easy lessons, when a glance at the astounded faces of those nice Britishers stayed my reckless tongue. This, one felt, was not a moment for airy persiflage. There was in the air a feeling of strained relations which did not abate until after the second round or possibly the third.

Next day we were taken, each one chaperoned by a disabled junior officer, on a sort of Cook's tour along the back edges of the front, staying just close enough to the combat zones to be able to smell the smell of war and hear the voices of war, but not close enough actually to taste it. And, of course, we skirted only comparatively quiet sectors. From the head of the table at dinner that night Major Norrie asked whether the first day's trip had measured up to his boarders' expectations.

"Very satisfactory jaunt—in most regards," said Brother Broadus, graciously taking it upon himself to speak for all three of us. "But since I've been asked, I must say I was disappointed in one respect."

"Oh, I'm very sorry, very," said Norrie. "I hate to think any of us have been remiss in our obligations."

"Oh, I'm not finding fault, exactly," stated Brother Broadus, "but I was hoping I'd witness hostilities at close range instead of being kept all day so far in the rear. I spoke about it, but it didn't seem to do any good."

"Well, you see," said Norrie, quirking a sandy Scotch eyebrow, "we are held responsible for the safety of the distinguished gentlemen who honor us with their presence. We would be soundly scolded, if nothing worse, if one of you met with an injury while in our care. Of course there are no absolutely danger-proof spots in the fringes of this war, but we do our best."

"Perhaps so," persisted Brother Broadus, "but I have looked

forward to the sensation of being under shellfire so that I might describe it to my Sunday-school classes when I get home. I'm told that after the first moment or so it is positively exhilarating." A sort of ripple ran round the table, instantly to be politely checked. "Mr. Cobb, you seem to enjoy having new experiences. Don't you think you'd enjoy the thrill of being under shellfire?"

I took my time about answering. Because I was puzzled. In spite of his get-up—Casper Milquetoast trying to pass for Jesse James or, anyhow, his brother Frank—our compatriot had not until now impressed me as being on the bloodthirsty side. Offhand I would have said that the only thing which conceivably might quiver at his menacing approach would be a mould of apprehensive aspic. But all transformed, here he was, a short-coupled war-charger, that champed and stamped and, with wide-nostriled desire, sniffed the battle from afar.

"Well, I tell you, Brother Broadus," I said, "in the early part of this war it so happened that once or twice I was where some shelling was going on. Understand, I didn't intentionally go where the shelling was. The shelling seemed to come where I was. I moved out fairly briskly. I wouldn't exactly say I ran but, as the fellow says, I passed quite a number of people who were running. And I got cured right away of any notion I might have had about the tonic and rejuvenating effects of being shot at by heavy artillery. That's considerably more than three years ago and I may say I'm still cured." (Subdued applause.)

So that was that. For the second morning our chaperons took us up on Vimy Ridge. We left the cars at the foot of that steep hill whereon so many thousands of brave men had died, and climbed the slope afoot, passing hundreds of holes; here troops had denned in the ground like badgers and foxes. It was a raw, snowy, gusty day and the way was steep, so my companion, a friendly but obviously bored young captain named St. John and I fell behind the rest. Brother Broadus had pressed briskly on ahead. For this grim height was literally carpeted with the debris of past fighting—empty cartridge cases, rusted trenching tools, smashed rifles, broken helmets, scraps of equipment—and he was a persistent souvenir collector. Already he had crowded his overcoat pockets with lesser junk. Now, with an ingenious webbing of strings, he was draping larger relics over his person, so that he clanged and rattled as he went.

Vimy had been quiet enough when we got there. Only the sullen crunching sound of intermittent bombardments on beyond around the beleaguered city of Lens disturbed the peacefulness where we were—if a spot so soaked with human blood and so salted down with human bones could be said to have any peace. But a German observation balloon must have spotted our halted automobiles, for all at once, fat nine-point-fives from a hidden enemy battery somewhere north of us began to drop. The first one to arrive hit just to our left and sent a geyser of clods and stones a hundred feet aloft and peppered us with frozen grit particles and left a hole in the harrowed hill big enough to bury a smokehouse in. And the next one struck just behind us and the third one took a bite out of the crest on above where we last had seen Brother Broadus and his guide, crouching against the skyline.

"I imagine," said St. John, as the reverberating echoes died away and the tortured earth ceased from its quivering, "I rather imagine that our friend's desire to be under shellfire is being gratified. Shall we get out of this?"

He needs must yell that last sentence above the cry of the keening wind because I already had started to go entirely away from there. He made a masterly job of catching up. He had been wounded but not in his legs. As for me, I had, on somewhat similar occasions before that, made the cheering physiological discovery that, given the proper incentives, a fat man can travel just as fast as he has to.

We were taking long sincere leaps when behind us arose a brisk clattering, like a runaway milk wagon, and Brother Broadus passed us, shedding souvenirs at every bound. His hat was gone, his mane streamed straight out behind, his arms and his legs were making swift little swastikas, one dissolving into another. He passed us without looking right or left, passed us as though we had been tied. And we weren't trying to throw that race, either.

When we reached the foot, he was huddled down and panting in one of the cars. He had come hither in an open car but now he was in the back seat of the only closed car of the three. Moreover, the lap robe was pulled up to his chin and he was making himself small and inconspicuous. If the hateful foe claimed him with its high explosives nobody would be able to say afterward he hadn't taken all possible precautions. He was uttering broken parts of speech indicating that he regarded war as both an inhuman abomination and a grave mistake.

He was still in a shaken state when we lunched, twenty kilometers distant, with a general commanding a Canadian contingent—Canadian, but sprinkled thick with Yankees who, before we joined in, had slipped across the line and enlisted under patriotic false pretenses. After lunch we drove a little farther and presently found ourselves down in a half-buried dugout, with a domed roof of sheet iron over it, being entertained by the staff of a battalion of the illustrious Princess Pats. By now the snow flurries had changed to driving volleys and above our heads we heard the big 'uns passing with noises like the roaring of freight trains, for the Heinies' heaviest guns were strafing the lines somewhere far behind us. But it was snug and warm inside there and you couldn't ask for better company than that of Major Hughie Nevin and Major Charley Stuart and Captain Arthur Chipman and the lesser immortals of that hard-bitten, battle-tested outfit. So we toasted the silver-framed photograph of the lovely Princess Patricia which stood alone on the mess table and we were thinking up other good reasons for drinking toasts when all of a sudden the Pats' splendid kiltie band of forty pieces let go where they quietly had stationed themselves just outside.

I ask you: If you were a Kentuckian four thousand miles from home in the war-racked land of France, and all of a sudden, between the banshee wailing of a bitter wind and the spat-spat of great snow crystals on the metal roof just above your head and, splitting the higher welkin, the shrieks of infernal projectiles as those brazen capsules of potential death went hurrying past; if unexpectedly, in the very midst of this, you heard for the first and only time in your life, forty bagpipes skirling and shrilling forth the opening bars of "My Old Kentucky Home," what would you do?

Well, so did I, and used up two pocket handkerchiefs and quite a quantity of Scotch doing it.

35

MINE EYES HAVE SEEN THE GLORY . . .

SPEAKING of emotional splurges sets me to thinking of the greatest thrill I ever got out of any of my platforming endeavors. Un-dimmed, I've carried the bright image of it in my mind, for it's going on twenty-one years now. It may be my memory of it is the keener because it was thought up and carried out where so many treasured recollections are centered—in my old home town.

While I was stalking copy in and out of the lines of the A. E. F. I wrote two mail articles under the heading, "Young Black Joe," both of them dealing with our colored contingents, and notably with Colonel "Bill" Hayward's New York regiment which in May and June of 1918 manned a sector just north of Sainte Menehould. Most of the American correspondents already had taken their whack at our negro soldiers, but until then much of these writings had to do with labor battalions crapshooting at Brest and bewildered cotton-pickers from the Deep South doing unconsciously funny things along the serpentine trail of the Service of Supplies. But I had seen black men actually under fire and despite that it was their debut at that scary sort of thing, had seen them acquitting themselves as men, too. It struck me that the color of a man's skin might not altogether determine the color of his soul and, purely as a biological proposition, that a black man might die just as pain-fully—and just as gamely—as the white comrade dying alongside him. So, in fairness to a race, I shaped my scripts into that current.

Not that I altogether overlooked the humorous side. For in-stance, I gave what I thought was a well-deserved paragraph to my fellow Kentuckian, Private Waterson Hightower, a stranger to me until that auspicious moment, who came along driving a truck and gave three of us a lift on to Chermont from where a staff car

had broken down with us on a powerfully lonesome stretch. I
climbed up into the seat beside him and he told me how the draft
had caught him up out of a Warren County tobacco patch and
shunted him along to this strange and unaccountable land of France
and set him behind a steering wheel. He hadn't enjoyed the crossing; in fact, he said that when the time came to go back home, he
infinitely would prefer returning by way of New Orleans, thus
avoiding another sea voyage. So I asked him whether he was prepared to endorse the war, what he had seen of it?

"Huh, boss," said Waterson, "don't come astin' me that. All
I'se seen the whole endurin' nine months I have been over heah is
mud an' kilo*meters*."

On reaching New York in the early fall I learned that colored
organs over the country had, by permission of the *Saturday Evening Post*, reprinted copious extracts from these two papers of mine,
with endorsing editorial comment. They appeared to be especially
gratified that I, a Southern-born man, confessedly having most of
the prejudices, hereditary and acquired, touching on race issues
which beset the average Southern-born man, had seen fit to give
the negro trooper credit for soldierly qualities displayed under
heavy cannonading as well as under snipers' bullets. I realized how
my stock had gone up in the Harlem wing of the Republican party
as I walked into the waiting room at the Grand Central and "Cap"
Williams, the courtly grizzled commander of the porter crew, lined
up his redcapped battalion for a guard of honor while I, feeling
mighty pleased but a trifle conspicuous, marched on into the train
shed. Until I had been lifted almost bodily aboard the coach which
would carry me to my station of Ossining, I figure other patrons
of the New York Central road wrestled their own baggage or
else just sat down on it and waited a spell.

On the heels of this reception I journeyed to Paducah to see my
mother and my two sisters. Upon the night of my arrival, the new
cook, wearing a proud yet mysterious grin, came from the kitchen
wing to announce that a committee craved to see me. She didn't
specify what sort of committee it was, but her happy grinning
was understandable when I left the living room and went aft.
There were five in the party awaiting me—George Ethridge, the
only negro member of the local bar; and a colored physician, a

colored undertaker, a colored grocer, and my old friend and well-wisher, Kelley Avant, prominent in the barbering profession. As chairman, Lawyer Ethridge explained that the Baptists and Methodists, along with the scattering few colored Presbyterians and colored Episcopalians and colored Catholics, had buried doctrinal differences—for the time being at least—and would unite in a mass meeting that following Sunday afternoon at "Pappy Dupee's Kingdom on Earth," the Washington Street Colored Baptist Church, which was the church having the greatest seating capacity of any church of any denomination, white or black, in town—provided I would accept their unanimous invitation to come there then and talk for so long as it might pleasure me upon the subject of the negro soldier's effort across the water. I have rarely felt more flattered, and I was never the one to sneak furtively around, dodging opportunities of being flattered.

During the intervening half of the week I frequently was in communication with the sponsoring board. Did I prefer a limousine to ride in from my mother's home to the church or would I favor an open carriage drawn by two white horses? I knew where that white span would come from; on occasion they hauled the colored undertaker's fanciest hearse, the one with the paneled sides and the black ostrich plumes at its four corners. The distance was not great; I said I would walk. What might my choice be touching on the proposed choral program? I left those decisions to Lawyer Ethridge's comely, highly educated wife, knowing her to be a skilled musician. On the night before the big day her husband slipped in by the side gate to bring word of the final arrangements.

"Mr. Cobb," he said, with half a smile on his face and half a wink out of one shrewd eye, "there are five pastors of five flocks cooperating in tomorrow's to-do and to keep anybody from feeling slighted or being jealous—and if you don't mind?—it's been decided to let all five of 'em introduce you, starting off with the oldest—and Lord knows that old Shoutin' Methodist man is plenty old and plenty long-winded. I reckon it just can't be helped though. So us committeemen are askin' you, please suh, to be patient and just quietly sit through the whole rigamarole and when they all five get through, then I'll introduce you the way which it should be done; and that'll be your signification to stand up like

John the Revelator and shower down hot coals of language out of
the book of the Gospel truth!"

To go along with me and sustain me, I invited six individuals,
four of them men of approximately my own age and, as representing the memories of our greatest war, two white-topped cronies of
my dead father, Captain James Koger, ex-Confederate, and Captain
Ed Farley, former Unionist; and these two caught the spirit of
the thing and turned up in their smartest veterans' regalia. We had
one o'clock dinner at my mother's and my sisters designed the
menu, so that, among other things, there were two kinds of pie,
pumpkin pie on Captain Farley's account, sweet-potato pie as
better suited to Captain Koger's palate; and Boston baked beans
were offset by smoked hog jowl with turnip greens, west Kentucky
style, and I may say that a pleasant gorge was had by all.

Going along Sixth Street, which lay in the white residential district and bordering the business district, we saw no signs indicative
of a communal turnout but as we came to the corner of Washington
Street it was as though we had stepped into a different town. For
three blocks westward the sidewalks were blocked with black
folks. Stretched in parade formation along the graveled roadway
within these flanking multitudes were colored lodges in uniform
with flags and emblems—the Masons, the Odd Fellows, the Daughters of Ruth, the Sisters of the Mysterious Tents; and colored Boy
Scouts and colored Campfire Girls, and a brass band of many pieces
and the consolidated choirs of half a dozen congregations. Places
were made for us at the head of the procession and then all hands
forward-marched, with the trumpets and the drums and the singers
bringing out the rich values of one of my favorites among the
spirituals, "Joshua Fit the Battle of Jericho."

In the church, where presently we seven whites were
squeezed together on the lip of the platform, just below the pulpit,
I looked upon a sight which instantly brought a lump into my
chest. Every inch of space was occupied—pews, aisles, entryways,
doorways, chancel, window ledges, odd corners. On the flat roof
latecomers were stretched upon their stomachs and peering through
the oblong ventilators that extended along a center ribbing, so that
from within each of these openings made a frame for a picture of
intent dark faces, pressed in, cheek by jowl.

Out of the mass below other faces—almost forgotten, some of them; faces I hadn't seen for many a year—suddenly stood out before me. I saw the huge black head of Bill Jordan who, with his brother Sam and his hound-dog Sounder, took me on my first 'coon hunt and got us lost for the whole of a chilly October night in the wet woods on Terrell's Slough. I saw other half-forgotten friends: "Tallow Dick" Evans the boatstore drayman, now bent and feeble; Will Marable the trusty hackman; spry Dave Turner, who had waited on the game away back yonder when I was learning the rudiments of draw poker; Johnny Montjoy, son of the deceased Tom who had stood at the tail gate of the ice wagon and served out the frozen chunks while I, at fourteen, swung the reins over Frank the morose white mule and Henry the cheerful gray mule; Uncle Arthur Woolfolk, the champion shoat-barbecuer and catfish-frier of Jackson's Purchase; Sist' Melissa Enders and her octogenarian husband, B'rer Zach, from out in the Blizzard's Pond section; and I recognized them, of course, for in former times before those homely arts went out of style, as the can and the can opener came in, Sist' Melissa had spent many a day in our back yard, making strong lye soap in a big black kettle and leaching out the lye hominy at her ash hopper or, in the steamy, fragrant kitchen, helping with the "picklin' an' pusservin'"; while in the appointed seasons for such wares B'rer Zach came bringing shuck doormats woven with his own nimble fingers and splint-bottom hickory chairs; and charcoal for filtering rain water into the family cistern; and bundles of dried "pennyrile" to fend off mosquitoes with; and faggots of the red sassafras root to be made into tea for curing spring fever among the young and thinning their blood of its winter sluggishness; or wild fruits or wild berries, nuts, papaws, ripe haws and the native crab apples, trapped 'possums and baby squirrels for potpies.

I saw younger friends: Will Lot, sexton at my mother's church; and dapper, brown-skinned Alvin Logan, he of the perfect manners, who inevitably was butler at everybody's wedding or anybody's reception; and smiling up at me from the edge of the rostrum, Mattie Copeland, a humble Christian but the best cook, I'll always declare, in seven counties, who lately had come into our service. (She'd cooked the dinner for us that Sunday and washed the dishes afterward and yet somehow had beaten us getting there.) She remained in that employ, loyal and loving, for fifteen years until my mother died and after my mother my older sister—which broke up the household, or I figure Mattie would be there yet.

Next, and all of a sudden, right down in front of me, I beheld a ghost—or for a moment thought I did. For lo and behold, here, desiccated and age-warped now into a shriveled mummified shape, was Donie Rucker, my first remembered nurse, in whose lap I learned the alphabet and at whose knees, a little later, I spelled out *Robinson Crusoe* and *Swiss Family Robinson* and, further along, read *Stanley in Africa;* as an outcome of which Sir Henry M. Stanley became my idol and continued as such until my father told me the man actually had deserted the Southern Army to join the Yankees, whereupon I foreswore him and readopted Israel Putnam and Davie Crockett and my Uncle Bob as demigods who never could be toppled from their pedestals. I had thought Donie to be dead and gone, but there she was, and spry as a cricket, too.

From out of her puckered pale face—Donie almost could have passed for white—she stared warmly up at me with a pair of squinted bright eyes. Although the weather was clear and Indian summerish, she carried one of the largest umbrellas I have ever seen in any clime. At the beginning she held it stiffly before her like a pikestaff, but almost immediately it became a proof of exultation to be threshed about in the air without regard for the safety of those neighbors jammed in about her. Whenever I said anything she liked—and she liked everything I said—she would cry out in a high-pitched crackling tone: "Tha's my chile! I learn' 'im his letters! An' now jest harken at 'im, you folks—harken an' heed!"

At each time of saying this she would swing her tight-furled weapon, inflicting various minor casualties, until the nearermost victims overpowered her. But even after being disarmed, she kept right on with her running fire of proud approval.

I also was aware—but that was not until I got underway—that Donie had a rival commentator in the person of a huge tar-colored woman stationed well back in the body of the church. Now this one had a full, far-carrying voice, even in the conversational style which she employed, and a pair of broad hands which she clapped to punctuate her statements. Whenever I paused for breath, in a familiar, almost intimate fashion, and yet somehow with reverence, she would come forth with such advices as these: "Heah him, Lawd!" . . . "Savior, sweet Savior, lissen to him tellin' it!" . . . "Please suh, Gawd, draw nigh an' heah this wisdom spoke!" . . . "Jesus, now ain't them the facts in the case?"

"Amens" and "Hallelujahs" might be for others to utter—and most abundantly were. But here, you might reckon, was a communicant who felt herself to be on close and confidential terms with the Deity.

Five times was I introduced in due form by five men who had the natural native eloquence of their color and the facility of their common calling. And then Lawyer Ethridge introduced me and, as he had boasted it would be, his speech was bright ore from the mother lode. I remember a line which had been spoken a year before by a noted orator of his race and which he now quoted:

"They say the negro won't fight for the flag which set him free. They say the black man's courage can't endure the strain of high explosives. People, hear me: Recruit our young men, officer them with the sons of Grant and Lee, Sherman and Sheridan and Stonewall Jackson. Send them across the sea, with the bearers of those great names to lead them, and I tell you they'll break the Hindenburg Line or report to God Almighty the reason why they failed."

I know of nothing more hypnotizing to the eye, or paradoxically, more stimulating to the tongue, than for a speaker to stand before a great audience every member of which, in perfect harmonious unison with every other member, is thrusting his or her tense body from side to side, and at each completed swing joining in a medley of restrained grunts, small panting sounds, and muffled, fervent exclamations. Almost instantly I found myself picking up mood and tempo from this stirring thing that was taking place there before me. The very walls seemed to be keeping pace with us. It was as though the building heaved to the rhythmic promptings of those swaying humans who filled and over-filled its interior.

For my start I went back into history. I told of Crispus Attucks, the half-African, half-Indian who fell a martyr in the Boston rioting against the British; and of the color bearer in Shaw's black regiment from Massachusetts who, falling of his wound on a Southern battlefield, bragged, "I never let the old flag touch the ground, boys"; and of the behavior of the Tenth Cavalry in Cuba, and of the recent exploits of Needham Johnson and Henry Roberts of Hayward's command when German raiders came over to rout them—and most emphatically didn't.

At the mention of that outfit I could feel the heartbeat of my audience quicken as clearly as though I had my fingers on one vast collective pulse. For from this, these listeners were aware that I neared the climax toward which through these preparatory stages, I had all this while been approaching.

"And now," I said, "the moment has come to tell you about a boy of your own color, from this, your own town, a volunteer soldier personally known to all or nearly all of you and certainly through reputation known to everyone, white or black, in this entire city by reason of the rewards for gallantry and fortitude which he won in the heat of battle and on the field of honor."

A hush suddenly had fallen, even Donie and the big black woman going silent for a moment. The movement of bodies was checked almost to a standstill and I could hear the taut breathing. I went on:

"And that same young soldier, wearing now the *Croix de Guerre* for leading a successful attack on a German machine-gun nest and taking, almost singlehanded, that machine gun's crew—that soldier whose deed reflects such eternal credit upon you, who are his people, and upon this community and upon his race and upon the banner of our country—"

The spell of the silence was broken. From high up in a window enclosure at the back came a shrill voice which hysterically cracked on the words:

"Name the boy!"

But the owner of that voice, being a negro and therefore having, as all his fellows there had it and as all his color everywhere have it, a primitive but proper sense of dramatic values, knew that not yet would I name the boy. The plea had been wrung from him by the boiler pressure of his own emotions—that was it.

So I continued:

"I myself remember seeing that soldier when he was a handsome, mannerly little chap living in the yard immediately behind my

mother's home and was the playmate of a young distant kinsman
of mine who later drowned while heroically doing rescue work in
a steamboat disaster which many of you doubtless recall. And
later I remember him as a worker at a store over here on Broadway,
enjoying the confidence and the good will of everyone because of
his conduct and his bearing. You remember all that, don't you?"

Again came the shriek from the window shelf:

"Sho' do! Name the boy!"

And three, four, a dozen, maybe twenty picked up the plea and
from then at every pause in my speech made of it a sort of chanted,
rightly spaced accompaniment:

"Name the boy! That's all we asts you—jest kindly name
'im!"

Next I told of a spring night, at regimental headquarters in
northern France where I sat with the colonel commanding—and
all this, as it so happened, was true—when word was brought by
an orderly that a certain noncommissioned officer waited outside,
craving opportunity to pay his respects to me, since he too was from
Paducah, and the colonel, nodding permission, had said: "Cobb,
you're about to meet one of the smartest-looking, smartest-acting,
most dependable soldiers in my regiment. I'm proud to have you
size him up."

"Dat colonel knowed—so name the boy!"

I went on to tell that when that Paducah-born negro entered,
how he was slim, like a lance, and poised, like a bronze panther,
and how snappy was his salute and how stiff was his spine and how
his buttons shone and his tunic fitted his wide shoulders and his
narrowed waist like a glove.

"Always wuz dressy frum a chile up! Please, suh, go on, an'
name 'im!"

"Seem lak we can't wait no longer—so name the boy!"

Yet had I named him then, I would have broken their hearts.
From now on I may have drawn on my fancy for scenic and atmospheric effects, indeed may have done some outright romancing.
But I've never been ashamed of having painted the picture with
colors squeezed from imaginary tubes.

"And now we come to another day. Not so very long ago, it
was my privilege to stand with a group of my fellow correspond-

ents on a recaptured, war-ripped battlefield in France and I was
gladder than I can tell you to witness that scene and glad that
today it is my further privilege to be able to describe it to you, so
that through my eyes you may see it as it was.

"For on that sunny afternoon, with the distant roar of the can-
nons in their ears, the picked forces of three great allied armies of
three great nations formed three sides of a great hollow square.
Over here showed the horizon blue rows of veteran French poilus.
Across there were the hard-fighting British. And yonder at the top
of the square, lined up the khaki-clad ranks of the Yanks. At the
opening at the bottom of the pocket, near where I was, were three
older men standing abreast. And one of these men was General
Sir Douglas Haig, Field Marshal of Great Britain, and another was
the beloved 'Papa' Joffre, Generalissimo of France, and the third
was John J. Pershing, Commander-in-Chief of the American Expeditionary Force.

"And then a command rang out like a bugle, and with a mighty
rattle of weapons all these soldiers came to salute and the trooped
colors of twenty regiments whipped in the air as the massed bands
of these twenty regiments blared forth in the strains of the Marseillaise Hymn. And on that, from the front row of the Americans,
there stepped forth the erect figure of one negro soldier. He
marched the length of that oblong until he came to a halt and stood
at attention facing those three great commanders. Then white-
haired Papa Joffre took from among the glittering array of decorations on his own breast the scrap of metal alloy with its adornment
of red and green ribbon—the tiny emblem which, whenever fighting men get together, stands for gallantry in the highest; and with
his own hands he pinned this badge of glory on the breast of that
lone soldier and kissed him upon both his cheeks. And that soldier—
blood of your blood, bone of your bone—was none other than—"

From two thousand sets of lungs it burst and swelled:

"PRAISE GAWD, HE GOIN' NAME 'IM NOW!"

Now all through this I had been watching a thin, tall old
mulatto woman sitting in her Sunday best, three rows back from
my place—watching her and, if the truth must be known, striving
to work on her. But her rigid face had betrayed no sign that she
heard a word of what I was saying; it was like a face scrimshawed

on yellow ivory. But now as I named him—Sergeant William Kivil, her grandson—she rose up, still frozen by an induced catalepsy and went over backward, stiff as a board, with her arms extended and her tranced eyes staring straight toward the ribs of the roof.

But all the rest were up and clamorous on their feet; and the nearermost rank of them came at us like a wave from the sea, threatening to trample us down and crush us. And at that moment Ethridge's wife—trust a negress to know her theatrical values—signaled to the consolidated chorus behind us and from those velvety African throats came the jubilant, triumphant bars of Julia Ward Howe's "Battle Hymn of the Republic" which begin with:

"Mine eyes have seen the glory of the coming of the Lord."

So we whites escaped out a back window and I went home, and went to bed and stayed there in a drained and flabby state for the next ten or twelve hours.

36

TONGUES IN TREES . . . SERMONS IN STONES

HERE not very long ago a very charming woman editor wore down my resistance and got my promise to do a piece on a subject most dear to both of us.

So I began thus:

I am minded to write of my love for the out-of-doors. Many times before I have been thus minded. But I choked down the inclination for a very good reason, namely, the realization of my utter inability to find the language which fitly might convey a measure of what my love for the out-of-doors is. There's a very good dictionary on my desk. It contains a great many thousand words. But nowhere in it have I ever been able to discover the words which express and define what wood and field and marsh and desert and swamp—and most of all, the beasts and birds that live there—mean to me. To that extent the English glossary is inadequate.

Now since writing is my chief trade, offhand one would say that after some faulty fashion or another, I should be able to set on paper a sense of my feelings. Perhaps the fault lies in me and not in the lexicon. Seeking an alibi for the shortcoming, I have come to the conclusion that none of us has the gift properly of describing that which to the heart is the dearest of all sentiments. The belief of a son in the goodness of the mother who bore him, the love of a father for his child, the force within which inspires a man to die for his country or for his faith or for an ideal—these are things which call for no lip service. We take them for granted; we do not seek to analyze and dissect them and resolve them into their chemical constituents, knowing, as we do, the utter hopelessness of such an undertaking.

446

To me the lure of the out-of-doors, with what goes with it—peace, content, sportsmanship, coming to grips with the wilderness—falls within the list of the passions which may not be translated into speech, so deeply are they rooted in the very sills of the soul. I never knew a real woods guide but had in him plenty of this inarticulate veneration for Nature. His wholesome idolatry enriched his competency with modesty, with unselfishness, with gentility. It made him frugal of the resources which Nature had provided to the end that he might earn his living. It gave him understanding of the splendors of his heritage. Nearly always it made him tactful, clean-mouthed, chivalric, considerate. And housed-in mortals, such as we are, amateurs at the game, taking our out-of-door pleasures by snatches and bits, on week ends or in vacation time, we too know in a lesser degree, that there is no religion healthier for a man's inner being than the pagan worship of the woodsman, no creed more cleansing or purifying than that which traces texts from campfire smoke, finds lessons in rippling waters and helps us read our title clear to earthly happiness in the scrollings of a lichened rock.

I got that far and then I booted my balking pen into another pasture. For one thing I had begun foraging after fancy language, fine writing, which was ever a bad sign. For another, I foresaw that I would do as most writing folk—and others—do when under the spell of a really compelling subject: go on a spiritual jag; get drunk on metaphor and emotion, swigged half-and-half; pile up the rhetoric until it topples from its own redundant tipsiness. See, even while making these labored excuses I'm repeating the original offense.

But I meant all I had said. I shall go on meaning it until I have to do my pathfinding in a wheel chair and confine my trophy-hunting to such specimens as may be garnered by superior marksmanship with a fly swatter. Especially I meant what I said about guides.

Going largely by what casual intercourse I have had with members of their craft, I would claim for railroad engineers that, collectively, they probably are the most admirably poised, most controlled and, by temperament, training and test, the best-equipped for their jobs of any like group in America. Before I board a train I like to stroll under the flank of the engine and take a peek up at the overalled chap in the cab. I have yet to see a man there whose very expression and bearing—his dignity, his air of sober efficiency, his radiation of responsibility—but convinced me that, with his eye on the way ahead and his fist on the throttle, I would be in the best of all possible hands. What is the curious sifting-out process by which a railroad segregates such admirable material for its loco- motives and—frequently but not always—such dull material for its information booths? A republic which in the one hundred and fifty-odd years of its existence, has chosen just one businessman to run a business government, and twenty-odd lawyers, those para- sites who prey on business, might not do so badly if it tried the experiment of adding a railroad engineer to the list of our presidents. A politician naturally would insist that the candidate hail from the right geographical division, but just on his looks alone I'd be willing to cut out all partisanship and sectional issues and take a chance by nominating the next fellow I meet straddling homeward after his run, with car grease on his nose and a lunch kit under his arm— provided of course, he's a good Democrat.

For skill at his calling, for accuracy in its execution, for all- around capability and resourcefulness under unpredictable condi- tions, I am sure the average forest-bred guide measures up to the same standards. With no exceptions, I have yet to meet a seasoned professional guide out of the tall timbers who was not a real stu- dent of nature and a real lover of nature, a conservationist, a believer in the protection and the propagation of the very game he hunted. Oscar Wilde said it—"Yet each man kills the thing he loves." However, in the case of the true man who makes his living by hunting down some of the wild creatures, he doesn't slaughter for the love of the slaughter—an atavistic blood lust from which the city man who hires his services not always is immune. He kills within moderation, not wastefully nor with a wanton greediness. He obeys the game laws of the land as he obeys the unwritten laws of the wilderness.

Whenever I have myself been off the main-traveled roads— and that means in more than half of the states of the Union and in nearly all the provinces of Canada and in northern Mexico and along the Panama Canal—I have enjoyed the companionship of, and profited by, contacts with men of this caliber and this character.

I tally off a long roll of such men, true sportsmen and good comrades, all of them—smiling Miguel, major-domo at Hal Mangum's marvelous ranch of LaBabia in Coahuila; Jack Brewster up at Jasper National Park in Alberta; John Flint,* who was an acknowledged kingpin among registered Maine guides; Tom Roberts, dean of Long Island baymen and his ally, wise, witty old Nelson Verity, with ten generations of Long Island Veritys behind him and nearly all of them baymen, too; Raymond Sabattis and Jim Lane, skilled deer-stalkers on the splendid Brandreth estate in the Adirondacks; C. M. Palmer's sweet-humored, storytelling "Garry" at Saranac; Elder Pindar, the bone-fishing expert of the Florida coast and the unpaid pastor of the little flock on Metacombe Key; Tammanee DeMarets, of the Cajun colony below Lake Charles; the Garretts, father and son, at Bob White Lodge in North Carolina, who talked to a bird dog in his own language— or at least that was what you could half-believe, seeing them work-

---

* On a memorable three-week canoe trip down the Allegash and the St. John's from Moosehead Lake to Port Kent on the Quebec border, as guests of the Forestry and Conservation Department of the state of Maine, there were eight of us and eight picked guides, besides the cook and his helper. The thing was done in style, this same John Flint being the boss of the convoy.

The eight guides included an Indian, courtly, gentle and soft-voiced, and three French-Canadians, all of them lithe, nimble chaps; but the remaining four were typical Yankees with the Down-East twang in their voices and the inborn conservatism of the true New England at the back of whatever they said.

I remember a certain speech of one of them. He delivered it between pauses, while he puffed his pipe and pondered his statements, testing each brief sentence for truth before he uttered it.

"Knew a feller onc't 'at p'izened hisself eatin' tainted salmon out of one of these here tin cans out of a store," he began. "Leastwise, they said ez haow twuz tainted." Pause. "Eatin' it didn't do him no real good, ez you might say." Pause. "They figured that eatin' it wuz enough, jest by itself, to kill him." Pause. "Fact is, I don't know but whut it did." Pause. "I wuz to the funerel."

ing the stubble fields or among the red clay gullies and the pine scrub; Harry Allen, president of the New Brunswick Guides Association, a gentleman and a scholar and a thoroughly devout man.

In a cold October drizzle which very soon turned to rain, Harry and I left his main camp, still-hunting for moose. By the time we reached one of his outlying cabins seven miles away both of us were sopping wet. We stripped off and put our clothing to dry by the fire; and while I crawled in a bunk and napped on fragrant balsam boughs, he prepared lunch from the store of food which he kept in a cache there. In midafternoon when we started on the back track it was snowing hard—big clingy flakes that turned the tamaracks into white sugarloafs and caked up on the almost leafless boughs of the hardwoods. I wondered why he kept ahead of me and was so silent; it wasn't like Harry to be so silent. Nor did he stop once to study the lay of the land although we traversed much good hunting country, and that was an even more curious thing. As the early twilight of that northern latitude came hurriedly on, he mended his gait until he traveled at a heavy-footed jog. It was quite dark when we scaled the brow of a low hill. Below us, a quarter of a mile across the intervening swale, was the gleaming from a row of fire-lit cabin windows. "That's the home camp," he said, and fell on his face in the snow and lay there writhing. At midday he had tapped a fresh can of condensed milk for our tea but by mistake had poured for himself from a can which previous occupants had left open and which, after three weeks of exposure, had gone bad. We barely had begun our return journey when the gripes seized him. Because he knew I would be lost in that waste of bogs and pine thickets if he collapsed, he had, by almost superhuman grit, forced himself to keep traveling until we were within sight of help. That was why he had hurried so; why he so persistently held the lead. He knew if I saw his face I would know his grievous plight. Three days we dosed him with home-made remedies for ptomaine poisoning before he was able to trudge the sixteen miles out to the railroad.

I think of five or six who, if you are one of a favored few, will do the guiding, not for pay, of course, but for love of the sport of matching their wits against the wily game and for love of their fellow man. Let's see: There's Jake Smothers, the manager host of the famous and most dependable Eagle Lake Rod and Gun Club near Houston, acknowledgedly a skilled ornithologist and a student of nature in all her moods—and how Jake can reach up with that weather-beaten little old sixteen-gauge of his and pull down some air-burning teal or a bullet-fast "blackie" or a spiraling jacksnipe; and there's Norman Jacobson of the High Cascades in Oregon, a past graduate at woodcraft; and pretty Mrs. Harold Johnson in Kerr County, Texas—Harold is a fair hand himself but Mrs. Harold has a keener eye for a buck in the brush or a gobbler skulking through the scrub than anybody, man or woman, with whom I ever went afield; and there's A. J. Thompson, Hal Mangum's closest neighbor—the two ranches adjoin and it's only forty-six miles from one front door to the other; and when you stop at the Tules for a meal or a night's lodging (which you surely will have to do if ever you journey that way) you'll agree with me that there's nothing more captivating than the slow, quizzical grin on A. J.'s lean face, unless it be the bubbling laugh of plump, hospitable Mrs. A. J. as she insists on you taking a third helping of the pepper-fed wild turkey, with Southern hot biscuits and Mexican frijoles to come along.

Also, if you don't mind having a millionaire pole your bateau through the swamp grass or coax down for you shy pintails and bullheaded mallards from the high flocks, I can recommend Will Hogg's brother, belovedly known as "Cap'n Mike" to half of the white population and all of the black in his corner of the state. Mike can take you for dove-shoots to historic Varner plantation on the Brazos; for quail to one prairie in the coastal country and for duck to another; for deer-shooting deluxe—in a station wagon— at the Rancho San Rodriguez below the international boundary south of Del Rio, or for winged game and finned game among a series of shallow bays off Port Aransas in the Gulf. And there's Rex Beach and also Fred Stone, and likewise Stan Murphy up in the Redwoods country.

If my prowlings into natureland had not taken me so widely to and fro, the possibilities are I might never have known such representative sportsmen as "Prent" Atkins and "Trab" Oliver of northern Louisiana; or Ben Ames Williams and Courtney Riley Cooper, who'd rather flycast than write books and who did both jobs exceedingly well; or Bishop Woodcock of the Episcopal Diocese of west Kentucky;* or Stuart X—yes, that's the name—up on Rogue River; or Charley Heddon, whose fishing tackle made Dowagiac famous; or that Ben Franklin of big league magnates, waddling, sweet-tempered Wilbert Robertson, manager of the Brooklyn Nationals; or the noble John Kirk clan in New Mexico; or George Walker of Los Angeles, who was the best dialectician in the state and the storytelling prodigy of Walgas camp out Mohave Desert way; or Harry Hanszen and John Crotty of the gold-mounted, oil-anointed Tejas Club in Houston; or Colonel Orie Johnson in upper California. Also under this category must be lumped a complete set of desirable members of the Hogg Brothers' entourage, a coterie capably headed by the famed raconteur, Major Raymond Dick-

---

* On his first diocesan journey to our end of the state the bishop was the overnight guest of my friend George Goodman at Goodman's home on Grundy's Hill out in the county. I happened to be in Paducah and Goodman and I took him quail hunting behind Goodman's dogs. For a man of sixty-five or more, our clerical companion made a good showing on coveys and scattered birds but the yellow clay of our countryside and its frequent barbed-wire fences rather did him in. He was pretty well fagged when we got back to the house in the dusk of a November evening and eased him into an armchair beside a blazing hearth. Goodman, who had been a whisky magnate before the Eighteenth Amendment fell on our necks, beckoned me out into the hall. He wanted to offer his reverend visitor a bracer, but dreaded the risk of offending a churchman of high degree by making the offer. I wasn't so timorous; it wasn't my house and I didn't belong to the fold. (As it developed he believed in moderation and therefore was heartily opposed to sumptuary Prohibition.) "Bishop," I called out, "would it make you mad if George brewed you a hot toddy out of some eighteen-year-old Bourbon, aged in the wood?" "Yes," he answered briskly, "it would—if he stopped at one." So without having to use force, we got two of them down him and he went upstairs. Presently Goodman, with his finger on his lips, came and beckoned to me and silently I followed him aloft. We tiptoed to the door of a bathroom, which was ajar. Cautiously peering in, we could see in a wall mirror the reflected image of Bishop Woodcock. He was stretched in the tub and his slender white hands gently were paddling the soapy water and with a beatific smile on his face he dreamily was humming, "What a friend we have in Jesus!"

son, and by Harry Brigham, who loves bird dogs to distraction and is himself distracted when a pup of his training misbehaves; and by all means, the group must be stretched to include black Ike Rhodes, that skillet wizard whom Will used to praise as the best "garbage-cook west of the Mississippi River," and yellow-skinned Mose Walton—twenty years, boy and man, on the same job—who described the first dachshund he ever saw as a "snake on roller skates" and who, delicately referring by indirection to a family suffering from a prostrating attack of acute prosperity, said: "Seems lak, Cap'n Mike, white folks that gets their money sudden, is got sech a *clumsy* way of spendin' it."

Certainly I should have missed knowing Will's old playmate, Bassett Blakeley, whose fame is more or less local but who if caught young and trained for the place might very well have succeeded Will Rogers as a philosophic jokester of rare merits. It was Bassett who, being for the moment over-extended at the banks as a result of a disastrous flurry in the cattle market, went as a last resort to a fellow townsman having plenty of cash and a reputation for hanging onto the same. "No, he didn't lend me any money," said Mr. Blakeley in recounting the affair, "but just as I was leaving he gave me some advice absolutely free of charge. 'Bassett,' he said, 'don't ever feed stock dry shucks in March. I did that once and one shuck blew away on me.'"

Certainly it is true that save for my poking about into new territories I should never have known a scad of McAlpins in New York or a slew of Duncans in Texas or vast numbers of the Broussard family in the Bayou country. Only the Broussards are more than merely a family; they're a species.

I keep on recalling more outstanding figures among the professional guides I have known: There was Robert the full-blood Abenaki Indian in the Laurentian Mountains of Quebec, who literally would coax a diffident brook trout out of water and do more things with a double-bitted ax than some could do with a whole kit of tools and a card in the carpenters' union. With that ax of his I believe he could mend a wrist watch. I can testify that with it and his pocket knife and some chips and dried branches and some birchbark, he could set you up at housekeeping in the woods—with candle-holders, cups, forks, spoons, platters, coat-hangers, gun rests, what not—and all in no time at all, it seemed like. Give him an hour more and he'd turn out a rustic table and a couple of benches, too.

There was Holt Collier, the champion bear-killer of Mississippi, who came one time with his pack of hounds—the same pack that President Theodore Roosevelt rode behind—to Colonel Jeff Snider's big permanent rendezvous at Lake Bruin on the lower Mississippi while a party of forty of us, from North and South, were being entertained there. Here was one of the finest gentlemen, black or white, I have met. He was the only negro regularly enlisted in the Confederacy. He served—with courage and fortitude—as a private in the Fifth Texas Cavalry. Harris Dickson the author not long ago wrote me from Vicksburg: "Nobody was more loyal and brave than Holt. The finest white men in our Delta were proud to have him for a friend because he never took up with the wrong kind. Singular, isn't it, that white men should have regarded his friendship as a sort of endorsement of their own standing?"

And inevitably I think of Louis Harlow up in Nova Scotia.

If exquisite and perfected knowledge of all that pertained to his business and its various ramifications be accepted as qualifications, then this stumpy, smiling, bowlegged, little half-breed man, who neither could read nor write, was the best educated man I ever saw. He was admittedly the deftest canoeman in the maritime provinces; he was the craftiest moose-caller in all of Nova Scotia, so they said; he had powerfully few equals in the whole Dominion at reading sign or trailing or fly casting, at trapping or at camp work. From his Scotch-Canadian father he got steadfastness and honesty and a sturdy, stout heart. From his Micmac mother he had bodily agility, and an incredibly keen vision, and a brain competent to outwit the creatures among whom he had lived all his life.

Louis was assigned to me when a caravan of us, all from the States, struck off into the wilderness beyond the finnan haddie drying racks and the laden apple orchards leading upcountry from the Bay of Fundy to Annapolis Royal. Our hosts were the provincial government and the Canadian Pacific Railway and together they made the outing most exceedingly agreeable for a heavyweight squadron, which included Colonel Tillinghast Huston, chief owner of the New York Yankees, and Harry Leon Wilson, the novelist, and the Four Horsemen among sporting writers: Damon Runyon, Bozeman Bulger, Bill McGeehan, Bill Macbeth; and Frank Stevens whose army of helpers at race tracks and ball parks feed more individuals daily than any other catering firm in the world does.

About the main camp there seemed to be no passionate desire to reduce the native mammalia of Nova Scotia by any appreciable extent. So four of us who thought we craved something with horns on it to be stuffed and hung up over the living-room mantel-piece—if our wives would let us—took pup tents and by pack and paddle adventured deeper into the woods. Louis and his fellow Micmac, Sam Globe, guided our footsteps thither. Now Sam was a master camp cook but when the moose steaks were done and the flapjacks were browned to a turn and the gravy was a poem in sepias and tans, he would catch up a cold tin plate from where it had been lying on a frosty bank and slam the food on it, so that instantly the steaks became as rubber blowout patches and the gravy was just so much stiff suet and the flapjacks turned into a low grade of sole leather. For dessert there would be half-congealed marmalade and domestic cheese, which was very good cheese, but from exposure to the cold had gone crumbly and almost tasteless.

So after the first supper at the outpost I introduced some flavory gadgets which were utterly foreign to the understanding of our attendant aborigines. First off, I heated the plates until they almost scorched a fellow's knees. They had never heard of heated plates. I spread cheese on hardtack, added dashes of red pepper and splashes of Worcestershire sauce, and toasted these primitive confections before the coals of the campfire and served them, sizzling hot and runny. They had never heard of improvised Welsh rare-bits, either.

After my tentmate and I had been for hours in our sleeping bags we could see the Indians still at the fire, making melted cheese snacks, and eating them, a whole cracker at a gulp. Next morning, of a four-pound cheese there remained only a rind and a memory, and the sauce bottle was almost empty. After breakfast Louis came to me:

"Some white people purty dam' smart," he said. "But you smartest white man yet. You think up about hot plates, you think up about cookum cheese. All out of your own head, huh? And all at same time, too! Injun never think up that much fine thoughts in whole lifetime. Shake hands, boss."

Simple, eh, that guileless child of the forest? But wait.

Two days after that, Louis and I—that is to say, I was along—
followed a set of great splayed hoofmarks for miles across an archipelago of shallow ponds and brawling, nameless little streams and
tiny shrubby islands into a watery and mossy bog where we lost
the tracks at the foot of a fair-sized height of land. We had left our
canoe at the foot of the last portage and that would be long, rough
miles behind us. The very thought of retracing our way over the
roundabout course by which we had come made me wheeze like a
pair of leaky bellows. Yet night was coming on fast. Louis read
my mind.

"Maybe so we takeum short cut," he said, indicating the stubby
dense-timbered mountain looming in front of us. Knowing that in
that country the average guide was badly bewildered once he got
away from the familiar interjoining waterways into any strange
territory, I said, "Have you ever traveled that route before?"

He shook his head. "Maybe so I find the way. No path
though—no trail. Much bad woods."

There was no moon that night. Pretty soon we were stumbling
along in a blackness so utter that only by hanging to an end of his
tump strap could I follow him at all. Down-stuff trapped my tired
legs and jagged dead limbs snatched at us, and tree trunks did not
show until our noses almost were scraping the bark. But by watching the stars I could tell that, the obstacles of the terrain considered,
we were pursuing a direct line up over the crest of that difficult
knoll and down on the farther side. After hours we came out into
the clear on the verge of a smallish bluff. I looked down. The
tents of our encampment were right beneath us, a friendly glow
shining through their canvas walls. I do not exaggerate when I
say that I could have spat on the roof of the nearermost tent.

After the thoughtful Louis had tucked my exhausted frame
into a nest of blankets, I said:

"Louie, how in the name of heaven did you do it—fetch me
straight back here through pitchy darkness and across a hogback
that you'd never climbed before?"

"Lissum here, boss," he said. "How does horse know? How
does dog know? How does t'ings what live in wood know,
huh? ... Well, that's how Injun know. Can't tell you no more than
that. ... Goo' night, boss."

37

I DECIDE NOT TO BE A MILLIONAIRE

Before he was caught up to what presumably was an exclusive and closely restricted Heaven—else he must have been woefully dissatisfied with those celestial accommodations—I knew a certain rich man who, in the matter of sportsmanship, lived out a parable of his own. He went in for the out-of-doors on the largest and most opulent scale possible to conceive of. There was a lot of the out-of-doors and apparently he coveted it all for personal use. He owned outright a shooting box in the Black Forest and a grouse moor in Scotland, a great tract of timber in Ontario, a trick ranch in New Mexico, a duck-hunting preserve on the Eastern Shore of Maryland, a restored plantation in tidewater South Carolina. He had under lease the fishing rights on several miles of a trout stream in Colorado, a dog-training establishment in Alabama and a sizable stretch of salmon water up a Norwegian fjord.*

When you were a guest at one of his estates it was his delight to tell you that every duck you knocked down from behind the tailor-made, flunkey-serviced blinds stood him five dollars, regardless of said duck's size, age or species; and that when you ate a ring-necked pheasant under that roof, it cost the establishment somewhere around ten dollars. You felt as though you were taking the bread right out of the mouths of his private yachts. Oh, I forgot to mention the private yachts, didn't I? There were two of them and I think he'd have had a private ocean for them to sail about on if he could have found out who owned all the land around the edges. Flickering about the least palatial of his lodges were more lackeys than there used to be drummer boys of Shiloh in a soldiers' home.

---

* Pronounced by the English "Ferguson."

The place would be downright foggy with butlers and footmen and off-bearers and things.

Now this gentleman was a fair enough wingshot and at whipping a pool I've seen worse than he, but I couldn't rate him a sportsman and I don't believe many others did. For the poor wretch had never trained a pointer pup, nor put up his own brush lean-to, nor fashioned his own balsam bed; had not even lacquered a trout rod. He kept all those noble properties of his in order to be able to talk about them. In short, he was a show-off with a typical plutocrat's itch for possessions, except he differed from the average run of his kind in that he went in for acquiring treasures of the open air rather than old masters and young wives or one of the more expensive ambassadorships.

On the other hand I have seen woods and water, and wind and weather—those diverse outpourings from Nature's cornucopia—work miracles upon many a rich man. Now this I would regard as the greatest of all the humanizing miracles which the communion of sportsmanship works upon our breed, since so many contrariwise impulses and influences constantly conspire to warp the rich man's soul—sense of power; suspicion born of the indubitable fact that most of those he meets hope to get something for nothing out of him; the sheer ossifying and numbing weight of that much money.

Mind you, I have no such deep-sealed grudge against money in mass that it couldn't be cured by a large legacy from some grateful unknown admirer. Money may not be everything, as some are prone to say, but I have noticed that it will buy quite a large number of desirable things as one goes along.

The point I'm trying to get at though is that it is harder for very affluent persons to be sane and normal creatures, loving simple things and doing natural things, than it is for lower-bracket people. If a rich man prefers to live simply they call him stingy. If he behaves naturally the critical multitude say his very lack of pose is a pose. Moreover, I claim—and I don't believe it is the voice of jaundiced envy that I am lifting—I claim that, taking them by and large, the great money-getters do not constitute a wide-visioned group nor even a reasonably smart group. They are the beneficiaries of a single undiversified talent, a sort of sublimated knack for acquiring money; and unless I'm wrong, the business of acquiring money in quantities does not call for the exercise of any particularly high grade of intelligence. It is a soul-hunger, a mania for acquisitiveness, whetted by practice and made keen by indulgence of that hunger. Without disparagement to either of the contrasted parties, I'd liken such a man as I've pictured to a rat terrier. A rat terrier goes along until he comes to a crack in the wall and he takes one sniff at it and starts scratching. A dozen or a dozen dozen other dogs have passed that way without smelling anything. But the terrier digs and digs and pretty soon he has added another gem to his earthly crown. He has harvested a hidden rat. His fellow type among the humans digs out a nest of dollars. It isn't intellect, it's instinct. For one, I could do with a smidgen of that instinct.

I'm afraid though it's too late for me to be getting started. I'll be sixty-five next birthday and, what with one thing and another, I've about decided to drop my life's ambition. It *was* my intention to be a retired millionaire.

The most attractive companions among rich men that I have known in my time, those with the greatest capacity for friendship and the most tolerant outlooks upon life, were sportsmen. They were real sportsmen, not purse-proud dilettantes buzzing about upon the outer hulls of sportsmanship but never, through the sweat of their own efforts or by their own craftsmanship, tasting of the savory and delectable kernels within. For a conspicuous and exemplary illustration of the attractive sort, I conjure up the memory of the late Charles R. Flint to whom in earlier chapters I referred briefly.

This Charles R. Flint came of a race of builders and owners of Yankee clipper ships, and to the end of his days the smell of salt water was spice in his nostrils. Inasmuch as he had a conspicuous part in welding the big industrial combinations which were so popular around the turn of the century, the papers dubbed him "Father of the Trusts" and bestowed on him much notoriety, which he enjoyed. He was an indomitable explorer into new fields of commercial adventure. Between these forays he qualified as a great sportsman. He owned and skippered the *Arrow*, the fastest yacht built before gasoline-driven pleasure craft were developed. Until he was far along in his seventies he rode spirited horses, trained his own retrievers, had a true eye for a snap shot in the brush and cast a smart trout fly. As an octogenarian widower, he sought legally to adopt for his foster-daughter a sentimental lady who was considerably less than half his age. Obstacles being raised here, he circumvented the opposition by marrying the clinging young romanticist, subsequently celebrating his eighty-third birthday and the second anniversary of the wedding simultaneously. When he passed on he was putting together—in his somewhat muddled mind—his largest trade consolidation yet. He'd been a mighty long time going senile though.

Earlier intimates of his were James G. Blaine and Samuel J. Tilden and the senior J. P. Morgan. As he passed out of middle age he began cultivating the company of men much his junior, saying the only way for an older man to feel like a younger man was to associate with younger men. I counted myself lucky to be included among his closer friends in the last fifteen years of his life. Money meant powerfully little to him. It was the game of getting it which lured him; that, and the frolic of spending it. He told me that once he walked out of a deal which would have netted him a quarter of a million in cash because he had an engagement to shoot big game in the Rockies with Major North, "Little Pawnee Chief," famous leader of Indian scouts in the Sioux and Cheyenne uprisings. "Never regretted it," he said, in his clipped State of Maine accent, "I didn't need the money and I did need a buffalo head for my game room. *Exactly!*"

When Mr. Flint said, "Exactly," which he did at the end of about every other paragraph and frequently halfway through it, the word seemed to explode all over the place like a Fourth of July bomb.

Having wearied of forming trusts, he took on what for him was a characteristic sideline. He sold munitions and secondhand military equipment to filibustering and revolutionary groups, mainly in Latin America, but occasionally to troubled nations elsewhere over the globe. In the Russo-Japanese War the Czar was his patron and the Czar's army was his very good customer. When the officers and men of the Brazilian Navy revolted and by a coup seized all Brazil's fighting ships it was Flint who, on a blanket commission from the despoiled government and with a cabled account of three million dollars to draw upon, within the space of twenty days, and working under cover because of fear of technical interference on the part of our Federal authorities, sent to sea a complete battle fleet of hastily armed merchantmen, manned by the trashy sweepings of the New York and Boston waterfronts, and staffed by cashiered naval officers of half a dozen nationalities and by maritime soldiers of fortune and hard-fisted bucko mates, who until they unsealed their sailing orders outside Sandy Hook didn't know what flag they were to hoist nor to what waters they would go nor for what country they would fight when they got there, and didn't care a hoot, either.

At the historic Wyandanch Club on Long Island he had a leasehold upon *The Miller's Cottage*, a shingled, low-eaved pre-Revolutionary relic. Daniel Webster used to be a frequent guest there and there was a legend that, while in his cups, the statesman occasionally fell overboard in Stump Pond and was hauled out by his boatman. Here, along with Bob Davis and Owen Davis the playwright—no kin to Bob except by appetite—I spent many a happy day and many a gorgeous night. Other visitors came and went. It might be a Chinese prince, or a visiting lady novelist, an exiled dictator of some banana republic, a foreign diplomatist. It might be Admiral Sir Guy Gaunt, chief of the British Intelligence Service here during the first World War; or Holbrook Blynn the actor, or Barton Hepburn and Jules Bache and Coleman Du Pont, the financiers, or William M. Ivins, the great corporation lawyer; or Thomas J. Watson, president of International Business Machines and at present distinguished as the highest-salaried commercial executive in America, and earning every penny of it, too. But the two Davises and C. M. Palmer and his son Dean Palmer, who looked like Dickens' somnambulant fat boy and sometimes, but not in business hours, behaved like him—were standbys. I was a consistent free boarder, too. Bob, that master concoctionist of tasty dishes, did the cooking and Owen and the Palmers and I did our share of the eating. Nor was Bob backward there, but on the contrary, frequently was well out in front. In the matter of food he was, as it were, a great hand to clean up after himself. Seeing him from behind when he was under full headway you might have been pardoned for thinking he was playing a snare drum. Dean Palmer made every stroke count, too; no wasted energy, no false motions there. The chief drawback about the average volunteer cook, however greatly admired he may be while in the kitchen, is that you have to put up with him between meals. But Davis could be induced to master his indigenous reticence and converse brilliantly for five or six hours continuously. Or, with a bass plug, thresh the waters of some peaceful cove to a lather, meanwhile sagely discoursing upon a cosmic range of topics.

Mr. Flint, the deviser of all these happy week ends, was nearing a proper time for retirement—only we could never imagine him retiring—when in 1917 we came to grips with the Central Powers. Immediately he moved to Washington. Being an intense patriot, he had the notion of serving his country and, as a secondary consideration, his pocketbook. A very good notion it seemed, too. Among the cranks and fanatics who would flock to the capital with all manners of fantastic contrivances for winning the war there would, he figured, be some with plans which might have real value for offensive purposes or defensive purposes. In the hurly-burly and confusion which would arise with a bewildered and unprepared people going to war, like a drunken Simple Simon going to the fair, it was certain that many such worthy inventions would be overlooked. For testing these ideas he proposed to provide a proving ground and a laboratory and a clearing house, meanwhile maintaining contacts with the War Department and the Navy Department. Very quickly he set up an organization, with a roster of engineers, scientists, chemists, highly paid specialists in various technical fields, and into the scheme put the bulk of his personal fortune. Having counted on a long war, he calculated his outlays accordingly. The Armistice came just as he was getting into stride, so the new business failed and he salvaged practically nothing out of its failure.

He never complained though. Only once, and then indirectly, did I hear him mention the loss.

"Doctor Cobb," he said, "I wish to offer you a word of advice. Patrick Francis Murphy, you know, says advice is what older men give to younger men when they no longer can set them a bad example. *Exactly!* Nevertheless, I'm offering you some. Doctor, never put all your money in an umbrella store unless you know it's going to keep on raining indefinitely. . . . *Hem!* We rode out here today in a Ford instead of a Rolls Royce. Well, what's wrong with a Ford? Gets you there, doesn't it? And a man can only wear one suit of clothes at a time or one set of false teeth, eh?" And he grinned to show his own extremely and most obviously artificial set, "*Exactly!*"

I can shut my eyes and re-create the scene where he made the reference to his financial reverses. The two of us—or the three of us if you counted Mr. Flint's constant companion, a sage, dignified little cocker spaniel named Dot, were together in a broad skiff on the lake. We were close up under the "New Dam," so-called because it was only a hundred and fifty years old. Just beyond the spillway stood the ancient Blydenburg Mill, still staunch after a century and a half. According to tradition it was in that mill that John Jay, as grand master for New York State, instituted the first Masonic Lodge on middle Long Island. I was rowing while he picked up a mess of fat yellow perch for Bob's waiting fry-pan, and Dot squatting between his knees as always. Our resident pair of fish hawks were ranging overhead for fingerlings, and some of the summer ducks which nested in the protection of the club woods were scooting by like little enameled jewel caskets. There were fat bullfrogs among the lily pads and on the dead tree trunks just above the water's edge thick rows of painted turtles warmed their backs and stretched their skinny pied necks in the slanted sunshine of a September afternoon. There might have been a dog fox barking up on the ridge or a young mink gliding along shore like a slim, brown streak. I wouldn't guarantee the dog fox and the baby mink, they being only occasional visitants, but the others surely must have been there as always they were in the proper season and at the right hours. We were forty-five miles from New York and less than two miles along a sandy, brier-bordered lane from one of the busiest suburban highways in America, but so far as the looks of that lovely spot went might as well have been a thousand miles away.

Through many months Mr. Flint wrote a book, *Memories of an Active Life,* for which I did the foreword and Bob revised the galley proofs. The reason it took him so long to write the memories was that he was so busy extending the span of the active life. I like to remember that he died in what he fondly imagined was the harness he so competently had worn in his prime, those golden days before dotage came, when the money was pouring in—and in big streams pouring out—and the mighty ones of the land besought his counsel and abided by his judgments.

That Wyandanch Club was an institution, the oldest chartered sports club along the eastern seaboard. In a Colonial farmhouse, only slightly altered, the members maintained the ancient customs, the ancient civilities. The cooking was old-fashioned; a man wrestled his own luggage, stocked his own cartridge pouches, mixed his own drinks. Electricity had been installed, but the routine of leaving for each person a candle in a candlestick on the second-floor landing was religiously maintained. For years modern plumbing and bath facilities had been available, but just the same every room was equipped with a washstand set, including the slop jar and the vessel under the bed. If a member complained of some feature instantly he was made chairman of the committee having that detail in charge and continued to fill the frequently exacting post until some other unfortunate made the mistake of criticizing. As a result there was powerfully little faultfinding and that little confined to green-horns.

Until he died in his nineties and for nearly all the time that I was a member, General George Washington Wingate was president of the Wyandanch Club. We never had any elections; somebody just notified him he was president for another year. Here was a grand old man, of a race of Americans now almost entirely van-ished. He had been a captain in the Civil War; I never heard him utter a disparaging word of those against whom he had fought. Once some hidebound Rebel-baiter, seeking to curry favor with him, spoke in unpraise of the spirit of the Confederates. Up bounced the old warrior with his chin whiskers bristling like the quills of the fretful porcupine. "My dear sir," he thundered, "when you say that, you offer me and all my comrades a gratuitous insult. Do you think it would have taken the North four long years to defeat an army of cowards?" When he got too old to walk around in our scrub-oak coverts and our cedar brakes after pheasants and wood-cock he took a stand and hoped that some birds would be driven his way. And if one did come whirling over generally he would scratch it down. After he grew too feeble to climb in and out of a rowboat he was lifted in but always he disembarked unaided. On his all fours he would crawl out upon the planks of the skiff landing. "Did that all by myself," he would chortle in his cracked voice.

One afternoon when the two of us were sharing the same blind waiting for the evening push of black duck to come in off Long Island Sound with the sunset, I said to him:

"General, nobody loves this sort of thing more than I do. But from the time I was sixteen until I was nearly thirty-six I never had a gun in my hands, except to fondle it. Now I'm trying to catch up. I like, each fall, to hunt in some place where I haven't been before. Next month I'm giving myself a month's vacation. I know you've hunted and fished pretty much all over this continent. I wish you'd tell me where to go this time—where the prospects should be the best?"

Through his glasses his old eyes began to dance. "Cobb," he said, "I'm going to tell you of a certain long ago time. When I was a boy in Brooklyn one of my father's closest friends was a certain Judge Brady. Let's see, I probably was about ten years old. He then was about ninety, so that as of this date the span of our combined ages would be approximately one hundred and eighty years and carry his memory back long before the Revolution. He had been a great nimrod in his day. So I, a youngster of ten, asked him substantially the same question that you just asked—where on the explorable fringes of the continent was the best hunting grounds and fishing waters that he'd known in his youth? And he said to me that for variety and abundance of game and provender within a circumscribed and compact area—for fresh-water fishing and salt-water fishing; for oysters, crabs, scallops, lobsters; for shad and sturgeon and salmon and mackerel and bluefish; for upland shooting, pond shooting, rough shooting and shooting from the shores, for geese and swan and ducks and cranes and lesser wading birds; for all the big game except the buffalo to be found in eastern North America, for small game—grouse, quail, heath hen, curlew and snipe, he'd have to hand the prize to—guess what, Cobb? It's only a short distance from here—Manhattan Island. But I guess I'll have to route you a little farther west than that, unless you're going to gun for fur-bearing push-cart peddlers on the East Side and black-birds in Harlem."

In the Wyandanch Club we had a number of very rich men, but you'd never have guessed it by anything which any one of them said or did. Eversley Childs was a big public utility magnate; and the hunting coat he wore was a raggedy scandal. Fred Erickson controlled a great advertising agency but when away from the clubhouse he smoked a five-cent cigar which should have been called the Burning Shame brand. Or possibly Sackcloth and Ashes would have been an even more suitable name? The only strictly enforced club rule was that the incendiary Erickson couldn't ignite one of the arsonous things indoors.

Once I almost qualified for admission to the ranks of the excessively affluent. Only the equation of quirkish circumstance deprived me of affectionate mention in the rival publications of the Messrs. Bradstreet and Dun. It came to pass in the early part of the second decade of the century. I still was toiling in the *Evening World* city room but my old running mate there, "Winnie" Sheehan, had quit newspaper work to become secretary to Police Commissioner Rhinelander Waldo. One summer night—it was the summer of the Rosenthal murder—Sheehan invited me to go on a tour of Manhattan Island aboard a new fire-patrol boat. Ed Hill of the *Sun* staff, afterward to become internationally famous as a radio commentator, was along; and another member of the party was Gaston Plantiff. At that time Plantiff served as publicity man for and intimate adviser to Henry Ford, who was beginning to be heard of as a manufacturer of low-priced automobiles. Plantiff steered Ford away from plenty of pitfalls, but when Ford persisted in going on that grotesque Peace Ship voyage of his to the European Front— "get the boys out of the trenches by Christmas"—the shrewd Plantiff quit in disgust. Had the relationship continued, it is reasonable to assume that Ford never would have committed himself to the vagary of trying to be elected president—an ambition in which he stood practically alone—or the folly of suffering the use of his name for fathering the utterly silly anti-Semitic campaign that was launched in his personal organ, the Dearborn *Independent;* or bringing a most disastrous suit for libel against the Chicago *Tribune*, this being a super-imposed and culminating error which further convinced the general public that while he might be able, singlehanded, to lick Wall Street when the biggest buccaneers there undertook to take his properties away from him, and while he was one of the great mechanical geniuses and great industrialists of his time, Mr. Henry Ford was not equipped for statecraft, or as an international interventionist, nor yet for literary pursuits and for appearances on a witness stand, at least not when Clarence Darrow was doing the cross-examining.*

---

* The first Cabinet dinner for President Wilson and the second Mrs. Wilson after their marriage was given by Secretary of Navy Daniels at his house. Mrs. Cobb and I went down from New York for it. Mr. and Mrs. Henry Ford also had been invited. It was the first time Mr. Ford and the President met, also the first time I had ever seen Mr. Ford. Instinctively you felt that, give him a monkey wrench and a screw driver and a balky engine to tinker with, and he'd show you some wizardry. So if sometimes he appeared a bit bemused when the conversation became general, what of it? If a man knows one useful thing better than any other man alive, that's enough for him to know, isn't it? Take my own case—I probably knew more silly big words than he did—words being the tools of my trade, but I'd get a nut-pick out of order and to me a shoe buttoner will always be a baffling piece of machinery while anything as intricate as an egg beater thwarts my powers of understanding. I regard a patent zipper—especially a zipper that seals a woman's frock up the back—as probably the greatest single boon which inventive science has conferred upon my sex since the dawn of civilization, but its mechanical complexities leave me groping in utter darkness. The first time I ran across a non-refillable bottle I just sat down and gave up. That a fellow couldn't pour something into the same opening from which he'd just poured it forth seemed one of the daunting mysteries of the ages. Then I caught myself saying to myself: "And yet why not, since nature showed the way? Did you ever see an egg come out of a hen? Well then, did you ever try to get an egg back in a hen?" In that spirit I accepted the phenomenon of it and ceased to worry.

But I was speaking of Mr. Ford, wasn't I? He had just bought a seagoing yacht; presumably because somebody suggested that one of the signs of affluence was the ownership of a seagoing yacht. He had never seen the yacht. Shortly he was going to Cuba on her. With a winning innocence, he asked questions about Cuba. That it lay close to our Florida peninsula, that it formerly had belonged to Spain and had a bloody history, that it was a lizard-shaped island, that its principal exports were tobacco and sugar, and its principal

But now Plantiff was in full command of Mr. Ford's advertising budget. As we sat on the deck of the patrol boat he said he was beginning to believe automobile advertising was too dull, too commonplace. He thought a lighthearted note might be indicated and he had converted his chief to the notion of a tentative experiment in that direction. I had been doing a series of signed articles for the *Evening World* and at that time still was doing a page spread called "The Hotel Clerk Says" which ran in the magazine section of the *World's* Sunday edition. (It ran, by the way, for more than five years and never missed a Sunday.) Following the same vein which I used for these special contributions, how would I like to write five short tracts to be put out in pamphlet form by the Ford Company; price five hundred dollars for the set?

Before he got the words out I was shaking hands with him to bind the bargain. In the hope of establishing myself as a free lance I had, only a few days before, asked for a leave of absence without salary, to follow my regular two weeks' vacation. Moreover, I had booked meals and lodgings for Mrs. Cobb and our little daughter and myself at a cottage on Chazy Lake up in the Adirondacks. Five hundred dollars on top of what small sums already I had saved up, would enable us to stay on until I had sounded the prospect of selling material in the periodical field.

Hardly had we reached the mountains than I was fulfilling my contract with Plantiff. I did all five of the screeds in three days—a most lucrative half-week, judged by the prevalent standards. I called them "Talks with the Fat Chauffeur"—why, I don't know,

---

manufactured products were cigars and uprisings—all this, one judged, was news to him. Before the evening was over he had invited several of the guests, all new acquaintances of his, to go on the first voyage. A fellow felt like whispering to him that it might be inadvisable to travel on the same ocean with a rank stranger, let alone on the same yacht, until he knew you better and you knew him better. Repeatedly he made mention of what he called the "hospitilities" then raging in Europe. Well, "hospitilities" is a good word. You could use it two ways to express two different things, one having to do with the horrors of war and the other having to do with one of the pleasures of peace. Since then I've been tempted to use it myself, and may yet do so.

unless it was on the theory that a fat chauffeur would be more good-natured than a thin chauffeur would. I'm not proud of it, but I think in that little booklet I coined the first out-and-out Ford joke, thereby inaugurating the primary trickle of what became a great torrent of Ford jokes which inundated the face of the nation until some patriot thought up a Ford joke to end all Ford jokes. For good measure, I threw in a slogan which was used extensively for a time, "You Can Afford a Ford."

I sent the batch of copy off and in a very few days got word from Plantiff that he liked the stuff and that the big bosses liked it, too. In fact, my scripts had such a favorable reception that as an evidence of appreciation, the company would give me all or any part of my honorarium of five hundred dollars in stock of the company, which shortly would undergo another capital reorganization, probably with a cutup of additional numbers of shares to be exchanged for existing holdings. Privately Plantiff urged me to accept the offer. He was putting all the funds he could rake and scrape together into the venture, he said. So were others inside the corporation. They felt sure of large profits ultimately. It wasn't a speculation; to them it looked like an ironclad cinch.

But all over the map automobile factories were withering on the vine and dying in the bankruptcy courts. I answered, thanking him for his kindness, but would he please send along the check? I never regretted my action either, even though Ford securities soon skyrocketed into the financial skies. By taking the cash I was able to hang on until a definite magazine connection was made. During that summer I wrote the first installments of the Judge Priest tales and I did a short horror yarn called "The Belled Buzzard" and one called "An Occurrence up a Side Street," both of which were translated into various languages, and that made talk and widened my market in other countries. True, I used to have a sinking sensation in the pit of my stomach when roughly I calculated how many hundreds and hundreds of thousands in dividends and bonuses I would have drawn down from my little investment in Ford stock—had I made the investment—and how many hundreds of thousands more the pyramided, piled-up stock would have been worth had I held it until Mr. Ford, paying fabulous prices, bought up the holdings of his smaller shareholders. Opportunity had knocked at my door, as she is said to knock at every man's door—once. But I let her get away and the sly jade never came back to knock a second time or if she did, there was nobody at home.

A few years back—and a good long time after all this Ford business happened—I was at Bob White Lodge in North Carolina as a guest of the late Charles Penn, first vice-president of the American Tobacco Company and by common consent the best blender of cigarette mixtures then alive. One night after supper and before the seven-up game started, I was moved to tell the assembled company, nearly all of them outstanding Croesuses and Midases, of the occasion when, by so narrow a squeak, I overlooked my opening to get into their ratings, financially speaking. They gave me the close attention which moneyed men always do give when the subject is the fascinating one of money.

When I was through and was receiving murmured condolences, Penn spoke up and said:

"Now that you-all have heard from this Jeremiah—and you'll recall that it was Jeremiah who bellyached so loud about his misfortunes—kindly listen to Job, who had ten times as much grief as that derned whiner Jeremiah ever dreamed of."

He went on:

"When my daddy moved his little one-hoss tobacco factory from Martinsville up in Virginia to Reidsville in this state, my brother Jeff and I came along to keep the shebang alive—pretty tough sledding it was, too, for a while. My other brother, Harrison, had a job with a wholesale firm in Atlanta. One day he wired me to expect him next morning. He was coming up from Atlanta with what looked like a nice little in-on-the-ground-floor proposition. Almost before he was off the train he started spouting about a young fellow in Atlanta, a pharmacist, I believe he was, who'd concocted a formula for a new soda fountain drink—a drink which seemed to be catching on. A drugstore owner who was a friend of Harry's had an option to buy the recipe. To swing the deal and start popularizing the stuff in a modest way would take six thousand in cash. The drugstore man had three thousand. If Harry could dig up the remaining three thousand, why everything would be hunkadory. So his bright idea was that I put up fifteen hundred for a quarter interest and lend him fifteen hundred so he could come into the picture on an equal basis with me.

"I had the money; had saved it a dime at a time, but we needed it to expand our own plant with. And I did know a little something about the tobacco business—or thought I did—but I didn't know the first thing about the soft-drink business. So I told Harry to quit dreaming and go back to Atlanta and attend to his knitting and we'd just forget the whole scheme. But pretty soon things began to occur which kept me from forgetting it."

He paused, with his back to the great fire of crackling six-foot hickory logs, and there was an added sparkle in his flashing brown eyes.

"Gentlemen," he told them, "look your full upon the sagacious and farsighted party who turned down a chance to buy a quarter interest in Coca Cola for fifteen hundred dollars."

For a space the circle sat in a silence so profound that outside in the hall you could hear Percival Hill's pet pointer bitch thumping her tail on the floor boards. For, as I have said, this audience was made up of rich men, and rich men, wherever found, have a proper reverence for the mere mention of augmented sums of money and especially for those elusive and augmented sums of money which, like scared rabbits, have escaped from the huntsman's clutches.*

---

* Nowhere below the Mason and Dixon Line, I'm sure, was the spirit of the Old-South-befo'-the-War atmosphere more jealously preserved than at Bob White Lodge. As the car which had brought you out from Greensboro deposited you, a newcomer, at the battered door of the flat-fronted homy clubhouse, a black face would be smiling into yours and a friendly voice would be saying, "Boss, whilst you's here I waits on you—jest you an' nobody else. Anytime you wants somethin' an' don't see me, jest holloa fur Gabe"— or Roscoe or Oscar or whatever the name was. And during your stay that's how it was. Your boy served you alone, building fires for you to get up by on cold mornings, drawing your bath, waiting upon you at the table, ready with slippers for your chafed feet and grease for your muddied boots when you came in from the covers. There were forty bird dogs, some of them field trial champions, in the kennels at the back; there was an icebox big enough for a hotel and it full up. There was a gifted cook to deal com-

[*Footnote continued from previous page.*]

petently with such knickknacks as "br'iled pattridge" and black-eyed peas and mulatto rice and country ham steaks and homemade smoked sausages. But "Uncle Sammy," a dried-up little old expert, would have been imported from Durham expressly and exclusively to lord it over the outdoor barbecue pit, he bringing along with him the holy secret of his own flavory barbecue sauce and the proud manners of an *artiste*. Once I came upon a stranger in the kitchen wing. "Yas, suh," he explained, "I fries the fried cawndodgers—tha's all. Mista Penns an' Mista Hills an' Cap'n Kings an' some of the other genelmen laks the way I fries the fried cawndodgers. So tha's pracly all whut I does."

38

ALL GOD'S CHILLUN GOT KINFOLKS

It is with regret that I confess I cannot tell much about the real Hollywood—if there is any real Hollywood. I have only been living here on the edge of the vortex for a trifle of six and a half years, approximately. In one week a reasonably alert investigator may compile a fair enough conception of Hollywood as at that particular moment it is reflected in its outward and more superficial aspects. But it will require a lifetime to pierce its inner cores, to read its true meanings; and by then Hollywood either will have become a ghost city and the hoot owls at eventide will flitter amongst its ruins, or it will have so changed that the original summaries won't fit the ultimate evolution. Since its main intent is to keep step with popular taste, and since popular taste is a fickle, shifty and unpredictable thing, it is inevitable that change must follow on change, always without rhyme and frequently without seeming reason.

Turn your head to violate the anti-expectoration laws and when you look back there's a new plan in parturition, a new campaign aborning, a new purpose stirring in the womb of idealistic fancy, a new caravan of uncles, brothers, nephews, aunts, nieces, daughters, sons, sons-in-laws and cousins arriving to take the places made vacant by other uncles, brothers, etc., who have been retired or fired or interred in the populous enclosure which proudly advertises itself as "Los Angeles' fastest growing cemetery." For when all is said and done, a producer is likely to be one who believes that charity should begin at home and, occurring frequently enough to constitute case history, an assistant producer is a connection by marriage. In these parts the word nepotism may not always be pronounced properly but it religiously is practiced. The surest sign of depression in the industry is not the cutting-down of stars' salaries or the dropping of contract players or the reductions of technical crews. The surest sign is when a major studio begins laying off relatives.

Distant kinspeople may not attain the organization's pay roll, but in number amounting to dense masses they have access to the lots and to the offices of writers and the dressing rooms of actors and the stages where the casts assemble; and here, without let or hindrance, they peddle all things from endowment policies and mortuary crypts to neckties, book subscriptions and Scotch by the case. Try to imagine General Motors or the Standard Oil Company engaging an expert in some highly specialized field at a salary of from two to five thousand dollars a week, and then suffering him to be pestered at his work and thrown out of his concentrated stride by constant processions of persistent invaders seeking to sell him commodities he doesn't want. In Hollywood you don't need to imagine it. It happens. It happens every working day. Probably it happens every working hour.

That, however, is merely but one side of the moving-picture game and this, mark you, is a game which has a hundred sides and abundant lesser facets for every one of its sides. In it great artists mingle with arrogant pretenders; modest gentility is nuzzled up against by blatant vulgarity; and out of a welter of seeming insanity and misapplied energy there pours forth a constant stream of popular entertainment, much of which is marked by flares of genuine splendor and practically all of which is better than a body might expect, the incoherent nature of its source considered. To one who has seen the giddy dynamos grinding and heard the gears shifting, the abiding wonder is not that so many bad pictures emerge from the mad powerhouse but that so many good pictures emerge from it.

My first experience as an employee dates back to 1926 when everything about a lot was very much noisier than it is now; so that afterward, when sound came in and the tumult was drowned in order that the microphones could operate, they called those boisterous days the silent days. This may give you a rough idea both as to past and prevalent paradoxes. Before that I had sold the cinema rights to various short stories and in the subsequent adaptations had seen my poor little pets battered out of all recognition even for their once-proud parent. However, I had been well paid for the mayhem and anyhow it had been my observation—and still is— that the name of the author of the tale as briefly flashed on the screen just before Reel One starts unreeling, means little or nothing, either for praise or for criticism, to the average audience. Even the name of the supervisor, though shown in type five times as tall, doesn't really score anywhere except in that gentleman's exultant soul. For this business abounds in overlords and deputy overlords who, like a cockroach in a cup custard, mistake prominence for popularity.

Before that summer of 1926, as I was saying, I had trafficked with the movie folk only at long distance. But now, by arrangement, I was to go to California's fairyland to fulfill a commission on the spot, in fact, to fulfill three commissions, for hardly had the principal deal been closed—with the Metro-Goldwyn-Mayer Company, when there bobbed up a chance to turn out a couple of stories for Cecil B. De Mille, who was operating independently. Mr. De Mille having bought two titles in a title contest, my bushelman's job, starting from scratch, would be to run up scenarios to fit the titles, as counter-distinguished from the somewhat commoner custom of paying a fancy price for a title already made famous on the covers of a successful book or by publication as a magazine serial, and then throwing it away—frequently along with the original theme—and making an altogether different yarn under a different title and ignoring the author insofar as is possible. Yet the author's name, especially if it be a more well-known name, presumably might have some small advertising value, were it more copiously displayed.

For M. G. M. a much larger canvas must be filled in. Having scored tremendously with *The Big Parade*, the studio hoped to follow up this great money-maker with a picture which would be as expressive of a notable national achievement in peace as *The Big Parade* had been emblematic of our effort in the first World War. So naturally the digging of the Panama Canal had suggested itself to the master intellects as the properest subject and priority claims to the use of it had been filed at the Hayes office. But although fourteen separate writers manfully had wrestled with the chosen topic, still the powers hadn't been satisfied with any of the completed

scripts. The deal with me provided that I have all my expenses de-
frayed and a drawing account of so much a week while actually
engaged on the preparation of Script Number 15, and, at the end
of a specified period, if I had turned in a satisfactory yarn, I would
receive a very nutritious lump sum, less the amount of the installments previously paid. Also under the system then—and now—in
vogue I could lift from the versions already on hand any episodes
or incidents or indeed any sustained sequences and incorporate such
portions into my own treatment with no credit going to the man or
woman who had conceived them. Since my script, if not used in its
entirety, would likewise be available to subsequent adaptionists, the
plan seemed fair enough. But I elected to work out my own synopsis
first. Afterward I would go through the stories of my predecessors
in the same category and borrow at will, but until then I didn't want
to be influenced by the viewpoints or the achieved performances of
others.

On the train going west I read the data which had been compiled
by M.G.M.'s research department and a magnificent example of
thoroughness it was, historically, geographically and topographi-
cally.* Then I sketched in a skeletonized working sheet, embodying

---

* It would seem that no matter how earnestly the research
bureaus strive for accuracy in investitures and local color, little slips
keep on creeping into the finished merchandise. While he personally was handling *Cosmopolitan* films, Mr. W. R. Hearst went to
great pains and heavy costs to make sure that no such errors would
occur in that elaborate feature, *When Knighthood Was in Flower*.
But in almost the very first scene women wore woven stockings
and diners in an inn ate with forks; the facts being that woven
stockings would not be thought of, nor forks invented until a much
later period than the period to which the play pertained.

The starlet playing the Christian maid in *The Sign of the Cross*,
a piece laid in ancient Rome, wore a form-fitting princesse gown
captivatingly buttoned down the back with large gold buttons,
thereby anticipating the use of buttons, not to say princesse gowns,
by several centuries, at the very least. In *The Covered Wagon* the
heroine made the pilgrimage across half the continent in the roaring
Forty-niner days, and among other hardships endured while en
route Indian attacks, a kidnaping, dust storms, floods, weeks of
blazing sunshine on the treeless prairies, snowdrifts, avalanches in

my notion of a suitable tale and while so doing hit upon a title which I thought vividly appropriate. Since this saga of the Panama Canal was to be a companion-piece to *The Big Parade* why not call it *The Big Ditch?*

I devoted the final day and a half of the journey to skimming through the bale of earlier manuscripts which had been turned over to me when I boarded the steam cars at New York. Here I found proof that two schools of thought had hatched out brain babies on what might be called a fifty-fifty basis. Seven writers had based their plots upon the machinations of a sinister international spy striving to defeat America's mighty project through one or another or a whole set of the nefarious devices fictionally attributed by the E. Phillips Oppenheim school of romance to practically all sinister international spies. By a remarkable coincidence the remaining seven had hung their plots on the perfidious conduct of an official, uniformed or otherwise, in the service of our government who, having been seduced from his patriotic duty by a beautiful but perfidious lady of alien birth, and having accepted the Judas gold of a jealous and secretly hostile power, strove to undo all that our loyal forces meant to do. But now the tally would stand at eight

---

the mountains and a few other things, but came triumphantly through without having mussed her hair or rumpled her frock or damaged her maidenly complexion. Indeed none of her fellow emigrants got weather-beaten or travel-stained.

Not so long ago an eminent star underwent shipwreck and, after that, life as a castaway on a remote South Sea island amongst savages, but when rescued some months later, every carefully coifed tress on her lovely head was in place and the shellac of her beautifully manicured fingernails shone with all its pristine brilliancy. Still more recently an Apache chieftain, who somehow succeeded in being warlike and winsome at the same time, went blood-thirsting and scalp-lifting through six dreadfully long reels attired in a Sioux headdress; a breech clout of the Northwestern plains people instead of the tribal kilt of the Southwestern desert country; beaded Kiowa moccasins not in the least resembling the characteristic toe-lifted, high-legged Apache bootees—and a Navaho squaw's necklace. His costume appeared to give general satisfaction, however, possibly because the wardrobe master who assembled it for the gentleman had avoided taking sides. Those who sort out the fan mail which

to seven because I too had picked on the traitor treatment. My "heavy" was a naval commander in the drafting department who, being inspired of the Devil, had by a trick not yet clear in my own mind brought on the great slide in Culebra Cut and generally had messed up things until retribution overtook him and his betrayer, that siren who hailed from a vaguely outlined foreign land.

Aside from its being on the majority side, it now appeared to me that my clever idea had not been such a clever idea after all. Nevertheless, I clung to it, and meanwhile expanded my formulation into fuller shape until during a story conference at the end of my first half-week in Hollywood, by the medium of a telepathic spark

reaches the studios in ton-lots every week will tell you though that, judging by the letters, fully thirty per cent of those who go to moving pictures in America do so not for edification, nor yet for education, but to discover flaws like these and then to write in about them, tauntingly or complainingly.

In the field of misapplied enthusiasm the all-time high was scored just before we got into the World War. Spending capital presumably furnished by the Berlin Government, an ardent German propagandist made a picture purporting to deal with American valor in crucial hours, but really aimed at discrediting the British for ill-treatment of patriots in the Revolution and again in 1812. Eventually this gentleman landed in a concentration camp for the duration and the Washington authorities confiscated his masterpiece, but I always contended it should have been preserved for posterity as an example of one fascinating inaccuracy superimposed on another through thousands of feet of film. For example: Paul Revere, riding across the New England landscape to rouse the Minute Men, drove up to "Joe's Garage" and wakened the boys there with the word that the Red Coats were coming. George Washington, crossing the icy Delaware on Christmas Eve to surprise the Hessians at Trenton, certainly must have surprised them with the flag he carried in his rowboat: it had forty-odd stars on it. Abraham Lincoln signed the Emancipation Proclamation in a room containing typewriting machines and a whole battery of steel filing cabinets. And as Andy Jackson's riflemen hurried out of New Orleans to mow down Packenham's Peninsula veterans from behind the cotton-bale breastworks, they marched along a macadamized highway with trolley wires overhead, and past quite a lot of hot-dog stands and soft-drink emporiums.

shuttling between the two persons present, the real scoundrel, the true antagonist simultaneously and instantaneously was revealed. My confrere was Irving Thalberg, one of the most brilliant men the cinema ever produced, who was to have overseership of the film, if, as and when made. In that one fleeting flash both of us realized that the only plausible and the most nearly perfect villain of the piece would be the tropics—jungle, fevers, heat, insects, snakes, muck, native superstitions, diseases, death. Here was not one enemy. Here were a dozen enemies, just made to order.

I had invaded the picture colony during perhaps the crowning cycle of Babylonian excesses and almost childish cutting-up amongst the inmates. Through the country "Hollywood parties" had come to be a synonym in the public mind for extravaganzas which on comparison made the fabled revels of the late Emperor Nero seem as mild as a wigwag drill by the Campfire Girls at Weeping Willow, Nebraska. To be sure there was much exaggeration in these accounts but even so the behavior of the more outrageous exhibitionists justified some of the be-adjectived descriptions that went out over the wires and through the mails—with now and then a nice messified murder or a juicy suicide stirred into the bacchanalian broth to give it a special flavoring, while divorces were a dollar a dozen. What else was to be expected in those wild undisciplined days? Take a soda-water jerker or a collar-ad model; take a bathing beauty or a comely manicure girl or a milliner's apprentice and suddenly elevate that inexperienced youngster to a spurious but transiently a worldwide fame and jump his or her wage from ten dollars a week to perhaps ten thousand a week and what else would you expect except that this sensational and fantastic notoriety, this incredible income, would produce a form of emotional insanity? As well give a six-year-old child a pint of brandy to drink and then wonder why the poor little wretch got drunk. The more opulent producers went in for seagoing yachts—on which they got seasick—and for strings of polo ponies that they rode very badly, if at all. Model ranches out in San Fernando Valley and mountain lodges and Palm Springs villas were to be the flourishings of a later era. If you were a female star it was expected of you that you load yourself with diamonds until you suggested the ice jam going out of Hudson River in the January thaw. If a male star and desirous of being in the fashion, you bought a highly expensive chassis and then retained an expert who was supreme in his confined and exclusive field to design and super-impose thereon an automobile body to suit your personality. This gifted gentleman first studied the various fascinating angles of your character and then went cunningly to it—regardless of expense. Among others, Rudolph Valentino, Tom Mix and Fatty Arbuckle— or so I was told—had automobiles built to suit their personalities. Then there was the important matter of the swimming pool. Did your neighbor install a swimming pool at a cost, say, of ten thousand dollars, you tore out yours, which represented but a puny outlay of five thousand or some such piffling matter and installed one paved with porphyry and jasper, with onyx curb-linings and platinum-plated stepladders. In this manner you established the permanency of your social position. Also you hired that mathematical magician "Margie" to fix up your income-tax returns in such a way as not to give greedy, grasping old Uncle Sam any the best of it. All she charged you was a percentage of what she saved you. It may be recalled that "Margie" subsequently went to a Federal penitentiary and some of her distinguished clients had flinchingly close calls from going there, too.

Things are different today. Ostentation is taboo; so is open misbehavior. Democratic simplicity is the motto of the hour and a seeming decorum in public the mode of the moment. I claim that, proportionately speaking, you'll find as many gentlemen and ladies—nor do I use the term in any snobbish sense—among the movie people as in any like group in any other modern setting, and the downy newcomers take pattern for outward conduct from these dignified sophisticates. So you'll kindly observe that I'm referring now to an earlier period, midway of the gay and riotous twenties.

In the sacred sanctums of the high muckymucks of the realm the King's English was being taught to take a joke. The word "epic"— generally pronounced *upik,* as in hiccough, and signifying any picture costing over a quarter of a million—was going out, having lost its vogue through being overworked; and as a modestly descrip-tive term "super-colossal" no longer was treated with the respect which once had been its proper due. Impious rascals had begun to make japery of it. "Functional," to denote almost any phase of

activity about some delirious plant, had attained a temporary popularity. But the real favorite was "motivation." Ah, there was a
linguistic bonbon to roll upon the tongue and dissolve against the
grateful palate. "Yes, yes," would say a reigning magnate who
originally was, by profession, a mere uncle, but now spoke with
weighty syllables, "you got maybe the rough ungredience for a
pitcher—good characters and menaces and climaxes and suspenses
and all like that. But where's your motivation?"

There was an impressive sub-mogul rating high in the graduated
cousin class, who said to me one day:

"Cobb, I ain't against the new slant you got on this here now
Big Ditch stuff. Somebody was telling me about it last night and it
don't sound so bad the way he tells it. But one thing you gotta
remember all the time: Make it Dinah-Mick."

"I beg your pardon?" I said, being momentarily dazed. I didn't
quite see how I was going to fit some Irish vaudeville team—possibly
song-and-dance sharps or mayhap a comedy patter act—into a
composition dealing with the construction of the Panama Canal.

So I said, "I beg your pardon?"

"You know, make it Dinah-Mick," he repeated. "From start
to finish." He clarified his meaning by a composite gesture denoting
intensity, forcefulness, strong pressure. With his command of
gesticulation he needed naught else.

And I told him it surely would be my aim to do so and from that
point on stressed the dynamic possibilities. And between times and
on off days I would play hookey and sneak down Culver City's
main thoroughfare three-quarters of a mile to where, in a white-
pillared structure built in imitation of a typical Southern mansion—
nearly everything then was built in imitation of something else—
Mr. Cecil B. De Mille, bringing to the task a wealth of affectionate
imagination and a reverent regard for the inherent greatness of his
subjects and especially for his mastodonic main subject, was engaged
in producing Cecil B. De Mille and various less massive conceptions.
Here, within the very shadow of brooding genius, I found the
impetus and the inspiration to cut out and paste together, first,
Turkish Delight, then *Ladies Must Love*. Later one of these tailored
conceits was put through the mill and marketed without creating
any absolutely epochal upheaval in the amusement world, but the

other bright little number presumably was done to extinction in the
dungeons below the supreme master's suite because I never heard of
it again, nor could I find anybody else who ever heard of it. The
catacombs of Hollywood are full of unmarked graves of the
Unknown Dead.

In due time I submitted the completed draft of the chief opus.
For this important and portentous proceeding I introduced two
finaglings which I believed to be of my own devising although they
may not have been. About once in so often I broke up the monotonous reading of the text, to pitch the typed pages aside and in my
crude fashion act out a scene. Or I would employ the conversational
and the colloquial rather than the literary forms to picture proposed
stage business. To my way of thinking, a more effective trick was
my trick, which I have employed since but then was trying out for
the first time, of calling my characters by the names of the actors
I mentally had assigned to the roles. I would speak of John Gilbert
as doing this and Hobart Bosworth as doing that and Norma Shearer
as doing so and so. This, I was pretty sure, fixed the separate personalities in the minds of my small audience in the conference room,
whereas, had I used stock names, the chance was that some among
my auditors might find it confusing to distinguish between "Larry"
and "Spencer," or be left in doubt as to whether "Maizie" was the
woman lead or the ingénue.

I was pleased—and somewhat amazed—at the warmth of the
reception my undertaking was given. Those present, there being
only three of them, including young Mr. Thalberg, said with an
enthusiastic emphasis that they liked it. There were changes to be
made, naturally; revisions, expansions here, excisions there. But
taking the first draft as a whole they liked it so much that it should,
they agreed, go into production at the earliest possible moment,
should be scheduled as one of the chief releases, perhaps the chiefest
release among the outstanding features of the ensuing winter. I had
performed my share of the undertaking as specified in the contract,
and a check in full for my story awaited me at the cashier's wicket,
but a supplemental and continuing salary arrangement must be set
up. I must stay right there—for co-operative services with King
Vidor who would direct the picture; for expanding and elaborating
the dialogue in collaboration with a trained builder of continuities;

for preparing subtitles as the production took shape. I explained that I couldn't tarry any longer no matter how generous the remuneration. Mrs. Cobb was abroad, awaiting my arrival. My own passage from New York to Genoa was booked, the sailing date being less than ten days away. Our daughter, living then in Italy, was expecting her first-born. I was sorry but I must be off.

Well then, would I promise to steam for home at the very earliest possible moment and hurry back to Hollywood to aid in the enterprise? To that I agreed. Already a tentative list of principals was being discussed. Negotiations, so I gathered, would at once be opened with the United States Navy for the inclusion of the Pacific fleet in divers spectacular action shots. Scouts would be seeking suitable locations in California for outdoor scenes. A site must be found for one built-up set showing the Canal in process of construction and for another set depicting a completed section of it, replete with practical locks and workable water levels. A camera crew—and some of the members of the cast—would shortly be off for the Isthmus to get background photographs. I had provided for sequences showing ten or twelve steam shovels at work. A mere ten or twelve?—why, the notion was preposterous. There would be fifty steam shovels, maybe a hundred steam shovels stretching away in a seemingly endless vista of steam shovels.

I went away contritely feeling that the mighty operations of a mighty studio would practically be at a standstill until I returned. At the Santa Fe station while waiting for my train—and it a Sunday at that—I was overtaken by a breathless emissary, direct from headquarters, desirous of knowing what I thought of the merits of Miss So-and-So for one of the secondary parts—secondary, but in a way, pivotal. To the best of my knowledge and belief I had never before heard of this lady, so without reservations of any sort, I could give my unqualified endorsement of the choice—and heartily did so. The next afternoon at Albuquerque I was intercepted by a long-distance telephone message dealing with some technical phase with which I was presumed to be familiar. I have forgotten the actual purport of the call but I do recall giving my counsel and advice—at so much a minute for tolls—even though I was hazy through the entire transaction.

Our grandchild did not arrive in the world on the anticipated date.* She stubbornly delayed the event for nearly two weeks past the scheduled time but, I might add, gave general satisfaction to all concerned when she did arrive. Through the delay my conscience gnawed at me like a persistent hidden termite. As soon as our daughter was out of the hospital, Mrs. Cobb and I sailed for America. From the docks I sent a cablegram to Hollywood giving the approximate date of disembarking at New York. I already had sent a cablegram saying we shortly would be on our way. No reply had reached me but, as I figured it, no reply was necessary, nor was one expected.

As the liner was being eased into her berth in North River, I told Mrs. Cobb, for the twentieth time, that she must be prepared to start with me for the West Coast almost immediately, and probably within a few hours. No doubt a representative from the New York branch of the studio would be on the pier with the tickets and the sleeper reservations. But he wasn't there, nor was there any

---

* The afternoon before the great advent there was a tea-fight upon the lawn of the little villina which my daughter and her household occupied in the Tuscan Hills above Florence. In the midst of the party, Buff, with a sudden whiteness about her lips and her jaws clamped on the first warning pangs, quite casually remarked: "If you'll all excuse me, I believe I'll go have a baby."

Which accordingly she did—after twenty-four hours of travail. She still was under the influence of anesthetics when Mrs. Cobb and I and two women friends were admitted to a room in the local Swiss nursing home. Here we were introduced to a tiny pink morsel called by an excited Italian serving maid, *"una bella piccolo bambina."* While the womenfolk flutteringly were discovering manifold beauty points in this young person, from the bed by the wall came Buff's drowsy voice saying: "Where's that brat of mine?"

Mrs. Cobb put the mite in its mother's arms. But Buff's eyes still were clouded by the fumes she had inhaled.

"What is it?" she asked, cuddling the small bundle to her breast. "Male or female?"

"Oh, Buff," exclaimed Mrs. Cobb, "it's a lovely little girl!" She noted that the baby's infinitesimal fingers were fluttering over its screwed-up face, and with pardonable grandmotherly enthusiasm added a somewhat overly enthusiastic descriptive line: "And, oh, Buff, she's so smart—she's trying to get her hand in her mouth!"

"Well, if she's a true Cobb she'll get it in," said Buff as she drifted off again into the ether fog.

telegram from Hollywood awaiting me. At our apartment there was no telegram, nor any letter, either.

I called up a friend of mine, a prominent functionary at M.G.M.'s local offices. I didn't want to unpack our trunks if the trip across the continent impended. Strangely enough, he hadn't heard a word from any source touching on a production dealing with the Panama Canal since the original negotiations on that score had been opened with my resident agent in the forepart of the summer—and this now was the middle of the fall. He said this unaccountable reticence puzzled him. I told him I was in the same state. He then said that he would be telephoning Hollywood on routine matters during the afternoon and he would take occasion to find out the present status of my picture.

His tone still was mystified, when toward evening he got me back on the wire. Irving Thalberg was away but so far as his assistants, his secretaries and his associates knew, the studio had not started preliminary work of any character on any picture dealing with any canal whatsoever nor, so far as they knew, was such a proposition in contemplation or being casually considered, or being discussed or even being mentioned. It seemed the departmental heads were concentrating on an altogether different line of pictures at present—costume pictures, historical dramas and so forth. However, if later he could ascertain any facts having a possible relation to my affair, he would let me know.

From that hour to this hour—and that covers a scope of approximately fourteen years, six months and some odd days—I have never heard a breath about the project except that in 1930, I think it was, I did read a paragraph in a movie gossip's column saying Donald Ogden Stewart was dickering with M.G.M. over the possibilities of scripting a picture pertaining to the Panama Canal, but seemingly nothing came of it and all the rest has been silence. So R.I.P., says I.

Onlookers who have been admitted to the studio during the filming of a big feature are likely to be appalled by the seeming waste of time—which means money, and by the expensive and tedious process of taking the same sequence over and over again, first from this angle and then from that, with long shots and close-ups and all, so far as they may judge, at the whim of an imperious director or possibly at the request of an apparently finicky cameraman. What they do not realize is that on the set the camera is, so to speak, the eye of the spectator as he views the finished product on the screen. The lens must go where the look of a bystander would go were the bystander spying on an occurrence in real life. If the lens fails to do this; if it fails to shift with lightning-like rapidity from this participant in the scene to that participant as the action progresses, while Tracy is saying this or Carrillo is doing that, confusion inevitably results in the mind of the theater patron. The photography may be perfect, the acting smoothly convincing, the lighting perfect, the lines clearly spoken, but still Mr. Customer senses a baffling indefinable defect somewhere in the product. The answer is that at some crucial moment, when the plot was being developed or a climax approached, the camera failed to travel back and forth in the same swift cadence that the human eye naturally would travel in. To prevent such blundering and insure harmony and a balancing of effect is where directorial ability attains its peaks. But after the director is done much yet depends upon the work of piecing and patching and assembling which goes on in the cutting room, for the exhibited reel, which seems a thing of continuity as it runs through the projecting machine, is really an amalgam of minute bits of negative, most skillfully jointed and co-ordinated and pasted together. Viewed in perspective the tessellation of your bathroom floor may be to you an unseamed pattern, but it was put down a tiny scrap of mosaic at a time. The same thing applies to a properly assembled moving picture.

Rather than those of the high-salary brackets, to me the real wizards in the fashioning of film-stuff are, in order, the cutter, the set designer, the boss stage carpenter, the property man. To the stage carpenter the supervisor says: "Bill, this Washington monument your gang has built is out of scale. Tear it down and knock me together another Washington monument half again as big at the base. Have it ready tomorrow at shooting time." And Bill says, "O.K., boss, you're the doctor," and he summons a double crew for all-night service and, lo, in the morning the utterly and obviously impossible magically has been accomplished. Or it's the director speaking: "Listen, Props," he commands, "we're hurrying through these shots in the cellar of the haunted house. So when the folks get back from lunch this afternoon I want you to have two hundred assorted spiders, fifty rats, a dozen bats, and a couple of bullsnakes waiting. Oh, yes—and a swarm of bluebottle flies. Got that?" Without turning a hair or sweating a single sweatlet, Props allows that he's got that and heads for the telephone to call up the purveyor of live vermin and the dealer in disagreeable insects.

One day at the main Fox lot in Westwood I went with Will Rogers and the chief scene technician to inspect an outdoor set showing the public square of a smallish American community back in the sloven eighties. It recently had been used for *David Harum*. Now the tentative intention was to adapt it for the shooting of a picture laid in the South, a picture for which I had fabricated the theme.

"Looks kind of Yankeefied," said Will dubiously as we walked through the empty streets and past the false fronts of homes and shops and the like.

"Come back here in forty-eight hours," said the designer, "and you won't know the old place. You fellows will take one look and involuntarily start humming 'Dixie.'"

It was even so. Two days later, by invitation, we revisited a spot transformed. "City Hall" was where "Town Hall" had been engraved over the façade of a squatty structure of brick—bogus brick pasted on in strips like wallpaper, if you must know a trade secret. "Livery Barn" was "Livery Stable" now. A stone church—make-believe stonework—had become a frame building and by some mysterious juggling of effect was no longer First Unitarian; it indubitably was Southern Methodist. Faded awnings had sprouted on store fronts. The courthouse strangely had taken on a weather-beaten aspect. Trim hedges had vanished; replacing them were picket fences, and some of the fences lacked for paint. Recently neat curbings had broken down here and there, and a thick crop of artificial weeds had sprouted on the near-by common, and for special touches of local color, curled-up watermelon rinds were strewn broadcast in the gutters and the town sow was rooting her way along the edges of a dilapidated wooden sidewalk.

"She's orthodox now," said Will. "I can almost smell the dog fennel and the tobacco stems. Say!" He pointed to a distant equestrian figure in the middle of the transmogrified public square. "Say, there's something kind of familiar about that statue yonder and yet there ain't. Where have I seen that mounted cavalryman before?"

The set designer grinned.

"Right over in the middle of that old French village layout across the creek," he told us. "She was Joan of Arc on horseback then. But we moved her over here and mixed up some plaster and turned her armor into a general's uniform and her helmet into a slouch hat, and gave her a nice long set of chin whiskers and stuck on a few other touches and now Joan wouldn't know herself because she's Stonewall Jackson, getting ready to lead a charge."

About once in so often a committee from one of the New York banks comes to Hollywood hoping to find out where the millions that have been loaned to some studio went to. Having a proper reverence for money—else they'd not be bankers—these gentlemen are agonized by the profuseness with which their dollars are being slathered about. They cannot understand the frittering away of precious days and half-days, while actors and extras and crews idle about; cannot understand why these expensive hired hands should not be made to pull time clocks and keep regular hours, as the clerks do in a bank; why an apparently inconsequential bit of business should be rehearsed interminably and then shot over and over again. They rend their garments, figuratively speaking, and show their great concern.

There are times when one who has been in a measure initiated into the inner mysteries of the industry feels deeply moved to say to these troubled delegates:

"Esteemed sirs, prithee harken: Leaving out of the argument various fixed factors and unavoidable considerations which are not visible to the naked eye, pray remember that in this curious business the promoters thereof are confronted with certain unescapable considerations, to wit, namely, as follows:

"First, unpredictable climatic conditions involving such matters as fog, rain, cloudiness, lightning, sand storms, desert glare, sunshine, murkiness, light and shadows which defeat the best-laid plans of smart men and upset the financial budget and cause them to regard the official prognosticators as exponents of a brilliant but untrustworthy school of fiction writing.

"Second, the potential that operations are at the mercy of

sound recording machines, cameras and lighting devices—perhaps the most temperamental, the most mercurial and the most unaccountably freakish mechanical appliances ever invented.

"Third, the still more significant fact that for their basic element, their original raw material, the producers must rely upon human beings, no two of whom are alike and no two of whom will react alike to the same impressions and contingencies and all of them subject to crotchets or bodily disabilities or ill health or ill humor or bad dispositions, so that if a leading man falls down and breaks his beauteous but fragile nose a picture in process of being made may be tied up for six weeks or some such matter at a cost of thousands upon thousands of dollars; and a fit of self-induced tantrums by some hysteria addict of the supposedly gentler sex may throw everything out of kelter at a crucial moment. You'd be surprised, gentlemen, how some of these doe-eyed, flower-faced soubrettes can turn the high-strikes on and off like a faucet and shriek like infuriated switch engines and use language right off the back wall of the boys' grammar school.

"Finally, gentlemen, I invite your attention to an underlying supplemental clause. To be sure and on occasion, the lavishness of some authority-swollen producer or the vanity of some director suffering from delusions of grandeur and ready to gratify them—so long as somebody else foots the bills—may run up the cost of a picture far beyond normal and proper limits. But, on the other hand, the pioneers in this enterprise and, to a degree, the present leaders in it graduated out of highly competitive small businesses where every penny was made to count, where every possible economy must be practiced if the proprietors hoped to survive. Moreover, the majority of them either were Hebrews or Irishmen—members of two races proverbially thrifty and frugal at their early merchandising ventures, however prodigal and generous at spending they might be after affluence were attained. This being conceded, don't you agree with me, gentlemen, that if there was any way by which the tremendous overhead could be reduced and the incredibly large running expenses might be curtailed, these canny people would not have gone along as they have, after this costly fashion for thirty-odd years without putting sound saving methods into effect? They'd have found out what the trouble was and the cure for it within thirty days after they broke into this chancy game. Indeed some of them would have smelled it out in the first thirty minutes."

It is the habit of some here in Moviedom to laugh at a lack of so-called cultural background and certain grammatical idiosyncrasies as observed among divers of the outstanding executives. Their mispronunciations are laughed at—privately. Jests are made in print of their personal extravagances. But while sometimes they may not be articulate to express what ripens in their brains, you may be very sure that they have an elemental feel for simple dramatics, an innate sensibility for emotional values, a judgment for what the average man is likely to favor in amusement—all the things which make up what we call the theatrical instinct. They may tell it with pantomime rather than with language, but they wouldn't have climbed to where they are and couldn't have maintained their hold on the upper rungs of the ladder after they got there had they not had true showmanship and plenty of it.

And besides all that, they certainly are mighty good to their families!

39

WHERE WEST ISN'T WEST

THE MORE you try to define the unbelievable commingling of contradictions which is known as Hollywood, the harder you work to classify and cross-index its hypothetical complexes, the more hopeless becomes the task. To begin with, it largely is a figment of the imagination. Politically, there is no such community. It is not a separate corporation, but lies altogether within the maw of that greediest of all cannibals among the cities, Los Angeles. It has a post office of its own, a sort of glorified substation, but that is only for the convenience of its dwellers. Strictly speaking, it neither is an outskirt, an excrescence, an overflow, a taxing district, a nucleus, a dependency, nor a municipal appendix. No longer do many of the big companies maintain plants within its more or less loosely defined boundaries and the homes of the upper movie classes are now nearly all remotely elsewhere, and Sunset Boulevard has ceased to be a *plaisance* and a loafing range for the masses of movie folk. Hollywood is in effect a name for coagulated namelessness, but since it has come to mean what generically it does mean all over the world—the axis of the world's greatest amusement machine—it is one of the most famous and most alluring words in modern geography. Mention of it conjures up an entrancing picture before the eyes of an infinity of people but when the tourists come a-seeking the picture, it isn't there any more. It has burst from its original frame and the sundered fragments—and their robust outgrowths— are scattered all about: in Culver City; over the ridge in the San Fernando Valley; at Studio City; at Universal City; down in Los Angeles proper. So you see that actually the thing doesn't exist at all, which is both suitable and typical, seeing that this more or less mythical Hollywood is in nearly all respects a collection of acute anti-climaxes.

It is the spot where Heartbreak House is right next door to Hallelujah Hall; where shoddy mediocrities and fustian misfits and crafty plagiarists seem sometimes to be plucking the juiciest persimmons while their betters take their leavings. The popular composer who has a memory for old tunes and hopes nobody else has; the script writer who is not necessarily a good writer but makes up for that by being indeed a very close reader; the extra who may be either a star who was exposed or a star who not yet has been discovered—all these are to be found, cheek by jowl under the same tents with gyps and geniuses; with wing-clipped failures who should have succeeded (but the forces of puffed-up and complacent ignorance defeated them), and bogus successes who most deservedly should have failed; with dreamers of dreams and cutters of cheeses; with potentially gifted unknowns fighting to gain a foothold or even to get a hearing and notorious imitators apparently safely ensconced at the top of the heap; with men and women who have it in them to make great visions come true—if only their taskmasters would let them, and once in a while do make these visions come true, in spite of Hell, high water and Hollywood.

Though this place is in Los Angeles it is not of it. A metaphysical wall a mile high separates the compacter segments of this chambered nautilus of a place from the great cellular monster which long ago engulfed it. But though Los Angeles swallowed Hollywood, it never has digested it and probably it never will. Its ardent membranes are powerless against that brassy morsel which has remained unabsorbed, like a Hindu girl's bracelet in a crocodile's belly; corroded but still intact. There are millions of people in Los Angeles County who have yet to look upon the inside of a studio although they'd mightily like to; this morbid impulse of theirs will remain forever ungratified.

In the spraddled larger compound there is a plaguing curiosity to know what goes on t'other side of the fence so that unregarded mash notes are thrown over the palings and wasted kisses blown through the cracks. And coupled with this is an only partly concealed envy—the big top being jealous of the side show; the dog wistful to wag the way the tail does.

In the inaccessible lesser corral there is indifference and a spicing of contempt for Los Angeles' lack of metropolitanism, for its sprawling unshapeliness, for its fumbling efforts to find itself and to become in esthetic values what already it is in population—the fifth largest city in the nation. Your paper each day carries on the same page two society columns, one limited exclusively to the doings of the elect of Los Angeles proper, excepting that rich Pasadena's stogy formalities are stewed in for an added flavoring. The other column is devoted to the sprightlier gaieties of the thirty-two thousand who constitute the encysted foreign body. It must be that few among Hollywood's aloof Smart Setters aspire to consort with the snuffy Towsers and the fluttery Fifis of Southern California aristocracy, for it is sure they gladly would be welcomed to those flexible inner circles. For they do say it takes an athlete to keep out of society and an Old Family is one which has been here long enough to sell its trailer. Upon the other hand, there isn't much doubt but that those stately dowagers and those palpitant debutantes who are listed among the Blue Book entries hereabouts would delight to scale the tall partition which hedges them off from the moving-picture precincts. However, except at large charity functions and at the local race tracks, the groups rarely mix. Anyhow they wouldn't have anything to talk about to each other. There are vastly different tribes on those adjacent reservations and their scalp dances aren't pitched to the same key.

Things weren't always so. No sooner had the first invasion of the fathers of the baby industry got under way than the entrenched burghers of the bustling young city took steps to show there was no welcome here for such itinerant raggle-taggles and bobtails as these. If they couldn't actually throw the brash vagabonds out, at least they could prove to them that there were two sides to this California hospitality business. Early comers to Moviedom's future capital like to tell of these difficult primitive days when apartments bore the sign:

> No Children,
> No Dogs,
> No Picture People.

The founder of one ambitious realty development publicly took steps to make his property impregnable against the assaults of the motley undesirables, save that along with actor-folk he included Semitics among those to whom his agents would never sell lots nor rent homes. The other day the wife of the head of a big production unit who owns an estate in that once cloistered spot, told me every householder on her street admittedly was either Jewish or actorish— or both.

Save as providing transportation facilities for expeditiously going elsewhere, Hollywood doesn't need her great neighbor and could get along quite well without her. But the proximity of the colorful annex is of enormous advertising value to Los Angeles. Her architecture (borrowed), her horticulture (adopted), her civic center (confused), her social inhibitions (imported), her Mexican quarter (commercialized), her Oriental quarter (synthetic), her fashionable promenades (there aren't any), her shopping district (scattered, characterless and woefully jumbled together, where drive-ins and glary billboards and all manner of cheap john shops snuggle up against magnificent retailing establishments), her seaport which is twenty-odd miles away—and a dreary long trip to get there, too; her manufacturing districts which are leagues apart from one another and leagues away from everywhere else; her made-to-order lightheartedness, the same being utterly alien to the instincts of a naturally staid and sober-minded peasantry; her landscape effects which are sufficiently spectacular, with a garish sort of beauty following the winter rains but other times are brutally austere and never, at any season, are friendly and inviting after the fashion of mountainous scenery in the East; even her much-vaunted climate— all these, for attracting visitors who may tarry, as annually scores of thousands of them do and become permanent inhabitants, are but minor assets alongside the drawing power of Hollywood.

The trouble with Los Angeles is that she wriggled right out of diapers into long panties. She suffers from growing pains and childlike uncertainty, along with a lusty overdevelopment. Maturity is a long way off; a floundering adolescence still abides with her. She is a thyroid case with persisting glandular disturbances. Yet it is as sure as any human calculation can be that, within a few decades and next only to New York—and possibly Chicago—she will be the largest city on the Western Hemisphere and, furthermore, unless the signs fail, will be a main production center for native art and domestic handicrafts and, besides that, the greatest style mart and the greatest resort for all-the-year-round sports in the United States —a veritable talent factory. At present though she has to a distressing degree the red-ant fixation common to most American communities, being madly desirous to crowd the already overflowing home nest with more red ants, regardless of their uncongeniality for intimate association with the original red ants; going drunk on a heady tipple of census figures and rejoicing when the happy buglers of the Chamber of Commerce trumpet forth estimates of a future expansion which will eclipse all the intoxicating statistics of the past.

Being situated about as far west as one can go without wading into the Pacific Ocean, Los Angeles does not in any notable regard suggest the West as it reveals itself on both slopes of the Rocky Mountains. The pioneering feel has vanished, if indeed it ever existed, about the site of the straggly Pueblo of Our Lady the Queen of the Angels of Rio Porciuncula. The old Spanish influence which reverently has been fostered in Santa Barbara, a hundred miles up the coast and which, without any artificial stimulus, congenially has endured in the adobe-walled purlieus of San Diego, a slightly greater distance below, entirely is lacking here. Scattered over the domain are some of the largest ranches in the United States, but they never seem as ranchified as do similar estates in Arizona or New Mexico or Wyoming or even Oregon. Somehow we do not associate the notion of a citrus grove inside the same boundary lines with a cattle range. One or the other seems to be misplaced.

Various volunteer diagnosticians have endeavored to define Los Angeles' pathological and psychological symptoms. Joe Frisco the stuttering comedian, called it, "P-P-P-eoria with p-p-alms." Hendrik Van Loon described it as "seven suburbs in search of a city." I always have thought of it as a newly built and still unfinished hotel where a vast number of bewildered strangers are spending the night on the American Plan.

The processes of radical change follow along so swiftly, one treading upon the heels of another, that Los Angeles is in a continual state of flux. Take her political complexities: The first predominant wave of settlement at the end of the last century and through the first twenty-five years and more of this century was out of the Middle West. This inflowing and infiltrating race was a conserva-

tive, agrarian-minded race passionately addicted to state picnics*
and voting the straight Republican ticket. The G.O.P. counted on
the lower half of the state as one of the most reliable Old Line
bailiwicks this side of the Great Divide. But later came the inunda-
tion of refugees from the heat-blistered, tree-denuded farming areas
of southwestern states, notably from wind-blown Oklahoma and
Arkansas and the Panhandle of Texas; penniless pilgrims seeking that
happy land where poor folks could sleep out-of-doors in any month
and pluck a meal off the nearest fruit tree and, when not pleasantly
on relief, work at luxurious wages in the ever-bearing sun-kissed
truck patches—as cruel a pack of lies as ever deluded a frightened
people, fleeing like hunted fugitives from their own agricultural
mistakes and their climatic miseries. So the Dust Bowlers, who
mainly were New Dealers, trampled down the Corn Belters or
converted them or ate them alive or something. For lo, the Republicans that once in countless herds ranged the high plateaus of this
Southland have gone, sharing the fate of the buffalo and the passenger pigeon, the great auk and the mustache cup and other vanished
species. Among the desert fastnesses of the Imperial Valley a few
furtive heads—a pair here, a lone buck there—are reported as hiding
and in partisan quarters hope is entertained that they may mate up
and bring the breed back again. Meanwhile there prevail almost as
many preachers of weird economic panaceas and sociological experi-
mentationists—Epic planners, Townsend planners, Ham-and-Egg-
ers, political Holy Rollers and fad jugglers—as there are curious
religious cults and faith-curing ologies and theological loose screws
and self-elected Messiahs on the nut-bearing side streets of Los
Angeles—which is to say, practically all the varieties there are and
all there ever will be too, until more and madder doctrines are
thought up.

Yet with this great multiplicity of isms and prisms to choose
from, with so many of these creeds and cults and fol-de-rols and
ferments to divert the resident emigrees, Los Angeles somehow
continues to be rather a commonplace and unexciting town, too
busily concerned with fattening up and broadening out to exercise
its imagination much. This intellectual stodginess has infected

---

* "Michiganders Bask Under Soft Skies While Folks Back Home
Shiver In Zero Temperature"—Standard Headline.

Hollywood where one might logically look for a continual three-ring circus performance, an unending street parade of spontaneous antics. Not by any means though. In fact, not at all.

With me it is as an open question whether Hollywood caught dullness from Los Angeles or Los Angeles' high blood pressure is due to the proximity of Hollywood.

However, in the case of the latter citadel, there may be contributory causes. The fact that they constantly are immersed in their own professional affairs to the exclusion of the affairs of the outer world tends to make people provincial and insular; there's no denying that provincialism prevails here within the fortress, although not to the extent which once it did. The knowledge that a bright sally or a quirkish speech, uttered casually, will instantly be stolen by some wise-cracking master of ceremonies at a night spot or some hired gag writer of the films—that also is a thing which makes for reticence in mixed company. The phrase-coiner has learned to keep his mouth shut until he has sold the wheeze himself. Silence is sure-enough golden in these parts. Then, too, the constant striving to be ultra-respectable has a tendency to choke off pleasant rowdyism. So the intruder who comes seeking after sinful merriment and unbridled ribaldry takes away the baffled sensation of having made a mistake in the address, as though he had aimed for a house of joy and found himself breaking in on a prayer meeting. Barring a few people with weak kidneys, there is no night life to speak of in the section where this family lives.

Soon after we moved out here my daughter and I went to a very staid, very elaborate dinner, indeed a regular high church dinner, at the ocean-front castle of one of the keymen of the Colony. I shan't call the roll of those present because that was more than six years ago and by now, of course, most of them are gathering dust in the discard. On the guest list, along with some of the most distinguished stars and executives, were a number of sojourning financiers from the East. They were out here looking for lost, strayed or stolen dividends, I would say. To be sure the costumes of some of the women were a bit over upon the far side—heavy masses of their portable jewelry on display and regal coronets and things like that. I recall that my eating mate, a queenly but robust lady, was encased in a low-necked gown of scarlet satin and looked a good deal like a magnificent radish. (P. S. The radish was peeled about one-third the way down from the top.) Another lady, a famous—for the moment—ingénue, seemingly labored under the impression that this was a fancy dress party. She was made up as Juliet. On the other hand the proceedings were marked by a classic dignity. With each course the appropriate wine was served but in strict moderation. By hard endeavor you might get slightly moist but without prospect of a thorough saturation.

For her table partner my daughter drew one of the outlanders, a Boston banker, the bearer of as old a name as you'll find recurring each generation on the muster books of Harvard. During the preliminary stages there was, she reported, an expectant eager gleaming behind his rimless nose glasses. It was obvious that through the stately prelude he was poised and waiting for something thrillful to happen. Nothing thrillful did happen except that for dessert we had a blazing rum cake. You might call this the high spot, and after the head butler, officiating as volunteer fire laddie, had extinguished the conflagration, the babble of discreetly low conversation was resumed right where it had left off. When the coffee came on this gentleman put his lips close to my daughter's ear and in a tense whisper—I'm telling the unvarnished truth—he asked:

"Do you think there'll be an orgy tonight?"

"Well," said Buff, "our hostess hasn't taken me into her confidence but if I know my social onions—and I think I should after two months out here—there'll be at least one table of stiffish bridge and the rest of us will see a picture. Since the majority of these people eat, drink, think, talk, act, produce, criticize and applaud pictures all the time they're awake and dream about pictures while they're asleep they naturally look at pictures when they want to relax. It'll be either a private preview of a new picture which hasn't been released yet or the revival of some good old picture which everybody is familiar with but is supposed to revive fragrant ancient memories. So, Mister, hold onto your hat! . . . Wait, I forgot this: On account of some of these hard-working folks having to get up so early, we'll nearly all jog home to shut-eye not later than 10:45."

From that point on disappointment claimed the visiting alien for her own. It was evident that for him the glamour had all come unglammed.

With some of the quickest wits and cleverest epigrammatists in America already domiciled in its midst—and more coming in all the time to sign term contracts and to cuddle down like pampered dormice for a somnambulant and generally an undisturbed hibernation in their respective padded cells at the studios where the smartest ones seem to be the first ones that are forgotten by the very men who hired them—with all this, nevertheless and to the contrary notwithstanding, depressed and blighted Hollywood seeks afield for its own peculiar divertisements. Hence the impulse of one smallish group of thinkers (persons who do feel things so intensely!) to dabble on the sly with the tenets of Communism. The Pink who would be a Red if only he weren't so yellow—he occasionally is smoked out from amongst the secret "fellow travelers" and has an unhappy hour before the grand jury or a congressional investigating body.

Those more sportively inclined turn for entertainment to endowed cutups and imported clowns. Hence also the presence of such exotic importations as Mike Romanoff and Maxie Rosenbloom and Elsa Maxwell, and the professional "ribbers," those rarely gifted humorists who'll gladly insult or humiliate your more timid guests all evening, which same is regarded out here as the very top of polite jocularity.

A few years back there also was Wilson Mizner. But Mizner was more than a copycat, infinitely more than a sidewalk Grimaldi or a hired contriver of mildly naughty entertainment to satisfy the somewhat infantile tastes of jaded and blasé movie folks. Here was an authentic wag, an artificer of darting and devastating repartee. But when he went in for verbal dueling this gaunt stinging hornet picked on somebody his size. He didn't show off his smartness at the expense of some agitated bus boy or self-conscious novice.

Literally, Mizner died laughing. For months before the end he dragged himself about Filmland so consumed by the mysterious illness which racked his wasted body that his skin, which always had shown a curious pallor, was now of a ghastly lifeless cast. His naturally sepulchral voice had become a forced graveyard croak and his great staring brown eyes burned with a febrile fire. Yet his customary hailing cry for friend or foe of "Hello, sucker!" was as explosive as ever and his tongue as keenly barbed.

He took to his bed only when he grew too feeble to drag himself

out of it. In the very last hour of his life he came out of a coma
to find sitting beside him a popular clergyman. This good man, who
had been summoned by a devout woman friend of Mizner, offered
his ministrations. "Part of my trade is giving such spiritual consolation as I may to those in extremity," he said. "Without offense,
please let me say that if there is anything I can say to you in this
hour or anything you'd care to say to me, I shall be only to glad to
serve."

"Much obliged, Padre, much obliged," wheezed Mizner. "But
why bother? I'll be seeing your Boss in a few minutes."

The fabulous Mizner brothers, of whom Wilson was the most
famous, grew up in San Francisco, which was fitting, since from the
very beginning of her cultural life San Francisco has been begetting
comic colts and quick-witted fillies. It is hard to conceive of San
Francisco and Los Angeles as being on the same continent, let alone
being in the same state. San Francisco is everything which Los
Angeles isn't or vice versa, should you care to put it that way.
Some day Los Angeles will grope her way into her own; will develop savor and a personality and the individuality which now she
almost altogether lacks. But I think San Francisco must always have
had the qualities of a complete and unique distinctiveness, even
when she was no more than a huddle of shanties among the sand
hills and the sand fleas.

For my money she is the most civilized city in North or South
America. She also is the most tantalizing, the most urbane, the most
mirthful and, figuring her comparative youthfulness and her size,
the most fecund mulching-bed for sprightly ability in the world.
Picturesque scoundrels and civic heroes; great actors, great painters,
great sculptors; journalists and playwrights and novelists; pugilists
and playboys; orators and singers; great ladies and great courtesans;
and most of all, a petted and encouraged school of uniquely charac-
terized types—these in multiplying hosts have grown out of her
inexhaustible soil through every period of her speckled, bedazzling,
besmeared, regrettable, resplendent history. Her people have the
greatest capacity for being carefree of any people I know. Any
time, with provocation or without it, they'll just haul off and enjoy
themselves.

To me she is unapproachably fascinating. No matter in what

shifting temper she is seen—as a worldly-wise yet forever juvenile hoyden swinging on her Golden Gate; as a somewhat shabby empress, proud though and self-content with a gorgeous justifiable vanity, where she sits enthroned, with the bronzed buckler of her mountain at her back and the silver lance of her bay aimed at the breast of the sea; a gay but tattered grass widow in the mood to reminisce about the various charming but undependable husbands she has had; a Babel's tower of clashing contrasts where the prettiest women live in the ugliest houses, and all the streets nearly run steeply uphill, excepting those that run precipitously downhill, and the sons of the dauntless Argonauts suffer their sea-borne commerce to be crippled and their water fronts to be made desolate by radical labor agitators and camouflaged Communists and racketeers sniping at industry from behind the ranks of decent American unionism. And these men had the Vigilantes for their grandsires!

They say San Francisco is dying. I don't believe it. If there were only two native San Franciscans left among her abandoned ruins she still would be a city and one of these survivors would be a booster and the other would be a prankster and between them they'd carry on the ancient traditions and man the last of the creaky cable cars while the friendly fog blew in from off the Farallones.

But admit that San Francisco is dying? Then when she's dead what a lovely corpse she'll make! And what a happy ghost!

Los Angeles may be California's diamond stomacher, but San Francisco is the poppies in her hair.

40

THE TOWN OF TOUCH AND GO

If I were enlisting the woman most competent, in my opinion, and above and beyond that, most willing at some undertaking calling for compassion; for unstinted unselfish labor to soften human distress or lift human need; for money, if money were needed, but more than money, for personal service freely and graciously bestowed, I'd have the choice of three great-hearted women whom I regard as very great ladies besides.

For the eastern seaboard my choice would be Fannie Hurst; for the West Coast, Marion Davies, and for the country at large, Kathleen Norris, whose soul is so universally maternal that she tries to mother all America and comes as near to fulfilling that self-appointed contract as any one person reasonably could be expected to do.

By the same token, were I choosing just two communities out of them all, whose people are the readiest to give and yet ask no questions, whose pocketbooks and whose check books will open widest to the call for help no matter how or from what quarter the call comes, one of my choices would be this same inchoate whirlpool of Hollywood about which I've mostly been blathering in preceding chapters. This is a strange thing, too, seeing that the members of Hollywood's Who's Who—and Whose Ballyhoo—are most assiduously and continually preyed upon by all fashions of extortionists, deceptionists and impostors. At the risk of making a bad pun in defense of a frequently maligned and often misunderstood spot, Hollywood might fitly be called The Town of Touch and Go— they touch you and then they go and they don't come back unless there's a lingering hope of another touch in case the victim should have a short memory or be of a forgiving disposition. I am sure more devices for wringing money by false pretenses out of generous souls successfully are practiced in the movie maelstrom than in any like area of the world's surface. For where the big money is supposed to be there the big chiselers flock—and fatten and thrive. For the fact stands out that every appeal, legitimate or dubious, seems to garner the shekels. Perhaps the psychology of it is that actor-folk and amusement caterers in general are an emotional species, wearing their sympathies on top of their nervous systems and easily moved even by vacuous pleas.

The other town where, according to my experiences and observations, charity is the quickest and the most free to flow, is a town which those who know it only by passing contact with its seemingly brazen indifference, its frigid outer shell, look upon as frozen up, like a dead fish in a cake of ice, against individual solicitation for help on behalf of individual causes. I'm speaking—prepare yourself, reader, for a small shock—to the town of New York and notably that borough of it which includes the sentimental island of Manhattan; and I'm taking my text from a case of which I had direct knowledge, an instance typical and characteristic, I claim, of a true generalization: the case of the late Morgan Robertson.

When I came to know him Morgan Robertson was on the way to be one of the forgotten men of the writing game. In his youth he had been a bucko mate on a Down-East clipper. He sickened of the brutality which harsh custom decreed should be the lot of foremost hands aboard sailing ships. He told me that one day when he finished working on a recalcitrant seaman he stared down a hatch through which he had thrown his victim and the fellow lay there bleeding like a stuck pig and looked as though a keg of pig lead had been rolled across his face. Robertson said to me, "I went to the rail and was sick over the side. I walked ashore that night and except as a passenger I never set foot on shipboard again. But I've never quit being a sailorman—at heart."

Having walked ashore, he learned the watchmaker's trade—he had always been nimble with his fingers—and spent the next few years hunched in the front window of a jeweler's shop in a State of Maine coast town, with a microscope screwed in one puckered eye and a table before him littered with pinions and mainsprings and little cogwheels. On a night he sat with some cronies talking of this and that and drinking in between. He fell to complaining of the mistakes of people who wrote seafaring tales. "I could write a better yarn about life on a windjammer than any of them," he said. "Because I know windjammers and these lubbers don't."

"Well, why don't you, then?" asked one of his hearers.

"By dern, but I will!" he said.

And he did. Before he went to bed that night he had whittled out the beginnings of a short story which was destined to be the first of a series dealing with the rude and sometimes violent adventures of a certain "Sinful Peck" and his dissolute friends. The great Captain Cuttle was no more picturesque a figure than Sinful, and Long John Silver might have admired to know him and beyond doubt some of W. W. Jacobs' dock-side folk would have felt at home in his mischievous company.

For the next few years Morgan sold his stuff to the magazines as fast as he could turn it out, which was pretty tolerably fast. Mostly the tales were loaded with a salt and tarry humor. But occasionally he sent his muse down some macabre and grisly alleyway. "The Grain Ship" was a compressed thing, but I think one of the greatest concentrations of hair-lifting horror that I ever read. Wyeth and Howard Pyle illustrated his wares and he rode a high wave and spent the money as fast as it came in. Even for those frugal times he never got top prices though. He was better at milling the grist than at chaffering with editors over taller rates. He was a sailorman at heart all right, I reckon.

The crest on which he coasted flattened and left him in shoal waters. He lost his vogue. Perhaps he lost the knack, for, sooner or later, does he but live long enough, every fiction writer pumps himself to a musty sterility. He became that most melancholy of figures in literature—the spot marked X where a vanished talent was last seen. Considering the quality of the work he had wrought, there was an amazing and a lamentable swiftness in the way Robertson passed out of popular remembrance. One thing about him: When he was done he knew he was done. He quit trying to pump life back into the cold corpse of his creative faculty.

When I first met him he was living somewhere in the festering jungles of Harlem—he and his wife. He used to sit with us of afternoons in the press box at the ball park. None of us seemed to know—perhaps none of us cared—where or after what fashion he spent the rest of his waking hours. He was short, stocky, rather silent even when he'd had a dram too many. He was shabby, but always precise and neat, with the primness of a man who had lived for long in cramped quarters. Regarding his fallen state he was quite philosophic and very gallant. From time to time he borrowed small sums, always suiting his demands to the pocketbook of the other person—a dollar here, two dollars there, rarely as much as five dollars; and when he carefully had entered the date and the amount of the loan in a little grubby notebook which he carried, the creditor figured the transaction was closed forever. He didn't know that to this little aging man these were debts of honor. Sometimes—but not often—Morgan tippled a wee bit too much.

We were living on the West Side then, in One Hundred and Tenth Street. One evening Bozeman Bulger, who newly had graduated out of sports-writing into a free-lancing job, raised me on the telephone.

"How much cash have you got on you?" he asked. His tone was urgent.

"Enough to go along on but not enough to stand much of a touch," I parried. "Why the mad rush, Brother Bones?"

"Keep it intact until I can get down there," he said. (He lived six blocks farther up Riverside Drive.) "A little while ago I got a telephone message from Morgan—with the charge reversed. He didn't even have the nickel to pay for the call. I went to the address he gave—a back room in a crummy old flat building on the edge of the Black Belt. Dam' it to hell, Cobb, that pair literally have been starving to death and too proud to tell anybody about it. They've sold or pledged everything they had, down to their extra clothes and the bed they slept in and the gas stove they cooked on—when they had anything to cook on it—and every stick of plunder that they could raise as much as a thin dime on. They had a pallet on the floor and boxes to sit on and another box for a table and that's about all. There wasn't a bite to eat in the place. And there's a dispossess notice tacked on the door. Unless they can raise rent money by tomorrow the wolves will be throwing those brave hungry old people out on a dirty sidewalk. I had enough spare change to rustle up a market basket of groceries and I got some scraps of necessary furniture out of hock, but we'll need still more money in the morning. I'll be right down."

I remember that the next afternoon was a hot, muggy afternoon in July and how Bulger and I sweated as we panhandled north on Broadway from the Flatiron Building to the top borders of the old Tenderloin, as it existed then, up in the mid-Fifties. We tacked back and forth from one side of the street to the other, stalking people from behind, buttonholing people on the sidewalks, invading bars and cafés and other likely coverts. Then we caught the el and rode to the Polo Grounds and canvassed the grandstand and the playing field for likely prey.

Our manner of approach didn't vary much. To each prospective subject we applied the same formula. One of us would say:

"Listen, there's a good fellow—and his sweet little wife—in a tough jam through no fault of their own. You probably wouldn't remember him but in his day he gave joy to millions of people. We're organizing a club to give that couple temporary relief until a bunch of us can figure out a way to get 'em back on their feet. This is a club with only two rules: Five dollars pays your initiation fees and your dues forevermore. A candidate can buy only one five-dollar membership, no more and no less. And the other rule is that nobody must ask the name of these people or where they live or any single solitary blamed thing about 'em. Are you in or are you not?"

Out of those we halted and there were close to a hundred of them, and all, we figured, amply able to contribute, just two failed us. One man said—and we could tell by the look out of his eyes he was lying—that he didn't have the money on his person but would see us later on, vaguely, like that. We told him that later on would be too late and so would he kindly forget it? The second said he would join up only on condition that he knew who the proposed recipients were and we broke the sad news that automatically and by acclamation he already had been blackballed. We relaxed the regulations slightly on George Cohan's account. We accepted from him a ten-dollar bill only on his solemn promise that he collect a rebate of five from his partner, Sam Harris, whom we accordingly admitted, sight unseen, along with Cohan. Before sunset we had collected upwards of five hundred dollars. It came from gamblers, actors, actresses, confidence men, ball players, promoters, writers, agents, dramatists, brokers, vaudevillians, businessmen, professional men, newspapermen, wasters, grafters, theatrical producers, chorus beauties, pugilists, one college professor, and two sporting clergymen—a Catholic monsignor and the rich rector of a swanky Episcopal parish uptown.

The fund didn't last long. It couldn't, seeing the uses to which Morgan put most of it. First, in celebration of his renewed and fortified fortunes, he went on a gentlemanly and restrained tour of various grogshops and had a drink in each one. And then—but I'll tell about it in Bulger's language to me:

"You know what that lovable, stubborn old fool is doing? He's batting around with that funny little account book of his in his hand, hunting up every chap that he's ever touched, and repaying the loan—with interest. If anybody refuses to accept the money he gets mad as the Devil. Well, what are we going to do next?"

From experiences which he made Robertson repeat to him he wrote two articles entitled "I Was a Sailor." I helped a little in the revisions. Lorimer bought both of them for the *Saturday Evening Post* and, being made aware of the circumstances, paid better than customary rates. The checks went to Bulger, but were by him endorsed over to Morgan. The yarns were printed anonymously and made talk.

With funds on deposit, the Robertsons had moved out of the slum into comfortable quarters and Morgan turned up for a World Series wearing a new toppiece in place of the crippled and infirm derby hat which through constant wear had become almost a part of him. But such succor as we had given the two of them was only a makeshift and a stopgap. A sort of committee on ways and means was formed, made up of writers and publishers, and the committee set to work on a plan for a permanent and, hopefully, a safe and profitable endowment to be raised in a way which would bring neither unpleasant notoriety nor embarrassment to its beneficiaries.

From the various publishing concerns which had published Morgan's works in book form we obtained releases on copyright assignments held by them. Only one house balked—an old and most respectable publishing house. From this firm we got a letter saying that on such of his stories as they controlled, they must receive a proportionate share of the profits derived by any proposed republication. During the preceding year the total of royalties paid by them to Morgan on account of sales had amounted to exactly thirty-seven cents! We called their attention to the co-operation cheerfully extended by fellow publishers of theirs. They still insisted on their measly pound of flesh. We then committed plain blackmail. We notified them of our intention to ask one of the leading New York dailies to print the correspondence, together with an explanatory statement to be signed by a number of well-known ladies and gentlemen—some of whom, incidentally, had publishing affiliations with their establishment. By return mail and special delivery came a letter in which the company said there had been a misunderstanding and it gladly would waive any proprietorial interests it might have in the matter.

At actual cost one publishing house printed a uniform edition of Morgan's completed writings. At actual cost another concern, specializing in subscription sales on a premium basis, loaned us the expert services of its corps of canvassers and distributors. On the day before the edition went on sale nearly every daily newspaper of consequence in the United States carried in its literary section or, more commonly, on its sporting page, something—a paragraph, a column, an illustrated special even—telling of the rediscovery of a great American writer and pointing out that his collected stories, now for the first time available, would have an irresistible appeal for all lovers of outdoor adventure and more particularly for those who went down to the sea in ships—or hoped to. The federated baseball writers of the town had conspired together to fire this broadside of publicity—an advertisement which could not have been bought for any imaginable sum of money. Oh yes, each volume carried an eulogistic foreword done by a distinguished author—Tarkington, Ade, Rex Beach, Richard Harding Davis, Charley Van Loan, and so on.

People who never before had heard of Morgan Robertson, or if they ever had, had forgotten him, fell over themselves to buy his books. People bought them who possibly never read them afterward. But they bought them and they paid for them, which was what counted with the promoters of our scheme. In the height of the campaign Charles M. Schwab, as president of the organization, asked me to speak at the ensuing annual dinner of the Pennsylvania

Society in New York and wanted to know what my fee would be. I told him I never accepted money for talking across a dinner table unless it was announced beforehand that I came, not as an invited guest, but as a plain hired hand. Howsoever, in purely a social capacity I'd come to his banquet and talk a spell provided he bought some of Morgan Robertson's books for distribution among his friends. He told me to send along as many sets as I thought he ought to have. Before dark a truckload of sets had been delivered at his great mansion on Seventy-second Street. Well, the Pennsylvania Society had plenty of money and Charles M. Schwab was doing fairly well, what with a salary of a million dollars a year—and pickings—from the United States Steel Corporation.

Through the sales a nourishing sum totaling well up into the thousands was forthcoming. A wealthy Wall Street operator—I wish I could recall his name now and print it here—volunteered to take a considerable part of the proceeds and see whether he couldn't fatten them up by a quick turn in the market, he practically guaranteeing us against any loss. As bread cast on the waters—the waters of speculation—the money came back, heavily buttered with a fifty-per-cent increase. And that Wall Street man had never seen Morgan and knew of him only through what some of us told him.

Next a fund was created, with a bank as trustee to invest and guard it and pay out monthly installments for life to Morgan and, if she should survive him, to Mrs. Robertson through the remainder of her days. But so wisely was the money administered that presently the accumulated dividends exceeded the payments and the bank was empowered, in its discretion, to hand over these surpluses to Morgan. However, he would not apply for such extra remittances unless this had the joint approval of Bulger and myself, whom he regarded as his unofficial but—bless his trustful old soul—his competent financial advisers.

In the following year I had a call from Bulger. There was a grin on his homely face—and just a suggestion of moistness in his eye. And his voice was a bit husky.

"Morgan won't come to you direct," he said; "afraid you might laugh at him, I reckon, or think he was being too extravagant in his old age. So he sent me to find out how you stand. All his life, he says, he's had an ambition to follow the example of the richest man in the Yankee town where he lived when he was a kid growing up. He's always wanted a fur overcoat and a gold-headed cane. He thinks he can afford these luxuries now. He won't buy them though unless we give our consent."

Through the good offices of a brother of a famous Jewish comedian, a smart merchant who knew the peltry market from the hair roots up, we got, at a sacrificial price, a garment with at least two kinds of dead animal skins on it. One kind, I suspect, was dyed rabbit; it might not have fooled other rabbits but it fooled Morgan. Nevertheless this undoubtedly was a bargain, even though purchased in the middle of an August hot spell when the overcoat market would be seasonably sluggish. The kindly captain of our precinct station house escorted Bulger to the shop of a professional fence masquerading as a pawnbroker and, under police pressure, the proprietor dug out from a stock of what undoubtedly was stolen goods, and sold at a ridiculously low figure, a heavy ebony stick adorned at the handle end with a great clump of scrolled gold. The gold bore some stranger's initials but a handy engraver remedied that small matter and cut the new owner's name into the massy bulb.

I think it was about three weeks after that when Bulger got me on the telephone. He was sniffling and before he finished with what he had to say, was blubbering over the wire:

"Morgan's gone," he said, "but gee, Cobb, what a swell finish! Yesterday he slipped away and went down to Atlantic City all alone and took a room at a cheap hotel on the Boardwalk—a front room so he could see the ocean from his window and hear the waves hitting the beach. They found him there this morning, cold and stiff. He was sitting in a chair at the open window. He had that ratty fur overcoat over his shoulders with the sleeves pulled around him like as if they were hugging him and the gold-headed cane was across his knees—and his eyes were staring out at the sea. So the last thing he ever saw in this world was the thing he'd loved most in this world. Gee, Cobb, could you beat it for a finish?"

Well, Bulger had a happy dispatch, too. He came in after playing eighteen holes of golf, ate a supper of the Southern dishes he loved, got up from the table saying he was tired but never felt better, went singing upstairs to his bed and lay down there and peacefully, quietly, just quit breathing. He didn't leave much of an

estate but what a turnout of people—all kinds of people—there was
at the funeral!*

---

* Bulger came from Dadeville, a small Alabama community.
Once when he had gone back to the old home on a visit, the leading
barber waylaid him.

"Mist' Bozie," he said, "I wrote me a poem fur my shop an' ever
sence I put it up, the w'ite folks been hurrahin' me 'bout it. You's
a big New Yawk writer now an' I knows you'd know ef 'twuz all
right or not. Please, suh, come 'long wid me an' pass jedgment."

Bulger accompanied the proprietor to his establishment. Upon
the wall, done in colored letters and enriched with floral embellishments and ornamental scrollings, was framed the criticized verse.
Bulger took one glance.

"Tobe," he said, "let these people laugh if they want to. But
you leave that effusion of yours where it is. Not only is it real
poetry but it's loaded with sound business principles."

So through the years the legend remained in full view, reading
as follows:

> Roses is Red
> Vilets is Blue
> Don't ast me fur Credit
> 'Cause I'll have to say No!

41

CHOICE OF JELLO OR STEWED PRUNES

As I COME near the end of this thick writing (that being the name my friends, the Blackfeet, have for a sizable book), I find myself moved to fluff out the tail of the manuscript with recitals of various and sundry happenings—or impressions—which mainly are unrelated to one another and only vaguely are related to the purpose of the narrative, that is, if it has any purpose except the egotism of a man moved to put down on paper the tally of experiences that have acquired merit for him because they were his own experiences and because they stick in his mind. To the extent of at least this chapter, I shall yield to the urge. It is as though one concluding an already unduly long letter felt impelled to tack on a whole string of postscripts. Or, since the reading of these matters is in no wise compulsory, perhaps a better simile would be to say the customer is being offered his choice of desserts at the finish of a drawn-out table d'hôte dinner.

Out of the rag bag of my small adventurings through life and out of a scrap pile of lesser reminiscences I mean to rummage for this material. Always things have stuck in my mind; things perhaps of no especial pertinence except to a professional scribbler who, sooner or later, expects to make use of nearly everything he ever saw or heard or did. And always I have been vain about my retentive powers. In certain regards all the members of my family have had freak memories. Mine is a lopsided faculty. I cannot remember telephone numbers nor house addresses, my own included; and I forget persons' names, even the names of persons I have known intimately. But not often do I forget places or physical settings or the governing circumstances or the faces of those I have met. Yet in my time I have shaken hands and swapped commonplaces with as many persons as the next one. If the meeting was more than swiftly incidental—if it covered hours or days—I automatically set one particular lobe of my brain to work the moment I see approaching me this former acquaintance. And quite frequently, by the time we are confronting each other, I have re-created in my head a mental likeness of the original background and the original conditions.

I am fortified then should this newcomer put to me the accusing question: "You don't remember my name?" which is a very cruel question indeed, because if I admit I don't remember his name and he turns out to be an important individual, that is a reflection on my intelligence and therefore is humiliating to me, whereas if he is not important, he is likely to be all the more sensitive and his feelings are hurt and again I am distressfully embarrassed. But this time I am organized to edge around that awkward corner. If it be a man I say:

"What talk have you? Why, I'll never forget that bully afternoon we had when we ran into each other on a train going from Winnipeg to Calgary—let's see, that would be all of eight years ago? —and we chinned about the North American Indians, both of us being nuts on that subject."

Or if it be a woman:

"Not remember you? Why, my dear lady, I've been trying to forget you so I could go on with my life. I often recall that grand day at the Fair in Chicago when somebody introduced us and we all had dinner together at the Belgian Village. And how smart you looked in that outfit of yours—brown tweed, wasn't it?—and that little trick hat of yours with the green rooster feathers on it. It must be in the wearer: that hat was mighty becoming to you. But I bet it would look like the dickens on me."

I'm out of deep water then. If I remind a man of what we talked about or describe to a woman her costume on a bygone occasion, I need not scrape around among the lees at the bottom of my mind for the names. The parties of the second part naturally assume that I know them.

In the case of a man I have a trick for making him tell me his name with no suspicion on his part that he is being tricked. This useful artifice was taught to me long years ago by the late United States Senator Joe Blackburn of Kentucky who through his tremendous acquaintance and his seeming familiarity with the intimate affairs of his constituents, as much as through his oratory, spent practically all of his active life from the time he was mustered out of the Confederate Army holding public office.

Somewhere along in the conversation I remark to my man, "Say, apropos of what we were just discussing, I want to mail you a clipping out of a magazine that bears on that very point." I haul out a pencil and an envelope and poise the pencil. "I need your address? And, by the way, what's your middle initial?"

Now it is a fact that no man, however modest or however inconsequential, can think of himself as a single letter of the alphabet—as K or M or J. He never has done so and he can't do so here.

Either he says, "John K. Ferguson—the K's for 'Knox' you know." Or he says: "Well, I rarely use the initial. Just plain Patrick McGaffey will reach me."

Not once in twenty tries will this small ruse fail and then only in the instance the man who purposely dropped his middle name or never had one.

I like to cite an example for proof of my ability—an inherent ability to begin with, but strengthened by diligent practice—to revive physical reproductions out of the remote past. Very early in my fictioneering days I wrote a short story having for the locale of its climax, Paducah's oldest theater and, in my childhood, its only theater. St. Clair Hall it was called and it stood facing the old Market Square building, a tumble-down ante-bellum shed of a structure about which much of community life centered in those early times, because then nearly every householder did his or her own marketing and the place was a clearinghouse for gossip and a swapping ring for political discussions.

It was there, at St. Clair Hall, that I saw *Humpty Dumpty* which was my introduction to the glamorous world of make-believe. And there also I saw *Nip and Tuck, The Widow Bedott, Box and Cox* and Lew Schoolcraft's minstrels, with Milt Barlow and Willis Sweatnam for the premier endmen. The building was cleared away when I was about ten years old, I'd say; and it was fully twenty-six or twenty-seven years later that I wrote this short story. For local color, I described in some detail the old drop curtain. This curtain greatly had impressed itself on my infantile susceptibilities because the center breadth presented a briskly colored scene of the Grand Canal of Venice and my juvenile conclusion naturally had been that this was a view on the main street of some town which was inundated, as Paducah lately had been, by the great flood of 1884, only in this town the people lived in bigger houses and wore gayer clothes than Paducah people did. I told also of the squares and oblongs in the friezes of the picture which bore advertisements of leading stores. There was a regular framework of them.

Shortly after this short story was published, I went down home on a vacation and the leading photographer, Will McFadden, came calling at my mother's house and without much preamble he said to me, "My father was the pioneer photographer of this town— daguerreotypes and tintypes first and afterward photographs. Mostly for his own amusement he loved to dabble in oil paints. He did portraits of a few of the old-timers and away back yonder, not long after the Confederate war, I think it must have been, he did the curtain for St. Clair Hall. And he was so proud of the job that he photographed it. After his death my brother and I found that old photograph in his files and I kept it as a souvenir of those early times. I thought it was the only copy in existence—didn't dream you or anybody else had one."

"I haven't," I said.

"But look here," he countered, "that yarn of yours, 'A Judgment Come to Daniel' that came out here a few weeks back—and that stuff you wrote about that old curtain—why, man, see here—" and he began tugging at an age-mottled faded cardboard square which was wedged in his coat pocket.

"Hold on," I bade him. "Don't show it to me yet. Let's see, from memory, how near I can come to drawing the same composition that your father painted?"

I made a quick pencil sketch which we compared with his treasured photograph. Except that I placed five human figures on the marble steps of the palace in the foreground, when there had been six, and provided four black-and-white, goose-necked hitching posts to which the waiting gondolas were tethered instead of three, which was the rightful number, I had made no outstanding mistakes. And of the fifteen or eighteen advertisers in the borders I correctly had listed eight—Dr. Pitcher the sporting dentist, Guthrie

& Johnson, dry goods, Abe Anspacher the hatter, Kirchoff the family baker, Wallerstein Brothers, clothiers, Langstaff & Orm, sawmillers, Thompson-Wilson, distillers, Little Williams' Marble Hall Saloon. I like to brag of that performance; I'm bragging now.

Excusing the chances of casual risks in various tamed and untamed parts of the world and at least one occasion when I suddenly was faced with the prospect of mortal extinction at the hands of a temporarily estranged and violently inclined individual, I have twice been about as near to death as a human being can go and yet come back to make a palaver about it. Through one of these ordeals I entirely was clear-witted, indeed it seemed to me that my perceptions sharpened as my bodily resistance lessened. What I suffered from was a profuse gastric hemorrhage which came upon me with no preliminary illness to speak of, so that physically I had not been worn down or mentally blunted by shock or by the exhaustion of prolonged invalidism. It is a fact that except for a great and increasing lassitude I never felt better in my life. Certainly I was organized to observe the processes of imminent dissolution as painlessly I drifted right up to the hereafter's threshold. I think I can best explain my sensations by saying that it was as though two individuals were concerned in the event—one being engaged in the act of passing out for good and the other, a trained reporter, engaged in recording the various stages of this highly interesting proceeding.

In the second seizure—a recurrence after seventeen years of the same attack of internal bloodletting—I was, through the critical periods, under the influence of morphine, but even so I had clear-headed intervals when lucidly I was able to appraise, for remotely possible future references, what went on within me and about me. So speaking, as it were, from the depths of inside information I am trying to comfort those who some day may be circumstanced as I was by stating that for the patient there is neither fear nor even apprehension of what may hereafter follow. On the other hand, as strength fails and the will power wanes, a passive resignation, an untroubled acceptance, takes the place of his first struggle and rebellion against fate so that there is a palpable desire, almost an alluring curiosity to see what may lie beyond those dark curtains which swing only one way. I figure that this is the emergency where if he altogether gives up the fight he is gone. It is, I take it, to the credit of most of us that feebly we do continue the fight. After the first attack, which occurred during a lecture tour, I wrote a magazine article about the processes I had undergone. I wrote that at no time did it seem to me either plausible or proper that I should appeal for help to any source except my own forces. On the contrary, I felt that to expect the Almighty to leave untended the conduct of the universe, including the ordering of the firmament, and such other details, in order to inaugurate a rally on the fourteenth floor of the Copley Plaza Hotel at Boston, Massachusetts, for the express benefit of the inconsequential atom which was myself, would be highly unbecoming, not to say downright impertinent on my part. For making this admission I ferociously was fired on in print or from the pulpit by a whole congress of God's gunmen, those self-appointed theological terrorists who, it would appear, most eagerly covet the opportunity to turn their consuming blasts of hell-fire and damnation upon anyone reckless enough to defy doctrinal gangsterism. Mob piety can be mighty murderous sometimes. And always it is pitiless.

What though I'm really getting at is this: In each of these times of critical illness, and usually at the lowest ebb, I've had a certain vision. Or perhaps it would be better to call it a phenomenally clear and distinct mental conception. It cannot be a dream, for it never came to me in my sleep or when I was in that indefinite hazy state between dozing and wakefulness. I should hesitate to call it a recurring hallucination, induced by drugs or weariness, because it invariably is vibrant with tone and hue and invariably, too, it is exactly reproduced. Yet it has no traceable association with anything that ever occurred in my life.

By unmistakable evidences I know that the setting must be the familiar section where I was born and where I spent my days until I reached voting age. I am walking alone on one of the old county turnpikes which long ago were replaced by a system of modern highways. The pike must only lately have been recrowned for where the fresh gravel is spread the middle breadth is the color of raw ocher. But along the verges the old metaling has bleached out to a faint tawny, so that the road is like an endlessly stretched

garter snake, a pale yellow garter snake with a streak of red down
its spine.

It is very hot and very still. Even the commoner birds—the
mockers and the mourning doves and the cardinals and the brown
thrushes—are mute in the woods of the flatland which border the
right of way. Not even the blue jays are vocal. I walk along until
I come to where a dirt road, no more than a narrow lane, meets
the pike at a sharp angle on the left. I turn into this lane. There
must have been a long dry spell, for dust, as fine as ground talcum,
spurts up almost to my knees as I put my feet down. The ruts and
the wagon tracks are brimful of dust; the surface seems treacherously smooth until I stumble into a small hidden hole or against a
concealed ridge. The trees overhead are powdered with dust and
there is a thick sifting of it on the blackberry briars at the roadside
and the wilted leaf pads on the mullein stalks have become long
drooping tongues, all coated and furred, as though the mullein suffered from the very fevers which its juices are esteemed to cure.

I cross a narrow wooden bridge over a sluggish, half-dried creek
and in the shallows its shrunken surface has turned from the customary healthy saffron to a dreggy brown, like bad coffee, and the
stagnant pools look dead and dusty. At the farther end of the
bridge a water moccasin, torpid and fat with the summer fatness
of its kind, is sunning itself on the right-hand shoulder of the road.
It always is the same dormant big snake and always encountered
at the same spot. It is so swollen that it seems more like a legless
lizard with a dropsical body and a spindly short tail than a water
moccasin. Instead of sliding down the bank away from me, it throws
itself into an awkward half-coil and its mouth gapes open to show
the cottony white lining, and the two fangs projecting from the
corpsy membrane of the jaws are like little curved prongs of ivory.
I do not molest it, nor it me.

As I go on past that unpleasant creature, all at once the air is
heavy with a great humidity; so heavy that I scarcely can breathe.
As though it had density, it clogs my nostrils. It is like trying to
breathe through pledgets of damp warm wool. And suddenly I am
aware of clouds in the sky and a quick sharp wind blowing. The
dust is whipped off the tree limbs and the weed tops in skeins. It is
lifted up from the road in whirling funnel shapes. In the next instant

I am so enveloped that I can see nothing but dust, taste nothing but dust grit, hear nothing but the silky swish-swish of all those spiraling dust clouds—and at that identical juncture the whole fantasy is dissolved away.

I wonder whether I shall ever travel through to the other end of that dust storm? For I am powerfully inquisitive to find out what may be on beyond.

Unexpected and acutely grave peril plays strange tricks on the prospective victim sometimes. I'm thinking now of what happened in Flanders away back in August of 1914 when the runty Prussian sergeant with the curiously speckled face got the spiteful notion that blowing a hole in my midriff would be quite a good notion. But I must preface the tale by explaining how I happened to be in that particular place on that particular afternoon.

About a week earlier, four of us, all American news writers, had been at the fall of Louvain. While the Germans, swinging slantwise across from Liége and Namur, approached the helpless town from one angle, we were riding toward it from the other side in a chartered taxicab. It was this same taxicab in which we were supposed to have cruised for three weeks behind the invading columns as they drove on down through Belgium and into France, with the meter running all the time and piling up a mountainous debt account. As a matter of truth we occupied this dilapidated vehicle less than three hours; had trouble occupying it that long. Because when we still were a considerable number of kilometers short of Louvain our driver, a red-nosed Walloon, put on the brakes and throttled his motor to an abrupt standstill and, with one hand cupped behind an ear and a startled look on the broad face which he turned upon us, said in a troubled tone: "Boom, boom!"

Now that his engine was stilled, we could hear the distant faint pounding, too—the first big guns any of us, with the exception of McCutcheon, had ever heard fired in anger. So, in scraps of French, with Yankee slang thrown in and some pantomime, our spokesman said: "Nix on the panic, brother! What's a little old faraway *boom-boom* among pals? Scoot along, kid, we'll take every care of you," or words to that tenor, and tactfully, in the same moment, slipped a ten-franc note into a receptive palm and flipped the cork out of a quart bottle of brandy which had been carried along strictly for medicinal purposes. Subsequent events conclusively proved that for ten francs and a deep swig of the brandy our chauffeuring friend would go forward half a mile. Eventually—but this was when the bottle practically was empty—an especially vehement *boom-boom* rattled the cab windows and something scalped the roof right off an old sugar-beet factory away to the east. That was where we left our charioteer and walked in, incidentally being the only pedestrians moving in that direction that morning although thousands of fugitives passed us, hastening the opposite way. He promised, by gestures, to wait for us there. We never saw him again. I doubt he waited very long.

That was on a Wednesday. Saturday afternoon the Germans, who had held us until then in a sort of semi-captivity, let us go and late that night we got back to Brussels which had capitulated on the day after Louvain was taken. The much advertised German efficiency machine was clicking all over the place, as we discovered Sunday morning when we set out from our hotel on a joint visit to our friend and protector, Brand Whitlock at the American ministry.

At the corner of the street an over-zealous non-com arrested us, presumably on suspicion of our being Englishmen, and his squad surrounded us and marched us to an improvised barracks, where a superior officer questioned us, examined our passports and the credentials vouching for us as deputized correspondents from a neutral country, then apologized and let us go. Before we had walked fifty yards farther another underling nabbed us. We traveled back to refuge by a series of progressive arrests.

Inside the hotel we hunted up one of our compatriots who had been staying in Brussels to witness its occupation.

"How does a fellow move around this town without an escort of bayonets?" we demanded. "We are simple private citizens and this military attention is extremely distasteful."

"Oh, that's easy," he said. "When the Germans first got in somebody pinched us every ten feet or so. So all the American press representatives who were here went to see the military governor, and he gave each a pass so we could move around without being nabbed by *Feldwebels* and second lieutenants and things."

"Where is this accommodating commandant?"

"Just over at the Hôtel de Ville."

"Lead us to him."

To the Hôtel de Ville we went and there we met the military governor, one Major General Thaddeus von Jarotsky, an elderly Franco-Prussian war veteran. In appearance and manner he was a typical Prussian, with the gun-metal eyes and loppy dewlaps of his breed. We showed our credentials and asked for passes similar to those which our confreres had secured of him.

"With pleasure," said the general, in excellent English. "But, gentlemen, I am just on the point of going to lunch. I am late for my appointment now. Besides, I have let my staff go. My secretaries and my clerks have been working night and day, and I have given them a few hours of rest." He considered a moment. "As I recall, one of your fraternity speaks and writes German, is it not so?"

"I am the man, General," spoke up the correspondent who had piloted us hither.

"Ach, good! Will you be good enough to make for each of these gentlemen a pass similar to the one you carry, merely substituting their names where your own name appears. Have these passes here at two-thirty o'clock, when I shall return, and I shall then validate them."

Back to the hotel we hurried and our sponsor unlimbered his typewriter. He took his pass out of his pocket and laid it down alongside him.

It was a sheet of paper with two typewritten lines in German on it. Translated the lines read:

> Mr. James So-and-So, writer for the American press, is entitled through all German lines to pass, in Brussels and its suburbs.

There was no signature, but the stamp of the Imperial Government and the stamp of the military government which the Germans had set up here were affixed to it.

"Hold on," said one of us, "isn't this General von Jarotsky rather a fussy bureaucratic sort of person?"

"You've sized him up," said the man at the typewriter. "He's sure a stuffed shirt. But what's the idea?"

"The idea is this," said the inspired one. "When you make out my pass just leave off the words 'in Brussels and suburbs,' see? I'm going to take a risk. If the old boy stamps my pass without reading it closely I'll have a document in my pocket that'll take me anywhere the Germans go—unless I have the bad luck to run into somebody above the rank of a major general."

"But suppose he does read it?"

"Why, in that case we'll tell him that in your haste to make out our passes before eating lunch you must accidentally have left something out. We'll ask him to let us come on back here and get corrected copies made." He turned to the other three:

"How about you fellows? Are you willing to gamble, too? The worst that can happen is that we'll be tied up here, and as things stand we're just the same as prisoners, anyway. The best that may happen is that we can slip out of here and possibly follow the Germans clear to Paris—if they get that far."

By acclamation the motion carried. At two-thirty o'clock we were at the Hôtel de Ville, each with his little typewritten joker in his hand. The trick worked. Old von Jarotsky barely glanced at the papers. In another minute they had been stamped and returned to us, and we were bowing ourselves out of the presence.

In five minutes more we had engaged a couple of open carriages, each drawn by a pair of crowbait horses. Ten minutes later we had passed the sentry posts of the environs and were sliding through the rear lines of the main German column ostensibly on our way to Waterloo, but really headed toward where heavy cannonading made noises like summer thunder. And before night we were in the back eddies of a battle which historians today list among the great battles of the world—the Battle of Mons.

Thereafter we traveled along with or close up behind the conquerors along two sides of a triangle through war-wracked Flanders—traveled afoot, to the damage of our poor feet; on second-hand retinkered bicycles, which were stolen from us; in a crippled dogcart, drawn by a venerable mouse-colored mare in a delicate condition, and answering to the name of Bulotte but because of her structural contours we called her Gray Gables; which outfit we bought at ruinous prices and lost when eventually the Germans wearied of our company and sent us off to German soil as quasi prisoners, aboard a train loaded with real prisoners and lightly wounded men.

Early on a peaceful Sunday in September our warders turned us loose, on a sort of probation basis, in the incredibly neat, demure little border city of Aix-la-Chapelle—a city which looked as though it were taken indoors every night and dry-cleansed and then put out again next morning. Our frowzy band of itinerants had grown now to a membership of six Americans and one horribly frightened Flemish photographer. Every available car at the station was being used to carry disabled men off for hospitalization so we climbed aboard a trolley car. It was comfortably filled with plumped-out citizens and their families on their way to Mass at the ancient Dom. As we got on by the back door most of these passengers disembarked by the front door, sniffing the while in a significant manner. For days we had been herded together; we had got used to one another. But by that sudden exodus we were made cognizant that we had become social outcasts.

McCutcheon and I had further proof of this—not that we needed any further proof—when we entered the ground floor arcade below Nagel's Hotel. At the foot of the stairs leading up to the bureau for travelers we peremptorily were halted by a slim but determined porter in a bright parrot-colored uniform. Neither of us found it in our hearts altogether to blame him for barring our way. I regard myself: For a week then I had not taken off the silk shirt and the blue flannel suit in which I had left Brussels allegedly for a sight-seeing ride to Waterloo, and for the past forty-eight hours I neither had washed my face and hands nor combed my head. Having literally walked a pair of light shoes off my feet, I was wearing a pair of home-knit carpet slippers which I had purchased from an elderly villager somewhere back behind us. They rather suggested two altered Maltese tomcats which, having died of a swelling, had then been skimpily embalmed. I also was wearing a greasy butcher's smock which lately I had acquired to save myself from the rain. My New York model straw hat was my own but four nights before, while sleeping in a cow shed where no self-respecting cow would willingly sleep, I had rolled over on it and mashed the top out of it so that my hair stood up through the opening in a very picturesque way. But I still clung to the brim and what remained of the crown as a man will cling to the last remnants of a one-time respectability. At that, I think I was better dressed than McCutcheon. At least I wore my things with an air.

"Postiffly you gouldn't gome here," stated the porter, with a rigid pea-green arm uplifted. "Der blace alreaty is gefull—mit officers und udder guests."

In my pocket was a buckskin bag containing twenty golden sovereigns. About my ample waist, under my shirt, was girthed a money belt loaded with many more sovereigns. Anywhere in Germany at that time gold was precious even though it be that the hateful British Government had coined it.

Taking my time about it and jingling the pouch, I sifted out one of those delectable coins and slid it into the tyler's receptive hand.

"Brother," I asked softly, "would it make any difference in your attitude if I told you I was absolutely upholstered with these attractive little keepsakes?"

His bow, as he pouched the glittering disk, almost took me in the chest.

"Ach, gentlemen," he begged, "oxcuse, blease! Ten tousand pardongs. But your gostumes"—diplomatically he switched—"please you be so goot und follow me?"

We got the best double room—with twin sleeping alcoves and a huge bathroom—in the house. First though, by our own request, we repaired to an emergency delousing station which had been fitted up in the hotel garage for the benefit of persons newly returned from the battle fronts. I do not wish to boast, but I believe I am warranted in the assertion that at that moment I was as densely inhabited as anybody my size in all of Continental Europe. Every time I scratched myself I got results and every time I shook myself the center of population shifted.

Each of us was invited to stand upon a large sheet of paper within a sprinkled ring of coarse salt. There was a belief that cooties were so opinionated they wouldn't crawl across salt. Privately I discounted that theory. It had been my recent experience that they'd go anywhere. First we removed our outer garments and bundled them up in one sheet of paper to be baked in an improvised oven and we made another bundle of our more intimate garments, but these were sacrificial offerings for the incinerators. Then a hostler came with a whitewash brush and a horse bucket overflowing with some foamy mixture of a sky-blue tint. This turned out to be suds made from mercurial soap, and he painted us with the compound until we looked like overgrown robins' eggs. After that, with a garden hose, he sluiced us down as though we had been a couple of buggies in a livery stable. Meanwhile our now devoted well-wisher, the tactful porter, had been buzzing about like an overgrown Lima bean and he had found the owner of a near-by haberdashery shop and induced him to come and fit us with underthings and bathrobes and sandals. Thus spruced up, we went to a barbershop in the arcade—also opened for our exclusive use by special persuasion—where a tonsorialist sheared our shaggy locks and shampooed and shaved us and explored my eyebrows which were thick, for any refugeeing little strangers; and a manicurist put our neglected digits in order. (Lacking a pencil, I could have written with my fingernail before I had this service.) A curious double feature was that the barber was a woman, but the manicuring operator was a man and very coy and kittenish he was, too, and gave our paws little roguish pats while he worked on them.

It was lunchtime when we got up to our chamber to find it done, walls and woodwork and all, in red Russian leather so that we had the feeling of being domiciled inside a freshly killed cow. In the courtyard below our windows people were having their luncheons and the clatter of dishes and the smells of hot dishes came up to us. But incredibly, we weren't hungry. It had been upwards of a fortnight since we had eaten a regular meal; it had been at least forty-eight hours since we had swallowed anything worthy to be called food; and through that dreary train trip we had talked about food and chose menus of the food we would eat when we reached a place where eating still was being carried on as a regular practice. But now neither of us wanted a bite. We stretched in languid ease on the beds—the only beds we had seen in a week or better—and in hopes of resuscitating our slumbering appetites we drank steins of the local Rhenish lager. A Pilsener type, it was, and the color of clear amber and very refreshing after the sour cider-like Belgian beer we had been having—when we could get it.

We swigged and loafed until after one o'clock before I called across the great open spaces of our quarters, "John, I'm beginning to brood."

"You and me both," he answered back. "I'll bet we're brooding on the same thing."

"Ham—" I began.

"And eggs," he joyously supplemented.

"Fried country style," I proceeded.

"Absolutely! All mixed up together in a pan the way they fix 'em in this part of the world."

"With buttered toast," I suggested.

"And plum jam," he amended. "As I recall from former visits, the natives around here throw a very tasty plum jam."

"Not to mention coffee," I went on.

"Or what these poor benighted people think is coffee," he added, correctingly. "I think they boil it about a week; brings out the full flavor of the chicory. And, naturally, one more tall pitcher of that good beer."

"By all means, at least one more. And probably after that mayhap still another and eke yet another."

"Stay right where you are," he cried. "Leave me ring for the lifesaving corps."

It was the head waiter, no less, who answered the call. He co-operated freely in hurrying the victuals along and we partook thereof to the bottom-most sip and the ultimate crumblet.

We lay down again then to smoke German cheroots, made out of chopped straw and pressed autumn leaves with some tobacco. But not enough to hurt. I think fully an hour must have passed before McCutcheon murmured:

"Irv, I'm meditating again."

"Mr. McCutcheon," I said, "you take the words right out of my mouth. Personally, I would nominate a light bait of the same as heretofore."

"When you hit on the one perfect lyrical unification, why tamper with your luck?" he said dreamily. "Surely it must have been a true poet who first made fried eggs rhyme with fried ham."

But the third time the affable *Oberkelner* didn't wait for us to speak. He stuck his head in the door and caroled joyously:

"Ya, ya. Shinken mit eure, nicht wahr?"

Between then and suppertime I had one more reorder of the ham and eggs, with the ordained trimmings, making four sets in all, but John, the quitter, stopped after his third. And naturally for supper we had ham and eggs and beer and toast, but instead of the plum jam we had apple marmalade. There's nothing, I find, like a change of diet to produce a stomachic fillip. Or anyway, it sounds like that, coming up.

So ever since then when people begin talking about what a starving American preferably will eat when finally he does get a chance to break his fast, I'm qualified to tell them. Because I am the one who knows.

It was four days earlier than this, during one of the periods when we walked—hobbled, rather—that I had my to-do with the dappled-faced under-officer whom I mentioned some pages back. We were nearing the famous lace-making village of Binche and somewhere on beyond there the retreating Allies fought a smart rear-guard action; the rumbling of the heavy artillery was almost constant. Myself and Roger Lewis of the Associated Press were going along perhaps a hundred yards in advance of our straggling compatriots and making a pretty slow job of it by reason of foot-soreness. That night when I got my shoes off dribbles of blood ran out of them. Along with the soles of the shoes I'd almost walked the soles off my feet; big blisters had formed and burst and eaten into the flesh. There were oozing raw patches as big as a dime. Had I known how badly damaged I was I probably couldn't have traveled another furlong. Sometimes we are better off for not knowing too much.

A string of military camions began passing the two of us, going slowly and with frequent checks. Why these camions should be going in empty unless they had been impressed for ambulance service to fetch out casualties, I wouldn't know. The driver of one of them hailed us. Even in uniform he still looked the typical German farm boy.

"Amerikanisher?" he asked.

Yes, we told him, American journalists, although we might not look it.

He waved to us to climb on. Lewis got on one running board,

I on the other. We started rolling over those bumpy stone blocks, it was all I could do to hang on. Our benefactor glanced nervously back—he had heard something we hadn't heard—and now a distressing uneasy look was on his face and he began repeating an urgent sentence. We gathered that one in authority immediately behind us had challenged his right to give us a lift. He kept telling us that something was *verboten*—very much *verboten* indeed. Lewis hopped off. I was poising myself to follow suit when at that precise moment that lumbering truck started down the only really steep, really long hill in that part of Belgium. Instantly it picked up a speed of perhaps twenty miles an hour. Traveling at that rate and with my agonized feet, I wouldn't have jumped off to alight on those big cobbles for all the watermelons in Georgia. With the driver still vehemently importuning me to take the leap, we coasted down to the foot of the grade, a distance of probably a quarter of a mile. Here the procession stopped and I stepped gingerly down and peered back through the dust for Lewis. He was running toward me, obviously concerned about something.

The driver of my camion was pointing rearward and frantically crying out in fright. I looked where his jabbing finger aimed. Two camions back, a short man in the uniform of a sergeant was tumbling down from a perch alongside his driver. He was, it turned out, the person in charge of that section of camions. And his shouted orders had been flouted by an untidy person who obviously was neither French nor Belgian and who might be a *verdampt* English spy. At that early stage of hostilities every foreigner who wasn't a native of one of the invaded countries was suspected of spying by the Germans and especially by overly officious underofficers.

He rushed at me, spilling his cap as he came. He was spitting frothy threats and imprecations. In that flash of time I took note chiefly of his face and his hair. His skin was a curious piebald—dead white but mottled with bright crimson dots as though a Dalmatian coach dog had had a cross of Easter egg somewhere back in its breeding. And either from rage or because it grew that way, every hair on his close-cropped scalp stood erect in a stiff bristly effect, like so much yellow wheat stubble. For the moment, strangely enough, those details scored more deeply in my mind than the fact that he was dragging at his belt, was tugging free a blued-steel, stub-nosed Luger.

He jerked it free. He poked the muzzle of it in my stomach. I think he pulled the trigger. I thought I heard the mechanism click, although that p——y have been imagination. He stepped back a pace and upen—d the gun and with his clubbed left fist pounded at its butt. ' getting it out of an oversnug holster he must have dis-—ngaged the magazine from the firing action and now was trying to hammer the cartridge clip back into place up the hollow handgrip.

And then I came ungalvanized. With both my hands I grabbed his right wrist and turned the short barrel of the weapon straight up in the air. He struck at me with his left—clawed at me, I should say, for the German is not a good fisticuffer until he has had some lessons; but I knew that he could never get that pistol down and directed again at me so long as I was free of attack from some other quarter. Out of the tail of my eye I could see soldiers closing in on our rumpus. My chief fear then was that one of them, seeing a comrade wrestling with a disheveled civilian, might fire on me first and ask questions afterward.

I was aware, too, that Lewis had about-faced and was legging it back up the hill. He wasn't deserting me though. Realizing that more than anything else I needed moral support—and an interpreter—he was seeing reinforcements for me in my plight from the only available source. As the remaining members of our group, taking the alarm, came running forward, he was telling them, in the fewest possible number of words, the facts in the case and my innocence of conscious wrongdoing. All this, you'll understand, occurred in much less time than it takes for me to describe it.

As they surrounded the interlocked pair of us, the foremost of the rescuers began explaining to my frenzied adversary, his syllables tumbling over one another, that I meant no offense when seemingly I had disregarded his commands. But he could speak fluent German—and he was doing his explaining in English.

Over my shoulder I remember throwing a plea at him. I urged that he say what he had to say in German else I might not be there to hear the conclusion of the conversation. This might not have been my exact remark, but it was the fervent purport of it. So he switched languages and when his meanings had sunk into the con-

sciousness of my enemy, the latter said, between pants and grunts
and hoarse cuss words, that if I would release my hold on him he
would refrain from killing me—on this occasion, anyhow. But it
better not happen again!

Never in all my life had I hated to turn loose of anything as I
hated turning loose of that little Prussian's wrist. But I did it and
he sheathed his automatic and gave me some more hard looks and
a farewell outburst of warnings, and climbed aboard his camion
and rode off, mouthing and still menacing us in dumb play until
he was a hundred yards away.

Again Lewis and I paired off, except that now we crippled along
in the wake of our companions. They also limped, but they were
better limpers than we were. A warm glow filled me. I was puffed
with a pleasant conceit. Under difficult circumstances I had kept
my head; had carried off the situation rather cleverly, I thought.
Mr. Cobb was exceedingly well pleased with his favorite author.

Perhaps half a mile farther we came to an angle in a stone fence
where cavalry horses had been fed. There was trampled hay on
the turf. Both of us dropped down here and for twenty minutes
lay in the attitude best suited to rest a wearied frame—flat of our
backs, with our arms and legs outstretched at angles.

I started to get up. I was halfway up when both legs gave way
under me and down I went on my hands and knees. Magically
those legs of mine had turned to twin columns of soft rubber. Their
bones had dissolved into jelly, their flesh was putty and the cartilage
was mucilaginous. Involuntarily I clapped my hand to my back,
saying to myself, "In the scuffle somebody shot me and I never
noticed it. He got me in the spine and I'm paralyzed from the hips
down." I brought my hand away, half-expecting to find blood on
it. Then second judgment told me that this was foolishness. I felt
my pulse; I held out my hand to see if it trembled, which it didn't.
So far as I could tell the upper part of my body was in a perfectly
normal state. But why—I recall laughing foolishly up into Lewis'
astounded face—why should my legs be limp and floppy, like loose
strings?

I brought my will power to bear on the misbehaving members
and we rubbed them and massaged them. But it was fully ten minutes before they became dependable enough for me to get upright

and trust my weight upon them. The first few steps were shaky and wobbly and little tremors kept running through the muscles, but that soon passed and I made the remaining laps of my journey into the occupied town of Binche in fairly good order—except for my flayed feet.

Years later I told a famous surgeon of my experience and he said:

"Uncommon but easily explained. When that crazy Heinie stuck that pistol up against you and pulled the trigger your principal nerve ganglion telegraphed the news to your brain that you had been shot. What's more, as far as your nervous system was concerned, you'd been shot right smack in the solar plexus. So you behaved accordingly. You went along until the imaginary bullet in your guts had its effect on your locomotive apparatus and then down you went on all fours—and down you stayed, until your brain decided it was all a mistake and sent back down word to the over-excited reflexes to behave themselves."

Why, at this place, I should be moved to start reviving long slumbering memories of the hangings of "Henry the Cat" and "Devil" Winston I'll not try to explain, because I can't. I just discover myself doing it, that's all. And I long ago learned that when my pen goes targeting off on a contradictory slant of its own, the easiest thing for me to do is to trail along.

Charley Hamilton, a big, good-natured, thrifty brown man, a truckman by trade and a contractor in a small but prosperous way, was the first human I ever saw in the very article of death. I was about fourteen, I figure, when my uncle-in-law, Judge Bagby, awakened me one midnight to go with him to write down Charley's will. The judge had a palsy of the hands, which made his own writing illegible and while he owned a typewriting machine, the first one, by the way, that was ever brought to Paducah, it was too cumbersome and heavy to be moved about easily.

So before daylight of a spring morning, by the light of a coal-oil lamp, I took dictation in longhand while, with the labored breath whistling through an open wound in his lungs, Charley gasped out the terms of his will and my uncle translated them into legal language; and six months later. as an uninvited but approving spectator,

through a knothole in the jail fence I witnessed the hanging of
Henry the Cat, that vicious yellow man who treacherously had
knifed poor old Charley between his shoulder blades from behind.

It was in a cold February dawning that they fetched The Cat
forth for his hanging and the sweat of his terror was standing out
in beads on his scalp and running in trickles down his face. As the
sharp air struck him that sweat gave off a little blue fog which
enveloped his head like a veil while they led him stumbling up the
steps of the gallows.

So the occasion of the execution of the law on the coal-black,
stumpy Devil Winston was not my first experience in this line—
besides, there had been one or two lynchings in between—but it
was my first attendance upon a hanging in an official capacity, as a
newspaper reporter. Moreover, it linked my current job with the
earliest job I ever had held, for Devil once had worked for the
firm with which my father was connected. At times, spelling Tom
Montjoy or Tallow Dick Evans, the regular helpers, Devil had
ridden at the tail gate of the same ice wagon which I steered, and
had handled the frozen product. He was a powerful stocky darky,
always polite and respectful in his dealings with white people, but
a black terror among his own race. Now he was about to be hanged
for cutting a negro woman into ribbons and I was to write the
story of the hanging for my paper.

With my fellow cub of the rival paper and two other witnesses,
I spent the night before the big doings at the jailer's house. We
played nickel-limit poker until three o'clock in the morning; then
we had a fried fish breakfast, and about an hour before daylight
we went to the jail. The condemned man was already up and
dressed in a new suit of black clothes. He wore a stiff white collar
and a black tie, probably the first collar and the first tie he had
ever worn in his life—and his hands were encased in white cotton
gloves, and his brand-new shoes had been given an extra polish by
one of the trusties. The suit and the shoes were a gift from the
sheriff; the white gloves had been Devil's own idea.

In a corner stood a preacher, a dark little round-shouldered nub-
bin of a man, in color and shape like an overbaked corn pone. He
was holding before him an open Bible and with his free hand he violently was smiting it and at each resounding slap, would cry out

shrilly, "Look on the Word! Look on the Lamb of God! Look on the Book of Truth!" Over and over again he repeated it, but nobody there gave heed to him. This was Devil's hour.

I can shut my eyes and see the picture of him as he paced the narrow jail corridor in the half-light of flickery gas jets. I can see his eight-dollar suit bunching in the back; see his gloved hands fluttering like restless white pigeons as he chanted snatches of hymns and broken prayers—working himself up to the state of exaltation that sent so many of his race to the gallows shouting-happy. Plastered against the barred cell doors beyond, like bats, hung ten or a dozen negroes, their eyeballs standing out from the shadowy background like so many pairs of shiny china marbles. In time to the cadences of Devil they crooned and groaned in a sympathetic chorus.

Suddenly the doomed darky paused and began a moving exhortation for all sinners within sound of his voice to take warning before it was too late, and repent of their sins. And those others promised him they would, promised him with sobs and amens and camp-meeting shouts. He warmed to his theme.

"Dis time tonight I'll be in Glory!" he told them, his voice rising in a long swing and then sinking low again. "I'll hab a shimmerin' robe upon me an' golden slippahs on my feet. An' I'se comin' back to dis yere world to hant de wicked an' de lost!"

From the cells came a long, shivering groan, and through the bars we could see his scared audience quaking.

"Yas, suh," he went on, "an' dat ain't all—I'se comin' back to dis yere jail!"

A howl of piteous entreaty arose, so loud that it reached the ears of the negroes gathering in the gloom outdoors, and they took it up and the whole air everywhere seemed filled with the sound of their wailings. A voice from one of the cells cut through this.

"Devil," pleaded a little prisoner, "please don't do dat! Come back to dis world ef you wants to, but don't come back to dis jail! 'Cause effen you does, Devil, I warns you right now I'se gwine make doors in this w'ite folks' jail whar they ain't no doors."

The time came to read the death warrant—a needless cruelty imposed by our statutes. There was a hitch here. The sheriff had been made ill by the task ahead of him and was violently nauseated in the jail office. One of his deputies was outside testing the rope and the trap. The other deputy was so nearsighted that in the bad light he could not make out to read fine print; but the death warrant must be read aloud in the presence of the condemned—the law so provided. Somebody shoved a paper into my hands and I found myself stumbling through the awesome document, while Devil stood facing me with his hands crossed flat upon his breast. He was drinking in the big, impressive words and glorying—visibly glorying—in his own importance. And when I was through he thanked me!

"Young Cap'n," he said, giving me my old ice-wagon title, "I always knowed dat ef ever you could do pore ole Devil a favor you suttinly would. Thanky, suh, kindly."

It was after they started the march to the scaffold that, for the first time, he showed a mortal distress. His forehead suddenly contorted until a deep V of ridged flesh appeared between his eyes. It was still there when they cut his body down.

Hundreds of negro women outside, seeing his head rise above the high fence, set up a dismal quavering lamentation; and, as though in defiance of them, a group of reckless young negroes began singing "The Devil Song"—one of those weird chants which guitar-picking minstrel bards among the Southern negroes write to commemorate a notable crime or a great tragedy. This one dealt with Devil's life and his crime and his trial; and now there were added verses, made up on the spot, to describe his finish. I remember the first verse:

> "Devil left Nine Hund'ed, wringin' wet wid sweat,
> Gwine kill pore Viney Stubblefield 'bout a Duke's
>   cigarette."*

Just as the drop fell a negro stretched on the limb of a tree over-hanging the enclosure fainted and tumbled off right at our feet. And either the rope was too long—as it so often is—or it stretched under the weight; and poor Devil's feet touched, and he made a long, sickening job of dying.

---

* "Nine Hundred" was a negro groggery at the corner of Ninth and Washington Streets.

We assisted in that hanging—the other cub reporter and I. I had already read the death warrant; now both of us served the ends of mercy. We stood together under the gallows. The dangling figure swayed and swung within a yard of us. We saw how the tip of one of Devil's toes was poised exactly upon the tip of a big piece of gravel which protruded above the surface of the jail yard. It sustained his weight—that and the rope about his neck. Something must be done and done quickly else the man would choke by degrees of slow torture; he was making hideous muffled sounds in his throat and twitching and jerking through all his frame. So one of us caught his bound legs at the bend of the knee and raised them clear and the other kicked the jagged pebble away. His feet did not touch after that although, even so, the margin was so narrow that you could not roll a lead pencil along the earth beneath him without scraping the soles of his shoes.

Aboard the old liner *Baltic*, now ferrying troops and supplies across the Atlantic, we were having, on a calm February evening of 1918, a poker game. It was our farewell poker game because, if nothing happened meanwhile, we would be at Liverpool docks when we waked up in the morning. Only not many counted on doing much sleeping that night.

All that afternoon we cautiously had been plowing through wreckage—an empty lifeboat, fragments of small craft, two bodies sustained in upright posture by life belts, so that those dead men seemed to be staring across the waters as they bobbed stiffly by. During the whole war that, as it turned out, was to be the worst week for Allied shipping in the channels about the British Isles.

The cabin where our poker games had been staged was on one of the lower decks, just above water line. The regular players were there—three officers of the Princess Pats, returning to active duty at the front in France after having had leaves at home; two members of the British Food Commission who had been over here dickering for provisions; a Canadian businessman in service as a sort of commercial liaison officer between the Mother Country and the Dominion provinces, a young military surgeon, and I, the only American-born one.

Through the long trip we had had daily bouts; all jack pots, fifty cents limit, dollar bets for a round of roodles; and by now I almost had quit marveling that Englishmen, who were so shrewd for other things, should show such lamentable dumbness touching on the rudiments of draw poker. Before one of them tried a bluff you could see him winding up like a baseball pitcher. He advertised his intent as plainly as though he had been a sandwich man walking down the Bowery.

We heard, outside the ship and up forward somewhere, a sharp clattering sound which drew nearer.

"Hark!" said somebody and everybody quit studying his cards to listen. It was a jumpy time anyhow.

The clamor increased swiftly, reached its climax for us when it passed along the hull just below the sealed and darkened portholes of the cabin, and dimmed out astern. The sound, gigantically exag-gerated, was as though a boy ran along a picket fence, rattling a stick between the pickets.

"What the devil was that, now?" asked someone.

"No doubt a torpedo knocking for admission," said somebody else; a grim joke and a poor one, but the best the joker could do, the state of his nerves considered.

"Well, why didn't the fool thing come on in, then?" said the first speaker. There was a strained little giggle.

"Whose bet is it?" put in a third man. "Go ahead; probably we just scraped against another chunk of floating debris. The sea's full of it."

But it was the second man's guess which had been the right guess. Perhaps five minutes later a major of an A. E. F. contingent that we were taking across, poked his head in at the door.

"The *Tuscania's* been hit, right behind us!" he said. "Come along quietly. Not many on this boat know yet what's happened."

From the time our squadron was made up at New York—with additions at Halifax—the transport *Tuscania,* so giddily camou-flaged that she was a veritable painted Jezebel of the sea, had fol-lowed us, her nose to our tail. In the formation on the journey over, there had been twelve ships, two of them converted liners, each carrying a regiment of our boys, and the rest commandeered merchantmen; with H. M. S. the cruiser *Cochrane* leading the way and keeping directly ahead of us. The *Baltic,* as the largest craft in the lot, was the front ship of the middle line. Two days out from land on the farther side, six English destroyers had joined the convoy, traveling three on either flank.

As we headed for the mouth of the Mersey, the *Cochrane*, our shield until then, swung away from her place. She was going to escort the detached *Tuscania* into Glasgow. At that precise moment, as later came out, a German submarine rose directly ahead and fired its torpedo at the now unprotected *Baltic*.

At the bow was our skipper, the famous "Tubby" Finch, who was only five foot four, but weighed three hundred pounds. Earlier in the war he had commanded the *Adriatic* and when an enemy sank her, true to the traditions of the sea, he stayed at his post on the bridge and went down with the ship. But he was too fat to sink and bobbed about, half-drowned, until a whaleboat picked him up.

Now, through the gloom, he saw the torpedo coming, so he made the helmsman aim the *Baltic* right at the approaching parcel of deadliness and signaled for full speed ahead, he figuring that a straight-on collision would blow the forepart of his ship to smithereens—and him with it—but perhaps the watertight compartments of her main hull might keep her afloat and in any event, leave her engines intact, and thus give his first officer a hope of beaching the crippled craft since there the shores of the narrowing estuary of the Mersey were only a few miles apart.

Head on, the hard-driven ship and the explosive snout of the torpedo met. The great wave thrown up by our prow sheered the torpedo slightly off its course so while it scraped the hull of the *Baltic* for her full length, its touchy contact cap was pointed outward. And then, going aft from us, the vicious thing, like a blinded sea adder, bit into the flank of the *Tuscania* which, as luck would have it, had at that identical moment and for the first time in the entire voyage turned broadside to us, with intent to trail the cruiser into Glasgow. At least that afterward was the accepted theory and certainly it was the thrashing propeller of the diverted torpedo which, passing almost within inches of us, had interrupted our valedictory poker party. Next day we saw where the whirring metal blades had scored deep marks in our iron plates, so that big scalloplike scars showed through the paint.

When we got topside there was the *Tuscania*, wallowing in our wake and not half a mile away. All her lights were on, tier upon tier—the only time in three weeks when we had seen a fellow ship lighted up. But those rows of lights already were slanted downward toward her bow, and visibly slanting more and more. From her drifting bulk a succession of red rockets—the mariner's cry for help—was going up, spilling red sparks like a Fourth of July show. And at our best zigzagging gait we were running not toward her but away from her. We were obeying the wartime law that an unarmed vessel must not go to the rescue of a stricken sister craft but should herself endeavor to escape. Yet I never felt such a coward in my life as I stood at the stern of the *Baltic* and watched those banks of lights dim out, one by one, and saw the last of the rockets fired and knew that we were abandoning a shipload of our boys to what might befall them. After we landed we learned, with a tremendous surge of pride, that as the waters rose around them, those green troops, soldiers from far northwestern states mostly, stood in ranks on the canted decks singing a popular song of the war, "Where Do We Go from Here, Boys?" And how the English destroyers had managed to save all but two hundred and odd Yankee youngsters out of more than two thousand.

As silently we started down an aft companionway our purser, a Londoner named Goldensleeve, hailed us. Four of us sat for meals at the purser's mess.

"I've been seeking you gentlemen," he said in a cautious undertone. "We've a good many ladies aboard, you know—all these nurses and Red Cross workers and the wives of military officers—and the captain is anxious to keep this thing from them, if possible. So the captain's compliments to all you gentlemen who are at my table, and he asks will you kindly say nothing to anyone of what's just occurred, and that at dinner tonight you be quite cheery and bright, you know? You see—" and here he employed a triumph of understatement which, I think, only a Britisher seriously might coin—"you see, in a manner of speaking, we're in rather awkward waters."

Awkward waters was right. Before daylight the raiding Germans scored hits on three more of our squadron which, with the *Tuscania*, made four out of a possible twelve. They blew up an ammunition ship, killing all her crew; they damaged the *North-*

umberland, a supply ship, and another freighter whose name I forget. These latter two managed to crawl ashore and there was no further loss of life.

According to orders, our squad was cheery and bright that night at dinner—or tried to be. There were corks popped and toasts were drunk and patriotic songs were sung and most of the women, I think, remained in ignorance of events until after we docked. Indeed there was more of outward calmness in the dining salon than in the smoking room or at the bar afterward.*

Here was a curious detail of byplay which impressed me at the time and often since has bobbed up as a subject for speculation, although I think I know the answer. Seafaring men who had spent their professional lives afloat and presumably were used to the ordi-

---

* Publisher's Note: To demonstrate how an incipient flight was checked on that momentous night in the *Baltic's* smoking room the publishers have dug up a narrative told in the *Bookman* in 1925 by Colonel William A. Bishop, V.C., D.S.O., M.C., D.F.C., of Canada and the British Royal Flying Corps, who in the World War was the outstanding surviving aviator of all the armies and who in 1939 became Air Marshal of the Canadian forces. This little tale is here incorporated without Mr. Cobb's prior knowledge—or consent. It is as follows:

"Colonel Bishop, returning to England in the early part of 1918, crossed on the same boat which carried Irvin Cobb. In convoy their ship was directly followed by the camouflaged troopship *Tuscania*. Their last night of the voyage, when the convoy was nearing port and after the *Tuscania* had been torpedoed, a danger signal was sounded.

"It had been arranged that five blasts of the *Baltic's* steam whistle meant a submarine and a quick exit to the lifeboats. After two stammering blasts had sounded great confusion raged on the ship, when at its height Mr. Cobb was seen looming above the scene. With a noble gesture he raised his hand.

" 'Wait,' he said impressively, 'remember, three more to come'—and for the moment calmed the excited party.

"Another hesitant hoot, then another, and then silence; the expected fifth blast hadn't followed. Mr. Cobb's hand descended.

" 'O.K., only I wish the dam' thing wouldn't stutter so!' he remarked, and, in the laugh that followed, his hearers forgot their rising panic."

nary perils of the sea, appeared noticeably more uneasy through that experience than did the landlubbers among the enlisted ranks.

I observed the same small phenomenon, starting homeward six months later on the *Leviathan* when a sub took a couple of quick shots at us as we were passing Penzance on the way out from Brest. One torpedo passed just back of our mighty stern and the other missed our nose by forty yards or so. However, we were all busy then watching our port battery of nine-inch guns trying to sink a second sub which boldly had risen and was driving a course parallel to ours, in a gallant effort to divert our fire upon her while her mate breached on the starboard side and loosed the contents of her loaded tubes at our great mass. So only a few on the *Leviathan* were cognizant of the attack and fewer still betrayed a jittery feeling. Anyhow, that affair was not long drawn out. Everything was over and done with inside of fifteen minutes, including the dropping of a depth charge by one of the two destroyers accompanying us, above the spot where the daredevil decoy craft finally submerged.

42

THAT WILL BE ABOUT ALL

For more reasons than one I've had cause ever since to remember that long-ago night of June 28, 1914. But one of those reasons was its beauty.

Spring was late that year coming to the lake country of lower Quebec. In these last few hot days the wildflowers—those which ordinarily would have finished blooming before this and those which now were in season—had burst out together. They brocaded the swales with colors that were like the patterning of some old prayer rug, and on the shoulders of each gentle terrace in the meadows they put Spanish epaulettes—crimson from fireweed and yellow from dandelions, and tasseling Indian paintbrushes for the fringes. Through the afternoon Mrs. Cobb and our young daughter and I had ridden in a venerable borrowed buggy through the fields and among the patches of woodland, drinking in the excellence of all this lavishness.

That night, it seemed to me, was the most perfect night that ever was. There was scarcely a breath of wind and the quiet was so deep that the small waves washing the shore below our cabin where it sat among the white birches and the balsam firs were like so many little amorous mouths, kissing the lips of the bank; and when a foraging black bass splashed in the shallows it sounded like a walrus turning over. The moon was nearly full and she came up grandly above the tree line of the opposite shore and then for a space she seemed to hang there, like the half of a great ripe muskmelon. She was tilted a bit so that the trails of radiance on the ripples of the lake were like the melon's spilt seeds dropping down along the water. The others had gone indoors and I was sitting there alone on the porch steps when a neighbor from the next camp

541

came through the grove to tell me that across in the village an extra
of a Montreal paper had come saying that in a town called Sera-
jevo—a town of which neither of us ever had heard—the Archduke
Franz Ferdinand of Austria-Hungary and his wife had been assas-
sinated by a fanatical student; and because of this, there was talk of
a clash between the Austrian Empire and Serbia.

But what the hell? They'd take it out in talking and then
there'd be arbitration or indemnities or something, and everything
would blow over. Those Balkans—potential trouble always was
smouldering amongst them, but never breaking out. Wasn't the
Roumanian situation chronically fraught with—well, with Rou-
manians? And, likely as not, the next disturbance you read about
merely would mean that a lot of Bulgars had been demonstrating
against a lot of Bulgars for behaving like a lot of Bulgars. Nasty
thunder forever was muttering in the Ural Mountains or the Cau-
casus Mountains or whatever they called those nests of mountains
over yonder in that far corner of the map. So why would this
newest quarrel in these inaccessible parts involve any of the greater
powers? A hip-pocket war there could never get out of the hip
pocket; how could it? The Hague Tribunal would take care of that
little problem, all right. And anyhow there were such things as
treaties and solemn covenants to bind the big nations together and
guarantee the territorial integrity of the minor nations. Civilized
peoples were about ready to quit raiding for the scalp locks of other
people.

To be sure there were the Prussian Junkers, those comical persons with Frenchified uniforms and English monocles and Sing
Sing haircuts. But the mezzanines of flesh on the backs of their
bulging necks and the *Schlager* scars on their jowly faces were their
own. These parties were much given to drinking to the toast of
Der Tag and swanking about, clashing their cutlery and their
expensive hardware. And Lord Northcliffe in London and old
Lord Roberts were bidding the British make ready against an onrushing day of wrath. And in Paris, about once in so often they'd
get together and sing the Marseillaise Hymn and demand revenge
for Alsace-Lorraine. But what of it? Alsace and Lorraine remained
quite calm; and anyhow the French were an emotional lot, much
addicted, as the primary geographies said, to light wines and

dancing. But at heart they were the most logical race in the world and they knew that fighting didn't pay dividends any more. As for Northcliffe, the man was an incurable jingo and a professional alarmist, seeking circulation for his daily journals. He was after subscriptions; that was what ailed him. And Lord Roberts might have done pretty well in South Africa against the Boers but that was a long time ago and now he was a doddery octogenarian, an imitation John the Baptist, calling feebly in the wilderness of his senile imaginings and awakening only echoes to mock him. And the Kaiser, that poor, sickly, deluded man, was a leftover from the armor-wearing, sword-rattling centuries—as old-fashioned as a halberd and as futile as a tin soldier. It was to laugh as he went strutting about Potsdam, playing with the obsolete fetish of the Divine Right of Kings and such like trumpery baubles of medievalism. Englishmen had no feeling against Germany, except in the matter of trade competition and German hate for England was manufactured and synthetic and the kindly German masses had no part in it. All the informed students of Continental politics agreed on these matters.

But, for the sake of argument, just suppose one or two countries did get themselves involved in a mess of hostilities? It was incredible that any war over there could ever get across over here directly to affect us. The United States would be safely out of it, Canada too. On a night like this why, in heaven's name, think of anything but peace?

So my neighbor and I agreed that it was too bad about the Grand Duke and the Duchess, but then royalty had to take those chances; and we had a dram together and he went home and I went up to bed and fell asleep watching through my window the moon riding higher and higher in the heavens, a tarnished silver platter now where it had been a split canteloupe when it came up.

How befooled we were! How utterly befooled we all were on this side of the Atlantic Ocean! An ax had been laid at the roots of Old World civilization and a flame was kindled which would burn away millions of lives and billions on billions of treasure all over the habitable globe. And from the malignant smouldering ashes of that flame, after twenty-five years or more, would spring up in 1939 a second and an even more hideous shape of devastation.

The beginning of the end of the Jubilee Age of this earth was at hand and nobody knew it.

Yes, I'm quite sure I lived through the Golden Era of all the eras since first man began to record the tally of the lean years and the fat ones. For us, I'd say it dated, roughly, from the time when the docile, lovable, machine-made McKinley was succeeded by Roosevelt, the Liberal—that is to say, liberal in spots, but no absolute bigot about it, you understand, and a most practical man where his own destiny was concerned. It continued, according to my count, for nearly two decades and for America, it came lamentably to a close with our entrance as active belligerents into the first World War and with the passage of the Prohibition Amendment to the Constitution of the United States.

Of course, standing today in the befouled debris of all that followed since that pleasant time, we are apt to coat over what lies behind us with a smooth patina of content and confidence which after all may really not have amounted to as much as we let on it did. Retrospection is a cheat of a mirror by which, looking over our shoulder, we behold our bygones as purer, sweeter visions than any we see about us, and blessedly free from most of the ills that plague us now.

That much being admitted, I still maintain that my chosen Golden Age was veritably the Golden Age for our people and, for that matter, for the main parts of creation as well. Briefly, let's capitulate: Steadily in this country the standards of living, the standards of human comfort, were going up; medical research and surgical skill were lengthening the human span. Religious bigotry wasn't dead—that poison snake never dies, never effectually is scotched—but at least it was in one of its torpid spells; A. P. A.-ism had languished and K. K. K.-ism would be the future hatching from one of the serpent's vilest eggs. Master devices for peoples' betterment and for their edification were being discovered; were being developed to greater usefulness: the automobile, the moving picture, the airplane, the wireless, the radio. Transportation had been simplified, made cheaper and pleasanter and speedier and as the years went on would be made speedier still.*

---

* I'm inclined to go peevish and fretful when I hear somebody proclaiming that modern highways and improved automobiles en-

Living was pitched to a less feverish, a less hurried, a less killing pace than the pace by which we since have learned to move. Thus far we hadn't been regimented into a monotonously common—and commonplace—resemblance. The individualistic spirit of the pioneers which had carried this Republic through its uncertain youth, the independence in thought and action which had set the men of

---

able Americans to see America. In one hour of leisurely jogging in a buggy behind Dobbin, or in two hours of aimless ambling afoot, any observant American can see more of America—its intimate little pictures, its pleasant nooks and glades, its friendly vistas, its panoramic scopes, than he can in two days of dawdling across the continent at from fifty-five to eighty-five miles an hour, the gait which has been the constant ambition of the average automobilist to achieve ever since the populace took to worshiping that murderous, child-killing monster, the Great God Haste.

Also some of us are prone to take issue with the benefactors who think they have improved vehicular transportation facilities in our cities. Consider how, for example, New York has improved it. It has been improved almost to death. Formerly, with the methods available in that slow-paced period, either by trolley power or by pedal propulsion an average progress of eleven miles an hour could be made through the traffic-congested areas and in a horse-drawn cab one could go almost as swiftly. Today the automobile, or any other rig for that matter, which makes six miles an hour over the very same route, is doing as well as could be expected. It is about as satisfactory—and there's infinitely less nerve strain—if the traveler just gets out and walks.

I might say though that I admire the saintly, the almost angelic guilelessness of automobile manufacturers who spend millions annually for advertisements urging purchasers of their cars to obey the laws against speeding, they, of course, being utterly ignorant of the fact that their selling agents and their district demonstrators lure prospective buyers by pointing out that these makes of cars may easily be driven at one hundred and ten miles an hour and what's more, proving they can by what the speedometer says during a trial spin.

But why the rush? I keep asking myself that question. As I catch a fleeting glance at the typical gasoline sot madly skyhooting by I say to myself that surely nobody will be glad to see him when he gets to where he is going although I'll concede it's understandable why folks may have been in a perfect swivet to hurry him

the severed states of the Union to cutting one another's throats for four bloody years of civil war yet stubbornly persisted amongst the inheritors. The Melting Pot spewed up sometimes and vomited out some uncongenial and unassimilable elements, but it hadn't begun to boil over. Labor was pushing upward toward its proper dignity and its deservedly greater deserts; while capital, in some quarters, was coming to have a realization of the moral responsibilities of its stewardship. Not all the great employers were delaying until sumptuary statutes would force them to a more equitable division of the profits with those who toiled to produce those profits. Some, of their own volition, were practicing common decency and common fairness in their dealings with their workers and with the public as well, and more of them would soon be following the example of these forerunners. We had fewer laws but more respect, I think, for the laws we did have.

Not yet were we afflicted with neutered pacificists, nor with pampered half-baked young radicals who in the next generation would burgeon forth as the prize pullets of coop-fed Communism. Taking us as a whole, we believed that representative government was something for us to support rather than a thing graciously conceived to support us. Uncle Sam was still Uncle Sam; he wasn't Santa Claus. Taxes were an annual event, instead of being for the majority of wage earners an enforced incentive for going on earning and scrimping—and giving up. We didn't hear talk about Right Wing movements and Left Wing movements and Little Left Wing

---

off from where he started. You wouldn't choose to keep that person on the premises any longer than possible.

I might add I'd rather be late for supper in this world tonight than to be in some other world on time for breakfast in the morning. But then I am an aging person, full of old-fashioned whims and antique crotchets. Indeed I must be very aged. I can remember when the first white Republican I ever saw in my childhood I thought must be an albino. And I was well along toward middle age before the young of the species and, Lord help us, some of the older ones, succumbed to the delusion that nudity, except in a raw oyster or a right young baby, is a thing beautiful to look upon. Still there must be something to this vogue for going about half to two-thirds naked in public. Because the only ones who seem to object to it are those who haven't tried it yet.

movements. The American Eagle had only two wings and when they flapped, they flapped together. National legislation might be selfish and in places venal, as legislation always is, but generally it was guided by experienced hands and neither academic reformers nor sophomoric uplifters nor amateur experimentalists—or anyway not in number—were being encouraged to tamper with the fabric of the institutions which the founders had set up, and among themselves blandly bent on improving the structure by knocking it apart first. What was best of all, so it would seem, as we look rearward and compare the past with the present, was that we were not beset, beleaguered and bedeviled by official snoopers, by governmental proctors and bursars and, worse than these, by busybodies bearing authority to pry into our private affairs, spy into our safety deposit boxes, regulate our way of carrying on professions and callings already sufficiently licensed and legitimatized, and generally empowered to overturn habits of living which conformed to the established and hitherto acceptable American model. You could mind your own business then; indeed, strange though it may seem now, you even might be left with some business of your own to mind.

And there was no school of political philosophy holding it as expedient that we should burn down the Temple of our Fathers in order to destroy a few cockroaches in the basement.

I am glad that for my mother her latter placid years should have coincided with the apogee of the Goodly Time. To the end of her days she took such a savor out of life, although because of the Scotch reserve which was her inheritance, you might not always have guessed it. Either great grief or great joy would freeze her to immobility. Afterward, in privacy, she might give way to her emotions but never while outsiders looked on. Long after bodily infirmities overtook her, indeed up to the very hour of her death, her brain functioned with the clarity and the precision of her maturity and her eyes were keen and her hearing perfect and she practically was bedfast before she lost her teeth. With avidity she read everything that was readable, discussed everything that was discussable—for a Southern-born woman—and kept abreast of the world's doings. Books, newspapers, magazines, pamphlets—she sat in a great nest of them; and for company she preferably chose young or youngish people. She was frank to say old infirm people bored her to distraction; they wanted to discuss their symptoms, wanted to waste their time—and hers—on small gossip and petty chitchat.

And she had, her four children thought, such fine small vanities. When she was in her eighties her complexion was that of a healthy schoolgirl. Privately she was very proud of this. And although in the sorrows of mid-life her hair turned snowy white, it never did take on that brittle, lifeless look which so often comes with age. It curled on her head and shone with a lovely luster. She loved little adornments of dress, loved bright colors, she who had walked most of her married life in the heathenish deep mourning decreed for women of her generation who had lost relatives. On the provocation of a special occasion—or lacking it—she would spend hours picking becoming effects in costumes—"primping up" she shamelessly called it. She had a positive gift for creating comfort and the feel of luxury out of simple possessions. Living in an attic or a basement, she somehow would make it homelike.

Without being offensive about it, she never avoided speaking her likes and dislikes. She had her social prejudices—she belonged to a so-called "old family," you'll remember, and she had political prejudices and certain race preferences—as who, to tell the truth, does not? And she had her sectional prejudices. Once I said to her, "That was a very attractive woman that called on you today." Her reply unwittingly was characteristic and behind her back my sisters and I exchanged grins. But we didn't laugh aloud; we didn't dare to. "Yes, son," she answered, "she's a very charming woman—although a Northerner."

But she was absolutely free from religious prejudice. I think she hated religious bigotry above every sin in the Decalogue, yet she was reared in the strict confines of Old Line Presbyterianism and for doctrinal purposes abided always within the creed. She thought it abominable that any American should be for or against any candidate for public office, solely on the grounds of the candidate's brand of faith—or the lack of it. Almost the last out-of-doors journey she ever made was when Al Smith was the nominee for the presidency and she caused herself to be carried to the polls to vote for him. Naturally, she supported him; wasn't he a Demo-

crat? And, as she would have put it, hadn't he come up from a
nobody to be a somebody? But the fact that within her own party
and among her own townspeople many opposed him solely because
he was a Catholic—that above all else enraged her. "I'll cast my
ballot for the man if it puts me on the flat of my back for the rest
of my days," she said. "Children, it's time for real Americans to
show their intolerance for intolerance."

My second sister Manie and I hurried from New York for her
funeral. As we approached the house Father Connolly, the old
pastor at St. Francis de Sales on the corner beyond, was just coming
down the front steps, wiping his eyes as he came. He had been
upstairs to say a prayer for the repose of her soul. They had been
friends of long standing. And Dr. Fletcher, the Episcopal rector,
was there with my mother's own minister. During the evening the
young Jewish rabbi and his wife came, showing real grief, both of
them, and the little local squad of the Salvation Army passed reso-
lutions of respect.

Her death was such a death as pious people ask for. A week
before, she had fallen and fractured two ribs but she rallied and soon
seemed out of all immediate danger. On this night for the first time
since the accident my older sister Reubie went out for a breath of
air and Mattie Copeland, the cook—and practically a member of
the household—had gone to her little cottage in the colored district
up on Jones Street. Left with the invalid was a trained nurse and
"Janie," who had been for several years past my mother's personal
attendant. At her request the nurse raised her so that she might
take a sleeping potion and Janie brought a glass of water. She
looked into the nurse's face. "Honey," she said, "you're the only
one who can lift me without hurting my side. Thank you." Her
glance included the gentle little brown woman, kneeling alongside
her. "Everybody has been so good to me," she said, and closed her
eyes and was gone.

Here, right at the windup of these wandering remembrances,
it has occurred to me that I have omitted one matter which no
person writing about himself and particularly no professional
writer should overlook. It is in the ordinances that this positively
should not be overlooked. This incumbent duty is to tell an expec-

tant public what writings by other people have exerted upon his life and his future career the most formative pressures. To begin back at the beginning, I might say that the little volume which in my early youth was most helpful to me was a prayer book bestowed by my dear Sunday-school teacher. Probably I'd be saying it too if I thought anybody would believe me. My most helpful work was a slim, small volume—a rough directory of all the street addresses west of the I. C. tracks, which I borrowed from the assistant postmaster. By reference to this useful folio I was enabled to build up my ice-wagon route and amass the funds with which I bought my first double-barreled shotgun, a Parker twelve gauge with hammers that stood up like a pair of mules' ears. The scope of my reading when first I was thinking of turning author myself is a confusion of likes and dislikes. I had an abundance of favorites—Clemens, Melville, Poe, Shakespeare, Hugo, Dumas, Wilde, Balzac, Stevenson, Dickens, Thackeray, Swift, Voltaire and anything about Nick Carter—and I had almost as many pet aversions. I would say that my chief aversion was anything written by Bulwer-Lytton, the blanket reason for this being that Bulwer-Lytton wrote it. Along here I rather avoided most of the formidable tomes recommended to me as classics. Mainly they seemed so overlastingly stilted and so dull. Anyway I felt it would be more agreeable—and much more profitable—to wait until the mood took me and then turn out a few classics for my own generation, not to mention a grateful posterity.

After having spent the greater part of thirty years spinning out fiction I find now in these times that I favor prints dealing with actual beings and palpable facts and plausible reminiscences rather than with the figments of the author's dream, howsoever feasible and captivating these latter may be. Perhaps it is the lurking hope of reaching a like-minded group among the buying public that is in some degree responsible for this elaborated effusion of mine.

I must qualify that preceding paragraph though by saying that the work I read oftenest—a book which is in part authentic reporting but obviously in a greater degree purely apocryphal—is the Bible. I don't mean all the Bible. I mean selected portions of it. Between these covers is my favorite compilation of splendid imaginative writings, my unapproachable budget of creative grandeur. For me the Book of Job is the finest piece of fiction in all literature. There, dressed in exquisite language, in the noblest of metaphors, is the most brutal story that ever sprang from an inspired but a perverted brainpan: The story of a God so cruel He deliberately makes a bet with Satan that by visiting unutterable miseries and unspeakable sufferings upon the most loyal, the most devoted man in the entire jurisdiction, He can drive that one good and perfect man to curse His name and then He'll win eight dollars and seventy-five cents or some such sum from Old Nick.

I like to re-read the Songs of Solomon and the Chants of David for the sensuous rhythm, the voluptuous cadences which fill them as a jeweled cup is filled with the sweetness of honey or a chalice with spiced wine. I find solace in the Twenty-third Psalm, for therein is a lovely promise and promises are rarer than threats in Holy Writ. And in it is no smell of death or of earthly decay or corruption. It makes my soul to lie down in green pastures beside the still waters, and take stock of itself.

I read the Gospels and then I know why when men go to war they pray not to That Man but to the vengeful, bloody-minded Jehovah of the Old Testament that, with an unrelenting sword and an unquenchable torch, the foe may be destroyed, root and branch, that his home may be made desolate, that his wives shall go to concubinage and his children to be enslaved. Reading after the evangels, I see a picture of the only world conqueror who came with clean hands—and these the same hands which the soldiers pierced with their iron spikes as they nailed the Nazarene to the tree.

And surely the Sermon on the Mount embodies the finest ethical creed, the purest preachment of idealistic Socialism—and the most absolutely suicidal code of business policies—ever spoken or penned. The Golden Rule is a perfect principle but, mind you, only for application by and for some already perfected race. And there are no such animals, nor ever were. Precious beatitudes, yes; moralities beyond compare, granted.

But on the other hand what a succession of acts and advices calculated to undermine the very foundations of all settled industrial rules and banking rules. Those Gadarene swine were the property of someone else; sending them rushing down to the sea probably meant bankruptcy for the unoffending swineherd. And scourging the money-changers from the Temple was in defiance of one of the oldest of financial precedents. Hasn't hypocrisy, that mask which the usurer wears and which the thimblerigger finds his most congenial disguise, always thriven best in the perfume of orthodox sanctity and under the rooftrees of the doctrinal formulas? Ask any hymn-singing collector of chattel mortgages. Ask any adept at foreclosure proceedings or any pious promoter of dubious stockjobberies.

Go further than that: Call the miracles myths; say the healings were hysteria or hypnotism or hypochondria or hallucination or describe them by any other aptly alliterative word that fits the skeptic's pliant tongue. Point out the biological impossibility of virgin birth. Let science disprove the fabled sophistries of a physical resurrection. Suffer logic, doing its merciless work, to strip away the believer's belief in divinity, even though it be as if a harsh hand had snatched away from some poor blind halting one the crutches upon which he hobbled on toward eternity—snatched them away because by this reasoned analysis they were such faulty crutches—and left the cripple forlorn and despairing in the dust. Apply the chemical test of plain common sense to this tangled-up equation and unravel the riddle of it to prove that when logic steps in by the door faith flies out of the window. Proclaim that the two may never abide together in the house of a man who asks rational questions and requires practical answers. But that, in so many cases, is not true. I've noticed that those who have sufficient faith can get along very well indeed without logic, while a majority of those who have logic demand some form of faith.

So much for so much. Speaking as an innocent bystander, who, without prejudice views this ageless controversy from the sidelines, I nevertheless and most reverently submit this—and this for my spiritual purposes is amply sufficient—that if humility and humanity and utter lack of snobbishness; if thoughtful consideration for fellow beings and compassion for their weaknesses and forgiveness of their transgressions; if graciousness and gentleness, charitableness, dignity and courage, simplicity and a regard for duty be the marks—and they are—then Jesus Christ was the first great gentleman of recorded history and the greatest gentleman that ever, in any age, walked upon this earth. And if that be blasphemy, I'm proud of it.

This morning I had a letter from my friend of long standing and happy acquaintanceship, Fred G. Neuman. I claim for him that he is a very valuable citizen in the old town, for he is the most authentic historian it ever had and he is a persistent, discriminating searcher-out of early traditions and communal folklore which otherwise might be forgotten. He sent me a clipping he had written for the paper dealing with "Honest Jim" Magnor, who at ninety-five is the senior native-born citizen of Paducah and, since the death of another, one of the three veterans of the War between the Sections left in our county. I remember when I could have checked off the names of hundreds of living veterans.

The patriarch enjoys another distinction. When hostilities broke out in 1861 he drilled with General Lloyd Tilghman's locally raised regiment, the Third Kentucky Infantry, but on account of his youth was rejected as a recruit when the regiment left for training camp below the Tennessee line. Soon the Confederacy was less particular about the ages of volunteers. As has already been mentioned, my mother's brother, Lewis Saunders, got in at fourteen by swearing he was eighteen. I recall having heard "Honest Jim" tell the sequel to his failure:

"After the Yankees captured the town a squad of 'em came to our house, hunting contrabands, I reckon, or just to pester us because our family were such strong Confederate sympathizers. There was a captain with 'em, a lippy, overbearing scoundrel from 'way up north somewheres and he was especially nasty to Ma. She sassed him right back though. I was only a kid, but I swore a paralyzed oath to myself that I'd kill him for low-rating my mother, if it was the last thing I ever did. So, by cracky, I up and offered to join the Union crowd, first making sure I'd get into his company. And sure enough they didn't suspicion anything and took me in. The first time we went into action I was going to shoot him from behind. But right away he was transferred or discharged or something and my chance was gone. By then I'd got to liking the fellows in my outfit so I stayed on with them the full four years and was mustered out with an honorable discharge. But all through those four years my feelings were all mixed up, in a funny way. My body was buttoned up in blue clothes but my heart was with my own people. I kept hoping we'd win every battle we went into, but that in the long run either the South would win the war, or else that it would be a dogfall."

I think it fitting and somewhat emblematic that the last of all that shadowy band of old soldiers at my home should typify, in a way, both sides of that great internecine struggle which split our country asunder and, at the end, reunited it in an eternal federation.

This book began, in the first page of its first chapter, with mention of Will Hogg. For my own sake I am bringing him into its last chapter.

I think I know the test for a man's personality. The thing depends on how long his memory abides in the thoughts of his friends after his body dies. It has been ten years now since Will left here, yet today, as I write these words down, the picture of him is as firmly fixed in my brain and the love that I bore for him is as definitely a part of me, as on the day when we buried him beside his father, the great governor, at the old capital cemetery in Austin. Surely they have liked him Over There—the Real Ones who traveled on ahead.

Will Hogg was like an iceberg. Not that he was cold or inaccessible, but that, as with an iceberg, only the craggy tip was revealed to the stranger's casual eye while the submerged seven-eighths carried along an unseen, irresistible force and solidity. His love for the state which sired him and which his people for three generations before him conspicuously had helped to build into strength and grace, was more than a love. It was an idolatry almost terrifying in its intensity. To his unpaid, frequently anonymous and often unsuspected service for Texas and for his home town of Houston, he added an unstinted, unselfish, unending devotion which was as rare as it was splendid.

He was a bundle of contradictions that clashed like cymbals. He had a consuming admiration for esthetic precious things: for architecture, for jewels, for flowers, for fabrics, for furnishings, for gardens and groves and parks; but he delighted to speak in the

lurid and crackling vernacular of the cattle camp and the border
cantina. His language never was dirty, any more than his thoughts
were; it was just his willful fancy to dress up speech in gaudy
swearwords. Beyond any man I ever knew he had a graphic faculty
for clothing a ripe philosophy, a keen judgment and a discerning
fine appreciation for beauty, in stinging and astringent profanity.
His gentlest, most gracious deeds were often so disguised. Once
some of the ladies of Houston came in his office to solicit a contribution to start a fund of fifty thousand dollars for a new W. C.
T. U. building. With a violent outburst which frizzled the hair on
their heads he demanded to know why they asked for a slice when
they deserved a whole loaf, and he strode out on the street and
in five minutes had under way a subscription which amounted to
just ten times what these good women had hoped for. His was probably the largest single donation, but his name did not head the list.
(It never did head lists; sometimes it wasn't on them at all, and
sometimes only there to encourage other donors, but a fat check
always was forthcoming.) Afterward a leading minister said Will
Hogg was the only man who cussed a half-million-dollar building
for a worthy cause right out of the ground, and he, for one, thanked
God for such cussing.

Will Hogg's temper was explosive and unpredictable, but the
flame died down as quickly as it flared up, instantly to be succeeded
by an equally intense repentance. Only where he thought someone
designed to smirch the honor of Texas or by schemes of skulduggery
to prey upon her citizens was he unrelenting in his rage. Then he
was a vengeful lion standing in the path of the plotters. And such a
fight as this he never quit until he had won that fight, no matter how
much time and money and energy—and vituperation—it cost him.
The soil of Texas was littered with the broken political bodies of
men who had opposed him in his battles for civic righteousness. He
could have had any office in the gift of the people to bestow but he
would take none. He preferred to keep a jealous guard upon those
who did hold the offices.

He left the bulk of his estate for popular education in the state.
How many millions he privately bestowed for education, for acts
of individual charity and for worth-while movements not even his
executors have ever been able to find out, but the total must have

amounted to a tremendous sum. His right hand never knew what his left hand did; maybe the right hand was too busy to keep the tally. He used to say that if he knew in advance when he would die he wouldn't leave enough, after his funeral expenses and his just debts were paid, to buy a dish of chili beans. He said Texas had given him money out of her lavish bounty—the Hogg fortune was founded on oil wells—and while he was here he was going to pay her back something on account.

His monuments, some of them tangible and some of them spiritual, dot the state and Texas, you'll please remember, is a sizable state. They are expressed in public betterment, in cleaner government, in communal art, in a fostered sense of cultural refinement, in lovely buildings, in scientists, musicians, college professors and physicians and the like, who got their professional training by his help. And the heart of every man and of every woman who ever stood close to Will Hogg will be a throbbing monument to his memory for so long as one of those men or one of those women lives.

For courage, for spontaneous generosity, for measured thoughtfulness, I never saw his equal. He was among the wisest, the quickest-witted and the most resourceful men I have encountered. He could be as winning and as companionable, and on occasion, as aggravating a creature as ever lived, I'm sure. Taking him as he was, with his little faults and his blazing big virtues, he was the most lovable human being I ever knew and I shall go on missing him until the time comes for me to follow along where he went.

They say every human being who writes an autobiography or anything resembling an autobiography, inevitably exposes himself, no matter how craftily he strives to make out as good a case for the defense as possibly he can. But which one of his selves does he expose? Which one of my own selves have I herewith unwittingly revealed? For, by my own way of figuring, there is in each one of us three separate and distinct selves and in the cases of some of us the relationship between Self Number I and Self Number II is too thinly drawn to be called a distant kinship even. I'm checking them off: There's the first self. That's the self which really is our own self, with the faults which we strive to conceal, with the naked shortcomings which we cannot conceal, so strong are they; with all our twisted bad thoughts and our misshapen inner biases and our secret skewed inhibitions of which, in self-analyzing moments, we privately are ashamed but which perversely we cherish and nourish all the same. Second, there's the self which each one fondly hopes the world may be cajoled into believing is he, accepting his stubbornness for resolution, his greediness for commendable thrift, his selfishness for proper self-protection of his earthly interests, his rudeness for a rugged individualism, his egotism for a proper and seemly appraisal of true worth—and so on and so forth. Third, and last, there is the self which discriminating mankind discerns, giving me the benefit of a doubt here, reading through my pretensions there; balancing off what palpably is artificial against what these judges decide may be wholesomely natural. This is a composite self put together by my shrewder neighbors, my kindlier friends, and my critical enemies. I'd be afraid to ask the Gallup people to take a poll amongst the readers of this book with a view of finding out just where, in this final estimate, I stand; I would so.

I wish my ulcers and I could get together on a mutually satisfactory diet. What suits me seems to disagree with them. I claim a stomach ulcer should be like a tapeworm or a boardinghouse guest—take what's put before it and raise no rumpuses. A touch of goutiness also seems to require quite a good deal of pampering. Altogether it is rather as though a fellow has a kennel of highbred dogs that are too fussified and persnickety to eat the same fare that the family lives on. All this constitutes another reason why I pine for that departed Golden Age, when anything I could eat I could digest. P. S. I could eat anything.

In the old days when I went campaigning, first for Woodrow Wilson and again for Al Smith, the job was comparatively easy. A fellow wrote a speech and tried it out and retouched it and polished off the rough corners and sweetened up the contents to taste, and then delivered that same version to as many audiences as would listen to him. But what with national hook-ups and regional hook-ups, the radio has killed this pleasant practice. Now one must have a new speech every time one broadcasts which is none too easy a task for anybody. I found that out for myself in the presidential campaign which newly is ended as I write this. Perhaps it helps to explain why some of the 1940 crop of speeches didn't seem to be so very high-grade even to those of us who uttered them. A different show for every night used to be pretty hard on seasoned repertoire troupers.

One aftermath of that election should be gratifying, I'd say, to all of us, no matter what our several party leanings may be. There was offered renewed and abundant proof that Americans are not greedy winners when they win, nor bad losers when they lose. Without surrendering their principles, the minority showed that they could go on displaying good sportsmanship which, I claim, means good citizenship, good sound patriotism, good, real Americanism. And the victorious majority have been neither vindictive nor arrogant about it.

It looks as though—with careful nursing and close watching— this country might last quite a spell yet. At least it always has. So it seemingly behooves those who backed the losing ticket to forget what's lost and fight for what's left.

Well, I reckon that will be about all. . . . But I make a motion that we depart from the rule of tacking on for a finis those two uncompromising words, "The End." Who knows what the end of anything is? Who knows where a thing begins or when it may end? By your leave then, we will put down here that line which sometimes is to be found in the stage business of a play to cue a character who is leaving the stage, and may or may not be back again:

EXIT LAUGHING

INDEX

INDEX

Adams, John, President, 22
Ade, George
  alumnus of sports page, 260
  father of, 355
  boulevardier, 363
  and Morgan Robertson, 508
Adriatic, 537
Albert, headwaiter at Palmer House, 348-349
Alger, Secretary of War, 302
Alien and Sedition Law, 22
All Aboard, 86
Allen, Ethan, 22
Allen, Gracie, 261
Allen, Harry, famous guide, 450
Allen, Private John, 270
Allison, J. Murray, 208
American, New York, 360
American Newspaper Publishers' Association, 284
American Visitors' Château, description of, 428-429
Andy the hackman, 54
Anna Christie, 366
Appetite Bill, confidence man, 254
Arbuckle, Fatty, 480
Arlen, Michael, Cobb's opinion of, 393
Armstrong, Paul, alumnus of sports page, 259
Arnold, Dorothy, mystery of, 177
Ashcraft, Major J. H., pallbearer for Uncle Jo, 86
Atkins, "Prent," 451
Attucks, Crispus, 441
Avant, Kelley, member of negro committee, 437

Babson, Roger, 421
Bache, Jules, Flint's guest, 461
Back Home, 359
Baer, "Bugs," prolific humor writer, 118, 260
Bagby, Judge, uncle of Cobb, 54, 531
Bailey, Frankie, 361
Baker, George Barr, admirer of Roosevelt, 281
Baker, Colonel John, great-grandfather of Mrs. Cobb, 218
Baker, Laura Spencer, *see* Cobb
Baker, Marcus S., father of Mrs. Cobb, 219
Ballowe, Pilot Eph, tall story of, 84-85
Baltic, Cobb aboard on dangerous crossing, 536-539

Barlow, Milt, 514
Barnum, P. T., 230
Barrie, Sir James, guest with Cobb, at Northcliffe luncheon, 192, 392
Bartlett, Uncle Gip, and the scalps, 32
Bartlett, Jane, great-grandmother of Cobb, 29
Beach, "Harry," recommends Cobb for job on *Tribune,* 111-112
  A. P. star, 208
Beach, Rex, 451
  and Morgan Robertson, 508
Beard family, 78
Beatty, Clyde, 341
Beck, "Eddie," city editor of Chicago *Tribune,* 111-112
Beckham, John Crepps Wickliffe, Goebel's successor to governorship, 215
Beecher, Henry Ward, 273
"Beefy" (Savoy bar attendant), 189
Belasco, David, 361
Bell, Digby, and O'Reilly, 237
Bell, Dr., encounters with Mr. J. Shrewsbury, 85, 90-92
"Belled Buzzard, The," Cobb, 469
Benchley, Bob, 261
Bennett, Arnold, and Cobb, 353*ff.*
Bernstorff, Count von, activities in America, 184, 190
Bessemer, Henry, and Cobb-Lyon furnace, 24
Bickel, Karl, president of U. P., 284
Big Parade, The, 475, 478
Bilkinson, Bishop, of Wall Street, 259
Billy the Kid, 38
Bishop, William A., Air Marshal of Canadian forces, 539
Bishop, Judge William S., in *Judge Priest,* 333-337
Black, Mr. Justice, contrasted with McReynolds, 307
Blackburn, Senator Joseph Clay Stiles, 209, 513
Blaine, James G., 460
Blakeley, Bassett, and Will Rogers, 453
Block, Paul, 263
Blossom, Henry, 254
Blynn, Holbrook, as Flint's guest, 461
Blythe, Sam
  editor and correspondent, 118
  a Great Reporter, 253
  and Brady, 361
"Bob Davis," 409